Blanche of Castile, Queen and Regent of France, 1188-1252

by

Élie Berger

Translated by Dr. Frank H. Wallis from

Histoire de Blanche de Castille, Reine de France (Paris, 1895)

Blanche of Castile, Queen and Regent of France, 1188-1252

Translation Copyright © 2015 by Frank H. Wallis. All rights reserved. Permission is granted to make and reproduce direct quotes, but not more than a total of five hundred words, with complete scholarly attribution. Excerpts and direct quotes longer than this must receive permission from the publisher. Paraphrasing of this work is encouraged, but must be acknowledged in a footnote, end note, or parenthetical reference, with name of author, title of work, date of publication, and page number(s).

Published in the United States of America.

Table of Contents

Translator's Note v

Preface vii

Chapter One 1

Chapter Two 45

Chapter Three 103

Chapter Four 143

Chapter Five 199

Chapter Six 253

Chapter Seven 315

Chapter Eight 373

Translator's Note

Blanca de Castilla was a Spanish princess who became the most powerful human being in France as Regent and Queen, from 1226 to 1252. From Élie Berger's, *Histoire de Blanche de Castille, Reine de France* (Paris, 1895), there can be no question that Blanche was ruler of France during a critical period of Capetian expansion, even imperialism. Berger's biography remains the best scholarly treatment of the manuscript sources.

Élie Berger (1850-1925) was born on 1 August 1850 in Beaucourt (Haut-Rhin), and died on 3 April 1925 in Paris. He was a doctor of letters, member of the École française de Rome, archivist in the Archives Nationales, professor of paleography in the École des chartes, and conservator in the Musée Condé. At various times Berger was a member of the Académie des inscriptions et belles-lettres, and the Comité des travaux historiques et scientifiques, Président of the Société de l'École des chartes, and Président of the Société de l'histoire de France.

Some of Berger's important works must include *Recueil des actes de Henri II, roi d'Angleterre et duc de Normandie concernant les provinces françaises et les affaires de France* (Académie des Inscriptions et belles lettres,1916-1920); *Recueil des actes de Philippe Auguste, roi de France* (1916); *Histoire de Blanche de Castile reine de France* (1895); *Les dernières Années de saint Louis d'après les layettes du Trésor des chartes*, (1902); *Les Registres d'Innocent IV* [1243-1254] (1884-1921).

This translation of the *Histoire de Blanche de Castille, Reine de France,* generally makes use of Berger's original spelling of place names and proper names. My task was to translate and not to revise. The major exception is of course Castille to Castile, along with English place names and proper names. In the days of Blanche the name Henri III d'Angleterre was not yet known to history as Henry III, King of England, but for English speaking readers of the twenty-first century the distinction is more convenient, if not more efficient. There are some terms which are difficult to translate, and these have been left in italics, with the English equivalent in brackets. Anything contained in parentheses is Berger's. His footnotes have been converted to end notes.

Dr. Frank H. Wallis

Monroe, CT

Preface

Blanche of Castile has several biographers, but most of them seem to be disposed to celebrate her merits rather than to recall her history; they especially try to clarify her piety, charity, and courage, to address her role as the mother of a great King. She was something more, appearing at the forefront of those who contributed to our national unity, and her political skill was still more remarkable than her private virtues or other qualities. Of all those who spoke of her, the best known is undoubtedly Le Nain de Tillemont, historian of Louis IX; but in his work, considered with justice as the starting point of all our studies on a grand epoch, facts relating to Queen Blanche are scattered in the midst of a quantity of information in which she fails to occupy the first place. The life of Blanche deserves a special and thorough study. To carry out a good end to this enterprise, it should be recognized that we are more favored than our predecessors. It is known that Le Nain de Tillemont joined together all the documents which one could use to write the history of Louis IX. His book is the work of a scientist, an observer, a very impartial judge. It was with a patience worthy of praise that he examined chronicles, collections, more varied publications, and the recognition that we owe him is very great, for you cannot approach even one of the questions relating to Queen Blanche without resorting to this abundant source of information. But it is necessary to ask whether Le Nain de Tillemont knew all the texts or all the collections of which we could make use.

We now have at our disposal, in the supplement of the *Trésor des Chartes*, a rather great number of important pieces for the history of Queen Blanche that Le Nain de Tillemont did not see; several have been published, but others are new. Archives of the departments and collections of the Bibliothèque nationale also provide more information on Blanche of Castile. In this respect, it will be enough to cite a letter by which a burger of La Rochelle, before the war with Poitou, informed the mother of Louis IX about a plot formed by Count de la Marche. This text, which throws a sharp light on the political role of Queen Blanche, was published, as one knows, close to twenty years ago by Léopold Delisle.

Le Nain de Tillemont, who did not know about this piece of spectacular value, did not have occasion to extend his research to the registers of the popes, some of which have entered, over the years, into the public domain. He had not been brought to examine the collections preserved in the archives of England and which contain, with regard to the time of Louis IX, a quantity of documents concerning the relation of France to England. More fortunate than he, I could work during long weeks in the Public Record Office, and study in their entirety, for the years during which Blanche was regent, the pipe rolls, letters patent, and others still. I believe that I must discharge a debt to the liberal traditions of this great establishment, while paying homage to the erudition and kindness of those who direct it; I request them to receive this expression of my very sincere gratitude for the very benevolent reception which they made for me.

The English, who have in London archives not only rich but well organized, acquired an undeniable fame in the scholarly world by the care with which they published, during this century, chronicles and documents interesting to their history, in particular in their large collection *Rerum Britannicarum medii ævi scriptores*. It was in this collection that I consulted, at any time, the *Royal and other historical letters illustrative off the reign of Henry III*, published by Shirley, the chronicle of Roger of Wendover, published by Hewlett, the large edition of *Chronica majora* by Mathieu de Paris, and the *Annales monastici*, due to the indefatigable activity of Henry Richards Luard, a friend I regret and for whom I venerate the memory.

The collection of the *Monumenta Germaniæ*, and especially the *Recueil des historiens de France*, contain, it goes without saying, a quantity of texts that our precursors did not know about, or they had to consult manuscripts, maybe in defective editions. I will mention in passing the Chronicle of Primat and especially the *comptes royaux*, whose last volumes of our large collection contain final editions.

Those devoted to the study of the Middle Ages know that the Académie des Inscriptions et Belles-Lettres recently completed publication of texts relative to the royal inquests of 1247 and 1248. The Commission of the *Recueil des historiens de France* authorized me to quote material, from the best pages of this edition, depositions of testimony relevant to Blanche of Castile and the agents of her government. I must pay homage for this.

I would be remiss if I did not admit of how much time I consulted the book of Wallon on *Saint Louis et son temps*. I make a point of also recognizing that my task was facilitated as well, in certain points, by the work of Arbois de Jubainville who, in his history of the dukes and counts de Champagne, discussed and set in context evidence relating to Thibaud IV and his relations with Queen Blanche. Auguste Longnon, with his well-known kindness, often helped with his counsels, and I owe him for the indication of important documents. Mr. A. de La Borderie agreed to transmit identifications to me relating to several Breton place names, encountered in the English documents. I also received invaluable information from Paul Guérin, secretary of the National Archives, and from A. Morel-Fatie, secretary of the École des Chartes.

Geffroy, after all the marks of benevolence that he has given me, wanted to accommodate this book in the Library of the French Schools of Athens and of Rome. One will understand how pleasant it is to see the tightening, if possible, of the bonds which connect me with the French School of Rome, where I passed many happy years.

Chapter One

Birth of Blanche. — Her parents. — Noble Houses from which she was descended. — John Lackland and Philippe Auguste decide to make her marry Prince Louis of France. — Blanche comes to France; her marriage. — She lives at the court of Philippe Auguste. — Hostilities between Castile and England. — First children of Blanche; her oldest son Philippe. — Prince Louis receives Artois. — Battle of Las Navas de Tolosa. — Blanche loses her parents. — Birth of Saint Louis. — Expedition of Prince Louis against England; efforts of Blanche to assist him. — Birth of Robert Artois; death of Prince Philippe, birth of the princes Jean, Alphonse et Philippe Dagobert. — Death of Henry I, King of Castile ; succession of Ferdinand III. — Coronation of Louis VIII and Blanche at Rheims; their entry in Paris. — Negotiations for the release of Ferrand, Count of Flanders. — Some noble Castilians offer the crown to Blanche and Louis VIII. — Arrival in France of Cardinal Romain, legate of the Holy See. — Last children of Blanche. — Expedition of Louis VII against the Albigensians. — His death.

Among the queens of France for which one preserves the memory, several made themselves famous for their spirit, their talents or their courage, but there is little which, from one end to the other, leaves an impression of grandeur. In a country where only men had the right to succeed to the throne, the wife or the mother of the sovereign, when she managed to exert royal authority, seldom maintained it beyond a few years, and if we want to enumerate those who controlled the state in the name of their sons, we would find rather more who finished under a poor or even an obscure condition. One remembers that Marie de Medici dominated Louis XIII, but one knows too that she made a sad end; the regency of Anne of Austria is well remembered, thanks to the great minister who did everything on her behalf, but few people are interested in the unobtrusive role that she played during her last years. The biography of these princesses and several others only concern history for certain brief periods; one can still doubt if they left on events or upon institutions any trace of a truly personal action. Such was not the case with Blanche of Castile; she ruled by herself, twice reprized; she raised, educated, and formed one of our greatest kings; she preserved, even when she did not hold anymore power, large and legitimate influence. It may be that she had help, but she was not dominated by anybody, and one does not know what would have become of our country, during the dangers of a long minority, without the help of this spirit full of resources and experience, of this character who never relaxed. Her life, during most of the thirteenth century, was the life of France, which she pacified; her history is that of royal power, outside of which there was no fatherland.

France, illustrated with so many great characters, can rightly be proud of this foreigner who was so useful; one hardly remembers that she was born in Spain, when it is known that she made France her fatherland by way of adoption, and nobody would have thought of reproaching her origin. But she assumed government at a time of disorder, during fights of the parties, the private interests, generally enemies of the public good. The men who hardly thought of the prosperity of the greater number, found it extremely convenient to treat her as Spanish in an attempt to discredit her among the French. They would have readily forgotten that she was Castilian, if she was less devoted to the happiness of the people. The people of her country, numerous at the court of France, did not rise with the great lords of the state nor to the rank of intimate advisers; they received marks of generosity that servants desire of their master, and remained without influence.

It appears that Blanche was born in Palencia, in the first months of the year 1188, before 4 March.[1] Her father, Alphonse VIII [the Noble One], was one of the most famous representatives of this valiant house which provided to Castile, at the time of its first increases, a whole line of intelligent princes and brave men. He managed to control by himself, after a minority long and agitated, in difficult circumstances, with courage and obstinate will, struggles against the Christian kings of the peninsula, but never prevented him from fighting the Arabs; each time that he carried out attacks on his neighbors left him little respite, and one saw beginning again a fight against the common enemy of Spanish Christians, a war which was to end in victory. Eleanor of England, wife of Alphonse VIII, was the daughter of Henry II [Plantagenet]; she carried the name of her mother, the famous Aliénor of Aquitaine, but hardly resembled her; a contemporary historian declared her pure, noble and of good council. Blanche had no brothers when she came into the world; Fernand, destined for an early end, did not exist yet; prince Henri, who after Alphonse VIII wore the crown of Castile for three years, was born only in 1204. The royal succession, while waiting for a male heir, belonged then to Bérengère [1181-1246], eldest of the family.

In France one hardly knows these Castilian princes of the twelfth and thirteenth centuries; separated from us by the mountains, their peculiar quarrels and the wars against the Moors, who always called them to the south, generally made them foreign to our interests and to the events of our history. Bérengère, born several years before the mother of Louis IX, had like her sister all that could make a great queen. First, she was heiress of Castile, then Queen of Leon and mother of several children, obliged to leave her husband and the throne, and after her parents died, protected young King Henri her brother. Removed from this role by the intrigues of her enemies, she reappeared in Castile to ensure her son Ferdinand III the crown which was his and which she scorned to carry. This son, who made an excellent prince, was canonized like his cousin the King of France; he owed much to his mother, as Saint Louis to his.

Blanche had several sisters; Urraque, was her elder by one year; she was given in marriage in 1208 to prince Alphonse of Portugal, who soon after became King; the brother of this Alphonse II, named Ferrand, Count of Flanders, is famous in our history for his revolt against Philippe Auguste, for his defeat at Bouvines, and for his long captivity, came to find himself one day in reconciliation with Blanche of Castile, his sister-in-law. One of the younger daughters of Alphonse VIII married, several years after the death of her parents, the King of Aragon, Jacques the Conqueror, who later repudiated her. Some time after, a daughter of Queen Bérengère became the wife of the King of Jerusalem, Jean de Brienne; she bore the name of her mother and preceded her into the tomb.

To Plantagenets, Blanche was as closely related as to the house of Castile; Richard Coeur-de-Lyon and Jean sans Terre [John Lackland] were her uncles, Henry III of England was her first cousin. Her aunt Mathilde had a son defeated at Bouvines, Otto of Brunswick, at first Count of Poitiers, then Holy Roman Emperor; another aunt,

Jeanne, married a second time Raimond VI, Count of Toulouse, and was the mother of Raimond VII, the last representative of the house of Saint-Gilles. Lastly, a first cousin of Alphonse VIII, Blanche of Navarre, Countess of Champagne, played a role in these states similar to that which Bérengère played in Castile and Leon; she controlled government for many years in the name of her son; thanks to her, Thibaud IV, Chansonnier, kept his heritance; he gained the throne of Navarre. Blanche of Castile and Thibaud IV were thus first cousins; this kin relationship, in default of other reasons, would sufficiently explain a mutual support in difficult times, between the young Count of Champagne and the dowager of France. [2]

The first years of Blanche are not known to us. Almost all her life passed at the court of France; she came as a strong young person and never left. In Spain she was only seven years old, when her father was vanquished by the Arabs in the bloody Battle of Alarcos (1195); he then resolved to approach his cousin Alphonse IX, King of Leon, and, for the sake of making an ally, gave him his oldest daughter, the Infanta Bérengère (1197). This union should have had for Spain the happiest consequences, but it was hardly consummated than the opposition of the papacy prevailed against the interests of Castile on a principle of which today we have trouble understanding. The King of Leon was first cousin to the father of this woman, and Pope Innocent III, severe defender of the doctrines professed by the Church, was absolutely opposed to these kinds of unions. One might obtain, with this close degree of sanguinity, exemptions for marriage, granted later, without difficulty, for the majority of those who requested it. Bérengère de Castilla, her parents and her husband, learned differently; threatened, beaten down by the agents of the pontifical court, the King and Queen of Leon refused for a few years to make the rupture that the Pope wanted to impose on them; but in 1204 they finally separated and their marriage was annulled, in spite of the children they had had, in spite of their feelings, under the contempt of more serious interests.[3] This painful fight was not finished yet, when Alphonse VIII, disappointed in the hopes he had based on the marriage of Bérengère, found for his third daughter a party of unique advantage.

The King of France, Philippe Auguste, fought against the English dynasty of Plantagenets a struggle sometimes interrupted with peace treaties or truces, but unceasingly renewed.[4] Louis VII and Henri II had bequeathed to their children this war, become inevitable because of the question whether or not Normandy and the western provinces of our country had to remain in the hands of a foreign sovereign. Suspended by the Third Crusade, hostilities renewed with violence after the return of Richard Lion-Heart, and since fought without resolution. Arrangements more or less durable were concluded with various treaties between the King of France and his adversaries, and in the negotiations they quite naturally sought to consolidate attempts at peace by matrimonial unions. In 1195 peace was made at Issoudun, and it was proposed to marry Prince Louis, heir to the throne of France, and then eight years old, with Aliénor, daughter of Geoffrey Plantagenet, sister of Arthur of Brittany, and niece of Richard.[5] Four years later, in 1199, the name of this young prince was again proposed when the two kings, whose violence resumed again, thought of disposing of them; but it was no longer a question of alliance. Richard Lion-Heart had other nieces, the daughters of his sister Aliénor, Queen of Castile; they agreed that one of these young princesses would be given to the son of Philippe Auguste, and would bring to him in dowry, along with twenty thousand marks of silver, the castle of Gisors.[6]

The execution of this project was delayed by the quite unexpected death of Richard; delivered from a frightening enemy, Philippe Auguste continued the war, seized Evreux and the surrounding country, and supported the claims of Arthur, nephew of John Lackland, brother and successor of Richard, on most of the fiefs which the Plantagenets had in France. Two truces had been concluded in 1199; the second, which dated from October and was to last until 14 January 1200, was not yet expired when John and Philippe met, shortly after Christmas, between Andely and Gaillon. In this conference, they included the project to marry Prince Louis to one of the daughters of Alphonse VIII; it was agreed that John would give to the son of Philippe Auguste, intended for his niece, the city and the county of Evreux, with all the strong places and castles that the French occupied in Normandy at the death of Richard; he promised to give him moreover thirty thousand marks of silver. The conditions of this agreement were to be carried out before Midsummer's Day, 1 July 1200.[7] The King of Castile had two unmarried girls, Urraque and Blanche, and the negotiators had not indicated which one was to reign in France. John charged his mother, Aliénor de Aquitaine, to go to seek in Spain the promised one of Prince Louis. Blanche, while waiting to be a most excellent mother and great queen, had the innocence and grace of her youth, but was brought to her new fatherland and perhaps designated for her role by her grandmother, one of the most wicked and most disreputable women of which history has left us the memory. It is said that French ambassadors sent to the court of Castile were put in the presence of the two girls to choose one for marriage with their master's son; Urraque appeared to them more beautiful, but she had too hard a name, which would not please the people of France; they preferred her younger sister Blanche.[8] Perhaps this judgment, strangely enough, and yet not unreasonable at bottom, was carried to the old Queen of England, who knew the French well, her former subjects. Perhaps Aliénor, charged to bring back a grand-daughter, was preceded or accompanied the envoys to which one entrusted the responsibility to make so important a choice. She had been able to leave France before January; she was to return to Bordeaux at the beginning of April. Aliénor and the young Blanche stopped in this city to celebrate Easter there; the following day (10 April 1200), a famous mercenary named Mercadier, come to Bordeaux to greet the Queen, was murdered by a man in the service of another *bande*. It may be that this murder made a major impression on the spirit of Aliénor; she was very old, very tired from a long voyage; she retired to the monastery of Fontevrault, and left the Archbishop of Bordeaux, Élie of Malmort, with the other people of her retinue, to bring a small girl to the King of England, then in Normandy.[9]

Peace, for the conclusion of which they had made a young princess from Castile travel a long way, was signed on 22 May 1200, on the banks of the Seine, between the castle of Boutavant, belonging to John, and that of Goulet, which belonged to Philippe Auguste; it was there that the conference took place in which the two Kings adopted their final conditions.[10] The King of England gave up the city of Évreux and the Évrecin, which Philippe seized in the previous year; in Vexin he kept only the lands at one time held by the Archbishop of Rouen, at a time when this archbishop had yielded Andely, by way of exchange with Richard Lion-Heart; all the remainder of Norman Vexin remained in the hands of the French King. John yielded to Prince Louis by virtue of giving away his niece, the fiefs of Issoudun and of Gracay, those which André de Chauvigny, Lord of Châteauroux, held in Berry from the crown of England. He still promised that, if he died without legitimate children, he would give up to Louis tenure of the fiefs that Hugues de Gournay, the counts of Aumale and Perche, held from him on the continent; but this last condition was not long in being cancelled by the birth of children that John had with his third wife, Isabelle of Angouleme. The last clause which related to the marriage of Blanche allotted to her new husband twenty thousand marks of gold.[11]

The conditions of this treaty were immediately carried out. The following day, 23 May 1200, John wrote to André de Chauvigny about conveying to the King of France the fiefs of Berry. The marriage took place the same day; they could not celebrate it on the territory of Philippe Auguste, because Innocent III, in consequence of this prince abandoning Queen Ingeburge, attached an interdict upon all of his estates. It was at Portmort, on the right bank of the Seine and within the limits of fiefs left to the King of England, that the Archbishop of Bordeaux married Louis de France and Blanca de Castilla, in front of a great number of bishops, men of the Church, French counts and barons. While Louis was on the another side of the border, John was remitted between the hands of the King of France [as a mere vassal].[12] At once afterwards, the two children whom policy came to unite, left for Paris, whose marriage was to have so great an influence on the destinies of France and England.[13]

The dowry of Blanche was assigned to her on the three *châtellenies* of Hesdin, Bapaume, and Lens.[14] That is all we know of this marriage; chroniclers and manuscripts say nothing more. Among moderns, certain authors speak of brilliant festivals celebrated at the foot of Château Gaillard, and even of a tournament in which Prince Louis seems to have been a casualty.[15] Louis was not even a teenager; born in September 1187, he was twelve and a half years old; the English chronicler who called him "a child with a happy nature" appears much more faithful to us with the truth.[16] One could add that he was blond and fair, like the family of his mother Isabelle of Hainaut, the first wife of Philippe Auguste.

His wife was a few months younger. She promised to be pretty; one or two contemporaries, while speaking about her marriage, praised her beauty. The name Blanche and the frankness of her childhood led to a play on words that one could not miss; one was consequently right to suppose that she would one day inspire faithful sentiments or great passions, but no one could guess the height of intelligence and force of spirit which time had not yet made to appear.[17] Prince Louis was a very attentive companion for his young wife from the very first days. It was at her request that Hugues,

Bishop of Lincoln, came to pay Blanche a visit on his way to Paris; the sainted man, being returned to the house where Louis had come to see him at the palace of the King, found the small princess in tears. I am unaware of the cause of this sorrow, that the consolations of Hugues were able to dissipate.[18]

Blanche had been princess of France for barely three months, when she became kin to a woman who one day became her enemy. In the month of August of the that same year, King John married Isabelle of Angoulême. To arrive at this marriage he had had to make back-to-back villainies which another would have been too ashamed of, but from which he would hardly recoil; he was then married a second time to Havoise, daughter of the Count of Gloucester; the [genetic] affinity which existed between them served as a pretext to break this union. Secondly, Isabelle was still a child, married to Hugues de Lusignan, Count de La Marche; their marriage had not yet been consummated, and Hugues held Isabelle in his guard while waiting for her to become nubile, when the Count of Angoulême ordered him to convey her to the King of England who sought her; John therefore did not hesitate to plunder one of his own vassals. The Archbishop of Bordeaux, this same Élie de Malmort who came to link Blanche of Castile to the son of the King of France, came to Angoulême to sanction by his blessing this double cowardice; Isabelle then went to England for her coronation.[19]

In the summer of 1201, her husband returned with her to France; they passed through Normandy, and from thence John went to Paris. Philippe Auguste made him the most flattering reception: he received John at Saint-Denis in solemn procession; gave him a sumptuous hospitality in the palace; it was filled with presents.[20] But at the moment when John seemed to realize the object of all his attentions, the King of France found, says one, a good opportunity to ask on behalf of Blanche of Castile for the domains located in on this side of the Andelle; they were the last remainders of Norman Vexin which remained to be stripped. The chronicler to which this account is due adds that John, not daring to resist the request of his niece, promised her, confirmed soon enough in a charter. This anecdote, if true, does not honor the generosity of Philippe Auguste.[21] What is certain, is that the marriage of Blanche hardly served her uncle and the house of Plantagenet; this union, on which he undoubtedly had hoped to restore harmony between two rival houses, did not prevent Philippe Auguste from placing in his hands, a short time after, the majority of the domains that the last son of Henri II possessed in France.

Perhaps Philippe Auguste, while inserting into his house a princess of Castile, had had a secret concern to create with the King England some new difficulties. Alphonse VIII had, in right of his wife Aliénor, claims on Gascogne;[22] he could be tempted to make him yield, and to attack John at the southernmost border of his estates; it had been for the King of France, in the event of war with England, a useful diversion. Be that as it may, John did not have the satisfaction of remaining a long time on good terms with his brother-in-law, and two years were not past since the marriage of Blanche, than they became enemies.

It is not known if the King of Castile came to a rupture by himself, or in answer to a provocation, but it was for him to resist when at the end of 1201 John approached King Sanche of Navarre. On 4 February 1202 these two princes signed in Angouleme a solemn treaty, by which Sanche promised to conclude neither peace nor truce with the Kings of Castile and Aragon, so much that they would not have given satisfaction to their ally.[23] Delayed by difficulties to the interior, Alphonse VIII took the offensive, without doubt in 1204. Either by the weapons, or in virtue of alliances concluded with the Gascon lords, he seized Saint-Sebastien, Orthez, Sauveterre, Dax, and several other strong places;[24] on 26 October of this year, he entitled the Lord of Gascogne in a charter relative to the Bishop of Dax, subscribed with the bishops of Bayonne and Bazas, the Viscount Gaston de Béarn, the Count of Armagnac, the Viscounts of Partas and Orthez.[25] The following year, Alphonse and John still disputed Gascogne;[26] in 1206 the father of Blanche came to besiege Bordeaux, and when he withdrew all the country was, says one, in his hands, with the exception of this city, Réole and Bayonne.[27]

This last assertion, which emanates from a Spanish historian, is perhaps an impressive exaggeration, but it is indubitable that England and Castile were then at war. To defend himself against this new adversary, John negotiated, in the summer of 1207, an alliance with King of Leon.[28] It is probable that this arrangement was concluded in 1208; but if John, by marrying his niece to the son of Philippe Auguste, had intended to shelter from attack his possessions on the continent, he was to be very disappointed; this alliance with Gascogne had not prevented invasion from Castilians, while Normandy and several other provinces, torn way from the

Plantagenets, passed under the heritance of Prince Louis.[29] By political needs and material interests Blanche of Castile moved away each year from the royal house of England; by giving heirs to the crown to France, she drifted into an attachment to her new family by the most powerful of affections.

Louis de France and Blanche de Castile had several children before Louis IX. It was a girl first, who appears to have been born in 1205; she lived a short while, since even her name is not known to us.[30] Four years later, on 9 September 1209, Blanche gave birth to a son, which they called Philippe in honor of his grandfather the King of France;[31] this young prince, that his elder intended for the crown, and who in 1215 was promised in marriage to the daughter of the Count of Nevers, died at the age of eight or nine years; one knows almost nothing of his short life; one mediocre versifier, to which we owe the date of his birth, said that by giving the world a son Blanche gave one lord for the French and the English; this allusion could authorize one to believe that Prince Louis then had consequent claims on the throne of the Plantagenets, but Philippe had neither time nor occasion to put them forward. When his parents carried him to Notre-Dame de Paris, the place of his burial, they had already lost two other children, born without a doubt in Lorrez-le-Bocage, in Gâtinais, on 26 January 1213; these two twins appear to have received the names Alphonse and Jean.[32]

Louis was in his majority when Blanche gave him his first son shortly before 17 May 1209, Pentecost [Whit Sunday]; his father had conferred the knighthood of Compiegne, in grand solemnity;[33] the moment had even been a territorial situation: Philippe Auguste, who did not diminish without necessity crown lands, was satisfied to give him the usufruct of the domains of Poissy, Lorris, Chateau-Landon, and some other fiefs located in Gâtinais.[34] It is true that Prince Louis had since the age of four years, as heir to his mother, Queen Isabelle de Hainaut, the nominal possession of the land of Artois: undoubtedly the King chose the moment when he became a knight to give this fief to him, which he had dismembered in 1200, by the Treaty of Péronne, the cities of Aire and Saint-Omer, restored to the Count of Flanders.[35] Louis was not late in placing a hand on this part of his maternal legacy.

The Count of Flanders [Baudouin IX], with whom had been concluded the Treaty of Péronne, and who was the brother-in-law of Philippe Auguste, had died as Emperor of the East, leaving only two daughters behind. The eldest, Jeanne, was Countess of Flanders and Hainaut, and remained, during her minority, in the guard and under the supervision of the King of France, her uncle and suzerain. Mahaut of Portugal, countess dowager of Flanders and aunt of the first wife of Philippe Auguste, used her influence to marry [Jeanne] to her nephew Ferrand of Portugal.[36] The King did not oppose this marriage, which put one of the great fiefs of the crown into the hands of a prince allied with his sister-in-law; indeed, the older sister of Blanche, Urraque de Castile, had married, in 1208, Alphonse, crown prince of Portugal, who ascended the throne about the time when his brother was established in France. Ferrand and Jeanne of Flanders were married in Paris, in the chapel of the royal palace; but it seems that Philippe Auguste, for the price of his assent, required the retrocession of Aire and Saint-Omer, not long ago removed from the fiefs which had formed the dowry of Queen Isabelle. This condition was strongly to the advantage of Prince Louis, who hastened in profiting from it. One week was not past when he appeared before Aire with an army and a siege train. It is said that, during this time, Ferrand of Portugal was retained in Péronne by order of his new cousin; it appears certain at least that he was not with Prince Louis, among whom were the Count of Saint-Pol, the Count of Ponthieu and several other barons. The bourgeois were summoned to open their gates, by calling upon the right that Louis de France held of his mother; they promised to make it when Saint-Omer would have been taken. At once this city was invested; its inhabitants, yielding to their fear, conceded and were accepted in grace. On the advice of their new lord, they increased their fortifications, and Louis, to be able to enter the city and to leave there to his liking, built a tower in the middle of the rampart, close to the gate which faced Boulogne. The Count of Flanders had to accept the accomplished fact; on 25 February 1212 he gave up forever to Prince Louis the two cities of Aire and of Saint-Omer, with their dependencies and all fiefs of the domains that Philippe Auguste had formerly held because of his marriage with Isabelle of Hainaut.[37] This event makes rather well know the character of Louis; it was decided promptly with dispatch. What is even more interesting is the singular prudence of which the King of France made proof on this occasion; to prepare for the possibility that his son would miss feudal duties, he demanded oaths of fidelity from Michel de Harnes, the chatelaine of Lons, the solicitor of Béthune, from other nobles, from mayors, aldermen and jurists of Hesdin and Aire.[38] The lords of the manor of

Aire and of Saint Omer, aldermen of Saint-Omer and Bapaume engaged the King by similar letters, in which a clause was inserted reserving the rights of Blanche of Castile, in obvious allusion to her dowry.[39]

In this business of Artois, Prince Louis acted in liaison with Philippe Auguste, and Blanche did not have occasion to put in his service the qualities of which she made proof a few years later; but she had at the court of France an important position; Pope Innocent III wrote to her at that time to recommend one of his legates.[40] In her new role, she remained faithful to her family and was made current to serious events which occurred then in Spain. Her father Alphonse VIII, formerly overcome by the Muslims, had passed long years preparing for revenge; the death of Prince Fernando, heir to the throne of Castile and younger brother of Blanche, did not stop the movement the head of which Alphonse was placed, and which involved against the infidels the majority of the Spanish Christians.[41] On 16 July 1212, the King of Castile, with the Kings of Navarre and Aragon, assisted by some French crusaders and Portuguese troops, gained a victory over the Moors, in Las Navas de Tolosa, one of those victories which change the destinies of people.

It was for the Catholic Church and for Christian Spain an immense triumph. The news spread at once throughout France. Archbishop Arnaud de Narbonne, former Abbot of Cîteaux, who had taken part in the battle, addressed to the general chapter of his order a detailed account of this memorable campaign.[42] Queen Bérengère, who for a long time lived separate from the King of Leon, had written to her sister Blanche to announce the first successes of Alphonse VIII;[43] learning of the battle, she forwarded to Blanche a letter full with pride and giving all glory to God and her father: "I inform you of joyous news; thanks to God, from whom all virtue proceeds, our King, our lord and father, overcame on the battlefield the Emir Almouménim, in what seems to me a good and great honor, since to date it is without example that a King of Morocco was defeated in a pitched battle. However, you must know that a servant of our father came in bringing the news, but I refused to believe it until I saw the official letters of the King." Bérengère told of the first combat, the preliminaries of battle, then described this great day while giving each one his share of honor. This letter, dictated in legitimate enthusiasm, reveals some exaggerations favoring the Castilians, allotting to her father a truly amazing triumph: the Arabs had lost 70,000 men and

15,000 of their women had perished; the spoils collected in their tents were inappreciable; among javelins and arrows they also took 20,000 animals. Alphonse VIII had wanted nothing for himself; he divided the loot between the King of Navarre, the King of Aragon, and their people and their other allies. Bérengère, in conclusion, requested her sister to communicate this great news to the King of France. When this letter came to Blanche, she already knew of the victory; in any case, she hastened to communicate the news to her cousin Blanche, sister of the King of Navarre and countess-dowager of Champagne.[44]

The victory which the father of Blanche had gained over the infidels was to some extent the last act of his life. Two years later (6 October 1214), he was carried off by disease at the age of 58, too early for his country, a death which threw it into disorder. Blanche of Castile did not witness his last moments. Alphonse VIII, feeling death approach, had had time to call near him Queen Aliénor his wife, and Prince Henri, who was for three years to wear the crown, Queen Bérengère and her two sons. They carried the body to the monastery of Las Huelgas, close to Burgos, of which he was the founder, and while the Archbishop of Toledo, the celebrated historian Rodrigo, gave the burial rites, the valiant and wise Bérengère gave up in front of the tomb of her father to a mortal pain. One month was not past, before Aliénor of England followed to the tomb the companion of her life (31 October 1214).[45]

The emotions and the great events followed one another *coup sur coup* in the life of Blanche; the year 1214, during which her parents died, was glorious for France, her second fatherland. John, to reconquer his French provinces, formed against Philippe Auguste a coalition, much more dangerous if he had found the means; between this coalition were two vassals of the crown. He had entirely gained to his cause one of those whom the King of France had supported, the Count of Boulogne, Renaud de Dammartin; the other one was the Count of Flanders, barely installed in the kingdom, dissatisfied and hostile. At the assembly of Soissons, convened by the King to prepare a descent on England, Ferrand of Portugal had insolently required the restitution of Aire and Saint-Omer and rejected compensation offered by the King; then he withdrew without wanting to subject himself to the obligations of feudal service;[46] a short time afterwards, he had refused to appear at Gravelines before his suzerain, and favored the invasion of Flanders by Renaud de Boulogne and the Count of Salisbury, helping to destroy part of the royal fleet; finally, on 31 May

1213, he formally allied with King John. Following this defection, the King of France had had to give up passing the sea, to launch a war in Flanders. The events which followed the treason of Ferrand are well-known; the Emperor Otto IV, nephew of John, having come to join him, France had to push back, in 1214, a double invasion. But the energy of Philippe Auguste and the valiancy of his subjects was equal to the height of danger: meanwhile, in Anjou Prince Louis inaugurated a brilliant campaign by forcing the King of England to precipitately raise the siege of Roche-au-Moine; the Emperor, the counts of Flanders, Boulogne, and Salisbury underwent in Bouvines, on July 27, 1214, an irrevocable disaster. Otto of Brunswick barely escaped; Renaud de Dammartin, who deserved death, went to finish his days in prison: Ferrand of Portugal, chained and brought back to Paris by his triumphant King, was placed in the castle of the Louvre, where he passed more than twelve years.

One may well wonder about the intimate feelings of Blanche during this war which put at odds her uncle John and Prince Louis her husband, Otto her cousin, and the King of France of whom she was daughter-in-law, at the court in which she passed her life. Ferrand of Flanders was also the brother-in-law of her sister the Queen of Portugal. No historian of that epoch took care to tell us about her feelings when she learned that the King of England and the Emperor of Germany fled before the French armies; but it is easy to guess. She knew this uncle very little; she had never seen this cousin; all her interests were in France, the throne of Philippe Auguste was for her and her children; it was her destiny, with the future of her children, decided at Bouvines and Roche-au-Moine. Without speaking about misfortunes which threatened France, the sons of Blanche would have met a sad fate if Philippe Auguste had succumbed. The affection of a princess married to a foreigner can prove for parents brought together more or less, weakens naturally by the absence; often opposed to the needs of policy, it loses its reason when duties of mother and wife come into play. With regard to John, the heart and the conscience of Blanche had to be at ease; since for fourteen years she lived in France, they had to take care to inform her about this poor wretch of a prince.

Three months before the Battle of Bouvines, Blanche of Castile had given to the house of France a new heir. On April 25, 1214, the day of Saint-Marc, she bore in the royal residence of Poissy, a son named Louis.[47] They celebrated this saint's day with the procession of Black Crosses, instituted to remember a plague under

Gregory the Great, during which he covered in black the altars and crosses. The arrival in the world of this child, who was then a junior, does not appear to have caused a great impression; hardly anyone took note, although in our time serious people claimed, based on specious reasons, that Saint Louis was born in 1215. This comes from memoirs collected, after a long time, from the piety of his admirers; they are uncertain anecdotes or even pure fabrications. Some said that this birth was due to the intervention of St. Dominique, but they forget that Blanche had one other son, and that Louis was her fifth child.[48] Others tell us that the princess, after her delivery, was made to transport out of the place where she had been confined, because she observed that to manage her repose they had ceased ringing the bells of the collegiate church of Poissy;[49] we have reluctance to believe it, the piety of Blanche having always been without exaggeration. In Poissy the infant Louis underwent baptism;[50] his parents gave him a nurse, Marie la Picarde;[51] there is no truth to the legend that Blanche was seized with jealousy after seeing her child nursed by another.

Shortly after the birth of the eventual Saint Louis, very serious circumstances provided Blanche the occasion to show that she was not only a good mother. The energy of which she made proof during the expedition of her husband to England was, for those who did not to know her yet, a true revelation.

In 1215 King John, overcome in France, scorned and hated by his own subjects, saw himself constrained to grant the Magna Carta to the English barons who were leagued against him; concessions that he made to them in this celebrated act were too humiliating for him not to seek their revocation, and to do it he relied on the Holy See. The Court of Rome, devoted to this irreligious person since the moment John declared himself its vassal in a fit of desperation, cancelled the promises that the barons had torn from him, and John, strong in this approbation, refused to carry out his Charter. The English nobility answered this act of bad faith with a formidable uprising, and this year full of disorders finished for England in the midst of a civil war during which the most outstanding event was the siege of Rochester castle, besieged by the King nearly two months; on November 30, the defenders of this place had to capitulate, although armed barons remained concentrated in London.[52] But nobles had not revolted only to seek help from a foreigner, without which their cause would be lost; this help came to them from France, and it was in Blanche of Castile that they endured it.

From the moment when they wanted to reverse King John, where he ignored the rights of his children, they had, in order to expel the dynasty of Plantagenets, to raise to the throne some other issue from Henri II. The English barons do not seem not to have thought of Emperor Otto of Brunswick, who by his mother Mathilde was nephew of their King; but another daughter of Henri II, Aliénor, had been Queen of Castile; they called to England neither her young son, King Henri I, who then occupied the throne; Alphonse VIII, nor the former queen of Leon, Bérengère, entirely absorbed by the business of Spain, nor Queen Urraque of Portugal. Blanche was closer, Prince Louis, her husband, was the natural enemy of John, and they could hope that Philippe Auguste would be brought in to support the pretensions of his son and his daughter-in-law. He had as well, at the beginning revolt, written to the English barons to encourage them and to promise as help much as he could, given the truce which existed then between England and France; he was pledged not to allow his subjects to give aid to John, and had even sent the rebels some machines of war.[53] The English barons thought that if they gave the crown to Louis, John would be abandoned by the French vassals and subjects of Philippe Auguste, who were numerous in his army.

It was undoubtedly during the siege of Rochester castle that they resolved to call the prince to England. Their ambassadors came to the court of France, charged with letters which carried seals of all the confederated English nobles. It is not certain that consequently Philippe Auguste was opposed formally to the cause in which they wanted to engage his son; but one is right to think that he could not or dared not launch such a hazardous adventure. To start it required, for surety, the handing over of a certain number of hostages who had been sent to the continent and imprisoned in Compiegne. The crown prince, not being restrained by the same obligations or same fears, accepted the throne, promised troops, and made known to his new subjects, perhaps as of this time, that he would take passage to the sea during Easter week. The first relief was joined at Hesdin, having left Calais and disembarked in England just before the capitulation of Rochester; another body arrived in London, by the Thames, at the end of February 1216. During the winter these troops were maintained, with the English barons, against Johns troops.[54]

While these events occurred in England, Innocent III excommunicated, in the Lateran Council, those who sought to cast off the throne his unworthy protégé. One has even recounted that during this time (November 30, 1215), Louis was included in the sentence pronounced against the enemies of John;[55] however it is probable that the Pope did not come to this end before he tested negotiations. By his order, a legate of the Holy See, Guala, came to find Philippe Auguste; but he failed in his mission, following two interviews with the court of the King, without declaring for his son, raised against the claims of the pontifical government, while Louis made a report to his representative about the rights of Blanche. The legate had to withdraw himself, after having requested from the King of France safe passage to England, and finally, on April 26, 1216, Louis came to Melun to request his father not oppose his project.[56] Philippe, while refusing him, because of the dangers that he envisaged, a formal approval, showed himself ready to help;[57] however a chronicler worthy of consideration mentions that he confiscated the domains of Louis and his partisans, and declared himself ready to prevail against all of them, saying that he was required to do so by the Church. This forced severity, of which the effects did not have to be quite so serious, is explained by the threats of Innocent III, who in his anger, was not content to launch anathema against Prince Louis and those who served his cause, but apparently wrote the Archbishop of Sens and his suffragans, a letter in which he declared the King of France excommunicated.[58]

Nothing permits one to believe that Blanche was tainted by the sentence which struck her husband. The prince, who could not abstain from making a plea to the Pope, sent ambassadors to the pontifical court, but did not delay his own departure; he united at Calais his flotilla and army; on May 20, 1216 he put to sea; the following day he disembarked on the island of Thanet, where soon he was joined by the majority of his vassals, whom foul weather had diverted. While John left Dover castle with the guard of the Justiciar of England Hubert de Burgh, he withdrew in front of his happy adversary, and Louis made his entry to London on May 20, 1216; his success appeared certain.[59] In Rome, they once again discussed the title of Blanche to the succession in England; the Pope that even if King John and his children had been stripped of the English succession, before passing to Blanche of Castile it would fall to a division among the niece of John, a daughter of Geoffrey Plantagenet, to Otto of Brunswick, son of his sister, King Henri of Castile, his nephew, or to Queen Bérengère, oldest daughter of Alphonse VIII and Aliénor of England. French envoys objected with reason that these heirs had not even tried to assert their rights; they could undoubtedly have added that they had not been called upon by the English barons.[60] Such a discussion, which focused on issues, was to be sterile; events spoke more powerfully: they condemned Prince Louis. When Innocent III entered the grave on July 16, 1216, one could consider the King of England as lost; three months later, Jean died, given up by all; his death, which seemed to ensure the triumph of Louis, was precisely the cause of his defeat. Those who had invited him to get rid of a hateful tyrant remembered then that he was a foreigner; little by little they joined with the oldest son of their mortal enemy, with the young Prince Henry of England. The crowning of Henry III, celebrated at Gloucester on October 28, was the prelude to a reverse after which Louis had to be constrained to give up his hopes.

Consequently, his party weakened quickly. After having a first time failed before Dover castle, he went to France, with the favor of a truce, during Lent 1217, to find his wife and ask for help from the King;[61] but Philippe Auguste, less and less willing to compromise himself, refused to discuss it.[62] The Prince however succeeded in gathering a certain number of great lords and knights, and, on March 25, took to the sea from Calais;[63] this business went from bad to worse. In this serious situation, the only help he received came to him from Blanche;[64] as from this moment she supported him in his bad fortune, with a constancy that could not be doubted. She did not let him become discouraged either by the failure of the flotilla that left Calais in May, or by the news of the defeat at Lincoln, in which the Count of Perche, lieutenant of her husband, received a mortal wound, while the Prince was for a second time that year stopped by the defense of Dover castle.[65] Louis hastened to inform his father and his wife of the disaster; the King, who could not support him openly, charged Blanche with all that related to the English adventure.[66]

In Calais, where she had gone to establish herself, Blanche did not delay to form a small body of troops, at the head of which was, with some other lords, Robert de Courtenay, and a flotilla, whose control was given to Eustache le Moine. This sailor, famous for his seamanship, was then the terror of the English. After having served King John, he had given up, in hatred of the Count de Boulogne, for attaching himself to Philippe Auguste.[67] He was the one that this prince had charged, in 1215, to bring machines of war to the barons ranged against John;[68] when the legate Guala proposed to pass the English Channel, and had asked a safe conduct from the King of

France.⁶⁹ At this time, Eustache seized the islands of Normandy.⁷⁰ We have incomplete and rather dubious information on the adventures made so long ago, but the fear he inspired and an idea of his skill are attested to in a strange poem, where he appears, in the middle of the fables and of the most singular adventures, as a man at the same time nefarious and brave, devoted to magic, a master of feints, and capable of all audacities.⁷¹

The expedition at the head of which Blanche of Castile placed him did not bring her happiness.⁷² On 24 August 1217, the flotilla left Calais, and was confronted by the English off Sandwich [Kent]. After fierce combat, the French were put to rout; Eustache, whose vessel had been taken, was decapitated. There is no agreement on the losses experienced on this unhappy day of battle intended for Prince Louis, but it is certain that it was partly destroyed.⁷³ No more help could pass to England, Henry III was triumphant, and the cause to which Blanche had devoted herself was obviously lost. The son of Philippe Auguste, hard pressed in London, accepted an honorable capitulation and returned to France.⁷⁴

The energy that Blanche demonstrated during the expedition to England struck her contemporaries, and undoubtedly she was therefore considered as a woman who would not yield anything for the maintenance of her rights and the achievement of her duties. The Ménestrel de Rheims, author of charming accounts where history blends agreeably with legend, shows her coming to ask Philippe Auguste about subsidies for Prince Louis, who was near the end of his resources. The King had remained deaf to his entreaties; he declared, "by the lance of Saint Jacques," that he wanted to provide nothing and worried about being excommunicated.

> When Madame Blanche knew this, she came before the King and said to him: "Will you thus let your son die, my lord, in a foreign country? My God, he must reign after you; send him that which he needs, at least incomes from his patrimony." – "Indeed," said the King, "Blanche, I will do nothing." – "Nothing, Sire?" – "Truly not," the King answered. – "In the name of God," said Madame Blanche, "I know well enough that I would." – "And what exactly would that be?" – "By the holy mother of God, I have beautiful children of my lord; I will pawn them and will find someone to make a loan upon them."

Then she left the King like a madwoman; and, when he saw her leave thus, he believed that she told the truth; he called to her: "Blanche, I will give you my treasure as much as you want; do what you will like with it and what you believe good; but know, in truth, that I will send to him nothing." – "Sire, said Madame Blanche, you speak well." Then the large treasure was delivered to her and she sent it to her lord.[75] True or false, this history deserves to be considered; those who lent to Blanche these proud words knew her character well.

The years which followed were quieter: with the hopes that she had been able to base on the succession in England, Blanche had seen many dangers, fatigues, and emotions, disappearing. Prince Louis had returned to his country, reconciled with the Church, which had no reason to detain him, at the moment when he saw Henry III crowned. Pope Honorius III hastened to confirm the discharge which his legate had granted to Louis when he had given up the throne of the Plantagenets, and the prince, on his side, was not long in giving to the Holy See a proof of his good intentions while going, for the second time, to make crusade in Languedoc.[76] He had already, in 1215, taken part in the war that partisans of the Church made, under pretext of heresy, with the Count de Toulouse, Raimond VI. Since then, the Lateran Council, after having stripped this unhappy prince, had allotted to Simon de Montfort most of his domains; but this spoliation had not put an end to the disorders which bloodied the Midi. When Simon was killed at Toulouse, his son Amaury found himself in a very perilous situation, and the Pope, extremely eager to save him, in 1219, towards Ascension [Holy Thursday], Prince Louis, by order of his father, set out again with many crusaders to make war against the Albigensians; he took Marmande, but failed in front of Toulouse, and withdrew for the remainder of the summer.[77] The Church could not wait for a man who had just been branded as an enemy.

As for the Princess, she seems to have remained outside affairs of state for the period which preceded death by Philippe Auguste; she was then extremely occupied by her duties as mother. At the time of the English expedition, at the end of September 1216, she had had a son to which they gave the name Robert, and who was to be one day the first Count of Artois;[78] but soon she was cruelly struck by the death of her eldest, Philippe, who was undoubtedly carried off in 1218;[79] one can only envisage what this painful event, in passing the crown to Louis IX, would be worth to France for one of its better kings. For the rest, Blanche was soon consoled by the birth of several children: Jean, born 21 July 1219; Alphonse, born on 11 November

1220; Philippe Dagobert, born 20 February 1222.[80] Jean and Philippe Dagobert were not to arrive at adolescence, but Prince Alphonse, to whom she had given the name of his grandfather the King of Castile, was reserved for higher destinies. The last children of Blanche were born after her accession; a bull of Pope Honorius III allows us to guess the concern she had on several occasions over the health of her sons: during the diseases of which they were afflicted, she had often made vows to him; because she feared not being remembered, she wrote to the Pope and obtained, by letters of 22 December 1220, the permission to make charitable works, to carry out engagements that she had been able to make in similar circumstances.[81] Though Blanche, when she held power, was not always in agreement with the clergy, nor even with the Holy See, her piety was not questioned; from time immemorial she demonstrated special devotion to the order of Citeaux, which, in 1222, accorded her the right to be associated with its prayers and good works.[82]

The events to which Blanche was most directly interested had not made her indifferent to what occurred beyond the Pyrenees, in her fatherland. In 1217 her young brother Henri I of Castile had been killed by accident, after a short and agitated reign. Become heiress upon his death, Queen Bérengère, older sister of Blanche and Henri, scorned to wear the crown, and placed it on the head of her son Ferdinand, the eldest of the children of her marriage with Alphonse IX, King of Leon.[83] After having given to the world this example of abnegation, the noble and valiant Bérengère did not cease to continue to be at the side of Ferdinand III, assisting his councils; thanks to her the King of Castile, according to a Spanish historian, could without fear devote himself to the war against the Moors, because she managed the Kingdom with wisdom and strength as no other.[84] Ferdinand, who however was a very remarkable king, and whose virtues had been worthy of the name of saint later, never ceased showing his mother the obedience of a child.[85] By reading the history of this great queen, who, after having ensured the throne to her son, controlled Castile during a struggle against the infidels, one remembers her sister Blanche quite naturally; and when one hears of this victorious king, who gave so much deference to his mother, one cannot refrain from thinking of Saint Louis.

The beginnings of Ferdinand III were not easy, and we shall see some of his subjects propose Blanche for the crown of Castile; but it does not seem that this singular and vain attempt was former to the reign of Louis VIII, and it is impossible to believe that Blanche ever supported it. What one knows of his relationship with Bérengère excludes this assumption. When in 1219 Princess Béatrix de Souabe, bestowed in marriage to the young King of Castile, passed through France to be presented in Burgos, Philippe Auguste accepted her with honor, which would not have been made, if he had regarded Ferdinand III as the rival of his children.[86] A short time after the marriage of her nephew, Blanche lost her sister, Queen Urraque of Portugal.[87] In 1221 she became the sister-in-law of Jacques I, King of Aragon, who married Princess Aliénor of Castile.[88] One is in the right to think that she did not regard this time in her life any less interesting, because she did not have then to occupy herself with public affairs. Soon she was altered by an event more important for her than all those to which she witnessed; the death of Philippe Auguste happened on 14 July 1223, making her Queen of France. Philippe Auguste had not made Louis the crown prince; he had, the first of his race, dropped this usage, in favor of the regular transmission of the royal power. Perhaps he was jealous to see a second king exerting the sovereign authority beside him; his kingdom was very powerful, his authority uncontested; the crown prince, who had age and experience, had given evidence of rather obvious energy so that no one could have tried to put himself across his path when he would have the chance to acquire the paternal succession. For this reason Louis VIII and Blanche of Castile were not invested with the royal authority before 1223. They were crowned in Rheims on 6 August, in the midst of a brilliant assembly of lords and prelates, and in the presence of Jean de Brienne, King of Jerusalem. The phial for holy oil was, according to tradition, brought to the cathedral by the Abbot of Saint-Remi, under escort of two hundred knights, and it was the Archbishop of Rheims, Guillaume de Joinville, who celebrated the ceremony. To avoid disputes between great vassals of the crown, of whom several claimed the honor to carry the royal sword during the anointing, they entrusted it to the brother of the King, Philippe Hurepel, son of Philippe Auguste and Agnes de Méranie, recognized as legitimate by the Pope while cancelling the marriage of his mother, and who was thus first prince of the blood.[89]

    Shortly after this day, finished by a sumptuous feast, the King and the queen took to the road for Paris where they made their solemn entry; they crossed, in the middle of the flowers that people threw to them, the streets of their capital, acclaimed by the festive population and by the students of the Université. When the King, and the princes who the accompanied him, had gained the royal palace, the bourgeois offered presents to him, in the midst of which was an ornate cup. Louis could not dissimulate the pleasure that he experienced in seeing himself received so brilliantly and surrounded with well-wishers. This day had to be quite merry, as much as one can judge of it by the obscure words of the poet who described it; one must regret that he was not a narrator less pretentious and more precise to tell us how the minstrel at the royal table welcomed his sovereign. The festivals lasted eight days; the King gave presents to the lords, freed serfs and gave pardons to prisoners, but his generosity did not extend to returning freedom to the counts of Flanders and Boulogne who, since the battle of Bouvines, had not left prison.[90] Blanche of Castile could not suspect when her reign started so well that it would be of very short duration, and that three years from thence she would assist, in quite painful circumstances for her and quite serious for France, with another coronation.

Louis VIII did not reign a long time, but he was a very active prince. His wife, undoubtedly happy not to put herself in front, assisted in every way; assisting the great fight with England, to whose succession the Kings of France had been transmitted the heritage. The war began again in 1224, in spite of the requests of Pope Honorius III; in answer to the claims of Henry III, who claimed the provinces removed from his father while being based on an alleged promise of the King of France, Louis VIII advanced on Poitou. He allied with the Count of La Marche, Hugues de Lusignan, who had finally married Isabelle of Angouleme, widow of King John. Niort capitulated; Savary de Mauléon, who delivered it, went to La Rochelle, which was invested on 15 July 1224 and fell on 3 August. The day before this city opened its doors, they had made in Paris a great procession, to Notre-Dame with the abbey of Saint-Anthony, to ask of the heavens a victory for the King of France. Three queens appeared in this procession, Queen Blanche, Queen Ingeburge, widow of Philippe Auguste, and the Queen of Jerusalem, Bérengère of Leon;[91] niece of Blanche and daughter of the famous princess who controlled Castile, come to marry Jean de Brienne, King of Jerusalem, who the one had brought back to France. Master now of La Rochelle, Louis VIII pushed to the Garonne and returned to triumph in Paris.

The Queen of France, satisfied with a modest role, exerted upon her husband an influence of no small account. Honorius III knew it, when he requested her to intervene with Louis VIII in favor of Robert de Courtenay, Emperor of the East.[92] The house of France, to which Robert belonged, could not be indifferent to the dangers which by its origin a very French empire ran. The Pope certainly had recourse to Blanche when he requested the delivery of the Count of Flanders.

Since the Battle of Bouvines, Ferrand of Portugal was prisoner in the Louvre, where the intercessions of Innocent III and Honorius had not been able to secure his release.[93] His wife, Jeanne the Countess of Flanders, was however cousin of Louis VIII; he had as a sister-in-law the Queen of Portugal, sister of Blanche. The Queen of France, for whose relations the family was crowned, linked her authority with those of the Pope and the cardinals, and thanks to their combined efforts that is; in April 1226 the unhappy Count finally had hopes of freedom. The King promised Jeanne to deliver him by Christmas for a ransom of 25,000 *livres parisis* [pounds] whose payment was to be guaranteed by temporary transfer of several cities; serious precautions were taken to guarantee the fidelity of Count Ferrand.[94]

At the same time Jeanne promised, in the presence of the King and of Cardinal Romain, legate of the Holy See, to again marry Ferrand before the next Fête des Rameaux [Sunday before Easter]; for want of that, the King was to be free of engagements to which he had just subscribed.[95] This bizarre act is likely to make one believe that the countess had not always had a sincere devotion for her husband; it was rumored that they had had annoying quarrels in the first times of their marriage, and later the Count, hardly liberated from prison,[96] had a care to abolish all the gifts that the countess had made during his captivity.[97] He even alleged that Count Pierre of Brittany, having formed the ambitious project to marry Jeanne, had obtained from Honorius III letters cancelling the marriage of this princess and Ferrand; this intrigue, by causing the indignation of the King, would have determined the freedom of this prisoner.[98] Such singular allegations should not be accommodated with other than an extreme reserve; Ferrand had hardly expiated his faults, and Blanche, in working for him, made a good work. Whom she had drawn from prison was one day a devoted ally.

Since his succession, Louis VIII confined himself to solve problems which were posed during the life of his father. The heritage of Philippe Auguste was heavy to carry; it was not a sinecure to succeed this great King who had undertaken so many things. The English, though overcome, were always to fear; all the provinces of the South continued to be agitated; the royal authority, in spite of its astonishing progress, still met resistances; in similar economic situations, it is not probable that the King of France seriously thought to launch, apart from his states, new conquests. His expedition to England had taught to him how hazardous it was to seek a foreign crown, even one offered by large and powerful party; also it is difficult to believe that he ever had a serious claim on Castile, in spite of the call which was sent to him in last months of his life.

Some noble Castilians, not very concerned to obey Ferdinand III, remembered or claimed to know that Alphonse VIII had made on his deathbed a declaration by which he cancelled possible rights of his daughter Bérengère. Envisaging the case where her son Henri might suddenly die without heir, he had, said one, decided that Blanche and her children were to assume the succession to the detriment of the former queen of Leon. This assertion, impossible to verify, appears quite suspect: he wanted to thus destroy the hopes of his oldest daughter, Alphonse VIII showing a poor policy, since it was to prevent the union of Castile and Leon, intended to pass one day to his grandson Ferdinand III; he would have been thus acting in bad faith towards Bérengère, who was very devoted to him; she was present at his last moments and showed at the time of his funeral a touching sadness. Be that as it may, a Castilian baron, Rodrigo Diaz of los Cameros, with some of his kinsmen and friends, informed Louis VIII of this real or supposed substitution and declared himself ready to recognize the rights of Blanche. The King of France appears to have asked Rodrigo Diaz and his partisans for sealed letters, which were sent to him, and whose originals were preserved with the Trésor des Chartes [royal archives]. In these acts, which are nine in number, the dissatisfied Rodrigo Diaz and followers declare themselves vassals of Louis, by the grace of God King of France, of the famous Queen Blanche and their children, their very excellent seigneurs; ready to face death for their cause, they affirm to have heard the declaration of Alphonse VIII. Not wanting to expose to dishonor to leave on the throne a foreigner when the legitimate heir was displaced, they addressed the King and begged on bended knees to send his son to them, that they would make Castile and Tolèdo under his reign.[99] It is quite probable that Louis VIII neither had the time nor the will to take seriously the devotion of these unexpected servants; in any case

Queen Blanche, clear-sighted and practical woman that she was, aspired neither for herself nor for her children the crown of Castille. Those who knew little about her heart and her intelligence sometimes reproached her, and that is what the poet Sordel did later, when, in a famous satire, he put Louis IX in the number of those who, to give courage, might have divided the heart of the valorous Blanca: "He also eats, the King of France, and he recovers Castile and loses it by silliness; but if that displeases his mother, he will not eat; who knows it well knows that he does nothing without her."[100]

Instead of desiring all the Kingdoms in Spain, Louis VII prepared to return under his authority all Languedoc. The man who came, on behalf of the Holy See, to push this project, played beside Blanche a very important role: Romain Frangipani, cardinal deacon of Saint-Ange, issue of a noble family, and likewise, so it was claimed, a distant relative of Louis VIII, an adviser who was going to be paid close attention to, a close collaborator.[101] By naming him, in the month of February 1225, legate in France and in the Kingdom of Arles, Honorius III was especially interested in destroying heresy in valley of the Rhone and on the edges of the Garonne; but the action of apostolic legates was always complex; beside the business which constituted the main object of his mission, the powerful individual representing Rome generally invested capacities of great extent, to have the eye on many things which interested the Church: questions of discipline and of ecclesiastic administration, favors and exemptions granted to laymen, canonical complaints against members of the clergy and against civil society, re-establishment of peace among sovereigns. It was thus that Romain, newly arrived in France, intervened once more, in the name of the Pope, in favor of the young King of England; it is true that Louis, engaged to restore domains once conquered by the Plantagenets, did not hold large account of this desire; encouraged by the King of Jerusalem, Jean de Brienne, he answered that he would keep all of the heritage of Philippe Auguste and would give up not a foot of ground.[102]

From Touraine, where he had been to find the King of France at the end of June, the legate returned to Paris, and, on his first stay in this city, had become the adversary of the Université, which was to return later in a fight with him and to continue its hatred of him. [103] This body already so important had the right to seal acts, in spite of the prerogatives which belonged to the chapter of Notre-Dame; chosen for referee, Romain broke the seals, defended, under pain of excommunication, in never doing another, and rescinded a privilege that the Masters of the Université had presented to them. At once a riot burst out; schoolboys, armed with swords and clubs, went to attack the house of the legate; blood ran, and the King, just returned from Melun, arrived in time to release by force of arms the representative of the Holy See. Romain fled Paris and excommunicated his attackers; at the end of the year, a great number of masters who had, following this annoying business, incurred canonical sentences, came to council at Bourges to ask to the legate for a discharge and they obtained it.[104]

It was a poor beginning; but in the business of the Albigensians the legate obtained all that he wanted. The Council of Bourges, that opened on 30 November 1225, opposed an end of accepting protests and the professions of faith from the Count of Toulouse, Raimond VII, and declared a crusade was needed to exterminate heresy, expressing the wish that it be directed by the King, and granted a ten-per-cent tax intended to provide for the expenses of holy war. By learning of these decisions, Honorius III promised to recognize all territory that this King could conquer from the Albigensians, and to guarantee to him throughout the war all domains in his possession. Encouraged by the legate, by his barons, by the bishops, Louis took the cross on 30 January 1226; he engaged to leave after Easter and to prolong the fight according to necessity for seven years; the cardinal, several bishops, and the chapters promised subsidies, during which time Honorius III admonished the King of England not to molest a crusading prince, and to support his cousin the Count of Toulouse; at the same time, Jacques I of Aragon returned to Barcelona prohibiting his subjects from giving protection to the heretics. Louis VIII, assisted with so many resources and supported by such good dispositions marched on 17 May.[105]

The Queen was resolved to this new separation; it is probable that she did it willingly; she had too much intelligence and experience to know that in a situation like hers personal feelings must pass only after reasons of state.[106] However she was to regret the departure of Louis VIII, with which she shared a faithful affection. The King left her to care for his many children: Louis, become heir to the crown by of death his brother Philippe, Robert, Jean, Alphonse, Philippe Dagobert, all five born before their parents were on the throne; others had been born since: Isabelle mentioned in the will of her father, dated June 1225; was spoken of; a sixth son, Etienne, was born in Paris in

1225, and raised on the font by the legate of the Holy See;[107] if this child lived, then one must change to eight the number of those whom Blanche had raised by the time she became a widow. A text, which is worthy of confidence, seems to indicate that Charles Anjou, the last of all, was born at the end of March 1227;[108] it would thus have been posthumous, if one believes that Louis left his wife before 17 May 1226, the date on which he left Bourges for his last campaign. As of the previous June, Louis had regulated by a will the fate of those that he left behind.[109] The eldest of his sons, intended to succeed to him, was to have at his disposal, for the defense of the Kingdom, the treasure preserved in the tower of the Louvre. The second son was to receive the fief of Artois, and all the land that he [Louis] took from Isabelle de Hainaut, with the reserve of the dowry of Blanche, except a clause of reversibility to the crown failing the male heirs; it was the share which later fell to Robert of Artois. The third son was to have Anjou and Maine, which seemed thus reserved for Jean, but the untimely death of this young prince gave it to Charles d'Anjou, the name under which it is known. The fourth son of the King, who then was Alphonse, received by the will of his father Poitou and the Auvergne. The fifth and younger brothers were intended to become clerics. The King still stipulated that failing his heirs the prerogative of his brother Philippe would give him the crown; he bequeathed to Blanche thirty thousand *livres*, and twenty thousand to his daughter Isabelle.

     From Bourges, where he had joined together his troops, the King gained Nevers, Lyon, and passed on the left bank of the Rhone. Arrived in the first days of June before Avignon, which was then under the Holy Roman Empire, he was constrained to undertake a siege. While under the walls of this place, whose resistance lasted nearly two months, the royal army received in one of the greatest lords of France a dangerous example. The Count of Champagne, Thibaud IV, had joined the besiegers a few days after the investment; a close relative of the Queen, allied to the King by his wife Agnes de Beaujeu, it seemed that this powerful baron, more than any other, brought to the joint undertaking an active and devoted contest. However, at the end of forty days, having satisfied strict obligations, which fell on to him because of feudal homage, he announced to Louis that he had an intention to withdraw. It was later said, that having intelligences in Avignon, he had in vain tried to convince his sovereign to raise the siege, and that irritated by the reproaches of the

King he decided to leave. Three days later he suddenly departed in the night, under a disguise; he was quickly followed by his knights.[110] This defection, whatever may have been the motives or incidents, was insulting to Louis VIII, who was made indignant at it; the conduct of the Count of Champagne, severely judged, attracted accusations that were as strange as they were libelous, to which the name Blanche of Castile was odiously attached. Such an act of disobedience showed how little the King could Count on his great vassals; one author claims that during this same campaign the Count de Bretagne, the Count de La Marche and several others, agreed with Thibaud de Champagne, to support the Avignonnaise and the Count of Toulouse, and formed a true conspiracy, whose secrecy was revealed by the dying Count of Namur; the son of Philippe Auguste was strong enough to contain them.[111] After the capitulation of Avignon, which fell at the end of August, the war was vigorously pursued; the royal army advanced to within four miles of Toulouse, and when the King returned, leaving behind a body under the orders of Imbert de Beaujeu, almost all of Languedoc had made submission.[112]

It was the last success of Louis VIII; in making progress against the English, whom his father had despoiled, profiting royalty by lowering the house of Toulouse, he was a worthy successor to Philippe Auguste, and whom the French formerly and for a long time called Philippe the Conqueror. Arrived at Montpensier, Louis acquired, on 29 October 1226, a case of dysentery and a fever so serious, that without delay he was given, in forecast of a catastrophe, last rites.[113] Seeing that he would cease to live before the arrival of the Queen, and fearing the dangers to which the dynasty was going to be exposed, he brought together the archbishops, the bishops, the barons, and the knights who surrounded him, and made them promise without delay, after he died, to Louis, his oldest son, to lend faith and homage to him, and to crown him as soon as possible. They engaged, moreover, to make for Robert, second son of the King, if the crown prince suddenly died, that which they had promised to make for his older brother.[114] In these supreme moments, the confidence that the King had never ceased to have in his wife inspired him to ensure the safety of his family and monarchy. He declared that Prince Louis, destined to succeed him, "as well as the kingdom and his other sons," would be under the supervision of Queen Blanche, and that she would exert this function until the majority of her children. The Archbishop of Sens, the bishops of Chartres and Beauvais, notified, by an act that we still have, this important decision of their master.[115]

The King still recommended his son to Mathieu, Constable of Montmorency, of which the name, for an unknown reason, is not in the acts where the other witnesses of his last moments appear; "he requested to take his child in guard, and Mathieu promised it while crying." Jean de Nesle gave him the same insurance, as well as the chancellor, Guerin, the valiant and faithful Bishop of Senlis, who was mad with grief.[116] During this short disease, which hardly lasted more than one week, Louis sent new expeditions into Languedoc, and recommended to those people who had remained in this country to hold firm and to defend well the authority of his son.[117]

It was on 8 November 1226, or the night before, that Blanche of Castile became widowed.[118] The death of a man she had so valiantly supported in the fights of his life experienced a dreadful misfortune. In addition to qualities derived from his race, and which came to make of him an excellent king, he had a pleasant character and a faithful heart: "He was of beautiful appearance, though of intermediate size; his face was calm, his complexion fair; he was not annoyed with the inconsiderate, but then he would suffer to alleviate it; he was devoted neither to luxury, nor to drink, nor to vice; his wife was enough for him."[119] Several historians spoke about the love that he had for Blanche: "They were so attached the one with the other, that they were always seen agreement, and never did a queen love her seigneur so much."[120] The author of the verse chronicle from which are borrowed these expressions recalls, in more than one place, the affection that Louis VIII and Queen Blanche had for their children; as for the marital fidelity for which several of his contemporaries honor him, the King gave, some say a few days before its death, a singular proof; the trait, however strange that it appears, merits reporting. Archambaud of Bourbon, who was near him, said that sex with a woman could attenuate the violence of the evil to which he succumbed, and sought out a pretty girl of good family. She came to offer herself to the King, by explaining to him that she gave herself to him not because of the pleasure that she could bring, but to cure his disease. While Louis slumbered, in full day, she was introduced next to him. The King, awaking, asked her who she was, how she had entered; but on learning why she had come, he thanked her and said to her: "I do not have need for you, my daughter; for no price would I like to make a mortal sin." Then he called for Lord Bourbon, and ordered him to marry her.[121]

The sudden death, almost unexplainable, of this man who, who some days before, marched at the head of an army and whose disappearance could benefit many people, gave rise to sinister legends. Some did not fail to say that Louis VIII had been poisoned, and when one wanted to find the author of this claimed crime, it was not necessary to seek very far. The suspicions went naturally to Count Thibaud de Champagne, who was so badly disposed towards his suzerain and was to fear his anger; he was shown to be not very faithful and of relatively scant devotion; the credulity of some, and the ill will of others, gave him a reputation of an assassin.[122] This was a hateful invention, and yet it found credit, especially during the time when Thibaud, become at the same time the defender and protégé of Blanche of Castile, exposed to the hatred of almost all the great vassals. Then there was the rumor that he had been, during the life of Louis VIII, the lover of the Queen, and that this passion, which his poetry made it possible to believe, had pushed him to crime. The English had care to spread this miserable legend, thinking of harming the reputation of an enemy which made them afraid; but all the filth that was thrown on him failed to sully him. Regarding the Count of Champagne, one has extremely judiciously remarked that the effect of poison was quite slow, if administered before Avignon at the end of July it had not killed their man before 7 or 8 November.[123] He was, in reality, strongly above similar allegations, and was certainly the opinion of Louis IX, the day when he gave one of his daughters in marriage to the son of Thibaud Chansonnier.

It was to be some time before some thought of hating Blanche; for the moment, one could only pity. The servants and companions in arms of Louis VIII placed his body on a litter and brought back it to Paris. On her side, the Queen, who did not suspect anything, was put en route with her children, traveling by wagon, to join the King; little Prince Louis rode in front. Chancellor Guerin, left first to announce to his sovereign what was to arrive, met her and made her turn around. When Blanche learned the fatal news, her pain was so violent that many believed her liable to commit suicide; it was a sad return: the brother of the King, Philippe Hurepel, was inconsolable, and the Queen cried so much that her people were very concerned.[124]

The King was buried beside his father, in Saint-Denis, and it was Gautier, Archbishop of Sens, who officiated at the funeral. During this sad ceremony, the Countess Jeanne of Flanders, niece of Philippe Auguste, was remarkable for her tears.[125] It is certain that around the tomb where Louis had just been buried, many friends and servants testified very sincere regrets. Others, free to give vent to their secret joy and unhealthy hopes, hastened to forget that Blanche of Castile was widowed and her children orphaned.

1   Fierez, *Memorias de las reynas catholicas*, t. I. Madrid, 1790, in-8°, p. 411 ; Schirrmacher, *Geschichte Castiliens im 12. und 13. Jahrhundert*, in-8°, p. 686. The date to which one attributes the birth of Blanche is given in a charter of Elvire, governess of her elder sister the *infanta* Bérengère : *Acta Sanctorum*, May, t. VII, commentary of P. Papebrock on Saint Ferdinand, p. Ml, col. 1.

Several authors have refuted the opinion that Blanche had been the eldest daughter of Alphonse VIII : Le Nain de Tillemont, *Histoire de saint Louis*, I, 156-157; Florez, Memorias, I, 400-403; Schirrmacher, *Geschichte Castiliens*, 681-689. Blanche was the third daughter of Alphonse; a charter proves that Urraque was the second ; as for Bérengère, the most authoritative contemporary historians give her the title of elder : Rodrigue de Tolède, *Acta Sanctorum*, May, t. VII, p. 313, col. 1 (I cite designedly so, when I can, this partial edition of Rodrigue, which is easy to find); Luc de Tuy, in Schott, *Hispaniæ illustratæ auctores varii*, IV, p. 77 (corrigez 107) and p. 112; Aubry de Trois-Fontaines, *Monumenta Germaniæ historica*, scriptores, XXIII, p. 895; Roger de Wendover, ed. Hewlett, II, 188, and Mathieu de Paris. *Chronica majora*, ed. Luard, II, 660. It is probable that Bérengère was born a little before January 1178 (Schirrmacher , p. 684); Urraque is named for the first time in a charter of 28 May 1187 (Id., 686).

For the history of Alphonse VIII , see *Memorias historicas de la vida y acciones del rey D. Alonso el Noble*, by the Marquis de Mondexar, in-4°, Madrid, 1783, and the history of Castile by Schirrmacher. Florez made a knowledgable panegyric to Queen Aliéner, mother of Blanche (*Memorias*, t. I).

2 Aubry de Trois-Fontaines, *Monmenta Germanæ*, XXIII, 837.

3 Schirrmacher, *Geschichte Castiliens*, 264-266, 273-274; Florez, *Memorias*, I, 349-376.

4 In the first chapter, I tried to speak, in diverse passages, of Philippe Auguste and of Louis VIII; I de so from necessity, freeing others to recount the history, with a competence beyond mine, the reigns of these two princes. I realize that the history of Philippe Auguste has been thoroughly treated by Achille Luchairo; as for the history of Louis VIII, by Petit-Dutaillis, this was finished before the *History of Blanche of Castile*; I direct the reader to these two works, whose knowledge would certainly have been a great help to me, if I had been able to consult them before the completion of this book.

5   Le Nain de Tillemont, *Histoire de saint Louis*, t. I., p. 5.

6   Roger of Hovedon [d. 1201], ed. William Stubbs (collection of the Rolls Series), IV, 80-81.

7   Roger of Hovedon (IV, 97) indicates 14 January 1200 as the final term of the second truce concluded between King John and Philippe Auguste; see, on this truce, the report of Kigord (ed. Delaborde, p. 110, n. 129). It was doubtless at the expiration, or a little before, that the two Kings fell out (Roger, IV, 106-107).

8   Florez, *Memorias de las reynas catholicas*, I, 412-413, after the *Chronica*

General de Castile ; Mondexar, *Memorias, etc., d'Alonso el Noble*, 239-240; Nostradamus (*Histoire de Provence*, p. 19C) admits this anecdote, which Le Nain de Tillemont (I, 6) refuses to take seriously.

9 Roger of Hoveden, IV, 114; Le Nain de Tillemont, I. p. 6 and 7.

10 Le Nain de Tillemont (I, p. 7) allows a date of 22 May. Roger de Hoveden (IV, 114-115) is correct, when he says that in 1200, 22 May was a Monday, and the 23rd, the wedding day of Blanche, a Tuesday. In reporting that the two kings collided « *in octavis nativitatis Sancti Johannis Baptistæ* », on 1 July, he says without doubt, the negotiations ended before this date, at the time of the interview which took place in January; the expression « *infra octavas* » had been more correct. Following Rigord (ed. Delaborde, p. 148, n. 132), the peace was made « *mense maie, in Ascensione Domini* », which indicates 18 May; without a doubt, he designated the week of Ascension, rather than the very same day of this festival. The text of the Treaty of Goulet was not given a date other than that of the month of May 1200 (*Layettes du Trésor des Chartes*, I, n. 578), but on 23 May, King John wrote to André de Chauvigny from the castle of Andeley to inform him about an article of the treaty which concerned de Chauvigny.

It is Roger of Hovenden who tells us the exact location of this interview; the terms employed by Rigoud are more imprecise; they do not contradict those of the English historian; Roger: « *inter Butavant, castellum regis Angliæ, and Guletun, castellum regis Franciæ* » ; Rigoud: « *inter Vernonem and insulam Andeliaci.* »

11 A copy of the treaty, in the name of King John, was given to the King of France (*Layettes du Trésor des Chartes*, I, n. 578) ; another, in the name of Philippe Auguste, was intended for the King of England (Kymer, ed. of 1816, I, p. 79). See the bibliographical indications relating to the Treaty of Goulet and the various parts which relate to it, in the catalog of the acts of Philippe Auguste by Léopold Delisle, articles 604 to 615 (615; 23 May 1200, notification of the treaty, made by Jean sans Terre to André de Chauvigny). One will have to also consult, on this subject, the *Atlas historique de la France* of Longnon and the explanatory text (p. 231-232).

The conditions adopted in the Treaty of Goulet were reported in an extremely incorrect manner by several authors; one says that Auvergne and Berry were ceded to Philippe Auguste : *Chronica Johannis de Oxenedes* (ed. Ellis, Master of the Rolls), p. 110; *Radulphi de Diceto Ymagines historiarum* (same collection), II, p. 168. Others, with Rigord, affirm that John promised, if he died without legitimate children, to abandon to Prince Louis all the domains of France : Rigord (ed. Delaborde, p. 148, n. 132); *Les Grandes chroniques de France* (*Historiens de France*, XVII, 387); Guillaume de Nangis (*Chronique*, ed. Géraud, I, p. 113); Nicolas Trivet (Achery, *Spicilegium*, in-f°, 111, 179). Le Nain de Tillemont (I, p. 8) has refuted this error.

12 *Hist. des ducs de Normandie and des rois Angleterre* (*Soc. de l'histoire de France*), p. 91.

13 Roger de Hoveden, IV, p. 115. Les annales de Waverley (*Annales monastici*, ed. Luard, II, 252) recount that the marriage took place in Rouen.

14   See what I say about this dowry at the commencement of chapter VII.

15   Lecointre-Dupont, *Jean sans Terre*, etc. (*Mémoires de la Soc. des Antiquaires de l'Ouest*, XII, 1845), p. 122-123; Doinel, *Histoire de Blanche de Castilie*, p. 19-21.

16   *Chronica Johannis de Oxenedes*, ed. Ellis, p. 110.

17   *Anonymi continuatio appendicis Roberti de Monte* (*Historiens de France*, XVIII, 341); *Historia rerum Francorum* (same report, XVII, 426) : Gilles de Paris, *Carolinus* (same report, XVII, 292); *Annales Marchionenses* (*Monumenta Germaniae*, scriptores, XVI, 616).

18   Rev. James F. Dimock, *Magna vita S. Hugonis* (collection of the Master of Rolls), p. 305. I must note the citation of this text to the graciousness of Petit-Dutaillis.

19   Roger of Hoveden IV, 119-120; Rigord (ed. Dolaborde), p. 153, n. 138.

20   Roger, IV, 164; Rigord, n. 135; *Chronicon Turonense* (*Historiens de France*, XVIII, 295) ; *Addenda chronico Andegavensi S. Albini*, ibid., 328.

21   *Histoire des ducs de Normandie and des rois d'Angleterre* (*Soc. de l'histoire de France*), p. 91.

22   Mathieu de Paris, *Chronica majora*, ed. Luard, V, 658.

23   Rymer, ed. of 1816, I, 86. See, at page 85, the pieces relative to the preparation of this alliance (14 October and 24 November 1201).

24   Luc de Tuy, in Schott, *Hispaniæ illustratæ scriptores varii*, IV, p. 109; Pierre de Marca, *Histoire de Béarn*, p. 506.

25   Marca, p. 507, col. 2; 26 October 1204.

26   Marca, p. 505; 1205.

27   *Ex chronico Burdegalensi Sanctæ Columbæ* (*Historiens de France*, XVIII, 245); Rodrigue de Tolède, book VII, ch. 34, in Schott, t. II, p. 128. The Abbé Monlezun, in his *Histoire de la Gascogne*, t. II, p. 249, considered the assertions of Rodrigue on this point to be exaggerated.

28   Rymer (1810), I, 96; 7 August 1207.

29   Rymer, p. 100; 8 March 1208 : John delivered a sfae conduct to the *chancelier* from the King of Castile. See Schirrmacher, *Geschichte Castiliens*, p. 274-275.

30   Scévole and Louis de Sainte-Marthe, *Histoire Généalogique de la maison de*

France, I, 510. It is certain that Blanche had an infant before Prince Philippe, in the manner indicated in verse of which we speak lower down (*iterato nomine matris*). A Flemish chronicle says that Louis VIII had two daughters, of which one died young (*Chronijke van Nederlant van den jaere 1021 tot den jaere 1525*, publiée dans la *Collection de chroniques belges*, parmi les *Chroniques de Brabant and de Flandre*, par M. Piot, 1879, p. 10-11).

31   Six verses, transcribed in the *Premier registre de Philippe Auguste* (heliotype reproduction published by Léopold Delisle, Paris, 1883, f° 93 verso), indicated the day of birth; published by Jean Besly (see *Archives historiques du Poitou*, IX, 1880, p. 6-7) and by Sainte-Marthe (*Histoire géneologique de la maison de France*), who has devoted a dissertation to the elder children of Blanche, (ibid., I, p. 511-512).

Several writers speak of the young prince : *Historia regum Francorum ab origine gentis ad annum 1214* (*Historiens de France*, XVII, 427); *Abbreviationes Gestorum Franciæ regum*, ibid., XVII, 433 ; *Fragmenta chronicorum comitum Pictaviæ and Aquitaniæ ducum*, same rec., XVIII, 244; *Fragmentum de vita Ludovici VIII* (Du Chesne, *Scriptores*, V, p. 289); Philippe Mousket, verse 24249-50; *Récits un ménestrel de Reims*, n. 308. Aubry de Trois-Fontaines (*Monumenta Germaniæ*, XXIII, p. 902) reports the betrothal with Agnès, daughter of the Comte de Nevers; on this subject see the papers by Du Chesne, in his *Histoire de la maison de Châtillon*, preuves, p. 40-41. Guillaume le Breton (ed. Delaborde, *Philippide*, livre X, verse 95-98) says that in 1214 King John had obtained the hand of Agnès for his son.

Philippe died in 1218 and was enterred at Notre Dame de Paris (Sainte-Marthe, *Maison de France*, p. 512).

32   Chronique de Bernard Iticr (*Historiens de France*, XVIII, 231 a), and *Chronique de S. Marital de Limoges*, published by Duplès-Agier (*Soc. de l'histoire de France*), p. 86. See, on the subject of these twins, their epitaph and their names : Du Chesne, *Hist. Francorum scriptores*, V, 442; Sainte-Marthe, *Histoire géneologique de la maison de France*, I, 505; Du Cange, *Glossaire*, on the word *Bustum* ; Le Nain de Tillemont, I, 421. This is a problem that I propose to resolve one day.

33   Guillaume le Breton, ed. Delaborde, p. 226, n. 149; Roger of Wendover, II, 50; Jean Ypres, *Historiens de France*, XVIII, 603 a.

34   Le Nain de Tillemont, t. I, p. 11.

35   Idem, p. 12 etc. Longnon, *Atlas historique de la France*, planche XII, and explanatory text joined to this atlas, p. 230-231.

36   *Genealogia comitum Flandriæ, Monumenta Germaniæ*, scriptores, IX, 330; Meyer, *Commentarii sive annales rerum Flandricarum*, Anvers, 1561, liv. VIII, f 64 V; 1211.

37   *Genealogia comitum Flandriæ*; *Willelmi chronica Andrensis* (*Monumenta Germaniæ*, scriptores, XXIV, 754); Meyer, fol. 64; Chronicle after Baudouin

Avesnos (*Mon. Germ.*, XXV, 419). It was then that Prince Louis confirmed privileges and customs of Saint-Omer (*Musée des archives départementales*, p. 109, and planche XXVIII).

38   *Layettes du Trésor des Chartes*, I , no. 982 to 987; *Catalogue des actes de Philippe Auguste*, 1353-1354, 1355-1358.

39   *Layettes*, I, 1004-1007; Léopold Delisle, *Catalogue des actes de Philippe Auguste*, 1359-1362.

40   Potthast, *Regesta pontificum Romanorum*, 4712; 19 April 1213.

41   14 October 1211.

42   Ughelli, *Italia sacra*, 2nd edition, I, 164; *Galia christiana*, VI, proofs, col. 53; *Historiens de France*, XIX, 250.

43   « *Sicut vice alia mandavi vobis.* » *Historiens de France*, XIX, 254.

44   Letters of Bérengère and Blanche on the Battle of Las Navas de Tolosa have been published several times; see, among others, *Recueil de Historiens de France*, XIX, 201 and 255. In the address of her letter to Blanche de Navarre, Blanche de Castile titled herself *reine de France*. One knows that the title of *reine* was generally carried, in Spain, by the daughters of the King. See, in this regard, what Guillaume le Breton said about the Comtesse Mahaut de Flandre, daughter of the King of Portugal, who called herself queen (ed. Delaborde, p. 295, n. 202).

45   Schirrmacher, *Geschichte Castillens*, 320-322.

46   April 1213 : Guillaume le Breton, ed. Delaborde, n. 165, p. 245; see, what follows, in this same edition, notes on pages 249, 250, 260, 263 and 264.

47   Many have written on the birth of Saint Louis; I believe with de Wailly, that this event took place on 25 April 1214, and not in 1215; I will not repeat here the arguments made by the illustrious savant in his *Mémoire sur la date and le lieu de naissance de saint Louis (Mémoires de theAcadémie des Inscriptions*, t. XXVI, 1 partie, 1867, p. 173-202); with texts enumerated and discussed by de Wailly joining together a new testimony, that Léopold Delisle agreed to supply us; this is a passage from annals written in Flanders in the thirteenth century: « *MCCXIIII. Loéis li flux Loéis fu nés. Li rois Phelippes venqui la bataille à Bovines contre Ferrant.* » Bibliothèque nationale, ms. français 6447, fol. 8 V, col. 1.

I propose to summarize soon, in a special report, what we know today about the children of Blanche of Castile and the dates of their births.

48   The Bollandistes have refuted this error : *Acta Sanctorum*, Aug., t. V, p. 284, *b*.

49   Pierre Mathieu, *Histoire de saint Louys*, 1618, p. 14, and other authors, report this anecdote, the origin of which I am ignorant.

50   Geoffroy de Beaulieu, *Historiens de France*, XX, 19-20.

51   It was Huillard-Bréholles who has rediscovered the name of this woman; note on the *Lieu de la naissance de saint Louis* (*Bulletin de la Société des Antiquaires de France*, 1859, p. 174-177); see memoir written in 1867 by de Wailly, p. 202, note.

52   The principal events of the civil war which afflicted England from 1215 to 1217 were summarized by Le Nain de Tillemont in his *Histoire de saint Louis*, t. I, preliminaries, ch. V to XII, p. 21 to 52. The castle of Rochester was besieged by King John from October 11 to 30 November 1215. I forced myself to speak as little as possible about the expedition in which Prince Louis failed to capture England, wanting by no means to cover a subject which only indirectly interests the history of Blanche de Castile. I extremely regret not having been able to consult, for the drafting of these pages the history of Louis VIII, by Petit-Dutaillis, currently in the course of publication.

53   Raoul de Coggeshall, ed. Stevenson (collection of the Master of Rolls), p. 173.

54   It is after having recounted the investment of Rochester castle that the *Histoire des ducs de Normandie and les rois d'Angleterre* (from the *Société de l'histoire de France*, p. 160) speaks of the first negotiations between Prince Louis and the English barons. This same chronicle (p. 161 and 162) gives details on the two bodies of troops sent by Louis to England. Raoul de Coggeshall (ed. Stevenson, p. 176) said that the first of these relief troops landed during the siege of Rochester.

The negotiations between Louis and the barons have been recounted by Roger of Wendover (collection of the Master of Rolls, t. II, p. 17'2-176) and, after him, by Mathieu de Paris (same collection, ed. Luard, t. II, p. 646-650). These two authors (Roger, t. II, p. 176; Mathieu, t. II, p. 680), and the *Histoire des ducs de Normandie* (p. 160) report that Louis promised to find himself in Calais around Easter. Roger of Wendover, of which the text is reproduced by Mathieu de Paris, said that the *châtelains* of Saint-Omer and Arras, and others with them, arrived in London via the Thames, 28 February 1216. This sending of reinforcements must undoubtedly be identified with that about which they speak of in the *Histoire des ducs de Normandie*.

Guillaume le Breton (ed. Delaborde, p. 305) said that, from the first, Philippe Auguste was opposed to projects of his son : « *patre suo penitus dissentiente.* »

55   Following the chronicle titled *Flores historiarum* (collection of the Master of Rolls, ed. Luard, 1890, t. II, p. 154), Louis was excommunicated at the Lateran Council, on Saint-André's day, 30 November 1215. Raoul de Coggeshall reports simply that the excommunication was pronounced at the time of this council, against the enemies of King John (ed. Stevenson, p. 179). Innocent III, in his *bulla* launched against the barons on 16 December 1215, restricted himself to recall that he excommunicated them at the council (Potthast, *Regesta pontificum Romanorum*, n. 5013). It is not necessary to raise here the various *bullæ* by which this excommunication was launched or renewed.

56 Roger of Wendover, t. II, p. 176-180, and Mathieu de Paris, t. II, p. 650-653; Guillaume le Breton, ed. Delaborde, p. 306-307.

57 Mathieu de Paris, II, 653.

58 Guillaume le Breton, ed. Delaborde, p. 307-308.

59 Descent of Louis on England; his first success: *Histoire des ducs de Normandie and des rois d'Angleterre*, p. 165-171; Guillaume le Breton, ed. Delaborde, p. 309-10.

60 Roger of Wendover, t. II, p. 183-190, and Mathieu de Paris, t. II, p. 656-663.

61 Roger of Wendover, II, 206; Mathieu de Paris. III, 13; Raoul de Coggeshall, ed. Stevenson, p. 185; *Chronicon anonymi Laudunensis canonici. Historiens de France*, XVIII, 719; verse chronicle of Philippe Mousket, ed. Reiffenberg, verse 22625-22627.

62 Guillaume le Breton, ed. Delaborde, p. 312; *Histoire des ducs de Normandie*, p. 187.

63 *Histoire des ducs de Normandie*, etc., p. 188.

64 Jean Ypres, *Chronique de Saint-Bertin* (*Historiens de France*, XVIII, 606-607) : « Uxor tamen ipsius Ludovic, domina Blanca, sibi de pecunia prout potuit destinavit. »

65 *Histoire des ducs de Normandie*, etc., p. 191-193.

66 Roger of Wendover, II, 220-21; Mathieu de Paris, *Chronica majora*, III, 25-26, *Historia minor*, II, 216.

67 Annals of Dunstable (*Annales monastici*, collection of the Master of Rolls, ed. Lnard, III . 34).

68 Raoul de Coggeshall, *Chronicon Anglicanum*, ed. Stevenson, p. 172.

69 Roger de Wendover, II, 179, and Mathieu de Paris, *Chronica majora*, II, 653.

70 Annals of Dunstable, p. 46.

71 Francisque Michel, *Romans, lais, fabliaux, contes, moralités el miracles inédits du XIIe and du XIII siècles*. Romance of Eustache le Moine, a poem preceded by an historical dissertation.

72 The chroniclers who recounted the expedition in which Eustache le Moine perished are in accord that it was organized by Blanche de Castile: Annals of Burton (*Annales monastici*, I, 224); Annals of Dunstable (ibid., III, 50); *Histoire des ducs*

de Normandie (*Société de l'histoire de France*), p. 198 and p. 200. Philippe Mousket attributes to Robert de Courtenay the command of the relief expedition of Prince Louis, v. 22691-95.

73 The sea battle of 24 August 1217 has been recounted by several authors : Guillaume le Breton, ed. Delaborde, p. 314; *Hist. des ducs de Normandie*, etc., p. 200-202; Mathieu de Paris, *Chronica majora*, III, 26-29; two relations, of which the first is imputed to Roger of Wendover (ed. Hewlett), II, 221-223; Annals of Worcestor (*Annales monasttci*, IV, 408-409); Annals of Waverley (ibid., II, 287); Annals of Winchester (ibid., II, 83); Annals of Tewkesbury (ibid., I, 62-63); this last chronicle I append is about the battle at sea, between Sandwich and the Isle of Thanet. See also the *Roman Eustache le Moine*, p. 82-83, v. 2200-2306.

74 11 September 1217; Rymer, *Fœdera*, ed. of 1816, I, 148.

75 De Wailly, *Récits un ménestrel de Reims* (*Societe de l'histoire de France*), 01-302.

76 Le Nain de Tillemont, t. I , p. 50-51; ratification of the treaty of peace by Honorius III and absolution, 13 January 1218; Potthast, *Regesta*, 5667 and 5608.

77 Ibid., 68-70.

78 Annales de Saint-Denis, 1st edn., *Bibliothèque de l'École des Chartes*, 1879. p. 280.

79 Louis and Scévole de Sainte-Marthe, *Histoire Généalogique de la maison de France*, in-f°, t. I, p. 512 ; Le Nain de Tillemont, *Histoire de S. Louis*, i. I, p. 419.

80 *Annales de S. Denis*, p. 280.

81 Honorius III to the prior of Saint-Victor de Paris, 22 December 1220, *Historiens de France*, t. XIX, p. 714; Potthast, *Regesta pontificum Romanorum*, 6453.

82 Teulet, *Layettes du Trésor des Chartes*, t. I, p. 556, n. 1557.

83 Le Nain de Tillemont, *Hist. de S. Louis*, t. I, p. 163-64; Schirrmacher, *Geschichte Castiliens*, p. 330.

84 Luc de Tuy, in Schott, *Hispaniæ illustratæ auctores varii*, IV, 115.

85 Ibid., p. 112.

86 Rodrigue de Tolède, 1. IX, chap. 10, ed. de 1545, f° lxxxr verso; Schirrmacher, *Geschichte Castiliens*, p. 343.

87 Urraque died in Coïmbre, 3 November 1220; Florez, *Memorias de las reynas*

catholicas, I, 415.

88 Schirrmacher, p. 349.

89 Le Nain de Tillemont, I, 288-91; Philippe Mousket, verse 24181 ff; *Ménestrel de Reims*, 309 ff.

90 Poem of Nicolas de Bray, *Recueil des historiens de France*, t. XVII, p. 313-316, verse 65-262.

91 *Gesta Ludovici Oclavi, Historiens de France*, XVII. 305-306; *Chronicon Turonense*, ibid., XVIII, 305; Guillaume Guiart, *La branche aux royaux lignages*, ed. Buchon, t. I, verse 7953-7971.

92 *Historiens de France*, XIX, 754-755 ; Potthast, *Regesta*, 7258; 20 May 1224.

93 Negotiations with Comtesse Jeanne : Delisle, *Catalogue des actes de Philippe Auguste*, 1509; Guillaume le Breton, *Chronique*, ed. Delaborde, n. 204; Intervention of Honorius III : *Historiens de France*, XIX, 730; Potthast, 6988; 9 April 1223; Démarches of Honorius towards Louis VIII, *Historiens de France*, XIX, 752; *Layettes du Trésor des Charles*, II, 1644 ; Potthast, 7224; 22 April 1224; Intercessions of Queen Blanche: Meyer, *Commentarii sive annales rerum Flandricarum*, Anvers, 1561, I 71 recto.

94 *Layettes*, II, 1761; *Musée des archives départementales*, p. 115, document 65; planche XXXIV.

95 *Layettes*, II, 1763.

96 *Richeri gesta Senoniensis ecclesiæ, Monumenta Germaniæ historica*, scriptores, XXV, 293.

97 Philippe Mousket, v. II, verse 27789.

98 *Chronicon Turonense* (*Historiens de France*, XVIII, 316).

99 Letters of Rodrigo Diaz de los Cameros and his partisans have been published by Teulet (*Layettes du Trésor des Chartes*, t. II, p. 97-98, no. 1813-1814). The editor endeavored to specify the date; I would not dare to do as much; however some expressions « *Dei gratia Francorum regi* » seem to indicate that these are subsequent to 14 July 1223. The words « *responsionem vestram* » (n. 1814) prove that Louis VIII had already written Rodrigo Diaz and to the other malcontents, in response to the first letter.

100 Paul Meyer, *Recueil anciens textes*, 1st part, p. 93.

101 "*S'iert parena le roi d'auques loing.*" (Philippe Mousket, t. II, verse 25379.)

102   Romain was recommended to the laity and clergy of his legation by letters apostolic of 13 and 14 February 1225 (Potthast, *Regesta*, 7.158 and 7360; Toulet, *Layettes*, t. II, no. 1603-1694). Honorius III wrote to him, on 27 February, to make haste with the King of France in favor of the King England (Potthast, 7372), but from the Annals of Dunstable we learn that Jean de Brienne urged Louis VIII to reject the complaints of Henry III (*Annales monastici*, ed. Luard, collection of the Master of Rolls, t. III, p. 100). In the current of the year 1225, the Pope strongly reproached Louis in his conduct regarding the English (Potthast, 7510). In spite of his joy over news of Louis VIII taking up the cross, and of which we find the proof in a letter to Cardinal Romain, dated February or March of 1226 (Potthast, 7542), he did not continue any less to defend with all of his power the son of King John, as he proved in comminatory letters addressed, 8 January 1226, to Hugues de Lusignan and to other nobles who had abandoned the party of Henry III (Potthast, 7515).

103   Le Nain de Tillemont, t. I, p. 356.

104   This incident is recounted in detail by the *Chronique de Tours* (*Histoire de France*, XVIII, p. 309). Following Aubry de Trois-Fontaines (*Monumenta Germaniæ*, scriptores, XXIII, p. 917) and Philippe Mousket (ed. Reiffenberg, t II, verse 25351 to 25380), it is a privilege of the Université which the legate would have destroyed, and not its seal, as in the *Chronique de Tours*; he had to make one or the other. See Le Nain de Tillemont, t. I, p. 373-375.

105   Le Nain de Tillemont, t. I, p. 375-389.

106   "*Madame Blance L'otroia, La roïne, c'on moult proisa.*" (Philippe Mousket, ed. Reiffenberg, t. II, v. 25451.)

107   Scévole and Louis de Sainte-Marthe, *Histoire Généalogique de la maison de France*, I, 510.

108   *Annales de Saint -Denis* (*l'École des Chartes*, 1879, p. 280).

109   Testament of Louis VIII, June 1225; Teulot, *Layettes du Trésor des Chartes*, t. II, p. 54, n. 1710.

110   Le Nain de Tillemont, t. I, p. 404, p. 446-4-17; Arbois de Jubainville, *Histoire des ducs and des comtes de Champagne*, t. IV, 1st part, p. 199-208. It is Philippe Mousket who gives us the most detail on this incident (t. II, verse 26173 ff.); see also the *Gesta Ludovici Octavi* (*Historiens de France*, t. XVII, p. 309), and the poem of Nicolas de Bray (ibid., p. 338, verse 1529, and p. 322, verse 577).

111   *Chronicon Turonense* (*Historiens de France*, t. XVIII, p. 316 a, 317 d).

112   Le Nain de Tillemont, t. I. p. 406-411.

113   Ibid, p. 413.

114   Act of Louis VIII, dated Montpensier, in November 1226, by which he informs all trusty and well-beloved friends that in forecast of his death he assembled his prelates and barons, and made them swear that, if he suddenly died, they would lend faith and homage to Louis, his oldest son, as to their lord and their King, and carry him to coronation as soon as possible. Those who pledged this were the archbishops of Bourges and Sens, the bishops of Beauvais, of Noyons and Chartres, counts of Boulogne, Montfort, Sancerre, and Jean de Nesle. This act, extracted from the *Liber principum*, cartulary of Champagne in the Chambre des Comptes de Paris, was published by Du Cange, in his *Observations de l'histoire of saint Louis*, 1668, p. 53.

Letter addressed to Thibaud, Archbishop of Rouen, and to his suffragans, by which the prelats and the barons were acquainted with the promise that he had made to Louis VIII. This document, in addition to the barons named in the preceding one, bears the names of the Count of Blois, the Lord de Coucy, and Archambaud, Lord de Bourbon : Teulet, *Layettes du Trésor des Chartes*, t. II, n. 1823. Similar letters were addressed to a certain number of bishops and nobles; same collection, no. 1824 to 1827.

Charter by which the prelates and the barons, on 3 November 1220, announce the promise that they made the King about his son Louis, and making, if Louis suddenly died, the same engagements in it concerning Prince Robert. This part carries, after the names which are in the preceding one, those of fourteen nobles, of which several officers of the crown, among others Jean de Beaumont and Marshal Robert de Coucy, in which are sealed as well as Marshal Jean Clément: *Layettes du Trésor des Chartes*, II, 1811.

Commitment similar to the preceding, undertaken by Simon, Archbishop of Bourges. Montpensier, November 1226; *Layettes*, 1812.

115   Teulet, *Layettes du Trésor des Chartes*, t. II, n. 1828.

116   Philippe Mousket, ed. Reiffenberg, t II, 27251-27258.

117   Philippe Mousket, verse 27261-27274.
118   Le Nain de Tillemont, t. I. p. 413-14.
119   *Chronicon Turonense* (*Historiens de France*, t. XVIII, p. 317); *Gesta Ludovici Octavi* speaks equally to the austerity of the King : « *Nam nunquam carnem suam maculavit, praeterquam cum unica uxore sua sibi legitimo matrimonio copulata.* » (*Historiens de France*, t. XVII, p. 310.
120   *Qimr il cntramoient si fort*
         Que tout lurent à l acort,
         onquos mais roïne anaa
         Son signor tant, ne reclama.
         (Philippe Mousket, verse 27145.)
121   Guillaume de Puy-Laurens, *Historia Albigensium* (*Historiens de France*, t. XIX, p. 217).

122   The idea that Louis VIII had been poisoned was very widespread in the thirteenth century; they even believed, in his army, many people had had the same fate:

> *Si quida on par vérité*
> *Thaton theeuist là envenimé ,*
> *Et les autres barons de theost ,*
> *Qui mort i estoient si tost.*
> (Philippe Mousket, t. II, v. 27283).

«*Rex vero Ludovicus and mulli alii tam clerici quam laici in regiono illa veneno perierunt.*» *Epitome Andrese Silvii priori Marchianensis* (*Historiens de France*, t. XVIII, p. 558).

«*Et inde reverions, toxicato vine, sicut creditur, multos suorum amisit.*» *Chronicon Turonense*, ibid., p. 317.

«*Tolosam vadit, ubi venenatus, ut dicitur, obiit.*» Richard de San Germane » *Monumenta Germaniae*, scriptores, t. XIX, p. 340, ligno 30.

Roger of Wendover formally accused the Count of Champagne to have poisoned his sovereign : « *procuravit regi venenum propinari ob amorem reginæ cjus, quam carnaliter amabat.* » (ed. Hewlett, t. II, p. 313); Mathieu de Paris does nothing but copy it, ed. Luard, t. III, p. 116. This opinion was current in England, thanks above all to Mathieu; it is found in the *Flores historiarum*, published by Luard in the collection of the Master of the Rolls, t. II, p. 180. The *Historia Minor* of Mathieu de Paris, published in the same collection, carries in the margin, for 1226, the *écu de France*, with this note : « *Clipeus Lodowici, filii Ludowici , potionati apud Avinionem* » (t. II, p. 290). The pretended crime of the Count of Champagne has been reported by other authors : « *procurante, ut dicitur, comite Campaniæ toxicatus* », speaking of the *Abbreviattones gestonim Franciæ regum* (*Historiens de France*, t. XVII, p. 433).

123   D'Arbois de Jubainville, *Histoire des ducs and des comtes de Champagne*, t. IV, 1st part, p. 209.

124   Philippe Mousket, t. II, verse 27293 ff.

125   Philippe Mousket, verse 27451 ff.; see Le Nain de Tillemont, t. I, p. 414. Following the *chronique de Tours*, the funeral was celebrated in Saint-Denis on 15 November, « *XVII kalendas decembris.* » *Historiens de France*, t. XVIII, p. 318.

Chapter Two

The Advent of Louis IX and the First Revolt of the Barons – The work of Philippe Auguste compromised by the death of his son.– Devotion of the nation to royal power. – Philippe Hurepel, uncle of the King; doubtful feelings of the high nobility. – Chancellor Guerin and servants of the crown. – Blanche of Castile regent by the will of Louis VIII; legitimacy of her power. – Crowning of Louis IX. – Deliverance of the Count of Flanders. – Death of Renaud de Dammartin. – Pierre Mauclerc, Count de Bretagne. – Relations with England; Henry III gains some Poitevin barons. – Hugues de Lusignan, Count de La Marche, Pierre Mauclerc and Thibaud of Champagne are united. – Blanche attacks them. – Submission of the Count of Champagne. – Treaties of Vendôme with the counts of Brittany and La Marche. – Suspension of hostilities between the French and Richard, brother of Henry III. – Pope Gregory IX at first favorable to the English. – Truce with England. – War in Languedoc; Raimond VII of Toulouse. – Romain, legate of the Holy See, fights against the chapters who refuse the King subsidies for war against the Albigensians. – He returns to Italy. – Capture of Labécède. – Difficulties between the Crown and Thibaud, Archbishop of Rouen.

After a few years of calm, Blanche of Castile had a terrible crisis, when she was suddenly charged to raise a king and defend a throne. Seldom had France been in a more serious situation.

Philippe Auguste had been a conqueror, a great prince; he had taken beautiful provinces once again from the enemies of his kingdom and of his family; under his reign, sovereign power increased to such a height that over the centuries in our country, such an authority one had been made to accept or to impose on the others; but he had been removed from his work before it was consolidated, and his son, who appeared worthy to succeed to him, had lived too briefly. The death of

Louis VIII placed all in question; Louis IX was a child and Blanche a foreign queen; one did not know him yet enough to fear him and believe themselves obliged to obey him. What was going to become of the docility of the great barons and the other vassals, now that they no longer felt themselves to be under an iron hand? Time would tell if several of them would give up ideas of independence or inclinations of revolt. The defeat of the Midi was hardly completed, and in the old domains of the Plantagenets, in Normandy, in Poitou, many people could be prevailed upon to return to their former masters. The Holy See, natural guardian of the weak, had interests opposed to those of France, and one was hardly in the right to count on it since a strange bond of suzerainty linked it with England. Blanche would have to defend this heavy crown resting on the head of a mere child.

She was at the height of danger; she accepted resolutely and supported without weakness a fight which appeared unequal, in which some thought to cast her down; from where she would leave in triumph. The role that she played during these hard years of regency was truly grand, and one cannot say this enough; it needed courage to maintain the traditions of French royalty. It is right to recognize that she did not fight alone; around the throne there were valiant men and intelligent servants, trained in the school of Philippe Auguste, of which they defended the heritage, and on more than one occasion public feeling was declared for a King who represented order and national unity, against turbulent feudality and enemies from outside.

In the first years or the first months which followed the advent of Louis IX, one of those naive poets who are always there to cry the death of kings and to welcome their successors, Robert Saincereau, expressed in one rhymed lament the fears that all faithful subjects must have felt for their young prince and his kingdom.[1] This elegy is a disagreeable invoice; the composition is awkward; the monotony of the form and the poverty of ideas grates unceasingly; the author shows involuntary and deprived repetitions of art; but the feeling which makes him write is simple, profound, and truly touching. One believes to see and hear the crowd of those who, in spite of miseries and the sufferings of this time, found themselves to be a little more tranquil or a little less unhappy since the King started to be strong. This poor versifier, on the same point, by lamenting his master, working as courtier, not having less sincerity when he regrets the prince who has just died, and made, while trembling, best wishes for his far too youthful successor. "I pray the Virgin, mother of God, by the saintly love that she had for her sons, I pray it by her pity to keep the King of France, to move away from sin. And the good queen: how the Lord of the heavens comforts her! You gave her, fortune, a great wrong, to her and her beautiful children (that God defends!) for the good King their father that you took too early from them."

And then the famous poet moved to virtuous terms by this valiant master in whom all the world had so great a confidence, he returned unceasingly with new wishes that he addressed to the small King, his mother, and his brothers: "That the Lord God our father, by his command, confuses those who betray him; that they live in torments they do not want to amend, the traitors let them become felons. That from God and the country they have a curse." Obviously one realizes already that royalty will be exposed to bad and unpleasant company. Robert Saincereau, who had composed the first sermon in rhyme soon after the funeral of Louis VIII, finished it a few months later, at the moment when Chancellor Guerin, Bishop of Senlis, just died; he had a whole page of regrets for this wise and honest defender whom his young master had just lost: "Blessed are those who will love you and who in *bona fide* will advise you; he was a strong support you had in the good bishop Guerin; by God and thanks to his great direction, you had many friends; he was man of honor, he was honest; they will certainly know it, because your father knew it well, liked him extremely so." He forever considered the good bishop since the time of Turpin and Charlemagne to have the friendship and the confidence of Philippe Auguste, King Louis, and Queen Blanche; "noble King, you must remember well this valiant man, because never did a better person die." Then the good panegyrist called the devotion of Philippe Hurepel, uncle of the King, of the Count of Flanders, who had just left his prison. Robert counts also on the other great vassals to defend the crown: "That God gives the Count of Brittany peace, harmony and great love towards the King; all those know well who will be faithful to him in this world and in the other they will have a high reward for it; that God, by his holy name, grants to the Count of Champagne peace and good alliance with the King and the barons."

The concerns which this small poem reveals were to be divided by a great number of those over whom Blanche of Castile was going to have to control. In the uncertainty of the first days each one wondered to whom Louis IX and his mother could turn to for support. Was it Count Philippe de Boulogne, first prince of the blood? Some hoped for, and he was shown extremely promising at the beginning, Pierre Mauclerc, the ambitious Count de Bretagne. Was it the Count de Champagne, at one time scarcely loyal to the King? No one could, before the facts had spoken, base solid hope on doubtful feelings. On the other hand, there were advisers to the crown, Chancellor Guerin, still alive in November 1226, the true chief and inspirer, showing enough devotion to the father and grandfather of their master so that for their share they had hope and nothing to fear.

  At the head of those who appeared intent to support with their devotion the new King there appeared the second son of Philippe Auguste, Philippe Hurepel, the Count de Boulogne. The son of Agnes of Méranie, of whom the marriage had not been recognized by the Holy See, Philippe had been solemnly legitimated by Pope Innocent III at the same time as his sister Marie, on 2 November 1201;[2] it was thus by an error they were sometimes treated as bastards. While he was still in the cradle his father occupied himself to ensure a worthy establishment for the son of a King: Count Renaud de Dammartin, later famous for treason and captivity, had by his wife Ide of Boulogne an only daughter, Mahaut; back in 1201 she was promised in marriage to Philippe, who did not have to marry her until fifteen years later. It was a brilliant alliance; the brother of Renaud, Simon de Dammartin, had married the Countess de Ponthieu, niece of the King; this was an especially good heritage, because Renaud had, as well by him as by his wife, the domains of Dammartin, Boulogne and Mortain. It is true that after his defeat at Bouvines, the infidel Count of Boulogne, thrown in prison for the remainder of his days, lost all his possessions, and it does not seem that Philippe Auguste gave them to his second son. He knighted him in 1222. The following year, when an untimely death had removed the King of France, Prince Philippe was present at his funeral, at the side of his older brother who, barely King, put in his possession the county of Boulogne. Soon afterwards, Philippe went to seize this beautiful stronghold. A few years before (1218), the death of Thibaud, Count of Blois, had added to the fiefs of which he already had the pleasure of, while also expecting the county of Clermont in Beauvaisis. Lastly, in February 1224, the King's brother confirmed to him the rights that he had on the counties of Mortain and Clermont, on a quarter of Dammartin and the county of Aumale. Philippe was thus a powerful seigneur. His contemporaries called Hurepel or *le Hérissé*, not, as some claimed, due to a roughness in manners which no text makes known to us, but rather because he had, like his father, shaggy and bulky hair.[3] He owed much to King Louis his brother, who had been for him a true benefactor; also he appears to have been very devoted to him; he was the companion of his last days and was remarkable, upon the death of Louis, for the sincerity of his pain.

In spite of the narrow relationship which linked him to Louis IX, Philippe Hurepel was not always to be devoted to the true interests of his nephew. Blanche could trust even less the princes from the house of Dreux, descendants of Louis VI, who were not brought closer to her sons by the links of blood so that their situation in the feudal world intended them to be great vassals. The elder of this family was Robert the Count of Dreux, but it was represented with a very particular flair by his brother Pierre Mauclerc. This dangerous and turbulent man, who by his revolts was soon to roil the kingdom, controlled Brittany, from whence he had married an heiress, while waiting for his son Jean to come into majority. He had two more brothers who were spoken of during the youth of Louis IX, Jean de Braine, Count de Mâcon, and Henri, treasurer of Beauvais, soon to be Archbishop of Rheims. The house of Courtenay, also resulting from Louis le Gros, and most faithful to the feelings of family, played a much less important role in the kingdom. Finally, the royal blood of France was represented, to a degree extremely remote, by the young Duke of Burgundy, whose family was well disposed towards kings in general. The Queen had too many reasons to consider with mistrust the other great vassals; before having seen their work, she had no right to expect they would allow her to hope they would be let themselves be dominated by reason of honesty towards their sovereign; however Countess Jeanne of Flanders, spouse of Ferrand of Portugal, on the issue which they worked then, was the niece of Philippe Auguste, and one could believe in her faithful feelings. The high clergy, by tradition and need, was more devoted than the great nobility to the cause of royalty, under the influence of the Holy See, and even the nature of its power brought frequent conflicts with the sovereign; it was necessary that all the archbishops and all the bishops were willing to support Blanche and to facilitate her task; they did not all have the good will of the Bishop of Sens, Gautier Cornu; he was a man of fidelity; he belonged to one of those families which populated the dioceses with good bishops and the royal court with excellent advisers.

It was especially in the immediate entourage of the King that one met with true merit, and devotion without mental reservation. The *Capétien* princes of the thirteenth century, who were self-made, were also good servants. Faithful to their practices of vigilance and activity, with their policy almost always well followed, they gave to those who knew them closely, who were already obliged and who had any interest to work on the progress of the sovereign power, examples of which it was easy to profit. From this relatively large number came devoted and quite select servants, from whom a small dynasty of advisers and civil servants came, formed of good part by noble families of ancient domains, where one inherited from his parents, with the confidence and the favor of the King, with often important responsibilities, a real attachment to the house of France. When one traverses the lists of witnesses inserted, at the time of Louis VIII, in the public acts concerning royalty, one sees, beside the archbishops, the bishops and powerful vassals, with the great officers of the crown, so many people, less important by their feudal situation or their political role, but who, for various reasons, belong to the house of the King; it is not rare to Count, in the same act, several of the same name or even family. When one surveys the reign of Louis IX, one will find them in the charters, in the household accounts, in the chronicles, being used as witnesses, following displacements of the court, invested in administrative offices or operations managers, but treated at the same time familiarly. They were useful and faithful collaborators of the royal capacity; beside the chancellor, chamberlain, constable, the small number of large lords of which with the need arose; support was never lacking, they were ready to give to the contest their activity and their experience.

    Among the barons who, by their traditions of family or personal attachment, formed to some extent part of the court, it is necessary to cite at the head of the list Archambaud de Bourbon. During the malady of Louis VIII, this lord was a devoted friend.[4] Imbert, Lord of Beaujou, whom the father of Louis IX had left in Languedoc at the head of the royal troops, was still one of those in whom Blanche of Castile could place her confidence; he was always faithful to his prince; his talents and services that he not had ceased returning were later worth the sword of a constable.[5] Count Amaury de Montfort, who preceded him, was with Louis VIII in November 1226, and since then his devotion was not contradicted. Son of the famous Simon de Montfort, who had broken the power of the counts of Toulouse, he had to give up the conquests of his father; but though circumstances had brought him to yield to the King all claims and the hopes to which he was heir, he remained a very good vassal.

For their part and above all those to whom was delegated, in an unspecified measurement, royal authority, there was one man of high intelligence and past services intended to play in the court of France, if he had lived longer, a role of great importance. Chancellor Guérin, so influential under Philippe Auguste and Louis VIII, appeared able to help the Regent in the middle of difficulties and dangers. He was Knight of the Hospital when the King of France, at the end of 1201, had taken him for vice-chancellor; the office of chancellor being for a rather long time vacant, Guérin had consequently exerted, under a modest title, the most difficult functions that there had been in the kingdom.[6] The product of a military clan who produced so many good soldiers and skilful administrators, he had continued to wear the costume of the Hospitalers as bishop elect of Senlis, and, even after his consecration, he continued to call himself Brother Guérin. Bound in friendship with Philippe Auguste and intimate adviser of this great prince, "his skill, the incomparable value of his intelligence, the variety of his talents, positioned him well at court, so he was like a second king and treated, without ever making a mistake, the businesses of state."[7] Very informed, always occupied in taking care of the interests of churches, he was still, and over all, a very good general. In 1213, after the naval defeat of Dam, he was one of those whom Philippe Auguste charged with burning the remainder of the royal fleet; a little time afterwards, he was placed, with the Count of Saint-Pol, at the head of an army which regained Tournay and devastated the seigniory of Mortagne. The morning of Bouvines, while the royal army was withdrawn to Lille, Brother Guérin, left in command of the rear-guard with the Viscount of Melun, stole a march before the army united; he hastened to inform the King, and in the council of war that Philippe Auguste assembled at once, he insisted on attack. He then returned to place himself at the head of the right wing, which faced the troops of the Count of Flanders, left behind those of whom he was the least sure, and shouted for the bravest, who formed the first rank: "The battle field is broad, extend yourselves straight for the plain for fear of enemies; it is not necessary that the knights line up one behind the other; place yourselves in order to be able to strike on one line." Then he launched the sergeants ahead on horses, by which he engaged the action. At the end of the day, it was with him that Count Renaud de

Boulogne went. In 1219, he accompanied Prince Louis in Languedoc; he went to the funeral of Philippe Auguste, who had charged him to take care of the execution of his will. Louis VIII, barley King, appointed him chancellor, but it did nothing but change his title: his influence and the credit which he had enjoyed for a long time could only increase. He took part in the interrogation of an impostor who had wanted to pass for Emperor of Constantinople, Baudouin of Flanders, killed in the East; one does not have to broach all the documents and historical texts where he appears as negotiator, arbitrator, or as his own counsel.[8] Guérin was one of those invaluable men who are fit for anything and to which one can entrust all; but he did not have time to make for his new master all the good that they expected of him. His death on 19 April 1227 had been for the crown a true misfortune, if Blanche of Castile had been unable to repair by her own merit losses even more acute.

The Chamberlain of France, Barthelemy de Roye, who survived ten years under Chancellor Guérin, was also justified by his eminent qualities and the constancy of his devotion, enjoying royal favor under the two preceding reigns. A long time before the autumn of 1208, during which he became one of the great officers of the crown, he appears in royal acts as an important character.[9] His good fortune is explained by the services he rendered in councils, in negotiations, in wars. One finds him with the army of Flanders during the campaign of 1213 and of 1214, and the biographer of Philippe Auguste knew as that he was already of an advanced age when he fought at Bouvines. At the end of this great day, when Emperor Otto IV made his escape, chased in his rout by Guillaume des Barres, Barthelemy did not want to abandon his King, who avoided terrible dangers; he was safe at the side, with Gautier of Nemours and Guillaume de Garlande, "whose lances were broken and swords stained with blood."[10] After having been the familiar of Philippe Auguste, who indicated him as one of his executors, he became the adviser of Louis VIII, then the defender of his son, and alluded to by the author of the *Chronicle of Tours*, when he represents France as controlled, during the youth of Louis IX, by a child, a woman and an old man;[11] but this old man was a person of great experience and good counsel, really worthy to preserve near his sovereign a privileged situation.[12]

The office of Bouteiller of France belonged in 1226 to Robert de Courtenay, first cousin of Philippe Auguste, and whose elder brother, Pierre, had been Emperor of the East; one of his nephews, Robert, reigned then in Constantinople; another, Baudouin II, was to be the last sovereign of this Latin empire, threatened with ruin soon after its advent. During the expedition to England, Robert de Courtenay was shown to be very devoted; after the defeat of Lincoln, he had answered the call of Blanche of Castile; but the vessel on which he was with Eustace the Monk had been captured in the naval battle of 24 August 1217. Barely King, Louis VIII had recognized the devotion of his cousin in raising him to the dignity of *bouteiller* [cup-bearer].[13]

The Constable, Mathieu de Montmorency, to whom historians of his house give the nickname of "Grand", had taken part in the Third Crusade; one finds him at the siege of Château-Gaillard and especially in Bouvines, where he performed his duty bravely. He had then accompanied the son of Philippe Auguste against the Albigensians. The King, who employed him in the negotiations, gave him the office of constable, of which he was in possession since 1218. He was with Louis VIII against the English, and joined the King at the siege of Avignon.[14] Blanche of Castile and her son could be happy to have this man close to them.[15]

The marshal Robert de Coucy is known only as having been present at Montpensier, the moment when the dying King of France required a promise from those who surrounded him to be faithful to his son, but another Marshal of France, Jean Clément, Lord of Mez and d'Argentan, displayed military qualities which were a tradition in his family. The office of which he was title holder, and was to belong later to his son, had been successively illustrated by his uncle Aubry, killed at the siege of Saint Jean-d'Acre, and by his father Henri Clément, who, in the saying of a contemporary, "had in his small body the heart of a giant". Philippe Auguste, after Henri was lost, made a point of recognizing his service by conferring the *maréchalat*, which however was not hereditary, upon his son Jean, then too young to exercise it.[16]

It would necessarily be excessive to enumerate all those who were known for their devotion to the late King, or the loyalty to which he addressed, on his death bed, a final appeal. It is sufficient to cite Jean de Beaumont, who was under Louis IX one of the best commanders in the royal army,[17] Adam de Beaumont,[18] Guillaume des Barres le Jeune, son of the celebrated brother in arms to Philippe Auguste, and Pierre des Barres,[19] Jean de Nesle,[20] Jean de Vallery,[21] of which the name was so gloriously carried by Érard de Vallery, the vanquisher of Tagliacozze, Guillaume Ménier, baillie and *châtelaine* of Étampes,[22] Adam de Milly, baillie of Arras,[23] Hugues d'Athies, counselor to Philippe Auguste, and *panetier* [quarter master] of France from the beginning of Louis IX,[24] Simon de Poissy, who after the defeat at Lincoln restored to Prince Louis the rest of the French army.[25] Chamberlain Ours, Philippe de Nemours, and Guy de Nemours, lord of Méréville, with Louis VIII in the days which preceded his death, also belonged to one of those families that the King had loaded with favors, and which on the other hand brought to them, with each generation, new evidence of their fidelity.[26] One cannot enumerate these good and honest servants of the crown without falling into repetitions, but it remains that almost all were distinguished by the same qualities, in some of those serious and decisive circumstances where there appears true courage and sure sentiments; when they are passed in review, one is at every moment obliged to recall that they fought at Bouvines, another took part in the English expedition. It is necessary to acknowledge that this monotony has something imposing. How much was in the case of the brave man Michel de Harnes, who successively served and advised three kings. After having translated into French the legendary exploits of Charlemagne and Roland,[27] and before seeking new dangers in England,[28] he received in the battle of Bouvines a thrust of a lance which, going through the thigh, nailed him to the saddle of his horse.[29]

The panoply of able and devoted servants was better for Blanche of Castile than undeniable rights. She relied on them to resist the enemies of royal power, and they supported her with a fidelity which never weakened; her energy, intelligence, and the high idea that she had of her mission made up the remainder. It is certain that she would have been reversed, if she had to rely only on the capacity and will of her husband. However, the intentions of Louis VIII did not lend any doubt; before dying, he had declared "that his successor, with the kingdom, and all his children, until their majority," were to be in the guard and under the supervision of the Queen.[30] In saying this, the late King had not only entrusted to Blanche the education of Louis IX, he had placed in the hands of the Queen the government of the state. One could not dispute his right to do so; because no use, no precedent, authorized the barons to intervene in the constitution of a regency. It was believed that Philippe Auguste had asked the approval of the barons when they assembled in Vézelay, before leaving for the

Third Crusade, that he had entrusted the government of the kingdom to his mother and his uncle; but the words *accepta licentia*,[31] on which this opinion is founded, means simply that he took leave of his nobility, and it is thus that one interpreted them, as of the thirteenth century, in the official texts.[32] When Louis IX, in his turn, got under way for the Orient, he remitted full sovereignty to his mother without consulting a single one of his subjects.

Blanche was thus at the head of the kingdom, in fact as well as by right, and if she had never taken in official acts the title of regent, that was because this title was not employed by those to whom the kings of France delegated their authority.

It is known that Suger, charged to control our country in the absence of Louis VII, was not qualified as regent, and Blanche herself, when she replaced her son, from 1248 to 1252, was called the Queen of France, without anybody thinking of disputing the legality of her power. Later, Mathieu de Vendôme and Simon de Nesle, left in charge of the kingdom two times, were entitled lieutenants of the King.[33] It is necessary to go up to the fourteenth century to find the title of regent at the head of acts promulgated by Philippe le Longue[34] and Philippe de Valois[35] after the death of Louis X and Charles IV, by the Dauphin Charles during the captivity of Jean le Bon.[36] The usage had changed since the time of Saint Louis, and under the successors of Philippe the Beautiful it was resolved to define in precise terms the functions that existed for a long time, without which one had been worried to give them an invariable name.

The powers conferred on Blanche were as regular as possible; but for how long was she to exert them? In other words, the young Louis IX, in the idea of his father, was to have supervision starting from his sacring, his entry into adolescence, or only after coming into majority? As regards the sacring, it does not seem that under the Capétiens the kings of France were regarded as major by the fact of having received holy unction. Philippe I, anointed King in 1059, a long time before adolescence, had remained for several years under the supervision of Count Baudouin of Flanders. One could crown a young prince in order to make his person inviolable, without claiming that by this fact he became able to govern; such was the case with Louis IX. It remained to be seen if he would reach majority at fourteen years or seven years later. This question would not be difficult to resolve, if one had the right to affirm that our kings were, under this aspect, submitted to the usage observed in the French nobility.

In France during the thirteenth century, the majority of lords arrived at their majority, *ætas legitima*, at twenty-one years. It is what Prince Louis, husband of Blanche of Castile, declared implicitly in March 1215 when he recalled a legal exemption established by the habit in favor of nobles who did not reach this age.[37] Hugues IV, Duke of Burgundy,[38] and Thibaud IV, Count deChampagne,[39] were not major until twenty-one years; it was thus with Jean, Count de Bretagne and son of Pierre Mauclerc.[40] In the house of France this same usage was in force for the sons of kings. Louis, son of Philippe Auguste, was knighted only in his twenty-second year, and it was probably then that a kind of prerogative was constituted to him. Those of his sons who arrived at the age of manhood were not differently treated; Robert, born at the end of September 1216, became Count of Artois and was made knight at the time of his marriage, in June 1237; Prince Alphonse, born 1 November 1220, became knight and Count of Poitiers in 1241; Charles, probably born at the end of March 1226, accepted the counties of Anjou and of Maine at Pentecost of 1246. With the treaty of Vendôme (1227), it was agreed between Blanche of Castile and Pierre Mauclerc, Count de Bretagne, that this one would hold certain strongholds until the moment when Prince Jean de France, intended for Yolande of Brittany, would have reached his twenty-first year.[41]

There could well be countries, like Flanders, where this regulation was not applied, and under this aspect I will restrict myself to cite the cases of Jean and Baudouin of Avesnes, considered as men when one was sixteen years old, and the other fifteen.[42] But their example proves only that in certain strongholds one did not conform to the French use.

As for the King, one is tempted to believe that he obeyed the common rule, by seeing Louis IX and Thibaud de Champagne make arrangements which must remain in force as long as Louis would not have achieved his twenty-first year.[43] However, the Capétien rulers did not always regard this age as being for them that of the majority. Philippe I was not thirteen years old when he formally declared that he had left tutelage.[44] After the death of Saint Louis, Philippe the Bold decided that, as he had suddenly died before his heir was fourteen years old, the guardianship of the kingdom was to belong to the Count of Alençon.[45] In the presence of texts very few and contradictory, we cannot solve this question of right. Perhaps contemporaries of Queen

Blanche, regarding this, were not better settled than us.

If it had been established that the King was to be in his majority at fourteen years, the nobles confederated against Blanche of Castile would not have failed to put forward this reason to get rid of her. However, what were their arguments? They repeated on every turn that they did not want not to obey a woman, foreign at that; they represented Blanche as poisoning her husband, the mistress of the Count de Champagne. It had been simpler to declare that she had no role to play in the life of the Prince, and this they did not do. It was essential to them, moreover, that their young King was able or unable to control affairs by himself; the fact alone interested them, and this fact, Blanche controlled until the day when her son, left adolescence, and was found in full possession of his authority and faculties. For this reason I am obliged to say that the regency of Blanche of Castile lasted nearly ten years. When the Queen felt it essential, it was withdrawn, giving up little by little the business of state to her son; the transition was so soft that nobody managed to discover the moment when she abdicated power to keep only its influence.

The life of Blanche merges with French history from 1226 to 1235, and so for this period the mother of Saint Louis did not take the title of regent, it not being a secret that she was mistress of the kingdom. There are many documents in which foreign princes, French persons of all ranks, nobles, priests or people of the cities, associated in public acts her name with that of Louis IX.

To strengthen as much as possible the authority of the new King, it was urgent to crown him. Once brought back to Paris, they found the Countess of Flanders, Jeanne of Constantinople, and two of her vassals, bearing a ransom for the Count, their master. The delivery of Ferrand was decided, but it was resolved to defer it until Louis IX had been crowned.[46] Without delaying more, the archbishops, bishops, and vassals who had been present at the death of Louis VIII, sent letters throughout the kingdom alerting prelates and nobles about the last will of the prince, and commanding them to meet in Rheims on 29 November, the day of coronation.[47] Commoners also accepted this order to be in this city at the date indicated;[48] but those who should have come did not answer the call of the regent. Joinville undoubtedly exaggerated when he said that, except for Spain, she had neither parents nor friends in all kingdom;[49] it is certain that, among the vassals, more were delighted by the misfortune which had struck.[50] Several barons abstained on pretext of the pain that the death of Louis

VIII had caused them.[51] Others objected that it was necessary, according to the use, to return freedom to the prisoners, especially to the counts Flanders and Boulogne; in 1223 the King had not drawn from their dungeons these two grand culprits, although he had given the proof of his generosity by slackening other prisoners. Finally, there were feudatories who claimed, as prerequisite for their presence in Rheims, the restitution of strongholds which Philippe Auguste and his son had placed in hand.[52]

One did not have to take account of all these requirements if one did not want to inaugurate the reign by dangerous marks of weakness. Blanche of Castile encouraged in firmness by the legate of the Holy See, maintained the day fixed for coronation and got under way with her son. In Soissons, the King was armed as a knight;[53] he made the voyage in a wagon, surrounded with an escort of barons; when they entered Rheims, he was bestowed a large *dextrier* [war horse]; he went down to the palace which was to be used by him as residence without the city being in festivities; they were too much delivered over to thoughts of mourning to give themselves to pleasure.[54] How had the most powerful feudatories behaved at this point? The Count of Brittany, Pierre Mauclerc had not come; at this time he combined with the King of England, who made common cause with the Count de Toulouse, enemy of the King of France.[55] The Count de La Marche and many lords of Poitevin had answered the royal convocation only with insolence; in place of returning homage to Louis IX, they did not think other than being with Henry III.[56]

In spite of these abstentions and bad premonitions, Blanche and the King saw around them a rather brilliant suite of prelates and vassals. At the head of the topmost clergy were the patriarch of Jerusalem and Cardinal Romain, papal legate. Among the representatives of the nobility, there was the Count de Boulogne Philippe Hurepel, the young Duke of Burgundy, Hugues IV, and undoubtedly also the King of Jerusalem, Jean de Brienne; Robert Count de Dreux and Henri de Braine, treasurer of Beauvais, who was going to be Archbishop of Rheims, protested by their presence against the disobedience of their brother the Count of Brittany; Jeanne of Flanders, Blanche de Navarre, mother of the Count de Champagne and cousin of the Queen, had come to make good relationships. The Lord de Coucy and his two brothers, the Count de Bar and the Count de Blois, several knights of Normandy and the country of Hurepoix, the Lady de Beaujeu, were also among those who curried support.[57]

The Count de Champagne, Thibaud IV, who had been unfaithful at the siege of Avignon, lent credulity to the public malignity shown to him over the rumors of his poising of Louis XIII, but he was on the road to attend the coronation; Blanche could not tolerate him coming closer without discrediting herself and disgracing the memory of her late husband. Informed of his approach, she ordered the provost of Rheims and the common people to prohibit him access to the city. He had sent his people in advance to prepare an entry, but they protested in vain; they wanted to await their master; the mayor of Rheims made them cut down their banners and throw their baggage outside the city. The Count, who prepared to make his entry, met his servants just driven out and returned, furious.[58]

The privilege to crown the King of France belonged to the Archbishop of Rheims; but the metropolitan seat was then vacant, and the brother of the Count de Dreux, Henri de Braine, was not elected yet; and Jacques de Bazoches, Bishop of Soissons, in his capacity as first bishop of the province, had the honor to officiate.[59] The sacring was celebrated according to rites devoted by usage; the Abbot of Saint Remy, escorted with three hundred knights, brought the ampoule of holy oil, and because there was no Archbishop of Rheims, it was Gautier Cornu, Archbishop of Sens, who accepted it on entry to the cathedral. The Bishop of Soissons proceeded to the sacring, assisted by Chancellor Guerin, Bishop of Senlis, and Louis IX, when he had received this anointment, charged the Count de Boulogne with holding the royal sword; the countesses of Flanders and Champagne, representing two peers of France, both emitted a claim to carry it; this difficulty was resolved by entrusting it to the uncle of the King. The day when Blanche brought her son back to Paris, she had to remember with bitterness the entry that she had made, three years before, in this same capital, where nobody thought of putting themselves into festive dress; but in the middle of sorrow, she was supported by the pride of seeing one of her children as King, and to feel that the fate of a great kingdom depended only on her.[60]

However, Blanche could not be unaware of the dangers of her situation, and to deal with them she did not have a day to lose. Surrounded by dissatisfied vassals and enemies, she first had to insure herself with powerful allies. The Count de Boulogne, her brother-in-law, appeared the natural guardian of Louis IX, and until then he had shown fidelity; to recognize his devotion and to encourage his favorable disposition, he was given as of December the castles of

Mortain and of Lillebonne, with the homage of the county of Saint-Pol.[61] At the same time the Queen, by an act of clemency and loyalty with which she would soon be pleased, took all necessary measures to free, without delaying anymore, the Count of Flanders from prison. During the life of Louis VIII, in the month of April 1226, it had been agreed that the captivity of Ferrand would end at Christmas; his ransom, fixed at twenty-five thousand *livres parisis*, double the sum equal to that guaranteed to the King by the temporary transfer of Lille, Douai, and Ecluse.[62] These were rather rigorous conditions; still Jeanne of Flanders did not obtain them other than by intervention of the Queen, assisted in her efforts by the prayers of the King of Portugal and the frequent pleas of the Count of Blois.[63] The sacring of the young King did not delay more than a few weeks the execution of the promise made by his father; at once returned from Rheims, Blanche occupied herself with finishing this business which interested her doubly, as a relationship and as a Queen. Countess Jeanne, who managed to gather the stipulated sums, had brought them to Paris; the payment was undoubtedly carried out in December, but Ferrand was not delivered until the first days of 1227.[64] Blanche of Castile, however benevolent were her provisions, made a point of taking the most serious of precautions.

By her order, two advisers of the crown, master Aubry Cornu and the *panetier* [royal bread steward] Hugues de Athies, were sent to Flanders to collect oaths from all the subjects of Ferrand before he was freed.[65] From 6 to 21 December they pressed the nobles and cities; engaged, by sealed letters, to give neither assistance nor council to their suzerains they did not carry out their engagements.[66] At the same time, Jeanne made an oath to swear with her husband the conditions of the treaty, that she would be in Flanders; in default of that, the Count and the Countess were to pay a fine of five thousand *marcs*, the guarantee of which was given by several great barons.[67] Jeanne and Ferrand promised finally that they would ask the Pope for letters to excommunicate them and to throw the under interdict all of Flanders if they did not observe the treaty.[68]

It was before the end of December when the articles relating to the delivery of the Count of Flanders were promulgated in Paris. Ferrand and Jeanne gave to the King the castle of Douai, for ten years, beginning 1 January 1227. Pointing out the oaths lent to the King by their vassals and middle-class men, they were compelled to prevail against those who dared refuse to pledge similarly. They renounced any action based on facts former to the treaty, left the King, his brothers and his mother, in peaceful possession of all that Louis VIII had held on April 1226, during the first arrangements; they promised to live in peace with Louis IX and he to them, and to harm them in nothing, as long as the King would be ready to render them justice in his court by the judgment of the peers. Moreover, it was agreed that no fortress could be built nor provided with new works in the part of Flanders located on this side of the Escaut.[69]

All in all, Blanche had notably reduced the obligations at one time imposed on the Count. Ferrand preserved Lille, Ecluse, and the town of Douai, which in the charter of April 1226 were left to the King until payment of a large sum.[70] The King did not inflict expiations, but only took guarantees, and this was only just. It is true that these guarantees were not of purest form, and one realizes their value when one sees Louis IX, two years later, authorizing Ferrand to raise the gates of his cities, but by reserving stone only for the foundations; what was above ground had to be built of wood, and the ditches could not be wider, in such a way that the cities thus closed were only shelter from a *coup de main* [surprise attack]. By the same act, Ferrand was granted permission to establish in Gravelines, around his manor, a ditch and palisades.[71]

Nothing more opposed the carrying out of the measure prepared for so long a time by Blanche, and Ferrand of Portugal regained freedom towards Epiphany (6 January 1227).[72] He returned to his country and hastened to promulgate in Lille, the treaty to which he owed his deliverance.[73] Consequently, he again resumed his life as a great large feudatory, and soon one saw him appearing in the Diet of Aachen, as Comte de Hainaut, before the King of the Romans, Henri VII, son of the Emperor Frederic II.[74] The treason of 1213 was forgiven, and moreover Blanche of Castile had an ally.

The Queen had no reason to extend compassion to the accomplice of Ferrand, Renaud de Dammartin, the former Count de Boulogne. This one was a true traitor; he did not deserve pity, and the memory of his actions did not allow forgiveness despite the Count's repentance. Elsewhere, he was not allied with Blanche, and his delivery would have caused worry to Philippe Hurepel, and this was important to consider. Shortly after Bouvines, after the terrible scene that Philippe Auguste had made in Bapaume, Renaud had been immured in the new tower of Péronne castle. He had more or less a lamentable life; in his first dungeon, there had been care to attach heavy and narrow chains to his ankles so that he walked in pain.[75] The King made a transfer later to castle Goulet on the lower Seine, "so he could see Normandy," says the Ménestrel of Rheims in referring to the criminal hopes that the Count de Boulogne had conceived at the time of his conspiracy with Otto IV, Ferrand of Flanders, and King John.[76] I would prefer to believe that in this new prison the unhappy one was treated with more humanity. He had to have a moment of cruel disappointment, when he learned of the Count of Flander's freedom and did not see his own pardon arrive, and it is undoubtedly despair which killed him a short time after, towards Easter; one recounts that he was given death.[77]

    During the last years of his life, Ferrand of Portugal was always a faithful vassal, and as long as the King could count on the good will of his uncle Count Philippe de Boulogne, he found in the alliance of these two great lords a resource that was quite necessary for him: more than ever the turbulence of the nobility threatened the royal power. In the first rank of those who, after the death of Louis VIII, rather thought of conspiring than in serving their master well, was a man of ambitious character and violent destiny intended to be the inspirer and the true chief of all revolts, Pierre Mauclerc, Count of Brittany. Younger brother of the Count de Dreux, and consequently descendant of Louis the Great, close relative to Louis IX, and until then treated very well by his sovereigns, Pierre seemed to have more of a reason to remain faithful to the dynasty. Thanks to Philippe Auguste he married, in 1212, the heiress of Brittany, Alix, oldest daughter of Constance of Brittany and of Guy de Thouars; it was a brilliant marriage:[78] the father of Alix died in 1213; himself removed in 1221, after having given Pierre three children, Jean, Arthur, and Yolande; while waiting for the majority of his oldest son, Pierre had the guardianship, or, as one said then, the lease of Brittany. He was in fact the true master of the country: the title of duke that he carried was recognized by the King of England, of which dukes or counts de Bretagne were vassals for the county of Richemont, while the King of France, popes, and others still, were limited to him Count. Recognizing Philippe Auguste, he served with valiancy, and showed warlike qualities of which he did not make, at first, a good employment. In 1213 he commanded, in Flanders, with the combat of Dam, the avant-garde of the royal army; then he defended Nantes against King John, encamped in Anjou with Prince Louis (1214), joined him in England (1216), departed with him against the

Albigensians (1219). In 1215, when Prince Philippe, older brother of Saint Louis, married Agnès of Nevers, Pierre was selected for guarantor of the clauses stipulated in their contract. Louis VIII, who he followed to Poitou, preserved his favor to him, giving him the seigniories of Champtoceaux and Montfaucon and two fortresses which had been for some time the first ramparts of Brittany, Bellême in Perch and Saint-James de Beuvron.[79] If Pierre de Dreux had died in 1226, he would undoubtedly have left regrets in the court of France; one year later, this prince of the blood, this companion in arms of Philippe Auguste and his son, was the most frightening enemy of royalty. It is true that a long time before the advent of Louis IX his dominating temperament, his hard and pitiless tenacity, were expressed in struggles against the episcopate and the nobility of Brittany.

History sometimes features bizarre generosities: a man who was at the same time valiant and crafty, impassioned to the point of becoming rapt and cruel, that led to treason and ambition to defeat, is judged nowadays with a flattering indulgence. Violence of which he gave the example are allotted to deep calculations; it passed for a great policy, because he was shown insatiable and twisted, and some say that he was certainly the first man of his time.[80] All that resembles an extreme legend; though Pierre of Dreux had intelligence and courage to achieve great things, he placed his natural gifts in the service of a hateful cause, always ready to sacrifice his duties as subject to the desire to be sole master of his place, to escape the authority of his sovereign, to establish in Brittany absolute power and to break all resistance. Among those who wanted to restrain him, especially the clergy, he abused without pity, and his relationship with the churches proved of such constant hostility, that some wanted, wrongly, to allot this origin to his surname of Mauclerc.[81]

The grievances of the Breton clergy went far: from the siege of Nantes, in 1214, Pierre had sacrificed churches and cemeteries to the needs of defense. These rigorous measures could be explained by the state of war, but soon he opened for the church of Nantes an era of true persecution. Violence of all kinds on the part of the Count of Brittany was perpetrated against the clergy lands that were under the authority of the Holy See. Once alleviated, the fight began again under the reign of Louis VIII. One would have been astonished to see the Count of Brittany in December 1225, unite with Hugues de Lusignan and several lords of the west to protest near the King against the abuses of the clergy;[82] a spirit of hostility towards the churches was then general in the laic community, and Saint Louis had on more than one occasion, taken the defense of the civil world against the encroachments of the religious power; but Pierre Mauclerc did not hold himself to words. In 1226, in Nantes, he reversed permission for churches to build walls or trace ditches on ecclesiastical lands and cemeteries;[83] he defrocked and imprisoned clergy, locked them up in holy places where they had taken refuge.[84] Three years later, he buried alive a priest with the corpse of an usurer to which this unhappy priest had refused to give burial rites.[85]

As hard on his vassals as he had been with his bishops, Pierre Mauclerc, as early as the reign of Philippe Auguste, created irreconcilable enemies in the nobility of Brittany. He despoiled and threw into revolt the viscounts of Léon;[86] attacked about same time by Amaury de Craon, and the counts of Nevers and Vendôme, who invaded his estates at the head of a large army, but drew from the business a victory at Châteaubriand (1222).[87] Some time thence, he was in Poitou to make war with Savary de Mauléon.[88] In Brittany, he did not have a worse enemy than his relative Henri de Avaugour, chief of the house of Penthièvre, and soon we will find among his adversaries his brother-in-law André de Vitré. The death of Louis VIII, after which some believed the royal power to have fallen into weak hands, was to excite the ambition of the Count de Bretagne, though undoubtedly he had never raised claims against the crown. Formed however, at this time, was a legend which had Robert, first Count de Dreux, as ancestor of Pierre Mauclerc and his brothers, who would have been elder brother of Louis VI. Drawn away from the throne for weakness of mind, he had, said some, reverted rights to his descendants, who formed the elder branch of the royal house.[89] Mauclerc, who could not seriously believe this remarkable fable, was quite capable of exploiting it to weaken and discredit the royal power. From the advent of Louis IX he showed his disposition to revolt in abstaining from the coronation. Grand feudatory, tested man of war, he saw France full of lords as disturbed as him; finally he was ensured of finding against Blanche of Castile, without even leaving the kingdom, the support of a foreign prince.

Peace had never been restored between France and England since Philippe Auguste had taken from John the best share of his continental possessions. In the eyes of young Henry III this humiliating spoliation could not be final, and the English awaited an occasion to return provinces that they had lost. Blanche of Castile knew that one day or the other the King of England would link up with those in France who sought the lowering of the royal power. While waiting, the relationship between the two countries was bad and prone to continual changes. At every moment, for a hope of revenge, a project of which the execution was still dubious, maritime relations were chaotic on the English Channel; vessels on one side or the other were seized or expelled; especially in England the French sailors were threatened unceasingly and their freight placed in danger. The most rigorous ordinances were promulgated, then rescinded, according to the whim of those who controlled England.

This state of affairs, perpetuated during all the reign of Louis VIII, did not improve with the advent of his son.[90] Louis IX had just risen to the throne when Henry III, in execution of previous orders, told the mayor and the viscounts of London, along with the bailiffs of Southampton and Sandwich, to arrest French merchants and to put their goods under sequestration.[91] This measure was carried out in December 1226 at Hartlepool, and in January 1227 at the fairs of Stanford, Saint Yves and Saint Botolph.[92] However the prohibition was raised, in the current of the same year, in favor of vessels loaded with wheat, wines and victuals.[93] Nothing was arbitrary; subjects of Henry III, foreigners against whom he had no grievance, were the same victims of these violent processes, when, suddenly, they authorized vessels held in the English ports to leave and, until a new order, to make trade where they saw fit.[94]

I do not know if Blanche of Castile and her agents treated with as much rigor the English sailors; it is certain however that in 1227 a merchant of Harfleur seized cargo from a ship of Bordeaux.[95] In the current of the same year, the deacon of the chapter of Rouen and two of his canons were authorized to go to England for the business of their church, but only after having made an oath promising to undertake nothing against either the King nor against the kingdom.[96]

All these facts indicate an extremely delicate situation. The severity of the English government was slackened however, in a certain number of circumstances, in consideration of commercial interests or for political reasons. The Normans, in particular, were saved, perhaps because the King of England still counted on the feelings of these people who for a long time had belonged to his family. In 1224, while French goods and vessels were sequestered throughout England, a Norman boat, arrested in Newcastle, was authorized to go to Dieppe.[97] In December 1226, exceptions were made in favor of ships bound for this port and a branch of the Somme.[98] Soon, a boat from Rouen was freed at Kings-Lynn, and Shoreham, the Dieppois were authorized to take the sea again, on condition that they pledged to return at Easter to serve Henry.[99] Safe conducts were delivered, in November 1226 and May 1227, for the Rouennais, and on 13 April 1227 for eight vessels of Barfleur.[100]

The death of Louis VIII, by putting the house of France in a perilous situation, seemed to support the hopes and claims of the Plantagenets. While Blanche of Castile found herself occupied with the ill will or the hatred of several great vassals, a worrying movement occurred on the borders of the provinces occupied by the English. Henry III dominated without question in Gascogne; he had sent there in 1225 his brother Richard, who he styled the Comte de Poitiers.[101] From the first days of the new reign, several Poitevin lords, at the head of which was Savary de Mauléon, abandoned the King of France and decided to run the country for themselves, to plunder on sea and land; they were attached to the party of the King of England and called Richard to come with them to attack Rochelle.[102] At the same time, the brother of Henry III and the Count of Toulouse intended to fight the French, their common enemy.[103] In Poitou, French domination was not yet well established; events were soon to show that the lord of Parthenay, Guillaume the Archbishop, and Hugues, Viscount of Thouars, were not for the crown of France vassals worthy of confidence, but it was especially on the Count de la Marche, Hugues X of Lusignan, that Henry III could hope to restore his authority in this area. Though this great feudatory was at one time loyal to the father of Louis IX, he remained closely related to the royal house of England by his marriage with the widow of King John, the ambitious Isabelle of Angouleme. He had, in addition to the domains of La Marche and Lusignan, the county of Angouleme, dowry of his wife; to the west his possessions extended from Saintes all the way to the island of Oloron.

With the assistance of the Poitevin lords the King of England could have the hope to push back the border of his French fiefs all the way to the lower Loire. Normandy, treated hard, after the conquest, by the agents of Philippe Auguste, was still very ravaged from these treatments under its new masters. The King of England had Pierre de Dreux of Brittany on his side, and one was going to see being formed against Louis IX and his mother a frightening coalition extending from the Pyrenees, along the Ocean and the English Channel, until the island of Cotentin. However, the Count of Brittany then seemed determined to make common cause with the enemies of France.

The disposition of Pierre Mauclerc had changed for the better since the time when Philippe Auguste mentioned him as a sound vassal and ally in the truce concluded between him and the Crowns of England.[104] On the another side of the sea he had, from his wife's inheritance, the county of Richemont, on the subject of which he had, a few years before, reached an agreement with Henry III and thus had on him a very powerful means of action, and the Count of Brittany, ambitious and unruly, was attached to the English alliance by serious interests.[105] Since 1224, the hand of his daughter Yolande had been sought by Henry III, who addressed himself to the court of Rome to obtain an exemption for this union.[106] It is true that shortly after the King of England had made steps to marry the daughter of Leopold, Duke of Austria; but this project, remained without progress, and did not make him give up the Breton marriage.[107] On 19 October 1226 he promulgated a notice of his intention to take Yolande for his wife, having received from the Pope the necessary authorization. Once the marriage took place, King Henry was to help Pierre to defend or put forward his rights; he engaged to deliver to him in entirety the Richemont fief he had suddenly lost in France; after having referred to an agreement previously concluded between him and the Count de la Marche, Henry III promised, on the faith of his oath, to cross the sea when Mauclerc would give him the council of it.[108]

The most powerful lords of Poitou, then, were won over to the English cause. The Count de La Marche, Hugues de Lusignan, the Viscount of Thouars, and the Lord of Parthenay treated, on December 18, with the enemies of France.

The Count de La Marche, to whom Henry III was son-in-law, obtained for him and his children advantageous conditions. The King of England gave him Saintes, Saintonge, Pont-le-Abbé, and the island of Oleron. Henry gave up all the rights that he could hold from his mother in the city and the county of Angouleme, infeuded in his ally Merpins and Cognac on the Charente.[109] The English felt assured of victory, because at the same time their King yielded Niort to his mother, and after it Lusignan; however this city since 1224 was occupied by the French; Queen Isabelle was to keep Niort until the day when she would claim her rights over Issoudun.[110]

To the Viscount of Thouars the King of England yielded the

fief of Loudun and its privileges, then in the control of Louis IX; in awaiting this seizure, the Viscount was to take, on the treasury of Henry III, a revenue of five hundred *marcs*.[111] In preparation for the case where the King of France would carry the war to Poitou, Henry agreed to maintain in Thouars a hundred knights, two hundred sergeants with horse, and twenty-five crossbowmen, and these forces were to be almost doubled, as from the moment when the French would have passed the Loire. It was, moreover, agreed that at once after having lent homage to Henry III, the Viscount would receive a gift of a thousand *marcs*, with the approval of the counts La Marche and Brittany.[112]

The same day yet Henry III, with the prayer of the Count de La Marche, granted financial benefits to Guillaume the Archbishop, Lord of Parthenay, by guaranteeing the possession to him of his castles and his strongholds. He engaged moreover to assist him in strengthening Partheuay, which had, in case of hostilities, to receive a garrison maintained by the King of England.[113]

From the end of December, Henry requested money from his barons, who promised it to him;[114] one month later, he made known his intention to cross over to France, established a levy on London, the cities of England, inhabitants of the boroughs and others places in his domains.[115] At the same time, owners of the boats which had to cross the Channel accepted an order to be in England by mid-Lent (18 March 1227), to be held for the provision of the King;[116] Gascon vessels, arrested in English ports, were authorized to leave, but on condition that they return at Easter.[117] On 13 January 13, the King of England wrote Pierre of Brittany to stimulate his zeal, with his Poitevin allies to announce the next arrival of ambassadors with whom they would have to meet.[118]

In the presence of growing dangers each day, Queen Blanche did not remain inactive; but she failed in her efforts to detach Count de La Marche from the league.[119] Not only Hugues de Lusignan and Pierre de Dreux were with the English, but the coalition of Mauclerc became even more frightening with the accession of the powerful Count de Champagne. At one unspecified time, but which cannot be posterior to the first months of 1227, Hugues de Lusignan engaged by oath to help Thibaud IV against all his enemies, with the reserve of the faith that he made to the Count of Brittany, and not to conclude with the King of England any arrangement prejudicial to his new ally. Thibaud accepted from Pierre Mauclerc a similar promise.[120] At the same time as the Count of Champagne, the confederates inserted in their party the Count de Bar.[121] Thus the movement which propelled the great feudatories to revolt was trending eastward in the kingdom.

In Poitou, these confederates had their the most advanced positions with Thouars and Parthenay; they occupied Bellême en Perhce, and in lower Normandy Saint-James de Beuvron, that the Count of Brittany had fortified and provisioned with victuals.[122] Some of the most recent conquests of royalty, especially La Rochelle, were lost in the middle of enemies. Count Richard, who had received from England money and the help of five hundred Welshmen, held the country from the rebel Poitevins, whose courage was supported by the hope to see Henry III soon arriving in person.[123] As for the reasons of this revolt, they could only be poor excuses; perhaps some of the vassal rebels reflected ahead the claims to be made on fiefs; in general, the clergy of the kingdom disapproved of their enterprise.[124]

Blanche of Castile, advised to go to Chinon to hear the rebels, set out at the head of a large army; she had Cardinal Romain with her, legate of the Holy See, the Count de Boulogne, Philippe Hurepel, the Count de Dreux, Robert Gâtcblé, brother of Pierre Mauclerc, faithful in his duty to the King, like his other brother, Henri, who came to be elected Archbishop of Rheims.[125] On 20 February 1227 they were in Tours, where Louis IX and his mother were solemnly received in the monastery of Saint Martin, then in the cathedral church of Saint-Maurice.[126] They arrived at Chinon the following day and went from there to Loudun. A very short distance separated the royal troops and the rebels, who were in Thouars; they stopped to negotiate, and during close to twenty days conferences were held halfway between the two armies, close to Curçay, in a place called Charièrre.[127] While the rebels, unable to attend themselves, sought to treat every man for himself, the Count of Champagne and the Count of Bar, who had come to the talks with a safe conduct of the King, were withdrawn near the confederates and camped under the walls of Thouars. It is necessary to believe that the English and the Poitevins did not have great confidence in them, because Count Richard and Savary de Mauléon, waiting remotely and observing events, tried to take them by a sneak attack. Thibaud and the Count of Bar had hardly time to escape and to take refuge in the midst of the royal army.[128] This failed attempt had one result; the Count de Champagne, already shaken in his resolution at the sight of royal troops, checked by the respect that he still had for his sovereign, subjected himself entirely to the King, who made him a benevolent reception, and the Count de Bar followed his example.[129] I am unaware of the moment at which the disposition of Count Thibaud was revealed to the confederates; on 2 March 1227, Pierre de Dreux and Hugues de La Marche were authorized to conclude a truce with the King which was to last until the fortnight of Easter and to end the moment when Louis IX and his army passed Chartres or Orléans.[130] This return to obedience, which was undoubtedly worth forgiveness of the Count de Champagne's fault, cost him little; in the March, finding himself in Paris, he abandoned to the King all that could belong to him in the fiefs of Breteuil, of Millancay en Blésois and of Romorantin.[131]

The influence of Blanche contributed to rehabilitate Thibaud. At the moment when her allies of the day before did not think to treat her as an enemy, he found in closeness to her and Louis IX a sincere devotion and a lapse of memory of offences. Blanche was thirty-eight years old, had been beautiful and certainly remained so; it is probable that the Count of Champagne felt carried towards her by the recognition of a more intimate feeling, and it was said, not without reason, that his passion for her consequently inspired in him some of his more gracious poetry;[132] verse such as this, written by a grand and powerful prince, could only address a Queen.[133]

One is obliged to recount how the defection of the Count of Champagne rendered the counts of Brittany and de La Marche more tractable; however, they did not decide at once to resort to arms; they undoubtedly hoped for English help. Summoned to appear before the royal court, they did not take the trouble to show up and made an offer to the King to come find him in Chinon; but this was undoubtedly a ruse to gain some time; at the fixed day, Mauclerc and Hugues did not show themselves and neglected to send representatives. They had to be summoned a second time; then, going to councils of their close relations, they declared themselves ready to appear before Louis IX in Tours. They waited in vain; finally the Queen lost patience and addressed them, on the opinion of the barons, a third summation. Now it was necessary to obey or accept war; the two counts announced the intention to come before their sovereign at Vendôme. The royal army had already been moving in retirement as envisaged in the arrangements made with the Count of Champagne, and the King was at Vendôme, when on 16 March 1227, Pierre Mauclerc and Hugues made their tender. It was there, after having made homage in the presence of the legate, that they subscribed to the conditions offered by the Regent.[134]

One can say that Pierre de Dreux made a good deal when, yielding to the solicitations of his brother the elected Archbishop of Rheims, he accepted the proposals which were made to him.[135] Culpable among all, he obtained unmerited advantages; but, under another relationship the treaties concluded at Vendôme between Louis IX and his unruly vassals deserves to be studied. While making good the counts of Bretagne and de La Marche, Blanche removed them from English influence to place them under her dependence and devoted to her family.

The Regent, in the name of the King, promised to marry the daughter of Pierre Mauclerc, Yolande of Brittany, to her third son, Jean, heir to Maine and Anjou, on condition however that the Church granted this union.[136] Until the moment when this young prince, born on 21 July 1219, achieved his majority, Pierre de Dreux was to hold Angers, Baugé, and Beaufort, with their dependencies, and to enjoy, in these domains, all seigniorial rights, along with the *droit d'host et de chevauchée* [right to call men to arms and have them serve in military expeditions of the lord], and *régales et des hommages* [the right to receive ecclesiastical revenue, i.e., *régales*, and the right to have men swear homage to him alone, i.e., *hommage*]. Saumur, Loudun, their dependencies and parts of Anjou located near the diocese of Angers, remained alone in the hands of the King and his mother. Moreover, if Queen Bérengère, widow of Richard Coeur-de-Lyon, suddenly died before the majority of Prince Jean, Pierre de Dreux was to have Le Mans and its *châtellenie* [like a *seigneurie* and the jurisdiction of a *seigneur*].

If Jean de France did not reach his twenty-first year, or even if his marriage with Yolande should be broken, Pierre of Brittany would no less preserve the fiefs indicated above during the number of years agreed to. On the other hand, the death of Mauclerc, if it arrived for during this period, was to make them fall into the hands of the King.

Saint-James de Beuvron and Bellême in Perche, which Louis VIII had given guardianship to Pierre de Dreux, were yielded to him on a purely hereditary basis, with the forest of Bellême and the castle of Perièrre, located at some distance from this city, on condition however of not raising new works or new fortresses. If the Count had suddenly lost rights to Bellême, Perièrre and their dependencies, the incomes of these strongholds were to be established for him to be paid in property.

For his part, Pierre promised to give in dowry to his daughter Briecomte-Robert, Champtoceaux, all that he could acquire in Anjou, plus Saint-James de Beuvron, Perièrre, Bellême and their belongings, while reserving all to himself during his life.

He swore to the King and the Regent that he would always serve them well, to never combine, either by marriage nor otherwise, with the King of England and with his brother Richard, with those who might be at war with the King, and not to be engaged nor to marry his daughter, as long as Prince Jean would not have achieved his fourteenth year.

The Queen, Chancellor Guerin, and the Count de Boulogne engaged to evaluate the incomes of Angers, Baugé and Beaufort, to be used for Pierre during his life, as from the moment when he would have lost the lease of these fiefs. It was further stipulated that if Jean, son of Pierre Mauclerc, died before his father, Prince Jean de France could not, as long as Pierre would live, take advantage of any right on Brittany of the inheritance of his wife. On the other hand, any infringement of the subscribed engagements by the Count was to involve the loss of domains which were allotted to him by the treaty, unless he did not make satisfaction before the court of the King forty days after having been requested.

Finally, Yolande was to be entrusted, before the fifteen of Easter [25 April 1227], to Philippe de Boulogne, uncle of the King, with the elected Archbishop of Rheims and with the Count Robert de Dreux, brothers of the Count de Bretagne, with his relative Enguerrand de Coucy and the Constable of France, Mathieu de Montmorency, except on being returned to her father if Jean de France had suddenly died. We still have the act by which five grand seigneurs were to act as guardians for the daughter of Pierre Mauclerc.[137]

Such was the first Treaty of Vendôme, at the same time equitable and intelligent, which increased the great honor of the political sense of Blanche of Castile and her advisers.[138] While ensuring to Pierre de Dreux certain strongholds and important incomes, the Queen attached him to the crown of France by the prospect of an advantageous union. It gave him much, but took, in a preview of new infidelities, serious guarantees. The treaty concluded with the Count de La Marche was no less skilful.[139]

Two marriages were decided, between Alphonse de France and Isabelle de Lusignan, daughter of Count Hugues and Isabelle,

Queen of Angouleme, the other between Hugues de Lusignan, their elder son, and Isabelle de France, sister of the King. It was agreed that if young Hugues suddenly died, his replacement would be heir in his place and would marry the daughter of Blanche. Prince Alphonse was to receive, as dowry, Saintes and the island of Oleron, but the King reserved to his liking the dowry of his sister Isabelle.[140] Louis IX promised, as compensation, 10,000 *marcs* if by default these two marriages, authorized by the Church, would not be accomplished. It ensured the Count de La Marche, for ten years, a revenue of 10,600 *livres tournois*, very important for the time, representing a double allowance. Louis VIII had formerly promised to the Count de La Marche, by a treaty concluded in Bourges in May 1224, to give him Bordeaux; the abandonment of this possible right was represented by part of the revenue promised.[141] The remainder was intended to compensate Isabelle of Angoulême, who renounced his dowry; only this lifetime allowance, was to be reduced by half if the King could make Henry III return to Isabelle the part of the dowry established in England.

Hugues promised to the King and Blanche to help them "against all men who could live or die," not to give asylum to their enemies; in the event of war, he engaged to make it possible to supply the places belonging to the King; this article aimed especially at La Rochelle. The King authorized Hugues de Lusignan to leave, in preparation for his death, the lease of its domain to his wife, Queen Isabelle, or to any other person who would be king or would not be at war with France. Lastly, a pledge later cancelled by Pope Gregory IX, had Louis IX promise not to make either peace nor truce with the King of England without the approval of the Count.[142]

Queen Isabella renounced, by a special act, her dowry.[143] As of 17 March, in other words, the very same day or shortly after when the treaty was signed, the Viscount of Brosse was concluded, the Viscount of Châtellerault and three other vassals of Count de La Marche guaranteed the conditions to which they had just subscribed and promised to constitute themselves hostages in Bourges in case of infringement.[144] Blanche of Castile took care to accurately implement its engagements, and three years later Hugues de Lusignan recognized that until this date sums promised by the treaty of Vendôme had paid been to him regularly.[145]

Remaining only with Savary de Mauléon and some noble Poitevins, Richard of England was in a less advantageous situation;

some have recounted that after the treaties of Vendôme the Count of Brittany went to join, to fight, Imbert de Beaujeu, who led royal troops then in the Midi.[146] This assertion would deserve to be confirmed, but it is certain that the brother of Henry III, abandoned by his allies, could not for the moment continue the war. He accepted without delay a truce which was to last until at Easter (11 April , and which, with its expiry, was prolonged until about Midsummer's Day (8 July 1227).[147] The Viscount of Thouars followed his example, and it happened that in a very short time, without spreading one drop of blood, Blanche of Castile reduced to nothing a frightening coalition.[148]

It is true that the King of England had not taken to arms yet; whatever his illusions, and he preserved some, he was to receive hard attacks. As of 21 March, he had written to Count de La Marche to inform him that some advised him to conclude a truce or make peace;[149] one must think that he did not know yet, at this date, the treaties that his confederates had just signed with Louis IX and Blanche of Castile; but, at this time, his envoys in France, the Archbishop of York, the Bishop of Carlisle and Philippe of Aubigny already knew the turn of events; when they came in the name of their master to ask for Yolande of Brittany, Pierre de Dreux answered them that he had made his peace with King.[150] They returned to England and Richard de Cornouailles followed, accompanied by Savary de Mauléon. He returned to his country some time after Easter, and probably in the first days of May, to seek the money necessary to pay his troops.[151] His title of Count de Poitiers was not to be more for him than a qualification without value, but soon he accepted a compensation, when Henry III, after a momentary estrangement, gave to him goods which in England had constituted the dowry of their mother Isabelle, with the removed fiefs of Pierre of Brittany and those which at one time had belonged to Renaud de Dammartin, Count of Boulogne, uncle of Louis IX.[152]

While Henry III prepared to better support a badly engaged war, there arrived help from Rome that he hardly deserved. Honorius III had died on 18 March; the new Pope, Gregory IX, elected on the following day and intalled almost at once, openly took the defense of English interests. The Holy See was disposed to spare France and to treat with regard a King from which the father came to die on return from a crusade against the Albigensians; but how to give up, in embarrassment to whence he was thrown, this King of England who claimed to be the suzerain? Gregory ordered Cardinal Legate Romain to remain in France, to advise the young King on the subject of his relationship with the English and Poitevins, and to supervise the crusade against the heretics of the Midi.[153] On 10 May, in one laudatory letter, he wrote Louis IX, his mother and her brothers, that he took them under his protection; but soon recriminations followed praises, when he learned that the English were going to see themselves threatened by an enemy that they had imprudently attacked.[154] In a rather sour tone that is, he reproached the King of France for the campaigns of his grandfather and his father against King John and Henry III; the Holy See, believing he had not wanted to proceed against them as he should have done; he had shown them much moderation, and here he advised their successors to remove from the King of England as little as possible that which remained to the English in France. Gregory entreated Louis IX to restore English possessions that he held unduly and not to raise a hand against the others (25 May 1227).[155] He also wrote Henry III that by taking Louis IX under his protection, because of his war against the Albigensians, he in no way had encouraged him to seize the English domains in France.[156] At the same time, Cardinal Romain accepted a pontifical letter which prohibited him to pronounce, unless under special order, excommunication or interdict against the King of England or Richard de Cornouailles.[157]

It is necessary to believe, for the honor of Gregory IX, that he had been badly informed. With his injunction, Blanche of Castile was right to answer that the King of France was a child and an orphan, and that the King of England, at the moment when this young suzerain had no means to attack, benefited from this critical situation to plot with vassals of the crown. It was not from Louis IX, but from Henry III that aggression had come.

However persecuted, this King of England, who pled for a cause with so much ardor, and without bothering himself to know if he had been first to disturb the peace, dreamed of warlike expeditions. On 15 April 1227, Henry III ordered the bailiffs Dover and several other ports to join together for the fortnight from Easter (25 April) all the vessels they were able to lay out.[158] Then, new armaments were announced for 23 May, and for the fifteen days to follow Pentecost (31 May - 13 June).[159] On 2 June, Henry notified all of his resolution to pass through Gascogne and Poitou, and readied a large fleet at Portsmouth on 25 July, the festival of Saint Jacques.[160] In June, he delayed his departure, but without stopping preparations; sums issued fro the aid levied on the English clergy for the war were sent to London for the disposition of the King, who was to leave on 1 August.[161] On this date, the King was to be joined in Winchester by his vassals, while supplies intended for the expeditions were to be gathered in Portsmouth.[162] But at the same time the Bishop of Carlisle and Philippe d'Aubigny crossed the Channel, undoubtedly briefed to negotiate an arrangement with Blanche of Castile.[163] Lastly, about the middle of July, the truce between the two kingdoms was concluded. It was to last until 24 June 1228;[164] it was claimed, probably wrongly, that it was bought by Henry III at the price of two thousand *marcs*.[165]

Peace, for all that, was not restored; Henry III would soon return to his military projects. While waiting to gain advantages more meritorious, he deprived his French vassals who had fiefs in England. It was seen that Pierre of Brittany and Philippe Hurepel, heir to the former Count de Boulogne, Renaud de Dammartin, had been dispossessed to the profit of Richard de Cornouailles; the Count Robert de Dreux expiated in the same way by losing his English fiefs for the fidelity with which he had served the [French] King.[166] Blanche of Castile hastened to give him, as compensation, fiefs located in Normandy, which were to remain with him as long as his English fiefs would remained unrestored.[167] In a moment where treason seemed so convenient, where true devotion was rare, the Queen had great interest to recognize, by advantageous concessions, services rendered to the crown. As of March, Philippe Hurepel had been granted a life annuity amounting to six thousand *livres tournois*.[168] The Rochelois had held firm when they seemed abandoned in the middle of enemies; she confirmed their privileges, and the fidelity with which they had made proof was rewarded by important exemptions.[169] In Anjou, Blanche was given homage, at the beginning of the year, by Jeanne de Craon, daughter of Guillaume des Roches, for the responsibility of seneschal of Anjou, Maine, and Touraine, which had been reserved for him.[170]

The Queen of France attached to her son those to whom she believed had a capacity to assist the royal power. She endeavored to satisfy everyone. In August 1227, by an act of leniency not contrary to her interests, she returned to freedom the former chief mercenary Lambert Cadoc, who had once served Philippe Auguste as a soldier and bailiff. After having been made odious by his exactions, he had been thrown in prison for a sum of 14,200 *livres parisis* that he owed to King Philippe. Blanche, on releasing him, required him to give up all his fiefs, some of which however were returned, and he was told that the Bishop of Évreux would excommunicate him if ever he contravened his engagements.[171] The Chamberlain Barthélemy de Roye appeared with some other crown servants in the charter that the Bishop of Evreux returned in this circumstance; one sees chancellor Guerin appointed; he had died on April 19, devoted to the service of his young master.[172] His disinterested fidelity did not remain without reward, because he had seen, with the treaties of Vendôme, the first success gained by Blanche of Castile over the enemies of royalty.

The treaties of Vendôme and the renewal of the truce with England gave a little respite to Blanche; for some time she was disencumbered from part of her enemies. This temporary pacification was more necessary as royalty had a war to support in the south of France. The unexpected death of Louis VIII and the advent of his young son had renewed the business of the Count de Toulouse and his partisans. By leaving Languedoc, King Louis had been able to believe that his authority had made important progress; beyond his kingdom and in the domains to which the Emperor claimed to extend his capacity, he had lowered the pride of Avignon.[173] The humiliation of this powerful city had been so great, that in the month of January 1227, to obtain from the legate Romain Saint-Ange [Romano Frangipani] his discharge, he had to subscribe to hard conditions: help defend the counts of Toulouse and Foix; an obligation to lend assistance to the King of France against his enemies, leveling the ramparts of Avignon and to filling its ditches, which could not be restored without the permission of the legate and the King, and to give the King all machines of war found in the city.[174] Louis VIII had established a seneschal in both Beaucaire and Normandy; he had left in Languedoc, to complete the subjection and control of the country, his relative Imbert de Beaujeu with five hundred knights.[175] Among those who held on at the edges of the Garonne for the party of the King there appeared in the first rank the brother of celebrated Simon de Montfort, Guy, Count of Sidon and of Castres.

The death of Louis VIII surprised but did not discourage those he left behind.[176] A few days after the advent of their young King, they delivered to the partisans of the Count de Toulouse a heroic battle, whose news came to Rheims during the anointment of Louis IX.[177] This advantage, on which I do not have precise information, was not to be very important, because the situation of royalty in Languedoc remained extremely difficult.

Blanche took measures to help them: in December 1226, the King wrote to his knights, burgers, and good people of Béziers, to announce that he was going to send in "Albigois" money and supplies of all sorts.[178] At the same time, Blanche sent troops to the Midi in the midst of which rode several bishops and a great number of knights.[179] In January 1227, the King took under his protection the town of Saint-Antonin en Rouergue and conceded for life to Béraud de Mercœur the castle and the viscounty of Grèzes in Gévaudan.[180] Thus royalty did not recoil to make its authority prevail in Languedoc, but it is necessary to point out that far from triumphing, one is misled when it was said that the reinforcements sent by Blanche of Castile reduced to obedience the city and all the county of Toulouse.[181] Far from being cut down, Raimond VII was then in a relatively favorable situation.

It is probable that in lower Languedoc the Count of Toulouse and his adherents were in progress, because we know by the acts of the Council of Narbonne, which was held during Lent of 1227, that at that time Limoux, at one time submitted to Louis VIII, had in fact defected.[182] In the valley of the Ariège, the crusaders took Varilhes, between Foix and Pamiers, but this conquest cost the life of Guy de Montfort (31 January), and elsewhere, Raimond VII quickly carried Auterive; the defenders of this place had to capitulate before anyone could go to their aid.[183] Guillaume Bernard and Pierre Gros, lords of Najac in Rouergue, had forgotten their recent submission to Louis VIII and returned their obedience to the Count de Toulouse; in May 1227, they promised him not to make peace with the King of France, nor with the Church, nor with any other of his enemies.[184]

In the middle of all the difficulties which accompanied the advent of her son, Blanche of Castile found the war in Languedoc imposed heavy financial burdens, and perhaps she had been forced by Raimond VII to make some not very advantageous arrangements, if she had not been strongly assisted, in the business of the Albigensians, by the legate of the Holy See, Romain, cardinal-deacon with the title of Saint-Ange. Since his return to France, this energetic man of good counsel had returned with more than service; charged by the Pope with completing the war against the Albigensians, he had been extremely useful for King Louis, in the service of which Honorius III had him accredited. His devotion appeared to double upon the death of this prince; at the time, he was not concerned only to make the interests of the Catholic Church prevail, and he also took in hand the cause of Blanche and Louis IX. Without doubt he thought that while placing at the service of the King of France his intelligence and any capacity with which he was invested, he defended against religious anarchy which threatened to tear off the southernmost provinces of our country; it is probable also that he took a genuine interest in this courageous woman and this child against which so many hatreds and ambitions were united. He followed them to Rheims, at the time of the coronation, and accompanied them in their path along the Loire, until they had to reduce the first revolt of the barons. To ensure money necessary for Languedoc, he carried out with proud tenacity a forced subsidy from the clergy that had been promised for this purpose the at the Council of Bourges.

This assembly, which was held at the end of 1225, granted to Louis VIII, for his direction of the war against the Albigensians in person, a ten-per-cent tax raised on all the ecclesiastical incomes of the kingdom; this subsidy was to last for five years, if however the war lasted this long. Under the terms of this decision, Romain, while Louis VIII lived, had written his prelates and clergy of his legation to pay, for the current year, a half of the ten-per-cent tax at All Saint's Day (1 November 1226), and the other at Easter (11 April 1227). Nobody opposed; the majority of chapters carried it out, as the remainder of clergy, paid for first half of the year and were subjected partly, after the death of the King, with the levy which was to take place at Easter. But soon, in the ecclesiastical provinces of Rheims, Sens, Tours, and Rouen, chapters of the cathedrals, which had started to contribute, refused to continue. The royal government addressed complaints to the legate. Romain, considering that the King could be ruined, while satisfying the business of the Albigensians, and that his council pressed him to give up if the churches paid him no subsidies that they had agreed to, authorized Louis IX to be paid by seizing the goods of recalcitrant chapters. He was justifiably irritated with their insubordination. He notified all these facts in a circular dated Monday before Ascension, 17 May 1227, and concluded while saying: "Those who fear that ecclesiastical jurisdiction is not enough to address evil, will be the least constrained by the secular power."[185] The same day, by letters addressed to the archbishops, bishops, abbots, other prelates and all the ecclesiastics, he gave an account of resistance by the chapters of the four provinces and defended no one, on this occasion, for promulgation of the excommunication, suspension, or interdict against the King, Blanche, their bailiffs, their clerks, their men or their land.[186]

Those who engaged in this fight did not accept defeat. The dissenting chapters addressed to the Pope a petition, more remarkable, to tell the truth, for its pretentious style than for the precision of its ideas;[187] but another letter, that the deacon and canons of Notre-Dame de Paris wrote at the same time to Gregory IX, had to give him pause. Telling in their manner of all the disputes relating to the ten-per-cent tax, the authors of this skillfully written memorial showed Blanche and the legate to have constantly acted, since the death of Louis VIII, without consulting the chapters. They reproached the legate for having told the Queen that, to make them pay the ten-per-cent tax, he would give her the very capes of the canons; Blanche did not want, said they, either to state a termination date for the war against the Albigensians, or to stipulate the number of the troops that she intended to devote to it. Moreover, if the chapters called upon Rome, it was to safeguard their freedom, rather than to escape the revocation of a subsidy.[188]

However the legate, without stopping this opposition, promulgated an ordinance in which he threatened various sorrows upon those that he regarded as rebels, and, on 5 June, he wrote to the Archbishop of Tours at Sens and to his suffragans to read and publish, recommending to them to give neither the original nor the copy to the delinquents.[189] The Pope gave him grief: in answer to a new address from the chapters of Sens and Paris, he enjoined Romain to revoke his ordinance.[190] Gregory IX had been misled by exaggerated complaints; he had reacted too soon; while waiting, the Cardinal continued his fight. The French episcopate does not appear to have been contrary to him; several of its members were personally attached to the crown; at the head of these stood the Archbishop of Sens, Gautier Cornu, member of one of those families who responded with unalterable good will to the interests of the sovereign. In the month of August, this Archbishop and the Bishop of Chartres, testamentary executors of Louis VIII, promised by letters patent to pay the King and Blanche, or their heirs, during four years, a sum of 1,500 *livres parisis* for the chapters of cathedral churches of the province of Sens.[191]

It was at this time that Romain left France for the first time. He paused on his voyage to attend the chapter general of the order of Cîteaux, which was held every year in September; then he recovered on the way, taking into his suite some abbots of Cîteaux and Clairvaux, some bishops and abbots recently named by him and the Archbishop of Sens, who accompanied him at the pleasure of the

Queen. He left the kingdom thus and went to Rome, preparing to take revenge on those whom he had fought. It did not take a long time to convince the Pope; the chapters of the province of Sens had yielded, while those of the provinces of Rheims, Tours, and Rouen were only more obstinate in their resistance. After having heard their prosecutors and received the explanations of the cardinal, Gregory IX wrote to the King of France, on 13 November 1227, approving the conduct of his legate and ordering the entire payment of the ten-per-cent tax, according to a promise made by Romain to Louis VIII.[192] All ended in a compromise. After much expenditure and miscalculations, the adverse chapters were authorized to replace the payment of the ten-per-cent tax, for the four years which remained, by a contribution of 100,000 *livres tournois*.[193]

In all this business, the Cardinal of Saint-Ange was led to regard Blanche with a full devotion of abnegation and courage, exposing himself to attacks and paying for a cause he found just. Thanks to him, Gregory IX, who at one time still supported the King of England against the crown of France, was finally briefed on the true situation of the kingdom. As for the chapters of which the opposition had been so difficult to overcome, it does not seem that their dealings were of an irreproachable frankness. They undoubtedly did not soon forgive the legate and the Queen who made them see reason.

Romain still had other enemies amongst the masters and students of the University of Paris, that he had so harshly treated at the time of his arrival in France. Also, it is hardly possible to know which among those malevolent insinuations in circulation reflected the true nature of his relationship with the Regent. "When he raised," says Mathieu of Paris, "a shameful matter that one should not repeat. It was said that lord the legate comprised with regard to Blanche a not very decent way. But it would be impious to believe it, this noise having been spread by the enemies of the Queen. In doubt, a benevolent spirit must rather believe the good."[194] Elsewhere, the same historian says that many great lords did not come to the coronation and refused to sit at the council of the Queen beside the legate, who was a hundred times soiled by his relations with her.[195] Mathieu of Paris was so credulous, so hostile to France and its princes, that he could not wait to see assailed without reserve as a calumny launched against Blanche of Castile; if he was himself stirring up a serious charge, his doubt would be worth an absolution.

The levies of money granted to King of France by the Council of Bourges allowed Blanche to continue the war in Languedoc. During the summer of 1227, Imbert de Beaujeu, accompanied Pierre Amelh, Archbishop of Narbonne, and Folquet, Bishop of Toulouse, the siege of Labécède castle in Lauragais, to the north of Castelnaudary. Raimond VII had entrusted this fortress to good garrison, that ordered Pons de Villeneuve and Olivier de Termes. One day Bishop Folquet passed with his people near the walls, while the besieged continued abusive cries: "Do you Hear? They call you the bishop of the devils. " "Certainly," Folquet answered, "and they tell truth, since we are, to them, devils, and me, their bishop." When the walls were no longer in a state to hold, the place was carried. Many knights and people on foot flew to the favor of the night; those who remained were massacred; the Bishop made it possible to save women and children. Géraud de la Mote, "deacon of heretics," and several unfortunates who partook of his belief, were burned to death.[196] This cruel war was continued thus, with alternatives of success and reverse. After taking Labécède, the Lord of Beaujeu left Languedoc for some time; Raimond VII continued the war, and during the winter it retook Saint-Paul-sur-l'Agout, halfway between Castres and Toulouse.[197]

It is probable that due to the recent war in Languedoc the King's men wanted to put their hands on the county of Melgueil, stronghold of the Roman Church, that Innocent III had pledged to the bishops of Maguelonne, after having stripped it from the Count of Toulouse. It was on this subject that Gregory IX wrote, in May 1227, to the King of France, the archbishops of Bourges and of Narbonne, to point out the rights of the Holy See and the validity of infeudation. This incident does not appear to have raised serious difficulties.[198] At some time after, the Pope, wanting to prevent the Queen of Cyprus, Alix, from addressing to the King of France against Count Thibaud IV her claims to the Champagne succession, wrote Louis IX and Blanche of Castile to remind them that since the time of Honorius III, of Philippe Auguste and Louis VIII, Rome reserved to itself the examination of the rights of birth on which Alix based her claims. As long as her legitimacy would have been recognized by the Holy See, in this respect no lawsuit could have been made before the royal jurisdiction.[199] No one could ignore, in this business, the prerogatives of the Papacy, and elsewhere it acted to defend its feudal interests which for some time it had sought to return to obedience. Lastly, since the settlement of incidents raised by the question of the ten-per-cent tax and the return to Italy of Romain, relations between the royal power and of the Holy See had a character of reciprocal good will. Thus, Blanche of Castile having expressed to Gregory IX her scruples on the subject of votive offerings that she had made more in good will than upon reflection, the Pope wrote the Archbishop of Sens to relieve them or authorize a change in the nature of them.[200]

Among the clergy of France there was more than one prelate to which the Pope could have given lessons of moderation. There, as among the nobility, was carried a resistance, opposite a young sovereign and a disputed capacity. It is true that Louis IX and his mother found among the archbishops, bishops and clergy of the kingdom, some of their most able and faithful advisers; devotion to royal authority and the respect of the duties which it imposed on subjects were frequent among those who were at the head of churches. But the instinct of resistance to civil authority also had representatives in this large body where, all in all, ideas of conciliation and traditional obedience dominated. The Archbishop of Rouen, Thibaud of Amiens, was one of these men with whole and inflexible character, who readily fought those who dispute their more or less real rights, and who did not know how to stop when once launched into opposition.[201] By an annoying coincidence, the inclinations of proud independence, which were not shown under Philippe Auguste and under Louis VIII, appeared when the throne was occupied by a child.

Thibaud carried structural timber to Rouen, that he had the right to take from the forest of Louviers, but only for his manor of Louviers, to the exclusion of others. The Bailiff of Vaudreuil, having learned of it, seized this wood, and thereby received a sentence of excommunication from the Bishop of Évreux. Blanche of Castile, in her turn, ordered the Archbishop of Rouen to appear before her son to answer about several objections. The King showed him to have excommunicated the Bailiff of Vaudreuil without having first referred to the King about it; to have levied a tax in the Villette, close to Louviers, and of which the baron belonged to the crown; to have misused the right that he had about the timber taken from the forest of Louviers; to have excommunicated the senior and several canons of Gournay, who were under the protection of the crown and its employees; of not coming to justice before the exchequer of Normandy, as had the other bishops and barons of this province.

Thibaud d'Amiens appeared in Vernon, undoubtedly in the month of July 1227, but declared that he did not make excuses for these various matters because the spiritual mixed with the secular. The young King and his mother showed extreme irritation over such insolence, and the Archbishop withdrew himself without giving any satisfaction.

After having consulted several barons on the matter of the Archbishop of Rouen, Louis IX summoned him for a second time, and in the presence of several great lords assembled around him, demanded his answers before the royal court. The Archbishop declared that he did not know any case where he had to do it, holding himself responsible only to the Pope. The King, pushed to the limit, and on the opinion of his barons, seized the incomes and secular holdings of the Archbishop. On the other hand Thibaud, after having consulted his bishops, launched an interdict on all the domains and castles which the King held in the province of Rouen, with the exception of the cities; then he left for Rome. Detained in Rheims on account of his health, he sent representatives to the Holy See. This business had not received a solution in 1228, when Romain came to France for the second time. The legate then obtained from the King the provisional restitution of seized goods, and the Archbishop ended up having a win, since they brought to him in Rouen the timber confiscated by the royal bailiff, the occasion first of the quarrel.[202] It is probable that the Cardinal did not take a parallel measure without sparing the dignity of the King; one cannot doubt either his skill nor his devotion to Louis IX and Blanche of Castile. But the end of this quarrel, was extremely serious for an archbishop to benefit from a difficult situation where royalty was made to appear powerless in France before a man who did not have to account for himself.

All would have been well for Blanche of Castile, if unceasingly reappearing interior difficulties were had not united with complications which came from abroad. Without the requests addressed to him from various interests in Brittany and Poitou, the King of England, then in truce with France, would perhaps never have made a descent on France. Rome, during this unfavorable time, took a more benevolent attitude. From Germany, the Queen of France had nothing to fear; in spite of the efforts of Henry III and his ministers to approach the house to Souabe, relations between France and the Empire remained good. In March 1227 the Bishop of Beauvais, without a doubt sent by his sovereign, had come to find at the Diet of Aachen the King of the Romans, Henri VII, son of the Emperor.[203] In

August, Frederic II himself, being in Melfi, confirmed the treaty that he had concluded with Louis VIII, committing him not to ally with the King of England.[204]

It was neither the house of Souabe, nor even the Plantagenets, from whence true danger came. To discover it, Blanche of Castile did not have to leave the kingdom. Concessions made in the treaties of Vendôme had not disarmed the nobility of France; while the Regent supported an interminable war in Languedoc, scandalous defections followed new revolts, showing her that too often duties yield to interests, and that the best promises hardly hold, when one thinks it easy to violate them.

1 Sermon in verse by Robert Sainceriax (*Historiens de France*; t. XXIII, p. 124-131). « *Sacheis bien, cil qui cest cscrit tendront, que le mois que li bons rois Looys trespassa, Robert Sainceriax en fit ce sermon...* » The author had thus placed his hand on it in November or December 1226; but he had taken this poem much later; demonstrating, as the editors observed, passages relating to the death of Chancellor Guérin and the deliverance of the Count of Flanders. Du Cange, who had published this text following the edition of Joinville (in-f, 1668, p. 162), entitled it: *Sermon en verse de Robert de Sainceriaux sur la mort du roy S. Louys*. One scarcely comprehends how he could have made such an error. Whatever the name Sainceriax, Saincriau, or Saincereau, it reminds one of Sancerre, and the authors of *l'Histoire littéraire de la France* (t. XXIII, p. 420) concluded that Robert could certainly be the originator of this city; in this regard, nothing is demonstrated.

2 Potthast, *Regesta pontificum Romanorum*, 1499 and 1500.
    Léopold Delisle, in his *Recherches sur les comtes de Dammartin au treizième siècle* (*Mémoires de la Société des Antiquaires de France*, 1-69, p. 189), recounted the history of Philippe Hurepel and given that the catalog of his acts is mainly from memory it is necessary to have recourse to all that refers to the name, the birth, the life and death of the Comte de Boulogne. I can cite two passages from Le Nain de Tillemont (*Histoire de S. Louis*, t. I, p. 73 and p. 322), and a dissertation by Bréquigny (*Mémoires pour servir à l'histoire de Calais; Mémoires de l'Académie des Inscriptions and Belles-Lettres*, t. XLIII, 17b6, p. 722 ff.).

3 Henri Martin, in his *Histoire de France* (t. IV, p. 134), makes of Philippe Hurepel a not very flattering portrait : «he was...a young ignorant and fat man, as indicated by his surname of Hurepel (rude skin), etc. » This appreciation is absolute fantasy. The surname of Hullepiaus, or Hullepés, is equally applied, by the poet Philippe Mousket (ed. Reiffenberg, t. II, verse 19239 and 19242), to Philippe Auguste, who did not pass for an ignorant and fat man, although he had shaggy hair, so that I append a curious text published by Paul Meyer : « *Si me meubre de Monseigneur le roi Phelippe de France que l'on pooit bien apeler le vallet maupingné, quant il estoit jucnes, car il estoit tous jours hericiez*. » Romania, 1885, p. 7.

4 Guillaume de Puy-Laurens, *Historiens de France*, t. XIX, p.217.

5 By his mother, sister of Isabelle de Hainaut, Imbert de Beaujeu was the first cousin of Louis VIII.

6 See the *Catalogue des actes de Philippe Auguste*, by Léopold Delisle, Introduction, p. LXXXVI-LXXXVII, and consult the pieces set forth in this work.

7 Guillaume le Breton, ed. Delaborde, n. 175.

8 Guillaume le Breton, in his *Chronique*, made a superb eulogy on Guérin (ed. Delaborde, *Chronique*, nos. 170 and 182), and Philippe Mousket was in agreement with him on celebrating his merits (ed. Reiffenberg, verse 27907 ff.); Robert Saincereau represented him as the most faithful servant of royalty (*Historiens de France*, l. XXIII, p. 128, verse 131 to 168).

Guérin was ordered to burn the royal fleet at Dam (Guillaume le Breton, ed. Delaborde, t. II, *Philippide*, book IX, verse 534). He retook Tournay (same ed., t. I, *Chronique*, n. 181 ; t. II, *Philippide*, liv. IX, verse 710).

His role at Bouvines (Guillaume le Breton, *Chronique*, no. 182, 183, 190, 196). He left with Prince Louis for the war against the Albigeois (ibid., n. 233); he assited with the obseques for Philippe Auguste (ibid., continuation of the manuscript of Paris, n. 7); he was charged by this prince with diplomatic missions (*Récits d'un ménestrel de Rheims*, ed. of de Wailly, *Société de l'histoire de France*, nos. 269 to 272, and 276). Under Louis VIII, he signed royal acts ; in December 1226, he was named in an act relative to arrangements concluded with the Comtesse de Flandre (Teulet, *Layettes*, t. II, n. 1898).

For the time of his death, see Philippe Mousket, ed. Reiffenberg, t. II, verse 27907; Aubry de Trois-Fontaines, *Monumenta Germaniæ*, scriptores, t. XXIII, p. 919, line 38; *Gallia Christiana*, t. X, col. 1413 and 1414.

9 Barthélemy de Roye became Chamberlain in September or October 1208 (Léopold Delisle, *Catalogue des actes de Philippe Auguste*, introduction, p. LXXXIII. See, in the table of this book, the indication of documents where it is cited).

10 In 1213, Barthélemy was one of those charged by the King to burn the royal fleet at Dam (Guillaume le Breton, ed. Delaborde, t. II, *Philippide*, liv. IX, verse 534): in 1214, he campaigned in Flanders, ibid., book X, verse 538). He took part in the Battle of Bouvines (Guillaume le Breton, t. 1, *Chronique*, n. 184, « *vir provecte etatis et sapiens* », and n. 192).

11 Barthélemy was, with brother Guérin, one of the testamentary executors of Philippe Auguste (*Historiens de France*, t. XVII, p. 115 b). Philippe Mousket gave the number of Louis VIII's counselors (ed. Reiffenberg, t. II, verse 23955).

12 *Chronique de Tours, Historiens de France*, t. XVIII, p. 319: "*Videbant enim regni Francis pervasores per manus mulieris and pueri, necnon et cujusdam senis, scilicet Bartholomæi de Roya eorumdem consiliarii, rognum Franciæ gubernatum, and ob hoc credebant illud consilio and auxilio destitutum, juxta illud Ovidii*:

> Tres aumus imbeltea numero : sine viribus uxor,
> Laertesque senez, Telemachusque puer."

One of the most curious texts that we have, concerning this, has been published, in 1890, by Léopold Delisle : *Instructions adressées par le comité des travaux historiques and scientifiques*, n. 30, p. 65; *Eloge de Barthélemy de Roie, grand chambrier de France, mort vers l'année 1231*. I used this document upon mentioning the death of Barthélemy. His generosity towards the Abbot of Saint-Antoine, near Paris, was attested to by a charter of November 1227 (*Gallia Christiana*, t. VII. proofs, col. 99 and 100).

13 Du Bouchet devoted to Robert de Courtenay several pages of his *Histoire généalogique de la maison royale de Courtenay*, in-f, 1061, p. 15, and p. 103 to 117.

The *Layettes du Trésor des Chartes*, published by Teulet, tomes I and II, contain a certain number of acts relative to Robert or signed by him ; his seal and counter-seal have been examined by Douêt d'Arcq, *Collection de sceaux*, t. I, n. 274.

Guillaume le Breton spoke of his role in the expedition to England (ed. Delaborde, t. I, *Chroniqe*, n. 223); but it was above all the *Histoire des ducs de Normandie et des rois d'Angleterre* which in this regard gives the most interesting details (ed. Francisque Michel, *Sociéité de l'histoire de France*, p. 166. 198, 201, 202, 205).

14 The life of Constable Mathieu has been recounted by Du Chesne in his *Histoire généalogique de la maison de Montmorency et de Laval*, in-fo., 1624, p. 125 ff. Rigord reported that at Messine, Philippe Auguste gave him three hundred ounces of gold (ed. Delaborde, n. 72); Guillaume le Breton noted his presence at the siege of Château-Gaillard (*Philippide*, 1. VII, v. 273), and with the army of Flanders, in 1214 (ibid., X, 469): his exploits were recounted at Bouvines (ed. Delaborde, t. I, *Chronique*, no. 186 and 188; t. II, *Philippide*, t. XI, v. 112). In April 1216, the King sent him on a mission to the Comtesse de Champagne (Delisle, *Catalogue des actes de Philippe Auguste*, no. 1658). He waas Constable from July 1218 (ibid., p. 399, note). See the tables in the *Catalogue des actes de Philippe Auguste* and the *Layettes du Trésor des Chartes*, tomes I and II.

15 Philippe Mousket, verse 28345-46.

16 P. Anselme, in his *Histoire généalog9ique and chronolog9ique de la maison royale de France*, t. VI, p. 618-021, has detailed the history of four marshals from this family :

1.) Aubry Clément, seigneur of Mez en Gâtinais, marshal under Philippe Auguste, killed at the siege of Saint-Jean-d'Acre (Itigord, ed. Delaborde, n. 81, p. 115; Guillaume le Breton, same work, t. II, *Philippide*, 1. X, verse 361).

2.) His brother Henri Clément, seigneur of Mez and d'Argentan,
nicknamed the Petit Maréchal : « *corpore parvus, mento gigas* », says Guillaume le Breton (*Philippide*, t. X, v. 224); he is found in the army of Prince Louis when King John was defeated at La Roche-au-Moine, and killed a short time later.

3.) Jean Clément, son of Henri.

4.) Henri Clément, son of Jean.

The name of Jean Clément returns in the course of this report. Guillaume le Breton, after having recounted the death of Petit Maréchal Henri (*Chronique*, n. 180), expressed himself in these terms : « *Cui successit Johannes filius ejus adhuc impubes, cujus vices commisse fuerunt Galtero de Nemosio ad tempus, quousque ipse ad adultam perveniret etatem ; et hoc totum fuit de benignitate regis, quia hereditaria succcssio in talibus officiis lecum non habet.* »

17 Jean de Beaumont; Teulet, *Layettes*, t. II, 1639, March 1224; ibid., 1811, act of 3 November 1226.

18 Adam de Beaumont; *Layettes*, t. II, 1811.
19 Ibid.

20 Ibid.

21 Jean de Vallery; ibid.

22 Guillaume Ménier; *Layettes*, t. II, 1639, March 1224; ibid., 1713, July 1225.

23 Adam de Milly; *Layettes*, t. II, 1639, March 1224.

24 Hugues d'Athies; *Layettes*, t. II, 1639, March 1224; 1713, July 1225.

25 Simon de Poissy often appears in the acts of Philippe Auguste (Lêopold Delisle. *Catalogue*, no. 660, 1008, 1404, 1888, 1951, 1959, 2191; years 1201 to 1223). Guillaume le Breton, who called him « Simon Pissianita », speaks of the role he played at the siege of Lincoln and after the defeat suffered by the French under the walls of this city (ed. Delaborde, t. I, *Chronique*, n. 223) In January 1226 he figured, with Robert de Poissy, in the number of vassals who, on this date, had declared to have counseled the King to undertake the expedition against the Albigeois (Teulet, *Layettes*, t. II , n. 1742). He is named in the act of 3 November 1226 (*Layettes*, t. II, n. 1811).

26 Gautier le Chambrier, or sometimes "Chambellano," servant of Philippe Auguste, had by his wife Aveline, Dame de Nemours, seven sons, of whom three were bishops, namely : Etienne, Bishop of Noyon; Pierre, Bishop of Paris; Guillaume, Bishop of Meaux; the four others became knights; they were Philippe de Nemours, Gautier le Chambrier or "Chambellan," better known under the name of Gautier le Jeune, Ours, *chambellan*, and Jean. Aubry de Trois-Fontaines named them in his chronicle (*Monumenta Germaniæ*, scriptores, t. XXIII, p. 881, p. 922) ; Guillaume le Breton eulogized three bishops, none of whom survived Philippe Auguste (ed. Delaborde, t. I, *Chronique*, n. 176). Gautier le Jeune, charged by this prince to reconstitute the registers of the *Trésor des Chartes*, was one of his most faithful counsellors; he rendered numerous services and distinguished himself well at Bouvines (see the table from the edition of Guillaume le Breton). His brother, the *chambellan* Ours, was often named in royal acts (Delisle, *Catalogue des actes de Philippe Auguste*, docs. 424, 478, 977, 1406, 2034); he figures as a witness in a charter of Marie, Comtesse de Ponthieu, subscribed by several other officers and servants of Louis VIII (*Layettes*, t. II, n. 1713, July 1225); he took part in the editing of the letter that the barons and prelates addressed to Frederick II during the siege of Avignon (*Layettes*, t. II, n. 1789, June 1226) ; he was near the King on 3 November 1226 (*Layettes*, t. II, 1811). A certain Philippe de Nemours appears, under the title of witness, in this last piece, in a charter of March 1224, signed by the grand officers and men of the King (*Layettes*, t. II, 1639). Their relative Guy de Mérévillo is in the same case (*Layettes*, t. II, 1639, 1713, 1811); he was, with Gautier de Nemours, seigneur d'Aschères (Delisle, *Catalogue*, 1982), and is found, in June 1230, in the act of condemnation of Pierre Mauclerc (*Layettes*, t. II, 2056). I do not need to write a history of the "maison de Nemours"; like the families of Mez, Barres, Vallery, Milly, all of them established on the same corner of the world, they devoted themselves for several generations to the service of a dynasty, to which they gave a fortune.

27 In 1206; *Bibliothèque des Écoles françaises d'Athènes et de Rome*, fascicule VI, p. 25.

28 *Histoire des ducs de Normandie*, p. 169, 198, 201.

29 Guillaume le Breton, *Chronique*, ed. Delaborde, I, n. 188; *Philippide*, book XI, v. 105, 133, 144. See, on Michel de Harnes, the tables from the *Catalogue des actes de Philippe Auguste* and the *Layettes du Trésor des Chartes*, t. II. He lived only until 21 March 1235 (*Layettes*, t. H, 2356); Philippe Mousket made his eulogy, v. 28338.

30 *Layettes du Trésor des Chartes*, t. II, 1828. November 1226.

31 Rigord, ed. Delaborde, n. 69. Bréquigny, *Mémoires de l'Académie des Inscriptions*, t. L, 1808 ; *Recherches sur les régences en France*, p. 524.

32 "*la prist congié à ses barons*" says the *Grandes Chroniques de France*, ed. Paulin, Paris, IV, 68.

33 *Musée des Archives nationales*, n. 269, April 1270; ibid., n. 291, June 1285.

34 Archives nationales, K 40. no. 3 and 4.

35 Arch. nat., JJ 65, fol. 1-52.

36 Arch. nat., K 47, no. 52 and 54, etc.; K 48, no. 7 to 7 ter.

37 Arch. nat., KK 1064, f 20 verso and 235 recto; Compiègne, March 1215; letter from Prince Louis to Jean de Brienne : « *Scire vos volumus quod consuetude antiqua and per jus approbata talis est in regno Francie, quod nullus ante viginti and unum annos potest vel dcbet trahi in causam de re quam pater ejus teneret sine placito cum decessit.* »

38 André Du Chesne, *Hist. des maisons de Dreux*, etc., p. 272.

39 D'Arbois de Jubainville, *Histoire des comtes de Champagne*, IV, 198.

40 *Layettes*, t. II, 2057 and 2059 : « *quousque predicti heredes Britannie devenerint ad etatem viginti et unius anni, et fecerint nobis quod facere debebunt.*»

41 *Layettes*, t. II, 1922.

42 *Layettes*, t. II, 2331; January 1235 : « *et ibidem judicatum fuit ab hominibus comitisse predicte quod otas illa sufficiens erat, secundum consuetudines que in Flandria observantur.* »

43 *Layettes*, t. II, 1995; avril 1229 : « *donec vicesimum primum etatis sue compleverit annum.* »

44 « *exeunte me de Flandrensium comitis Balduini mundiburdie.* » Diplôme de 1065 : Luchaire, *Histoire des Institutions monarchiques de la France sous les premiers Capétiens*, t. I (1883), p. 74, note 2.

45 Dupuy, *Traité de la majorité de nos rois*, p. 142 (1270), p. 143 (1271). I do not reproduce here the arguments given by Charles V in his celebrated ordonance of August 1374 on the majority of kings. On finds it, among other editions, in Dupuy, p. 157.

46 Philippe Mousket, v. 27489-27502.

47 *Layettes du Trésor des Chartes*, t. II, 1823 to 1827.

48 Philippe Mousket, v. 27509.

49 Edition of 1874, n. 72.

50 Philippe Mousket, v. 27523.

51 Le Ménestrel de l'Alphonse de Poitiers, [in] *Historiens de France*, XVII, 432 : « But he still refused to go for the struggle of the father and for the discomfort of the Queen. »

52 Roger of Wendover, ed. Howlett (collection of the Master of Rolls), II, 315, and following him, Mathieu de Paris, *Chronica majora*, III, 118.

53 *Willelmi chronica Andrensis*; *Monumenta Germaniæ*, scriptores, t. XXIV, p. 766 : « *Suessionis promotus in militem.* »

54 Philippe Mousket, ed. Reiffenberg, t. II, v. 27577 to 27586.

55 Philippe Mousket wrote (v. 27561-65) that Mauclerc wanted to give his daughter to Richard, brother of Henry III. The fact is doubtful; he had just promised her to the King of England himself.
Annales de Dunstaplia, in the *Annales monastici*, published by Luard, t. III, p. 10'2 : « *Comes vero Ricardus and comes Tholosanus, confœderati, de die in diem prosperabantur.* »

56 *Chronicon Turonense* (*Historiens de France*, t. XVIII, p. 318).

57 Philippe Mousket cited, as having been present at the sacring : the Duc de Bourgogne, the Patriarch of Jerusalem and the legate (v. 27543-57); Robert de Dreux and his brother Henri, Treasurer of Beauvais (v. 27567) ; the brothers of Coucy, the Counts of Bar and Blois, the noble Normans, those of the Hurepoix (v. 27654-65); the Comte de Boulogne, the Comtesses de Flandre and Champagne (v. 27707). Roger of Wendover appears to be misled when he said that Count Bar was absent (t. II, p. 315; cf. Mathieu de Paris, *Chronica majora*, ed. Luard, t. III, p. 118).

As for Jean de Brienne, it is certainly to him that an allusion is made about the expenses involved in the coronation of Saint Louis, coming from the Chambre des Comptes, and published by Du Cange in his edition of Joinville, 1668, *Observations sur l'histoire de saint Louis*, p. 44 : « and for the king overseas, 400 livres. »

58 Philippe Mousket, verse 27587 ff; Arbois de Jubainville, in reportiing all of the facts recounted by Mousket, seems to doubt their exactitude (*Histoire des ducs and des comtes de Champagne*, t. IV, p. 210, and p. 211 to 212).

59 Le Nain de Tillemont, *Histoire de saint Louis*, I, 433; Numerous texts, which would be superfluous to cite here, prove that the Bishop of Soissons replaced the Archbishop of Rheims, due to the absence of the Archbishop. The report of the sacring is found in the verse chronicle of Philippe Mousket, verse 27627 ff. For a complete idea of this ceremony, one may refer to the texts on the sacring of Louis VIII and Louis IX, that Théodore Godefroy has published in his *Cérémonial françois*, t. I, p. 13-29.

60 Philippe Mousket, verse 27717 ff.

61 *Layettes du Trésor des Chartes*, II, 1909; December 1226.

62 *Layettes*, II, 1761.

63 Philippe Mousket, v. 27761 ff.; Chronique de Saint-Bortin, *Monumenta Germaniæ, scriptores*, XXV, 834, 1. 41 ; the intervention of Sancho II, King of Portugal, nephew of Ferrand and Blanche, is attested to by a Flemish historian : *Recueil des chroniques de Flandre*, t. I, p. 154-155 (Collection de chroniques belges); cf. Meyer, *Commentarii*, 1561, fol. 71 v.

64 Philippe Mousket, v. 27499. Texts relating to the payment of ransom for Ferrand are numerous : Martène, *Amplissima collectio*, I, 1205; *Willelmi chronica Andrensis*, Mon. Germaniæ, XXIV, 766; Vincent de Beauvais, *Speculum historiale, Mon. Germaniæ*, XXIV, 837; Ménestrel d'Alphonse de Poitiers, *Historiens de France*, XVII, 432.

65 *Layettes*, II, 1830; December 1226.

66 *Layettes*, II, 1831 to 1894; 6-21 December 1226; Archives nationale, J, 1022, n. 1. bis, letters of Ghislain le Roux.

67 *Layettes*, 1898; December 1226; ibid., 1899-1908.

68 *Layettes*, 1897-1898.

69 *Layettes*, t. II, 1895-1896.
70 Philippe Mousket, v. 27773.

71 Arch. nat., JJ 26, 231 r, col. 2, n. CCXII; Melun, August 1229. Cf. *Table chronologique des diplômes*, V, 352.

72 « *entor la Tiephanie,* » said the Ménestrel d'Alphonse de Poitiers (*Historiens de France*, XVII, 432), in agreement with several other texts. A Flemish author is more exacting : « *in vigilia Epiphanise Domini* », *Recueil des chroniques de Flandre* (Collection de chroniques belges), I, 155.

73 Arch. nat., JJ 31, f 118, col. 2; Lille, January 1227. Cf. *Table chronologique des diplômes*, V, 291.

74 *Annales Colonienses maximi* (*Monumenta Germaniæ*, scriptores, XVII, 840); *Ægidii Aureævallensis gesta episcoporum Leodiensium* (ibid., XXV, 121); *Annales Floreffienses* (ibid., XVI, 626); *Annales de l'abbaye de Saint-Ghislain*, Collection de chroniques belges, *Monuments pour servir à l'histoire des prou, des prov. de Namur, etc.*, VIII, 422).

75 Guillaume le Breton, *Chronique*, ed. Delaborde, n. 199.

76 Récits d'un Ménestrel de Reims, ed. N. de Wailly, n. 291. The transfer from Renaud to Goulet is attested by the *Philippide* de Guillaume le Breton, livre III, verse 90-92, and by the *Annales d'Anchin* (*Historiens de France*, XVIII, p. 554 a).

77 Mort de Renaud; *Annales d'Anchin* (*Historiens de France*, XVIII, 554 a); *Willelmi chronica Andrensis* (*Monuments Germaniæ*, scriptores, XXIV, p. 766); Philippe Mousket, verse 27815.

Aubry de Trois-Fontaines (*Mon. Germaniæ*, XXIII, p. 919) said, in regard to this death : « *Pro socio ejus Renalde Boloniensi comite quidam laborabant, scd in vanum. Qui interim circa sequens Pascha voluntaria, ut dicitur, morte vilain finivit.* » The death of Renaud has given birth to a strange legend about which it is adequate to mention : Collection de chroniques belges, *Istore and croniques de Flandres*, t. I, p. 132-133.

78 Alix had been affianced to Henri d'Avaugour (D. Morice, *Histoire de Bretagne*, preuves, t. I, col. 812).

Her mother, Constance, had been the first wife of Geoffroy Plantagenet, son of Henry II, by whom she had had two children, a girl, Eléonore, who died in England (1241), and a son, the unfortunate Arthur of Brittany, assassinated in Rouen by King John. United for some time with the Count of Chester, she was married, in 1199, to Guy de Thouars, by whom she had two girls, Alix and Catherine. Catherine was the wife of André de Vitré; when her older sister was given to Pierre de Dreux, Brittany was subjected to Philippe Auguste, and governed by Guy de Thouars, who held the lease.

79 D. Morice, *Histoire de Bretagne*, prouves, t. 1,852; register of the *Trésor des Chartes* JJ 26, f 182 V, col. 2; Nangis, *Vie de saint Louis* (*Historiens de France*, t. XX, p. 312.)

80 Michelet, *Histoire de France*, 1876, t. II, p. 335.

81 Mauclerc means, not enemy clerics, but bad cleric; perhaps the Count of Brittany owed his nickname after having embraced the ecclesiastical profession and then turned over to the military life and feudality; this opinion was adopted by the authors of *Histoire littéraire de la France*, t. XXIII, p. 684. Some have said he studied at the Université de Paris; I do not know the basis for this opinion (Bertrand d'Argentré, *Histoire de Bretagne*, f 217 V).

82 *Layettes du Trésor de Chartes*, t. II, 1734.

83 *Historiens de France*, XVIII, 331 (Ex *chronico Britanniæ altero*); D. Morice, *Histoire de Bretagne*, I, 155.

84 *Historiens de France*, XVIII, 318 (*E chronico Turonensi*).

85 Roger de Wendover, ed. Hewlett, II, 3N0 ; Mathieu de Paris, *Chronica majora*, ed. Luard, III, 191, year 1229. The annals of Dunstable recount that the curé was burned alive (collection of the Master of Rolls, *Annales monastici*, III, 115).

86 Guillaume le Breton, *Philippide*, book XII, v. 370 ff.

87 *Philippide*, liv. XII, v. 432; Chronique de Tours, *Historiens de France*, XVIII, 303; D. Morice, *Histoire de Bretagne*, I, 151.

88 Philippe Mousket, verse 23525-32.

89 *Récits d'un Ménestrel de Reims*, ed. N. de Wailly, n. 5; *Johannis Longi chronica S. Bertini, Monumenta Germaniæ*, scriptores, XXV, p. 799-800, 835.

90 Thomas Duffus Hardy, *Rotuli litterarum clausarum in Turri Londinensi asservati*, in f, t. II, p. 5, col. 2, 8 November 1224; p. 145, col. 2, 22 December 1225; p. 155, col. 2, 24 September 1226.

91 Ibid., p. 159, col. 1, 12 November 1226 : « *De arestandis mercatoribus*. »

92 Ibid., p. 162, col. 1 ; 18 December 1226; p. 163, col. 1, 26 December; p. 207, col. 1-2 ; 25 January 1227.

93 Ibid., p. 164, col. 1, 1 January 1227; p. 168, col. 1, 25 January; p. 204, col. 2, 5 November 1227.

94 Ibid., p. 158, col. 2, boats for Bayonne and Bordeaux; Ibid., p. 158, col. 2, p. 192, col. 2, provisional seizure of goods whose owners are subjects of the Comte de Toulouse; p. 205, col. 1-2; 16 December 1226.

95 Ibid., p. 181, col. 2.

96 *Inventaire des archives de la Seine-Inférieure*, série G, t. III, p. 390, col. 1 (ch. on Rouen); G, 4493, 1227.

97 T. Duffus Hardy, *Rotuli litterarum clausarum*, II, p. 5, col. 2; 8 November 1224; vessel of Jean Foulard, from Dieppe.

98 Ibid., p. 161, col. 2; December 1226.

99 Ibid., p. 165, col. 2; 10 January 1227: « *navem Radulphi de Rothemage.* » ; p. 173, col. 2; 20 February 1227 : « *De nave deliberanda.* »

100 London, Public Record Office, Patent rolls, rotulus 34, membrana 12 r, 28 November 1226 (merchants of Rouen); Ibid., membrana 6 r, 3 May 1227 (merchants of Rouen); Ibid., membrana 7 t, 13 avril 1227 (vessels of Barfleur).

101 The English then gave the name of Gascogne to their French possessions, whose capital was Bordeaux.

102 Chronique de Tours, *Historiens de France*, t. XVIII, p. 318; Philippe Mousket, v. 27739.

103 Annals of Dunstable, *Annales monastici* (collection of the Master of Rolls), ed. Luard, t. III, p. 102. Henry III was for a long time in agreement with Raimond VII (see Rymor, ed. of 1810, p. 179 : letter of Henry III from 14 August 1225).

104 Rymer, *Fœdera*, ed. of 1816, t. I, p. 158; truce between Henry III and Philippe Auguste.

105 Rymer, p. 153; 16 January 1219.

106 Rymer, p. 174 : letter from the Bishop of Lichfield to the Bishop of Chichester, including a letter to Henry III by three Cardinals, on the subject of his marriage project.

107 Rymer, p. 176; 1225 : letter of Léopold of Austria to Henry III. In 1227, he wanted to espouse the King of England with the daughter of the King of Bohemia (Rymer, p. 185). The annals of Worcester mention these three projects of marriage, nearly simultaneous (*Annales monastici*, ed. Luard, t. IV, p. 420).

108 Shirley, *Royal and other historical letters illustrative of the reign of Henry III* (collection of the Master of Rolls), t. I, 1862, p. 295-96; Rymer, p. 180-81, 19 October 1226.

109 Rymer, I, 183, 18 December 1226. I give here only the principal conditions of these treaties.

110 Shirley, *Royal letters*, I, 301 ; 18 December 1226.

111 Rymer, I, 183, 18 December 1226.

112 Ibid.; another act dated the same day.

113 Shirley, *Royal letters*, I, 302, 18 December 1226. On 20 December, the Archbishop of Canterbury and several English bishops promised to take care of the execution of the conditions granted to the Poitevins. Rymer, I, 184.

114 PRO. Patent Rolls, 35, membrane 2 recto; 22 December 1226.

115 *Rotuli litterarum clausarum*, II, 208, col. 2; 30 January 1227.

116 Ibid., p. 207, col. 1 ; 21 January 1227.

117 Ibid., p. 168, col. 2; 4 February 1227.

118 Rymer, I, 184; 13 January 1227. Roger of Wendovor, ed. Hewlett, II, 316 and 319. These envoys were the Archbishop of York, the Bishop of Carlisle, and Philippe d'Aubigny. Count Richard, who found himself in Gascogne, was warned to conform to their advice.

119 Shirley, I, 304; December 1226 or January 1227; Comte de la Marche to Henry III.

120 D. Morice, *Mémoires pour servir de preuves à l'histoire de Bretagne*, t. 1, p. 856. I have the most original of these documents, which date to 1226 ; they were after Easter 1226, and before 1227.

121 *Chronique de Tours* (*Historiens de France*, XVIII, 319).

122 Guillaume de Nangis, *Vie de saint Louis* (*Historiens de France*, t. XX, p. 313).

123 Philippe Mousket, v. 27804; *Chronicon Nicolai Trivetti*, d'Achery, *Spicilegium*, in-4, t. VIII, p. 577; Roger of Wendover, t. II, p. 316 : « *ipsum ad eos veniro cupientem.* »

124 Philippe Mousket, v. 27745; Joinville, edition of 1874, n. 72; Philippe Mousket, v. 27747.
The requests for fiefs about which Joinville speaks appear to be addressed to Blanche at the time of the first revolt. Undoubtedly the Seneschal of Champagne was erroneous in his recounting when he says that these complaints were contemporary with the plot of Corbeil.

125 Ibid., v. 27800; Guillaume de Nangis, *Vie de saint Louis* (*Historiens de France*, t. XX, p. 313).

126 *Chronique de Tours* (*Historiens de France*, XVIII, 319); today under the name of Saint Gatien.

127 *Chronique de Tours* (*Historiens de France*, XVIII, p. 319); *Vie de saint Louis*, par Guillaume de Nangis (*Historiens de France*, XX, p. 313); Guillaume de Nangis, *Chronique*, ed. Géraud, t. I, p. 177.

128 *Chronique de Tours* (*Historiens de France*, XVIII, 319).

129 *Chronique de Tours*; Guillaume de Nangis, *Vie de saint Louis* and *Chronique*.

130 In other words, 25 April.
   D. Morice, *Histoire de Bretagne*, prouves, p. 859; *Historiens de France*, XVIII, 319, note a.

131 According to the Annals of Dunstable, the King restored to the Count de Champagne two châteaus which Philippe Auguste had taken from him (*Annales monastici*, ed. Luard, III, 103); *Layettes*, II, 1921.

132 D'Arbois de Jubainville, *Histoire des ducs and des comtes de Champagne*, t. IV, p. 215-216.

133 Ibid., 215.

134 Guillaume de Nangis, *Vie de S. Louis*, *Historiens de France*, t. XX, p. 313, *Chronique*, ed. Géraud, p. 177; *Chronique de Tours*, *Historiens de France*, t. XVIII, p. 319. This *Chronique de Tours* gives a date of 16 March ; the poet Guillaume Guiart only translates and paraphrases, for his recounting of events, the *Vie de S. Louis* by Guillaume de Nangis (*Historiens de France*, t. XXII, p. 179-180). He affirmed that the royal army marched beyond « *vers Champaingne* »; nothing more is shown, unless Guiart wanted to indicate thus the counties of Blois and of Chartres, for whom Thibaud IV was then still the suzerain.

135 Mousket, v. 27875-77.

136 Treaty of Vendôme concluded with Pierre Mauclerc, *Layettes*, II, 1922; Yolande had recently been sought after by Henry III.

137 André Du Chesne, *Histoire Généalogique de la maison de Montmorency*, prouves, p. 89.

138 Everyone knew that the treaties of Vendôme were the work of Blanche : « *matre ejus partes suas interponente* », according to Roger of Wendover (t. II, p. 319), of which the receipt has been reproduced by Mathieu de Paris (*Chronica majora*, ed. Luard, III, 123).

139 Treaty of Vendôme concluded with Hugues X de Lusignan, comte de la Marche, published in the *Amplissima collectio* de Dom Martène, t. I, col. 1214, following register JJ. 26, *Trésor des Chartes*, f 189 r, col. 1 and 2.

140 The work opens : « *cum fromen. , cum pertinentiis, and insulam Oleronensem cum pertinentiis.* » This bad reading has its origins in the fault of a scribe, who wrote « *cu. fronen.* », which should read « *civ. Sconen.* », or « *civitatem Sanctonensem.*»

141 Treaty of Bourges, May 1224, *Trésor des Chartes*, side JJ. 26, f 182 r, col. 1.

142 Shirley, *Royal and other historical letters*, t. I, appendix V, n. 26, p. 548-549 : letter of Gregory IX to Cardinal Romain, legate of the Holy See, mentioned by Rinaldi, *Annales ecclesiastici*, t. I, p. 612, 2nd year of Gregory IX, art. 23.

143 Teulet, *Layettes du Trésor des Chartes*, t. II, n. 1924.

144 Martène, *Amplissima collectio*, t. I, col. 1209, after register JJ. 26, f 227 r, col. 2; 17 March 1227.

145 Teulet, *Layettes du Trésor des Chartes*, t. II, n. 2052, 30 May 1230, letters of Hugues de Lusignan. Letters analogous to Queen Isabelle, ibid., n. 2068, June l230.

146 Aubry de Trois-Fontaines, *Monumenta Germaniæ historica*, scriptores, t. XIII, p. 919.

147 There exists some doubt on the subject of the date which one can assign to this truce; the act, published in tome II of the *Layettes du Trésor des Chartes*, n. 1926, and previously in the collection of the *Historiens de France*, t. XVIII, p. 320, note, says : « *Actum anno gracie M·CC· vicesimo septime.* » It is probable that Count Richard, finding himself in France and concluding a truce with the King of France, dated this act according to the French style, in which the year begins with Easter; or this feast, in 1227, falling on 11 April; the truce would thus be later than 11 April, agrees extremely well with the account of Philippe Mousket, after which a first truce was concluded before Easter, then renewed at Saint-Jean (verse 27851, 27859).

But the act says that the truce was concluded with all those who held for the party of the King the Monday after Sunday *Lætare Jerusalem* : however this Monday, in 1227, was 22 March. Le Nain de Tillemont concluded (t. I, p. 462) that this was the truce date. It seems that one could give the following solution to this little difficulty : 22 March, was the first truce, until 11 April, the day of Easter; then it was renewed, after Easter, so let us accept that which was understood originally. The truce was to last until Midsummer's Day, 8 July 1227, as written in the act, and not until Midsummer's Day, as adverted to in the *Chronique de Tours* (*Historiens de France*, t. XVIII, p. 320). It cannot have been concluded after the end of April, because at this time, Richard was no longer in France.

The truce with the Vicomte de Thouars was mentioned in the *Chronique de Tours* (p. 320). The Viscount gave homage to the King in April 1226, old style, in other words, from the 1st to the 10th of April 1227 (*Layettes*, II, 1925).

148 « *absque humani sanguinis effusione* », Guillaume de Nangis, *Vie de saint Louis*, *Historiens de France*, XX, 311.

149 *Rotuli litterarum clausarum*, t. II, p. 149, col. 1; 21 March 1227.

150 Roger of Wendover, ed. Hewlett, t. H, p. 320; cf. Mathieu de Paris, *Chronica majora*, t. III, p. 123; *Historia minor*, t. II, p. 295.

151 Roger of Wendover, t. II, p. 319 : « *instante solemnitate paschali.* » ; « *post Pascha* » : *Annales de Theokesberia* (*Annales monastici*, ed. Luard, t. I, p. 70) ; *Annales de Wigornia* (ibid., t. IV, p. 419); « *mense maio* » : Roger of Wendover, t. II, p. 320; Philippe Mousket, v. 27885-90.

152 Le Nain de Tillemont, *Histoire de saint Louis*, t. I, p. 464; see Roger of Wendover, t. II, p. 322.

153 Philippe Mousket, v. 27897.

154 Potthast, *Regesta*, n. 7897; Marténe, *Amplissima collectio*, 1. 1, col. 1210, after the register of *Trésor des Chartes*, JJ. 26, fol. 190V, col. 1. The same day, 10 May 1227, Gregory IX wrote on this subject to the legate Romain; Potthast, 7898; Martène, col. 1211; 33. 26, fol. 190 V.

155 Rinaldi, *Annales ecclesiastici*, t. I, p. 599, LIV-LV.

156 Potthast, *Regesta*, 7920.

157 Shirley, *Royal and other historical letters* (collection of the Master of Rolls), t. I, appendice V, n. 25, p. 548; 27 May 1227.

158 *Rotuli litterarum clausarum*, t. II, p. 150, col. 1; 15 April 1227.

159 Ibid., II, 151, 8 May; convocations for 23 May, addressed to the baillies of Dover and other ports; ibid., II, 210, 30 May 1227; letters to the barons and to the baillies of Hastings and other places, etc.

160 Ibid., II, 211a, 2 June 1227.

161 Ibid., 211b, 9 June; letter to the Bishop of Lincoln.

162 Ibid., 211a, 8 June 1227; letter to the Count of Chester, etc.; 211b, 18 June ; to the Bishop of London; 211 a-b, 9 June; letters relative to supplies addressed to the baillifs and officials of Winchelsea, etc.

163 Ibid., 189a, 8 June; letter to the Viscount of Kent.

164 Ibid., 212a, and Rymer, I, 185; 17 July 1227; Rymer, 186; 17 July; Rymer, 186, and register of the *Trésor des Chartes* JJ. 26, 326 v, col. 1, letters patent du 19 July. One sees that the truce was concluded 17 July. Cf. Philippe Mousket, v. 27916-22.

165 *Annales de Wigornia* (*Annales monastici*, ed. Luard, IV, 420).

166 *Rotuli litterarum clausarum*, t. II, p. 189a, col. 1; 8 June 1227; ibid., 198a; 21 August 1227.

167 Royal diploma, dated at Vernon, July 1227; supplement to the *Trésor des Chartes*, J. 1020, n. 1; Charter of the Comte de Dreux, same date : André du Chesne, *Histoire de la maison de Dreux*, p. 269-270. The land given to Robert de Dreux was situated in the environs of Yvetot.

168 *Layettes*, t. II, n. 1920; Loudun, March 1227 : charter of Philippe Hurepel.

169 *Table chronologique des diplômes*, t. V, p. 300 (May 1227); Register of the *Trésor des Chartes* JJ. 26, fol. 120 V, Paris, June 1227 : three charters in favor of the Rochelois; the second has been published (*Table chronologique des diplômes*, t. V, p. 301), and all three have been noted by Amos Barbot in his *Histoire de la Rochelle* (*Archives historiques de la Saintonge el de l'Aunis*, t. XIV, p. 78-80).

170 *Layettes du Trésor des Chartes*, t. II, n. 1915; January 1227 : charter of Jeanne de Craon; Martène, *Amplissima collectio*, t. I, col. 1206, and D. Morice, *Histoire de Bretagne*, preuves, t. 1, col. 860 : charter of Louis IX, following the register of *Trésor des Chartes* JJ. 26, fol. 227.

171 *Layettes*, t. II, n. 1938; 10 August 1227 : charter of Lambert Cadoc; ibid., n. 1937, 9 August : charter of Richard, Bishop of Evreux; Martène, *Amplissima collectio*, t. 1, col. 1213 : charter of Louis IX.

172 Le Nain de Tillemont, *Histoire de saint Louis*, t. I, p. 467-468.

173 In 1226.

174 Dom Vaissète, *Histoire de Languedoc*, t. VI, p. 620-621.

175 Ibid., p. 612 (the first seneschal was Pèlerin Latinier): Aubry de Trois-Fontaines, *Monumenta Germaniæ historica*, scriptores, t. XXIII, p. 919, ligne 1.

176 *Chronique de Tours*, p. 318.

177 Philippe Mousket, v. 27727.

178 *Revue des sociétés savantes*, 4 série, t. V, p. 446.

179 Guillaume de Nangis, *Chronique*, ed. Géraud, t. I, p. 177. *Vincentii Bellovacensis memoriale omnium temporum* (*Monumenta Germaniæ historica*, scriptores, t. XXIV, p. 161), and several others.

180 Dom Vaissète, t. VIII, col. 825; January 1227; Martène, *Amplissima collectio*, t. I, col. 1206, after the register of *Trésor des Chartes* JJ. 26, fol. 226 V. The charter of

Béraud de Mercœur, relative to this concession, is in the *Trésor des Chartes : Layettes*, t. II, n. 1916.

181 Dom Vaissète, ed. in-4, t. VII, p. 72.

182 Labbe, *Conciles*, t. XI, 1st part, col. 308; article 17.

183 The siege of Varilhes took place in January 1227, as is proved in the chronicle of *Æclara Francorum facinora*, published by Catel (*Histoire des comtes de Toulouse*, in-f, 1623, preuves, p. 129), and the *Chronique de Tours* (*Historiens de France*, t. XVIII , p. 319). One is founded wrongly on a not very precise passage of Guillaume de Puy-Laurens for the report of the year 1228 (*Historiens de France*, t. XIX, p. 218); Guillaume de Puy-Laurens, p. 217.

184 *Chronique de Tours* (*Historiens de France*, t. XVIII, p. 318); *Layettes du Trésor des Chartes*, t. II, n. 1928, May 1227.

185 Dom Vaisséte, ed. in-4, t. VIII, p. 866. This document is found in register JJ. 26 of the *Trésor des Chartes*, fol. 327, and in the supplement of the *Trésor des Chartes*, J. 1035, n. 18.

186 *Supplément du Trésor des Chartes*, J. 1035, n. 19.

187 26 May 1227.

188 See this letter and the supplication from the dissident chapters in Rinaldi, *Annales ecclesiastici*, I, p. 600, art. 56.

189 *Layettes du Trésor des Chartes*, t. II , n. 1930.

190 Rinaldi, *Annales ecclesiastici*, t. I, p. 601; Potthast, *Regesta*, 7986.

191 Teulet, *Layettes*, II, n. 1942; Martène, *Amplissima collectio*, t. I, col. 1212; D. Vaissète, t. VIII, col. 868. Cf. Léopold Delisle, *Mémoire sur les opérations financières des Templiers* (*Mémoires de l'Académie des Inscriptions*, 1889, t. XXXIII, 2nd part, p. 42).

192 Rinaldi, *Annales ecclesiastici*, t. I, p. 602; ibid., note; Potthast, *Regesta*, 8053.

193 *Willelmi chronica Andrensis, Monumenta Germaniœ*, scriptores, t. XXIV, p. 766; *Historiens de France*, t. XVIII, p. 580.

194 Mathieu de Paris, *Chronica majora*, ed. Luard, t. III, p. 119.

195 Mathieu de Paris, *Historia minor*, t. II, p. 290.

196 Guillaume de Puy-Laurens, *Historiens de France*, t. XIX, p. 218. Le Nain de Tillemont, t. I, p. 466-467.

197 Guillaume de Puy-Laurens, p. 218.

198 Potthast, *Regesta*, 7910, 23 May 1227; letter to the King; 7914, 25 May letter to the Archbishop of Bourges; 7915, 25 May, to the Archbishop of Narbonne.

199 Teulet, *Layettes*, t. II, n. 1940; D'Arbois de Jubainville, *Histoire des ducs and des comtes de Champagne*, t. V, catalogue, n. 1777; letter to the King. The letter to the Queen is mentioned in this same work, n. 1778.

200 Teulet, *Layettes*, t. II, n. 1953; 5 December 1227 : Gregory IX to the Archbishop of Sens.

201 Guillaume le Breton, *Philippide*, ed. Delaborde, liv. XII, verse 669-670.

202 The history of this conflict is found in the *Chronique de Rouen* (*Historiens de France*, XXIII, 332-333). The letter from the legate, relative to the provisional restitution of seized goods, has been published by Martène (*Amplissima collectio*, I, 1226), after the register of the *Trésor des Chartes* JJ. 26, f 235 V).

203 Huillard-Bréholles, *Friderici secundi historia diplomatica*, III, 310, 27 March 1227.

204 Idem, III, 16; Martène, *Amplissima collectio*, I, 1195, note, following register JJ. 26, f 168 V, in the margin.

Chapter Three

New Revolts. — Submission of Languedoc. — Education of Louis IX. — Increased hostility of the great vassals. — They assemble in Corbeil to remove the King. — Parisians search for Louis IX in Montthéry. — Cardinal Romain returns to France. — The war continues in Languedoc; Raimond VII regains Castelsarrasin. — Devastation of the environs of Toulouse. — Poor situation of Raimond VII. — Prorogation of the truce with England. — Troubles in Gascony. — Ambition of Philippe Hurepel. — Intrigues of the Lord of Coucy. — Blanche demands oaths from certain towns. — Gascons and Poitevins vainly call Henry III to France. — New revolt; fidelity of the Count de Champagne. — Siege of Bellême. — Siege of Haie-Paynel. — Tortuous politics Henry III. — Disorders committed by students in Paris: the Université is dissolved. — Gossip on the intimacy of Blanche and the legate. — End of the war against Albigensians. — Treaty of Paris. — Legate Romain, returning to Italy, remits the marquisate of Provence to the guardianship of the King.

It was not only necessary take care of the safety of France; Blanche had many children; one carried the crown, and all that touched upon his education interested the future of the kingdom. In private life, one must accord the highest praise for a mother who undertakes to raise and to instruct her family; the widow of Louis VIII could not devote to this noble task any more than part of her time and energy; it was discharged in the middle of revolts and wars, in spite of the plots of nobility, and in spite of the English. In a time when she needed to subject the Count de Toulouse, to start again almost each year the war against Pierre Mauclerc, to fight and support in turn the

Count de Champagne, to hold forth against Henry III, she never lost sight of the education of Louis IX, his brothers and of his sister. More than anything, she made herself famous in this respect.

In Saint Louis there were virtues and superiorities of birth with which one must have been able to develop, and to raise to perfection with education. Blanche of Castile could not wish that her son become a saint; she sought to make of him a man without defects, a true king. One will see that without the exaggeration of luxury, she always had care for the behavior of her children worthy of the rank they occupied; Louis IX, from the beginning of his life, certainly bore a princely manner, and we know by the confessor of Queen Marguerite that his mother "gave nobility and noble bearing to the king." For the young King of France it was however a very serious and very simple existence that he carried out; his days were divided between work, physical exercise, and achievement of religious duties; "he made no time for himself to play, did not visit wood and river, and others places in like manner, being honest and serious in discipline."[1] A master, whose name is not known to us, was given to him when he was thirteen.[2] Louis subjected himself with humility to his severe authority; he lived in the midst of serious people, with a monk whom the Queen made a point of placing near him, and it is said that the Dominicans over all contributed to inform his development.[3] Blanche herself, by her lessons and examples, taught him how to be a Christian prince, and as he had a good memory, he remembered all of this easily.[4] The royal house was filled with good advisers, knights and clerks who were formed in the school of Philippe Auguste and whose devotion was up to any test; the young King liked to surround himself with their opinions. He had been struck by this precept, which one had taught him: "A bad emperor or a bad king is less to fear than bad advisers, because it is easier for several men to gain one, than for only one to gain several."[5]

For his time, Louis IX was an erudite man; he knew Latin.[6] His manners, from childhood on, were soft and polished; he neither addressed insults nor hard reproaches to anybody, "and to each one he always spoke in the plural."[7] Frequenting the churches every day, the strange ardor with which he followed the divine offices, had given him early on a perhaps exaggerated scorn for the pleasures of ordinary youth.[8] While advancing in age, he preserved very pure manners, and Blanche of Castile issued on this subject a declaration that shows very well which principles she had given him. A monk, misled by false charges, reproached the Queen to let her son live in disorder; it had been said to him that the young King maintained concubines, and that his mother pretended to be unaware of it. Blanche justified herself gently, and was satisfied to answer that if the King her son, who she loved more than any creature, was sick to death, she would not like to see him cured at the price of a mortal sin.[9] This affirmation, that Saint Louis had often heard from his mother, remained in his memory as long as he lived.[10] He made it one of the rules of his conduct; he liked to repeat it to Joinville, and was remembered in the counsels he left to his son.[11]

The predilection that Blanche had for her oldest son did not make her forget her other children; after the death of King Louis, even when occupied in public affairs, she redoubled her care in their favor.[12] Princess Isabelle tended from childhood, like the King her brother, to marks of great piety. Agnes of Harcourt, to which we owe the account of her life, wrote that one morning, at the moment when the royal family left in travel, Isabelle was put, to request in silence, under her covers, and one of the servants charged to carry the luggage removed it without seeing her, believing he was carrying a package of clothing and bed linen.[13] This anecdote, which Saint Louis preserved in memory, makes known the feelings and the practices that Blanche had inculcated in her children.

Religious ceremonies always held a great place in the life of the King. On October 24, 1227, he attended with his mother the dedication of the splendid church which Cistercians had built in Longpont.[14] This solemnity had to make a great impression on him, and it is said that he formed there, by the counsel of Queen Blanche, a project to create an abbey, to carry out one of the clauses contained in the will of his father. This new monastery, of which the establishment appears to go back to the beginning of 1228, was erected on the right bank of the Oise, in Cuimont, and gave to its founders the name of Royaumont. By an exemption in the will of the expired king, Louis IX and his mother, installed the monks of Citeaux in this place, instead of the regular canons of Saint-Victor.[15]

In the eyes of the people most poorly disposed toward Blanche of Castile she would have been quite a virtuous woman, worthy of all praises, if she limited herself to supervise the education of Louis IX. But she reigned, she had a firm hand, and in this role she could not please the partisans of disorder. Those who, upon the demise of Louis, had hoped for a lowering of the royal capacity, did not forgive him in placing an obstacle before their projects. Amongst the high nobility she had, beside some sincere friends, many secret or declared enemies. The Treaty of Vendôme had not satisfied Pierre of Brittany; others were ready to announce their ambitions, their instincts avid and turbulent. The Queen alone obstructed them; it was necessary for all to remove the guardian of the King and the director of affairs; they proposed this in 1227 which she had inaugurated by making an act of sovereignty.

It is necessary to read poems of this time if one wants to learn all of the bad reasons given by the great barons to put her out of their way: France was not made to be controlled by a woman, a foreigner; Blanche drew away the friends of Louis VIII from the young King. Her enemies went so far as to call her "dame Hersent," while giving her by derision the name which the she-wolf had in the novel of Renard.[16] A partisan of great barons, the poet Hugues de la Ferté, abused and insulted her :[17]

> Doubtless France degenerates,
> Affirm it baron, and understand,
> When woman has control,
> And such as one knows,
> They are not but pretend kings,
> With false crowns.[18]

In a pamphlet which dates from the time to when the Count de Champagne became the source of all hatreds, Hugues shows the Queen sending money from the royal treasury to Spain, to provide subsidies for Thibaud; as for her small boy :

> My lady, verily I say
> That people love this little boy,
> So dispose equity on this house.
> Leave quickly.
> Return to Spain....[19]

The King must truly recognize those who have moved away from him; his mother gave him a good lesson on hatred and disdain.[20] Instead of the nobles, who truly supported the crown, she called around him Spaniards and clerics. One must know that Gautier, Archbishop of Sens defended her: "Sire, continues the poet, send for your barons; hear them; reconcile the peers to one who partakes to direct France..."[21] Hugues de la Ferté knew very well those about whom he repeated objections with so much energy; the animosity of the great barons against the Regent was too real; one did not hesitate in seeing it.[22]

In the current year which followed the treaties of Vendôme, the bad dispositions of the large feudatories appeared in a new act of hostility.[23] For some time, several among them, encouraged in their opposition by the counts of Brittany and de la Marche, disputed in Blanche of Castile the right to exert regency : "and the barons against the King asserted, that Queen Blanche, his mother, came only to control the kingdom of France, …. And the King maintained against the barons that he was strong enough to rule, with help from the good people who were in his council."[24] It is not shown that Philippe Hurepel consequently put himself openly at the head of the dissatisfied lords; Joinville, who affirms it, wrote in his memoirs that a long time afterwards, and for the first years of Saint Louis his memories often lacked precision.[25] He acted to remove the King, to withdraw him from the influence of his mother.

Louis IX then traversed the country which borders Orléans; informed of danger, he hastened to return on horse towards Paris. But arrived close to the castle of Montlhéry, in Chârtres, he learned that vassal rebels were assembled in force in Corbeil.[26] Lightly accompanied, he dared not push further; he took refuge in the castle, and requested aid from Blanche, who was probably in Paris. The population of this city was very devoted to the royal family. Blanche was well liked there; some years before, she was received in Notre-Dame among the priests and burgers, a charitable association in which representatives of the Parisian clergy and the middle-class joined to make good works and to help one another.[27] She called the principal inhabitants to her and asked them to come and help her son. They answered that they were ready to do it; following their opinion, she convened by letters the surrounding communes. Soon, knights of the country and communal militia arrived and united with the people of Paris. When they were all joined together, they left the city, and went right to Montlhéry: "there they found the young King; they brought him to Paris..."[28] It was a beautiful return; Saint Louis never forgot: "he told me, says Joinville, that from Montlhéry, the road was very full with men-at-arms and without arms all the way to Paris, and that all shouted to Our Savior that He give him a good and long life, and defend him and keep him against his enemies."²⁹ The barons, assembled at Corbeil, not feeling strong enough to attack this year improvised, and withdrew each one to his domain. They supposed, says a chronicler, that the hand of God was with their King, and throughout the year they dared to make no attacks against him.³⁰

The fate of Louis IX had been not very enviable if *les grands* managed to separate him from his mother; Blanche saved him while remaining near him, and it was for the greatest good of the kingdom that she affirmed her authority. In February 1228, consuls and inhabitants of Limoges, the people of Saint-Junien in the Limousin, named the Queen, with her son, in charters by which they swore fidelity.³¹ When at the same time the Viscount and the Viscountess of Thouars made liege homage to Louis IX, they made an oath to help the queen mother to preserve the guardianship of the King until he was an adult.³² After the plot which so fortunately came to be thwarted, one could not have illusions on the intentions of great vassals; the Regent saw surrounding her an army of the dissatisfied growing larger; it was natural that she took precautions.

In the difficult situation where she was, she asked the Pope and obtained from him the return to France of Romain. No one, in or outside the kingdom, was more devoted to the house of France and to Blanche of Castile. At the time of his preceding legation, he had served the interests of the crown with so much address and fidelity, that the Queen was ardently to wish his return. The war on Albigensians continued to trail in length, the attitude of England was always threatening, in France the anger of the nobility could one day or the other lead to a general rising; the Cardinal of Saint-Ange was going to find opposite him all those he had already fought, and to defend against them the young person of the King of France, she brought to Blanche of Castile his councils, full devotion and energy, without speaking about the authority which he had as representative of the Holy See.³³ On March 21, 1228, by two distinct letters, the Pope informed Louis IX and Blanche that the legate had been named *a latere* in France, in Provence, in the ecclesiastical provinces of Lyon, Tarantaise, Embrun, Vienne, Aix, and Arles. Resolute for finishing with the business of the Albigensians, he [the Pope] recalled in his *bullæ* the devotion of Louis VIII and the efforts which the royal government had made since death of this prince to destroy heresy; it was to answer the pressing requests of the King, or rather of his mother, that he returned north back over the Alps a devoted friend of

Louis IX, of his family and of the kingdom of France, who thoroughly knew "in their nature even and in their circumstances" the business of Languedoc.[34]

At this time, fortune seemed favorable to the Count de Toulouse. About Easter, Raimond VII laid siege to Castelsarrasin, a fortified town located on the right of the Garonne, in the corner formed by the confluence of this river with the Tarn.[35] On this news, the Archbishop of Narbonne, the bishops of Toulouse and Carcassonne, were summoned to aid Castelsarrasin with the lieutenant of the King, Imbert of Beaujeu.[36] Simon of Sully, Archbishop of Bourges, who then traversed for his pastoral visits the diocese of Cahors, also rode with his nephew Henri of Sully, some French knights and a small body of troops.[37] But they sought vainly to establish themselves between the place and those besieging them; Raimond VII had raised a double line of retrenchments against the garrison and against the army of relief. The crusaders and the royal troops were spread across the country, and occupied, in Villedieu, a command post of Templars; but after some time, realizing they could not relieve Castelsarrasin, they went up the Garonne, and, after some days forced the surrender of Montech. Thrown upon their own resources, the defenders of Castelsarrasin were reduced by famine; they were spared by the besiegers.[38] They had made a beautiful defense, and we still have a complaint, addressed in 1247 to the royal investigators, in which a knight of the garrison, Hugues of Montaigu, asks for an allowance because of bad food that he had to eat during the siege.[39]

An English historian recounts that the royal army experienced, on May 18, a serious check near Castelsarrasin. They tried, if one believes it, to besiege in this place the Count de Toulouse; but Raimond VII, having gone to await his enemies in a forest, surprised them and put them to rout. Losses of royal troops would have risen, without counting deaths, to five hundred knights and two thousand soldiers made captive. One claims that the Count, after having made the latter strip off their clothing, mutilated them in various ways, and then let them carry throughout the countryside proof of their defeat. The author of this account adds that, in this same summer, Raimond VII beat the French three times; but this assertion appears exaggerated as well.[40] After successes of such importance, Raimond would not have been reduced, as he soon was, to hard ends. It is probable that an unfavorable combat to the crusaders was delivered close to

Castelsarrasin, but I know not at which moment it is advisable to place it; perhaps the royal troops were defeated when they advanced to attack the Count de Toulouse, when he besieged the city; it may be also be that they were unhappy in a renewed attack, after Raimond had already returned as master.

To repair their failure at Castelsarrasin, the lord of Beaujeu and his people resolved to recapture Saint-Paul-sur-l'Agout, which Count Raimond had taken some time before. For this purpose, they advanced until Lavaur. But soon, giving up their project, they fell back on the surroundings of Toulouse. This royal army had been joined by the archbishops of Auch and of Bordeaux, by bishops and Gascon lords who brought a whole population of crusaders. About Midsummer's Day (24 June 1228), the royal army and their auxiliaries were established in Pech-Almeri, east of Toulouse, and started to devastate the vines; then they turned to the south, camped in Montaudran, and continued with a pitiless regularity their work of destruction, cutting the harvests, demolishing the dwellings, razing the vineyards. Each morning at dawn, after hearing Mass and taking some food, those who were to proceed *à la taille* towards the walls of Toulouse, covered by a row of bowmen, supported by squadrons of knights, cut the vines starting with those which were most distant. They were withdrawn thus, under the protection of the troops, leaving desert everywhere they had passed. For nearly three months, those who were in the city witnessed the ruin of these plantations and these harvests which made their wealth: "We have an astonishing manner of beating our enemies while fleeing," Bishop Folquet quipped in jest; and, in fact, this rigorous and methodical execution contributed more than all the rest to shake the constancy of the Toulousains.[41]

When all the countryside around Toulouse had been ransacked, the Gascon crusaders withdrew and the royal army advanced, by the valley of Ariège, in the direction of Foix. The French occupied the defile of Pas-de-la-Barre, not far from this city, and camped for some time on the plain of Saint-Jean-de-Verges; then they withdrew and left behind garrisons.[42] In spite of the advantages that Raimond VII had gained in spring, the forces of Louis IX were strongly established on the high Garonne; it cut to his liking the communications between this area and the county of Foix; surrounding neighborhoods of Toulouse were ruined. Undoubtedly Count Raimond, seeing the gravity of his situation, had already thought of asking for peace; Blanche of Castile, wanted to end a horrible war, which could terminate only by her victory. She then spoke of marrying his daughter Jeanne to one of the brothers of the King; on 25 June, Gregory IX had written on this subject to Romain. Jeanne and the children of Louis VIII were cousins; Romain was informed that the Pope had resolved in favor of their grant, in preparation for this marriage, a dispensation in the event of *parenté* [consanguinity].[43] The Pope assisted the action of the cardinal: he recommended, on 26 June, to the Count de Champagne;[44] some days later, addressing thanks to the people and to the counsels of Narbonne for the help they gave him.[45]

It was undoubtedly in 1228 that Beaujeu and the seneschal of Béziers took Brusque, in the south-east of Rouergue, on the confluence of the Biterrois; on all sides the royal authority tended to prevail.[46] In the vicinity of the sea as on the edges of the Garonne, resistance seemed impossible; one had the proof of it when, on 21 November 1228, Olivier and Bernard de Terms yielded to the King the fortress of this name, to take it again into his hands.[47] This capitulation was done before Pierre Amelh, Archbishop of Narbonne, the Bishop of Carcassonne, and Guy de Lévis, marshal of the army of the faith; it was agreed it would be ratified by the royal lieutenant Imbert de Beaujeu. The war against the Albigensians was finished; Raimond VII was the only one left to submit.

From England, the danger was always the same. From one instant to the next a war could begin again and, in spite of the good will which both sides had shown to the other, there was no safety. Temporary conventions extant during the regime under which one lived were not always observed, and, from the autumn of 1227, Henry III complained to Louis IX about wrongs that he had made, in spite of the truce, in Savary de Mauléon.[48] Although the intentions of the King of England were peaceful, at least for the moment, on 11 March 1228, he informed his new seneschal of Gascogne, Henri de Trubleville, that if the truce had been infringed by the English, the King of France might obtain satisfaction.[49] Two envoys of Henry III were to go, fifteen days after Easter, to France, in a place named Lègue, to settle this question in liaison with the representatives of Louis IX. Henry III wrote on this subject to the King of France and to Blanche of Castile; at the same time he informed his people who had complaints, to forward them at the fixed date, before bailiffs appointed by the two crowns.[50]

The Pope, on his side, worked to restore peace. The truce

concluded the previous year was to end on 8 July 1228, and it was due absolutely to him that it was renewed. By his order, two of his chaplains, Pierre de Collemezzo and Master Etienne, started for the negotiations in France for this purpose, with Gautier Cornu, Archbishop of Sens, and the Bishop of Salisbury.[51] The King of England, who, without worrying about an unfavorable peace, was not in a position to start a war, lent himself to the desires of the Holy See. On 6 May 1228, he informed the four negotiators that two of his most influential advisers, Philippe d'Aubigny and the seneschal Raoul Fitz-Nicolas, were going to come for the signature of a new truce. The same day, he notified this determination by a circular to the King of France, Henri de Trubleville, Savary de Mauléon, and the Dauphin d' Auvergne.[52]

Gregory IX was rewarded for his efforts; on 6 June, Guillaume the Archbishop, Lord of Parthenay, who among the Poitevin vassals of Henry III was the closest to French possessions, signed a truce of one year, beginning with the octave of Holy Madeleine (29 July), with the King and Blanche. It was the Count de la Marche who was used as guarantee.[53] Two days later, the King of England yielded; he wrote Louis IX, and his mother, that Gregory IX had engaged to renew the truce, while waiting the conclusion of peace. The Bishop of Salisbury and Master Etienne, chaplain of the Pope, having already threatened him with ecclesiastical censures, he wanted to subject himself to the will of the Holy See. The King of France had received similar injunctions from the Pope, undoubtedly through mediation of the Archbishop of Sens and Pierre de Collemezzo.[54] Lastly, in the month of June, the conditions of truce were settled at Nogent-le-Roi; the Count de la Marche was understood to be a partisan of the King of France; commissioners were appointed for the establishment of reparations in case of infringement; the truce was to last until 22 July 1229; it was only on 6 July 1228 that Henry III informed his subjects of the truce.[55]

The disposition of Gregory IX had changed much since the time when he took up the defense of English interests, and it was probably due to the influence of Romain that he had returned to more equitable feelings. An English chronicler reported that in 1228 the counts, abbots, and priors of his domains were summoned, by authority of apostolic letters, to appear, some in Touraine, others in Champagne, and that Henry III was believed to call upon the Holy See; he could not to admit that anyone obliged his subjects to plead their businesses in enemy country.[56]

In reality, those who had been constrained to renew the truce had come to it before their desires. Far from being able at this moment to retake Anjou, Normandy, or Poitou, he [Henry III] he was only half certain of Gascogne. This province had been extremely agitated, as much as I can judge about it, between the departure of Prince Richard and the arrival of the seneschal Henri de Trubleville; perhaps even the Gascons had gone, in certain places, to plot in favor of the King of France. In Réole, several inhabitants had been expelled for having schemed to deliver their town to the enemies of the King of England, in other words the French. The arrival of the seneschal did not calm the dissatisfied ones. On 27 August 1228, Trubleville joined together in Langon the vassals and the representatives of cities, to take measures relating to pacification of the country and to publish the truce concluded with Louis IX.[57] In the midst of this assembly the Archbishop of Bordeaux and the Bishop of Comminges gave assistance, along with several barons, the mayor of Bordeaux Pierre Callan and several of his fellow-citizens rose and petitioned the seneschal in residence to pardon the exiled and restore their goods. Trubleville having answered that above all he wanted to advise his King and to consult the principal inhabitants of Réole, the mayor of Bordeaux and his colleagues overpowered him with insults and threats of death. Then they returned to their city, and as of the following day they occupied the castle, expelled the royal sergeants, took sums of money intended for the King of England, as well as pieces of furniture and the goods of the seneschal. Without wasting time, they wrote to the inhabitants of various localities to refuse the seneschal any obedience and any money. I do not know what was, in general, the attitude of the Gascon cities; people of Sainte-Bazeille hastened to write Henry III to tell him about the revolt of Bordeaux. Elsewhere, two noble Gascons, after the Langon meeting, denounced the malcontents of Bordeaux; it was, to hear them tell it, that the burgers had encroached little by little on the rights of the sovereign; they pressed the King to put them to rights.[58] The seneschal did not wait for action; letters of Henry III, dated 13 February 1229, apprize us that this prince took under his safeguard the burgers of Bordeaux and the nobles who, at the time of the disorders, had been faithful to his representative.[59]

It is necessarily so that in the English province the disorder was quite extensive, because immediately after prolongation of the truce Trubleville had asked for its recall. Henry III answered him, on 2 August, that he was extremely grateful for his services, but proposed to come himself to Gascogne. At the same time he wrote to him on the subject of the inhabitants of Rochefort, whom they could attach in their granting of customs and freedoms, the people of Saint-Emilion, who held for the party of the King of France.[60] These people were disposed so well toward Louis IX, that he had included them in his truce. Thus the one revolted in Bordeaux, or conspired with Réole; in Saint-Emilion, a few miles from the English capital, they were at war with the heir of Henry II and Richard the Lion-hearted. Knights of the King of England were believed to have license to make, under this full truce, an expedition against this city, and their master was obliged to punish them: "We alert you, he wrote to his seneschal, it is our will, to oblige them, by the punishment of their bodies and all other means in your disposal, to provide a reparation; it is necessary for any price that it is given; otherwise we could not obtain the indemnities to which we have a right." The King of France, for his part, did not give up the people of St. Emilion: he sent to claim an indemnity which was due from them, and on 21 September Henry III answered him, thus to Blanche, declaring himself ready to pay a hundred and fifty pounds sterling, instead of six hundred *livres tournois* which he had been asked to remit. On the other hand, he recalled that Louis IX had also some indemnities to be made; he requested his bailiffs be handed an order to parlay on this subject, with the carrier of his letters and the seneschal of Gascogne.[61] The indemnity of Saint-Emilion was regulated, as an order of payment addressed by the King of England, on 18 November, to his treasurer; the sums to be remitted had to be handed over to Robert of Sanford, commander of the Temple in London, bound for the treasury in Paris.[62] On the 19th, Henry III assigned from his treasury to Renoul de Talmont a gift of one hundred *marcs* to strengthen his castle.[63] One always prepared for war, while carrying out with honesty the clauses of a truce.

  Romain had necessarily played a very active part in the negotiations with England. He was at the same time the agent of the Holy See in France and a devoted auxiliary, the very influential adviser of Blanche. In the autumn, the Pope, renewing the indulgences granted to crusaders for the fight against heresy, had once more recommended him to the archbishops and to the clergy of France and kingdom of Arles.[64] Romain also played referee, beside Blanche, during the course of a pending transaction between Thibaud

IV and the Templars, in which the seneschal of Champagne, Simon of Joinville, had been given as a hostage.[65]

Cooperation with this foreigner was quite invaluable to Queen Blanche, now that she had so many enemies in France. At this time the first prince of the blood, Philippe Hurepel, who had at first shown devotion, passed to the party of revolt. Undoubtedly the dissatisfied barons had been able to make him believe that he was to have the upper hand in the business of the kingdom, and that the Queen usurped his rights by exerting control of the government. As long as Renaud de Boulogne, the prisoner of Bouvines, had been in homage to the King, Hurepel, whom he had supplanted, had been afraid that a return to freedom might not happen; in the event of estrangement, his sister-in-law would have held against him a frightening weapon. But Renaud had died in the spring of 1227; and from this side having nothing more to fear, the Count de Boulogne became more accessible to bad influences. He hastened to strongly establish himself in his domains; he transported by land and water large quantities of stone and timber; Boulogne, the castle of Ilardelot and other places were strengthened;[66] in Calais he raised an *enceinte* [enclosure] and a castle, for the construction of which the burgers lent eight thousand livres.[67] Since 1228, the son of Philippe Auguste was among the enemies of Blanche. Rumor was that he aspired to reign, but this claim had been so criminal, so contrary to the conduct he had displayed until then, that it appears difficult to attribute it to him. It is more probable that, pushed by ambition or jealousy, he wanted to have the regency. He certainly believed in his right, and who knows if once master of power, he would not have misused it to create in France, for his profit, one of those powers which more than once held royalty in check.[68]

Storytellers of the time reported that the Lord of Coucy raised his ambitious sights onto the throne of France. Great-grandson of Louis VI by his mother Alix de Dreux, and as such, first-cousin of Louis VIII, uncle, by his sister, of the Count de Dreux, Robert III, of Pierre Mauclerc, of the Count de Mâcon, of the Archbishop of Rheims, of the countesses of Bar and Roucy, Enguerrand III disposed then a true power; the superb castle which he built remains in our time the most imposing monument of feudal pride, and soon Enguerrand was going to show his power, while marrying his daughter to the King of Scotland. It was said that the barons, at the moment when they conspired to make the Count de Boulogne a king, had had a secret intention to put the Lord of Coucy on the throne; Enguerrand would have taken this offer seriously, and would have gone far to secure a crown.[69] This history is quite strange, and certainly it would have been insane of him to give up unreasonable hope. If Louis IX and his brothers had been disposed to favor civil war, then the sovereign power would have been naturally reserved to Philippe Hurepel. With his defection, there were no more princes of the house of Dreux, descendants of Louis VI, as the Lord of Coucy, and at their head the Count of Brittany, so from whose ranks and talents was there anyone ready to govern? Until the end of 1227, Enguerrand had been correct and respectful in his relationship with Blanche of Castile and the young King; in the autumn of 1227 one still sees him taking towards them the commitment to destroy on their requisition a bridge thrown across the Oise, in Beautor.[70] Whatever the nature of his pretensions, he was soon the most ardent to fight the Regent.

At the moment when the barons were going to deliver to the sovereign power a new attack, Blanche required, by letters patent, an oath of fidelity from the communes of all the parts of the royal lands between the Seine and Flanders. In the month of October, municipal magistrates and burgers of Rouen discharged this duty before Jean de la Porte, bailiff of Rouen, and Jean des Vignes, bailiff of Gisors; communes of Chambly, Beauvais, Chaumont-en-Vexin, Mantes, and Pontoise, acted similarly, to serve and defend with all their capacity the King, the Queen, and her other sons. In October and November an oath of comparable nature was lent by the municipal magistrates of Amiens, Bruyères-sous-Laon, Cerny-en-Laonnois, Chauny, Compiegne, Corbie, Crépy-en-Valois, Doullens, Hesdin, Laon, Montdidier, Noyon, Roye, Saint-Quentin, Senlis, Soissons, Wailly-en-Picardy, Verneuil, Athies, Bray-sur-Somme, Cappy, Ham, Lens, Montreuil-sur-Mer, Peronne, Pontpoint-en-Ile-de-France, Saint-Riquier, and Tournay.[71] They answered the hostile preparations of the Count de Boulogne, the Lord of Coucy and all their allies, in ensuring their services.

The barons, in a general meeting, had decided that Pierre Mauclerc would revolt first. Gathering for the army which the Queen would not fail to join together to march against the Count of Brittany, they agreed to answer the royal convocation personally, but each one brought only two knights.[72] It was treason in a form of obedience, a timid and dissimulated revolt; during the regency, the majority of barons, not daring to take direct action against royalty, did not cease to attack persons faithful to her, or to haggle over their help against her declared enemies.

French subjects of the King of England and the malcontents in provinces conquered by Philippe Auguste, who knew the dispositions and the projects of the nobility, came to be tempted to make a profit. With the festivals of Christmas (25 December 1228), the Archbishop of Bordeaux found the King of England in Oxford; sent by the lords of Gascogne, of Guyenne, and Poitou, he had the role of calling Henry III to France. Delegates of the Norman nobility were also found there; they ensured that if the son of King John landed in their country, the nobles would come to a meeting with their horses and their weapons and would bring all the population out for him to help to reconquer his heritage.[73] But Henry III was a young person, hesitant; he followed the councils of his minister, the dispenser of justice Hubert de Burgh, who persuaded him to postpone this expedition to some other time. Henry was not ready and the truce he had accepted the preceding summer was to last until July 1229; he had every reason to delay requests of the Normans and Poitevins. He gave them leave to return..

One is thus misled when one claims that he went down to France.[74] Nothing permits us to believe that Richard de Cornouailles, in the absence of his brother, brought at this time help with Pierre Mauclerc.[75] Henry III, had he acted in this manner, could some time afterwards, address to Louis IX complaints relating to the infringements of the truce, and the passage of chronicler Philippe Mousket, which relates that Richard came consequently to Brittany, appears only to apply to later events.

Pierre Mauclerc opened hostilities, but the hope of the barons was disappointed. The Count de Champagne, who sided with them in 1227, thwarted for the second time their calculations by filling with fidelity his duties of vassal. I know, by an unfortunately incomplete copy, the list of nobles, vassals of Thibaud IV, convened by their suzerain to go to war for the King. This document, of which the original was destroyed, carried more than eight hundred names, among others that of Geoffroy, Lord of Louppy, who appears in the midst of nobles convened by Marshal Champagne. However, Geoffroy could not have carried this title before July 1227; on the other hand, the list of convocation or *arriere-ban* mentions the dowry of Blanche, Countess of Navarre, mother of Thibaud IV, who died in March 1229. It was thus between July 1227 and March 1229 that the

Count de Champagne raised this army, and the expedition to Brittany was the only circumstance in connection with which he could take a similar measure.[76] By this fact even, it is shown that this campaign, during which Bellême was besieged, took place in 1229, and not in the following year.

It is probable that the lords of Champagne did not all of them answer the call of Thibaud, or that this prince had put himself in a position to join them together because Joinville relates that the Count joined the royal army at the head of three hundred knights.[77] It was enough to draw Blanche into the business at a time when the treason of these vassals threatened all.

The King of France had delayed Pierre Mauclerc in Melun, for the Sunday after Christmas, 31 December 1228. Pierre did not appear in person. His envoy, in the absence Louis IX, protested before the King's men that he had missed feudal uses by not giving him a deadline of forty days, and asked of his master a new summons.[78] While the Count of Brittany endeavored to save time, Blanche of Castile started herself at the head of a large army, to which the quotas provided by the cities and the countryside were joined by the communes. She took along with her the young King; it was the first campaign of Saint Louis. In full winter, in the month of January, the royal troops moved towards Perche.[79] The Count had occupied for several years the forest of Bellême, defended in the south by the fortified town of this name, with the west by the castle of Perrière. The treaty of Vendôme had recognized him, but on condition he was to raise no new fortifications. Undoubtedly, Mauclerc was well situated; to observe this restrictive clause, the castle of Bellême, defended by an excellent garrison, passed for impregnable.

The Count of Brittany had ordered all to evacuate the city and to concentrate all resistance in the castle, because parishioners about Saint-Saver and Saint-Pierre de Bellême complained later that, about the time of the siege, he had made them burn their houses. Close by Bellême was Sérigny, which had much to suffer; the neighboring localities were occupied or put to work by the royal troops; c' were the villages of Saint-Jean-de-la-Forêt, Nocé, Dame-Marie, Saint-Ouen-de-la-Coer, Eperrais, Courthiou, Vaunoise, Colonard, Igé, Courcerault.[80] The borough of Saint Martin-du-Vieux-Bellême, located at some distance, on the edge of the forest, was tested above all, and one would really arrive at considerable sums, if one made a total of the expenditure or the losses they had to undergo during the siege.⁸¹ The King was placed either in Bellême, or in one of the nearby places; Jean Clement, Marshal of France, undoubtedly also occupied a house, but most of the army camped under tent.⁸² It was necessary to have many supplies, fodder, and subsistence for many people and horses; they were taken a little everywhere, and later Louis IX returned, to Mans, a hundred *livres tournois* to the monks of Saint Martin-du-Vieux-Bellême, for the supplies which they had made over to him.⁸³ The leper-houses of Bellême and Mauves were not free from exactions which weighed on all the region: the war, then as always, had rigors against which one could do nothing.⁸⁴

Blanche had not only come to accompany her son; she had her eye on everything, took care of the wellbeing and the maintenance of her army. As the cold was excessive, she ordered men to light large fires in the middle of the horse parade, to guard against the freezing cold; she promised wages for all those who would go into the forest and by the countryside, to cut down trees to bring wood to the camp which they needed; she could thus heat not only the houses, among others that of the King, and the marshal, but also tents of the soldiers.⁸⁵ The servants who accompanied the army attended it by requisitioning wagons.⁸⁶ The work of approaches during a siege required a great quantity of wood; they cut down the trees of forests; they demolished houses in Bellême and in Sérigny to take the beams or to get the stones from them to be launched by machines of war.⁸⁷

On the day following the first attack, which was vigorously pushed back, the Marshal advanced the miners and ordered them to sap the bases of the castle, all the while protecting their work with his knights. At the same time as the attack began again on all sides, the garrison bravely answered by shooting the attackers; this obliged the sappers to move back, then to make an escape; but at the end of this hard combat, which lasted until three in the afternoon, the base of the ramparts had been extremely damaged. The next day, in the morning, the Marshal drew up two machines from which they launched large stones and some smaller. The first of these two *pierrières* dispatched to the interior of the fortress such an enormous projectile that the dwelling of the lord of the manor collapsed upon the people who found refuge there; at the same time the keep staggered on its foundations and collapsed. Then the garrison lost courage; they did not see any approaching help; the walls they had bravely defended were attacked at the base, already half destroyed at the top; soldiers of Pierre Mauclerc capitulated and the King granted them grace.⁸⁸

The castle of Perrière was undoubtedly retaken before Bellême; one named Hugues the Fair had delivered the keys to Louis IX.[89] It was a nice success that in the fall of these two fortified towns, and, while waiting for better, Blanche could be content to have carried out a so heavy a blow. Bellême was put into a state of defense and was furnished with supplies, while the victors returned to Paris.[90] Allies of Pierre Mauclerc dared not move; the only one who declared against the King was the lord of Haie-Paynel, close to Avranches, whose family, equipped with fiefs in England, were devoted to the former masters of Normandy. The news of his revolt came to Blanche of Castile the day when Bellême capitulated. At once she ordered the bailiff of Gisors, Jean des Vignes, to leave with a body troops raised in Normandy to put to reason the people of Haie-Paynel; they knew the royal army was occupied fighting the Count of Brittany and would not be attacked in full winter; the abrupt arrival of Jean des Vignes disconcerted them; they surrendered at the end of a few days.[91]

The King of England neither ignored the rising of Pierre Mauclerc, nor the plot of the French barons, nor especially the revolt of Haie-Paynel who were his partisans; but perhaps he did not know yet about the surrender of Bellême, or at least that of Haie-Paynel, when he wrote, on 6 February 1229, to the Count of Chester and of Lincoln: "I know that it often happens to us that noises of which we cannot, because of their innovation, inform you and our other faithful. Among others, there lately arrived to us a news item which interests our profit and our honor in particular, like yours and that of all our subjects. It will be to you, when we shall have communicated, extremely pleasant and welcome news." To speak thus, was obviously to refer to the events in France, from which Henry III hoped well to profit; without explaining more, he mandated the Count hold ready his horses, his weapons and all materiel for an expedition, to be able to cross the sea with him, which he hoped to make happen very soon. At the same time, he forewarned the authorities of Sandwich and several other ports to prepare their vessels.[92] How could such measures be reconciled with negotiations having as their goal the restoration of peace? Henry however made a pretence to wish it: the Pope, and the Cardinal of Saint-Ange worked in good faith; he left them in their illusions. The same day as he spoke to the Count of Chester about his quarrelsome projects, he wrote to the legate as if he had been seriously questioning how to arrange [peace] with France: why Louis IX had not announced certain proposals to be acceptable when brought to the Cardinal by the Abbot of Cleeve? Before entering into direct talks with the Holy See for the conclusion of peace, the King of England made a point of knowing on what conditions the King of France would like to treat.[93]

During this time, Henry III remained in a relationship with the Count de Toulouse, who had not yet made peace with his sovereign. At the beginning of March he sent his counselor Philippe d'Arderne and a burger of Bordeaux, on a secret mission that undoubtedly did not have as its aim the service of French interests.[94] They continued to negotiate about the indemnities to be paid for the infringements of the truce, but the letters that Henry III wrote on this subject to Louis IX, on 4 March and 1 April, are in a rather sour tone for reconciliation.[95] Philippe d'Aubigny and the other English agents in charge of the relationship with France came and went between England and the continent; but had they spoken sincerely, at the court of England, that their mission succeeded?[96] On 5 April, Henry III wrote to the legate, to the King of France and his mother, to accredit near to them the Bishop of Coventry and Lichfield, Raoul Fitz-Nicolas, and a third envoy; he charged these ambassadors to bring to France peace proposals, and at the same time gave them full powers to conclude a new truce.[97] However, what were these proposals for peace? He wanted nothing less than to claim for the grandson of Philippe Auguste all that his father and his grandfather had conquered as Plantagenets, with the exception of Normandy. Still the King of England claimed to include in this province the bishoprics of Avranches and Coutances, or at least one or the other. Passing to another mode of arrangement, the instructions given to the English envoys spoke about marriages to conclude between Henry III and the sister of Louis IX, between Louis IX and a sister of Henry III; but the King of France had nothing to be gained from a similar union, which was to be paid by the retrocession of Normandy; moreover the dowry of the English princess, formed by Maine and the part of Anjou located north of the Loire, was to be begun again if the sister of Henry III, became queen of France, and did not have children.[98] It would be painful to believe that the King of England and his advisers counted on success from such an attempt. It was advantageous for them to create, on any matter, new difficulties for Blanche of Castile. A few weeks after the capitulation of Bellême an unforeseen circumstance allowed the King of England and the Count of Brittany to once more support those who in France made opposition to the government of the Regent.

    The Université of Paris had received from Philippe Auguste privileges which would appear exorbitant, if one did not know how much the kings of France held to its prosperity. The honor that it was worth to the kingdom and the interest that they took to support it might explain the legal immunities which it enjoyed, even though its students did not always demonstrate their worthiness. It goes without saying that serious concerns and a taste for hard work were not always shared among those who came to Paris from everywhere, and often from afar, for their studies; in the student body, pleasure, and practices of disorder and idleness had to have many followers, and when one follows through the ages the history of this large and illustrious institution, one sees repeating in every century the same scenes and tumultuous adventures, starting with strange buffooneries and finishing in bloody affrays. Undoubtedly it had been easy to subject to a severe discipline the clerks of the University, but one made a point of preserving them, to attract them from all the provinces and from all the foreign countries towards Paris, which had become, in a short time, an incomparable center for studies. As far as possible one tolerated the noisy ones, not to push away the others, and it was at the end of the twelfth century when students often came there from the bourgeois of Paris and from the inhabitants of nearby villages. Towards 1192, they were caught in a quarrel with peasants of the abbey of Saint-Germain-des-Prés, and one of them was killed.[99] In 1200, a new brawl, of which I am unaware of the origin, cost the life of five men, clerks and laymen. What did Philippe Auguste do? This firm prince, so jealous of his power, prevailed with an extreme rigor against the provost of Paris and his people, who had undoubtedly intervened with too much energy at the scene of disorder; then he recalled in a royal decree the punishment inflicted on his agents, took the most serious measures to protect the clerks, declared that provosts and representatives of royal justice would only have to arrest any student, if it was for a crime or a very serious offense; if required, the arrest would have to be done without brutality; the delinquent would be delivered to the ecclesiastical authority, and if the hour was not too far advanced they could immediately turn him over to his natural judges, to be temporarily kept, without having to undergo ill treatment, in some house of students.[100] In 1210, the King repeated, by specifying them, provisions of this ordinance in letters addressed to the mayor and sworn by the communes.[101] From now on students, even if they were at fault, would be sure to escape, in the first moment, from the repressive powers which could be the consequence of their excesses.

Those who were supported in such usages with little moderation and relative impunity, ensured themselves with royal benevolence; the religious authority itself had arrived, during the first years of Louis IX, to find their ways intolerable. A few months after his elevation to the episcopal see of Paris, Guillaume d'Auvergne, in July 1228, was extremely irritated against students of Saint-Thomas-du-Louvre who, not content to work, and disturbing the studies of their comrades, had forced the doors of a convent.[102] It was worse the following year: Blanche of Castile returned to Paris, from the siege of Bellême, when disorders burst forth on the occasion of Carnaval.[103]

On Fat Monday, 26 February 1229, some students from the nation of Picardy went to drink, outside of the city, in Saint-Marcel; when asked to pay, they quarreled with the innkeepers; they traded blows, pulled hair; people of the village assisted their neighbors, thrashed the students and put them to flight. Overcome, they returned to Paris, furious, exciting their comrades to avenge them, and the following day (27 February), returned in force to Saint-Marcel, armed with swords and sticks. One cabaret was ransacked, then the youths spread through the village, and delivered blows to all those whom they met, without sparing the women. At once, the deacon of the chapter of Saint-Marcel, worried about his people, petitioned before Cardinal Romain, legate of the Holy See, and Guillaume d' Auvergne, Bishop of Paris; these two great persons referred it to Blanche, and engaged her to prevail. Whatever were the wrongs of the students, it should be remembered that Romain and Guillaume d'Auvergne were extremely badly disposed towards them; the Cardinal had not forgotten a riot that he had caused, at the time of his first arrival in France, by breaking the seal of the Université, and we have just seen that the Bishop was not going to tolerate the misconduct of the students. The Queen, with her characteristic energy and authoritative temperament, could be only of their opinion; she ordered the provost to leave the walls with a troop of armed men, that the historian of this adventure called mercenaries, to restore the authors of disorder to reason. However, it was during the holidays; clerks, in large bands, were spread throughout the countryside; the first who met the provost and his troops were not, as they claimed, those who mistreated the inhabitants of Saint-Marcel. The fight proceeded however; there were deaths and casualties; students were beaten without pity, and many, to escape, hid in the vineyards and stone quarries.[104] Were people of the King shown to be brutal? Those they had harshly abused were foreign to Saint-Marcel? Mathieu de Paris, who affirms it however, tells us that among the deaths was a Flemish student, belonging to the nation of Picardy, whose students caused of all this scandal. It is certain that students were killed; a chronicler even tells that several perished by drowning in the Seine.[105]

Upon learning what had just occurred, masters of the Université, after having proclaimed the closing of lectures and discussions, petitioned the Queen and the legate. They complained that persons had benefited from the disorder caused by some bad characters. It is certain that in being regulated on the schedule of Philippe Auguste they would have had to proceed with less rigor and precipitation, in arresting the guilty and stopping them without their doing evil; but Mathieu de Paris, to whom we owe the account of these events, was always subject to caution when it concerned the kings of France: is it certain that the provost of Paris attacked the innocent in error, that students did not cause by their resistance and the employment of weapons the conflict in which several among them found death? Actually, the system established by Philippe Auguste became inapplicable, at the moment when clerks of the Université convened from there to maltreat passers by and to plunder their houses. Blanche of Castile, whose power was then extremely disputed, was not to suffer similar abuses. Perhaps she acted with a little promptness to fight them; in this respect opinions remained divided.[106]

At the end of a few weeks, when the Université definitely saw that neither the Queen, nor the legate, nor the Bishop, would address their complaints, it passed from remonstrances to threats. On 27 March, its headmasters wrote a letter in which they declared that if within one month from Easter (15 April-15 May), no one had obtained satisfaction, no master, and no pupil would be authorized anymore, during a period of six years, to live in the city and the diocese of Paris; this time, no one would have rights to return if insults to the Université had not been repaired.[107] Then the students dispersed; they went to Rheims, others to Angers, still others to Orléans. Many crossed over to England, some passed to Spain, to Italy, and undoubtedly to Bologna.[108] The events in Paris benefited the new University of Toulouse;[109] they had especially pleased the Count de Bretagne and the King of England. Pierre Mauclerc was then master of Angers; the students went there as a group; it is true that soon the war drove out some of them.[110] As for Henry III, he wrote, on 16 July 1229, from Reading, a circular to the masters and students of Paris, to promise all kinds of facilities to them, and they came to be fixed in his kingdom.[111]

As the students liked to laugh, this conflict, burlesque in its origin, was enlivened by bad jokes. Those for whom the severity of Blanche had brought them to leave Paris vividly remembered the way that the legate was her adviser and friend; already enemies of the Regent had imagined that she lived on too good terms with Romain; clerks of the University took again for their account this insinuation, of which one cannot materially show the falseness, but which has no probability. They show up in the circulation of an epigram that the chroniclers repeated with pleasure; it is too improper for one to dare translate it; here is the paraphrase: "Alas! we die; we are killed, beaten, drowned, stripped; it is the lewdness of the legate for all that is worth."[112] This legend, which could not seriously compromise the reputation of Blanche, enjoyed for some time a certain credit; one finds a glimpse of it in the Minstrel of Rheims, this charming storyteller whose accounts reproduce the popular opinion of historical events of the thirteenth century rather well. He shows us the Queen, made pregnant by Cardinal Romain, and showing him quite naked with his prelates and barons to confuse his slanderer.[113] In this order of ideas, even the strangest inventions almost always find someone to amplify them.

The attacks whose object was Blanche did not prevent her from making an arrangement. To the solicitations of the King of England she answered while making confirmation of her son, in the month of August, in the privilege of Philippe Auguste, and it was undoubtedly at that time that was written, such as we know it, the oath imposed on the provost of Paris about his relationship with students.[114] This kind of capitulation did not bring back pupils and masters who had left Paris in great number who had left for the enemies of the King. They knew the Pope supported them; on 24 November 1229, Gregory charged the Bishop of Mans, the Bishop of Senlis and the Archdeacon of Châlons, to actively employ means of restoring peace. The same day, he wrote Louis IX and his mother.[115] His provisions with regard to the University were more than favorable; he had, the day before, censured in severe and probably unjust terms the Bishop of Paris, who was shown, in all this business, the defender of order and of discipline.[116] This attempt of the Pope did not alleviate the disagreement; it was to last a long time, but could not to occupy more than a secondary place in the concerns of Blanche. While the students of Paris made common cause with the Count of Brittany and the English, she had found a way to end, in very advantageous conditions for the crown, the long one and cruel war of the Albigensians.

The distress of Raimond VII and his partisans made peace inevitable.[117] Talks were, for some time, committed between the court of France and the Count de Toulouse, when, on 10 December 1228, Raimond gave well defined powers to Hélie Guerin, abbot of the Cistercian convent of Grandselve: wishing to return the Church to unity, to submit to the King his lord, to Blanche his cousin, he charged the abbot to regulate the conditions of an arrangement; he promised on the Gospels to observe a suspended agreement with Count Thibaud of Champagne; he declared moreover to have taken this decision with the approval of his barons and consuls of Toulouse.[118] While the legate held two councils to regulate the business of the Albigensians, one in Sens at Christmas, the other in Senlis, at Candlemas (2 February 1229), a truce had been concluded, and the Abbot of Grandselve, returned from the court of France, ending up in Baziège, between Toulouse and Villefranche-de-Lauragais, to bring a draft treaty.[119] This preliminary act, where Thibaud of Champagne seems mediator, and the Count de la Marche as referee, was accepted in January with the approval of Raimond VII.[120] He decided to continue the negotiations in France, and it was in Meaux, on lands of Thibaud IV, that Raimond went. They found the legate there, people of the King, the Archbishop of Narbonne and his suffragans.

After conferences which lasted a few days, all returned to Paris, and when the conditions of the treaty had been approved by the King, written, and sealed, Raimond was allowed to make an act of contrition and obedience. On Holy Thursday, 2 April 1229, this unhappy prince, who for so many years fought with courage for the heritage of his fathers and the independence of his people, had to lend himself to more mortifying formalities. He presented himself barefoot, wearing a hair shirt, before the portal of Notre Dame; there he promised, in the presence of Romain and the legate of the Holy See in England, to subject himself to the orders of the Church. Then Romain, recognizing this act of humility and devotion, lifted the sentences which had struck, and at same time, of his consent, he declared excommunicated again, if he contravened the conditions to which he had just subscribed. He was then led away. The following day, Holy Friday, he took the cross.[121]

No historian recounts that Blanche assisted in the humiliation of her unfortunate cousin. It was enough for her to have terminated with profit to royalty a long and dangerous war. Actually, it was especially the Queen who had just gained the victory. In spite of the devotion with which her officers had been useful in Languedoc, the tender of Raimond was her work as well, because the Count de Toulouse would not have been overcome if Blanche had not the courage of continue this fight in spite of the innumerable difficulties that it placed upon the government of her kingdom. Although she was not named in the act which put an end to the war of the Albigensians, it was Blanche who, in her capacity as Queen of France and friend of the Church, dictated the conditions of peace.

The Treaty of Paris is known to us by several specimens, the first dated 11 April 1229.[122] This document, in which so many questions are regulated, is characterized by its precision and its methodical clearness. Its writers, instead of mixing the various subjects, as was too often done, separated and approached one after the other, without ever returning to a previous clause. Here is the order in which the articles follow one another composed in a group.

The Count de Toulouse promised above all to remain faithful to the Church, to the King and his heirs; he engaged, under conditions as detailed as they were precise, to fight heresy. He was to keep the peace in his domains, while helping with this maintenance in the countries yielded to the King. He would expel mercenaries, defend and respect the churches, make certain that sentences of excommunication were observed, restore to churches all the goods and rights of which they enjoyed before the first arrival of the crusaders, pay and make to pay tithes, which were not to fall into the hands of laymen.

An indemnity of ten thousand *marcs* was to be paid to the churches and members of the clergy. Four thousand *marcs* were also divided between the abbeys of Cîteaux, Clairvaux, Grandselve, Belleperche and Candeil. The King was to receive six thousand *marcs* to strengthen and keep the Château-Narbonnese, citadel of Toulouse, and the other castles that he occupied during ten years for his safety and that of the Church. These twenty thousand *marcs* would be paid in four years, five thousand *per annum*. In addition, four thousand *marcs* were to be given to the Masters of the University of Toulouse.

The Count declared that after his absolution he would take up the cross, and go overseas for five years. The Count was not to make difficulties with anybody to have been party to the Church, the King, and the counts of Montfort; the King and the Church took from the partisans of Raimond the same engagement.

Louis IX agreed, by grace, to marry one of his brothers to the daughter of the Count de Toulouse, Jeanne, who was to be given by the King; the Church was to authorize this marriage by an exemption. In consideration of this union, the King left to the Count all the bishopric of Toulouse, except the domain known as the Marshal [Guy of Lévis], that this lord would hold it for the Crown. After the death of Raimond VII, the bishopric of Toulouse would belong to the prince that Jeanne will have married, or to her children. If Jeanne died without issue, Toulouse and its bishop would go to the King. Louis IX left Raimond VII the bishoprics of Agen and Rodez, with part of Albi on the right bank of the Tarn, except Albi and all the part which extended in the direction of Carcassonne were removed to the Count. Raimond was to preserve the bishopric of Cahors, except the town of this name, and the strongholds that Philippe Auguste held, at his death, in the aforementioned bishopric. If Raimond died without legitimate issue other than Jeanne, this princess and her heirs were to have all the fiefs left to the Count, but Raimond preserved the right to make pious donations to the Bishop of Toulouse from lands of which he remained the owner. Aside from this exception, donations of the King, his father, and counts of Montfort were not sustained. Raimond VII made homage to and took an oath of fidelity, according to the use formed by the barons of France, for all the lands which the King left to him. He admitted having given up to the King all the remainder of such that he had on this side the Rhone, to the legate and the Church the lands he had to the east of this river.

The Count was required to make war on those of his men who would not want not to subject themselves to the King and to the Church, in particular to the Count de Foix. If their lands were occupied, Raimond VII would keep them; but he was to destroy their castles and fortresses, unless the King wanted them for ten years, for his security and that of the Church.

Raimond VII was to destroy the walls of Toulouse and fill the ditches of this city. He was to cut down the ramparts of thirty cities and castles of which twenty-five are named in the treaty, and these same would not be able to be strengthened again without the consent of the King and the Church. The Count would not be able to raise new fortified towns; he was to employ, if necessary, the forces to ensure the dismantling of the places indicated above. Raimond VII attested to have lent his oath to observe these conditions, and promised to make his men swear to them, and in particular the burgers of Toulouse. If he missed these engagements, his subjects would be released from their duties towards him, and at the same time he would incur confiscation and excommunication. The oaths in question would be renewed every five years, at the will of the King. For more safety, the King would occupy for ten years the Château-Narbonnais, citadel of Toulouse, and eight other fortified places; during the five first years of this occupation, the Count would pay, for the expenses of the garrison of the aforesaid places, an annual rent of fifteen hundred *livres tournois*, without speaking of six thousand *marcs* for maintenance stipulated above. The King, without this sum being decreased, would be able to destroy four of the castles which were left to his guardianship. Finally, Louis IX relieved the people of Toulouse and the other subjects of Raimond VII from all engagements taken against him, his father, and the counts of Montfort.

This treaty, so remarkable for the importance of the adopted conditions, for the clearness of its drafting, the prudence with which all the details were regulated by it, is one of most beautiful works that Blanche of Castile left to us. It is just to add that the Cardinal of Saint-Ange, legate of the Holy See, brought into these negotiations so skillfully carried out and finished by wise arrangements, in their spirit, an order which distinguished her policy from the Roman court. Blanche returned peace to large provinces, put an end to the civil war, received the submission of a powerful vassal, and took all precautions necessary for effectiveness. She made available most of the forces which royalty had maintained for several years in Languedoc; she removed dissatisfied barons from the alliance which, among all, could best assist their ambitious projects; she deprived Henry III of confederates that were united in blood ties and a community of interests that seemed to intend support, one day or the other, for an English invasion. And of course she did not misuse the situation to push an unhappy adversary to the end. At the same time that Blanche had been assured of arriving one day at entirely destroying the house of Toulouse, the success of such an expedition would have cost many dangers, in time, money, and blood, and after the final destruction of Raimond VII and his partisans, it would have been necessary to carry to the end a hateful war, of odious and unjustifiable spoliation. This result itself was more dubious, and, in being constrained to seek it, one ran many risks. All things considered, the Treaty of Paris and its relative moderation, was quite preferable. Royalty, heir to a fight it had not started, restricted itself to preserve most of the conquests for which it had fought; it left the remainder to be overcome, but the heritage of this reduced power was partly ensured to the brother of the King; they could yet hope that one day the totality of the domains of Raimond VII would belong to a son of France.

The territorial clauses of the Treaty of Paris made over to the King, in the Midi, an excellent situation. The Toulouse heritage would consequently break up into four groups: 1.) east of the Rhone, the marquisate of Provence, nominally depending on the Empire as a fief of the Kingdom of Arles, became property of the Church. 2.) counties occupied by royalty, west of the Rhone and along the Mediterranean, were definitively given up to Louis IX; they formed the two *sénéchaussées* of Beaucaire and Nimes, Carcassonne and Béziers. In addition to this, Raimond VII renounced suzerainty over a certain number of fiefs which passed under the direct tenure of the crown. 3.) Toulouse and most of its bishopric became the heritage of a son of Blanche; Raimond VII preserved them only for the term of his life. 4.) Agénois, Rouergue, and most of Quercy, north of the Albigeois, were left to the Count de Toulouse, but they envisaged the case where this prince, having no new heir, would be reduced to bequeath them, as all that remained, to his daughter Jeanne, wife of a French prince. One can see that the conditions imposed on Raimond VII were still hard, and Guillaume de Puy-Laurens could say, without too much exaggeration, that only one of them would have been enough to pay his ransom, had he fallen, after a battle, into the hands of his sovereign.[123]

After the conclusion of the peace, Raimond VII, executing an arbitral decision of the Count de Champagne, gave as hostages five burgers of Toulouse, who remained in the hands of the King until this city razed its walls and filled its ditches to an extent of five hundred *toises*; this partial dismantling had to precede the complete demolition of the ramparts.[124] The Count remained temporarily in the Louvre while waiting for his daughter to be given to the representatives of Louis IX, along with the Château-Narbonnais, and four other fortresses, to be delivered to the King.¹²⁵ At the same time the Regent renewed with Count Amaury de Montfort the renunciation by which he had yielded to the Crown, during the life of Louis VIII, all his rights to the old conquests of his father Count Simon.¹²⁶ Lastly, the Treaty of Paris having partly for its goal the re-establishment of the Catholic faith in Languedoc, promulgated without delay a grand ordinance on the repression of heresy.¹²⁷

The sons of Viscount Aimery de Narbonne remained heirs of land belonging to their father on condition of their making homage to the Crown, and the King, in the month of June, wrote to the faithful of the diocese of Rodez to transport their homage to Raimond VII, to whom he had restored Milhau.¹²⁸ For his part, Romain and Thibaud de Champagne, as referees, decided that the Count de Toulouse, by means of the transfer of Saint-Antonin in Rouergue and the abandonment of his claims on Cahors and several strongholds of Quercy, would be exempted to pay the indemnity which the treaty had imposed on him for the maintenance of the castles delivered to Louis IX as guarantee.¹²⁹

When they had taken all precautions relative to the execution of the Treaty of Paris, the Count de Toulouse, whom the King had just knighted in Pentecost, returned to his estates, and the legate, based on the exemption previously granted by the Holy See, proclaimed the legitimacy of the engagement concluded between Jeanne de Toulouse and Alphonse de France.¹³⁰ In accordance with one of the articles of the treaty, troops of Raimond VII united with royal troops to march against Roger Bernard, Count de Foix, whose lands were occupied until Pas-de-la-Barre; shearing off part of the county of Foix located to the north of this procession temporarily left to the Count de Toulouse.¹³¹ Roger Bernard, who was not able to fight both against his suzerain and against the King of France, on 16 June 1229 accepted, at Saint-Jean-des-Verges, the conditions which were granted to him by Mathieu de Marly, lieutenant of the King in Albigeois, and by the vice-legate Pierre of Collemezzo, representative of the Church and lieutenant of Romain.¹³² In September he came to Melun, to settle with the King the final conditions of his submission.¹³³

However, Pierre of Collemezzo had proceeded, in Toulouse, to the ceremony of reconciliation; the capital of the country where heresy had thrived being thus purified, Romain came to visit; in November he held a council to establish the Inquisition.¹³⁴ His mission in Languedoc was accomplished. Romain proceeded to lower

Languedoc, then passed to the marquisate of Provence. The Church, to which the Treaty of Paris had deposited this stronghold of the Empire, had been, for the moment, extremely embarrassed in managing itself; on 29 December 1229, the legate gave it in guardianship to the lieutenant of the King in the province of Narbonne, Adam de Milly, and to the seneschal of Beaucaire; the following day, Romain heard Adam de Milly on the subject of goods confiscated from heretics; it was the last act of this legation, in which he had fulfilled the mission that the Pope had entrusted to him, while assisting Blanche of Castile with much devotion and skill.[135]

When Cardinal Romain crossed the Rhone, disorders had for several months returned again to France; Blanche was, once more, at odds with the barons. But the war in Languedoc was finished, and Raimond de Toulouse could no longer join those who combined their efforts to take power from the mother of Louis IX.

1   The confessor of Queen Marguerite, *Historiens de France*, t. XX, p. 65.

2   *Regis Francorum beati Ludovici canonisatio, Historiens de France*, t. XXIII, p. 155 « : *cumque... ætatis annum quartum decimum attigisset...* »

3   Ibid. *Gesta sancti Ludovici Noni auctore monacho Sancti Dionysii anonyme* (*Histor. de France*, XX, p. 46) : « *cepit... sub cura magistri humiliter proficere.* »

4   *Beati Ludovici vita e veteri lectionario extracta* (*Historiens de France*, XXIII, p. 160) : « *sub cura specialis magistri et consilio religiosorum, maxime ordinis fratrum Praedicatorum...* u 5. *Gesta Sancti Ludovici auclore... anonymo* (*Historiens de France*, t. XX, p. 46) : « *Ipsamet namque eum per exempla ad bona documenta informabat...* »

5   Guillaume de Nangis, *Vie de Saint Louis* (*Historiens de France*, t. XX, p. 312).

6   Geoffroy de Beaulieu (*Historiens de France*, t. XX, p. 15, chap. xxm) : « *proprie et optime noverat coram illis transferre en gallicum de latine.* »

7   The confessor (*Histor. de France*, t. XX, p. 66); L'anonyme of Saint-Denis (ibid., p. 46); *Beati Ludovici vita, partim ad lectiones, partim ad sacrum sermonem parata* (ibid., t. XXIII, p. 168) : « *proximis humilitatis honorem sedulus exhibebat.* »

8   The confessor, p. 66.

9   Geoffroy de Beaulieu (*Historiens de France*, t. XX, p. 4).

10   The confessor (Historiens de France, t. XX, p. 64); *Beati Ludovici vita e veteri lectionario extracta* (ibid., t. XXIII, p. 161).

11   1874 ed., § 71.

12   The confessor, p. 65 a : « *ainçois les fist plus diliganraent et plui curieusement après norrir, garder et enfermer.* »

13   Du Cange, ed. Joinville, 1668, in-f°, *La vie d'Isabelle, sœur de saint Louis*, by Agnès de Harcourt, p. 171.

14   Le Nain de Tillemont, I, 476.

15   Le Nain de Tillemont related many details of the foundation of Royaumont (t. I, p. 489 ff.).

16   « *Per lou conseil dame Hersent,* » said, in speaking of Blanche, the unknown author of a dialogue in verse (*Histoire littéraire de la France*, XXIII, 773, 4th strophe, verse 6).

17   Paulin Paris, *Le Romancero françois, second serventois de Hugues de la Ferté*,

p. 188-189.

18   On guard.

19   Paulin Paris, *Le Romancero françois, premier serventois de Hugues de la Ferté*, 2nd strophe, p. 182-183.

20   Ibid., 4th strophe, p. 183-184.

21   Ibid., *Le Romancero françois, troisieme serventois de Hugues de la Ferté*, 2nd strophe, p. 190

22   Same poem, p. 191-192.

23   « *anno subsequenti* », according to Guillaume de Nangis (*Vie de saint Louis, Historiens de France*, t. XX, p. 314 b), which follows that of the *Grandes chroniques de France* (same collection, t. XXI, p. 104; ed. Paulin Paris, t. IV, p. 233).

24   *Les Grandes chroniques de France, ou Chroniques de S. Denis* (*Historiens of France*, t. XXI, p. 104; ed. Paulin Paris, t. IV, p. 233).

25   Edition of 1874, § 72.

26   Châtres, today called Arpajon, « *apud Castra* », according to Guillaume de Nangis (*Historiens de France*, XX, 314).

27   Le Roux de Lincy, *Recherches sur la grande confrérie Notre-Dame aux prêtres et bourgeois de la ville of Paris*, Paris, 1844, *Mémoires de la Société royale des Antiquaires de France*, t. XVII, p. 217; see, concerning Blanche of Castile, article 5 of the statutes of this *confrérie* ; same dissertation, appendices, p. 282.

28   *Chroniques de Saint-Denis* (*Historiens de France*, XXI, 104; ed. Paulin Paris, t. IV, p. 235).

29   Ed. of 1874, p. 73.

30   Guillaume of Nangis, *Historiens de France*, XX, 314. For this episode, see Le Nain de Tillemont, t. I, p. 478-479.

31   *Layettes*, t. II, n. 1960; February 1228; Ibid., p. 650, n. 1959, 10 February 1228; Ibid., n. 19591, 1 February 1228.

32   *Layettes*, II, 1962 et 1963; February 1228.

33   Aubry de Trois-Fontaines, *Monumenta Germaniæ*, scriptores, XXIII, p. 921 ; 1228 : « *Romanus, a Roma regressas pro facto Albigensium et pro discordia*

principum Francio », etc.

34   Potthast, *Regesta*, 8150; Rinaldi, *Annales ecclesiastici* , t. I, p. 612, 2nd year of Gregory IX, g 21-22; 21 March 1228.

35   In 1228, Easter fell on 26 March.

36   Guillaume de Puy-Laurens, *Historiens de France*, t. XIX, p. 218.

37   *E mari historiarum*, same collection, t. XXIII, p. 108.

38   Guillaume de Puy-Laurens.

39   *Historiens de France*, XXIV, p. 66, n. 500 : Inquest on the vicomte d'Exmes.

40   Roger of Wendover, ed. Hewlett, t. II, p. 347, and after him, Mathieu de Paris, *Chronica majora*, ed. Luard, III, 156.

41   Guillaume de Puy-Laurens, *Historiens de France*, t. XIX, p. 218-219.

42   Guillaume de Puy-Laurens.

43   *Layettes*, t. II, n. 1969; 25 June 1228; Potthast, *Regesta*, 8216.

44   D'Arbois de Jubainville, *Histoire des comtes de Champagne*, t. V, n. 1841 ; Potthast, 8120.

45   *Histoire de Languedoc*, ed. in-4°, t. VI, p. 630; liv. XXIV, chap. xxxix, note.

46   *Historiens de France*, t. XXIV, p. 368, n. 42, et p. 376, n. 81. Other allusions to this siege, ibid , p. 338, n. 83; p. 340, n. 95 : p. 342, n. 105.

47   *Layettes*, t. II, 1980; *Histoire de Languedoc*, t. VIII, in-4, p. 877-78.

48   *Rotuli litterarum clausarum*, II, 215b; Rymer, I, 187; 10 October 1227.

49   See the list of seneschals of Gascogne, published by M. Shirley, *Royal letters*, II, 399. Gascogne was for some time without a governor following the departure of Prince Richard; On 6 November 1227, Trubleville had not yet crossed the sea, when Henry III ordered the Constable of Porchester to furnish gangways and supplies to trim his vessel (Record office, close rolls, 38, membr. 15 recto).

50   Rymer, I, 190; 11 March 1228; letters to Trubleville, to Louis IX, to Blanche, to the subjects of Henry III.

51   This person is often designated by modern writers under the name of Pierre de Colmieu (see Le Nain de Tillemont, t. II, p. 1 to 3). He appears to have originated in the village of Collemozzo, between Cori and Norma. I could cite several

contemprary texts proving, without a doubt, that he was Italian, and from the Campania.

52   *Layettes*, II, 1967. Rymer, ed.. of 1816, I, 190; 6 May 1228 : Henry III to the King of France. The other letters from the same day are in Rymer, I, 191.

53   The charter of Archbishop Guillaume is only dated June 1228. See Martène, *Amplissimia collectio*, I, 1224, following register JJ. 26, fol. 230 v; no. CCVI; that of the Comte de la Marche was dated 6 June 1228, *Layettes*, II, 1968.

54   Rymer, I, 191 ; 8 June 1228 : Henry III to Louis IX, to Blanche, to Gautier Cornu, to the Bishop of Salisbury, to Pierre of Collemezzo and to Master Etienne, to Henri of Trubleville.

55   Truce of Nogent-le-Roi or Nogent-l'Érembert ; June 1228: example of the name of Philippe d'Aubigny and of Raoul Fitz-Nicolas; *Layettes*, II, 1970, and Rymer, I, 192. Expedition in the name of Louis IX, register JJ. 26, fol. 229 r, col. 2, n. 199; letters of the Archbishop of Sens, of the Bishop of Salisbury, and the two pontifical chaplains, relative to the truce. Martène, *Amplissima collectio*, 1, 1223, after JJ. 20, fol. 230 V, n. 205. See Le Nain de Tillemont, I, p. 516; Rymer, I, 192; 6 July 1228.

56   *Annales de Dunstaplia* (*Annales monastici*, ed.. Luard, t. III, p. 108).

57   Sunday following the day of Saint-Barthélemy.

58   All that we know of this revolt is published in two letters by Shirley in his *Royal and other historical letters* : letter of Pierre de Landiran and his son, t. 1, p. 321, n. 2C4 ; letter of the artisans of Sainte-Bazeille, t. II, p. 1, n. 413.

59   Shirley, t. 1, p. 344, n. 283; 13 February 1229.

60   Shirley, t. I, p. 332, n. 274 ; 2 August 1228.

61   Shirley. p. 336-337, n. 278; 21 September 1228.

62   Archives of England, Liberate rolls, Henry III, anno 13, n. 491, membrana 13 r; 18 November 1228.

63   Liberate rolls, ibid,; 19 November 1228.

64   Potthast, 8267; 21 October 1228.

65   Arch. nat., J. 1035, n. 20; Arbois de Jubainville, catalogue, n. 1862; 28 October 1228.

66   *Johannis Longi chronica Sancli Bertini* (*Monumenta Germaniæ*, scriptores, t. XXV, p. 840).

67   *Willelmi chronica Andrensia* (*Monumenta Germaniæ*, t. XXIV, p. 767; *Historiens de France*, t. XVIII, p. 580); Archives du Pas-de-Calais, inventaire in-4°, p. 13, col. 2; série A, Trésor des chartes d'Artois.

68   Guillaume de Puy-Laurens, *Historiens de France*, t. XIX, p. 223, "*aspiranti regne*" ; *Récits d'un ménestrel of Reims*, ed. of Wailly, n. 339 and n. 347; Cf. *Johannis Longi chronica S. Bertini*, loc. cit., p. 836; *Chronique de Jean des Prêts* (Collection de chroniques belges), t. V, p. 189.

69   Récits d'un ménestrel of Reims, ed. of M. of Wailly, n. 347; *Johannis Longi chronica S. Bertini* (*Monumenta Germaniæ*, scriptores, t. XXV, p. 800); Du Chesne, *Histoire de Coucy*, preuves, p. 367: Extract of a latin chronicle from the reign of Charles V.

70   September 1227 : Enguerrand de Coucy prayed the King and Blanche of Castile to receive hommage from the Comte de Roucy for the fief of Sissonne; Archives nationales, registre JJ. 26, fol. 227 V, col. 2, n. 188; cf. *Table chronologique des diplômes*, t. V, p. 306. Teulet , *Layettes*, t. II, p. 138, n. 1959; January 1228 : letter of Jean, comte de Roucy, on the same subject.

Registre JJ. 26, fol. 227 V, col. 2, n. 190; cf. *Table chronologique des diplômes*, V, 306 ; October 1227.

71   *Layettes*, t. II , no. 1979. 1976 (p. 651), 1979 to 1979 (p. 651-654).

72   Joinville, ed. of 1874, n. 74. Joinville said that this assembly of the barons took themselves to Corbeil, and to mingle, without doubt, with those who preceded the affair of Montlhéry, and which took place the previous year; barons, having formed such a project, did not have to remain one year without carrying it out.

73   Roger of Wendover, ed. Hewlett, II, 355-356, and, after him, Mathieu of Paris, *Chronica majora*, ed. Luard , III, 164-165, and *Historia minor*, ed. Madden, II, 306.

74   Guillaume de Nangis , *Vie de saint Louis* (*Historiens de France*, XX, 316); the same, *Chronique*, ed. Géraud, I, 179; *Chroniques de Saint-Denis* (*Historiens de France*, XXI, p. 105; ed. Paulin Paris, IV, p. 236).

75   Le Nain de Tillemont, I, 526.

76   It was Longnon who indicated this document to me and who gave me the most precise information about this date.

The role of the *arrière-ban* [war summons] of Champagne formed part of a register formerly preserved in the Chambre des Comptes de Paris, and destroyed in the fire of 1737. Lévesque de la Ravalière had taken an extract from it, which is in the Bibliothèque Nationale (Champagne 136, fol. 122). It was there that Arbois de Jubainville copied it to insert in volume II of his *Histoire des comtes of Champagne* (documents, p. XXXVII - XLII; see the same volume, introduction, p. 12).

Longnon, having noticed in this text the name of the Marshal of Champagne, Geoffroy de Louppy, who did not take up duties before July 1227 (see

Arbois of Jubainville, t, IV, p. 512-513), concluded from it that the convocation of the *arrière-ban* [war summons] of Champagne, of which we have some knowledge, can be neither before this date, nor after March 1229, on which Blanche of Navarre, whose dowry was mentioned in the extract made by Lévesque of la Ravalière ("*De dotalicio Blanche comitisse*;" from Arbois de Jubainville, T. II, p. XLI).

From July 1227 to March 1229, Thibaud IV could only convene this *arrière-ban* to go with the King against Pierre Mauclerc. With the first of these dates, the first revolt of the barons had already ended. The attempt made then by *les grands* to seize the King was a simple *coup de main*, a surprise to which Thibaud probably had no part. Thus ended the expedition against Pierre Mauclerc. The convocation of the Champagne *arrière-ban* having taken place before March 1229, it seems that this expedition and the siege of Bellême, which was the principal episode, took place in January 1229, as Tillemont thought.

77 Joinville, ed. 1874, n. 75.

78 These facts have been exposed by the Count de Bretagne in his letter of declaration of war to Louis IX, 20 January 1230 : Du Cange, ed. of Joinville, 1668, observations, p. 44. The copies of this letter are found in the Bibliothèque Nationale (Dupuy, volume 702, pièce 30; De Camps, vol. 73, fol. 41).

79 The siege of Bellême, one generally admits, took place in January 1229. This date cannot be gleaned from the account of Guillaume de Nangis, which, in his *Vie de Saint Louis* as in his *Chronique*, muddles the chronology of events. The *Grandes Chroniques de France* or the *Chronique de Saint-Denis*, whatever interest in the details that they give in this respect, make, with regard to the dates, the same confusions. But from Guillaume de Nangis and *Grandes Chroniques de France* we learn that the siege of Bellême was done in full winter, in a cold that was intense. However, the route of Louis IX presents, between December 1228 and the first days of February 1229, a gap in which one can place the expedition against Bellême. It is true, similarly, that the King was far from Paris, and in Anjou, in January 1230, but I will show that the new seizure of weapons of Pierre Mauclerc, the cause of this campaign, should not be confused with that which brought the King under the walls of Bellême. Moreover, the charter by which Mauclerc defied the King is from 20 January 1230; Manclerc speaks there about the capture of Bellême and the protests that he forwarded to his sovereign; he says that since then he did not address a new adjournment. All these facts could only have happened between the end of December 1229 and 20 January 1230 (Le Nain de Tillemont, I, 534). Lastly, the convocation of the Champagne *arrière-ban* being previous to March 1229, tends to prove that Bellême was besieged in the month of January of this year.

80 "Enquête à Bellême," 1247 (*Historiens de France*, t. XXIV, p. 19, n. 126 bis) : « *ad reædificandas domos suas, quas comburi fecerat comes*. » ; wrongs committed against the inhabitants of Sérigny , same inquest, p. 20, n. 136; p. 21, n. 145; 21, n. 146; 22, n. 153; 23, n. 169; 24, n. 176; 24, n. 179; 25, n. 186; and pp. 22 to 26.

81 Saint-Martin-du-Vieux-Belléme, (ibid., p. 19 to 24, no. 126, 143, 147, 150-152, 154, 155, 158, 161, 166, 170, 175, 179. 183).

82   Ibid., p. 19, n. 126 : « *quse delata fuerunt ad domum domini regis*; » — « *in domo regis et alibi.* » ; ibid., « *marescallus Franciæ, qui in domo propria hospitabatur.* » ; *Chroniques de Saint-Uenis* (*Historiens de France*, XXI, p. 105).

83   "Enquête à Bellême," p. 20, n. 135.

84   Ibid., p. 22, n. 156; p. 28, n. 225.

85   Guillaume de Nangis, *Vie de saint Louis* (*Histor. de France*, t. XX, p. 316); *Chroniques of Saint-Denis* (ibid., t. XXI, p.105); "Enquête à Bellême," p. 19, n. 126.

86   Ibid., p. 27, n. 211 : « *quadrigam suam cum quatuor oquis et hernesio*; » ; p. 18, n. 122.

87   Ibid., p. 17, n. 115; p. 20, n. 132, n. 133.
     Windmill destroyed in Sérigny, ibid., p. 18, n. 118; « *destruxorunt quamdam domum suam in parrochia do Seriné, valontem of solidos, et marromium dictae domus attulerunt ad exercitum* » (p. 20 , n. 130); « *destrui fecit domum suam, si tam in parrochia supradicta, ia vico Heraut, quando obsessum fuit castruin Belimonse, ut posset habere lapides quae* (sic) *proici possent por petrariam, ad impugnandum diotum castrum* » (p. 18, n. 117).

88   Guillaume de Nangis, *Vie de saint Louis*; *Chroniques de Saint-Denis*.

89   "Enquête à Bellême," p. 18, n. 120 : « *Milesent, relicta Hugonis dicli Blondi, et Guillelmus, filius ejus, do Potraria, conqueruntur quod, cum maritus dictse mulions tradidisset domino regi claves castri dictse villae, tempore quo veniebat apud castrum Belismi,* » etc.

90   Ibid., p. 19-20, n. 128 : « *conqueruntur quod dominus rei, post capcionem castri Bellismi, fecit fossatum fieri in quadam terra sua.* » ; Ibld., p. 17, n. 114 : « *conqueritur quod quatuor sextaria famuli domini regis acceperunt, cum captum fuit castrum, ad municionem castri.* »

91   Nangis, *Chronique*, t. I, p. 179; *Historiens de France*, t. XX, p. 316; *Chroniques of Saint-Denis*, t. XXI, p. 106, ch. VII.

92   Record Office ; close rolls, n. 39; 13th year of Henry III, memrabrana 16 V; 6 February 1229.

93   Rymer, *Fœdera*, ed. 1816, t. I, p. 193; 6 February 1229.

94   Rymer, p. 194; 4 March 1229. On 28 February, Henry III had ordered his treasurer and men of his chamber to deliver ten *marcs* to Philippe d'Arderne, who he sent on a mission across the sea : Record office; Liberate rolls, n. 491; 13th year of Henry III, membrana 9, above; Rymer, I, p. 194; 7 March 1229.

95   Rymer, I, p. 193; 4 March 1229; Shirley, *Royal Letters*, p. 349-350, n. 287 ; 1

April 1229.

96   Rymer, p. 193, letter of 4 March : Philippe d'Aubigny envoy to France; Record office; *Liberate* rolls. n. 491, 13th year of Henry III, memb. 9, near the bottom ; 6 April 1229 : Bishop of Coventry and Raoul Fitz-Nicolas envoys to France; same roll, membrana 7 r; 7 May 1229 : new mission of Philippe d'Aubigny and two other envoys.

97   Rymer, I, p. 194; 5 April 1229 : six letters.

98   Shirley, *Royal Letters*, n. 288.

99   Denifle, *Chartularium Universitatis Parisiensis*, t. I, p. 47, n 47 of the 1st part.

100   Ibid., p. 59, n. 1; 1200.

101   Ibid., p. 72-73, n. 13; May 1210.

102   Guillaume had been confirmed by the Pope, as Bishop of Paris, 10 April 1228; Valois, *Guillaume d'Auvergne*, p. 10; Denifle, t. I, p. 116, pièce 60 ; July 1228.

103   Blanche was no doubt in Paris on 10 February : Le Nain de Tillemont, t. I, p. 534. The bloody affray of Saint-Marcel took place on 1229; this date is established in several chonicles, and above by the letter from the King of England the the papal bulls of Gregory IX that I cite later.

104   Mathieu deParis, *Chronica majora* , ed. Luard, t. III, p. 166 ff. After a bull of Gregory IX, of 18 April 1231, the leader of the inhabitants of Saint-Marcel had taken part in the death of scholars, « *in occisione scolarium* » ; Denifle, *Chartularium*, t. I, p. 142, n. 84.

105   Guillaume de Nangis, *Vie de saint Louis*, *Historiens de France*, t. XX, p. 318, and the *Chronique*, ed. Géraud , t. I, p. 181; *Gesta S. Ludouici noni, auctore monacho S. Dionysii anonyme* (*Historiens de France*, t. XX, p. 47); *Chronique de Fécamp*, same collection, t. XXIII, p. 429.

106   « *et inde culpabantur regina et ipse domnus cardinalis, scd quoi sunt capita, tot sentcntie.* » Aubry de Trois-Fontaines, *Monumenta Germaniæ Historica*, scriptores, t. XXIII, p. 923.

107   Denifle, *Chartularium*, t. I, p. 118, n. 62; 27 March 1229.

108   *Majus chronicon Lemovicense* (*Historiens de France*, t. XXI, p. 764); Bernard Guy (ibid., p. 695); *Mare historiarum* (same collection, t. XXIII, p. 108).

109   Bernard Guy, loc. cit.; Denifle, *Chartulariuim*, t. I , p. 129, n. 72 : « *multi scolares confluunt Tholosam.* »

110   Annal of Dunstable (*Annales monastici*, ed. Luard.t. III, p. 117), and the texts cited above.

111   Denifle, p.119, n. 64; Rymer, *Fœdera*, ed. 1816, t. I, p. 195; 16 July 1229.

112   Mathieu de Paris, III, 169 :

> *Heu! morimur strati, vincti, mersi, spoliait ;*
> *Mentula legati nos facit ista pati.*

113   *Récit d'un Ménestrel de Reims*, ed. of Wailly, no. 184 to 188. Wailly has refuted this fable in the critical summary placed at the head of his edition, p. LIV.

114   Denifle, *Chartularium Universitatis Parisiensis*, t. I, p. 120, n. 66; August 1229; Denifle, p. 122-123, n. 67.

115   Denifle, p. 127-129, no. 70-71; 24 November 1229.

116   Denifle, p. 125; 23 November.

117   For all that concerns the Treaty of Paris, its preliminaries and its consequences, see the *Histoire de Languedoc*, ed. in-4°, t. VI, p. 631 ff, Le Nain de Tillemont, t. I, p. 513, and t. II, p. 1 ff.

118   *Histoire de Languedoc*, t. VIII, col. 878-879 ; 10 December 1228.

119   Aubry deTrois-Fontaines, *Monumenta Germaniæ Historica*, scriptores, t. XXIII, p. 922; Guillaume de Puy-Laurens, *Historiens de France*, XIX, p. 219.

120   *Histoire of Languedoc*, t. VIII, col. 879-833, January 1229.

121   *Histoire* of Languedoc, ed. in-4°, VIII, col. 893; Guillaume de Puy-Laurens. Annals of Dunstabl (*Annales monastici*, ed. Luard, III, 115).

122   Examples of the treaty written in the name of the Church by Cardinal Romain, date from 11 April, with the exception of only one, which was on the 17th (*Layettes du Trésor des Chartes*, II, 1991). Raimond VII had promulgated, to my knowledge, two documents, on 12 April; one of them was sealed, on orders of the Count, by the archbishops of Sens and of Narbonne, by the bishops of Paris, of Toulouse, of Albi, of Maguelonne, and of Nîmes. The royal act, in the form of a *diplôme*, signed by the great officers of the Crown, mentioned only the month; it could therefore not be later than 14 April, Easter having fallen, in 1229, on 15 April (*Layettes*, 1992 and 1993).

123   Guillaume de Puy-Laurens, XIX, 223.

124   *Layettes*, II, 1994; April before Easter.

125   Du Chesne, *Historiæ Francorum scriptores*, V, 814.

126   *Layettes*, II, .2000; April 1229.

127   *Ordonnances des rois de France*, I, p. 50; *Histoire de Languedoc*, VII, 73, n. v, dissertation on the date of this document.

128   *Hist. Languedoc*, VIII, col. 897-898; on 17 May 1229, Aimery, consuls of the bourgeois, and knights of Narbonne, engaged to execute the ordinance on the business of heresy; Bibliothèque Nationale, *Mélanges of Colbert*, t. 414, n. 955; extract from *Hist. Languedoc*, VIII, 896-897; *Layettes*, II, 2011; June 1229; *Layettes*, 2010.

129   *Layettes*, 2008; *Histoire de Languedoc*, VIII, 901.

130   3 June; Guillaume de Puy-Laurens, *Historiens de France*, XIX, 223; *Layettes*, 2009; *Hist. Languedoc*, VIII, 900; June 1229.

131   Aubry de Trois-Fôntaines, *Monumenta Germaniæ*, XXIII, 923; Guillaume de Puy-Laurens, *Historiens de France*, XIX, 223.

132   *Layettes*, II, 2003-2004; *Histoire de Languedoc*, VIII, col. 903-906; 16 June 1229.

133   *Layettes*, 2019, letters of the Count de Foix; *Histoire de Languedoc*, VIII, col. 906, letters of the King.

134   Guillaume de Puy-Laurens, p. 223-24; Labbe, *Conciles*, t. XI, 1st part, col. 425-436.

135   *Layettes*, II, 2025; *Histoire de Languedoc*, VIII, col. 917; *Layettes*, 2026; *Histoire de Languedoc*, col. 918-919.

Chapter Four

War in Champagne. English Invasion.

Hatred of *les grands* for Thibaud de Champagne; love of the Prince for Blanche. — Most of the barons coalesce against him. — Pretensions of Alix, Queen of Cyprus. — The Duc de Bourgogne invades Champagne. — The Count of Flanders makes a diversion in Artois. — Intervention of Blanche obliges the Bourguignons to retreat. — Hesitations of the coalition. — Ravages in Lorraine and the Barrois. — War between Philippe Hurepel and Thibaud. — The English prepare to invade France. — Treason of Pierre Mauclerc. — Armaments of Henry III. — He disembarks in Brittany. — The royal army in Anjou. — Condemnation of Mauclerc. — The King abandoned by a part of his vassals. — Henry III proceeds to Gascogne, enters Brittany, and returns to England. — The baron coalition ravages Champagne; Thibaud is delivered to the Queen. — Submission of Philippe Hurepel; the coalition is dissolved. — New campaign against Pierre Mauclerc and the English. — Truce between England and France. — The Count de Ponthieu returns to grace. — Triumph of Blanche.

After two years of plots and revolts the great vassals were not more advanced than on the first day. The Treaty of Vendôme, to which two among them had been able to gain something, had only been useful to show how much it was difficult for them to listen; in Corbeil, they were unable to carry out with strength a simple attack; lastly, the fall of Bellême had reduced to nothing a formidable conspiracy. Again, the Count de Toulouse could no longer, since the Peace of Paris, bring his troops to aid the disaffected: for some time at least, he was *hors de combat* [out of it]. Blanche of Castile alone had shown skill, decision, a spirit of continuation. While waiting for more favorable circumstances, it was necessary to give up a frontal assault, unless all the top baronage of France did not want to openly combine with the English; the majority of the malcontents would have moved back before such manifest treason, and elsewhere one was not sure if there had been a defeat of Blanche and the disorganization of royal power. Better yet was to play a new game, and by holding with those who took to the party of the Regent, they recognized themselves too weak or too poorly led to attack her themselves.

Apart from the royal domains, high above the faithful subjects found in a great number of cities or among the second-rate nobility, Blanche of Castile especially relied on two large feudatories. In the north, the Count of Flanders, in case of revolt, could take the domains of the Count de Boulogne from behind, the Count de Saint-Pol, and the Lord of Coucy. To the east of Paris extended the vast estates of the Count de Champagne. Thibaud Chansonnier threatened Enguerrand de Coucy, Philippe Hurepel, and the house of Châtillon; he prevented them from combining their action with that of the barons who had their fiefs to the south of his. His knights, brought to the King at the time of the siege of Bellême, were ready to go against the Count de Bretagne or any other rebels that it pleased Blanche to indicate. Philippe de Boulogne, Pierre de Bretagne, and their united cohorts of the time had satisfied their resentments and had much reduced the forces that their enemy could oppose to them.[1] He [Thibaud] was feared, they were upset with him, they needed to destroy him; the hatred he inspired increased every day.

Thibaud was perhaps not a man of the most delicate morality, but though he had been gifted with the most irreproachable conscience and the noblest character, his adversaries would not be hesitant to attack him with blows of calumny, while waiting to have recourse to iron and fire. The great vassals could reproach him for having given them up before the Treaty of Vendôme and during the last rising of Pierre Mauclerc, to be the intermediary by which the Count de Toulouse finally came to parlay with the King, but these were not very credible objections, as in these three circumstances he was held to be an honest subject. The old charge was revived, poisoning, which went back to the siege of Avignon and the death of Louis VIII. This prince, having been suddenly removed, shortly after that Champagne had left the royal army in spite of his orders, the rumor had run that Thibaud, to avoid revenge, was removed from the scene. This ridiculous insinuation enjoyed a certain credit, and it is not impossible that Philippe Hurepel himself sincerely took it seriously. However, the Queen held Thibaud in the highest esteem, and this favor was very naturally interpreted against Blanche of Castile out of spite, or in bad faith.[2]

Thibaud Chansonnier was then in love with the Queen; the fact can hardly be disputed. It was probably the name of his beautiful sovereign that he referred to while letting escape this tender plaint:

> *Trop estes trouble, et s'aveis si cler nom.*[3]

The love for such a noble Queen was to have a very great attraction for Champagne, who elsewhere had known her when he was young; perhaps he longed for her for a long time. Historians and poets spoke about this love, some with an obvious ill will, others without putting in their accounts or their allusions a thought of blame. From the number of the latter it is necessary to quote the compiler of the *Grandes chroniques de France*; he represents Champagne, coming after his last revolt, in 1236, to submit himself to the court, and treated extremely hard by the Queen, who reproaches him for ingratitude. Then the passion of Thibaud awakes:[4]

> *Le conte regarda la royne, qui tant estoit sage et tant belle que de la grant biauté de lui il fu touz esbahiz. Si li respondi : Par ma foy, Madame, mon cuer et mon cors et toute ma terre est en vostre commandement ; ne n'est rienz qui vous poist plaire que je ne feisse volen tiers; ne jamais, se Dieu plaist, contre vous ne contre les vos je n'iré. D'iluec se parti touz penssis, et li venoit souvent en remenbrance du douz regart la royne et de sa belle contenance. Lors si entroit son cuer en une penssée douce et amoureuse. Mais quant il li souvenoit qu'elle estoit si haute dame, de si bonne vie et de si nète qu'il n'en pourroit jà joïr, si muoit sa douce penssée amoureuse en grant tristèce. Et por ce que parfondes poussées engendrent mélancolie, li fu il loé d'aucuns sages homes qu'il se estudiast en biaus sons de viole et en douz chanz délitables. Si fist entre lui et Gace Brûlé les plus belles chançons ot les plus délitables et mélodieuses qui onques feussent oïes en*

> *chançon ne en vièle. Et les fist escrire en sa sale à Prouvins et en cèle de Troies; et sont apelées les chançons au roy de Navarre.*

This account is of a charming form, but its author was certainly confused in not only one but two different facts. It is very true that in 1236 Thibaud de Champagne, after one moment of infidelity, made his submission, and that Blanche then pointed this out to him. Only, in 1236, Blanche approached around fifty years of age; it is difficult to believe that at this time the feeling of Thibaud still had such an amount of tenderness and power. Some said with reason, it seems, that the sorrow of the noble poet goes higher, at the first years of the reign of Saint Louis, in the years when Blanche of Castile could still seduce by nothing other than the charm of her deportment or the nobility of her character.

An author much less famous than the chronicler of Saint Denis, often a mediocre rhymester, but in this case quite inspired, has spoken, in recounting the events of 1230, of the devotion which Blanche of Castile had dedicated to her cousin Champagne, from news which the popular imagination drew from this unquestionable data and of the undeniable passion of Count Thibaud. At the moment when his enemies invaded the Champagne, the Count, to know what one says and what one thinks of him, disguised himself in "*ribaud*"; followed by only one companion as miserably dressed as himself, through the country; but listens in vain, collects only bad words everywhere; everyone, good and bad, small and great, speak about him as a traitor:

> *Lors dist li quens à son ribaut :*[5]
> *Compains, or voi j'en bien de plain ,*
> *Que d'une denrée*[6] *de pain*
> *Saouleroie tous mes amis ;*
> *Je n'en ai nul, ce m'est avis,*
> *Ne je n'ai en nuli fiance ,*
> *Fors qu'en la raïne de France.*
> *Cèle li fu loial amie ;*
> *Bien moustra qu'el le n'enhaiet mie.*
> *Par li*[7] *fu finée la guerre ,*
> *Et conquise toute la terre.*
> *Maintes paroles en dist an*

Comme d'Iseut et de Tristran.[8]

Here now are the enemies of the Count de Champagne. These do not limit themselves to speaking of love or passion that Thibaud did not hide; they denounce it and exploit it without measure. The poet Hugues de la Ferté, in favor of Pierre Mauclerc, in verses beautiful and violent, takes occasion to overpower with insults this man and this woman against whom hatred of the nobles broke out with an incredible violence.[9] France, if one believes him, was at the discretion of Champagne and the Queen: "He and her, side by side, hold it together." We saw what Hugues de la Ferté said of Blanche; here is how he treats her alleged lover:

> He who holds Champagne and Brie is not master by right; know it, it is after the death of Count Thibaud that it was generated; look at how he was well born! Such a man should hold a seigniory, castles, cities, after he refused his assistance to the King [Louis VIII], with the royal army gone? Know ye well that if the King had returned from there, no man born of mother could prevent him to be disinherited. By the son of holy Marie, who suffered on the cross, he made in her life such things for which he should be arrested. Lord God, you know it well; it could not be defended, because he seems guilty. Lords, barons, why do you wait? - Count Thibaud, gilded with envy, furnished with crimes, it is not for acts of knighthood which you are famous; knowledge of surgery is rather your fact.[10]

Thus Thibaud was a bastard; he betrayed his master; it was good that for the trade of doctor, an obvious allusion to his false reputation as poisoner; until scoffed for his stoutness.[11]

We must not read too much of Hugues de la Ferté: he was of his party, and he lived then in civil war. In the nobility of France, many people accepted more or less in good faith this legend of the Count de Champagne, murderer of Louis VIII, lover of Blanche.[12]

Nothing leads us to believe that the Regent ever yielded to the blandishments of her admirer, no matter what he said to encourage this, and the sincere attachment of which he gave evidence could not be suspect. The mother of Thibaud IV, Blanca de Navarre, was in close relationship to Blanche of Castile; she herself had passed part of her childhood at the court of Philippe Auguste. After a first fault, he was, in one serious strong moment, rejoined to the party of the King; since then, he was useful to the King. By defending Thibaud de Champagne, Blanche acted as she would have done had her son been of age to rule. Thus a legend is reduced to its just proportions born from the malignity of the one, the credulity of the others, embellished by imagination. The love of Thibaud, as real as it was, changed nothing in the policy of Blanche, and all is brought back in the last analysis to an extremely simple situation: a share, a coalition of great Lords ready to serve ends less creditable to reverse that which obstructed their claims; and opposite them, a Queen who fought for the throne, a mother who defended the rights of her son and who, to resist the attacks of his enemies, pressured two princes of her family, Ferrand of Portugal and Thibaud de Champagne.

The hatred of the barons against Thibaud IV was neither recent, nor accidental. A treaty he had concluded, in July 1227, with the young Duke of Burgundy, Hugues IV, and his mother Alix de Vergy, show that he was consequently in a state hostility with the majority of great vassals.[13] Hugues IV and his mother were engaged to support him against Guigues, Count of Nevers and of Drill, and all others, with the exception of the King and Blanche. Alix de Vergy and her son moreover had sworn that Hugues would not marry, without assent of Thibaud, any daughters, sisters or nieces of the Count of Dreux, Pierre Mauclerc, the Count de Go, Philippe Hurepel, Robert de Courtenay, Enguerrand de Coucy, Guy de Châtillon, Count de Saint-Pol.[14] This solemn act had been guaranteed by several vassals of the Duke of Burgundy who had, if the conditions would not be carried out, to constitute themselves hostage at Troyes, one month after they would have been required by the Countess of Champagne, the Bishop of Langres, or the new Archbishop of Lyon, Robert Auvergne, first cousin once removed of Hugues IV.[15] Champagne thus had as enemies, even before Bellême, almost all those who went, in 1229 and 1230, to make upon him a war of extermination. Philippe Hurepel was the heart of this party. In agreement with all those who went against Thibaud IV, he reproached him his pride towards the other barons, and strongly accused him of having betrayed and poisoned the King his brother.[16] A circumstance in which Thibaud was not the first wrongdoer soon gave to those who wanted to kill him the pretext which they needed.

The Archbishop of Lyon, who should have taken care of the

execution of the treaty of 1227, was not have scruples to push his young relative the Duke of Burgundy to take for a wife, in contempt of his promise, the daughter of Count Dreux. It was a scandalous lapse of memory. Thibaud had the problem, or at least the awkwardness, of authorizing an act of violence. Robert Auvergne returned from Paris, where he had gone to see the Cardinal of Saint-Ange, when he was kidnapped with several nobles, while crossing Champagne, by people or the partisans of Thibaud. During a few days, they were taken from castle to castle, transferring them at night, with blindfolded eyes. But they had an unexpected liberator: Count Henri de Bar, who had until then allied with Thibaud IV, was, by his wife Philippine de Dreux, the brother-in-law of the counts of Dreux and Brittany, and consequently uncle of the new Duchess of Burgundy. He took at once the cause of Robert Auvergne and delivered him, thanks to intervention of the legate and with the help of the payment of a large ransom.[17] Consequently, friendship of the Counts of Bar and Champagne was transformed into hostility. The party of those united against Thibaud increased all forces further than the Duke of Bourgogne had.[18] The war was from now on inevitable; it proceeded on conditions very favorable to the enemies of Thibaud, because the truce concluded between France and England expired on 22 July 1229, and one was to hope that Blanche of Castile, occupied in the west, could not intervene in favor of her relative.

Although the Duke of Burgundy took measures for the campaign which was soon to open, Thibaud IV made it possible not to be in the middle of danger.[19] The Duke of Lorraine, Mathieu II, was adversary of the Count of Bar; he was, by this fact, placed into alliance with Champagne; 11 June 1229 they renewed against their common enemies an old treaty.[20] A Lorraine baron, Conrad de Riste, was engaged to support Mathieu II against Henri de Bar.[21] Elsewhere, Thibaud ensured, on 21 June, the homage of Guillaume, Lord of Pesmes.[22] All that would have been of little effect, if Champagne had been able to count on the aid of the Count of Flanders, hoping that Blanche of Castile would come to his relief. The situation of barons united against him was formidable under all reports; not only could they plead, as reason for attack, the so-called poisoning of Louis VIII and the recent imprisonment of the Archbishop of Lyon, but they hoped as well to benefit from the claims raised against him by his cousin the Queen of Cyprus.

The rights of this princess to the Champagne succession were more contestable; however they were there just at a point to support the enterprise of the barons.²³ Henri II, Count of Champagne and King of Jerusalem, brother and predecessor of Thibaud III, consequently uncle of Thibaud IV, had died in 1197, leaving only girls, born from his illegitimate union with Isabelle, heiress of the throne of Godefroid de Bouillon. This Isabelle was the spouse of Honfroy de Thoron, until she was removed by the famous Conrad de Montferrat, Marquis de Tyr; her first husband, the only true one, still alive, when in 1192 she brought to Count Henri II of Champagne, at the same time as her hand, the crown of Jerusalem. The Church could not recognize the validity of such a union, and it nevertheless had seen the younger daughter of Isabelle and Henri, Philippine, wife of Érard de Brienne, aspire to the succession of Champagne. The war that Érard de Brienne had undertaken to put forward the claims of his wife had not been successful; in 1229, Thibaud IV had nothing more to fear on this side. But Philippine had an older sister, Alix, who was Queen of Cyprus by her marriage with King Hugues de Lusignan. Become widowed, he had resolved to remarry, but the Holy See was opposed to the realization of his projects. He was free, when in 1229 the barons resolved to use his quite contestable rights to dispossess Thibaud IV. Unfortunately for him, Pope Gregory IX, with example of his predecessor Honorius III, refused to recognize as legitimate the daughter of Henri de Champagne and Isabelle. On 30 August 1227, he had written to Louis IX and Blanche of Castile that Alix was not to be allowed to put forward her titles in the Champagne county, as long as the question of her birth would not have been decided in the court of Rome, and the same day he took Blanche of Navarre and Thibaud IV under his protection.²⁴ Next on 27 September he wrote in the same vein to the Archdeacon of Châlons and two other commissaries.²⁵ The enemies of Thibaud IV could not to know this, but signified little to them; Alix was from now on the true Countess of Champagne, in their minds; Thibaud, who they were going to fight, against whom so many objections and calumnies accumulated, became a usurper.

In early July, while Champagne gathered together his army at Troyes, the Duke of Burgundy and the Count of Nevers, who had made their junction with Tonnerre, passed Armancon and advanced out of Champagne. They went by Saint-Florentin, which was undoubtedly ransacked, and decided to raze the country, burning the castles, the cities and the villages.²⁶ After having, according to all appearances, put fire to Castle Ervy, which stood not far from Saint-

Florentin, they invested Chaource, and perhaps also Bar-sur-Seine.[27] Documents, in agreement with testimony of a historian, shows that as of July the hostilities were started; one sees the Duke Burgundy refer then, in a charter granted to the monastery from the Saint-Seine, to the war that he made on the Count de Champagne; at the same time, the town of Chablis, to escape devastation, was placed under the protection of the King.[28] What made the others coalesce? It may be that some had consequently invaded Champagne with Hugues of Burgundy and the Count of Nevers; however it appears more probable that the majority held to their fiefs by the diversion of the Count of Flanders.

In answer to a request which Blanche of Castile had sent to him, Ferrand of Portugal invaded the county of Boulogne. By July he crossed Gravelines and went on to Calais; bringing fire to the farm of Oye, which belonged to the Benedictine abbey of Capelle, set fire to the castle of Marck, destroyed harvests, burned houses, plundered all. The city of Calais, not feeling sheltered behind the fortifications which Philippe Hurepel had raised, compromised for fifteen hundred *livres* and twenty barrels of wine. Then the Count of Flanders crossed the small river of Nieulet, and passed the county of Guines, but had to beat a retreat, not without receiving four hundred *livres* from the borough of Wissant, which had been allowed to make an indemnity by mediation of the abbot of Saint Bertin.[29] In the autumn or winter he again took the offensive and went towards the county of Saint Pol., of which however he could not be made master. While the troops of Ferrand were spread everywhere to take spoils, the inhabitants of the country gathered and hunted them; many Flemings were killed in the woods and along roads, and Ferrand had to take the road to his county, leaving behind him, if one believes a historian, ditches full of corpses and fields drenched in blood.[30] I do not know precisely at which moment this second incursion of the Flemings took place. The first had been frightening; in letters of Henry III we learn that at the end of the month of August a vessel from Calais had to take refuge in Dover because of hostilities.[31]

Thibaud de Champagne had been indirectly protected by attacks of the Count of Flanders, but the Burgundians occupied a part of his estates. Extremely fortunate for him, the Queen of France was not far away. Upon learning about the invasion of Champagne and investment of Chaource, Blanche of Castile summoned the barons, by letters patent, to have to them leave her vassal in peace; then, as they refused to raise the siege, she put herself at the head of her army, took her son with her and came before Troyes. Hugues IV and his allies did not dare to come to blows with the King: abbots and monks were there to assist the actions of the Queen, and by their mediation finished by concluding a truce.[32] For this time at least, Champagne was spared.

Relief came to him from all sides; to defend him, the Pope joined the Queen of France. Learning that Pierre Mauclerc had formed a project to marry Alix of Cyprus, Gregory IX had written (21 July) to the Bishop of Mans, to remind him that this princess and the Count of Brittany were cousins in the fourth degree, and to order to him to oppose, where necessary, their union.[33] Since at the time he remained contrary to the ambitious Alix and her partisans, and in the following year, at the moment when the barons were going again to launch a war against Champagne, the bull of 27 September 1227, relative to the illegitimacy of the Queen of Cyprus, was solemnly promulgated by the Archbishop of Rouen and bishops of his province.[34]

The Burgundians had entirely evacuated Champagne; we find the proof of it in a charter going back to Saint-Florentin, in September, by which a Lord, Ponce Mount-Saint-Jean, engaged to return, if necessary, to Thibaud IV his Riel-les-Eaux fortress.[35] As of the next month, the Count detached from the league one of his more powerful adversaries, Count Guignes of Nevers and Forez; the cardinal legate of Saint-Ange, who prepared to leave France, was selected for referee by the two sides on 12 October, and two days later he rendered a sentence establishing the conditions of peace.[36] In spite of that Thibaud was now exposed to a renewed attack, and it was in forecast of imminent dangers that on 22 October he passed a new treaty with the Duke of Lorraine.[37] Against the Count of Bar he attracted to his alliance the Bishop of Metz, Count Henri de Grandpré (3 January 1230).[38] Against the Duke of Burgundy he concluded arrangements with Simon de Beaujeu (September 1229), Jean, Count de Châlon-sur-Saône (28 December 1229 and January 1230), and Jean de Seignelay (March 1230).[39] The war had started again in Lorraine before the moment when the majority of these conventions had passed, but on the side of France the partisans of disorder hesitated yet again to take up their weapons.

This is not to say that their provisions with regard to Thibaud IV and Blanche were doubtful: when in November it was learned that their true chief, the Count of Brittany, was in England and discussed an invasion opportunity with Henry III, it became clear that they were ready to reverse the Regent, and that in this interminable fight they directed attacks against Champagne. The Pope, carefully informed of what occurred in France, knew better than anybody to which end the business of the barons tended; he made sincere efforts to recall them to the feeling of the duty. The Duke of Burgundy was summoned by him to remain faithful to his sovereign, to hold himself aloof from the civil wars which afflicted France, to make it possible to alleviate them. The bishops of Senlis, Orleans and Meaux had orders to interpose themselves between the crown and the barons, and Gregory IX signified to them that he would take under his protection the young King of France and the Queen.[40] On 29 November, in a letter to the Archbishop of Lyon, he railed in severe terms against the audacity of *les grands*, who in their contempt of royal authority shook by their discords "a kingdom of blessing and of grace." Gregory, emphatically professing his predilection for the King of France, ordered Robert Auvergne to insist that Hugues IV remain apart from the coalition and work for peace.[41]

At the same time he removed from the barons the pretext that they had provided for imprisonment of the Archbishop of Lyon, while intervening in his favor. The Bishop of Paris, abbots of Cîteaux and of Ferté-on-Grosne, accepted, by a letter of the Pope, the mission to prevail against those who had stopped [the Archbishop] and against their accomplices, by summoning them to restore all whom they had removed with the Archbishop and with his people, and to then come to seek in the court of Rome their discharge. The end of this last letter aimed indirectly at Champagne, as the Pope ordered three commissaries to exhort "those on the land where the crime had been committed" to require a full reparation.[42]

Several of the barons leagued against Thibaud were to be highly embarrassed. They were not all of the same degree nor of the same interested reasons to put themselves in open rebellion. One song, composed during autumn of 1229, painted their tergiversations extremely well:

"Gautier, who comes from France and was with these barons, thus says to me if you know what is their intention. Their arguments will always last and we will never see them in agreement; they will never come to hand close enough to earn one *ecu*.

"Pierre, if one believes our Count Huré [Hurepel], and the

Breton, and the bold Barrois, and the Lord of the Burgundians, before they pass Rogations (13 May 1230), you will see the Basques pushed back so well, their boasting so deadened, that not even a king will defend them.[43]

"Gautier, they last too long a time, these threats; they are not worth granting. It does not seem that they have the desire to be avenged, and yet they have, by my faith. Each day, I see them to assemble; they come from afar, in large groups, to lose their goods, their honor, their money, as men who can neither speak nor keep silent.

"Pierre, one often saw arriving in misfortune per too much distress. It was advisedly that they honored the Cardinal and the King, who put them at evil by the council of Lady Hersent.[44] But from now on all would go up in smoke, and each one has more to think of oneself.

"Gautier, I dare to trust them not; I find them too slow to start. They let the good weather pass by, and now it will rain and snow. And when I see them provoke to anger, when by spite they move away to the court, they leave two behind or three of theirs, to work under hand to prolong truces.[45]

The Count of Bar was of all the least dubious or the first to act. In his treaty alliance with Mathieu of Lorraine, Thibaud was engaged to remove himself from his homage at Christmas and to leave in war forty days afterwards; Henri de Bar did not wait; at once after Christmas, he was thrown into Lorraine, where he set fire to more than seventy villages. In their turn, Duke Mathieu, Thibaud and the seneschal of Champagne, Simon de Joinville, invaded and devastated the county of Bar; they raised then a fortress at Montiers-sur-Saulx, not far from Joinville. It is true that, in this year, the Count of Bar returned and destroyed it. During this time the residents of Metz, combined with the Duke of Lorraine, entered Barrois and crossed, on the Moselle, the bridge of Maidières, thus removing from their enemy the communication with his castle of Mousson.[46]

The example of the Count of Bar was well calculated to give confidence to his confederates. An English historian claims that on several occasions the great barons asked Blanche to authorize to finish by a legal duel their quarrel with the Count de Champagne.[47] It is certain that idea of a similar provocation was rather widespread in their party.[48] The King was in Compiegne, in March 1230;[49] it was undoubtedly then that the great barons came to the city to express their objections to Blanche of Castile, who answered them with haughtiness :

> *Quar tout les het et desdaigne.*
> *Bien i parut l'autre jour, à Compaigne,*
> *Quant li baron ne porent droit avoir,*
> *Et nes[50] deigna esguarder ne véoir.*[51]

Then the Count de Boulogne sent two knights to defy in his name the Count de Champagne, under pretext of avenging the death of Louis VIII.[52] In answer to this provocation, Thibaud combined, on 22 March, with Érard de Brienne, husband of his cousin Philippine and her former enemy, against Hugues IV, Philippe Hurepel, and Henri de Bar.[53] Then he marched on Dammartin-en-Goële, seat of one of the domains of Philippe Hurepel, and put it to flames.[54] He waited for terrible reprisals. Dangers to Blanche of Castile and her son were not less important; in vain on 2 April, Gregory IX, "like a father of the orphans, as natural judge of the widows," wrote to the Bishop of Chartres that he take them under his protection, and enjoined him to defend them against their vassal *révoltés*.[55] A civil war, even more serious than the preceding, was going to break out in all of France, when the intrusion of a new enemy, while increasing the dangers which threatened the Crown, came to suspend the operations of united barons and afford some respite to the Count de Champagne. After long hesitations, Henry III had taken the decision to cross over to France.

For a long time the truce with England had come to an end. Since 22 July 1229, the war had begun again, and, this time, it appeared to be serious; Henry III decided to make a major effort to reconquer the lost provinces of his father. As of 5 July he had taken general measures so that no foreign merchant remained in England after the day indicated for the resumption of hostilities.[56] At the same time, on the other side of the English Channel, boats and French vessels assembled on the coasts, ready to start war again.[57]

Projects of the King England were threatening; he acted to stop boats and to confiscate goods, to excite from afar the revolt of the vassals of Louis IX and Blanche, or to make a small war in Poitou; it was an invasion of France which Henry III contemplated. At the end of July, he ordered the seizure of all the boats, English or otherwise, which were in the ports of his kingdom, on coasts of the south and south-east; to ensure that they would be at the disposal of the King fifteen days after Michaelmas, on 13 October, ready to leave in the direction which would be indicated to them. In each county was to be drawn up a list written in double, bearing the indication of all the vessels, mentioning how many horses that each one might contain, and the names of the owners or captains.[58] At the same time Henry made known, by letters of convocation, to all his counts and barons, bishops and abbots, that on opinion of his friends overseas and of his vassals he had resolved to be in Portsmouth, to embark, fifteen days after Michaelmas.[59]

Who were these friends overseas? Undoubtedly Pierre of Brittany, among the Poitevin Lords, and with them a certain number of knights and ship-owners or Norman sailors. Within the Norman nobility Henry III had another member; of this number was Paynel, who recently had taken up arms against the King of France. Others would stand up as a friend of the Plantagenets: Richard de Harcourt, who on 25 July 1229, after the resumption of hostilities, obtained the exceptional permission to bring from England to France two palfreys, and who, in June 1232, was accepted with regards to Dover, where he was to go with King Henry.[60] In this province recently conquered by the French and badly accustomed to its new fate, some lords were at the same time vassals of two crowns, and the Norman clergy, like the nobility, was constrained in its devotion to the King of France by the bonds which linked them to a former master. For example, Blanche of Castile could hardly count on Guillaume, Abbot of Fécamp, who held, as such, domains in England, and whose election Henry III ratified on the day when the truce expired.[61]

Moreover, those who controlled France could not be unaware that the King of England regarded as his the sailors of several Norman ports. During all the time that Henry III prepared his invasion, as relations between England and the adjoining countries were suspended, certain privileged people continued to deliver themselves to trade in the English ports, and in this category one discovers the names of a certain number of Frenchmen, almost all of them Norman. For example, among others, a merchant of Gisors, Rouennais, sailors of Barfleur with six vessels, the Dieppois, and men of the Archbishop of Rouen. Two vessels of Dieppe, charged with goods belonging to the latter, after being seized, one in King's Lynn, the other in Sandwich, were exempted against the promise usually required of them to be in Portsmouth within about the fifteen of Michaelmas.[62]

Henry pressed his preparations as much as possible.[63] Towards end of September, the commissaries who had been sent to Portsmouth distributed various lords to vessels for crossing.[64] The King of England had taken measures so that the fleet was equipped with supplies; he had already given letters of safeguard to those who were to accompany him concerning their men and their goods.[65] He did not hesitate to take to the sea, when unforeseen circumstances tried his patience with a test.

He who was given the responsibility to make an expedition to France the following year was precisely this Count de Bretagne whose support was needed to complete it.

Pierre de Dreux had definitely thrown off the mask. The role of malcontent vassal was not enough for him anymore; he was resolutely poised as an enemy of France. Without any doubt, his first attempts to make the English come to Brittany do not date to then. The writer of the *Grandes chroniques de France* represents him going, before the siege of Bellême, to propose to Henry III a descent on the continent.[66] It does not seem, however, that Mauclerc went to England before this siege, which appears to us to have taken place in January 1229, but the writer of the *Grandes chroniques de France* could have confused written proposals that the Count of Brittany would have made at that time and the interviews that he had in October with the King of England. The fact of his arrival at Portsmouth is not contestable, and one must add that he disembarked there in really serious circumstances.[67]

At the moment when the King England embarked, vessels at Portsmouth, though many, were far from being enough. Then the King betook himself against his principal minister, the Grand Justiciar, Hubert de Burgh, one of those to whom he owed the crown, called a "treacherous old man," shown to have done everything for 5,000 marcs that the Queen of France had paid him. He delayed until then to draw the sword against the dispenser of justice and was hardly retained by those who surrounded him.

He was there, when Mauclerc entered the port, 9 October 1229. It is probable that a few days still passed in hesitation, but the Count of Brittany soon tried to persuade a young inconsistent and irresolute prince that the season was advanced too much, that it was to better wait for the spring. He furloughed the army. Hubert de Burgh and his King reconciled themselves for some time; however Henry III kept a resentment and soon he had, in dramatic economic situations, his first project, the invasion of France.[68]

On 26 October, Henry III informed his vassals that he had just received the homage of Mauclerc for [the province of] Brittany and that, conforming with an opinion of the Count de Bretagne and with that of his barons, he had pushed back the disembarkation until the Sunday after Easter (14 April 1230).[69] The treason of Pierre de Dreux remained complete, though the effect was moved back; historians of the two countries are all in agreement in allotting to him the invasion that Louis IX and Blanche of Castile had to push back in 1230. While waiting, he received the price of his odious conduct; during winter, spring and summer, all the incomes and the fiefs were returned to him that he had lost in England as a subject of Louis IX, in particular the county of Richmond, and on 21 May 1230 we see Henry III give to him, in an act gone back to Nantes, the title of duke that the King of France did not recognize.[70]

While the loading of the English troops on boats was deferred, Blanche of Castile had before her a few months to occupy herself on these subjects, while waiting for enemies. She did not lose one moment. According to all appearances at this time, part of Anjou was occupied by royal troops; in any case, Louis IX was in Saumur in the month of January.[71] Pierre Mauclerc, at the height of fury, no longer restraining himself, on 20 January sent the King a letter designed in the most insolent terms, at the head of which he styled himself Duke of Brittany and Count of Richmond. After having pointed out all his objections, denials of justice, he took Bellême, seized from his Angevin domains, and declared to Louis IX that he did not regard himself any more as his vassal, withdrew himself from his homage, and understood by this declaration that he challenged him [Louis IX].[72]

The war, inevitable consequence of such an arrogant provocation, did not become serious on the borders of Brittany until the arrival of the English. In preparation for this frightening event, Blanche of Castile sought to decrease the number of enemies that she was going to have to fight. In Auvergne, the Crown was in a fight with two dynasties, coming from the same stock, who divided the country among counts and dauphins.[73] Since then, under Philippe Auguste, Guy de Dampierre, Lord of Bourbon and Constable Auvergne, had occupied, in the name of the King, a good part of the country, the son of the Dauphin, Guillaume, Count de Montferrand, had just made peace. His cousin Guillaume the Count of Auvergne had, admittedly, concluded on 25 July 1229 a truce with Archambaud de Bourbon, son and successor of Guy de Dampierre; but the Dauphin remained at war with the King.[74] In February 1230, this old baron and his small son Robert finally made a treaty with Louis IX by which they made homage.[75] At the same time Guillaume, son of the Dauphin and father of Robert, after having ratified the treaty, received from Archambaud de Bourbon the castle of Pontgibaud, on condition of not using it against their sovereign.[76] The reconciliation of this house with the Crown removed from the King England one of the allies upon which he could have counted.

On other points, the house of France gained ground in the vicinity of the provinces occupied by the English, and it was relevant that the dukes of Aquitaine, Archambaud, Viscount of Comborn, Abbot of Saint-Martial of Limoges, and Abbot Uzerche made homage to the King, or swore fidelities to him and to his mother and her brothers.[77]

However, the English prepared their invasion with an activity which reflected their intent, believing it to be the proper time, to erase by an easy victory the memory of their reverse. They set to work to ensure themselves success which was to have as a result the ruin of Blanche and the dismemberment of France. The armaments that they made then interests too directly the history of our country to exempt oneself here, on this subject, from some new information.

Henry III, for his descent on Brittany, had above all to equip a fleet, and under this heading his kingdom offered sufficient resources. However, there was not in England, a royal navy capable of transporting armies. The predecessor of those which dominate today on the seas had some vessels, but the number was very restricted. One of them, the *Grande-nef* (*Magna navis*), is often named in the documents of the English chancellery; those charged to take care of its maintenance carried the title of "*garde de la Grande-nef et des galées*," because Henry III had with him ships assigned, according to any probability, for regular communications with Ireland, the coasts England, and the countries overseas. The "*gardes de galées*," charged with taking care of the good operation of this service, often received orders to put one or two of their ships at the disposal of the royal envoys, or of the seneschal of Gascogne, when he went to its government.[78]

One needed something else to embark thousands of men and horses, with the provisioning and the material necessary for an army.

To charter a Genovese fleet, Pisan, or Venetian, was extremely expensive; this expensive process imposed, in truth, on the Western princes when they wanted to go to the Holy Land, to sail with thousands of crusaders on distant seas and little known to the people of the north. But the English could well dispense with employing foreigners, when it came to crossing the English Channel or to return from the Bay of Biscay, where they already had practice. Also, the Kings England, when they contemplated a descent on France, had recourse to the levy *en masse* of commercial boats belonging to their subjects, or the provisional confiscation of foreign ships collected in the English ports. All this improvised transport, of extremely varied sources, was not, as much as was necessary, of the same tonnage. However, it was important that they were not too small; in 1230, the King England and his officers let go, after having seized them, many boats which were not large enough to contain at least sixteen horses.[79]

It was by way of requisition that one had proceeded, in England, to constitute a fleet in the autumn of 1229; the expedition prepared against France having been postponed, they applied the same system in the months which followed. Beginning in November the agents of Henry III again seized vessels which were in English ports, except letting them go against the promise, given by the owners, to return either at Easter (31 March 1230), or, for some, after Easter (14 April.[80] At the same time the King of England, not content to follow viscount's list of all the vessels on which he could count, convened for his expedition the sailors of Dieppe and Barfleur (1 February 1230).[81]

To avoid a dangerous dispersion, Henry III had decided that two ports only, Dover and Portsmouth, would affect the passage.[82] But this last city was, for the expedition of 1230, the point of rallying for all the fleet. It was there that he concentrated the English army, representing, so it seems, a sizeable force, since Henry III, a few days before setting sail, granted letters of protection to three hundred eighty nobles to be left with him, and including some number who had brought other knights.[83] It goes without saying that the King of England had in his pay, in addition to the quotas provided by the nobility and the clergy of his kingdom, troops of sergeants and archers.[84]

As for the ships united at Portsmouth for transport of the English army, it was per hundreds that they amounted. One can have an idea of their number by seeing the letters patent that the King of

England, once arrived in Brittany, delivered to captains of his vessels, authorizing them to return. One of the documents in which these letters are analyzed mentions more than two hundred and twenty owners, the majority English, though several were from the Empire, in particular from Cologne and Staveren in Friesland.[85] One second list mentions seventy ships, of which many came from France, or, better to say, Flanders, Normandy, and Gascogne. The port of Barfleur only provided him with nine boats, but Saint-Valery, Caen, Bernières-on-Sea, Ouistreham, were also represented, like Berneval, between Dieppe and Tréport, Leure, at the current site of Le Havre, and Follet.[86] The lists from which we borrow these names do not include all the vessels assembled after the passage to Brittany, and elsewhere Henry III had to maintain at his disposal part of his fleet. One can consequently have an idea of the forces that he had joined together. After having enough vessels in autumn of 1229, he had the following spring too many, and we know that in this regard he did not profit, by leaving Portsmouth, all the forces of which he could deploy.[87]

He spared nothing to prepare the invasion of France. Money and material was brought to Portsmouth on carts that the King of England had requisitioned. The body of the expedition was abundantly provided with weapons and supplies. Henry III, not intending to let diminish the glare of royal majesty, had considerable baggage for his personal use. As a man accustomed to ostentation, he carried, even in the country, a vessel of silver.[88]

At the time of departure, he remembered that his cutlery and crockery remained behind, and he wrote to the Bishop of Carlisle, his treasurer, to forward to him without delay the sealed trunk which contained them.[89] He ordered a royal coat of white silk cloth, with a crown, a scepter, and a royal baton of gilded silver, without forgetting the sandals and gloves intended to supplement this costume.[90] What was the purpose of all of this, if not to solemnly recognize his overseas heritage despite the young King of France and Blanche of Castile? Henry Plantagenet triumphed in the future; he had forgotten King John already, like his grandfather, master of almost all the French provinces that bathed in the English Channel and North Sea. There was work to be done.

The English army was joined together towards Easter at Reading; a rather short distance separated it from Portsmouth.[91] Arrived in this city, Henry III, at departure time, visited the poor and the sick, kissed the lepers and gave them generous alms; these acts of external humility were like the prelude obliged to his proud company.[92] On 30 April 1230, the English embarked; on 1 May, on the feast day of St-Philippe and St-Jacques, they set sail.[93] The following day, Henry III, having with him about thirty vessels, stopped for the night on Guernsey, in order to give a little rest, in the middle of a painful crossing, for one of his sisters, who accompanied him.[94] On Friday 3 May he landed at Saint-Malo, with William the Marshal, Count of Pembroke, the counts of Hereford and of Gloucester. The dispenser of justice England Hubert de Burgh, it count de Chester and of Lincoln, the Count of Huntingdon, Philippe Aubigny, one of the principal advisers of the King, and some other barons, had arrived in this port as of the day before in the evening. But this was a weak part of the English army. The large part of the fleet, having at its head Count Richard, brother of Henry, was separated in Guernsey from the vessels which accompanied the King. Richard, the Count de Ferrers, the Constable of Chester, and almost all those who were going to invade France, disembarked on Thursday 2 May, in the harbor of Saint-Gildas, better known nowadays under the name of Port-Blanche, located at some distance to the north of Tréguier, and confined between the island of Saint-Gildas and the coast of Bretagne.[95] Henry III, as he learned of their arrival, ordered them to go to his meeting in the direction of Lamballe, gave appointment with Dinan, and sent to them carts intended for the transport of his treasure.

Pierre Mauclerc was then at the border of Anjou, intending to oppose the march of Louis IX, who was still on French soil and advanced towards Angers. He learned on his arrival of a powerful combined force, and went in all haste to Saint-Malo, where he arrived on 6 May; on the 7th, the King of England and the Count of Brittany had a meeting.[96] The majority of Breton vassals were then in agreement with Pierre; many made homage to Henry III and lent an oath of fidelity to him, while the Count delivered his fortified cities and castles. However, the nobility of the country on the whole was not devoted to this bad cause; the brother-in-law of the Count, André de Vitré, held openly for the party of the King of France.[97] The fidelity of this lord and of several others, who prepared their resistance, mattered very much to Blanche of Castile and her son; as from the beginning of hostilities, they had in Brittany some faithful subjects, while waiting for the day when all those who feared or hated Pierre Mauclerc were going to declare themselves against him.

Henry III did not propose to remain a long time on the edges of France nor to cross it to invade Normandy immediately. He tried to move towards Anjou, where the King of France had expelled the Count of Brittany, towards Poitou, whose nobility, always stirring things up, seemed disposed to rally for the Plantagenets. His stay in Saint-Malo was of short duration: on 4 May, he sent letters authorizing the Templars of La Rochelle to communicate freely with their states by means of their vessels the *Templière* and the *Busarde*.[98] He found five and seven more, and gave safe-conducts to several of the vessels which had followed; two among them, the *Bride* and the *Dameise*, were from Barfleur.[99] Before getting under way, he granted letters of protection and safeguard to the town of Saint-Malo and its inhabitants, who accepted the permission to trade with England.[100] Then he left (8 May) for Dinan, where he hoped to meet with his mother, Queen Isabelle. His intention was to pass then to Nantes, to try to gain for his cause the husband of this princess, Count de La Marche and Angoulême, Hugues X de Lusignan. Nicolas de Moles was sent ahead to confer with them, although, on the 9th and 10th of May, Henry III discharged the largest part of his fleet.[101] The 11th saw him still in Dinan; he only crossed to Bécherel (12 May, stopped two days in Rennes (13-14 May), crossed to Bain (15 May) and arrived at Nantes; he went there for six weeks (17 May – 30 June).[102]

While waiting for the large armies, hostilities continued in extreme cases for the lands occupied by the French and the English. Savary de Mauléon, who held for the King of England, made war on the inhabitants of La Rochelle, faithful to the King of France. On 26 May, Henry III wrote to Nantes to his bailiffs and trusted friends to not oppose this indefatigable warrior.[103] But great military operations were made to wait; Henry prepared slowly. On 7 June, he asked Pierre Mauclerc for twenty thousand arrows that he deposited in the castle of Rennes.[104] In May, in July, in August, in September, he asked for money. He wrote to the chancellor, the Bishop of Chichester, and to his minister Etienne de Segrave, to have for Trinity all the cash available, for Nantes, for Saint-Gildas, if he could not go up the Loire.[105] Then it became a question (1 July) of 3,000 marcs intended for Mauclerc.[106] Part of the royal treasure was brought by sea to Lannion and entrusted to Philippe Aubigny, then, on 8 August, in Gautier de Brackley.[107] At the end of the same month, Henry III still speaks of this treasure which, on 1 September, was deposited in Nantes.[108] In all this war, the English spent much to do little. It does not seem, elsewhere, that they sent to England for considerable reinforcements; those who, like Jean and Gerard Talbot, joined their prince in Brittany, were isolated.[109] Henry III had taken along with him almost all the troops that he could without danger to his kingdom; it was in Brittany, in Normandy, especially in Poitou, that he intended to find new soldiers.

At this time, the situation of Pierre Mauclerc was not bad; the movement of opposition trained against him among the Breton nobility was not yet marked. In June, Mauclerc came to an arrangement with the Viscount of Rohan.[110] For his part, Henry III endeavored to reconcile himself with the Church. The bishops of Rennes, Saint-Brieuc and Tréguier, whom Pierre had stripped and reduced to expatriation, had formerly pronounced against him the sentences excommunication and interdict, and, on 29 May 1228, Gregory IX in his turn had ordered Maurice, Bishop of Mans, with two of his canons, to publish this judgment again.[111] Undoubtedly, the Bishop of Mans and his two colleagues were still, in spring of 1230, among the number of adversaries with whom Pierre would have to contend, because the King of England wrote to them, from Rennes, a rather haughty letter. He sent the Abbot of Cleeve to them, charged to give them a communication the nature of which I am unaware, with the power of calling, he said, "that by chance, those whom God does not like, whom we do not want to believe, you warn yourselves to act against our right, our interest and that of our people."[112] This warning was without any doubt intended to preserve Mauclerc from rigors similar to those of which he had already been subjected. Soon the Pope answered: on 30 May, he enjoined three apostolic commissioners to appraise the Count of sentences against him by the bishops of his estates, and to promulgate this absolution.[113] The King of England could hope that all of Brittany was going to be in agreement with Pierre against the King of France.

In Normandy, Henry III was sure to find more than an ally. Foulques Paynel, whom Blanche of Castile had recently chastised for revolt, addressed the counts of Bretagne and of Chester to make proposals which they transmitted to the King of England. On 26 June, Henry wrote to him that he accepted these conditions, took him into service, and requested he come to find him later.[114] In answer to this invitation, Foulques Paynel and Guillaume his brother, acting as one, arrived in Brittany with sixty knights, pressing the King of England for the conquest of Normandy. The Justiciar, Hubert de Burgh, having diverted his master from this campaign, demanded two hundred knights, with which they were to force the men of the King of France out of their country. But Hubert protested that in yielding to this request King Henry would not make them send knights to their death, and the business remained as it was.[115] Perhaps Paynel was not wrong to preach bold resolutions in their interest. They knew the floating and dubious feelings that the memory of a still recent conquest and contradictory obligations in the feudal system maintained by many Normans was a quite difficult situation for ecclesiastical and secular Lords including a great number who were placed in homage to two enemy sovereigns. One could not have been more embarrassed than Isabelle de Crèvecœur, Abbess of the Trinité de Caen, subject of Louis IX, and at the same time obliged to come to serve the King of England, to render service to him that she owed because of her English fiefs; on 16 June 1230, Henry granted her a reprieve until Michaelmas, in consideration of the war that he made against the King of France.[116] Before the expiry of this time, Isabelle submitted and left for Brittany, to submit herself to the enemy of Louis IX in achievement of her obligations.[117] In another vein, while the French and the English fought in Brittany and Poitou, sailors of Dieppe, Barfleur, of Caen, of Rouen, of Quillebœuf, continued to be tolerated in English ports.[118] It is true that the subjects of the Count of Flanders generally enjoyed the same facilities. In spite of the fidelity of Ferrand to the King of France, the trade of England with his states had too much importance for him not to endeavor to safeguard it.

Without going too far to claim, like a historian of the time, that the great vassals of the crown of France had treated with the King of England, I can affirm that even in the presence of foreign invasion, their feelings with regard to Blanche and Louis IX had remained extremely tepid.[119] They were soon going to see up to what point it was possible to count on them. It is probable that the Count de Boulogne and several barons leagued against Thibaud de Champagne had come to line up under the royal banner to go against the English.[120] In any case, Louis IX and his mother were at the head of a large and beautiful army, when in early May they advanced towards Angers.[121] Concurrently, to people with dubious zeal or with openly hostile feelings, Blanche had in this army some great Lords of certain fidelity. More famous were the King of Jerusalem, Jean de Brienne, the Count of Flanders, the Count de Champagne, who appeared with the counts of Nevers, Blois, Chartres, Montfort, Vendôme, Roucy, and

Mathieu de Montmorency and several others, acting on the judgment pronounced against Mauclerc.[122] The names of Philippe Hurepel and his friends would be sought in vain. While many others prepared themselves to desert, Ferrand of Portugal and Thibaud de Champagne remained, in spite of the dangers to which their fiefs were threatened, but were so concerned about their role with royal army, that they disputed command of the avant-garde and rear-guard. On 8 June, they ended with an arrangement of this disagreement.[123]

At the start of hostilities, the Count de La Marche, in spite of his connections with the Plantagenets, was considered by the English as following the interests of the King of France. One however had a right to classify him among those whose feelings were most dubious: it was to him that Blanche first listened. In May 1230, by the Treaty of Clisson, the Queen of France and her son renewed an agreement which had been made between them and him, in 1227, with the Treaty of Vendôme.[124] Clauses relating to the marriage projected between Isabelle de France, sister of the King, and the eldest son of Hugues X, was preserved, but it was no longer a question of marrying Prince Alphonse of France to Isabelle de La Marche. The Queen, in her own name, took engagements to observe the conditions granted by her son, and the King made the Constable, Mathieu de Montmorency, swear it in his presence. Moreover, the King of Jerusalem, Jean de Brienne, the Archbishop of Sens, the Bishop of Chartres, and Thibaud de Champagne attested the oath which the Constable came to take.[125] The Queen dowager of England, Isabelle d'Angoulême, wife of the Count de La Marche, ratified for his part, in June, the Treaty of Clisson.[126] Moreover she declared, by a special act, that the King of France had yielded to her husband Saint-Jean-d'Angely, Montreuil-en-Gâtine, and Langeais, except returning to the crown if the marriage of her son and the Princess of France came to a conclusion.[127] Geoffroy, Lord of Argenton and Poitou, had, on his side, lent liege homage to the King by a charter dated at Clisson (May 1230).[128]

The negotiations continued, during June, between the Queen and the Poitevin Lords; soon it was the Viscount of Thouars, Raimond, who, with the camp close to the Ponts-de-Cé, made homage to the King for the fiefs belonging to his family more in Poitou than in Anjou.[129] He accepted the promise of a revenue of five hundred *livres tournois*, payable until the moment when he would have recovered his castle of Mareuil.[130] Guy de Thouars, Lord of Tiffauges and nephew of Raimond, became at the same time, at the request of his uncle, liege man of Louis IX.[131] Raimond, by an act gone back to Thouars in May, had requested the King and the Queen to transport to her vassal Robert de Maulevrier revenue of fifty livres to be taken on the incomes that they had constituted to him;[132] Louis IX declared, in the camp of Ponts-de-Cé, that he ratified this gift.[133] Blanche of Castile could be pleased to have destroyed, by these treaties, part of the hopes which the English based on the nobility of the West.

There could not be any discussion about bringing back the Count of Brittany; he was written off. The royal army was under the walls of Ancenis, undoubtedly occupied with the siege of this city, when Blanche pronounced through her prelates and barons the solemn condemnation of Mauclerc. The Archbishop of Sens, bishops of Chartres and of Paris, counts of Flanders, of Champagne, and of Nevers, all great lords and officers of the Crown present in the French camp, declared that Pierre, for his crimes against the King, was deposed by their judgment from the lease of Brittany. In consequence, the Breton barons and other vassals were released from their homage and their oath of loyalty.[134] The King, by notifying this sentence for the barons of Brittany, recalled to them that they and their ancestors had always been faithful to the kingdom, concerned with its honor; he asked them to be loyal, and promised them that, if they remained in their duty, they would be rightly praised.[135] Among all those to whom this declaration was addressed, André de Vitré was undoubtedly the first to ratify the pronounced judgment of prelates and French barons. He made liege homage for his fiefs of Vitré and Marcillé, while reserving the rights that upon their majority the children of Pierre de Dreux, Jean and Yolande, would have as heirs to Brittany. On the other hand, the King enfeoffed five hundred *livreés* of land, which was to be assigned to him either in Normandy or in Anjou, ensuring him compensation in case his lands would be removed from him, in all or partly, during the present war, promising to him to relieve his castles if they were besieged. The constable Mathieu de Montmorency said, for love of the King, that his master would not make peace with Pierre de Dreux without approval from Andre, and would not conclude with the King of England any treaty which had to replace him in homage of this prince. Mathieu made the same oath in the name of the Regent.[136] André de Vitré, for his part, promised to receive the King and his retinue in his castle, "in large or small numbers," and to leave them, if necessary, until the day when the heirs of Brittany, arrived at the age of twenty and one years, would have filled their duty as vassals.[137]

Modern historians, on the faith of a text which seems lost, say that after this judgment Blanche sent Guillaume d'Auvergne, Bishop of Paris, to the Breton vassals, to bring them together and parlay with them.[138] The fact is extremely probable, but it is not true that all the great lords of Brittany joined as of this moment in the royal cause. The French army, mistress of Ancenis, advanced towards Oudon, located at some distance, on the right bank of the Loire, and seized it; then they attacked Champtoceaux, opposite, on the left bank. The defenders of this place deserted; they brought their keys to the King, who granted them a pardon.[139]

The occupation Oudon and of Champtoceaux was a rather modest success, but Blanche of Castile, abandoned in war by a large part of her vassals, could not at this time dream of great victories. In such a serious situation, one could not move back. The nobles united against Thibaud de Champagne, when the King had convened them to come to fight the English, had made a truce which had to last until the octave of Midsummer's Day (1 July). Nearing this term, and nearing the forty days expiry during which they owed military service to the King, they took leave of Louis IX, and despite all his efforts and prayers, returned to their private wars. The King, who prepared himself to make a new siege, had to give up and follow his barons, to supervise them, and save the Count de Champagne if possible. He retrogressed to Anjou, then by way of the Isle de France came to Paris at the end of June.[140] Pierre Mauclerc took the offensive again and put himself in a good position to besiege Vitré.[141] Henry III had the loyalty of Geoffroy de Lusignan, Lord of Vouvant and Mervant in the Vendée; he returned to freedom with the help of the temporary transfer to him of these two places.[142] Aimery de Thouars, of whom Geoffroy was the vassal, stood as guarantor of his fidelity, and even placed him in the service of Henry III.[143] About thirty knights, among them Hervé and Pierre de Volvire, had been made prisoners either by the English, or by Pierre of Brittany: the King of England freed them, after being assured of their fidelity.[144] Was fortune going to turn? One could have believed it, by seeing the English flatter themselves to bring back to their cause the ambitious and conspiratorial Count de La Marche.[145] The moment seemed propitious for Henry III to go ahead of him, to push the point upon France. He did well. Vigorous resolutions did not concur with his character, and elsewhere the councils of his entourage did not care to risk themselves in a dangerous expedition. In this moment they were called in all haste to Gascogne, where disorder continued to reign.[146]

On the council of Hubert de Burgh, the King of England resolved to enter Poitou, and then advance, crossing this province, until his possessions in Gascogne.[147] This campaign, in the spirit of those who had advised it, was to cause a restoration of English influence between the lower Loire and the Gironde. It did not present any danger. Blanche of Castile and her son were far distant; the Poitevin nobility, interested, stirring up, seemed intent on approaching the English; in the army of Henry III, they counted on the traditional fickleness of the Poitevin barons, and the seneschal Raoul Fitz-Nicolas certainly expressed the hopes of his master, when he wrote to the Chancellor England: "I believe that the King our Lord will have the greatest number of the Lords of Poitou, who will come to his service, like Geoffroy de Rancon, Renaud de Pons, Etier de Barbozieux, Robert de Sablé, Aimery de Rochechouart, Aimery de Thouars and Benoit of Mortagne. Thanks to them, the King will be able to ride in safety through the land of Poitou unto Gascogne, and, if needed, return to Brittany."[148]

The best means of gaining the Poitevin lords to the cause of the English had been to inflict a good defeat on the troops of the King of France. Henry III found it more prudent to negotiate. During his stay in Nantes, attract to his party Guillaume Maingot, Lord of Surgères, and Guillaume Archbishop, Lord of Parthenay; at the same time, he concluded a truce with the Viscount of Brosse.[149] On 1 July 1230, he crossed the Loire, then advanced slowly through Poitou, attracting to his service, one after the other, Renaud de Pons, Hugues de Tonnay, Guillaume de Mauzé, and all the nobles for whom Raoul Fitz-Nicolas had tendered an offer, taking some guarantees, but especially making fair promises, giving much money. Poitevins were made to pay expenses; this war without battles cost as much as another, and to refill his chests, Henry III borrowed from several of his Gascon subjects, from the people of Bordeaux, Bayonne, Dax, and the Bishop of Bazas.[150]

From Pirmil, opposite Nantes, on left bank of the Loire, Henry gained Montaigu, Luçon, Marans, Vandré, attained by a detour to the east, not being able to pass under the walls of La Rochelle. He was in Tonnay-Charente from 11 to 13 July, in Pons from the 15th to 19th or to the 20th. After having crossed Plassac, the English, for the first time since their departure from Brittany, met resistance. The small fortified town of Mirambeau, located at the south of Plassac and in the direction of Blaye, closed its gates to them; it had to be taken.[151]

Mirambeau was besieged from 21 to 30 July. Soon after he invested it, Henry III wrote, for reinforcements, to his government in Gascogne, who were close-by. The burgers of Saint-Macaire had been ordered to come to the siege, and similar convocations were dispatched, at the same time, to inhabitants of several cities, among them Sainte-Bazeille and Bazas, to the people of Franchises de Bazadois, Hélie Rudol, Lord of Bergerac, to Bernard de Rioux, to the knights and good people of Entre-deux-Mers. The mayor and the commune of Bordeaux were informed to bring before Mirambeau three, or at least two, *mangonneaux* [stone throwing machines] and to send to their prince, for the archers, thirty thousand arrows.[152] Bernard de Rioux sent machines of war, a *trebuchet*, two *tombereaux* (*tumberellos*), two *mangonneaux*, and Henry III had to promise to return these to him in good condition; if these machines were suddenly ruined, the King promised to buy them, or to compensate Bernard de Rioux after an estimate made by third parties.[153] A fortress of little importance could not hold out a long time in the face of an army provided with sufficient material for a siege. After a resistance of a few days, the garrison ended up succumbing under the attacks of the English; it was made prisoner while attempting to escape.[154]

The King of England, master of Mirambeau, continued his march towards the Gironde. In Blaye, on 2 August, he promised to Geoffroy de Rancon two thousand marcs to attract him to his service and attain his homage.[155] During this campaign he had gained, in Aunis, a serious advantage while occupying Oléron; this island, which Henry III had at one time pledged to the Count de La Marche, which Louis IX and Blanche of Castile had promised to this same lord by the Treaty of Vendôme, was to remain some time in the hands of the English.[156]

Henry III crossed the Gironde, gained Bordeaux, but remained there at most a week. Gascogne was not his base operations, and he had come, so far, to visit the capital of his French domains, only to ensure the submission of Poitou.

Returning to Blaye on 10 August, he stopped in this city three days, then he retraced his steps, hardly stopping in Pons, Saint-Georges-des-Côteaux, and Tonnay-Charente.[157] He tried to regain Brittany without being out flanked by the King of France, who had returned towards the west. In July, Louis IX was in Saint-Maixont, where he granted a communal charter to the burgers of Niort.[158] In the month of August, one finds him in Poitiers, probably occupied with supervising the comings and goings of the English.[159] But Hugues de Lusignan and other partisans of Louis IX were nearer to the road taken by the army of Henry III. The day when the English left Tonnay, one of their Poitevin companions-in-arms, Guillaume de Fouquebrun, was attacked and stripped by "criminals" who appear to have been members of the French party.[160] It was by Surgères and Marans that Henry III arrived in Luçon, where he remained from 24 August to 6 September; finally, on 12 September he finished his not very glorious expedition whilst returning to Nantes.[161]

What had been the purpose of this military promenade? Could it not be said that by leaving Poitou he left in a good situation those who were compromised for him, those whom he had bought at a handsome price and not very sure devotion? Much between them had, after his departure, been rather exposed. This was the case of the Viscount of Rochechouart who, surrounded by enemies, had made at great expense an effort to surround his castle with strong walls, towers, and a deep ditch. He wrote Henry III that he would be, without his help, incompetent to hold on if the King of France came to his country; he recalled in pressing terms his expenditure, his need for money, called for his son Aimery upon a generosity like that which the Poitevins raised, except for their retreat back to Brittany.[162] We do not know if Henry III granted him subsidies. The King of England was not in a state to hold the countryside, and the results of his expedition were quite poor; without winning any serious advantage, without engaging in any important action, he was obliged to conclude a partial truce, while waiting for the final end of this enterprise.

The Count de La Marche, whose wife was the mother of Henry III, and who had remained faithful to the King of France, was chosen as the negotiator for suspension of hostilities. Between him and his son-in-law, the war had not been violent. As of 16 July, Henry had written to the masters of galleys, in Savary de Mauléon, to the Seneshal, Henri de Trubleville, to let go, with their wine that had been seized, the merchants of Hugues X.[163] At the time of his passage to Pons, on 15 August, he had, with permission of the Count, started talks with the King of France; peace reigned to the south of the Loire from 18 August to 1 September. The King of England requested the Count of Brittany and his most important Poitevin followers to subscribe to this truce, promising to explain to them, when he would see them, the reasons which had brought him to conclude it.[164] On 26 August, he announced that it was prolonged until 8 September; the 30th, he still wrote to Savary de Mauléon to order him to give freedom to vessels and men of the Count de La Marche who were provided with safe conducts.[165] If the Count and his people made infringements of the truce, Henry reserved making justice to his court, before which Hugues wanted his men to answer in such cases.[166]

It was not only by words that the King of England showed his reconciling intentions. Learning that two canons of Saintes were made prisoners of the night, in Saint-Pierre d'Oléron, in a house where they were placed, he asked if it was not appropriate to free them because of the truce. He wrote to the constable of Oléron to make them delay payment of their ransom and to send to him, after an inquest, those who carried out the arrest.[167] Three days later, he gave full powers to regulate all that concerned the truce to his brother Richard, Hubert de Burgh, the Count of Pembroke, the Constable of Chester, and Raoul Fitz-Nicolas.[168]

Henry III returned to Nantes and remained there from 12 to 23 September.[169] He found Brittany in the state where he had left it at the time of his departure for Gascogne; great lords of the country, or at least some of the most important, were still faithful to the party of Pierre Mauclerc. Henry III had care to appease them; he gave orders to his ministers to give Alain, Viscount de Rohan, and Henri Avaugour possession of the fiefs that their fathers had formerly held in England and of which they had been stripped at the time when King John lost Normandy.[170] The good provisions of the Breton nobility were to him more necessary than ever; his army was foundering. English troops, confined in the peninsula, had suffered much from heat during the summer; food and drink that they found in the country and to which they were not accustomed had caused diseases; the horses died, the supplies were exhausted, money spent. Counts and barons, not making battle, comforted themselves on their inaction by living "in the English mode"; as for the simple knights, they were reduced to selling their horses and their weapons to carry out a miserable life.[171] English knighthood was thus decimated without fighting; the King himself had been sick, and Prince Richard, injured, was not yet cured.[172]

At the time of his departure from Poitou, Henry III had announced his intention to cross again to England before Michaelmas, sent commissaries to the ports of his kingdom to ensure vessels necessary for the transport of troops and ordered all owners and sailors of his domains to come join him at Saint-Malo as of the first favorable wind.[173] Soon one saw noble Englishmen asking for and obtaining permission to cross the sea again: Roger of Quincy, fallen ill, was authorized to return, and with him several knights of his kinswoman Marguerite de Quincy, Countess of Winchester; similar edicts were made in favor of Henry of Hastings and several others.[174] Henry III pressed forward his own departure; faithful to standard procedure, he stopped ships in Saint-Malo and in nearby ports.[175] At the same time he said that the state of his health would not allow him to remain in France during winter, so it was agreed among barons and the Count of Brittany that his return was necessary. It was from the harbor of Saint-Gildas that he intended to set sail; the Count of Brittany, the Count of Chester and Lincoln, and William the Marshal, Count of Pembroke, would have to continue the war.[176] A letter of 2 October still shows us Henry III pressing for the arrival of English ships.[177]

On 26 September, he wrote to all his knights and sergeants remaining on the continent that William the Marshal was charged to direct in his absence all military operations.[178] Geoffroy de Lusignan was informed that the counts of Brittany, Pembroke, and Chester were under orders to take care of his interests and the business of the partisans that the Crown of England preserved in France.[179] Henry III promised subsidies and gave guarantees to those that he charged to replace. A thousand marcs were allotted to the Count of Chester to support the war.[180] William the Marshal reserved for himself the faculty to return to England at the time of Lent, but agreed to remain in Brittany until that time; it was promised to him that if he died before crossing the sea, his brother Richard would inherit him indisputably.[181] Henry III engaged to leave with Pierre Mauclerc four hundred knights and a hundred *sergents à cheval*, and even, after one historian, five hundred knights and a thousand bailiffs.[182] It was agreed that the Count of Chester and William the Marshal would be able to attract to the service of the King of England all those who wanted, without risking repudiation, and the Count of Brittany received full powers to conclude truces with Louis IX.[183] He was the true chief of the English party in France; he was made increasingly necessary; Henry III, always needy, had recourse to the interested generosity of this skilful and powerful ally who advanced six thousand marcs to him.[184]

Thus Henry III left for others the continuation of a war he had so badly managed. On 23 September he left Nantes: after a six day stop in Redon, he moved towards the north, passing by Guer, Saint-Méen, Jugon, Saint-Brieuc, Guingamp, Pabu, Tréguier, Lannion, Morlaix.[185] On 25 October at the latest he was in Saint-Pol-de-Léon; he was still found there the following day. Lastly, after having ordered freedom for the vessels of Saint-Malo and other Breton boats seized in preparation for his passage, he set sail and moved on to Portsmouth, where we find we him on 28 October 1230.

Henry had hardly imagined to be returned to this port as he had left it, a few months before, full of arrogant hope. His situation was not very satisfactory; that of his French partisans was much less still. Aimery de Thonars, Lord of Roche-sur-Yon, were not long in alerting him of their distress.[186] Another of his faithful, Renaud de Pons, wrote to him that to protect himself from the King of France he had spent much money to strengthen his city. He needed new funds to put his fortifications in a state of defense. Renaud begged the King of England not to leave him at the mercy his enemies: "The Queen of France," he concluded, "has declared, before the Count de La Marche and Geoffroy de Rancon, that she will disinherit me, or the King will lose France."[187]

While the grand expedition of Henry III ended in a piteous failure, barons united against Champagne, were constrained to renounce their hopes. It was to cut down Blanche of Castile that they had wanted to destroy Thibaud, and the Regent had had enough energy to save her vassal.

The Bishop of Langres wrote to his canons, that on 9 May 1230 the Duke of Burgundy and the Count de Champagne were ready to come into their hands; but at this time the English had disembarked; *les grands*, called by Louis IX to push back this invasion, had deferred execution of their revenge against Thibaud, authorized a truce, and taken the way of Anjou.[188] Then, at the forty days expiry during which they owed the King military service, they had left the royal army to resume their war on Champagne. Thibaud IV had had to follow them; the King and Blanche of Castile, also, hastened to return to Paris to closely supervise the serious events of which the kingdom was going to be the theater. The situation of the Count was alarming, almost desperate. Most of his vassals were at heart among the disaffected, to whom they soon delivered their castles.[189] Thibaud was reduced not to trust the people of the towns and countryside and to declare, in a day of distress, that Blanche of Castile was his only hope.[190]

From one end to the other they prepared a campaign which was to be decisive. While Thibaud, allied with the Count of Flanders, with the Duc de Lorraine, the Count de Chalon, authorized Erard de Brienne to build a fortress at Bagneux, the Duke of Burgundy held Châtillon-sur-Seine, ready to go, through Champagne, to rally his allies.[191] It was in effect on the north side which Champagne was especially threatened; there was a large army of malcontents, with the Count de Boulogne, the counts de Guines and Saint-Pol, Enguerrand de Coucy, Robert de Courtenay, and probably the counts Robert de Dreux and Jean de Mâcon, brothers of Pierre Mauclerc. Their other brother, the Archbishop of Rheims, held openly for the party of the malcontent coalition. Finally, the estates of Thibaud were exposed, on the east side, to attacks from the Count de Bar.

Champagne, threatened on three sides at the same time, hardly had natural defenses. In the north, on the Vesle, Thibaud had, in Fismes, a castle able to sustain a siege; then, after an open space, the invaders were to be opposite the Marne, on which were Vitry, Epernay, Damery, Reuil, Port-à-Binson, Château-Thierry. Behind this river was, not far from Virtus, the redoubtable stronghold of Mont-Aimé; then, passing to Sézanne, one arrived at Provins, where the Count had equipped it with new defenses.[192] On the side of Burgundy, the estates of Thibaud were protected by Chaource and Saint-Florentin, and in the second place by the line of the Seine, which furnished the Bar-sur-Seine, Troyes, Bray-sur-Seine and Montereau-faut-Yonne.[193]

The coalition of the north, under the orders of Philippe Hurepel, joined together at the *septentrionale* frontier of the Champagne country, probably at Braisne, patrimonial fief of the house of Dreux, and went on to Fismes, defended by Simon de Tréloup, who resisted them.[194] They marched around this and crossed the Marne, sparing the villages, the houses and the castles of nobles, although they seized goods from monasteries; it was thus that they ransacked, between Vesle and the Marne, Sergy, Favières, and some possessions belonging to the abbey of Saint-Médard de Soissons.[195] Historians of the time recount that they ravaged far and wide.[196] Thibaud IV destroyed an arch of the bridge of Binson, from which they would have been able to cross the Marne; the bridge, thus cut, had been fortified and provided with a garrison under the command of Count Hugues de Rethel; it was a strong position, that without doubt it would have been hard to approach; but the Count of Saint-Pol, going up the river, moved on Reuil, where he crossed it in spite of the resistance of approximately ten knights. On this news, the Count de Rethel gave up Binson and escaped; at once they united and crossed the Marne, which was low at the time, and devastated and extorted Damery, and then seized Epernay, to which they set fire, if as it was the Count de Champagne they had burned.[197] Thibaud was reduced to deliver to the flames those of his towns he could not defend : Virtus and Sézanne were thus burned, that is to say by him, that is to say by his enemies; he had to be satisfied to concentrate resistance on a few points.[198] Mont-Aimé, close to Virtus, had a strong garrison which held strongly; the Count himself waited for the coalition under the walls of Provins. It was undoubtedly there that he fought a battle; but fate was contrary for him: thirteen of his knights perished in action, and it is claimed that two hundred were made prisoners. Thibaud escaped, chased in his diversion by enemy parties who followed him to the very walls of Paris, where he sought refuge.[199]

It seems that the day was gained for the adversaries of Thibaud; they had crossed Champagne victoriously, and were close to grasping the hands of the Duke of Burgundy and their allies in the south; Thibaud in his escape, was separated from Troyes by the army which had just beaten him. But defenders of Mont-Aimé occupied in the middle of the country a position remaining until then impregnable, from where they sortied to cut communications between the army of the barons and Rheims. It was indeed from this city that the invaders drew their main resources, and by intercepting the convoys of subsistence that Archbishop Henri de Dreux sent to his allies, it was sure to put them in a great embarrassment.[200] The barons, short of supplies, returned to Champagne, spreading into the country and devastated more, dismantling castles, burning villages and cities, cutting vines and fruit trees, and leaving only the churches upright.[201] Their passage brought them before Ramerupt, under the walls of which they spent fifteen days.[202]

Champagne, reduced in resources, would have been lost; but while Philippe Hurepel marched with iron and fire between the Marne and the Seine, Ferrand of Portugal, with his Flemings, was again thrown onto the county of Boulogne.[203] On the other side, one of principals among the coalition, Henri de Bar, granted on 4 August, with the prayer of his friend Érard de Chassenay, a truce with Thibaud and the Duke of Lorraine; this suspension of arms was to last from 6 to 29 August inclusive but the effect was extremely mitigated by a clause which held for Henri de Bar and Mathieu de Lorraine the faculty to bring without restraint, the one to aid the barons, the other to assist Thibaud.[204] Invaders, to finish off their enemy, wanted to seize Troyes: they were preceded there by the seneschal of Champagne, Simon de Joinville; this Lord, who had joined his men, proceeded in only one night, by a forced march, from Joinville to Troyes. The coalition, seeing their surprise lost, went to camp on the left bank of the Seine, in meadows which bordered Isle-Aumont. They made their junction there with the Duke of Burgundy.[205]

All was soon changed by arrival of the Queen. Blanche of Castile, returned from Poitou, approached with Louis IX, at the head of a large army.[206] It camped within four miles of Troyes; from there she made an interdiction with the Count de Boulogne and his allies to make complaints about the Count de Champagne, vassal of the King, offering to those who held grievances to come expose their objections to her son. The barons protested that they would not plead, and some pushed with insolence to declare that it was a habit of this woman to prefer anyone for the murderer of her husband. However, the presence of the King gave them pause to reflect; they requested him to be withdrawn, offering to join battle with Champagne and the Duke of Lorraine with three knights less than their two enemies would have. Such a proposal could not be taken seriously by the Queen: she answered that they would not attack men of the King without his presence. The barons, increasingly intimidated, sent to say that if the King wanted it, they would readily hear with reason the Queen of Cyprus, for whom they affected to be partial, by stripping Thibaud; but acceptance of this offer was compatible neither with the rights of the Crown, nor with royal dignity. The Regent could not admit unjust claims of the Queen of Cyprus to the Champagne succession if discussed by rebels and their army close by. It meant that the King would accept no peace, and would not allow Thibaud to agree to it, before the Champagne country had been evacuated.

This proud attitude produced a salutary effect on the spirit of the Count de Boulogne; he remembered that he was first prince of the blood, and finally saw that putting himself at their head, but only for their interests, had thought that they would shake royal authority for their profit. He declared without turning on his confederates that he could not, without lying to the King, continue, in spite of his defense, with combat on Champagne: the King was his nephew, son of his brother, and his liege lord; Hurepel decided to leave the alliance of the barons to line up with the party of his sovereign. The barons protested in vain; he would have his peace with the Queen and they would lose their domains: "In the name of God," the Count de Boulogne answered, "better to leave than folly to pursue."[207] And without delaying more he wrote to the Queen that he was ready to submit and conclude a truce.[208] The Champagne war was finished; the coalition withdrew to Isle-Aumont at Jully-sur-Sarce, then to Chaource, and finally to Laigne, on the lands of the Count de Nevers.[209] There did not remain to them any more than to disperse: each one regained his fiefs. In this movement of retirement, *les grands* finally made Fismes capitulate; they mined the castle and burned it. "But the good tower was," records the Minstrel of Rheims, "although tilting over, still standing."[210]

      The King was in Compiegne in the month of September, when he made peace with his uncle.[211] The Count de Boulogne obtained all that he wanted; compensated for the losses which the incursions of the Count of Flanders had caused him; other compensations or other advantages without any doubt were ensured to him, but we do not know them.[212] I do not know either if Philippe Hurepel, in Compiegne, made an agreement with his confederates, or if he negotiated only for his own account. One historian recounts that in September the King of France and Blanche of Castile held with the barons a conference for peace, that Thibaud de Champagne, under the terms of conventions then agreed upon, was compelled to make a pilgrimage to the Holy Land with one hundred knights, that Louis IX and his mother swore to return to each one his rights and to give justice to all their men according to the right customs.[213] It is certain that the King of Jerusalem, Jean de Brienne, used his influence to help with the re-establishment of peace; elsewhere, by a declaration of Philippe Hurepel, it was on 25 September 1230 that the counts of Boulogne and of Champagne were made referees by their friends and their partisans, who accepted their decision.[214] The same act established that at this time Philippe Hurepel had already made peace with Ferrand of Portugal, and that the Count de Chalon accepted the mediation of the two referees; Philippe and Thibaud were to mark the conditions of peace that the Count de Chalon had made with the Duke of Burgundy and his mother, the duchess dowager Alix de Vergy, and the Count engaged to make homage to the Duke. Finally, the Count de Bar and the Duke of Lorraine, reconciled in Vitry, promised to subject themselves, for the later disputes, to arbitration of the counts of Boulogne and Champagne; if the latter were not of the same opinion, the Queen was to decide.[215]

Consequently, on 12 December 1230, Philippe Hurepel and Thibaud IV pronounced an award between the Duke of Lorraine and the Count de Bar. It was agreed, among others, that the bridge and the fortress of Pont-à-Mousson, belonging to the Count de Bar, would be rebuilt, and that Champagne would pay half of this repair; the price had to be fixed by Thibaud and Philippe Hurepel, estimated by carpenters and masons that they would send; in the event of disagreement on this subject, they must follow the opinion of the commissary delegated by the Queen.[216] The Count de Champagne paid moreover indemnities to various other people; Thomas de Coucy, brother of the Lord de Coucy, Enguerrand III, had been one of his enemies at the time of the first war, and Champagne had devastated, near Provins, the lands that he held from Count Rethel; Thibaud paid, to this chief, to Count Rethel, three hundreds livres, whose receipt Thomas gave him.[217] It is also known that Robert Auvergne, Archbishop of Lyon, obtained from the Count de Champagne, obviously as damages, the promise of three thousand marcs money, and that as of February 1233 part of this sum had been paid.[218]

The Count de Dreux, like his allies of the day before, made with the King his normal relationship of vassal to suzerain once again, and all had returned to order, when in December 1230 Louis IX held his court in Melun; he issued there, on the subject of Jews and usury, an ordinance which was subscribed by Philippe Hurepel, Thibaud de Champagne, the Count de La Marche, the Duke of Burgundy, the constable Amaury de Montfort, the *bouteiller* of France Robert de Courtenay, the counts of Bar, Saint-Pol, d'Eu, Chalon, the Viscount of Limoges, Enguerrand de Coucy, Archambaud de Bourbon and his brothers Guillaume and Guy de Dampierre, Jean de Nesle, and Guillaume de Vergy.[219] Among those who sealed the royal act was Jean de Braisne, Count of Vienne and Mason, brother of the Count deBretagne.[220]

The re-establishment of peace between Thibaud IV and his enemies was to have as a result the final failure of the English. Henry III quit the continent after having assisted from afar in the submission of Philippe Hurepel and his allies; to retake the old fiefs of his family, he had counted on the revolt of the great French nobility, and this revolt had been put down; his bad health, which he had pled in returning to England, was not the true reason of his departure; it was the progress of his enemy and the state of his affairs which gave him pause to reflect: he had lost confidence. Always hesitant, he neither acknowledged to himself that it was necessary to wait for his projects of revenge, nor began an effort that his subjects were ill disposed to assist. Without great sacrifices, he however continued to kill people and to spend money from his treasury for this war in Brittany which could not succeed.

In November, he collected great sums of money in Porchester, intended to be sent overseas;[221] five thousand marcs had been deposited there, including 4,680 marcs sent to Pierre Mauclerc, and 320 marcs to William the Marshal, Count of Pembroke, "to support the war of the King."[222] Another money transfer took place in the month of June, and they sent a cargo of squares there for crossbows.[223] Reinforcements were also sent, and, towards the end of winter, the King of England wrote to several of his Viscounts to come to London, in the month following Easter, all them providing sergeants with hauberks and good horses which would be used for his military on the continent.[224] Henry was generous towards the knights who devoted themselves in Brittany to an ungrateful task; they obtained, for the duration of his service, the pleasure of a manor;[225] Pierre Mauclerc was given possession of other manors, belonging to his English fiefs.[226]

At the same time, the English government took general measures to halt the disembarkation to England of all subjects and agents of Louis IX; Richard the Marshal, heir to the county of Pembroke, was liege man of the King of France.[227] His brother, Count Guillaume, had just left him incontestable rights after his death; but having to deliver his fiefs to him, Henry III wanted to know if he intended to withdraw the homage that he had lent to an enemy prince.[228]

After the death of Guillaume [William] the Marshal, English troops remaining in Brittany had as their chief the Count of Chester. Pierre Mauclerc made this lord return the fortress of Saint-James-de-Beuvron, returned to him in right of his wife. He had supplied it and placed it in a state of defense.[229] The English were under his orders to ride through Anjou; they traversed this country for fifteen days, advanced to the south of the Loire, destroyed Gonnord, whose castle was taken and razed, returned to north Angers where they seized Châteauneuf-sur-Sarthe, which was burned. A short while after this expedition, the Count of Chester made an assault near Normandy and set fire to the small town of Pontorson, whose castle was demolished.[230]

In spite of these advantages, the situation of the Count de Bretagne worsened; the nobility of his estates turned to the French party and, after January 1231, efforts of the royal government to detach them from Mauclerc obtained every success. To reassure the future of those that were thus won over, they [Blanche] authorized them to stipulate in their acts a homage reserved in favor of the heirs of Brittany from which rights were to be respected when they would have reached their majority. It was an excellent means of losing Pierre Mauclerc while saving the feelings of the Bretons. It was thus that Olivier de Coëtquen submitted himself to the King of France, that Raoul de Fougères delivered his castle to the King by this convention, acquired the right to put at Fougères a garrison, large or small, to his liking, according to the council of Andre de Vitré; on the other hand, he promised to maintain his pledge of thirty knights to the Lord of Fougères, either in this fortified town, or elsewhere, until the end of the war as heir to Brittany; Raoul was authorized to hold garrisons in his castle, but in leaving the command to people of the King, who on his side promised to relieve the place in the event of siege, and not to make any peace, or truce by which Raoul de Fougères was exposed to fall down in homage to the King of England or to Pierre Mauclerc.[231] Raoul still promised to make his knights swear that they would be against him until with full satisfaction, he defaulted on his engagements; his uncle Foulques Paynel, at one time so hostile to France, guaranteed him.[232]

Soon there was Guiomar de Leon and Henri Âvaugour, chief of the house of Penthièvre, which, after having made homage to Louis IX, entered in his service, one with fifteen knights, other with twenty-five, and accepted in preparation for war the promise of money.[233] Henri Avaugour obtained, for the duration of the war, the castle of Guarplic or Guesclin, not far from Cancale, and gave his two sons as hostages. If the King could have the disposition of this castle, which was then in the hands of Dreu de Mello, he was to give Avaugour another place, where he could withdraw with his wife and all his family. Before leaving with the royal army which had just assembled in Vincennes, Henri Avaugour recognized, in effect, that he had received the guardianship of the castle of Guarplic and that he was obliged to return it without any requisition.[234]

Tanguy, son of Tanguy, vassal of Guiomar de Leon, made homage in his turn, as Raoul of Tillay who was recognized for faithful services while returning fiefs to him that Philippe Auguste had given him to hold "in the customs and habits of Normandy."[235] Alain d'Acigné, also in the service of the King, accepted for liege homage forty *livres* of land.[236] Lastly, among those who adopted the royal cause, one counts Geoffroy de Châteaubriand, Gédouin de Dol, Geoffroy Ancenis, and Richard Marshal.[237] King Henry III punished these desertions better, and the reprisals were easy for him when those who gave up had fiefs in England. Henri Avaugour paid with the loss of land that he held in the domain of Waltham.[238]

It was claimed that on 1 June 1231 Louis IX held in Paris a conference for the re-establishment of peace with the Count of Brittany and the King England, and that a three years truce was arranged there.[239] The conference can have taken place, but in this case it was without result; the truce was concluded only the next month, and at this time even the King of France joined together in Vincennes an army intended for war in Brittany. He appears to have taken some of it under his command: he was seventeen years old, but this was not his first campaign; Blanche, who hardly ever left her son and who liked to arrange things herself, certainly left with him. A disbursing account made at Antrain on 23 July 1231 tells us that the troops gathered for this expedition included, at the moment when they reached the height of effective manpower, a hundred and forty six knights, one hundred thirty-five sergeants with horse, a certain number of archers on foot and horse, and three thousand sergeants on foot.[240] The infantry had with it more than fifty carts, without counting the wagon train of state money. In addition, the King was accompanied, as always, with feudal quotas. The Count de Champagne, Jean Afficamps, and Marshal Jean Clément had a big role in army, since considerable sums were allocated to them in this circumstance.[241] The Count de Bigorre, the Viscount of Limoges, Guillaume and Pierre des Barres, Henri de Sully, and many other nobles were there; Angevins and Breton enemies of Pierre Mauclerc had come in number to line up under the royal banner : Henri Avaugour and Guiomar de Leon had with them thirty-eight knights; at their side, and apart from their company, appeared Geoffroy de Pouancé, Olivier de Coëtquen, Alain from Beaufort, Jean de Dol,

Jacques and Philippe de Châteaugiron, Zaffre Alain; they received sums of varying importance, and the payment orders were made, sometimes in the name of the Queen, sometimes by Pierre de Chambly, Amaury the constable of Montfort, or the chamberlain, Jean de Beaumont; these two last were tested men of war. The constable, Mathieu de Montmorency, giving to the crown long and useful services, had died on 24 November 24, 1230, and it was Count Amaury de Montfort who succeeded him.[242]

The army, leaving Vincennes, moved on Brittany from Mantes, Anet, Mans, Brulon and Laval.[243] The counts of Brittany and of Chester, undoubtedly not being strong enough to attack frontally, threw themselves behind the convoys of weapons and of supplies, on wagons which carried the machines of war; they set fire to them and seized about sixty horses. One English historian, whose assertion cannot be verified, claimed that this bad beginning decided the French to make a truce.[244]

For some time Pope Gregory IX had already worked to reconcile the Kings of France and England; on 25 April, he had written to them to point out the dangers surrounding the Holy Land and to exhort them to make peace, or at least a truce. He indicated for his representatives in this business the Bishop of Winchester, Pierre des Roches, and Gautier Cornu, Archbishop of Sens; I know from another source that the Bishop of Winchester, being in France, took an active share of this work of appeasing and humanity.[245] The truce, negotiated for France by the Count de Boulogne and the Archbishop of Rheims, for England by the counts of Brittany and Chester, was concluded in Saint-Aubin-du-Cormier on 4 July 1231, for three years, to date from the last Midsummer's Day; hostilities with England were thus suspended until 24 June 1234.[246] During this long time of respite, Blanche of Castile was going to be free to regulate many interior difficulties, to work for strengthening royal power, without being threatened with a foreign war.

The majority of stipulations arranged between the two crowns related to Count de La Marche and his wife the dowager Queen of England, manifest proof expressions of the care with which the Regent made in defending the interests of those who had not flagged in their duties towards her son. During the three years of truce, the Count de La Marche was to occupy the island of Oléron, which the English had seized, or to receive in compensation an annual rent of eight hundred *livres tournois*; this question was thus regulated only in a provisional manner.[247] At the end of August, Henry III received in England Baudouin, prior of Saint-Martin-des-Champs, whom the King of France sent to him for the ratification of the truce. In the presence of Henry, this envoy and the Seneshal of England, Raoul Fitz-Nicolas, made the oaths; Richard de Cornouailles and the Justiciar, Hubert de Burgh, Count of Kent, also swore to take care that the truce was observed in good faith by their master.[248] The Count of Cornouailles, the Seneschal and the Justiciar gave on this subject three letters patent that were sent to Louis IX; that of the Justiciar is dated 31 August.[249]

After a document which I know only from second hand, it would have been agreed that the truce would be sworn by seven Breton barons, at the choice of the King; if Pierre Mauclerc made a violation of the truce and failed to repair it in forty days after being required by the conservators, these seven noble were to refuse any assistance to him. Pierre moreover would have delivered guarantees to the Count de Boulogne's castle of Saint-Aubin-du-Cormier, so that it was put in the hands of the King in case of infringement; he would have been committed to hand back to Viscount de Brosse two castles that he had removed from him; he freed it for the duration of the truce, in possession of the fortified towns that he had removed from his vassals, in favor of partisans of the King; only it was to serve the annual income of it to them.[250] What is more, it is that in July he shows in his account a truce whose final time limit was to be on 24 June 1234. He engaged by a special codicil not to return to France during these three years; the limits that it did not encompass were the counties of Mortain, Domfront, Vendôme, Loches, Saumur, Loudun, and Poitiers; access to the fortified towns and the castles held of the King was prohibited to him; finally he promised to spend the night, as long as the truce would last, in none the big cities of the royal domain, and to set foot inn the estates of Count de La Marche.[251] These obligations were to have the effect of making his quite difficult, if not impossible, relations with other great vassals of the crown.

The rapprochement between Blanche of Castile and Pierre Mauclerc was certainly facilitated by the efforts of Robert de Dreux, frightened with idea of the punishment of which his brother was threatened; but one undoubtedly goes too far in saying that the Count of Brittany, reconciled with his King, came to make homage and swear on the Gospels, never to be to disloyal again.[252] It was a simple truce, and not a final peace, which was concluded in July 1231.

Bellême, Angers, and their dependencies remained naturally in the hands of the King; this loss by Pierre de Dreux was the result most clearly of an inexcusable revolt and a completely unworthy treason.[253] A long time after reign of Saint Louis someone manufactured, to serve the interests of some Duke of Brittany, a false treaty, that was dated Angers 1231; this awkward falsification cannot be taken seriously.[254]

Pierre Mauclerc was so far from peace that he remained, even after the suspension of hostilities, in constant communication with the enemies of the kingdom. As of January 1231, he announced the intention to go to England at once after the conclusion of the truce, and crossed the sea with the Count of Chester and Richard the Marshal; he preserved for some time the confidence and subsidies of Henry III. The temporary appeasing which had succeeded the state of war did not prevent the two kings and their partisans to remain enemies; the new Constable, Count Amaury de Montfort, had to give up in favor of his brother Simon all the rights that he could have had on the English fiefs of his family.[255] Henry III, after the Constable of France notified this transfer to him, could not suspect that Simon de Montfort, the new Count of Leicester, would be one day be his most frightening adversary.

In France all returned to order; the large vassals had failed so well in their campaigns against the Regent that she could be generous without danger. In March 1231, she granted forgiveness to Count Simon de Ponthieu, brother of the traitor Renaud de Dammartin. Associated, under the reign of Philippe Auguste, with the plot which had cost Renaud his freedom, Simon had been stripped of his fiefs. His wife, Countess Marie, who was niece of Philippe Auguste and first cousin of Louis VIII, had obtained grace, in July 1225, that the Count of Ponthieu would be left, under certain conditions, in heritage with his children, but by promising that Simon would never return without approval of the King.[256] Since then, the Count had remained apart from his fiefs; this situation favored him to the King of England who, on 22 January 1230, gave him letters of safe conduct.[257] A few months later, Henry III lifted the sequestration order placed on a cargo of wine belonging to men of the Count de Ponthieu, proof that Simon was regarded by him as a friend.[258]

Blanche of Castile did not wait for the suspension of hostilities to draw the Count de Ponthieu from this annoying position. The Count obtained relief to return to his fiefs by ratifying conventions to which his wife had subscribed in 1225. Moreover, Simon and Marie underwent a whole series of conditions similar to those that Count Ferrand of Flanders had accepted before gaining freedom: commitment not to build nor to increase any fortress without consent of the King; promise not to marry their two oldest daughters before two years without permission of the King and of Blanche, and never to link any of their daughters to a declared enemy of Louis IX or his mother; and, an obligation to make their communes, their cities, their vassals swear to hold for the King and his heirs if the Count and the Countess violated their engagements. In case of infringement of the articles of the treaty, if the King did not receive satisfaction forty days after having sent to Simon an injunction, he would be able to seize the lands of the Count and of the Countess until they made amends. Simon was to provide guarantees of ten thousand marcs and would give liege homage to the King for the lands that Louis VIII left with Countess Marie. This act was, according to usage, written in double, in the name of Louis IX and of the Count de Ponthieu; five barons guaranteed it, until the stipulated sum and each for his quota, the execution of promises that Simon had just made. Finally eighteen vassals and thirty towns or communes relevant to the Count provided letters to the King attesting their oaths.[259]

 Thus the barons had all made their peace with the Queen, with exception of Pierre Mauclerc, who, while waiting for his final humiliation, remained isolated, condemned to inaction. They had been able neither to destroy the Count de Champagne, nor to get rid of Blanche of Castile, nor to reduce to impotence their young King; their revolts only called the English to France. It is true that by their fault several provinces were covered in ruins: the invasion of the Duke of Burgundy in Champagne; general devastation of this great stronghold by the united coalition; incursions of the Count of Flanders into the counties of Boulogne and of Guines; devastation of Lorraine by the Count de Bar and reprisals exerted against him by Thibaud IV; war at the western border of Normandy, in Brittany, in Anjou, in Poitou, in Saintonge; destruction of a quantity of castles, burning of several cities and innumerable villages, without counting money spent, blood spread, the result of which one was proud; here is what they made of their country, Philippe de France, son of Philippe Auguste, Pierre Mauclerc and his brother princes of Dreux, descendants of Louis VI, Enguerrand de Coucy, Hugues of Burgundy and so many other grand lords, famous representatives of the French nobility. The foreigner they had claimed to drive out was innocent of all these sufferings; she made war to defend her son and to put an end to odious campaigns. Deaf to insults, she continued her work in the middle of hatreds and plots, pushed back the English invasion, destroyed the league of nobles; each time that a new danger was shown, Blanche moved with her army, brought all into play to save faithful subjects and to reduce the others. She was going to govern with less emotion and difficulty; the most terrible difficulties were overcome, the King was made great; the regency, whose term Blanche foresaw, promised to finish well.

1 *Récits d'un ménestrel de Reims*, ed. of Wailly, n. 340.
2 Philippe Mousket, v. 27948
3 *Histoire littéraire de la France*, XXIII, 799; On that which concerns the passion of Thibaud IV for Queen Blanche, one should read and study the dissertations in which Paulin Paris and D'Arbois de Jubainville have treated this question with the highest authority.
      Paulin Paris, *Le Romancero françois*, 1833, in-12, p. 165 ff.; *Histoire littéraire de la France*, XXIII, 770-777; D'Arbois de Jubainville, *Histoire des ducs et des comtes de Champagne*, IV, 215-216 et 280-285. Paulin Paris does not absolutely reject the opinion in which the Queen had been good natured toward Thibaud (Romancero, p. 181). D'Arbois de Jubainville refutes with indignation accusations in which Blanche had been the victim.
4 *Historiens de France*, t. XXI, p. 111-12 (*Extraits des chroniques de S. Denis*); Paulin, Paris, in-12, t. IV, p. 254-55.
5 The Count.
6 The value of a sum of money.
7 For her.
8 Chronique rimée dite de Saint-Magloire, *Historiens de France*, t. XXII, p. 83, verse 52 to 64; ed. Buchon (tome VII), p. 8.
9 Paulin Paris, *Le Romancero françois*, p. 186-189, second serventois of Hugues de la Ferté.
10 Thibaud III, father of Thibaud IV.
11 In a play by Thibaud, Raoul de Boissons, on the girth of Count de Champagne: « *Que vos ventres gros et farsis.* » P. Paris, *Romancero françois*, p. 188, note.
12 Roger of Wendover, ed. Hewlett, t. III, p. 4 : « *Agebant autem contra comitem magnates quasi de crimine proditionis et reum lacsse majostatis, ut qui dominum suum regcm Lodowicum in obsidione Avinionis ob amorem reginse, quam amabat, veneno necaverat, ut dicebant.* » This passage has been transcribed by Mathieu de Paris (*Chronica majora*, t. III, p. 196), under the name of which it became famous. It is one support to prove that Thibaud was in love with Blanche before the death of Louis VIII; the fact is possible, but a history of poisoning the King of France by the Count de Champagne is a poor and wretched invention of great vassals and their partisans, collected and popularized by English historians.
13 D'Arbois de Jubainville, *Histoire des comtes de Champagne*, t. IV, p. 218; t. V, catalogue, n° 1773; Ernest Petit, *Histoire des ducs de Bourgogne de la race capétienne*, t. IV, p. 38; justificative documents, p. 229-231; catalogue, n 1872.
14 Killed in 1226 at the siege of Avignon.
15 For all that is relating to the fight of Thibaud IV against the great vassals, I cannot do other than to return to volume IV of the book of D'Arbois de Jubainville (*Histoire des ducs et des comtes de Champagne*). The historian of the counts of Champagne is, above all, one who gives the most order and clarity to this muddled question. Volume V of D'Arbois de Jubainville contains a catalog of acts to which I will often return in my brief to quote the numbers of documents.
16 Philippe Mousket, verse 27953-60; *Willelmi chronica Andrensis* (*Monumenta Germaniæ historica*, scriptores, t. XXIV, p. 770; *Historiens de France*, t. XVIII, p. 582); Cf. *Johannis Longi chronica S. Berlini* (*Monumenta Germaniæ historica*, t. XXV, p. 836).
17 Aubry de Trois-Fontaines, *Monumenta Germaniæ historica*, t. XXIII, p. 924;

Annals of Dunstable (*Annales Monastici*, ed. Luard, t. III, p. 116); D'Arbois de Jubainville, t. IV, p. 220-221.
18 Thomas de Coucy, brother of Enguerrand, and Count Hugues de Saint-Pol were again in the number of confederates. Aubry de Trois-Fontaines, *Monumenta Germaniæ historica*, t. XXIII, p. 924.
19 Petit, *Histoire des ducs de Bourgogne*, t. IV, catalogue, n. 1937-1938.
20 *Layettes du Trésor des Chartes*, II, n. 2002.
21 Dom Calmet, *Histoire de Lorraine*, t. IV, preuves, col. CCCCXL; Aubry de Trois-Fontaines, loc. cit. I have not been able to identify this seigneur.
22 D'Arbois de Jubainville, t. V, catalogue, 1910; Petit, *Histoire des ducs de Bourgogne*, IV, catalogue, 1941.
23 D'Arbois de Jubainville, t. IV, p. 223-24.
24 Letter to Saint Louis, 30 August 1227; *Layettes*, II, n. 1940; Potthast, *Regesta*, 8021; Letter to Blanche of Castile : Bibl. nat., 500 Colbert, vol. 59, fol. 89 r; *Layettes*, II, n. 1939; Potthast, 8022.
25 *Layettes*, II, n. 1944; Potthast, 8041.
26 Aubry de Trois-Fontaines, *Monumenta Germaniæ historica*, XXIII, p. 924.
27 D'Arbois de Jubainville, t. IV, p. 228, note c; Idem; Guillaume de Nangis, *Vie de saint Louis* : text in latin, *Historiens de France*, t. XX, p. 314; text in French, ibid., p. 315; *Chronique*, ed. Géraud, t. I, p. 177. It is in the *Chronique* that Guillaume speaks of the siege of Bar-sur-Seine, which, according to D'Arbois de Jubainville, had taken place. The poem of Guillaume Guiart had nothing, in that which concerns facts, original value.
28 Petit, *Histoire des ducs de Bourgogne*, t. IV, catalogue, 1942; July 1229; Layettes, II, 2016; Petit, toc. cit., 1943; July 1229.
29 *Willelmi chronica Andrensis* (*Monumenta Germaniæ historica*, XXIV, p. 769, and *Historiens de France*, XVIII, p. 581) ; cf. *Johannis Longi chronica Sancli Bertini* (*Monumenta Germaniæ historica*, XXV, p. 836).
30 *Willelmi chronica Andrensis* (loc. cit.).
31 Record office, Close rolls, 13th year of Henry III, roll 39, memb. 5 r; 23 August 1229 : « *De quadam nave de Kaleis.* »
32 D'Arbois de Jubainville, t. IV, p. 228-229; Guillaume de Nangis, *Vie de saint Louis*, text latin, *Historiens de France*, XX, p. 314-316; text French, ibid., p. 315-317; *Chronique*, ed. Géraud, t. I, p. 177. Aubry de Trois-Fontaines, *Monumenta Germaniæ historica*, XXIII, p. 924 : « *mediantibus tamen abbatibus et religiosis personis.* »
33 *Layettes du Trésor des Chartes*, t. II, n. 2014; Potthast, *Regesta*, 8434; A similar order was addressed to the patriarch of Jérusalem : d'Arbois de Jubainville, t. IV, p. 225; t. V, catalogue, n. 1924; Potthast, *Regesta*, 8435.
34 Bibl. nat., 500 Colbert, vol. 60, fol. 94 V-96 r; 29 June 1230 : the Bishop of Bayeux notified his clergy of a mandate dated 16 June 1230, by which the Archdeacon of Châlons, the cantors of Châlons and Langres, transmit to the Archbishop of Rouen and to his suffragans the *bulla* of Gregory IX on 27 September 1227.
35 Petit, *Histoire des ducs de Bourgogne*, t. IV, catalogue, 1948.
36 D'Arbois de Jubainville, t. V, catalogue, 1940-1942 ; Petit, t. IV, catalogue, 1952-1954.
37 D'Arbois, catalogue, 1943-1944.

38 D'Arbois, 1945-1948; Archives nationales, registre KK 1064, fol. 385 r ; *Layettes du Trésor des Chartes*, II, n. 2034; d'Arbois, catalogue, 1977-1978, et t. IV, p. 230.
39 D'Arbois, t. IV, p. 231; Petit, t. IV, catalogue, 1950, 1959, 1968, 1971. The last piece, which is the alliance between Thibaud and Jean de Seigneley, is found in *Layettes*, t. II, n. 2044.
40 Rinaldi, *Annales ecclesiastici*, t. II, p. 18, Gregory IX, an. 3, n. 56.
41 Ibid.; Potthast, *Regesta*, 8468; 29 November 1229.
42 Potthast, *Regesta*, 8469; Manrique, *Cistercienses annales*, t. IV, p. 391; 29 November 1229.
43 Thibaud was heir presumptive of Navarre.
44 Traditional name of the she-wolf; an insult aimed at Blanche.
45 *Histoire littéraire de la France*, t. XXIII, p. 773.
46 Aubry de Trois-Fontaines, *Monumenta Germaniæ*, XXIII, p. 926; D'Arbois, t. IV, p. 233-34.
47 Roger de Wendover, ed. Hewlett, t. III, p. 4, and, following him, Mathieu de Paris, *Chronica majora*, ed. Luard, t. III, p. 196.
48 Paulin Paris, *Le Romancero françois*, p. 187; 2nd s*erventois* of Hugues de la Ferté: « Tel chose a faite en sa vie, Dont déust estre apelez.»
49 Archives nationales, register ,JJ. 61, n° 475; false transcription, but of which the date is certain.
50 « *Ne les.* »
51 *Le Romancero françois*, p. 184; 1st *serventois* of Hugues de la Fertè.
52 *Récits d'un ménestrel de Reims*, ed. de M. de Wailly, n. 340; *Annals of Dunstable* (*Annales monastici*, ed. Luard, t. III, p. 116).
53 D'Arbqis de Jubainville, t. V, catalogue, 1991; Petit, catalog, 1970; 22 March 1230.
54 Chief town of the small county of this name, which had belonged to Renaud de Dammartin, comte de Boulogne, and had then passed to Philippe Hurepel. The burning of Dammartin is mentioned in the verse chronicle of Saint-Magloire (*Historiens de France*, t. XXII, p. 82): *L'an M. CC. et XX. et X. Fu Dammartin en flamble mis.*
55 Potthast, *Regesta*, 8513; 2 April 1230.
56 Shirley, *Royal letters*, t. I, p. 353-354; 5 July 1229.
57 Letters of Henry III, 17 July 1229 (Shirley, p. 354).
58 Shirley, p. 356; 26 July 1229. This circular was supplemented, the same day, by another royal mandate in the archives of England, in the roll of letters patent; Patent rolls, n. 37, membrana 5 r : « *Rex omnibus ballivis et aliis de portubus maris, etc.* »
59 Shirley, p. 356-57; 27 July 1229.
60 Public record office, Close rolls, 39, 6 r; 25 July 1229 ; Close rolls, 43, 8 r; 21 June 1232 : « *Pro Ricardo de Harecurt.* »
61 Patent rolls, 37, 5 r; 21 July 1229 : « *De abbate de Fiscampnis.* »
62 *Bibliothèque de l'École des Chartes*, 1893, p. 10-11 : Preparations for an English invasion and the descent of Henry III on Brittany. I have expounded in detail, in this article, on measures taken by the King of England with regard to his expedition.
63 *Bibliothèque de l'École des Chartes*, 1893, p. 11.
64 Close rolls, 39, 4 in dorso ; 19 Sep. 1229 : « *Mandatum est Willelmo Talebot,* »
65 Patent rolls, 37, 2 in dorso.

66 *Historiens de France*, XXI, 104; ed. Paulin Paris, IV, 236.
67 Annals of Winchester (*Annales monastici*, ed. Luard, t. II, p. 85).
68 Roger of Wendover, ed. Hewlett, II, 378-380, and, following him, Mathieu de Paris, *Chronica majora*, ed. Luard, III, 191-192 ; Roger of Wendover, III, 33; Mathieu de Paris, III, 222.
69 Shirley, Royal letters, I, 358-359; cf. Annals of Tewkesbury (*Annales monastici*, t. I, p. 73).
70 *Biblio. de l'École des Chartes*, 1893, p. 12-13 (*Les préliminaires d'une invasion anglaise*, etc.; I return to this article for the indication of English documents).
71 *Layettes du Trésor des Chartes*, II, 2037.
72 This piece is published by Du Cange in the observations which follow in the edition of Joinville (1668), p. 44-45.
73 Le Nain de Tillemont, t. II, p. 50.
74 Baluze, *Histoire généal. de la maison d'Auvergne*, t. II, p. 89.
75 Layettes, II, 2038-2041. Caution provided in this circumstance by Maurice de Bréon, Baluze, *Maison d'Auvergne*, II, 250, after the register of Philippe Auguste (Arch. nat., JJ. 26, fol. 208 V).
76 Baluze, loc. cit., p. 776.
77 Le Nain de Tillemont, t. II, p. 51-52; Du Tillet, *Recueil*, t. II, p. 174; letter of Raimond, Abbot of Saint-Martial, (Arch. nat., JJ, 26, fol. 313 v., col. 1., 26 March 1230).
78 *Bibliothèque de l'École des Chartes*, 1893, p. 17-18.
79 *Bibliothèque de l'École des Chartes*, 1893, p. 18-19.
80 Ibid., p. 14.
81 Patent rolls, 39, 6 r; 1 February 1230 : « *De navibus de Depe et de Barbeflé.* »
82 Patent rolls, 39,2 in dorso ; 7 May 1230 : Henry III recalled this disposition to Geoffroy de Lucy and to others.
83 Patent rolls, 39, 4 in dorso; 20 April 1230.
84 [Public] Record Office, Liberate rolls, 492, 4; 2 April 1230 : « *Liberate pro servientibus et balistariis.* »
85 Patent rolls, 38, 9 r; Dinan, 9 May 1230.
86 Without doubt S. Valery-en-Caux; Patent rolls, 38, 8 r; 10 May 1230.
87 *Bibliothèque de l'École des Chartes*, 1893, p. 19-20.
88 *Bibliothèque de l'École des Chartes*, p. 20-21.
89 Close rolls, 40, 10 r; 19 April 1230 : « *De quodam coffino mittendo ad regem.* »
90 Close rolls, 40, 11 r; 14 April 1230 : « *Pro quodam regali facicndo ad opus regis.* »
91 Roger of Wendover, II, 383 and, following him, Mathieu de Paris, *Chronica majora*, III, 194.
92 *Chronicon Nicolai Trivetti*, d'Achery, *Spicilegium*, in-f°, t. III, p. 190.
93 Roger of Wendover, Mathieu de Paris.
94 All facts relating to the crossing and the descent on the English were known to Roger of Wendover and Mathieu de Paris who, in this place as in many others, were constrained to copy Roger, and especially in two letters, the one from Nicolas Nevil and his companions to Raoul, Bishop of Chichester and Chancellor of England, the other, from Count Richard to Gautier, Bishop of Carlisle (Shirley, *Royal and other historical letters* , t. I, p. 364-365, et p. 362-363).
95 I owe this identification to the kindness of Arthur de la Borderie, member of the

Institute. The locality of Port-Blanche and the island of Saint-Gildas belong to the commune of Penvenan and the canton of Tréguier. The roadstead of Port-Blanc, still very frequented nowadays, was not less in the Middle Ages. Borderie has rediscovered it, mentioned between Morlaix and Saint-Brieuc under various orthographies, in the majority of the harbor maps preserved in the Bibliothèque National. Henry III, in one of his letters, indicated it as being at some distance from Lannion and Morlaix: « *Tune transferant se versus duo castra comitis Britannie, que sunt prope portum qui vocatur Sanctus Gildasius, quorum unum vocatur Lanniun et alterum Muntrélès* » (Record office; Close rolls, n. 41, 8 r).

96 Letter of Nicolas Nevil, Shirley, I, p. 364-365.

97 Roger of Wendover, t. II, p. 384 and, following him, Mathieu de Paris, t. III, p. 104-195. André de Vitré married Catherine, youngest daughter of Constance de Bretagne and Guy de Thouars, sister of the Comtesse Alix and sister-in-law of Mauclerc. Several interesting documents of this seigneur are found in the Archives nationales (AA. 00, dossier 1544); M. Campardon, who knew of them for a long time, agreed to divulge them to me.

98 Record office; Patent rolls, n. 38, 9 r; 4 May 1230 : « *De licencia concessa veniendi in terram et potestatem domini regis.* »

99 Patent rolls, 38, 9 r.

100 Ibid.; 7 May : « *De protectione.* »

101 Letter of Nicolas Nevil; Patent rolls, 38, memb. 8 r and 9 r; 9 and 10 May.

102 *Bibliothèque de l'École des Chartes*, 1893, p. 24.

103 Patent rolls, 38, 7 r, 26 May.

104 Close rolls, 41, 7 r; 7 June.

105 Close rolls, 41, 8 r; 11 May.

106 Close rolls, 41. 7 r; 1 July 1230.

107 Close rolls, 41, 5 r ; 8 August 1230.

108 Close rolls, 41, 4 r; 26 August; Close rolls, 41, 3 r; 1 September.

109 Close rolls, 40, 5 r; 17 July : « *Pro Johanne et Gerardo Talobot.* »

110 D. Morice, *Histoire de Bretagne*, Preuves, t. I, col. 869; June 1230.

111 Potthast, *Regesta pontificum Romanorum*, 8196.

112 Patent Rolls, 38, 8 r; Rennes, 14 May 1230. The two named canons, with the Bishop of Mans, in the *bulla* of 29 May 1228, are P. de Domfront and G. de Lavalle. In his letter Henry III called them Robert de « Damfrunt » and Geoffroy de « Daunval. » It was undoubtedly the case that monks transcribed the names badly.

113 Potthast, *Regesta*, 8560; 30 May 1230.

114 Patent Rolls, 38, 6 r; 26 June 1230 : « *Pro Fuleone Paynel.* » Another Norman is named at the end of this piece : « *Radulfus Normannus habet litteras de protectione,* » etc.

115 Roger of Wendover, t. III, p. 5 and, after him, Mathieu de Paris, t. III, p. 197.

116 Close rolls, 41, 7 r; Nantes, 16 June 1230 : « *Pro abbatissa de Cadame.* »

117 Ibid., 3 r; 16 September 1230 : « *Pro abbatissa de Cadame.* »

118 Numerous documents attest to the facilities accorded by Henry III to the people of these ports (*Bibliothèque de l'École des Chartes*, 1893, p. 27, note 2).

119 « *cum rege Anglorum Henryco fedus ineunt* » ; *Willelmi chronica Andrensis* (*Monumenta Germaniæ historica*, scriptores, XXIV, 770).

120 Philippe Mousket formally said that the Comte de Boulogne came with the royal army : verse 27988; it is in accord, on this point, with the chronicle of Saint-

Médard de Soissons : d'Achery, *Spicilegium*, ed. in-4°, t. II, p. 794.

121 « *Mais li rois et la roïne Blanche sa mère le desfendirent si bien que il l'en couvint raler en Engletière sans rians faire.* » Chronicon Hanoniense quod dicitur Balduini Avennensis (*Monumenta Germaniæ*, scriptores, XXV, p. 451).

During all the duration of the campaign, the English, whatever some might say, were never in possession of this city, which was from the very first the general headquarters of the King of France. The error was made by an English historian (*Flores historiarum*, ed. Luard, t. II, p. 199). The itinerary of Henry III belies this assertion.

122 *Willelmi chronica Andrensis* (*Monumenta Germaniæ historica*, scriptores, XXIV, p. 770); Archives nationales, KK 1064, fol. 272 V, and Du Chesne, *Histoire de la maison de Montmorency*, preuves, p. 92; *Layettes du Trésor des Chartes*, II, 2056.

123 Aubry de Trois-Fontaines, *Monumenta Germaniæ historica*, scriptores, XXIII, p. 926 : « *Nullus autem ita fideliter juvit regem Francic, sicut comes Campanie, ut dicitur, contra regem Anglie.* »

Charter of Thibaud : Archives nationales, KK 1064, fol. 279 V; d'Arbois de Jubainville, t. V, 2037; Charter of Ferrand; d'Arbois, 2037 bis : 8 June 1230.

124 Treaty of Clisson, 30 May 1230; *Layettes*, II, 2052.

125 Archives nationales, KK. 1064, fol. 272 V; Du Chesne, *Histoire de la maison de Montmorency*, preuves, p. 92; Clisson, 30 May 1230.

126 *Layettes*, II, 2008; June 1230.

127 *Layettes*, II, 2065; June 1230.

128 *Layettes*, II, 2053; Clisson, May 1230.

129 *Layettes*, II, 2060 : to the camp near Ponts-de-Cè, June 1230, charter of the Vicomte de Thouars; Archives nationales, JJ. 26, fol. 346 r, col. 2 ; charter of Louis IX.

130 *Layettes*, II, 2061; charter of the vicomte; Arch. nat., JJ. 26, 346 r, col. 1-2 ; charter of the King.

131 Guy de Thouars, *Layettes*, II, 2062.

132 *Layettes*, II, 2055, Thouars, May 1230.

133 *Layettes*, II, 2063; royal ratification.

134 *Layettes*, II, 2056.

135 Archives nationales, AA. 60, dossier 1544; vidimus of pieces relative to André de Vitré; fiftieth charter : in the camp before Ancenis, June 1230.

136 *Layettes*, II, 2057; Archives nationales, AA 60, 60th charter; *Layettes*, II, 2058; Archives nationales, JJ. 26, fol. 236 r, col. 1.

137 *Layettes*, II, 2059.

138 Among others Le Baud, *Histoire de Bretagne*, in-f°, 1638, p. 231, and *Chroniques de Vitré* (at the end of the same volume), p. 40.

139 In 1247, a parishioner of Saint-Jacques de Chinon complained about not having been paid for eight tons of wine which the steward of the King had purchased at a price of sixty livres, « *apud Ancenis in exercitu domini regis.* » The fact endorsed by this complaint shows without a doubt that it was June 1230. *Historiens de France*, t. XXIV, p. 193, n. 1131.

These two sieges have been recounted by Guillaume de Nangis, *Vie de saint Louis* (*Historiens de France*, XX, p. 318), *Chronique* (ed. Géraud, t. I, p. 180), and, following him, by the *Grandes chroniques de France*, called *Chroniques de*

Saint-Denis (ed. Paulin Paris, t. IV, p. 239), then by Guillaume Guiart. Roger of Wendover (ed. Hewlett, t. II. p. 384) speaks with disdain of this fight : « *quoddam debile municipium Hodum appellatum obsedit.* » Cf. Mathieu de Paris, ed. Luard, t. III, p. 195.

140 Letter of G. de Wulward to Raoul Nevil, Bishop of Chichester and Chancellor of England (Shirley, *Royal and other historical letters*, t. I, p. 377-378). Roger of Wendover, t. III, p. 1; Philippe Mousket, verse 27988; chronicle of Saint-Médard de Soissons (d'Achery, *Spicilegium*, in-4°. t. II, p. 794).

Cartulary of Philippe Auguste, Arch. nat., JJ. 26, fol. 207, n 145 bis.

141 Letter of G. de Wulward.

142 Ibid.

143 Patent rolls, 38, 6 in dorso ; Rymer, ed. of 1816, p. 196.

144 Letter of G. de Wulward; Patent rolls , 38, 6 r; 18 June 1230 : « *Pro Herveo de Volurio et aliis militibus, de eorum deliberatione.* » ; Hommage d'Hervé de Volvire, Rymer (1816), p. 197, after the Rolls of letters patent, 38, 6 in dorso.

145 Letter of G. de Wulward, Shirley, I, 177-178.

146 Geoffroy de Beauchamp to Henry III, Shirley, t. I, p. 367-368.

147 Roger of Wendover, ed. Hewlett, t. III, p. 6.

148 Shirley, *Royal and other historical letters*, t. I, p. 370-371; 8 June 1230.

149 Les préliminaires d'une invasion anglaise, etc. (*Bibliothèque de l'École des Chartes*, 1893, p. 32-33. One finds in this article an indication of documents relative to the negotiations between Henry III and the Poitevin barons.

150 *École des Chartes*, 1893, p. 33-35.

151 Les préliminaires d'une invasion, etc. (ibid., p. 35-36). I have demonstrated, in this article, that the town besieged by Henry III was likely Mirambeau, and not Mirebeau. The first idea for this rectification was suggested to me by Paul Guérin.

152 Public record office; Close rolls, 41, 6 r (lower); 21 July 1230 : « *Teste rege apud Mirebel.* » The King of England had reserves of arrowheads in Bordeaux, as in several other of his fortified places.

153 Patent rolls, 38, 4 r ; 26 July 1230 : « *Pro Bernardo de Royl.* ; » this baron is called Bernard de « Ryous » in the convocation of 21 July.

154 Roger of Wendover, III, 6, and, following him, Mathieu de Paris, *Chronica majora*, III, 198.

155 Close rolls, 41, 5 r : « *Pro Galfrido de Ranconio.* » – « *Teste rege apud Bleyve, secundo die augusti.* »

156 Les préliminaires d'une invasion, etc., p. 37.

157 Ibid., p. 38. I am not obliged to indicate here the English documents after which I have established, elsewhere, the succession of events.

158 *Layettes du Trésor des Chartes*, II, 2070; Saint-Maixent, July 1230.

159 Archives nationales, JJ 26, fol. 239 V, pièce 270; August 1230.

160 Close rolls, 41, 4 r.

161 Les préliminaires d'une invasion, etc., p. 38-39.

162 Shirley, *Royal and other historical letters*, t. I, p. 383-384.

163 Close rolls, 41, 6 r; 10 July 1230.

164 Close rolls, 41, 5 in dorso : « *Rex Petro duci Britannie,* » etc. Letter dated from Saint-Georges-des-Côteaux , 17 August, relating to the negotiation started on 15 August 1230.

165 Rymer, l, 198 ; 20 August 1230.
166 Close rolls, 41, 3 in dorso; 30 August 1230.
167 Close rolls, 41, 3 in dorso; 3 September 1230.
168 Rymer, I, 198; Luçon, 6 September 1230.
169 Close rolls, 4l, 2 in dorso; Nantes, 23 September.
170 Close rolls, 41, 3 r; 17 September 1230 : « *Pro vicecomite de Rohan.* » Ibid., 1 r; 14 October : « *Pro Henrico de Avaugor*; » mandate relative to the homage of the seigneur and the restitution of his fiefs; Close rolls, 42, 21 recto; 28 October : « *Pro Henrico de La Vagor.* »
171 *Willelmi chronica Andrensis* (*Monumenta Germaniæ*, t. XXIV, p. 770). Roger of Wendover, ed. Hewlet, t. III , p. 7, and, following him, Mathieu de Paris, *Chronica majora*, III, p. 199.
172 *Ex Walteri Gisburnensis cronica de gestis rerum Angliæ*; *Monumenta Germaniæ*, XXVIII, p. 632; letter from Henry III to Hugues de Lusignan : Shirley, *Royal letters*, t. I, p. 385; 29 September.
173 Patent rolls, 38, 3 r; Mareuil , to the north of Luçon, 6 September 1230 : « *De navibus.* »
174 Close rolls. 4l, 3 in dorso; 16 and 17 September.
175 Patent rolls, 38, 3 in dorso; 17 September : « *Rex ballivis portus de Sancto Maclovie,* » etc.
176 Patent rolls, 38, 3 iccto; 16 September : « *De navibus faciendis venire usque Sanclnm Gildasium.* » ; Shirley, I, p. 385.
177 Patent rolls, 38, 2 r; 2 octobre 1230 : « *De navibus faciendis venire usquo Sanctum Gildasium.* »
178 Patent rolls, 38, 3 r; 20 September 1230.
179 Shirley, I, p. 385 ; 29 September.
180 Patent rolls, 38, 3 r; 26 September 1230 : « *Pro comite Cestrie.* »
181 Patent rolls, 38, 3 r; 25 September : « *Pro comite Maroscalle.* »
182 Rymer, I, 198; 23 September; Roger of Wendover, III, 7; Mathieu de Paris, III, 199.
183 Rymer, 198; 27 September; Patent rolls. 38, 2 r; 8 octobre 1230 : « *De treugis capiendis.* »
184 Rymer, I, 198; 26 September 1230; letter of 8 October relative to the same subject, Patent rolls, 38, 2 r : « *Comes Britannie,* » On 10 March 1232, Henry III was still the debtor of Pierre Mauclerc; Patent rolls, 41, 8 r : « *De debito quod rex debet Petro comiti Britannie.* »
185 *Les préliminaires d'une invasion*, etc., p. 43-44. The route of Henry III after his departure from Brittany, such as I established in this article, must be corrected on two points. After erudite observations addressed by La Borderie to me, the locality of Saint-Pabu, about which the English documents speak on this occasion, is Pabu, at the gates of Guingamp and to the north of this city. As for the name of Saint-Tudual, mentioned by two letters of Henry III, it used to indicate Tréguier, thus named because of its patron and the term for its cathedral. Henry III remained there from 13 to 18 October 1230; La Borderie notices, not without reason, that the King of England would have had no reason to remain so long a time in the small village which today is named Saint-Tudual.
186 Shirley, *Royal Letters*, I, 386.
187 Ibid., 386-87.

188 *Gallia christiana*, t. IV, Preuves, col. 201.
189 Récits d'un ménestrel de Reims, n. 31; Willelmi chronica Andrensis (*Monumenta Germaniæ historica*, scriptores), t. XXIV, p. 770.
190 Aubry de Trois-Fontainos, *Monumenta Germaniæ historica*, t. XXIII, p. 929, ligne 35; Chronique rimée dite de Saint-Magloire (*Hist .de France*, t. XXII, p. 83).
191 *Layettes du Trésor des Chartes*, II, 206O, 28 July 1230; Petit, *Histoire des ducs de Bourgogne*, IV, catalogue, 1982, July 1230; Ibid., 1987, 30 July; Joinville (1874), n. 83.
192 D'Arbois de Jubainville, *Histoire des ducs et des comtes de Champagne*, t. V, catalogue, n. 2063.
193 The very complicated history of this war is so well-known that since the account that D'Arbois de Jubainville gave some time ago I decline to follow his account step by step. D'Arbois de Jubainville knew all the really important documents which relate to the fight of Thibaud de Champagne and the barons; he especially related the facts to their place and brought light to this chaos in the middle of which his precursors, Nain de Tillemont among others, were lost.
194 *Chronique de Sainte-Catherine du Mont* (*Historiens de France*, XXIII, p. 398); *Willelmi chronica Andrensis*, *Monumenta Germaniæ*, XXIV, p. 770; D'Arbois de Jubainville, IV, p. 243; Idem; *Récits d'un ménestrel de Reims*, 342-343; Aubry de Trois-Fontaines, *Monumenta Germaniæ historica*, XXIII, p. 926.
195 *Chronicon S. Medardi Suessionensis*, d'Achery, *Spicilegium*, ed. in-4°, t. II, p. 794.
196*Chronique de Sainte-Catherine du Mont*, loc. cit., Guillaume d'Andros, loc. cit.; *Le ménestrel de Reims*, n. 346; Roger of Wendover, t. III, p. 1 and 2; Mathieu de Paris, III, 190.
197*Le ménestrel de Reims*, n. 342-345; Idem, 345; *Chronique de S. Médard*, Achery, *Spicilegium*, in-4°, II, 795; *Chronique de Fécamp* (*Historiens de France*, t. XXIII, p. 429).
198The same ones.
199Roger of Wendover, III, p. 1-2, and, following him, Mathieu de Paris, III, p. 190. D'Arbois do Jubainville, t. IV, p. 245-246.
200 *Le ménestrel de Reims*, n. 346.
201 Roger of Wendover, t. III, p. 2, and Mathieu de Paris, t. III, p. 196.
202 D'Arbois de Jubainville, t. IV, p. 248.
203 Philippe Mousket, verse 27997; *Johannis Longi chronica Sancti Bertini* (*Monumenta Germaniæ*, scriptores, t. XXV, p. 836).
204 Dom Calmet, *Histoire de Lorraine*, t. IV, Preuves, col. 442. D'Arbois de Jubainville, t. V, n. 2053.
205 Joinville, ed. of 1874, n. 84; d'Arbois de Jubainville, t. IV, p. 248.
206 *Le ménestrel de Reims*, n. 348 ff; Joinville, n. 85.
207 *Le ménestrel de Reims*, n. 349-351.
208 Idem, 350-351 ; Philippe Mousket, verse 28007-28012.
209 Joinville, ed. of 1874, n. 86.
210 *Le ménestrel de Reims*, n. 343; *Chronique de Fécamp* (*Historiens de France*, t. XXIII, p. 429); d'Arbois de Jubainville, IV, 243, note.
211 *Mansiones et itinera* (*Historiens de France*, t. XXI, p. 409).
212 Philippe Mousket, y. 28015; Teulet, *Layettes*, II, 2227, act of January 1233,

making an allusion to the Peace of Compiègne.
213 Roger of Wendover, t. III, p. 7, and Mathieu de Paris, *Chronica majora*, t. III, p. 198-199.
214 *Chronique de Sainte-Catherine-du-Mont* (*Historiens de France*, XXIII, p. 398).
215 Bibliothèque nationale, 500 Colbert, vol. 26, fol. 266r-V; d'Arbois de Jubainville, catalogue, t. V, n. 2060. For all these negotiations, I take the opinion of D'Arbois de Jubainville, t. IV, p. 252-253.
216 *Layettes*, II, 2081; Arbois de Jubainville, t. V, catalog, 2073, 12 December 1230.
217 Aubry de Trois-Fontaines, *Monumenta Germaniæ*, scriptores, XXIII, 924; D'Arbois de Jubainville, V, n. 2072; 11 December 1230.
218 Idem, 2226; February 1233.
219 *Layettes*, II, 2084.
220 *Layettes*, II, 2083; Aubry de Trois-Fontainos, *Monumenta Germaniæ*, scriptores, XXIII, 927.
221 Close rolls, 42, 20 r (above); 15 November 1230 : « *De thesauro regis custodiendo apud Porecestre.* »
222 Close rolls, 42, 20 in dorso; mandate to Hugues de Saint-Philebert.
223 Close rolls, 42, 10 r; 10 June 1231 : « *De quarellis liberandis.* »
224 Closo rolls, 42, 16 in dorso; 3 mars 1231.
225 Ibid., 17 r; 13 February 1231 : « *Pro Hereberto filio Mathei.* »
226 Ibid., 17 r; 5 February 1231 : « *Pro comite Britannie, de mancriis de Ketelberghe et Netlestede.*»
227 Close rolls, 42, 15 in dorso; 15 April 1231 : letters to the baillies of Winchelsea and a great number of ports, to the Justiciar and to the Comte de Cornouailles.
228 *Annales de Oseneia* (*Annales monastici*, ed. Luard, IV, 72); Rymer, I, 199, 25 May 1231.
229 Roger of Wendover, III, 6, and following him, Mathieu de Paris, *Chronica majora*, III, 198.
230 Roger (III, p. 8), and Mathieu (III, p. 200).
231 D. Morice, *Histoire de Bretagne*, Preuves, t. I, col. 873; 31 January 1231.
232 *Layettes*, t. II, 2128; Athis-sur-Orge, March 1231; Ibid., 2129 : letters of Foulques Paynel; letters of the King on the same subject; Arch. nat., JJ 26, 236V.
233 Letters of Guiomar de Léon, May 1231 : *Layettes*, II, 2136; Letters of Henry d'Avaugour, May 1231; *Layettes*, 2135.
234 *Layettes*, II, 2139; Vincennes, June 1231.
235 Arch. nat., JJ. 26, 237 v°, col. 2; Paris, June 1231; Arch. nat., JJ., 237 V, col. 2, et 238 r, col. 1; Vincennes, June 1231, diplomas of Louis IX.
236 JJ. 26, 238 V, col. 1 ; Saint-Germain-en-Laye, August 1231.
237 Le Band, *Histoire de Bretagne*, p. 231.
238 Close rolls, 42, 8 r; 9 July 1231.
239 Aubry de Trois-Fontaines, *Monumenta Germaniæ*, scriptores, XXIII, 929.
240 *Historiens de France*, t. XXI, p. 220-226.
241 Jean d'Affricamps was seneschal of Carcassonne from 1236 to 1239; *Historiens de France*, t. XXIV, p. 368 j and note.
242 André du Chesne, *Histoire Généalogique de la maison de Montmorency*, p. 143, and Preuves, p. 93, extract from the obituary of the Abbot of Val.
243 *Historiens de France*, XXI, p. 223.

244 Roger of Wendover, t. III, p., 13; Mathieu de Paris, t. III, p. 204.
245 Rinaldi, Annales ecclesiastici, t. II, p. 50-51 ; Rodenberg, *Epistolæ Romanorum pontificum*, t. I, p. 353, n. 438; 25 April 1231; Annales de Dunstable, *Annales monastici*, ed. Luard, t. III, p. 127.
246 Roger of Wendover and Mathieu de Paris, loc. cit.
247 *Layettes*, II, 2141, 4 July 1231; in the camp near Saint-Aubin.
248 Arch. nat., JJ. 26, fol. 326 r; D. Morice, *Histoire de Bretagne*, Preuves, t. I , col. 875-876.
249 JJ. 26, fol. 326 i, col. 2; D. Morice, loc. cit.
250 Le Baud, *Histoire de Bretagne*, 1638, in-f°, p. 233.
251 *Layettes*, II, 2144; July 1231.
252 *Chroniques de S. Denis* or *Grandes chroniques de France* (*Historiens de France*, t. XXI, p. 106). Robert de Dreux being dead on 3 March 1234, his intervention, of which the Grandes chroniques speak, accords well with the events of 1231 and not those of 1234.
253 *E Mari Historiarum* (*Historiens de France*, t. XXIII, p. 108).
254 Copies of this false treaty are found in the Bibliothèque nationale : 1st Latin text, Brienne (Bretagne), 298, 3rd piece in volume, f ° 5 ; 2nd French text, De Camps, vol. 73, f° 47. D'Argentré had published it, and Le Nain de Tillemont demonstrated its falsity : *Histoire de S. Louis*, t. II, p. 104.
255 Rymer, ed. de 1816, I, p. 201; 16 January 1231, letter of Henry III to Pierre Mauclerc; Roger of Wendover, t. III, p. 13, and Mathieu de Paris, *Chronica majora*, t. III, p. 204; Layettes, II, 2151, August 1231; other letters of Amaury on the same subject, ibid., 2190, June 1232.
256 *Layettes*, II, 1713; July 1225.
257 Patent rolls, 39, 7 r; 22 January 1230 : « *De conductu comitis Pontifiensis.* »
258 Close rolls, 40, 5 r; 1 July 1230 : « *De navibus deliberandis.* »
259 Example of the treaty in the name of the Comte de Ponthieu; *Layettes*, II, 2121; Saint-Germain-en-Laye, March 1231; Letter of the King; Arch. nat. , JJ. 26, f° 183 r; Charters of the five guarantors, *Layettes*, II, 2122-2126; oaths of the nobles and towns; ibid., 2090-2120.

Chapter Five

End of the Regency

Accord re-established between the King and the Université. – Fortifications of Angers. – Death of the princes Jean and Philippe Dagobert. – The Queen opposes the marriage of the Count de Champagne and the daughter of Pierre Mauclerc. – Barons sustain the pretensions of the Queen of Cyprus to the succession of Champagne. – Death of Ferrand, Count of Flanders. – Death of Philippe Hurepel. – Blanche manages an accord between the Queen of Cyprus and Thibaud, who cedes to the King the tenure of Blois, Chartres, Sancerre, and Châteaudun. – Difficulty of Raimond VII; good will of the Queen to his consideration. – In vain she urges the Pope to render the marquisate of Provence to Raimond. – She reconciles the counts of Provence and Toulouse. – The King marries Marguerite de Provence. – Negotiations with Henry III. – Pierre Mauclerc and the Bretons. – Final expedition against Mauclerc; he submits. – New truce with the English. – Majority of Louis IX. – Intrigues of Thibaud de Champagne before the King of Navarre. – He gives his daughter to the son of Pierre Mauclerc and forms a coalition. – The King raises an army against him. – Submission and humiliation of Thibaud.

From 1231 to 1236 during the last years of the Regency and the commencement of the personal rule of Saint Louis, we see one after the other the resolution of almost all the problems which had been present since the death of Louis VIII. The violent hostility of the barons resolved itself little by little. Some died, as did Philippe de Boulogne; others finished by renouncing their resistance. Such was the case with the Count de Bretagne, who, after taking up arms at the expiration of the truce, finally recognized that the English alliance was not sufficient to assure him of an advantage. Henry III himself did not renew his grand attempt of 1230, which had piteously run aground; the war to which the English took part in 1234 was not the repeat of that which had been made in the previous invasion. Thibaud de Champagne, who remained for some time between active campaigning and intrigue, gave, in 1236, a new proof of infidelity, when he definitively renounced his role as vassal and less than grateful *protégé*. At the moment when these last plotters ended with a definite submission, Blanch no longer had the Regency; although one can say that this episode of the struggle against the great vassals still behooved her government. The transition was insensible between the moment when she stopped exercising sovereign power and the first acts by which she affirmed the activity of her son.

Of all the questions left unresolved at the time of the great troubles, that of the Université was first to be resolved. During the storms of the year 1230, the opposition of the Université was maintained, thanks to the grace and beneficence of the Holy See. The Pope, more favorable in this case, to his natural *protégés* than to their sovereign, had at first taken a real obstinacy to their defense. On 2 April 1230, while preserving, seemingly, provisions accommodating them, he had written Louis IX a letter scarcely encouraging, and a few weeks later he had enjoined the masters and scholars established in Paris and Angers to address envoys charged by him to settle their disagreement with the Crown; Guillaume of Auvergne, Bishop of Paris, and Chancellor Philippe de Grève, had also received their orders to go, for this purpose, to the court of Rome.[1] They finished by settling in the spring of 1231: while remaining rather firm, the Pope showed himself formally committed to conciliation; that is what a letter proves with Louis IX, dated 14 April, in which he affirms readiness to conclude all with amity.[2] It was true that at the same time he claimed the renewal of the privilege granted to the Université by Philippe Auguste, i.e., the establishment; an equitable tariff for the residences of the students, and finally the payment of authorized indemnities by the royal government.[3] On 18 April 1231, he ordered an investigation on the misdeeds charged to the leader and the inhabitants of Saint-Marcel, tasking the Archbishop of Rheims, the Bishop of Amiens and a third commissary to take care of the conservation of the privileges granted to the students.[4] About the same time, he mandated to the Abbot of Saint-Germain-des-Pres and to Guillaume d'Auvergne to force their men to act, in their reports on students, as the bourgeoisie of Paris were compelled to do by the royal decree.⁵ These letters show that consequently an agreement was concluded between the King and the Université. In the days which followed, Gregory IX took various intended measures to facilitate this reconciliation.⁶

The Université had to consider itself happy in finishing with an opposition without exit; it could, with rigor, be thankful for not having to capitulate. On another score, the Regent was certainly at ease with reconstituting this great center of studies to the profit of royalty, from whence science was spread by everyone, carrying to far distances the name and influence of France. Historians of Saint-Denis celebrated on this occasion the wisdom of Saint Louis; they wrote long enough after the events and did not reflect that the King of France was then seventeen years old, and that all was done by the authority of his mother.⁷

The reconciling intentions of the Regent were obvious; but, in spite of her good will, she still had too many enemies. The very provisional arrangement that she had just taken with the Count of Brittany and the English offered no safety. Pierre Mauclerc remained until the new order a declared enemy; Angers, of which the King had been rendered master, and which during the last war had been used as general headquarters of the French, was then, for the royal armies, an advanced station. Blanche of Castile took part in making it, against the Bretons and their allies overseas, an important place of arms.

All around this city, they raised a large flanking enclosure of towers; the old castle of the counts of Anjou was entirely transformed and became a redoubtable fortress that one sees, nowadays still, rising on the left bank of the Maine.⁸ It was necessary to upset many things to build it. Canons from Saint-Laud, on which the church was located on the site of the new castle, were transferred out of the walls; the majority of churches and religious establishments, which existed in number in the city, had to claim and obtain indemnities for the damage which had been caused to them, when they proceeded with the construction of the fortified enclosure and with the transformation of the castle.⁹ Two of these settlements are particularly curious. First, the abbot and the convent of Saint-Aubin admit having received from the King and his mother six hundred *livres tournois*, to their thinking a sum too paltry, in compensating wrongs that had been done to them: partial destruction of theirs vines and of their cemetery, on which was made to pass the trenchwork; demolition of several houses; employment, for construction of this enormous castle, materials borrowed from the walls of the convent, without counting the wood cut in the vicinity to the detriment of the abbey, and carts or barges that were torn apart to make frames.[10] The Bishop of Angers and his chapter, in their turn, recalled that two of their churches and several of their houses were destroyed; stone, lime, and beams prepared for the work of the cathedral were employed, by the royal agents, in the construction of ramparts; the Bishop and the canons claimed fifteen hundred *livres tournois* and obtained only nine hundred.[11] The King came to Angers to survey this great work, of which the execution was very expensive, since after all the expenditure made in 1232 one still finds the mention of it, in charters, two years later, and until 1262.[12] But the sacrifices that they made to ensure on the lower Loire and Maine a base for operations were nothing less than useless.

In waiting for the reprise of hostilities, previewed by the truce of 1231, Pierre de Dreux made a pretense more distant than ever for a definitive accord with the Crown. This same year 1232, during which they raised threatening works to the very gates of his domains, was marked by the death of he who, in one day of reconciliation, had been intended for his daughter, Yolande, Princess of Brittany. Born on 21 July 1219, Prince Jean de France, younger brother of Louis IX and Robert, elder of Alphonse and of Charles, indicated that summer, by the will of his father and the treaty of Vendôme, to hold in prerogative the counties of Anjou and Maine.[13] He was carried off at the age of thirteen years, in circumstances which are unknown to us, but certainly before the month of October, the time at which the general chapter of the order of Prémontré mentioned his very recent death, associating him in prayers that they had already promised to the royal family.[14] A historian of the time affirms that another son of Blanche, Philippe Dagobert, died the same year;[15] but this assertion should be allowed only under some reservation: Philippe Dagobert, born on 20 February 1222, is perhaps indicated in one account of May 1234.[16] He was buried in the church of Royaumont, where his epitaph was still visible in the seventeenth century.[17] It is hardly as if history preserved the memory of this double mourning, which had to reach Blanche of Castile cruelly; in the middle of the struggles that she had to support, these intimate events, even most painful, have passed almost unperceived.

All had changed since Blanche had wanted to ensure the alliance of the Count of Brittany with a marriage, and several years before prince Jean died, or had had to give up the idea to make him marry Yolande de Dreux. Pierre Mauclerc thought well of marrying his daughter, but that was to cause the Regent new embarrassments. During the summer of 1231, the Count de Champagne had lost his second wife, Agnès de Beaujeu; the inconstant mood of Thibaud was well-known; by a sudden transfer, his enemies, forgetting hatreds and violence of the day before, resolved to attract him to their party. Yolande was to be used as a pledge in this reconciliation, and they thought, with reason, that as of the first months of 1232 Champagne had accepted the idea of marriage.[18] This new intrigue of the dissatisfied was too contrary to the interests of the Crown for Blanche of Castile to let it succeed; it was undoubtedly with her prayer that on 24 April Gregory IX wrote to Simon, Archbishop of Bourges, to prohibit, due to incorrect consanguinity, the marriage projected between Thibaud and Yolande; on 4 June, the Archbishop noticed this decision to the Count de Champagne.[19] At the same time Blanche acted, according to her practice, with vigor. Parents of Pierre Mauclerc, and princes of the house of Dreux, who witnessed this unexpected amity between the Count of Brittany and Thibaud IV, brought the young princess to the abbey of Valsecret, of the order of Prémontré, which is close to Château-Thierry; Thibaud had just left this city to go to join his betrothed, when Geoffroy de La Chappelle came to find him on behalf of the King: "Lord Count de Champagne," said he to him, "the King learns that you are agreed with the Count of Brittany to take his daughter in marriage. The King commands you to do nothing, if you want to lose all that you have in the kingdom of France, because you know that the Count of Brittany was made worse off than any man who lives." Thibaud took the opinion of his people, reversed and returned to Château-Thierry. The blow had been averted.[20]

Pierre Mauclerc could seek another husband for his daughter; although it was not scruples which obstructed him. It is about certain that in this same moment he was in talks with the King of England to marry Yolande. Henry III himself alerts us, by a letter to the Count de Bretagne, dated 20 July 1232, that Mauclerc, after having promised him his daughter, stated the ability to hand her over before Michaelmas (29 September).[21] The adversaries of the Regent pursued a quite tortuous policy; Blanche had sufficient uprightness and practical sense to show them up.

Thibaud soon took his part in the sacrifice imposed on him by his protector. As of 22 September, he married Marguerite, daughter of

Archambaud de Bourbon.[22] This heiress was not from as noble a family as the Breton one, but she brought in a dowry of thirty six thousand *livres parisis*, a considerable sum for the time. Archambaud was elsewhere well known for his fidelity towards the King; the barons did not forgive Thibaud for having once more given up.

They still fought by diverted means. At the time of their great coalition against Champagne, the princes of Dreux, Philippe Hurepel and their allies had forced the claims of Alix, Queen of Cyprus, to the Champagne succession. This time they made Alix travel west; after leaving the Holy Land before the end of the year, she left Genoa, in January 1233, to go to France.[23] Her arrival could cause the Count de Champagne very serious embarrassment. Vassals of Champagne were not all in perfect fidelity of course, and perhaps there was the ulterior motive to have the King and his mother recognize rights that were allotted to the Queen of Cyprus. This was certainly, a quite chimerical hope. Furthermore, Champagne had in this business one powerful defender.

The Holy See, with various arguments, had refused to take seriously the claims of Alix and her sister Philippine, Lady of Brienne, as long as the legitimacy of their birth would not have been proclaimed in the court of Rome. Gregory IX, faithful to the traditions of his government, opposed, in this serious circumstance, what he regarded as an encroachment on the rights of the Church. On 16 April 1233 he wrote Ferrand, Count of Flanders, ordering him not to take part in any judgment that Louis IX and Blanche of Castile would like to pronounce, at the request of Alix, on the Champagne succession, before the Holy See had judged if the Queen of Cyprus was legitimate. While waiting, he prohibited Ferrand from giving her council, assistance or protection.[24] At the same time Gregory addressed in terms similar to Louis IX, the Archbishop of Sens, Count de Saint-Pol, the bishops of Langres, Laon, Châlons-sur-Marne, and Chartres.[25] Having learned that several nobles, vassals of Thibaud, threatened to recognize Alix, he gave the responsibility to commissaries to excommunicate them, if they carried out this project. Thus it was that the Church condemned the future of the Queen of Cyprus in homage due to the Count de Champagne; during the months April and May this prohibition was communicated by the Pope to the Count de Bar, Count de Châlon-sur-saône, Mathieu, Duke of Lorraine, Marguerite la Noire, Lady of Dampierre and sister of the countess of Flanders, the counts de Chiny, Chartres, and Nevers.[26]

One must admire the rigorous and sure method with which the court of Rome proceeded on this occasion, as in all those where its legal prerogatives could be threatened. While taking the necessary measures to prevent anybody from pre-empting his decision, Gregory IX launched in France and in the Holy Land a double investigation into the rights of the Queen of Cyprus;[27] he ordered the Abbots of Chézy, Saint-Jean-de-Vignes and Valsecret to invite Alix to appear before them to judge if she was legitimate; he ordered them to oppose, by ecclesiastical censure, so that her claims were discussed before the Holy See to solve this question of legitimacy.[28] On 24 June the three abbots, pursuant to the apostolic mandate, wrote to the abbots of Nesle and of Saint-Sauveur de Vertus to command Alix to present herself at the court of Rome, personally or by prosecutor, to plead against Thibaud de Champagne.[29] Lastly, on 31 July, the Abbot of Nesle informed them that the day before, at Château-Landon, he cited the Queen of Cyprus to appear before the Pope in the following February.[30]

The support of the Holy See was much more useful for the Count de Champagne, when in this moment he lost one of his best allies. Ferrand of Portugal died of the stone, in Noyon, on 27 July 1233. They brought his body back to Flanders, and it was buried in the abbey of Inlays, which his wife had founded.[31] This death, in the circumstances where it arrived, was a significant event; Ferrand was a powerful prince and a valiant man; recall his fight against Philippe Auguste and his long captivity, with all that happened, leaving little resentment; in any case, since his delivery, he was constantly shown faithful to Blanche of Castile and her son. In more serious moments, he had courageously held the party of the King, not hesitating to throw himself over the estates of those who attacked the Count de Champagne. In the event of war, Thibaud could no longer count on a diversion of the Flemings; it is true that his situation could hardly be compared with that in which it was found three or four years earlier. In 1233, there were undoubtedly hostilities out of Champagne, but the fight was neither general nor violent. The Count had to repress isolated revolts; we know that his faithful subjects had orders to assemble with weapons, on 28 August, at Montéclair, and to bring supplies for one month; that was undoubtedly when Thibaud besieged Nogent-in-Bassigny.[32] Nothing shows that the great vassals at this time made a new attack against Champagne. The Pope always held to the same line; in the month of October, his commissaries delegated in

Champagne took new measures against the Queen of Cyprus, who was once more cited in court of Rome the following summer.[33]

The enemies of the Count de Champagne could no longer claim to strip her, and all efforts tried in favor of Alix intended to make him obtain as strong an indemnity as possible. The Count of Boulogne was, of all his partisans, most powerful and most stubborn; that is to say he still believed in the poisoning of Louis VIII, preserved resentment against Thibaud IV, had always continued in his hatred, and remained until the end at the head of those who sought to defeat him. But his enmity was not to appear anymore than in the negotiations. He prevented the Queen of Cyprus from accepting advantageous conditions, when Thibaud offered 8,000 pounds worth of land and 20,000 *livres tournois*.[34] Alix had soon to repent for having refused this proposal.

At the beginning of 1234, towards 18 January, Philippe Hurepel died; he was buried in Saint-Denis, near his father, King Philippe Auguste.[35] Some did not fail to say that he had been poisoned, and the gossip even ran that this sudden death was the work of the Count de Champagne.[36] Thibaud IV had to be more at ease to see his adversary disappear, but all that was said obviously came from the bias that persons had to calumniate him. The chronicler Philippe Mousket affirms that all France cried for the Count de Boulogne; to tell the truth, I do not see what the country could lose with this death; another historian, worthier of faith, restricted himself to recall that Philippe Hurepel left as monuments of his power the castles with which he had covered his domains in the country of France, in Normandy, and Boulogne.[37] As for the legend that claims he was killed in a tournament, it does not deserve to be refuted.[38] The son of Agnes de Méranie had been for Louis VIII a devoted brother, but during difficult years of the regency he was shown to be extremely ambitious and wild, inconstant, not very faithful to Blanche, to the King his nephew, for whom he was however the natural guardian. With him disappeared a house which would have become threatening, had he lived longer. Soon after his death, Countess Mahaut of Boulogne made homage to the King, promised to give her fortresses to him upon any requisition; she promised at the same time to deliver to Louis IX, for ten years, the fortified towns of Calais and Boulogne, and to lend him as his vassal, the people of her communes and towns, with oaths guaranteeing their fidelity.[39]

Another enemy of Thibaud IV, the Archbishop of Lyon,

Robert d'Auvergne, had died on 6 January.[40] On 5 March, Count Robert de Dreux disappeared in his turn.[41] The coalition of 1229 and 1230 existed no more. In April, the Duke of Burgundy, who refused to engage himself with Louis IX to remain at peace with Champagne, had to make towards his sovereign an act of obeisance and of atonement.[42] A few days later, he who at one time was seen threatened with ruin ascended the throne of Navarre. King Sancho VII, uncle of Thibaud, having died on 7 April 1234, the Count hastened to go beyond the Pyrenees to collect his heritage, a throne and a fortune that was said to be extremely large. While his patrimonial fiefs were entrusted to the guardianship of the King of France, he made his entry to Pamplona and was crowned King of Navarre.[43] What could the imprudent Queen of Cyprus henceforth plan against him? Those with whom he had compromised had died or been reduced to impotence; the rights of his happy relative was supported by the Pope; the time of proud claims had passed; Alix could not depend any more but on the mediation of the Regent.

Negotiations undertaken in the name of the King to finally regulate the succession of Champagne are attested in the accounts of the year 1234; at that time Louis IX and his mother were in frequent communications with Champagne, when they made the Queen of Cyprus come to conferences, and we know the amount of the expenses allocated to those who several times brought her to the court.[44] But the desire to arrange all did not authorize Alix to have grand illusions; when she went, after death of Philippe Hurepel, to the interview which had been assigned to her, she saw how much her situation had been impaired.[45] They did not offer her any more than modest conditions; she was made to accept them.

In September, the Queen of Cyprus renounced in the presence of Louis IX, all the rights that she could have in the counties of Champagne and Brie, and invested these rights in the father-in-law of Thibaud, Archambaud de Bourbon. The Count paid for this renunciation by giving her 2,000 *livres* rent and 40,000 *livres tournois* payable in cash. He declared that if he died before he had ensured his cousin the 2,000 *livres* rent, the King was to proceed to this assignment. As for the 40,000 *livres*, which the representatives left in France by the new King of Navarre did not have at their disposal, they asked the King who, in exchange, was given tenure in the counties of Blois, Chartres, Sancerre, and the viscounty of Châteaudun.[46] This transfer was approved, two months later, by the Queen of Cyprus, and, on 11 November, Alix gave a receipt to the King for the sum which had been paid to her.[47]

By this negotiation Blanche put an end to the ventures of *les grands* against the Count de Champagne and removed any pretext for them to fight him. At this time the royal authority had made a notable progress, since from now on the counties of Blois, Chartres, and Sancerre, and the Viscounty of Châteaudun, did not raise more [money] than the Crown. The holders of these four fiefs no longer had anything on Thibaud; it was in the royal army that their troops had to fight, if ever the Count de Champagne was advised to revolt.

Successes of Blanche of Castile, in her fight against great vassals, were due partly to the isolation, to the irremediable weakening to which the feudality of the Midi was reduced. The Count de Toulouse himself, exhausted by war of the Albigensians, would have played too large a game if he had assayed to plot against the Regent with adversaries more or less declared against royalty. Since the peace of 1229, it was royalty which made the law on the edges of the Garonne, to the west of the Rhone and along the Mediterranean. The authority of Louis IX was well established in lower Languedoc, in the two seneschalsies of Beaucaire and of Nimes, Carcassonne and Béziers; this new part of the domain was regularly managed by royal seneschals, at the side of whom one finds the lieutenants of the King, Adam de Milly, then Eudes le Queux.[48] It is true that the occupation of the country and the exercise of the sovereign power involved duties and pressures: thus it is seen the Archbishop of Arles claiming the King owed money to him because of the castle of Beaucaire, pledged by his predecessor Simon de Montfort; the Archbishop complained to the King, holder of this castle for three years, having not paid anything, and requested the Pope support his complaint (*bulla* of 11 May 1230).[49] The power of the King was extremely great in the fiefs freed from the former masters of the countryside, and which were one day to fall to the Crown. Blanche of Castile could not forget the succession of the house of Saint-Gilles was mainly reserved for her son Alphonse. As of 26 April 1230, this young prince appears in a charter of the Bishop of Puy as heir apparent to the Count de Toulouse.[50] But if the one wanted to draw real advantages from the situation that the treaty of Paris had created for the house of France, it was necessary to do something to finally return prosperity to these countries, so cruelly tested by the war.

The Pope was preoccupied with restoring order there, but he

did it in his manner, by completing the extirpation of heresy. During the last years of the regency, he was represented in Languedoc by three legates, Pierre de Collemezzo, Gautier, Bishop of Tournay, Jean de Bernin, Archbishop of Vienne. The Count de Toulouse, by signing the peace, had undertaken serious engagements with regard to the Church, and Gregory IX did not have enough confidence in him to abstain from supervising and observing.

Blanche of Castile did not absolutely trust the Count de Toulouse; she was however not hostile to him, quite the contrary. Raimond VII was her close relative; she never forgot this. That did not prevent her from benefiting, for royalty, from the distress into which the civil war had thrown Languedoc. In this respect, she led Raimond VII, as with Thibaud de Champagne, as with Ferrand of Portugal, as a skilful Queen, without ceasing to be in a good relationship. Thibaud, son of her cousin Blanche of Navarre, had never been treated by her with rigor, even shortly after the least forgivable faults; always let him return, recalled him to duty, delivered him in the most critical moments, and all the while he was known to be not very faithful. It is true that in revenge the Queen supported him to resist the barons, and that in exchange for a pecuniary help she took him in again. At the beginning of the reign, Ferrand of Portugal did not seem to be quite a serious ally; but he was a relative of Blanche, he had had as a sister-in-law the sister of the Regent, and Blanche did not give up on his misfortune; she freed him from prison and Ferrand recompensed her; from 1227 to 1233, he was for her a very useful auxiliary. In the same way, she knew her cousin Toulouse enough not to allow herself any grand illusions, she never ceased making very serious efforts to finally ensure a tolerable situation for him.

Raimond VII, since his reconciliation with the court, had remained in a state of serious difficulties. He had opposite him the Church, sometimes benevolent, more often wary and severe. Languedoc was deeply disturbed, and there was an exaggerated tendency to make only Raimond responsible for all the violence, for all the infringements upon the engagements for peace that had been imposed on him. How could inhabitants of these unhappy countries soon forget the massacres, spoliations, prisons and butcheries, the bitterness of their defeats and the regret of their old prosperity, their autonomy, about the furies of 1209? Those who had accepted the mission to ensure in the fiefs of Raimond VII a final triumph of the

Catholic faith knew of course on which feelings they had the right to count; also the cardinal Romain, upon returning to the Pope, had considered it to be necessary to carry the parts relative to his investigation into heresy; they feared revenge, if the witnesses who had deposed in this business would come to be known. Since the peace, several of those who continued as heretics had been killed, and perhaps Guillaume de Puylaurens does not see a partial truth when he allots these violences to the desire that some people had to relight the war to benefit from disorder; for all that, he was to have even more resentment there than interested calculations. Raimond, who was not pressed to punish the culprits, was shown to be tepid before the Pope and the King. Bishop Folquet de Toulouse took his side and declared himself ready to take again the way of exile.[51] He could, as it appears, circulate without being made to be accompanied by armed men.[52] What were these objections, in comparison to atrocities which the Midi had just undergone during twenty years? Blanche of Castile and the Pope himself, realizing reality, sought appeasing.

In May 1230 the King, which is to say his mother, defended the Bishop of Cahors and allowed him to perturb Raimond VII about donations formerly made by the counts of Montfort and revoked since the peace of Paris.[53] At the same time, Gregory IX gave to the Count de Toulouse an undeniable proof of leniency. Raimond had promised to pay, in form of indemnities, 10,000 *marcs* to the churches, 4,000 to the abbots of Cîteaux, Clairvaux and others, 6,000 to the King, to put in defense the Château-Narbonnese, citadel of Toulouse, and other fortified towns. These 20,000 *marcs* were to be paid in four years, at a rate of 5,000 per year. Moreover, Raimond VII had taken the cross to spend five years in the Holy Land. He wrote to the Pope to ask deferments, pleading difficulties of his situation, and the exhaustion of the country. Gregory IX, appreciating an act of sincere devotion, informed the legate Pierre de Collemezzo that he had granted to the Count a delay in the payment of 10,000 *marcs*. As for his departure for the crusade, the legate inquired about provisions which animated the King and Blanche, to take in this respect the opinion of the prelates, the barons, and to refer it to the Holy See (9 July 1230).[54] Raimond VII had to be satisfied when a letter from Gregory IX, dated the same day, made known to him these benevolent provisions.[55] On 22 September, the Pope charged the Archbishop of Sens, the bishops of Paris and Chartres, to take information about the requests addressed by Raimond VII.[56] The legate Romain having at one time granted the Count permission to be given, for the sums that he had to pay, an assistance to levying on people of the churches, Raimond solicited authorization to raise taxes; he requested the Pope not to grant leave for the prelates to oppose the execution of this measure, and Gregory IX granted his request (letters of 13 and 25 September 1230).[57] At the same time the Pope wrote to the legate to examine himself, without leaving them to go further, lawsuits that they would have brought against the Count de Toulouse based on apostolic letters.[58]

Raimond VII made a point of giving a burial to a Christian woman with her father, who had been buried outside of holy ground: the Pope prescribed to his legate, to the Bishop of Toulouse and to the Abbot of Grandselve, to make an investigation on this subject.[59] Before this time he was concerned to restore harmony between the Count and his wife Sanche of Aragon. All of these measures proved dispositions which had nothing of hostility, and the situation of Raimond would have been good, if he had not had to consider the head of the Church and the Queen of France.[60]

But the clergy of the Midi did not disarm. It was on his request that in 1231 Gregory IX sent to Languedoc a new envoy, Gautier, Bishop of Tournay.[61] The successor of Pierre de Collemezzo was not yet in the country, when the Pope, returning with severity, wrote to him; to oblige, it was necessary for the Count de Toulouse to pay money, under the terms of the Treaty of Paris, to the abbey of Cîteaux and other religious establishments (2 January 1231).[62] Arriving at the end of March, Gautier started by assigning to Castelnaudary those who had to deposit complaints against the Count. Raimond answered this measure while promising to give satisfaction if possible.[63] In spite of that; the legate appears to have continued to be hard, because it was needed; at the beginning of the following year the Pope recommended to him to treat the Count de Toulouse with softness and not to let the prelates mistreat him, who had perforce too much eagerness to excommunicate him.[64] On 12 March 1232, Gregory IX wrote to his legate to preserve intact the rights of the Count.[65] Raimond VII made a zealous show with the Bishop of Toulouse hunting for heretics, then relapsed into indifference.[66] Bishop Folquet had died at Christmas, but his disappearance had not changed the feelings of the clergy in Languedoc or Provence. Shown by the legate, by the Archbishop of Arles and several bishops, not to carry out the peace of Paris well enough, Raimond had to appear in Melun before King. It was decided he would amend his wrongs on an investigation by the new Bishop of Toulouse and a knight that Louis IX would send. Gilles de Flagy left for the Midi, charged with a double mission: after having been to see the young princess in Provence whom her sovereign was soon going to marry, he went to Toulouse; there Raimond VII, in his presence, in front of the legate, the seneschal of Carcassonne and several barons, published, about heresy and its repression, the statutes which were carried by the seneschal of Carcassonne to be applied in his seneschalsy, and by Gilles de Flagy to be submitted to the King (20 April 1233).[67] At the same time the Pope, by a measure which was to have the most serious consequences, charged the Dominicans with proceeding against heretics in Toulouse and the remainder of the kingdom, especially in the ecclesiastical provinces of Bourges, Bordeaux, Narbonne, Auch, Vienne, Arles, Aix, and Embrun, that is to say, in the old Gaule Narbonnese and in all Aquitaine. The inquisition was consequently made into a regular jurisdiction.[68]

While Raimond VII, in spite of his apparent reconciliation with the Church, remained under the most irritating of surveillance, Blanche of Castile endeavored to render service to him.

The marquisate of Provence, that the peace of 1229 had removed from the Count de Toulouse to give to the Holy See, had been placed under the guardianship of the King by the legate. Yielding probably to requests of her cousin, Blanche wrote Gregory IX and made him write the King to give Raimond possession of this great fief. Gregory IX answered, on 4 March 1232, by two distinct letters, but at bottom identical, to the King of France and his mother. He protested that the Holy See had no desire to preserve for its own use the marquisate; but order was only imperfectly restored; religious pacification of the country was still not very solid. So well disposed towards Raimond VII, the Pope could not then yield the request which was expressed to him. He ordered the legate of the Holy See to gather the high clergy of the country to take opinion on the appropriateness of restitution.[69] Raimond accepted at the same time a letter of the Pope conceived in the same sense.[70] This question of the marquisate became complicated with difficulties born of the war that were made to the Count de Toulouse, combined with the town of Marseilles, and the Count de Provence.

In 1234, Gregory IX, having for some time given for successor the Bishop of Tournay, as legate, the Archbishop of Vienne, Jean de Bernin, showed himself again favorable to Raimond VII; on

13 January, he formally recommended him, with the other Archbishops and the bishops of "province."[71] Raimond had at the proper time believed himself renewed among the authorities about the marquisate, but he only obtained an evasive answer.[72] Blanche of Castile had to be dissatisfied to see that her steps remained without effect. In March, while Raimond was in Lorris, at the court of France, she wrote to the Pope, in the name of her son, a new letter in which Louis IX recalled his preceding complaint: Jeanne de Toulouse, sole heiress of Raimond VII, was intended to the brother of the King; it was thus a personal service that the King of France wanted from the Pope when he pressed to return the marquisate to the Count de Toulouse. As for the repression of heresy, the King knew, from the clergy of the country, that Raimond showed much vigilance; finally, on the opinion of his council Louis resolved to make this news tentative.[73] At the same time he informed the Pope that he could not preserve any more in his hand the domains located beyond the Rhone, entrusted to its guardianship by his "very dear friend" Cardinal Romain.[74]

Raimond VII did not obtain anything yet, but the moment when the King of France withdrew from the marquisate his officers, it seemed difficult that this country did not end up falling one day or the other into the hands of its former lord. At first, Raimond was not hasty; when, in the current year, Frederick II allied with the Pope against the Romans, the Count went to join the army of the Church in Italy.[75] But soon he changed roles, and addressing himself directly to the Emperor, he obtained from him, in September 1234, the restitution of Venaissin.[76] Perhaps the Pope had good reasons not to give up this country as long as heresy there was not extinct, but, in the interest of the Church, he had undoubtedly done better to return it to the Count de Toulouse, when Blanche of Castile took it urgently; he never obtained guardianship taken again by the King, and soon it was the Count de Toulouse and the representative of the Emperor who were made to submit.

The good will of Blanche of Castile with regard to Raimond VII did not contradict him. He had in March 1234, a new proof. Being then at the court of France, he felt grieved for, during several years, possessions he had lost, in his fiefs and against his will, by many prelates and religious establishments. The King, seeing validity in his request, wrote to the secular clergy and to the monks of Languedoc to enjoin them to release that which was taken; he gave them one year to carry this out, as from the moment when the Count would have required them, and prohibited them in the future from similar usurpations.[77] On the other hand, the Pope, not very satisfied with the support that Raimond found from Louis IX and Blanche, protested, in the month of May, against the control of the royal agents that he alleged to oppress the Albigensian churches and clergy. He noted in this respect an investigation made jointly by the Archbishop of Vienne, legate of the Holy See, and by a royal envoy.[78] Blanche had consequently to accustom herself to these recriminations, unceasingly renewed, from the court of Rome against the more or less apparent injustices of the bailiffs and the seneschals. I do not know if she answered Gregory IX at this time, but it is to be supposed that in her desire to please the Pope it did not make her change anything in the system of government that she had established in the Midi.

While treating the Count de Toulouse with much benevolence, she continued to gain ground in the valley of the Rhône. Domains of the Crown extended now until Beaucaire; but this great progress was not enough for the Regent; it went further, and despite being unable to conquer the kingdom of Arles, she definitively made the influence her dynasty prevail there. In 1234, she caused to marry Louis IX the oldest daughter of the Count de Provence; this union was not celebrated yet when the King, chosen for referee between the man who was going to be his father-in-law and the Count de Toulouse, restored peace in this area, which nominally paid homage to another sovereign.

The kingdom of Arles, subjected for two centuries to the authority of the emperors, was so well regarded as foreign land by the inhabitants of our country, that in 1226, at the time of the siege of Avignon, the barons joined together under the royal banner had solemnly affirmed, in a letter to Frederick II, rights of the Empire to this city. It thus seemed that French royalty had to remain absolutely indifferent to the war that the Count de Toulouse and the Marseillais made since 1230 with the Count de Provence, Raimond Berenger: but Blanche of Castile, who wanted to marry her son off, had conceived the thought to give him as a wife one from Provence. When this project was carried out, the emperors actually ceased dominating between the Rhône and the Alps, and the kings of France, without putting themselves absolutely in their place, for a long time not the masters of the country, dominated their policy. We had not possessed Provence until the end of the fifteenth century, but in the middle of the thirteenth, and thanks to Blanche of Castile, the Provençaux were more than allies for France.

Louis IX was only nineteen years old, when in 1233 his mother occupied herself with finding a wife for him. One of the biographers of the King says in all seriousness that she resolved to marry him off, not to satisfy his instincts, but to have children.[79] She acted indeed to ensure heirs to the Crown of France, and Louis was not treated differently than ordinary young sovereigns; only it is probable that the initiative, in this case as in so many others, belonged to Blanche. She had the care, elsewhere, to consult great persons and barons who surrounded her.[80] The princess on whom her choice was fixed was Marguerite de Provence.

The Count de Provence, Raimond Bérenger, had four daughters, Marguerite, Aliénor, Sanche, and Béatrix, who all were intended to become queens. Extremely powerful by himself, allied by his wife Béatrix to the ambitious house of Savoy, he concerned the Empire, but shared enough rare circumstances, his duties of vassal towards Frederick II were well in agreement with a state of almost total independence. As for the daughters that were sought then for the King of France, they were young and beautiful, very pious and educated.[81] Before taking action pursuant with her project, Blanche, in 1233, charged Gilles de Flagy to proceed to Languedoc, to pass through Provence to negotiate about Marguerite; the negotiation succeeded, and Raimond Berenger hastened to accept the offer which was made to him.[82] As his daughter was, by the house of Castile, cousin of the King of France, and they sent a request to the Pope for an exemption that he granted without difficulty.[83]

The Count de Provence could not be any more for Blanche than a foreigner, and like another example she held a sincere interest in her cousin Raimond de Toulouse, and quite naturally employed herself in giving an accord. The papal legate worked, from his side, on this work of peace, and on 13 February 1234 Raimond Berenger accepted the arbitration of Louis IX and his mother; he promised to carry out the conditions which would be imposed on him, as soon as his daughter would have married the King; Raimond VII followed his example.[84] Gautier Cornu, Archbishop of Sens, and Jean de Nesle went to seek in Provence the young princess, who came to the court, accompanied by her uncle Guillaume, elected Bishop of Valence.[85] She undoubtedly had a numerous retinue; in any case royal accounts speak on this occasion of a minstrel of the Count de Provence and of six trumpets, come with Marguerite.[86] Going towards Sens, the fiancée of the King stopped, on 19 May, at the abbey of Tournus.[87] At the same time, Louis IX came from Paris, by Fontainebleau, Pont-sur-Yonne and the abbey of Sainte-Columbe near Sens.[88] He had with him his mother, his brothers Robert and Alphonse, his cousin Alphonse of Portugal, nephew of Blanche, and who was raised with the young princes. Other children of Blanche of Castile, Isabelle and Charles, had remained in Paris.[89] In addition to the ladies of her house, the Queen had certainly with her a very great number; officers and great lords: *chambrier* of France, Barthelemy de Roye, the chamberlain Jean de Beaumont, Ferry Pâté, later marshal, are named, in connection with the marriage of the King, in the accounts of the hotel, like Raimond of Toulouse and the Jeanne countess of Flanders.[90] To transport her household, the Queen hired out, according to the use, boats and horses.[91]

The court was in Sens from 26 to 28 May 1234, and the marriage was probably celebrated the 27th; in any case, it was on this date that Louis IX settled the dowry of Marguerite, in a charter where he speaks of her as already being his wife.[92] Though at that time royal household expenses were not exaggerated, Blanche and her son deployed on this solemn occasion a fitting luxury: accounts of the household mention a crown made for the young Queen, a "*chapeau d'or*" adjusted for her use, two spoons and a gold cup, certainly intended for the royal table; the cup was given to the *bouteiller* of France.[93] They returned to the state the crown of the King, and jewels were bought from the goldsmith of the Countess of Flanders.[94]

One could make a long list if one wanted to enumerate the vestments, bed linen, objects of any kind that Blanche bought for the marriage of her son, robes for the King, those which were intended for the officers and great lords of the court, Prince Robert, Prince Alphonse, with their cousin the prince of Portugal, the Count de Toulouse, furs bought for the young Queen or given to the ladies of court.[95] Among the robes distributed for coronation, many were of silk and several were purple; these were distributed, according to custom, to those who were knighted on the occasion of the royal marriage.[96] The Queen prepared residences for the court in Sens, and by her order a house had been retained for the Countess of Flanders.[97] The city could undoubtedly not lodge all those who had accompanied the King, but tents had been brought.[98] They raised on high a house of branches (*feuillée*), of which the destination was not indicated in the accounts and which contained, for the use of the King, a throne covered with silk.[99] There perhaps was the venue for the minstrels, of which several belonged to the entourage of Prince Robert.[100] Finally, scaffolding was built in front of Saint-Etienne church, where the coronation of Marguerite was to take place.[101]

Several men of the court had been sent ahead of the princess; when she approached, the King, Blanche and the princes went to the meeting.[102] Shortly after the marriage, the young Queen was crowned by the Archbishop of Sens, who administered holy oil.[103] The Archbishop of Rheims, Henri de Dreux, had not followed the court; he could only be astonished by the preference which Blanche had given to Sens, and the Queen had not obeyed reasons of a secondary order when she decided that her daughter-in-law would not be crowned in Rheims. Henri de Dreux was the brother of the Count de Bretagne; in the disorders that transpired, he had been combined with barons leagued against Thibaud de Champagne, and in this moment he even declared opposition to the King by supporting against him the Bishop of Beauvais. On the contrary, the Archbishop of Sens, like all members of his family, was the devoted servant of the Crown.

Charity was not forgotten in the middle of these rejoicings consecrated to the happiness of princes. The sick were brought before the King, who distributed money to them; one poor fellow, whose horse had been killed during the festivities, accepted an indemnity.[104] The court took again the road to Paris, undoubtedly as of 29 May, by Montereau-faut-Yonne and Fontainebleau.[105] Marguerite had received in dowry the city of Mans and its environs, with Mortagne and Mauve-sur-Huisne.[106] Her dowry was 10,000 *marcs*, a very high sum, which perhaps was never entirely paid, because I know that in 1266 8,000 *marcs* were still due to Saint Louis by the fact of his marriage.[107] It is probably in guarantee of this payment that the Count and the Countess of Provence had engaged with the King the castle of Tarascon, in promising to make approval of this act by the Emperor.[108] Thus, the marriage of Louis IX came to conclude for royalty an immediate advantage; three months were hardly past when Count Raimond Bérenger, won over to the French policy, was designated as mediator by the Pope for difficulties that kings of France and Aragon had about Carcassonne.[109]

However, Louis IX had returned to Paris about 8 June, bringing back his young queen.[110] It is known that Blanche soon atoned for the new arrival, for hard injustices, her title of sovereign and the ascending that she had taken over the King. He who Marguerite came to marry had more spirit and virtues than she to necessarily make his wife forget the small miseries of daily life. Marguerite de Provence, who was never a great Queen, was always a courageous and devoted wife. I do not know at which point she took to the party of the all-powerful influence that Blanche of Castile exerted on her son until the end; but it does not seem that she ever reproached the King his filial devotion nor the strange exaltation of his Christian fervor. Saint Louis, from his youth, was not a prince like others; Marguerite could see this at the time of her marriage, when to inaugurate married life, before asking for the evidence of her love, he remained three nights in his prayers, accustomed to pass his religious duties before the even most legitimate satisfactions. No matter how long they lived together, in spite of the affection that he never ceased to display, Louis remained faithful to his practices of temperance and chastity during Advent and Lent, without counting certain days of the week, such as Fridays and Saturdays, the days before great feasts, these festivals themselves, and finally the days which preceded and followed those to which he had accustomed himself to receive communion.[111] It is certain, that this young princess, accustomed to the luxury of an elegant court, had to be astonished to see the rich and powerful King of France give up, hardly twenty years old, all games, to leave the hunting dogs and the hawks, so vital to the princes and lords of his era, to observe in his costume an extreme simplicity.[112]

    The King had not been married for one month, before it was necessary for him to go on campaign. He had only intended to prolong beyond the agreed term the truce with the King of England and the Count de Bretagne, and it was in Saint-Jean when hostilities were to resume [24 June 1234.]. During the three years which came before the expiry, the relationship between the two crowns had remained as they had almost always been since the last days of Philippe Auguste; Henry III, not being able to either make peace, or to again take the field, waited on events, going, according to his interests and his fears, with hostile measures; since he had ceased fighting, the subjects of Louis IX remained enemies; he did not make use of his rights when he ordered the bailiffs in English ports to keep in sight the French knights and archers who would have approached England.[113] His relations with Pierre Mauclerc had not changed: the Count of Brittany was always combined with the English; he corresponded with him by the mediation of Amaury de Saint-Amand, giving him a safe conduct to come to England to confer with the King; in compensation of the fiefs that he had lost in France he received manors taken from Richard Marshal.[114] The care that he spared was the best proof of hostility that he could give to France.

However, it was necessary to show peaceful intentions. The Pope, always concerned about helping the Holy Land, wanted to revive the agreement of the princes whose antagonism was prejudicial to the interests of Christianity; he did not wait for the truce to come to its full term in order to act in good faith. In the month of May 1233 he wrote the two kings praying for reestablishment of the peace, recommending as negotiators, the Archbishop of Sens, the Bishop of Paris, and the bishops of Winchester and Salisbury.[115] He knew that the King of England thought it necessary to take advantage of this initiative, and two months after the overtures of the Holy See, he informed Louis IX and Blanche of Castile that he had ordered his Bishop Henry of Rochester, Philippe d'Aubigny, and the seneschal Raoul Fitz-Nicholas to leave for Abbeville, in order to broach discussions with the French envoys.[116] But it was easier to set up a meeting than to make them lead to consequences; not much had happened by February 1234, when Gregory IX interposed himself, one more time, between the King of France and Henry III. The Pope demanded a renewal of the truce for a period of three years; the commissaries delegated by the Holy See remained the same except for the Bishop of Salisbury, replaced with the Bishop of Exeter.[117] Winter and the middle of springtime passed by; they approached a time when war would be renewed, when the King of England sent safe conducts for the Archbishop of Sens and Guillaume d'Auvergne, Bishop of Paris, asking them to supply English colleagues to represent the King.[118] He wrote in the same sense to the bishops of Winchester and Exeter, informing them that Philippe d'Aubigny, and the seneschal Raoul Fitz-Nicholas, then on mission with the Count de La Marche, would come to second them.[119]

During this time the Count de Bretagne, a man of practicality but few scruples, was not above saving appearances. It however seems that he had had to keep in regard to the King of France some caution, because his situation was not likely to inspire much haughtiness in him; Yolande de Bretagne was then in Coucy, in guarantee of the commitments entered into by her father; the Count de Montfort was sent to seek her in 1234, perhaps in order to bring her to Sens for the royal marriage.[120] Blanche of Castile had no reason to make this innocent [woman] expiate the wrongs of a man not very faithful to his word; also Mauclerc had not hesitated to be avenged, in full truce, upon those in Brittany who joined the party of the King. He was not man to forgive those who had pledged as certain their connection to him; in an interview that he had had in Ernée with the Count de Boulogne, he had, according to all appearances, promised not to allow his people to maltreat vassals whom he had fought.[121] Philippe Hurepel appears to have taken his role of mediator seriously, but he died in January 1234, and that is probably when Mauclerc again took to practices of violence. Those about whom he had to complain, clerks or laymen, tested one more time the effects of his anger. The lands of Henri d'Avangour were devastated in three attacks, back-to-back, first by the seneschal of Cornouaille and Normand de Québriac, marshal of Brittany, then by the Count in person, finally by his son Jean le Roux; these incursions took place, at least in part, towards Rogations, Ascension, and Pentecost (29 May – 11 June), i.e., before the expiry of the truce.[122]

The Bishop of Dol, Clement de Coëtquen, was not treated better. Already his predecessor, Jean de Lizanet, had undergone acts of spoliation; but it was quite another thing when the Count sent his marshal to occupy Dol. Normand de Québriac started by breaking the gates of the city and filling the ditches that the Bishop had ordered to be excavated by the burgers. The men under command of the Marshal sacked the house of the Bishop; they burned the frames of the windows, the pulpit, the tables, took the lead off the gutters to sell, and left this dwelling in such a state "that the house was said to be that of either a robber or a traitor." The abbey of Vieuville was also extremely maltreated by the garrisons of Rennes and of Saint-Aubin-du-Cormier, that he had sent against the Bishop of Dol, and depredations made on the goods of this monastery were evaluated at a thousand *livres* of damage. Finally, Jean de Dol, one of the Breton lords that one finds in 1231 in the army of the King, saw his domains and those of his men devastated, and twice by a knight of the Count, Robert de Sorel, came to burn the town of Combourg.[123] The bishop of Tréguier, the Bishop and chapter of Saint-Malo were obliged to exile themselves, and in June the Pope had to charge the Bishop of Orléans to provide for their needs.[124]

While overpowering the Bretons who opposed him, the Count prepared to start the war again, and tried to deliver Saint-James-de-Beuvron to Henry III. After the death of the Count of Chester, the

King of England had entered into possession of this fortress; in January 1233 he had written to the constable, or to the captain who had the possession of it, to deliver for Philippe of Aubigny crossbows, [crossbow] bolts, weapons which were found there, and this lord held for him a garrison with English knights; but soon Pierre Mauclerc established himself in Saint-James with the approval of Henry III, who, as of the month of April 1233, gave him 1,200 *livres* to maintain himself.[125] In spring of the following year, the sums to which Mauclerc had a right for this fact are mentioned in a letter of the King of England; at the same time the King promised to send to the Count sixty knights for the garrison of Saint-James.[126] Things were still in this state at the beginning of September, after the renewal of the truce between the Count of Brittany and the King of France.[127] Mauclerc had in Saint-James-de-Beuvron an extremely important advanced station, at the same time intended to cover Brittany and to threaten lower Normandy.

As for aid which the Count of Brittany could depend on from England, it was dispatched to him before the resumption of hostilities. On 20 April 1234, Henri de Trubleville had orders to be in Portsmouth by Ascension (1 June), with five knights gone up well armed, to pass to Brittany to be used in the pay of Henry III. Forty English nobles accepted convocations;[128] then it was Roger Stock and twenty-six other knights who, on 15 May, were warned to gain Portsmouth before 8 June.[129] It would take too long to enumerate the guarantees and the promises accepted by those who embarked then for Brittany.[130] They were provided with vessels (4 June); they collected money intended for their military pay; one of the documents relative to these preparations tells us that all was placed under the orders of Amaury de Saint-Amand and of one other captain, Hubert Heuse.[131] In addition, they had a body of two thousand Welshman sent to Brittany.[132]

To fight the King of France with any chance of success it would have required considerable forces, especially to help the Count of Brittany. But Henry III, in England, was overtaken with serious difficulties, and certainly the pecuniary resources he laid out did not allow him to make a serious effort against France. Some weeks before the day when hostilities were to begin again, he was still, according to his practice, in tergiversations. On 28 and 30 April 1234 he made general provisions against the French who tried to unload goods in England, then, on 25 May, he wrote the bishops of Winchester and

Exeter to open talks with the representatives of Blanche of Castile; he later added the Abbot of Westminster and Jean le Blond.[133] After having declared prolongation of the truce, he lined up the opinion of his council and authorized them to work on the re-establishment of peace.[134] On 21 June, three days before the end of the truce, the mayor and viscounts of London, bailiffs of Bristol, Southampton and of King's Lynn, and the Justiciar of Ireland, were informed that the subjects of Louis IX were authorized to trade freely in England until Pentecost of the following year.[135] They were in full war, when, on 17 July, orders were given for the lifting of the sequestration which had been put on vessels and goods belonging to Frenchmen.[136]

It is impossible for us today to know if there was some connection between all these apparently contradictory measures; but one might believe that the hesitations of Henry III were caused partly by financial embarrassments. Pierre Mauclerc, who had passed to England at the end of 1233, returned there next spring and spoke, in Westminster, with Henry III about sums which were due him.[137] After his departure, Henry III wrote to him, on 31 May, that the serious businesses of which he was occupied did not allow him to entirely discharge sums. He ordered the Bishop of Cornwall to explain his case to him, addressed to him by this Bishop 3,000 *marcs*, requested him to have patience until August for payment of the remainder.[138] About the same time, he sent 500 *marcs* by the Bishop of Durham to the Count de La Marche; he owed him 500 *marcs*, for which he asked a respite until Michaelmas.[139]

While the King of England prepared with indolence to recommence the war, Blanche of Castile assured herself in Brittany with allies and good positions. If Count Pierre possessed Saint-James-de-Beuvron, the King, for his part, held Pontorson, by an exchange concluded with Henri d'Avaugour and his wife Marguerite.[140] Avaugour had received from Louis IX the castle of Guesclin; but made him promise, under the guarantee of several noble Bretons, that he would deliver it on any requisition.[141] The castle of Guesclin was consequently given, in the name of King, by Dreu de Mello to Josselin, uncle of Avaugour.[142] On the coast of Normandy, provisions for the maritime population and of part of the nobility remained doubtful. During the years 1234 and the 1235 sailors and the merchants of Dieppe, Caen, Rouen, Caudebec, Honfleur, and Barfleur, the latter especially, traded constantly with England. Once granted safe-conducts, they returned their vessels to them and their goods, when they had been confiscated in virtue of orders given against the subjects of the King of France.[143] As for nobles of Normandy, their fidelity to the Crown of France was not always above suspicion, especially when they had fiefs in England, and, on another score, Henry III could hardly rely on them. Having seen, in the summer of 1234, that Richard de Harcourt had just made war against Pierre Mauclerc in the army of Louis IX, he placed under sequestration his goods, and those charged to carry out this measure handled it so awkwardly, that the blow they struck landed on the domain of another lord of the same name, an inhabitant of England. It was necessary to repair this error, and elsewhere Henry III, undoubtedly seeing that he was misled, was not long in reconsidering the decision that he had taken with regard to the Lord of Harcourt.[144] Obviously, this was a character upon whose devotion neither of the two kings could rely.

Accounts of the royal household show that Blanche of Castile waited until 24 June to put herself in train to act with strength against Pierre Mauclerc. One finds there, beside expenditure made for the marriage of the King, the mention of sums allocated to messengers who delivered, for the war, the royal convocation to vassals of the Crown. Among those for whom this convocation was addressed appear, among others, the Count de Nevers, the Count de Vianen, allied with the house of Courtenay, the Countess of Flanders, the bishops of Auxerre, Châlons, Amiens, Coutances, Évreux, Avranches, Troyes, Langres, and Autun.[145] There were undoubtedly bailiffs who, in many places, had the role of recruiting troops; Pierre le Ber, or Baron, bailiff of Touraine, was ordered to oppose anyone taking horses out of his bailliage; orders were addressed to him at this time, thus with the seneschal of Anjou; Berruyer de Bourron, one of the royal bailiffs of Normandy, was also convened, as well as the knights of the Étampois and the Orléanais, the surroundings of Senlis, Artois, Montdidior; it was the same for Paynel, these Normans at one time faithful to the English, of Guillaume de Mortemer and of nobility which lived in the country of Caux.[146] Mails were dispatched to Passy, Vernon, Mantes, Melun, Sens, and Crespy.[147]

It is probable that part of the royal army had orders to meet in Mans; in any case, the mayors of Corbie and Montdidier were to send their people to this city.[148] Others had Niort for their center of rallying; among this number were the knights of Loudunois and environs of Thouars, Poitevins, Tourangeaux, Berry.[149] The Duke of Burgundy also went to the royal army, and we have the proof of his passage to Tours.[150] Abbeys of Lions and Mortomer, various abbeys of Laonnois, communes of Crespy, Soissons, and Laon provided carts.[151] It was necessary that the forces intended for the expedition to Brittany were considerable, because one said, before the opening of the operations, that the Count would soon be reduced to throwing himself at the feet of the King.[152]

This forecast was to be realized; the resistance of Mauclerc was not long. The King of France marched against Brittany; after some preliminary operations in which the English, according to one of their historians, gained a partial success over the French, killed a certain number of horses and captured their convoys, Louis IX divided his army into three bodies, of which the weakest alone was able to reduce the enemy forces.[153] Brittany was invaded from three sides at the same time; undoubtedly the remaining corps of the army departed, the one for Niort, the other for Mans or rather for Angers, the third for lower Normandy.[154] Oudon and Champtoceaux, the most advanced fortresses of Brittany on the edges of the Loire, were newly taken; Châteaubriand was besieged and fell into the hands of the royal troops.[155] The English alliance that year had been of scant help for Pierre Mauclerc; he was abandoned to himself. While there was still time, he could have submitted.

In the month of August, he concluded with the King of France a truce which was to last until 15 November; it was said that to obtain it Mauclerc had been constrained to deliver three of his stronger places; it would have even been agreed that if the King of England did not come, before the expiry of this truce, to help Brittany, Pierre would give all his lands into the hands of Louis IX.[156] We do not know if these hard conditions, brought back by an English historian, were indeed imposed on the Count; concerning this arrangement I do not have an act containing additional stipulations. It is known that during the truce the barons and the Breton knights opposed to Pierre Mauclerc would remain in possession of all that they held when they were put at the service of the King. The Count submitted moreover to the decision of Louis IX and Blanche for payment of some business not indicated in the document, and there was care to stipulate that if either of them suddenly died, then Pierre would be subjected to a sentence pronounced by the survivor.[157] The Count de Mâcon, the Duke of Burgundy, the Count de Saint-Pol. and the oldest son of the Count de Soissons went as guarantors for the Count of Brittany, the first for guarantee of all his goods, the others for sums forming a total of 6,000 *marcs*. At the same time the Count de La Marche and his wife Queen Isabelle recognized the right of Louis IX and Blanche to make a truce with Henry III that was not to be prolonged, without their approval, beyond 8 November.[158]

This three months truce, following close to that which had ended at Midsummer's Day, bears in Breton documents the name of small truce (*minor treuga*). Pierre de Dreux did not respect it anymore than the first; one can understand this in reading the complaints addressed to the King, the following year, by the nobles and churches of Brittany.[159] However, he had no intention of continuing the war; after having returned to the King of England his knights and Welsh troops, he asked for a safe conduct and crossed in the month of October.[160]

Henry III, whatever were then his intentions with the regard to France, had neither the desire nor the means for making new sacrifices for the Count of Brittany. When Mauclerc told him the price he had paid for the truce, and when he claimed to have spent 15,000 *marcs* fighting the King of France, Henry answered that he neither had negotiated nor ratified this truce, that all the treasure of England would not be enough to defend Brittany. He could not place at the disposal of his ally, to continue the war in Brittany, four English counts and a number of knights and troops. Mauclerc withdrew furiously.[161]

Some claimed that he was presented to the King of France, a rope around his neck, acknowledging his treason and giving up all of Brittany with its fortified towns and castles. Following the author of this strange account, Louis IX would have declared that he agreed to spare him his life and that he left to his son the possession for life of Bretagne.[162] This obviously exaggerated account should not be taken to the letter; at most one might conclude from it that Mauclerc, in yielding to royal leniency, submitted without conditions. It is certain that he did not lose the government of Brittany, which still belonged to him for three years, until the majority of his son Jean. What is known is that he came to Paris, and in November 1234 he submitted to the decisions from on high which Louis IX and Blanche wanted to make.[163] Waiting for a ruling on questions which interested the barons and noble Bretons in the service of the King and Count de La Marche, he delivered as pledges Champtoceaux, Mareuil, and Saint-Aubin-du-Cormier; these places were to be restored to him, once conditions of the treaty were met, at Easter in three years time.[164] Pierre Mauclerc still promised to be useful to the King and his mother, not to conclude any agreement, any confederation, either in person or by his children, or by marriage or otherwise, with Henry III and Richard de Cornouailles. He gave up forever Saint-James-de-Beuvron to the King, all that he had received from him in Maine and Anjou, Bellême, Perrière and their privileges. The letters by which these domains had at one time been conceded to him were returned to Louis IX before Christmas.[165] It was a final abandonment; Pierre Mauclerc and his son Jean renewed it in 1238.[166] It is said, moreover, that the Count had to take the cross and spend five years in the Holy Land; he returned there indeed, some time after having given to his son the government of Brittany.[167]

Reconciliation of the Count de Bretagne with the court of France could only displease the King of England. During the winter, he wrote Gregory IX a letter in which were enumerated with bitterness his objections against Pierre Mauclerc.[168] However, rupture between Henry III and Mauclerc was not instantaneous, and the Count had already made his peace with Blanche of Castile, when Henry III, then occupied with negotiating for a new truce with France, wanted to know if the Count of Brittany wished to be included: "It seems to us," wrote he, "to us and our council, that it would be contrary to our honor to make a truce without the count, before having learned from him if he had left our service."[169] He had indeed left; he informed the King of England that he was withdrawn from his homage, and Henry III answered this notification while seizing the fiefs that his old ally held in England.[170] Mauclerc had the means of being avenged; by his order, hunting for English vessels in the English Channel. The English consoled themselves with catching pirates.[171] Elsewhere, they used reprisals; those who had been stripped at sea by people of the Count were authorized to compensate themselves while plundering the Bretons; what they would take in excess was to be given to the Crown of England.[172] It goes without saying that few spared the other; the English took to the conflict with so much spirit, that they seized on the coasts of Brittany the boats of Barflor, in spite of the safe conduct of Henry III.[173] It was undoubtedly this war of corsairs alluded to in letters patent of Henry, where he speaks about "captures and robberies made at sea since the end of the truce formerly concluded between us and the King of France."[174]

The final rupture of the Breton alliance put the King of

England in need of managing at least to conclude a truce with France. The Pope, flush with his ideas of crusade, had written Louis IX, as of 6 November, to urge him to restore peace, and to start by concluding a truce.[175] Soon Henry III, on his side, informed Louis and Blanche of Castile that he had given full powers to swear a truce to Simon Langton, Archdeacon of Canterbury, and to the Abbot of Sainte-Radegonde.[176] At the same time he named as guardians of truce Renaud de Pons and another of his vassals.[177] The seneschal of Gascogne, Henri de Trubleville accepted the order to disembark as soon as the English negotiators would have learned of a conclusion.[178] On 7 December, Henry III informed all his bailiffs and all his faithful that he had charged Simon Langton, the Abbot of Sainte-Radegonde, and Philippe de Arderne to bring to England the French envoys to whom the truce was to be sworn.[179]

Finally, on 27 January 1235, a project of truce was written in Westminster, and copies were sent to Louis IX and Blanche of Castile, with safe conducts intended for their representatives; but at this time there emerged new difficulties.[180]

The English were always masters of Oléron, and the Count de La Marche, then faithful to the party of Louis IX, required the restitution of this island as the price of his adhesion to the truce.[181] When, in January 1235, Henry III joined together in Westminster the Archbishop of Canterbury, high clergy and the nobility of England, to speak to them about negotiations in progress with France, all declared that the abandonment of Oléron to the Count de La Marche was contrary to the honor of the Crown. For any compensation, they agreed to offer to Hugues 200 *livres* per annum throughout the truce. Henry III, upon learning what happened from Simon Langton and the Abbot of Sainte-Radegonde, directed them to inform the Pope about provisions partly reconciling Hugues de Lusignan.[182] He himself wrote soon after this to Gregory IX (25 February); he did not charge in any way to the King of France nor to his mother the new difficulties which stood in the way of establishing a truce; he remained in correspondence with them, and announced to them he was dispatching new envoys, the Abbot of Beaulieu and Henry, Chancellor of Saint-Paul's, London.[183] The Pope was in agreement with the King of England to blame the processes and the requirements of the Count de La Marche. It is true that this lord was for the English a not very convenient neighbor; he advanced from there to seize Blaye, and to make captive Geoffroy Rudel and his son, vassal of

Henry III.[184] The talks for the truce continued, as attested in letters addressed in April, May, July, August 1235, by Henry III, as much to his agents and officers of his estates as to the King of France and his mother.[185]

It was only in July that the King of England arrived to parlay with Hugues de La Marche, while promising him during five years 200 pounds sterling.[186] The Hospitalers and Templars, ordinary intermediaries of the financial operations between England and France, were charged to carry out these payments; but the truce, the conclusion of which Hugues had delayed for some time, was not signed until the month of August, and sworn solemnly until February 1236.[187] The King of England included the Count d'Auvergne and his people, while the King of France included, for his part, Aimery de Thouars, the Count de Bretagne, the Count de La Marche, and Queen Isabelle.

From the moment when war could not produce anything but insufficient results, where it had no other effect than to ruin trade and to expose the subjects of the two crowns to vexations and violence, they came one way or the other to suspend it for a few years. Documents from the English chancellery seem to prove that Henry III had a real interest in restoring relations between his kingdom and France, and it was probably his need to conclude a final truce that led Blanche of Castile and her son, during the negotiations, to take some rigorous measures. By their order they made captive a knight of the King of England, named Guillaume, and arrested English merchants throughout France.[188] Their vessels were seized in Normandy, their goods sequestered by the bailiffs in Rouen, Caen, and Pont-Audemer.[189] Henry III made good use of reprisals in January and May 1235; but on several occasions slackened the severity, first in favor of fishing vessels, then in a more general manner, by ordering the setting free of all tradesmen or French sailors and their vessels (February, March 1235).[190] Despite everything, the hostility, the mistrust remained the rule; in March 1236, Henry III showed himself extremely dissatisfied with what the Count d'Eu had unloaded in England without prior approval, and gave instructions to the Constable of Dover, the Archbishop of Canterbury, and bailiffs of Southampton, for measures to be taken.[191] At the same time, in full truce, the Archbishop of Toledo, sent by the King of Castile to Louis IX, was detained in Guyenne, stripped of his baggage and of his mounts. It was an infringement much more serious as it happened to the representative of a neutral power; Henry III was alarmed; he sent Renaud de Pons and the seneschal of Gascogne, Henri de Trubleville, and took general measures so that the insult was suitably repaired.[192]

The war was only suspended; but for a few years they were going to dispense with raising troops, preparing expeditions, defending coasts and ports. The act of war and the expenditure which is its first condition returned in the summer of 1240. There was a five years respite that Blanche ensured her son, at the time when he began to govern by himself.

Louis IX had entered his twenty-first year on 25 April 1234; in fact, and probably in right, it was about this time that he was considered in his majority.[193] It was also when his mother, considering him ripe for power, let him take in hand, little by little, direction of affairs. No official document, no formula introduced into the drafting of the royal charters, marks the end of regency and the inauguration of a new mode. In a quantity of circumstances, the intervention of Blanche remained visible; in June 1235, when Louis IX could in no wise be considered a minor, the Queen was named in an agreement concluded between Raoul de Fougères and Guy Mauvoisin, and we will see that since then, until the voyage of Louis IX for the East, she had on the government of France an undeniable action; but the King was more in supervision.[194] The historians do not tell us when she had, at a given moment, given her son the supreme authority. The passage of her regency to the personal government of Louis IX was undoubtedly insensible. It hardly mattered, fundamentally, that Louis was declared major in the spring of 1234, at the time of his marriage, or in the year which followed. Blanche had upon her son an all-powerful influence, and nobody in France was going to impose an unspecified obligation on him; only Blanche had enough experience to know at which moment and in which affair the action of the King must substitute for hers, and Louis was too sensible to press his mother to yield power. I can say without being mistaken, that she did everything in the kingdom until 1235, and that from this year forward French history ceased merging with her biography. Consequently, I shall have to speak of cases, still many, where her personal intervention is attested by the documents and the accounts of historians.

At the moment when Blanche bestowed power into the hands of a great prince that she had formed, she was right to believe that her work was accomplished; it was indeed, and the last revolt of the

Count de Champagne showed soon enough that royal authority had left her hands more powerful than ever. Though the regency was then finished, the history of a new attempt, made by *les grands* to withdraw subjects and vassals from their duties, attaches too directly to the minority of Saint Louis to separate them .

The barons seemed to have given up their practice of mutiny when the anxious mood of Thibaud IV called in question the interior peace of the kingdom. Nothing however in the first days of the year 1235 could predict his share of hostile intentions; on 28 January he had concluded with the Duke of Burgundy an arrangement which was at the very least approved by the Crown, since the Duke, while subscribing to it, had the care to reserve fidelity to Louis IX and Blanche.[195] The King was made executor of this agreement, and in the month of April, Hugues IV, in spite of his engagements had refused accord with his old adversary, had had to subject himself to this chief with payment of a heavy indemnity.[196] From whence could come danger, at the moment when the Count of Brittany was reduced to impotence, when the Duke of Burgundy accepted royal decisions, while Thibaud de Champagne had recourse against him to the authority of his sovereign? The majority of barons had returned to their role of vassal; they did not think anymore of plotting against their enemy, now victorious; their thoughts were elsewhere.

Gregory IX had managed to divert the concerns of the French nobility towards the Holy Land. By his order, the Dominicans and Franciscans were for some time given to preach the crusade; it was in the name of Christian establishments in Palestine that in November 1234 the Pope insisted the kings of France and England conclude a truce, and a few days later he called all the faithful in France to the help the Holy Land.[197] His efforts were soon rewarded. Thibaud IV, who at the time of his peace with the barons had promised to take a hundred knights to the East, finally took the cross at the beginning of 1235.[198] A certain number Flemish knights made in the same way for Hesdin, in the midst of one tournament; among those who crossed this year, among others the Duke of Burgundy, Count Jean de Chalon, Count Guy de Forez and Nevers, Amaury de Montfort, Pierre Mauclerc, and Henri, Count de Bar.[199] The Pope, seeing that the idea of the crusade gained ground, stimulated the generosity of the faithful in making bishops encourage each man or woman, clerk or layman, to give for the holy war at least one farthing per week.[200]

The sense of security that this movement for crusade was to

inspire in the Queen could only strengthen itself when Louis IX, undoubtedly advised by her, promised in marriage his brother Robert to Marie, daughter of Jeanne, Countess of Flanders.[201] This was a new triumph for the Crown; this union, if it had been able to be carried out, would have made Flanders fall into the hands of a son of France, and no one could expect that the young princess upon whose marriage was founded such a hope would die before becoming the sister-in-law of the King. The situation, in France was thus excellent, when the King of Navarre was made principal author of a new plot. After a rather long stay in his new states, he returned to Champagne, in February 1235.[202] Without waiting for the end of negotiations entered into for the truce between France and England, he made with Henry III a private truce, according to which he was given by this prince, in June, a guarantee of one year.[203] Perhaps he consequently had impure thoughts, because soon after his return he gave new proof of his fickleness which, on several occasions, he had failed to lose. When he made a deal, at the price of money, with the Queen of Cyprus, he had given up to the King of France for 40,000 pounds, the suzerainty of the counties of Blois, Chartres, Sancerre, and of the visounty of Châteaudun; but now that he was rich, and wore a crown, he regretted not having in his vassalage these old fiefs of his house.[204] Scarcely concerned to observe conditions that his father-in-law Archambaud de Bourbon had accepted on his behalf and of which he could be unaware the nature of, he claimed that he had not definitively given up the homage of these four fiefs, that he had simply engaged and intended to repurchase them. If it is necessary to believe one historian, Louis IX, in answer to this communication, would have declared that the time of repurchase was expired; but it is much more probable that the homages asserted by Thibaud had been, originally, abandoned to the King; that is at least what the King himself formally declared later to Joinville.[205] Actually, he said to Thibaud that he was ready to subject his case to the judgment of peers.[206]

Thibaud did not have great illusions about the result of this injunction; he knew Blanche enough to know that she did not like to yield, when the interests of the Crown were concerned, and that she would not let her son give up dexterously acquired homages. Without anymore delay, he passed from dissatisfaction to hostility, began to prepare his fortified places and to ensure his allies. Since 1235, he built up the fortification of Nogent-en-Bassigny, Méry-sur-Seine, and above all Meaux.[207] At this time, he was isolated in the kingdom and without any another support than Blanche; it was at the instigation of Pierre Mauclerc, his former enemy, that he opposed the Crown, and one must believe that the Count de La Marche and Queen Isabelle were the instruments of his new reconciliation with the Count of Brittany.[208] Once launched on the road to perdition, he went ahead to press the execution of a project probably anterior to his unjust complaints.

The King of Navarre had a daughter named Blanche from his second wife Agnès de Beaujeu, formerly promised in marriage to the son of the Count de Bourgogne and since then promised to Prince Alphonse of Castile, oldest son of Ferdinand III and great nephew of Queen Blanche. Having an interest in allying Castile against Aragon, Thibaud had given to young Blanche the heritage of Navarre, by stipulating that children of his third wife, even if male, would not be entitled to his kingdom.[209] This arrangement had certainly been approved by the King of France; at that time, no vassal had the right had to marry his daughter without approval of the suzerain and it is certain that Thibaud, on several occasions, had made formal promises to Louis IX, on this subject, with the guarantee of three of his castles.[210] He soon forgot that he had given his word, as he believed himself to have assurances from the houses of Dreux and Lusignan. These two families at this time were closely linked, and soon they were going to confuse their blood and their interests by the marriage of Yolande of Brittany with Hugues le Brun, son of the Count de La Marche.[211]

On 16 January 1236, at Château-Thierry, Thibaud, without warning the King, not being concerned with the affront that he gave to the King of Castile, married his daughter to Jean le Roux, son of Pierre de Dreux, and intended to soon become Count de Bretagne.[212] Blanche accepted from the Breton princes a beautiful dowry, and, at same time, Thibaud granted the succession of Navarre to him.[213] It was necessary that he lost much to get allies against the King, to make with his daughter this exorbitant concession, which explained all the more his relationship with the Spanish dynasties. Pierre took the commitment to provide before Easter, as guarantee of these conditions, letters from the Duke of Burgundy, Count de Bar, Count de Mâcon, Érard de Chassenay, Simon de Château-villain, Enguerrand and Thomas de Coucy, the Archbishops of Rheims and Sens, the bishops of Châlons-sur-Marne and Langres, the counts of Soissons and Saint-Pol, Roger de Rosoy, Gerard de Durnay, and

Renaud de Choiseul.[214] All these characters had been named, with the counts of Grandpré and Roucy, in the charter of the Breton princes relative to the heritage of Navarre.[215] It is astonishing to see the Lord of Coucy and his brothers, kin of the Count de Bretagne, his brother the Count of Mâcon, his other brother the Archbishop of Rheims, in guarantee of an agreement with the noble Champagne completely contrary to the interests of Louis IX; but the roles of the Count de Blois and the Viscount of Châteaudun could give one pause to reflect; did they realize that they had been since 1234 direct vassals of the Crown?[216] How then to explain especially that the Archbishop of Sens, Gautier Cornu, this trusty servant of the house of France, gave his guarantee to an alliance made against the King?[217] Perhaps they did not understand from the first day that which was intended; their doubts, if they had any, were raised soon enough.

On 13 April, Hugues de La Marche and Queen Isabelle, in answer to the invitation of Pierre Mauclerc, engaged themselves to defend the King of Navarre against any enemy, without stipulating any reserve in favor of Louis IX.[218] It was the league of 1227 reformed.[219] This time the barons could count on the abstention of the Pope, or even on his benevolent disposition. Gregory IX, who at one time had prohibited the marriage of Thibaud IV and Yolande of Brittany, did not refuse exemption, a rather explainable favor, if one realizes that the relationship of Blanche and Jean le Roux was an extremely distant one.[220] Elsewhere, the King of Navarre and the Count of Brittany, who were crusaders, had by this fact the right to protection from the Holy See. Thibaud had no need to leave for war; at the end of May, he informed his people to meet in Meaux for 10 June; at least we know that men leaving the abbey of Molesme had orders to march on this date, armed and provided with two months of supplies.[221]

The King of France was not caught unawares. At the news of Thibaud de Champagne's preparations he convened his vassals; his two young brothers, princes Robert and Alphonse, were with him, and soon the royal army was joined together, either in Paris, or at Saint-Germain-en-Laye, where several lords, among others the Duke of Lorraine and the Count of Chalon, had received the order to be there on 8 June.[222] Without delay, Louis started himself, concentrating his forces in the forest of Vincennes; he took along *pierrières* and *mangonneaux*; a large *trebuchet*, that the Count de Boulogne had made, brought for the siege of Montereau-faut-Yonne; this place was undoubtedly one of those which Thibaud IV had promised to deliver to the King if he married his daughter off without authorization.[223] The two armies were almost in each other's presence, and they waited for battle.[224] The King of Navarre did not dare to deliver it; it is probable that the counts of Brittany and de La Marche had not joined, and that his friends were not very eager to fall into the hands of the King. In the final analysis Thibaud, after having easily concluded his alliances, had no power to use them; instead of moving against the royal army, he called upon the protection of the Pope. Gregory IX hastened to intervene; on 18 June, he ordered the bishops of Paris and Langres, with the Abbot of Clairvaux, to prohibit Louis IX from attacking Champagne, who was crusader.[225] As of this moment, Thibaud did not think anymore than to escape the revenge of his sovereign; he declared through the Pope that his person and his grounds, considering his wish for crusade, were as the shelter of excommunication and of prohibition, and that ecclesiastical sentences could not reach him until the day when he would have returned from the Holy Land, or upon his death.[226] During this time, many and powerful influences acted on the King to obtain for Thibaud a forgiveness that he hardly deserved.

Nobody was more helpful to him than Blanche. Without her support Thibaud was lost; she had pity on him. Thibaud, seeing very late that he was headed for ruin, was in greatest perplexity; he hastened to send to the court an embassy, charged to ask grace and to offer on his behalf a complete submission.[227] The Queen then, seeing the moment come, informed the Count to find her and promised to obtain peace for him; it was the end of summer.[228] The conditions to which she had to subject this man who deserved the most severe punishment were not too hard. He renounced, of course, his claims on the homage of Blois and Chartres, Sancerre, and Châteaudun; he gave up three places, in the number of which it is probably necessary to count Montereau-faut-Yonne and Bray-sur-Seine, of which the King took possession;[229] yet certainly the King returned these castles, simply delivered on guarantees of compensation to the Crown for the expenditure caused by his imprudent revolt.[230] As he was a crusader, the obligation to go to the Holy Land, which was imposed on him, had scarcely cost him; while waiting, he promised to withdraw himself to Navarre for a time about which we are unaware of the duration.[231]

Thibaud, who could be happy about drawing so little expense, did not have to complain about the reproaches that the Queen addressed to him when he appeared before her. It is recounted, she said to him:

> By God, Count Thibaud, you should not have been contrary to us; it would have been well for you to have remembered the great kindness that the King my son made you, when he came to your assistance to help your county and your land against all the barons of France, who wanted to burn everything to cinders. By my faith, Madam, the Count answered, my heart, my body and all my domains are at your command; there is nothing which you can like that I would not be eager to readily give you, and never, thanks be to God, will I go against you and yours.[232]

The historian who lends to Blanche of Castile and Thibaud de Champagne these well-known words is certainly misled, when he speaks about the sorrow which fills the heart of the King at the time when the poet took leave of the Queen, and I am sorry to believe that he then tested so many desires and regrets before this woman of forty-eight years, insensitive to his passion for such a long a time. This feeling, formerly very intense, was to be attenuated; but, in the entourage of the Queen, they had forgotten neither the unforgivable defections of Thibaud, nor perhaps the unjust charges of which he had been victim upon the death of Louis VIII and of the Count de Boulogne. Undoubtedly also his old love for Blanche had made him ridiculous. He was overcome; those who saw him reduced to this sad state would have had to abstain themselves from insult.

    Prince Robert, who all his life and until the day of his death was a man with a fierce and proud character, and who always had hated Thibaud, gave proof of his not very generous role. Thibaud was still in the room where Blanche and Louis IX had received him, or perhaps he had just left it, when people in service near Robert threw at his head a soft cheese, others say a bundle of tripe and rags; during this time servants, to insult him, cut off the tail of his horse.[233] The King of Navarre came before the Queen, still soiled with refuse of which he had been covered, and reproached her for the insult that they had just given him despite of the royal safe conduct.[234] Blanche was indignant; she imprisoned these sad defenders of the throne and the

King ordered that they be hung. But they were let go, when Robert declared that he was the true culprit.[235] "Never," as an author of the time related, "did one hear of treating either king nor count thusly."[236] Louis IX sent his barons to escort he who came to expiate his faults by such a miserable humiliation. Thibaud was taken along to Nantes by Pierre Mauclerc; from there, he left for Navarre, while Champagne, by an irony of fate, remained with the guard of the King of France.[237]

1 Denifle, *Chartularium Universitatis Parisiensis*, t. I, n. 74; 2 April 1230; ibid., n. 75, 10 May 1230.

2 Denifle, n. 82; 14 April 1231.

3 I do not see the utility of this objection; the privilege of Philippe Auguste had been renewed from 1229.

4 Denifle, n. 84; 18 April 1231; Idem, n. 85; 18 April.

5 Denifle, n. 80; 13 April 1231; n. 88; 24 April.

6 I do not have to provide the details of this affair; one may consult in this regard the cartulary of R. P. Denifle, pieces 89, 90, 92 to 94 and 95; May 1231.

7 Guillaume de Nangis, *Vie de Saint Louis* (*Historiens de France*, XX, p. 320), and Chronique, same collection, t. XX, p. 546, ed. Géraud , t. I, p. 181-183; *Les Grandes chroniques de France*, ed. Paulin Paris, t. IV, p. 250; *Gesta sancti Ludovici Noni, auciore monacho S. Dionysii anonyme* (*Historiens de France*, XX, p. 47).

8 Célestin Port, *Dictionnaire de Maine-et-Loire*, t. I, p. 38 and 49.

9 *Layettes du Trésor des Chartes*, II, 2311; September 1234; *Layettes*, 2198, 2200 to 2204, 2215 to 2220; September 1232, and 1232 (without indication of the month).

10 *Layettes*, 2215; 1232.

11 *Layettes*, 2200; 22 September 1232.

12 *Historiens de France*, XXIV, 118, n. 215 : « *quando venit Andegavis dominas rex, fortericiam suam ibidem facturus.* » ; *Layettes*, 2311; September 1234; Le Nain de Tillemont, II, 136; Archives nationales, J. 178, pieces 30 and 30 bis; 1262.

13 *Annales de S. Denis*, 1st redaction : *Bibliothèque de l'École des Chartes*, 1879, p. 280.

14 Aubry de Trois-Fontaines, *Monumenta Germaniæ*, scriptores, t. XXIII, p. 930 : « *Duo de fratribus regis Francie , Johannes et Dagobertus , moriuntur.* » ; *Layettes du Trésor des Chartes*, t. II, 2213, 2214. The general chapter of Prémontré has a reunion each year, at Saint-Denis : Le Paige, *Bibliotheca Præmonstratensis ordinis*, p. 251, col. 2.

15 Aubry, loc. cit.

16 *Annales de S. Denis*, loc. cit. ; Le Nain de Tillemont, t. II, p. 135.

17 André Du Chesne, *Historiæ Francorum scriptores*, t. V, p. 442.

18 D'Arbois de Jubainville, *Histoire des comtes de Champagne*, t. IV, p. 253-254.

19 D'Arbois, t. V, n. 2186; Potthast, *Regesta*, 8919; 24 April 1232; D'Arbois, t. V, n. 2191 ; 4 June 1232.

20 Joinville, ed. of 1874, 80-81.

21 Record office; Close rolls, n. 43, memb. 7 in dorso.

22 D'Arbois, IV, 256.

23 D'Arbois, IV, 256; Mas-Latrie, *Histoire de Chypre*, t. I, p. 306, note. For all of these events I can only recapitulate the account of d'Arbois de Jubainville and cite pieces which are found in his *catalogue* (t. V).

24 D'Arbois, t. V, n. 2238.

25 Rinaldi, *Annales ecclesiastici*, t. II, p. 95; D'Arbois, V, 2243 to 2246 and 2251 ; 22 and 26 April 1233.

26 Ibid., 2248-2250, 26 April 1233; 2258-2201, 6 and 7 May.

27 Ibid., 2240, 17 April 1233; 2247, 23 April.

28 Ibid., 2241; 17 April.

29 Ibid., 2272; 24 June.

30 Ibid., 2274, 31 July 1233.

31 Le Nain de Tillemont, t. II, p. 145; *Willelmi chronica Andrensis, Monumenta Germaniæ*, scriptores, t. XXIV, p. 772; *Chronique dite de Hugues de S. Victor*, continuation of Clairmarais, ibid., p. 101; Aubry de Trois-Fontaines, same collection, t. XXIII, p. 933. Philippe Mousket says that Ferrand died at Douai (verse 28154).

32 D'Arbois de Jubainville, t. IV, p. 257; t. V, n. 2276; 23 August 1233; Aubry de Trois-Fontaines, loc. cit.

33 D'Arbois, t. V, n. 2285; 24 October 1233; *Layettes du Trésor des Chartes*, t. II, 2297; d'Arbois, V, 2308; 3 August 1234.

34 *Chronique dite de Baudouin d'Avesnes, Historiens de France*, t. XXI, p. 162, and *Monumenta Germaniæ*, scriptores, t. XXV, p. 452.

35 Léopold Delisle, *Recherches sur les comtes de Dammartin au treizième siècle* (*Antiquaires de France*, 1869, p. 201); *Premières et deuxièmes annales de S. Denis* (*Bibl. de l'Ecole des Chartes*, 1879, p. 281 and 290); Félibien, p. 232.

36 *Willelmi chronica Andrensis, Monumenta Germaniæ*, scriptores, XXIV, p. 773; *Chronique dite de Baudouin d'Avesnes*, loc. cit.; Philippe Mousket, ed. Reiffenberg, t. II, v. 28132.

37 Mousket, verse 28136; *Willelmi chronica Andrensis*.

38 *L'Art de vérifier les dates*, t. III, p. 204; Bréquigny, *Mémoires pour servir à l'histoire de Calais*, *Mém. de l'Académie des Inscriptions*, t. XLIII, 1786, p. 732; Léopold Delisle, *Recherches sur les comtes de Dammartin* (*Antiquaires de France*, 1869), p. 203.

39 *Layettes du Trésor des Chartes*, t. II, 2266-67; January 1234.

40 D'Arbois de Jubainville, t. IV, p. 261.

41 Ibid.; *Chronique de Fécamp* (*Historiens de France*, t. XXIII , p. 429).

42 D'Arbois, t. IV, p. 261.

43 D'Arbois , t. IV, p. 268 ff; Aubry de Trois-Fontaines reported that Thibaud

found in the treasury of his uncle 1,700,000 *livres*; this figure seems exaggerated.

44 *Historiens de France*, t. XXI, p. 229 e, 233 k; Ibid., p. 229 9, 233 a, 234 b, 238 t.

45 *Chronique dite de Baudouin d'Avesnes* (*Historiens de France*, t. XXI, p. 163), and *Monumenta Germaniæ*, scriptores, t. XXV, p. 452.

46 *Layettes du Trésor des Chartes*, t. II, 2310, 2312 to 2314; d'Arbois, t. V, 2309 to 2314 and 2338 ; September 1234; Joinville indicated these conditions exactly (ch. 86-87) ; it is the same in the *Chronique dite de Baudouin d'Avesnes*.

47 Layettes, 2322-2323 ; November 1234.; Archives nationales, registre JJ. 26, fol. 69 r, col. 1 ; 11 November 1234; d'Arbois, 2316.

48 *Histoire de Languedoc*, ed. in-4°, t. VIII, col. 945; September 1231; Bibl. Nat., ms. latin 9071, piece 7; 1230; *Histoire de Languedoc*, t. VI, p. 678.

49 Potthast, *Regesta*, 8552.

50 Registre du Trésor des Chartes JJ. 26, fol. 141.

51 Guillaume de Puylaurens, *Historiens de France*, XIX, p. 225.

52 Ibid , XX, p. 764.

53 *Layettes du Trésor des Chartes*, t. II, 2054 ; May 1230.

54 Potthast, 8584; 9 July 1230.

55 Potthast, 8585.

56 Potthast, 8609; 22 September 1230.

57 Potthast, 8605; *Histoire de Languedoc*, t. VIII, col. 931-932; 13 September 1230; Potthast, 8613; *Layettes*, II, 2073; 25 September.

58 Potthast, 8598; *Histoire de Languedoc*, t. VIII, col. 931; 5 September 1230.

59 Potthast, 8608; letter to the legate; 18 September; Potthast, 8616; 25 September.

60 Potthast, 8589; 22 July 1230.

61 Guillaume de Puylaurens, *Historiens de France*, XX, p. 764; *Willelmi chronica Andrensis*, same collection, XVIII, p. 582, and *Monumenta Germaniæ*, scriptores, XXIV, p. 770-771; Le Nain de Tillomont, II, 89.

62 Potthast, *Regesta*, 8645; 2 January 1231.

63 *Histoire de Languedoc*, VI, p. 665; Guillaume de Puylaurens, *Historiens de France*, XX, loc. cit.

64 Potthast, *Regesta*, 8881; 18 February 1232.

65 Ibid., 8896; 12 March 1232.

66 Guillaume de Puylaurens, *Historiens de France*, XX, 765.

67 Guillaume de Puylaurens, *Historiens de France*, XX, 765; *Histoire de Languedoc*, VIII, col. 963-969; statutes of the Count de Toulouse against the *hérétiques*.

68 *Histoire de Languedoc*, VI, 673-674.

69 Potthast, *Regesta*, 8888 and 8889; 4 March 1232.

70 Ibid., 8890; 4 March.

71 Rinaldi, *Annales ecclesiastici*, II, p. 103; *Histoire de Languedoc*, VI, p. 675;

Potthast, 9365; 13 January 1234.

72 Ibid., 9367; 15 January 1234.

73 Rodenberg, *Epistolæ sæculi XIII e regestis Pontificum Romanorum selectæ*, t. I, p. 470, n. 577. *Histoire de Languedoc*, VI, p. 681.

74 Rodenberg, n. 576.

75 Mathieu de Paris, *Chronica majora*, ed. Luard, III , p. 304.

76 *Layettes du Trésor des Chartes*, t. H, 2309; *Hist. de Languedoc*, t. VIII, col.979.

77 *Layettes du Trésor des Chartes*, II, 2276; *Hist. de Languedoc*, t. VIII, col. 972.

78 Potthast, *Regesta pontificum Romanorum*, 9452; 2 May 1234.

79 Guillaume de Nangis, *Vie de Saint Louis* (*Historiens de France*, XX, p. 322).

80 Philippe Mousket, vers 28687; *Beati Ludovici vita, etc.* (*Historiens de France*, XXIII, p. 161 b).

81 Philippe Mousket, v. 28692; Guillaume de Nangis, *Hist. de France*, XX, p. 322.

82 Guillaume de Puylaurens, *Historiens de France*, XX, p. 765.

83 Layettes, II, 2263; Potthast, *Regesta*, 9358; 2 January 1234. Le Nain de Tillemont, II, p. 203.

84 Guillaume de Puylaurens, *Historiens de France*, XX, p. 765; *Layettes*, II, 2270 ; 13 February 1234; *Layettes*, 2275; March 1234.

85 Guillaume de Nangis, *Historiens de France*, XX, p. 322. The Archbishop of Sens and Jean de Nesle, sent on embassy to find Princess Marguerite, kept in constant communication with Blanche of Castile: *Comptes royaux* [royal accounts] of 1234 (*Historiens de France*, XXI, p. 235 k, 238 h, 239 d, 240 l). Following Philippe Mousket, it was the Archbishop of Bourges who had been charged with the negotiation (verse 28703); it was not, in any case, he who finished it, and I do not have proof that he went to Provence. *Historiens de France*, t. XXI, p. 245 a, 246 d.

86 *Historiens de France*, t. XXI, p. 246 § 16.

87 Chifflet, *Histoire de Tournus*, 1664, p. 462.

88 Le Nain de Tillemont, II, p. 206. *Historiens de France*, XXI, p. 228.

89 *Historiens de France*. XXI, p. 246 f.

90 Ibid., p. 241 h, 246 c, 247 f, 243, 247 e, 247 d, 246 c, 241 a.

91 Ibid., p. 241 h.

92 *Historiens de France*, XXI, p. 247 h; Tillemont, II, p. 206; Martène , *Thesaurus anecdotorum* , 1, p. 987; Arch. nat., JJ. 30, fol. 138 r; 27 May 1234.

93 *Historiens de France*, XXI, p. 247.

94 Ibid., 244 j. The text opens with : « *comitis Flandriae.* » There was no Count of Flanders; Jeanne of Constantinople was widowed, and did not remarry until 1237.

95 Ibid., p. 243 j; household accounts, in 1234, are full of anecdotes relative to the robes of the King, the princes, etc.; see above all, in this regard, p. 247; *Historiens de France*, XXI, p. 247 d; 246 c; 247 h; 246 e.

96 Ibid., p. 247; 244 a.

97 Ibid., p. 243 a; 241 a.

98 Ibid., p. 243 f, « *Pro vectura papilionum apud Senones.* »

99 *Historiens de France*, XXI, p. 247 a, f.

100 Ibid. p. 246, § 16.

101 Ibid.

102 Ibid., p. 245 b. p. 247 a; Le Nain de Tillamont, II, p. 206. 243 a. 241 d.

103 Guillaume de Nangis, *Vie de Saint Louis* (*Historiens de France*, XX, 322). The Abbot of Saint-Denis assisted in the coronation; *Deuxièmes annales de Saint-Denis* (*Bibliothèque de l'École des Chartes*, 1879, p. 290).

104 *Historiens de France*, XXI, 244 *l*; 245 *b*.

105 Le Nain de Tillemont, II, 207.

106 Arch. nat., registre 30, fol. 138 r; Martène, *Thesaurus anecdotorum*, I, 987.

107 *Layettes*, II, 2719; testament of Raimond Borengcr. See Tillemont, II, 204.

108 *Layettes du Trésor des Chartes*, II, 22801; 30 April 1234.

109 Rinaldi, *Annales ecclesiastici*, II, p. 105; Potthast, *Regesta*, 9517.

110 Vincent de Beauvais, *Speculum historiale* (*Historiens de France*, XXI, 72); « *juvenem reginam.* » Marguerite is often designated under the name in the accounts of 1234 (*Historiens de France*, XXI, 245, 246, etc.). « *Pro quadriga quæ adduxit de Senonibus hernesium juvenis reginæ* » (244 g).

111 *Le confesseur de la reine Marguerite* (*Historiens de France*, XX, p. 110 e).

112 *Historiens de France*, XX, p. 46 e.

113 Record office; Close rolls, n. 43, memb. 11 in dorso; 12 May 1232.

114 Close rolls, 44, memb. 14 r ; 12 January 1233; Rymer, ed. of 1816, t. I, p. 210; 9 October 1233; Close rolls, 45, memb. 32 r; 17 December 1233 : « *De commissis comiti Britannie Twyford[e] et Westkinton[e].*» ; Ibid., memb. 18 r;23 June 1234 : « *Pro comite Brittannie.* »

115 Shirley, *Royal letters*, t. I, p. 551; 14 May 1233; Valois, Guillaume d'Auvergne, p. 353, piece XXXVII; 15 May 1233 : letter of Gregory IX to the Archbishop of Sens and to three bishops.

116 Rymer, I, p. 210; 13 July 1233 : letter to Louis IX; Shirley, *Royal letters*. p. 416-417; 14 July 1233 : letter to Blanche.

117 Teulet, *Layettes*, II, n. 2269; 12 February 1234 : Gregory IX to the King of France; Valois, *Guillaume d'Auvergne*, p. 362, piece XLVII; 15 February 1234: letter of Gregory IX to the Archbishop of Sens and to three bishops.

118 Rymer, I, p. 211-212; 10 May 1234.

119 Rymer, I, p. 212; 10 May 1234.

120 *Historiens of France*, XXI, p. 229 m, p. 233 l; XXII, p. 574 b, accounts of 1234. A *bulla* of Gregory IX, dated 18 January 1234, proves elsewhere that at this time Yolande was still in the hands of Louis IX or, at least, among people who had been commanded to keep her following the Treaty of Vendôme (Valois, *Guillaume of Auvergne*, p. 360, part XLVI). These commissaries had been the Archbishop of Rheims, the counts of Boulogne and Dreux, and the Lord of Coucy; however, at the time of the marriage of Louis IX, the two counts had died and the Archbishop was the brother-in-law of Pierre Mauclerc. It was more natural than ever that guardianship of Yolande belong to the Lord of Coucy.

121 « *sicut creantaverat coram ipso comite in pallamento do Hernea.* » Testimony of the Bishop of Dol against Pierre Mauclerc ; Archives nationales, J. 240, n. 30. An insufficient extract of this document is found in Teulet, *Layettes*, II, n. 2419, and Dom Morice gives an analysis in, *Histoire de Bretagne*, preuves, I, 889-890.

122 These facts relate to an inquiry on the complaints of Henri d'Avaugour, of which only an extract has been given in *Layettes du Trésor des Chartes*, t. II, n. 2418. See the manuscript: Arch. nat., J. 241, n. 29; analysed in Dom Morice, *Preuves*, I, col. 888.

123 Testimony produced against Pierre Mauclerc by the Bishop of Dol, the Abbot of Vieuville, and Jean de Dol; Arch. nat., J. 240, n. 36.

124 Potthast, *Regesta*, 9477-9478; 26 June 1234.

125 *Annals of Dunstable*, 1233 (*Annales monastici*, ed. Luard, t. III, p. 132); Record office; Close rolls, 44, membr. 14 r; 12 January 1233 : « *De armis que fuerunt R. comitis Cestrio in castro Sancti Jacobi super Beveronem.* » ; Ibid., 13 January 1233 : « *De duobus militibus comitis de Ferr[ers] missis usque Sanctum Jacobum.* » ; Close rolls, 44, 10 r; 27 April 1233 : « *Pro priore Sancti Jacobi super Beveronem.* » ; Ibid., 8 r; 1 July 1233: « *Pro Henrico de Sancto Eylero.* » ; Liberate rolls, n. 493, membr. 7, and above, 25 April 1233.

126 Close rolls, 45, membr. 27 in dorso ; spring of 1234 : « *Sciendum est quod die mercurii,* » etc.

127 Patent rolls, 43, membr. 5 r, 2 September 1234 : « *De quingentis marcis mutuo capiendis de comite Britannie ad opus militum existentium apud Sanctum Jacobum de Beverone.* »

128 Rymer, t. I, p. 211; 20 April 1234; Also see roll 9, 12 of the Miscellaneous rolls (Record office, Chancery) : « *Nomina militum destinandorum in Brittanniam. Henricus de Trubleville se quinto,* » etc.

129 Rymor, t. I, p. 212; 15 May 1234.

130 Patent rolls, roll 43, memb. 12 r, 29 May 1534 : « *De protectione quorumdam militum qui profecti sunt in Brittanniam.* » ; Ibid., memb. 11 r, 3 June 1234 : « *Pro Roberto de Pavelly.* » ; Close rolls, roll 45, memb. 19 r, 12 June 1234 : « *Pro Alano filio Warini.* »

131 Close rolls, 45, memb. 20 r (lower); 4 June 1234 : « *De militibus destinandis in Britanniam.* » ; Ibid., memb. 17 r, 1 July 1234 : letter of Henry III to Pierre de Montgommery.

132 Roger of Wendover, ed. Hewlett, t. III, p. 93, and after him Mathieu de Paris, ed. Luard , t. 111, p. 297 : « *milites sexaginta et Wallenses duo millia.* »

133 Close rolls, 45, memb. 25 in dorso, 28 and 30 April 1234. On 25 June, Henry III gave orders for the expulsion of all French chevaliers and sergeants at arms who could be found in his domains; Close rolls, 45, memb. 18 in dorso.

134 Close rolls, 45, memb. 24 in dorso.

135 Ibid., memb. 18 r, 21 June 1234.

136 Ibid., memb. 15 r; 17 July 1234.

137 Close rolls, 45, memb. 27 in dorso : « *Sciendum est quod die mercurii,* » etc.

138 Shirley, *Royal letters*, p. 441-442; 31 May 1234.

139 Close rolls, 45, memb. 20 in dorso; Henry III to comte de La Marche.

140 Teulet, *Layettes*, t. II, 2253 to 2255, September 1233.

141 Ibid., 2289 to 2293, July 1234.

142 Ibid., 2308, Oudon, August 1234, letters of Henri d'Avaugour; Archives nationales, reg. JJ 26, f° 239 v, col. 1, guarantees furnished on this subject for several Breton lords; and, Archives de la Loire-Inférieure, série E, n. 218; letters of Louis IX.

143 English documents relative to Barfleur are particuliarly curious : Patent rolls, roll 44, memb. 16 r, 7 January 1235; Close rolls, 46, 20 r, 11 January : « *De nave deliberanda.* » ; Ibid., 18 r, 1 March, Patent rolls, 44, 11 r, 10 April : « *Pro mercatoribus de Barbeflé.* » ; Ibid., 9 r, 21 May : « *De conductu.* » ; Ibid., 5 r, 24 July 1235 : « *Pro Willelmo le Wignun preposito de Barbeflé.* »

144 Close rolls, 45, 15 r, 16 July 1234 : « *De terris Ricardi de Harecurt.* » ; Ibid., 14 r; 21 July 1234; mandated to the Viscount of Oxford, on the subject of the confusion made between the two Richard de Harcourts; Ibid., 5 r, 27 September 1234 : « *Pro Ricardo de Harecurt.* »

145 *Historiens de France*, t. XXI, p. 240 e-h. I cannot affirm that the other convocations mentioned in the same passage had been made in view of the expedition to Bretagne, p. 240 *a-c.*

146 Ibid. , p. 241 *a*; Ibid. , p. 244 *g.*

147 Ibid., p. 240.

148 *Historien de France*, t. XXI, p. 241 l.

149 Ibid., p. 244 *j-h.*

150 Ernest Petit, *Histoire des ducs de Bourgogne*, t. IV, p. 65.

151 *Historiens de France*, t. XXI, p. 241.

152 Teulet, *Layettes*, II, 2285; 13 June 1234 : letter of the precentor of Amiens to Jean de La Cour, canon of Paris.

153 Louis IX marched in person against Bretagne, as the testimony of Roger of Wendover proves. A deposition of the mayor of Huismes before the royal inquisitors, in 1247, equally affirms : « *ab annis XII citra, tempore quo dominus rex, propter guerram Britanniæ, ad partes ipsas accessit* » (*Historiens de France*, t. XXIV, p. 191, n. 1115). According to any probability, the King was in Oudon, or in front of this place, in August 1234 (*Layettes*, II, 2308). It is at the very least probable that his mother was with him.

154 Roger of Wendover, t. III, p. 93; Mathieu de Paris, ed. Luard, t. III, p. 297.

155 *Chronique de Saint-Florent de Saumur* (*Historiens de France*, t. XVMI, p. 329). This chronicle mentions the presence of Louis IX at the siege of Châteaubriand. The new siege of Oudon and of Champtoceaux, already taken place in the preceding war, was attested again by Philippe Mousket, verse 28321-28327. One finds in the inquests of 1247 many allusions to the siege of Châteaubriand (*Historiens de France*, t. XXIV, p. 31, n. 242; p. 82, n. 116; p. 83, n. 124). As for the facts relating to the siege of Oudon and of Champtoceaux, which one can glean in these same investigations, they appear to be ascribed to the campaign of 1234, without however affirming them with certainty (*Historiens de France*, t. XXIV, p. 25, n. 187; p. 104, n. 80; p. 107, n. 111. See also, for the siege of Oudon, the *Chronique d'Amadi, Documents inédits*, ed. René de Mas-Latrie, 1891, p. 183).

156 Teulet, *Layettes du Trésor des Chartes*, t. II, n. 2302, August 1234; Roger of Wendover, t. III, p. 93-94; Mathieu de Paris, t. III, p. 297.

157 *Layettes*, II, 2302.

158 *Layettes*, II, 2303 to 2307.

159 Archives nationales, J. 241 , n. 29 : « *tum infra treugam majorem cum infra minorem*; » ; « *de dampnis que facta fuerunt infra treugam, et prima et ultima.* »

160 Roger of Wendover and Mathieu de Paris; Record office; Patent rolls, 43, memb. 3 r, 9 October 1234 : letters of Henry III, notice of a safe conduct to Pierre de Bretagne.

161 Roger of Wendover, t. III, p. 94; Mathieu de Paris, t. III, p. 298.

162 Roger of Wendover, p. 95; Mathieu, p. 298.

163 Aubry de Trois-Fontaines, *Monumenta Germaniæ*, scriptores, t. XXIII, p. 935.

164 *Layettes*, II, 2319; Paris, November 1234.

165 *Layettes*, II, 2320; Paris, November 1234.

166 Ibid., 2705 and 2706.

167 Guillaume de Puylaurens, *Historiens de France*, t. XIX, p. 223 d.

168 Rymer (ed. of 1816), I, p. 215; 25 February 1235 : Henry III to the Pope. The *Annals of Tewkesbury* charged with treason the conduct of the comte de Bretagne (*Annales monastici*, ed. Luard, t. I, p. 95).

169 Close rolls, 46, mamb. 22 in dorso; 6 Dec. 1234: Henry III to Simon Langton.

170 Rogor of Wendover, t. III, p. 95.

171 Mathieu de Paris, ed. Luard , t. III, p. 298 : « *pirata factus execrabilis.* »

172 Patent rolls, 44, memb. 15 in dorso; 2 February 1235 : Henry III to the barons of the Cinque Ports.

173 Shirley, *Royal letters*, t. I, p. 464-465; 10 April 1235 : Henry III to the barons of the Cinque Ports.

174 Patent rolls, 44, memb. 4 in dorso; 29 August 1235 : Henry III to same.

175 Shirley, *Royal letters*, t. I, p. 557-558; 6 November 1234.

176 Rymer, I, p. 214; 22 November 1234.

177 Ibid., same date.

178 Ibid., 6 December : Henry III to Henri de Trubleville.

179 Patent rolls, 44, memb. 17 r; 7 December 1234. On 31 December, the Constable of Dover received an order to pay travel expenses for a canon who was going to France to join Simon Laugton: Close rolls, 46, memb. 21 r : « *Pro quodam canonico cunti (sic) in nuntium regis.* »

180 Patent rolls, 44, memb. 15 r; 27 January 1235.

181 Letters in the Close Rolls refer to a certain number of documents in which Henry III appears to make an act of suzerainty over Oléron; see, among others : Close rolls, 44, memb. 14 r, 12 January 1233 (Pro Roberto de Sabloilo); Ibid., 12 January (mandate to Hugues de Vivonne); Ibid., 13 r, 6 February 1233 (Wasconia, pro Rannulfo Bompar.). In 1236, Henry III abolished the right of *aubaine* [escheat] on the coast of England and Poitou, Gascogne, and Oléron (Rymer, I, 227).

182 Close rolls, 46, memb. 18 in dorso ; 27 January 1235.

183 Rymer, I, 215; 25 February 1235; Rymer, 216; 26 February 1235 : Henry III to Blanche and Louis IX.

184 Shirley, *Royal letters*, I, p. 559; 2 March 1235 : Gregory IX to the Archbishop of Bordeaux and to the Bishop of Bazas; another *bulla* relative to the resistance of the comte de la Marche is seen in Shirley, p. 559-560, 22 March 1235.

185 Shirley, I, 463; 10 April 1235: Henry III to Simon Langton; Close rolls, 47, memb. 6 in dorso, 1 May; in the same, Rymer, I, 217, 1 May; Patent rolls, 44, memb. 10 r, 2 May 1235 : Henry III to Louis IX, to Blanche, etc.; Potthast, 9954, 1 July 1235; Patent rolls, 44, 6 r, 8 July 1235 (*De treugis Francie*).

186 Close rolls, 47, memb. 3 in dorso : Henry III to the Prior of the Hôpital in France; Patent rolls, 44, memb. 6 in dorso, 10 July 1235 : letter of Thierry, Prior of the Hôpital in England; Shirley, *Royal letters*, t. I, p. 476-478, 12 July 1235 : arrangement of Henry III with the Hospitalers of England; Patent rolls, 44, memb. 6 r, 12 July 1235 : letter of Henry III to Gautier de Kirkeham, on the subject of monetary arrangements made with the Hospitalers (this letter has been cancelled; it was not peculiar to the arrangements made with the comte de la Marche); Patent rolls, 44 , 5 r and 4 r, 25 August 1235 : « Templum. De obligatione regis versus comitem Marchie et Engolismi. » ; Rymor, I, 218; 1235 : Henry III, the Templars and the comte de la Marche; Patent rolls, 44, 4 r, 25 August 1235 : Henry III to the Bishop of Chichester.

187 Rymer, I, 218; 25 August 1235 : Henry III to Louis IX; Idem, I, 221, 16 January 1236: letters of Henry III, on the subject of the safe conduct delivered to the anvoys of the King of France; Rymer, I, 221-222, 3 February 1236 : Henry III announcing the truce concluded with France from 15 August 1235; Ibid., p. 222, 3 February : letters of Richard de Cornouailles and others, on the subject of the truce that they juried; Close rolls, 48, memb. 18 r, 4 February 1236 : order related to the voyage of the French envoys; Patent rolls, 45, memb. 11 r, 16 February 1236 : Henry III alerts Louis IX that the Count d'Auvergne and his people are included in the truce; Close rolls, 48, memb. 15 in dorso, 8 April 1236 : complaint of Henry III to Louis IX, on the subject of the infraction of the truce.

188 Close rolls, 46, memb. 19 r, January 1235 : reprisals ordered in answer to the arrest of Guillaume, *écuyer tranchant* [royal meat carver] of Henry III, and of English merchants; Ibid., 18 r, 11 February 1235 : « *De mercatoribus deliberandis* » ; two letters relative to the same facts; Ibid., 10 r, 4 June 1235 : « *Pro Willelmo scissore regis.* »

189 Close rolls, 46, 5 in dorso, 16 August 1235 : letters relative to the truce, making allusion to the arrest of English merchants in Normandy; Close rolls, 46, 11 r, 10 May 1235 : « *Pro mercatoribus de Lenn[e].* »

190 Close rolls, 46, 18 in dorso, 20 February 1235 : Henry III to the bailiffs of Shoreham ; mandate relative to fishing boats; Patent rolls, 44, 13 r; 28 February 1235 : « *Littero directe ballivis comitisso Bolonie.* » ; Close rolls, 46, memb. 18 (en bas); 1 March 1235 : « *De mercatoribus et navibus deliberandis.* »

191 Close rolls, 48, 15 in dorso ; 12 March 1236.

192 Close rolls, 48, memb. 15 in dorso; 18 March 1236 : Henry III to Raimond, vicomte de Fronsac.

193 See Chapter Two.

194 *Layettes du Trésor des Chartes*, II, 2390.

195 *Layettes du Trésor des Chartes*, II, 2330.

196 Ibid., 2365.

197 Guillaume de Nangis, *Chronique*, ed. Géraud, I, 185; Potthast, 9761, 6 November 1234; Rinaldi, *Annales*, II, p. 108; Rodenberg, *Epistole summorum pontificum, etc.*, t. I, p. 491, n. 605, 17 November 1234.

198 D'Arbois de Jubainville, IV, 278.

199 Aubry de Trois-Fontaines, *Monumenta Germaniæ*, scriptores, XXIII, 937; *La Mer des histoires*, *Historiens de France*, XXIII, 109-110.

200 Potthast, 9951; 28 June 1235 : Gregory IX to the Archbishop Reims and to his suffragans.

201 *Layettes du Trésor des Chartes*, II, no. 2387-2388; June 1235.

202 D'Arbois de Jubainville, IV, 271.

203 Rymer (1816), I, p. 214; 3 January 1235; Rymer, I, 217; 2 June 1235.

204 For all that concerns the last revolt of Thibaud, I can only return to *Histoire des comtes de Champagne* by Arbois de Jubainville, t. IV, p. 271.

205 Aubry de Trois-Fontaines, *Monumenta Germaniæ*, scriptores, XXIII, p. 938; ed. of Wailly, 1874, § 87.

206 *Le ménestrel de Reims*, ed. de Wailly, g 357. See also the *Chronique de Jean des Preis* (chroniques belges), t. V, p. 200.

207 Chroniques de Saint-Denis, *Historiens de France*, XXI, p. 111; Aubry de Trois-Fontaines, *Monumenta Germaniæ*, scriptores, XXIII, 937, 1235; D'Arbois de Jubainville, t. V, catalogue, 2362-2364, August 1235; Ibid., t. V, 2344-2345, April 1235. *Le ménestrel de Reims*, g 357.

208 Philippe Mousket, verse 29128.

209 D'Arbois de Jubainville, IV, 270-271.

210 Philippe Mousket, verse 29140-45.

211 D. Morice, *Histoire de Bretagne*, t. I, p. 169.

212 Philippe Mousket, verse 29148; Guillaume Anelier, *Histoire de la Guerre de Navarre*, ed. Francisque Michel, p. 22; the act by which Pierre and Jean de Dreux organized a dowry for Blanche de Champagne (D'Arbois de Jubainville, t. V, catalogue, n. 2361), apparent in the edition of D. Martêne (*Thesaurus anecdotorum*, I, col. 991), the date : « *Actum apud Castrum Theoderici, anno Domini MCCXXXV, die mercurii post festum beati Laurentii.* » However the other parts relative to this marriage go back to Château-Thierry, in the year 1230, Wednesday after Saint-Hilaire. The scribe to whom we owe the copy published by D. Marténe poorly wrote "Hilarii," and to make of it "Laurentii," leads one to believe that this part, like the others, is 16 January 1236, and not 15 August 1235.

213 D'Arbois do Jubainville, t. V, n. 2361. D. Martène, *l. c.*; D'Arbois, 2377; 16 January 1236. *Layettes du Trésor des Chartes*, II, 2432.

214 D'Arbois, V, n. 2379. D. Morice, *Histoire de Bretagne*, Preuves, t. I, p. 896; 16 January 1236.

215 *Layettes du Trésor des Chartes*, II, 2432.

216 See, about the promises made by these various characters, the acts analyzed in the catalog of Arbois de Jubainville, t. V, 2391, 2392, 2395, 2403, 2409-2411; D'Arbois de Jubainville, V, 2393-94.

217 *Layettes*, 2432; D. Morice, *Preuves*, I, 896.

218 *Layettes*, 2443; D'Arbois, V, 2406; 13 April 1236.

219 Mathieu de Paris, ed. Luard, t. III, p. 366.

220 D'Arbois de Jubainville, V, n. 2634.

221 Idem, t. V, 2414; 23 May 1236.

222 *Le ménestrel de Reims*, § 357; *Chroniques de S. Denis* (*Historiens de France*, XXI, p. 111); Guillaume de Nangis, *Vie de S. Louis* (*Historiens de France*, XX, p. 322); André Du Chesne, *Hist. Généal. des ducs de Bourgogne*, Preuves, p. 135.

223 Guillaume de Nangis, *Hist.de France*, XX, 322; *Le ménestrel de Reims*, § 357.

224 Aubry de Trois-Fontaines, *Monumenta Germaniæ*, XXIII, 938.

225 D'Arbois, V, 2419; 18 June 1236.

226 D'Arbois, V, 2420-2427, 14 July 1236; Potthast, *Regesta*, 10207.

227 Guillaume de Nangis, *Historiens de France*, XX, p. 322; *Chroniques de S. Denis*, ibid., XXI, p. 111; Aubry, *Monumenta Germaniæ*, XXIII, p. 938.

228 *Le ménestrel de Reims*, § 358; Mathieu de Paris, ed. Luard, III, 370.

229 Aubry de Trois-Fontaines, loc. cit.; Philippe Mousket, verse 29156-29160; Guillaume de Nangis, *Historiens de France*, XX, p. 322; *Chroniques de S. Denis*, same study, XXI, p. 111, and several others; *Le ménestrel de Reims*, § 359.

230 Aubry, *Monumenta Germaniæ*, XXIII, p. 938; *Le ménestrel de Reims*, § 359.

231 Philippe Mousket, verse 29158-29160.

232 *Chroniques de S. Denis* (*Historiens de France*, XXI, p. 111-112).

233 *Le ménestrel de Reims*, § 358; Philippe Mousket, verse 29160-29171.

234 *Le ménestrel de Reims*, § 358.

235 Idem, § 359; Philippe Mousket, verse 29172-29178.

236 Philippe Mousket, verse 29188-89.

237 Philippe Mousket, verse 29179-29187.

Chapter Six

The royal family. — Blanche of Castile and Marguerite de Provence. — Expenditure made for the princes. — Alphonse de Portugal. — Spaniards employed at the court. — Gifts made to *les grands*, to new knights; minstrels. — Alms and bread to the poor. — Horses. — Relations with foreign sovereigns. — Rapport with the nobility, with the clergy. — Enlightened Piety and firmness of Blanche. — Conflicts of jurisdiction. — Difficulties with the Archbishop of Rouen. — Quarrel with the Bishop of Beauvais. — Relationship with people of the cities and the people of the country. — Sufferings of the population; exactions of the royal agents. — Repression of heresy; Robert le Bougre. — The royal army. — Command; the constable, marshals. — Other men of war; bailiffs and seneschals; role of Blanche. — Feudal quotas. — Service owed by the churches. — Troops; cavalry, infantry, archers. — Supply. — Cartage; machines. — Communal Militia.

At the moment when Louis IX left her supervision, Blanche of Castile, who had accepted the mission of taking care of the interests of France during his minority, could be satisfied after casting her eyes upon it. The King was master in the kingdom; the enemies of the throne were subjected or discouraged from fighting; the sovereign power was strong and well armed.

I will not go as far to claim that in all of France the population was happy. They emerged from a violent crisis, and if we want to study in detail what occurred in several provinces, we would see that under the regency of Blanche there were thousands of people who, mistreated by royal officers, underwent acts of injustice and spoliation. Does one have to charge these abuses to a princess who had to fight foreigners and her own subjects? It is rare that one makes reforms in time of invasion or civil war.

Elsewhere, if the royal administration had defects, one must recognize that they were former to the advent of Louis IX and that they remained a long time after the moment when this great king was found at the head of the government. It was especially in the last part of his reign that he could occupy himself with organizing and administration. We cannot thus study thoroughly the state of the people and the royal administration for a period restricted to the first regency of Blanche.

On the contrary, it is possible for us to know what were the resources of the sovereign power when calm of a relatively stable regime succeeded agitations during the years in which Blanche had been fighting. We are in a place where it is good to describe the life of the court and the royal family, and I must recall in few words what were, under the administration of Blanche and at the end of her government, the relations of royalty with the various classes of French society, with the nobility and clergy; what concerned the people of the cities and countryside is sadly rather less definite; one can however seize something. Lastly, in the midst of institutions of which progress was then not very visible, there was an element of power that Blanche of Castile developed, or at least maintained with obvious care. This Queen who herself went to war had at her disposal a well organized military force.

The respect and personal devotion that the King met among the majority of his subjects is attested by innumerable witnesses. There was already more than a century during which royalty gained unceasingly in popularity and influence. Since the first days of the reign, one had seen on many occasions that the King, in spite of the bad disposition of certain people, could count on the affection and fidelity of many. Had such feelings not existed, Blanche of Castile would never have overcome her adversaries and preserved intact the royal power; they affirmed more and more when the populations of France, accustomed for some time to consider the sovereign authority as a guardian power, discovered in their King Louis a defender of all good causes, a consolator of all miseries, respectful of all their rights, even when they were contrary to his apparent interest. Louis IX and his brothers had been raised seriously, and the spectacle outside the court of France, under the authority of Queen Blanche, could only inspire respect. The life of the royal family had something of patriarchy; those who composed it were truly plain; they carried out a rich enough train to cut a good figure before the eyes of the world, but abstained from a wounding luxury, such as the Valois who later gave so scandalous an example; neither exaggerated economies, nor insane expenditures. The King, his mother, his wife, his brothers and his sister, the princes and the lords of his house, had all that was necessary for them, but a charity of every day, very broad and known very well, ensured them; esteemed the humble and attenuated as much as possible so painful a contrast that produced before the eyes of the people the inevitable bringing together of richness and poverty.

It is impossible to know the sum devoted each year to the personal expenditure of the young King. In the accounts of the household, the objects bought for his intention are seldom enumerated separately; at any moment, one finds item such as these: "For six *hoquetons* intended for the King and for Prince Robert. – For four covers of silk for the use of the King our Lord, Madam the Queen, Prince Robert and Prince Alphonse. – Four carpets for the King and for Prince Robert.[1] – Five saddles for the King, five for his brothers and Lord Alphonse (of Portugal)."[2] However, it goes without saying that Louis IX, even in his first youth, had apartments and servants with him; the accounts of 1234 speak about his chapel and quote, on several occasions, women of the household of the King; they were well placed, paid only once, for their dresses, a hundred and seven *livres* six *sous parisis*.[3]

When Louis IX married, there were three Queens in France, Blanche of Castile, Marguerite of Provence, and Ingeburge of Denmark, widow of Philippe Auguste. An attentive study of royal accounts written at that time and during the following years seems to show that, in these documents, the title of Queen (*regina*), without qualifier, is in general used to indicate Blanche of Castile. The King's wife is generally called the young Queen (*juvenis regina*), and this name was still applied in 1237 and 1239.[4] It is known that Marguerite de Provence, in spite of serious qualities and her grace, scarcely met the affection which, in the eyes of everyone, was and remained par excellence reserved for the Queen of France. Joinville left us the memory of sad quarrels in which Marguerite did not have a bad role, or rather acts of hardness that Blanche of Castile, so great, so powerful, should not have made. One remembers the preference that Louis IX and his wife had for their house in Pontoise, because in this residence their apartments were above the other in communication. How singular that this King and this Queen of France, reduced to meet in a staircase, except to run away, as children who feel at fault, when ushers knock on the doors to inform them that Queen Blanche has arrived! One day the King was detained near the bed of his wife, sick under the covers, Blanche took him by the hand and while saying to him: "Come here. You accomplish nothing here." And the poor Queen said while swooning: "Alas! you will let me see my Lord neither dead nor alive."[5] Blanche of Castile was unwarranted; loved by her son until the point of weakness, her jealousy had no reason to be; she did not honor him. The most beautiful figures sometimes have unpleasant traits.

The third Queen, Ingeburge, did not reside at the court. Withdrawn to her estate in Orléans, she lived there until 1237.[6] They called her, in the royal accounts, "Queen of Orléans."[7] This princess, so unhappy for a long time, was certainly treated better and much less isolated from her husband, but she had her own existence.[8]

The other royal family members remained together, and it was Blanche of Castile who took care of them. In the middle of the greatest affairs, she always remained a mother, just as Louis IX, King of France, never ceased to be the older brother. The Queen and all them lived on common expenses; accounts of the household in 1239 have an article "for the shoes of the Queens, the countesses and the *enfants*," another "for the furs of the Queens and countesses."[9] Though each one of the princes had his particular servants, the accounts give us, confoundingly, the expenditure of all the royal family, not only in 1234, but several years after the marriage of Louis IX, in 1237 and 1239. It was thus that in 1234 one finds pell-mell the dresses made for Eudeline, one of the ladies of Queen Blanche, for Pierre de Chambly, Prince Alphonse of France, the Lady of Amboise, Jean de Beaumont, the Countess de Chartres, and Queen Marguerite.[10]

Whoever thus entered on the same page the expenditure of the King, his other children, his daughter-in-law, his nephew, of his cousins, all his servants, did not put aside, in the accounts, purchases made for himself. However, some of the supplies which were given to him clearly can be adumbrated. In 1234, a sum of one 150 livres was employed for his robes; he paid a hundred and eight *sous parisis* for a silver vase; carpets were bought for his room, as well as quilts, by Gautier de Poissy; Robin de Poissy bought, also for the room of the Queen, three *aumucelles*, undoubtedly a type of bed cover or coverlet.[11] Blanche had *dames* and *demoiselles* attached to her person;

of this number were the Lady of Amboise, a Spaniard named Mincia, a person whom the royal accounts call Miss Eudeline, come to Sens for the marriage of Louis IX.[12] Blanche had in her household a man especially charged to bleed her; she also had a cook and his kitchen, proof that she did not always eat, and perhaps not ordinarily, with the King.[13]

In spite of the relative simplicity which was the rule at court, the royal children of France were treated richly. Robert, who soon became Count d'Artois, often figures in the accounts, at the time of regency. We see his *valet de chambre* mentioned, his stable, and his falcons, which were given to the care of a servant.[14] Eight pairs of shoes were made for him at one time; he drank from a silver cup, and wore, like his brother Alphonse, a gilded belt with a buckle of gold.[15] In 1234, Robert was already a young man of seventeen years; he had a taste for luxury, and was extremely given over to weapons and horses, which he liked all his life. It was known that the Bishop of Chartres sent him a horse, knives, a sword and a buckler; the King and Robert were brought, for a use which is not specified, iron arrowheads.[16]

The name of Prince Alphonse, later Count of Poitiers and of Toulouse, is found at every point in the accounts of the household.[17] He had an entire suite at the age of thirteen and a half years. A man was charged to keep his falcon, and for only one season, they made him nine pairs of robes for his riders and six pairs of robes for his "boys."[18] His servants, as all those who lived at court, were extremely well treated; gratifications were allocated to them, especially in the event of disease or taking up the cross.[19]

There was another prince of the name of Alphonse at the court of France; he was the younger son of Queen Urraque of Portugal, sister of Blanche of Castile. Queen Blanche, who certainly had a predilection for this orphan of her family, raised him as a third son; they were both called "Alphonse," and when the Prince of Portugal appears alone in the accounts, he is generally named "Lord Alphonse the second."[20] With the marriage of the King his cousin, he received a robe of crimson; two knights were attached to his service, and the royal accounts speak about his people, to which they gave saddle horses.[21] We will see that after she treated him like a son, Blanche of Castile made him Count de Boulogne, while waiting for the day when he became King of Portugal.

He who was later celebrated as Charles d'Anjou was then a

strong little boy; he rather seldom appears in the accounts of 1234. They made him a trunk; a servant placed at his service received a sum of forty *sous parisis*, and accounts of the household say familiarly that this man was for Charles.[22] In general, Charles and the young princess Isabelle, in these accounts, are simply called "children" when it is a question of their shoes, or of their apartment (*hospitium*).[23] Yves the glove maker received thirty-four *sous* six *deniers* of money for gloves provided to the Queen "and children."[24] During the time of the royal marriage the "expenditure of the children remaining in Paris" formed an article of up to 673 *livres* three *sous parisis*.[25] In the account of the bailiffs and provosts for Ascension term of this year, one finds a small sum spent, in Paris, for the bourgeois "who sleep in front of children."[26] I do not know if the *enfants de France* had in general for the night, in their room or in front of their door, a bourgeois guard; perhaps it acted only as an exceptional mark of confidence that Blanche of Castile would have given certain people of Paris, when after leaving for the marriage of the King she entrusted Charles and Isabelle to them. The population of Paris was then in great honor; I note that two Parisian widows had been given as godmothers for Philippe Auguste; after Bouvines, the crowning of Louis VIII and of Blanche, the inhabitants of Paris had shown how sincere was their attachment to the dynasty, and they especially had had to preserve a memorial recognizing the memorable day when they had left with weapons to come seek at Montlhéry their young King, threatened by a plot of the barons.

    It would be difficult and tiresome to reconstitute the personnel which composed the house of the King, the Queen mother, and that of the princes. There are many examples enough to prove that people employed at the court, whatever was their condition, enjoyed good advantages. Benevolence was apparent, to give them money when they went to stay in their country.[27] The Spaniards who had joined Queen Blanche, and who were numerous at the court of France, had only to enjoy their lives. Blanche had enough political savvy to take care not to raise them up to important offices, but they profited from her generosity. The Spanish woman attached to her person, Mincia, is often named in the accounts of 1234; she had people in her retinue; when she left for Spain, after the marriage of the King, she was awarded money for the road, and for the carriages which accompanied her until La Rochelle; it was probably for this voyage that she accepted two saddle horses.[28] During the coronation of Queen

Marguerite, two Spaniards, Lord Fernando and Lord Roger, appear in the number of those who received robes.[29] Another received sixty *livres* for returning beyond the Pyrenees, without counting a cup with the price of ten *livres*, and eight *livres* paid to the clerk who was in their company to buy a saddle horse. The cook who served them remained at court after their departure.[30] These persons were unquestionably *gens de qualité*; I do not have any precise concept on the positions occupied in the entourage of the Queen and of the princes by several other Spaniards whose names are given in the royal accounts.[31] Queen Blanche did not spare gifts to those of her compatriots who came to find her, envoys or servants of the Queen of Castile, Spanish clerics, Spanish merchants robbed by Savary de Mauléon, and lay brothers and sisters from the same country.[32] A Spaniard, who wanted to enter to the service of the King as an archer, received an indemnity.[33] The favor accorded by the Queen to those whose presence pointed out their fatherland to her explains as much or better than anything.

The crossbowmen and sergeants with horse who appear in the last accounts of the household for 1234 were probably used as guards and escorts at court; the forging mill of the crossbowmen was cited in these same accounts, and we know that later crossbowmen and sergeants armed with lances were attached to the royal household.[34]

It goes without saying that they spent much for the great lords and important characters who followed the court. I cite among other expenses made for the old Chamberlain of France, Barthelemy de Roye, a breviary, reaching the sizeable price of fourteen *livres parisis*, given to Hugues de Athies.[35] Raimond VII of Toulouse, at once the great vassal and cousin of the Queen, received rich hospitality at court. Until he arrived there in 1234, he was defrayed for his stay, accepted textiles, a palfrey, and a riding horse.[36] One man was paid to keep his falcon for him; and they presented gifts to his people.[37]

The clothing of numerous personnel and distributions of robes made to a crowd of barons constituted one of the greatest expenditures of the household. These distributions of robes were given regularly on the occasion of grand religious festivals, important ceremonies, and marriages celebrated in the royal household.[38] New knights were created, who also received robes and gifts; it was especially Pentecost that served for dubbing, and we know from Aubry de Trois-Fontaines that in 1237, the day of this festival, a hundred and forty men accepted knighthood.[39] It was also at Pentecost that in 1239 knighthood was conferred on Baudouin II of Courtenay, Emperor of Constantinople, and to Prince Alphonse of Portugal.[40]

The minstrels, who played a great part in court festivals, cost much money, in 1237, when Robert d'Artois was knighted, distributing to all of them 220 *livres*.[41] They did not have to play instruments or sing, and it was told that on this same occasion several of them performed acts of legerdemain before the King and court.[42] Many lords had minstrels in their service, and it was customary to treat them liberally. The Count de Provence sent one along with his daughter when she married the King, and we find in the royal household those of Thibaud de Champagne, Guillaume de Chauvigny, the Count de Sancerre, Robert de Courtenay.[43] Prince Robert of France liked to make them gifts.[44]

Messengers, envoys of the princes, those of the Pope, people charged with missions, received gifts of silver or expense accounts which held a certain place in the expenditure of the court. With them I finish the enumeration of those to whom gifts and remunerations of all kinds were devoted. But beside these acts of generosity, of the payments for normal or accidental services, it is necessary for me to speak about the cost of charity for Blanche of Castile and Louis IX.

Among the most frequent gifts, there were cases of true alms-giving. Blanche came readily to aid some not very fortunate people who wished to marry; relatively modest and variable sums were allotted, not only to people in service, for their establishment, but for their children, their sisters, completely foreign women to the various courts and conditions.[45] A poor lady of the neighborhood of Anet received thus one hundred *sous parisis* for the marriage of her daughter; while returning from Angers, Blanche met a young daughter of the *châtellenie* of Nogent; she gave her fifteen *livres* to marry, an important sum.[46] In Paris, a girl who wanted to solicit a gift of this kind placed herself on the Grand Pont, during the passage of the King, and Squire Hugues, one of those who in the court had the mission of alms-giving, gave forty *sous parisis* for her marriage.[47]

The travels of the court did not have as their sole consequence the distraction of the King and his retinue. True, Louis IX and his mother changed residence unceasingly, but it was to see what occurred in the kingdom, to make themselves known to the population, to render justice to them and gain their affection. When one studies lists of the voyages and sojourns of Louis IX which were published, or the first chapter of the expenditure of the household in

1234, one is astonished to see that the court hardly remained in place and that it spent much time in ceaseless peregrinations.[48] These voyages served as an occasion to crowd good works together; in this respect, as under all the reports, Blanche and her son did not lose time in any way. On a brief stay that they made in Bourges in February 1234, shortly before the marriage of the King, they distributed money to patients and the poor, called after them Archambaud de Bourbon, with which they wanted to maintain, undoubtedly about the business of his son-in-law the Count de Champagne, to establish an accord between Henri de Sully and Robert de Courtenay, then in disagreement.[49] The royal accounts teach us that before arriving at Bourges, Louis IX had given a small sum to the priest of Isde, in the house of whom he had taken a meal.[50] In Bourges, Queen Blanche had made for herself a *chape* [cape or cope] and dress; prince Alphonse de France also spent there, for himself and his retinue, about thirty-two *livres*, without counting a gift for two of his servants who had then left his service.[51]

When it was learned that the King and his mother was approaching, the poor people came to put themselves on their path, and as the procession could not stop at all moments to give alms, people of the household, in general of the squires, were charged with this task; of them, the squire Herbert was to be extremely occupied with it. During the spring of 1234, on the travels of the court, they distributed in kind, at each stage, a series of small purses averaging from twenty-five to forty or even fifty *sous parisis*.[52] There were undoubtedly some exaggerated generosities, but once arrived in the place where they wanted to stop, Blanche and her son usually began the distribution of alms again, and then they proceeded grandly: twenty-five *livres* in Beaumont-sur-Oise, twelve *livres* to the poor of Issoudun; the Queen gave a hundred *sous* upon arriving at Pont-de-l'Arch, and four *livres* at Château Gaillard; in Vaudreuil, 300 poor people shared a hundred *sous parisis*; distribution of eight *livres* eight *sous* in Gisors, and the same sum in Vincennes, where 200 poor were helped; new alms of one hundred *sous parisis* were given at the court of Vincennes. The same amount was given to the inhabitants of Beaumont and surrounding parts, then to a hundred poor at Fontainebleau.[53] In passing by Asnières, Guillaume de Bray, one of the men attached to the court, gave ten *livres* to a poor lady of the Pontoise area; Squire Herbert gave forty *sous* to one other woman.[54] They made a gift of forty *sous* to a poor woman who had a debt to pay.⁵⁵ The lepers received help, and at the time of his marriage in Sens, the King give twenty *livres* thirteen *sous* to the patients who came to see him.⁵⁶ The sums distributed thus by Louis IX and his mother were considerable; for in examining accounts, there should be care not to forget that this money then had a value quite higher than that which it represents today.

All occasions were good for charity; they distributed alms for the birthdays of Isabelle de Hainaut and Louis VIII, at Easter, Maundy Thursday; and the King, having eaten twice the day of the Annunciation, gave money to a hundred poor; he was not satisfied to receive the unfortunate ones, so he would seek them out; people of the household brought alms to the poor of Normandy.⁵⁷

In addition to silver alms, they gave, at the court, bread to the poor, about a *livre parisis* per day; the bread was brought in bags made purposely for this use.⁵⁸ In Lent of 1234, the King distributed 45,000 herrings; to *carnaval* in Lorris, they had given pigmeat to the poor for a sum of nineteen *livres*.⁵⁹ Princes who demonstrated such a generous manner, so regular in their duties of charity, could without scruple spend the money necessary to the good behavior of their house.

Accounts of the royal household provide curious information on fabrics and furs, but precious stones rarely appear.⁶⁰ One finds dice and chess-men of the kings quoted there, and ivory chess-men, intended for a gift.⁶¹ Let me also cite the mention of a sum spent to buy and shave parchment.⁶²

Beside robes and other objects being used for costume, special attention must be made about the purchase of horses. Undoubtedly very important sums were expended at the court for mountings and attachments, and nothing can astonish me.⁶³ It was not only to cut a good figure; the *roussin*, the palfrey, the *diagrid*, the *dextrier*, were of a use so constant, that one was absolutely obliged to have a number of them, and of as good a quality as possible.

Roncins or *roussins*, were saddle horses for the use of household staff, for the mails, and for everyone on a journey, and cost in general from eight to ten *livres parisis*, seldom less, sometimes more. The price of sixteen *livres*, that one finds in an account of 1239, appears extremely high for a horse of this species.⁶⁴ They were bought unceasingly and in quantity.

Palfreys, horses of luxury, which were not employed in war, usually cost from ten to twelve *livres parisis*, but it was not rare to see them reaching higher prices. Prince Alphonse of France, who had one of twelve *livres* in 1234, accepted a palfrey in black poplar, or dappled gray, of twenty *livres*, in 1239, and this same year they bought two of them, the one of twenty, the other of twenty-two *livres*, for Count Alphonse de Boulogne, nephew of Blanche.[65] The King rode palfreys of black poplar, which cost twenty to twenty-seven *livres*; the most expensive horse of luxury that Louis IX, to my knowledge, rode in this period of his life, was forty *livres*, the year of his marriage.[66]

Chasseurs, or hunting horses, were of much less frequent use. Those of Prince Charles, Prince Alphonse, Alphonse of Portugal, and the King, appear in the accounts of 1239 prices varying between twenty *livres* to thirty-seven *livres* twelve *sous*.[67]

Sommiers [pack horses], large draught horses employed in the transport of material, cost in general more than the palfreys; they usually reached fourteen, fifteen and sixteen *livres*; one which was used in 1234 for transporting the King's bed, cost twenty-one *livres*.[68]

As for the *dextrier* (*equus* or *dextrarius*), the horse *par excellence*, the war-horse, its price varied according to different cases, but went far beyond that of the other horses (twenty-five, thirty, thirty-five, and forty *livres parisis*). In 1239, one bought for Aimery de Narbonne a *dextrier* for forty-five *livres*; that of Eustace de Neuville cost forty-seven in 1234; those which the emperor Baudouin II of Constantinople and the Count de Boulogne, Alphonse of Portugal, accepted when they were dubbed knights, undoubtedly reached exceptional prices of sixty and seventy-five *livres*.[69] The *dextrier* that one got for a similar sum must have been a superb animal.

When one adds to expenses caused by the purchase of horses the money spent for saddles, harnesses, clamps, one arrives, concerning the stable, at very high sums.[70] A forging mill followed the court, another was assigned to the service of crossbowmen, undoubtedly for those used to guard the royal family.[71] There were naturally wagons in the baggage service, for transport of sums of money, and we know that at that time the money, when one the carried it in great quantity, was loaded into barrels.[72] Princes and people who surrounded them traveled on horseback, so the number of vehicles which were useful in transporting the court was very restricted. With this singular exception, I found in accounts of the household in 1234, a cart for which they made new wheels and accessories; in 1239, a certain sum was expended to repair the cart of the young Queen and to buy a new one; it certainly appears, in this case, to be a cart that Marguerite de Provence had for personal use, and the accounts of this year speak about its coachman.[73] Blanche of Castile and people of her retinue often traveled by water; for example, they hired boats for a voyage to Vincennes, to return to Paris by Melun, and Beaumont-sur-Oise.[74]

The princes and important barons all kept falcons, birds of great price, that they entrusted to men especially charged to keep them. A falcon was bought, in 1234, for the large sum of ten *livres parisis*; at this price one could have had a good *roussin* or an ordinary palfrey of value. The court had its bird-catchers, a hunting pack and its keepers of dogs.[75] As for services of the kitchen and pantry, we cannot know what they cost during the youth of Saint Louis; it is only later that special articles were set forth in the royal accounts.[76] The final accounts of 1234, rather poorly classified if one compares them with those which were held thereafter, include, without speaking about receipts, seven subdivisions relative to expenditure: 1.) Travels. 2.) Gifts and harness, including, among others, alms, pledges and gratuities of all kinds, mostly various purchases. 3.) Robes. 4.) Expenditure of the *enfants de France* [royal children] left in Paris at the time of the marriage of Louis IX. 5.) Expenditure made on the occasion of this marriage. 6.) Horses and saddle horses. 7.) Crossbowmen and sergeants with horses.[77]

Under the government of Blanche of Castile, it was in the royal household as in all the rest; though controlled well enough, it was less regularly organized than at the end of the reign.

During the years which followed the advent of her son, Blanche of Castile interfered to the least possible degree in what occurred among her neighbors. Only occupied to consolidate the sovereign power, she hardly thought of making alliances, and foreign princes for their part, with the exception of the King of England, left her rather quiet. One can say that French diplomacy in the time of the regency was reduced to a little thing.

The relationship of Blanche to the Holy See had especially for its goal the regulation of interests of the French churches and their relationship with royalty; the Queen was committed to a variation of the fight between the Pope and the Emperor, and in this regard gave to her son an example he had the wisdom to follow. The letter of 18 July 1229, by which Gregory IX denounced to the King the intrigues of Frederick II, had no result; it was a kind of circular [letter], and without speaking about the sovereigns and foreign prelates who accepted it, I know that it was addressed to several French archbishops and their suffragans.[78] Gregory went further, when, on 28 and 30 September of the same year, he wrote the Archbishop of Lyon and the Bishop of Paris, to put them in resolution to go help raise forces.[79] At the end of 1234, archbishops of France, like other ecclesiastical and laic princes, accepted the circular, in which Gregory IX requested them to bring him troops to resist the tyranny of the Romans [Germans].[80] Lastly, next June, he thanked the Count and Countess de La Marche, the archbishops of Tours, Sens, Rheims, and their suffragans and clergy of their provinces, as well as the abbots and convents of the free monasteries located in France, for offers of subsidies that they had made him.[81] It is seen that the clergy of France and even certain French lords were ready to provide the Holy See with help against its enemies. In 1230, Miles de Nanteuil, bishop of Beauvais, had gone to find the Pope with a troop of knights; Gregory rewarded his zeal by naming him vice-chancellor of the duchy of Spolète, at the head of which he remained nearly three years.[82] Blanche of Castile could not be satisfied to see her subjects thus mingling with quarrels of which nothing interested the kingdom; however I do not see that she protested.

The adversary of the Holy See, Frederick II, had been from time immemorial regarded by the court of France as a friend; but relations that the French government maintained with him, from 1226 to 1235, did not have a real importance. A cooling, which however did not lead to an official rupture, occurred when, in 1235, Frederick sought Isabelle Plantagenet, sister of Henry III.[83] He invested Gregory IX in vain on the initiative of this project of marriage, on the subject of which the Pope wrote for his account to the King of France; one might consider him consequently as pledged to the English policy. He however remained in personal rapport with Louis IX, and in the summer of 1235, had the care to inform Henry III, but his sincerity was subject to caution.[84] After his marriage, which was celebrated on 15 July of this year, he was concerned so little about his ally of the past, that he went so far as to request the King of England to send his young brother, Richard de Cornouailles to him, to direct, on the side of Germany, the war against France.[85] This fanfaronade did not have consequences, and if he was upset, at the court of France, by seeing the Emperor to thus change dispositions, they could not conceive of concern. Frederick was very occupied with his own business, and the way of Bouvînes, fatal to his predecessor Otto IV, would not tempt him. The alliance with the house of Souabe had brought back nothing for Blanche of Castile, and the reversal which deprived Louis IX of this support passed almost unperceived.

As for England, its hostile attitude was not to change for a long time. The two countries were always at war, and all the efforts of those who tried to regulate their interests ended in periodic renewal of truces. In January 1236, Henry III married Aliénor, Princess of Provence, sister of Queen Marguerite, but it was certainly not a peaceful intention that had pushed them to seek union.[86] Perhaps it was on the contrary the hope of thwarting French policy in Provence. If it was thus, Blanche and her son did not make a show of it, and when the betrothed of the King of England crossed France, she was treated with honor by Louis IX, the young Queen, and Blanche of Castile.[87]

Other European states, especially Aragon, always hostile, in the Midi, to French interests, remained almost entirely foreign, during the regency, to what occurred on our soil. Blanche, on her side, thought so little about concluding alliances, that she did not do anything, so it seems, to engage Castile in her interests. Apart from her estates, she made only one serious effort to extend the influence of the Capetian dynasty; it was in Provence, when she married her son to the oldest daughter of Raimond Bérenger.

It was on interior matters that all the of attention of the Queen mother was concentrated; it was necessary as well, since all the danger came from there. Blanche had worked wonders in bringing the great nobles to respect the authority of her son and to defend the general interest against private ambitions. When Louis IX ceased to be in tutelage, nobody in France was, at least for the moment, in sufficient state to rise against him. The integrity of the royal domain, one moment compromised by the Treaty of Vendôme, had been safeguarded; Blois, Chartres, Sancerre, and Châteaudun, these old fiefs of Champagne, no longer concerned the King; by the Treaty of Paris, two new provinces were united with those which Louis IX had received from his father. The house of France, designated heiress of what remained of the Count de Toulouse, had become dominant on the left bank of the Rhone, and great feudatories, at one time threatening, had been transformed into respectful vassals.

The first of those whom Blanche had had to fight, her cousin Raimond de Toulouse, had become protected by the crown. After having removed from him Beaucaire and Nimes, Carcassonne and Béziers, after having named his heir Alphonse of France, Blanche of Castile tried to help him take the marquisate of Provence, which did not belong to the kingdom. The Church would have well wanted the guardianship of this country entrusted to [French] royal agents, but it was not returned, because she [the Church] felt impotent to preserve it; for the last time, in February 1235, Gregory IX insisted, to the King and his mother, not to withdraw from Venaissin their seneschal; it was in vain; soon Raimond VII again took possession of this land, which was to him again enfiefed by Frederick.[88]

The others feudatories were reduced to impotence. Pierre Mauclerc, definitively vanquished, prepared himself to give Brittany to his son Jean le Roux. The Count de La Marche and his wife Isabelle of Angoulême, who in the last crisis had held to the party of the King, were vassals of a doubtful fidelity, but several years still separated them from the moment when they combined with the enemies of the kingdom. Thibaud IV, if inconstant in his relationship with the Crown, received a hard lesson, and his attention was shared between Champagne and Navarre. The house of Dreux was more to fear; the count Robert de Dreux had died, and the county of Mâcon was soon going to fall into the hands of the King; Enguerrand de Coucy had returned to his role of *grand seigneur*. The Countess of Flanders remained as she had been in the bad days of the minority, a good vassal and a devoted relation, and her neighbor Mahaut de Boulogne, widow of Philippe Hurepel, was not in a position to create embarrassments for the crown; what remained then of the feudal power which the second son of Philippe Auguste had wanted to found? An untimely death had destroyed the ambitious projects of the Count de Boulogne, and it was Louis IX who, in 1235, occupied himself to regulate the succession.[89] In February, Mahaut announced that she promised to be faithful to the King as her liege lord, that she had not made any promise of marriage, that she would not marry nor would not become engaged without his assent and that of Blanche.[90] At the same time, she engaged not to marry and promised her daughter would not marry without their approval, to keep in places indicated by the charter that she delivered to the King, and to yield to him if it was necessary. Any infringement of these promises was to result in the seizure of her domains, and the many barons given as guarantors of her good faith delivered to the King letters mentioning the signatures of their guarantees.[91]

I noted that Blanche was often named, at the side of her son, in obligations and oaths of the nobles. She made use of this type, on many occasions, during all of her regency, as on 21 March 1235 when Hugues d'Antoing associated himself with the King in an act relative to his homage.[92] Furthermore, the precautions which the suzerains at that time took with the regard to their vassals were not specific to the government of Blanche of Castile. Thus the use, then frequent, in declaring that one would return to the King such or such castle, with large and small forces, if one was required by it, existed well before the advent of Louis IX, and the King was not only to profit from them.[93] It was the same promise that one often made not to raise fortifications without the assent of the King. Finally, we see that, in a great number of cases, Blanche, to ensure the execution of the contracts and arrangements passed with feudatories, was assured by various persons; these *pleiges* answered, each one for a stipulated sum, the fidelity which would be observed in clauses accepted by the interested principal. It goes without saying that these processes were not invented by Blanche of Castile; but too often she had applied them for her advantage in her relationship with the nobility.

The clergy was never, like the nobility, in open revolt against Blanche of Castile, but they created grave difficulties for her. The too frequent hostility of the archbishops and bishops was, it should be said, encouraged by the Holy See, which was often involved to support the representatives of the Church in claims completely foreign to religious interests. The mother of Saint Louis would have shirked one of her primary duties if she had not resisted, as her son did later, against inadmissible requirements, and in their opposition to her government, people of the church were much less excusable because they could not be unaware of her piety.

The Pope, who on several occasions defended her against men not very worthy of consideration, did not haggle with them in these external regards, nor upon these favors that the head of the Church granted easily to other sovereigns: permission to enter the monastery of Cluny during the general chapter, insurance that the chapels of the Queen Mother, as those of the King, would not be placed under interdict.[94] The clergy of France and monks from foreign lands were not aware of the enthusiasm of her feelings?[95] Blanche was always extremely generous towards the orders; it was not without her authorization that Louis IX, still a young person, founded the abbey of Royaumont; in 1233, she attended with her son the dedication of Saint-Anthony des Champs; in 1229, she contributed 300 *livres* to raise the church of Couture, or Sainte-Catherine du Val-des-Écoliers, founded, at the request of the sergeants-at-arms, in honor of the Battle of Bouvines.[96] The abbey of Saint-Denis figured naturally in the first rank of the monasteries that she supported; in 1231 the abbot Eudes Clément decided to rebuild the *chevet* [apse] of his church, encouraged by Blanche of Castile and by the King, who, without any doubt, took an active part in this work.[97]

Perhaps these good monks, so devoted to the house of France, celebrated with a little emphasis the emotion which their sovereigns showed, when they lost, then found, in 1233, one of their more invaluable relics, the Holy Nail. The historians of their abbey told of this event with passion, so serious for them, whose chancellor of Paris, Philippe de Grève, wrote an interesting relation.[98] It was necessary to make their pain known to the Queen and her son; the young King declared that he would prefer to see the best city of his kingdom destroyed; he promised a reward of one hundred *livres* for the discovery of the relic. For one month the Holy Nail remained lost; Paris and France were in mourning. It was found, and at once the abbot hastened to inform the Queen; Blanche, as a circumspect woman, recommended to him above all to precipitate nothing: it was necessary to be wary of impostors; then she found a pious excuse to avoid the ceremony at which only the monks of Saint-Denis would celebrate. She directed, elsewhere, to send three advisers to honorably represent her in a procession of the Holy Nail; the King having been unable to attend this solemnity, came a few days later to the abbey to revere the sainted relic. Blanche of Castile appeared to be strongly interested in this worthy object, but perhaps did not make a point of being personally engaged in the little factitious agitation that the monks of Saint-Denis created on this occasion. Saint Louis, in his devotion to relics, did not always show as much prudence.

Pious as she was, Blanche never sacrificed the interests of the Crown to those of the churches. Her son, whose burning piety could not be disputed, accepted this rule of conduct from her, which he observed all his life. During the regency, *droits de régale* [rights that belonged exclusively to the king] were charged to the churches when they pertained to the King; royal agents managed them as long as the replevin [procedure used to recover personal property] had not been granted to a new title holder. The King, or rather his mother, did not fail to announce the death, in timely fashion, of a bishop or prelate, the only means of knowing at which moment they were allowed *droits de régale*. Blanche had seldom been named in these acts by which the Church filled their duties of subjects; she scarcely held to them, at the moment when the authority of her son was sufficiently recognized.[99]

It was natural that the Crown required the clergy to meet their engagements with fidelity, whereas on her side she was shown to be extremely concerned to defend them, in case of injustice, against the laic lords and communes, even against royal agents. In the thirteenth century, as much as any other time, the protection of the churches was not a sinecure; then more that ever the civil element and the religious element were, at any moment, in absolute opposition, not only on questions of principles and general policy, but in the things of detail, in the practice of daily life. Great contemporary affairs of this regency, during which certain churches, wrongly or rightly, claimed themselves injured by the royal power, do not have to make us forget the mass of occasions Blanche of Castile and the young King had very scrupulously filled their duties towards the French episcopate and religious communities. This assertion can be justified enough by many examples.

In 1229 Adam, Bishop of Térouanne, Pierre de Collemezzo, provost of the chapter of Saint-Omer, and five abbots of the region officially noticed the reparation to which the royal bailiff of Saint-Omer subjected them, to have seized and executed a man of Arques, in the locality belonging to the Abbey of Saint-Bertin.[100] In 1231, the aldermen of Arques, having attacked in an ambush the abbot of Saint-Bertin, the prior of this monastery and their people, the King, in royal progress through Saint-Bertin with his mother and nobles of his court, rendered justice to the abbey.[101] It was in the presence of the King that in January 1230, Gautier, Lord of Autremencourt, made amends with the Bishop of Laon, and that in 1233 an agreement intervened between the bishop and municipal officers of this city; the King entrusted the payment of this business to Gautier, the Bishop of Chartres, to Geoffroy de la Chapelle, and to the bailiff Renaud de Baronne.[102]

Churches and monasteries were thus not abandoned by the royal power in their contentions with laymen; with protection of the King, who in any case was ensured to them, united in support of the

Holy See. Not only the Pope intervened with the King to denounce to him the wrongs caused by laymen against clerics, but he did not hesitate, if necessary, to take the defense of the French clergy against the agents of the royal authority.[103] In February 1233, Gregory IX denounced to the King the bailiff of Vermandois, who in the choir of the church of Saint-Prix, in Saint-Quentin, was carried to acts of violence on the chancellor of the church of Paris, Philippe de Grève.[104] In 1234 he complained to Louis IX about how, in lower Languedoc, his officers oppressed the churches, plundered them, and removed rights from bishops of Béziers and Agde, whose castles were held by agents of the King, and were constrained to plead before royal jurisdictions.[105]

It was especially in the conflicts over jurisdiction that the struggle became impassioned. Excommunication and interdict came into action quickly when representatives of the Church had to defend their rights or to put forward their legal claims, and then the King himself was hardly spared more than the others; they struck his servants and his domains, not daring to confront him personally. Saint Louis, during his reign, was opposed to this too frequent use of canonical punishment, whose clergy claimed to oblige him to sanction the effects, and, at first, he found himself in accord, in their resistance, to the most undisciplined of his vassals.[106]

During the first half of the thirteenth century one sees the nobles unite to oppose, as regards jurisdiction, the often exaggerated claims of the prelates. In 1205, under Philippe Auguste, in 1225, under Louis VIII, several great vassals confederated to resist the encroachments of the clergy, and it is with this movement, almost universal among the nobility, that they assembled in Redon, where Pierre Mauclerc, in accord with the barons of Brittany, took some serious measures against the churches.[107] In this great quarrel, the Holy See was naturally on the side of its bishop, while Louis IX and Blanche of Castile could hardly be opposite to resistance of the lords. At the moment when, hardly beyond his adolescence, he was still controlled under the supervision of his mother, Louis himself was involved in a fight with the arrogant ways of the Archbishop of Rouen and the Bishop of Beauvais.

We saw that, at the beginning of her government, Blanche of Castile had had to fight the Archbishop of Rouen, Thibaud d'Amiens, whom she reproached, among other things, for not to wanting to recognize the jurisdiction of the King. The successor of Thibaud,

Maurice, did not show himself more manageable.[108] On the occasion of difficulties which partly had the same origin, the Queen seized, in 1232, the Archbishop's palace in Rouen. Maurice twice requested in vain for the restitution of his property; the King, remaining deaf to his pleas, refused to give him a precise answer for the seizure. The Archbishop accentuated his opposition while removing images of the Virgin in the churches of his diocese, and ordering that if necessary the same measure would be taken, within fifteen days, for images of Our Lord.

The Queen not having yielded, the Archbishop returned to attacks. In addition to his preceding objections, he reproached the King for not wanting to oblige the abbot and several monks of Saint-Wandrille, who he had excommunicated, to appear before the metropolitan jurisdiction. This time, all the chapels of the King were placed under interdict in the diocese of Rouen, except in the case when Louis IX or his mother were found to be present. Throughout the diocese, the interdict was proclaimed against the bailiffs and under-bailiffs of the King, against their clerks, their wives, and servants of their houses. Maurice also interdicted the cemeteries, and decided that in all the churches, without excluding those of the monasteries, they would cease ringing the bells and singing the offices. At Mass, after the Lord's Prayer, the priest, the clerics and the people were to throw themselves on their knees and to pray for the church of Rouen. This was only the beginning of rigor; the King having resisted several monitions, a general interdict was proclaimed, with an exception for baptisms of children and penitences of the dying. While acting with as much violence as obstinacy, the Archbishop claimed to have no desire to wrong the King, only to defend the freedom of his church.

At this point the Pope could not miss the chance to intervene. On 29 November 1232, he wrote Louis IX a pressing letter, though moderate in its form, by which he informed the King that the bishops of Paris and Senlis had orders to force the royal officers to return the palace of the archbishop, and to enjoin, in the event of resistance, an interdict on the entire ecclesiastical province of Rouen.[109] Believing that the two bishops temporized, Gregory IX reiterated his command to them on 26 August 1233, and a few days after (1 September) he again addressed, in eulogistic terms, but with authority, to Louis IX, Blanche of Castile, and advisers of the King.[110] The next month (23 October) he had to write two more letters, to Gautier, Bishop of

Tournay, and to the Abbot of Pontigny, another to the Abbot of Savigny and to the Dominican Prior of Paris, to charge them with warning the King, and to engage for the return of confiscated possessions.[111] Lastly, on 25 October 1233, or perhaps in the following year, the interdict was raised, after the handing-over by the King of the palace and of the fruits received throughout the seizure.[112] We do not know if Maurice bought by an act of submission this restitution so obstinately required; he died in January 1235; his epitaph said that he had passed all his life in sorrows; with a little moderation and respect towards his sovereign, he could easily have saved himself these last tribulations.[113]

In Beauvais it was even worse.[114] In the province of Rheims, the entire episcopate, in August 1231, formally declared at the Council of Saint-Quentin against the doctrines and the intrigues of laic lords in the event of conflict with churches. After a struggle between lower class people of Beauvais and wealthy burgers of this city, the King had entrusted the functions of mayor to a burger of Senlis. However, Beauvais then had as a bishop Miles de Nanteuil, in a hurry for money, who gave up his diocese for three years to serve beyond the mountains in the cause of the Pope. Although he belonged by birth to the house of Châtillon, Miles supported the lower orders against the rich persons of his city. He had returned from Italy, and was at his house in Bresles, when on 31 January 1233 the people rose again against the aristocratic bourgeois; the mayor and his partisans, taken refuge in a house, were obliged to leave because the besieger had set fire to the house next door. Twenty of the principal inhabitants were killed, thirty were wounded in brawls; the mayor, whose clothing had been torn to the belt, fell into the hands of the insurrectionists, who paraded him through the streets while saying to him in derision: "It is now that we make you mayor."[115] The treatment inflicted on this man was a bloody insult to the majesty of the sovereign.

While these serious events occurred, a knight, Barthelemy de Fresnoy, went to Bresles to inform the Bishop, and recommend he not enter Beauvais without being sufficiently accompanied. The Bishop refused, and entered the city at night, and took council at once to know how he was going to prevail. Eighty of the principal culprits being presented to him, Miles required them to submit entirely to his justice, but the mayor, who he went to consult, having remarked to him that they were not sure of their lives, was withdrawn. When it was shown that the Bishop had not detained them, he answered that his people were not armed; but all those engaged in the business did not listen to this reason; the *sous-chantre* of the cathedral declared in his deposition that the Bishop had refused to meet out justice, and the King appears to have questioned the sincerity of his intentions.[116]

About midnight the Bishop learned that the King was en route to Beauvais. Louis IX was with his mother, at the moment when the Archdeacon and Barthélemy de Fresnoy said to him that the Bishop asked him for council, to make justice after his opinion. For any answer, the King, in agreement with his mother, declared that he would render justice himself, and on the same day came into Bresles.[117] It was there that the Bishop came to find him, to urge him not to enter Beauvais: "I will go to Beauvais," answered the young prince, "and you will see what I shall do."[118] Then he proceeded on the road with a troop of knights and militia of nineteen communes, belonging partly to the fiefs of his uncle the Count de Boulogne.[119] He entered the city, and established himself in the house of the Bishop. Miles saw him, asked for the second time not to encroach on his rights, read a charter of Louis VII relative to his jurisdiction, then addressed to him, as Bishop, a monition which the King did not answer, believing, "there was nothing of worth in it."[120]

Whatever were the rights of jurisdiction of the Bishop, he was a vassal of the King, as a peer of France and Count de Beauvais; on the following day Louis IX, acting as suzerain, made his proclamation of outlawry, and ordered all the population to meet on the market square.[121] It was probably when the children of those who had been killed and the casualties requested justice of him. The King showed himself very severe; some of the culprits had been thrown into the prisons of the Bishop; the others were locked up in the market hall; it is said that on this occasion 1,500 people were banished to Paris or elsewhere; many inhabitants from Beauvais were banished from the kingdom. Moreover, the King proceeded, in the name of the mayor and the commune, with the demolition of fifteen houses.[122]

The King, as suzerain, had to perceive, for the five days that he had passed between Bresles and Beauvais, the right of procuration, due in such a case by the vassal. Upon leaving, he taxed this right with 800 *livres parisis*, and as the Bishop refused to carry it out, seized his goods and left the city under Simon de Poissy and Pierre de la Halle, who brought with them a troop of knights and sergeants.[123] The house of the Bishop was occupied by two royal sergeants, who confiscated the wines of the Bishop and assumed his revenue.[124]

I do not propose to tell here in detail the long and serious difficulties from which this act of authority had it origin. It was especially at its beginning that the business of Beauvais interests us, because Blanche of Castile then exerted in her plenitude the sovereign power. The King was not yet nineteen years old, and, in all that he did in Beauvais, I find the hand of his mother. The quarrel lasted a long time; ranged successively before several provincial councils, continued with eagerness by Miles de Nanteuil, embraced with fervor by the Archbishop of Rheims, Henri de Dreux, this proven accomplice of great barons in their revolts and intrigues. I will recall only the interdict pronounced by the Bishop of Beauvais in his diocese, by the Archbishop and his suffragan in the province of Rheims, useless steps tried near the King, canonical monitions to which Louis IX and his mother refused to yield. In this obstinate fight, the King had for him the Bishop of Noyon, who refused to proclaim the interdict in his diocese, and the chapters, which never wanted to observe them, and then invited attention from the Pope, by pleading that he had omitted a consultation with them.[125] Their resistance and the lassitude of several bishops finally obliged Henri de Dreux to lift the interdict that he had placed on his province, and then Gregory IX charged Pierre de Collemezzo to settle the issue. The letters which the Pope wrote on the subject, on 6 April 1234, to Louis IX and Blanche of Castile, announced a temporary appeasement; however, Miles de Nanteuil, little prepared for conciliation, would undoubtedly have persisted in his resistance, had he not died soon after going to the court of Rome.[126] His successor Geoffroy took up the fight again; but the King did not capitulate. It was another Bishop of Beauvais, Robert de Cressonsacq, who had the honor to restore peace. Blanche of Castile followed this business to the end, in which the Pope still addressed her on occasion in 1236 and 1238.[127]

The business of Beauvais ended up merging partly with another quarrel no less famous, also caused by a conflict of jurisdiction, and in which the King clashed with the Archbishop of Rheims and his suffragans.[128] This time Louis IX was in his majority, and, though the Pope still had recourse to the intervention of Blanche, as a *bulla* of 4 April 1235 proves, the personal action of her son was too certain here to regard the Queen as having, in this case, played the primary role.[129] It was during the height of this quarrel between royalty and episcopate that the great vassals and officers of the crown, joined together in Saint-Denis near their sovereign, addressed to Gregory IX a collective complaint against the Bishop of Beauvais, the Archbishop of Rheims, and the Archbishop of Tours, who claimed to withdraw from the royal jurisdiction and to not appear before the civil judges. This memorable act, written in September 1235, does not belong to the history of regency, although it is narrowly related to Blanche's fight to maintain the legal prerogatives of her son against the high clergy.[130] Things change, and time, an ally of those who choose to resist and wait, often brings adversaries together on common ground. Blanche of Castile could note while observing, in the assembly of Saint-Denis, Pierre Mauclerc playing a game with royalty.

     Blanche of Castile, who during her regency had unceasingly taken into account the claims or the systematic opposition of the nobility and the high clergy, did not meet with, even in her worst days, hostility among the people of the cities and the countryside. She did not have to fight with the communes and was not obliged to ensure their support in their making of concessions. Charters granted by Louis IX, at the time of his minority, with Rouen, La Rochelle, Saint-Jean-d'Angely, Niort, hardly deserve mention, because they were only renewals of former privileges; however the fidelity of the cities had a real importance, and in certain cases Blanche was worried about assuring them to her son. It was thus that in October 1228, a time when the situation of royalty could be regarded as critical, she requested oaths from a great number of communes, Beauvaisis, Vexin, Picardy, and the surrounding area.[131] Oaths of fidelity were also lent, at the beginning of the reign, by the men of Saint Junien-de-Vigen, and those of Limoges.[132] As for engagements taken, in special circumstances, by the cities which concerned certain feudatories, they had another character; in December 1226 and January 1227, at the moment when Jeanne of Flanders negotiated the releasing to freedom of Count Ferrand, sureties were provided by the towns of his fiefs as also by his vassals; it was the same in March 1231, when the Countess Marie de Ponthieu returned her husband Simon de Dammartin to grace; mayors and aldermen of Abbeville and of several other communes took, on this occasion, engagements towards the King.[133]

     During the minority of Louis IX, the communes, on more than one occasion, faithfully met their duties, and I note that their militias answered the convocation of the King in time of war and expedition.

Royalty, although it was often rather harsh, was all in all a quite preferable power for people of the cities than was the authority of barons. It was in making people of the communes follow Blanche and Louis IX, in the disorders of Beauvais, inflicting on the people of this city a hard punishment, and soon after, when the King, in spite of the resistance opposed him by Archbishop Henri de Dreux, exerting his right of jurisdiction in Rheims, that the people of the city did not protest the rigor of the royal sentence.

Apart from certain cities protected by their privileges, their organization and their means of defense, people suffered, during the regency of Blanche, in the cities and in countryside. It should be recognized that royal agents were often brutal and unjust; to the miseries of every day life were added the devastations caused by war; certain countries had to be really unhappy, and they saw, in 1234 or 1235, the south-west kingdom afflicted by a horrible famine. This plague prevailed especially in the Limousin and Poitou. They died of hunger; grain made so expensive that men were reduced to eating grass, and epidemics having come to join the food shortage, mortality became alarming. A chronicler tells that in one day he saw burying, in a cemetery of Limoges, about one hundred corpses, and that in this city, during the famine, death usually took thirty and fifty victims per day.[134]

The mother of Saint Louis should not be regarded as the person in charge of all that her subjects suffered during troubles and war. To cite only one example, it is certain that royal troops partly devastated the environs of Bellême when this place was taken again by Pierre Mauclerc; but it was necessary, to reduce it, to demolish houses, to forage wood and food from the countryside. It was not Queen Blanche who had pushed the Count of Brittany to revolt. From 1209 to 1229, there was continual battle in the Midi, and when the Peace of Paris rendered the situation of this unhappy country less terrible, it happened that order and justice quickly succeeded anarchy and violence; but it was not Blanche of Castile who had unleashed the odious war of the Albigensians. The majority of evils about which one could complain under her government resulted from habits, from circumstances, rather than her will.

The state of the French populations during first half of the thirteenth century can be understood to a certain extent when we will have published in its entirety the great investigation that Saint Louis prescribed, in 1247 and 1248, in all the provinces attached to his fiefs since the reign of his grandfather. Then one will be able to realize the resources of the inhabitants of these countries, their material life, the injustices that they underwent, and wrongs which must be charged to the agents of royal power, quite serious wrongs, and whose rectification gave to the most just and charitable of our kings an imperishable celebrity. But in this respect the years of the regency cannot be the object of a special study. From the conquests of Philippe Auguste until the beginning of Saint Louis' first crusade, one finds the same processes, the same complaints. Bailiffs and seneschals, provosts, lords of the manor of the King, and their sergeants, did not act otherwise under the regency in 1220 as they did in 1240. Elsewhere, a great number of depositions made before royal investigators are without dates, and so much that one will not have drawn up a list, a succession of officers against whom voices were raised, so it will be at the very least difficult to know if the administration of Blanche, with regard to the interests and the rights of private individuals, was better than that of her two predecessors. Blanche had to fight too much for her to think much about organization, reforms, general repression of abuses. One can hardly devote time to other areas when one fights for one's life. Without maintaining a judgment which would be premature, I can at least cite some facts concerning the rigorous processes of which royal agents made use between the death of Louis VIII and the majority of her son.

One must note that, in a certain number of cases, abuses of power were obviously contrary to the intentions of the King of France and his mother. In 1229, the King remitted to Philippe Coraut, *châtelain* of Tours, silver intended to remunerate a carpenter of Saint-Pierre des Corps, employed in the building of the royal château, but the *châtelain* kept the payment.[135] The widow of another carpenter of Tours, who worked for six weeks on behalf of the King, complained about a sum due to her husband never paid by Adam Panetior, bailiff of Touraine, in spite of strict orders from Blanche.[136] The gatekeeper of the castle of Tours was frustrated by Philippe Coraut out of four *livres tournois* over three years of service that he had given beginning in 1231, and his widow came in 1247 to claim them before royal investigators; the Queen, undoubtedly, had not been aware of this injustice, but the *châtelain* Philippe had obstructed and despoiled people; he was jailed, until he made restitution; also an inhabitant of Tours, guilty of having claimed a quilt requisitioned for the service of the King.[137]

Complaints against the Queen Mother were quite rare in the investigations of 1247 and 1248; I must however cite one of them. It was a question of a Norman knight, whose son had married a goddaughter of Blanche; in 1234, the King, passing by Breteuil, ordered him, on the counsel of the Queen Mother, to give 500 *livres tournois* to his son, although he had profited from an advance of his inheritance. The poor knight, at once not being able to find this sum, was obliged to sell his belongings at a loss; in waiting, his manors were occupied by the King's men, who despoiled his goods. It was recognized elsewhere that Louis IX, following the opinion of Queen Blanche, exempted him from paying eighty-six *livres* and more, concerning the *droit de tiers et danger* [royal right to collect tax on lumber] from which he had been exempted.[138]

Blanche would be truly worthy of blame, if it was shown that she knew in detail the abuses of power of her representatives, because one must recognize that they were frequent, and sometimes scandalous. Some of it resulted, for the provinces recently acquired, in an undeniable state of suffering, and, even admitting the exaggeration of certain complaints lodged later made before royal investigators, one is obliged to recognize that the fate of the populations, from 1226 to 1235, was not enviable. Elsewhere, each country suffered in their way, because each royal agent, when he wanted to misuse power, had his own procedures.

Normandy, treated very harshly after the conquest of Philippe Auguste, was probably less unhappy in a period for which I recount its history; however it hardly lent itself, under the regency, to those for which one had entrusted its administration. In this province, a man still suspect due to his old attachment to the Plantagenets, could see at any moment royal agents seizing property of which the owner had crossed to England under Philippe Auguste or later; but he was not there, far from it, as the only pretext which served to cause too frequent confiscations; it was unfortunately true that they alleged with deplorable facility the most varied reasons to despoil the inhabitants.[139] Property of a man arbitrarily shown in flight, and loss without judgment, remained confiscated from 1226 to 1247; a woman who, reduced to poverty, could for two years cultivate her soil, was dispossessed because the King's men sequestered on this excuse the *redevance* [dues] or *champart* [field-rent paid in kind] that they were to deduct previously.[140] In the number of those who erected a system of confiscation there appears the bailiff Jean des Vignes, who was nevertheless a very valiant man, and who, in 1229, rendered to the Crown a great service in seizing Haie-Paynel.[141] In the viscounty of Exmes, seventy-two parishes remained subject to the levy of *fouage* [hearth money] which had never been collected before the conquest, and in these same localities Jean des Vignes, contrary to custom, took since 1229, on the sale of wine and cider, rights formerly required in only the case where vendors helped themselves to false measurements.[142] People of various localities complained of having lost forest rights, and the woodland of the King invaded the land of the inhabitants.[143]

I must restrict myself to give some examples; it would be easy to multiply them infinitely, if I wanted to prove it obvious that during the minority of Saint Louis Normandy was hardly happy. But it is important to repeat that, according to any probability, Blanche of Castile and her son were often badly informed on the injustices which were made on their behalf, and that they endeavored to repair them when they suddenly passed through the country. It was thus that Louis IX, passing from Bec to Pont-Audemer, gave orders to bailiff Jean des Vignes to remit a manor belonging to a man named Robin Louvet, and located in Condé-sur-Rille; this manor, which was in the guard of the King since 1227, had been entirely devastated and destroyed partly by the bailiff, who, once the King left, neglected to carry out his will.[144]

Whatever were the miseries of Normandy, it seems that things occurred even more badly in the provinces of the west. In Touraine, in Anjou, arbitrary imprisonments were frequent; inhabitants complained of have been thrown without reason into a dungeon reserved for robbers.[145] The royal investigations reveal to us, for these provinces, a quantity of monetary extortions; a parishioner of Saint-Pierre-Puellier, in Tours, deposed against the *châtelain* Philippe Coraut, who, in 1231, took from him eight *livres* and two *cuillières* of silver, falsely accusing him of having been in England during the war between Louis IX and Henry III.[146] In default of money, royal functionaries were paid in wheat, rye, oats; they confiscated meadows, lands of all kinds, gardens, houses. In Tours, in 1227, the *châtelain* removed people from their dwellings, because they refused to sell them to one of his sergeants.[147] A parishioner of Villaines, close by Azay-le-Rideau, deposed against the royal forester of Chinon, who, in 1229, took seven oxen under the false pretext that he killed a stag; he added that at the same time and for the same objection, the *châtelain* of Chinon burned three houses which belonged to him.[148] In addition to money and buildings, they removed from people according to a complaint about clothing, dresses, capes, fur-lined coats, surcoats, quilts, and carts. In 1235, Philippe Coraut took from an inhabitant of Tours his cart and three horses, to transport to La Rochelle sums of the King's money.[149] Still more: horses, oxen, sheep, pigs, that the agents of the King seized for reasons as varied as they were contestable. One of the royal provosts in Touraine had a practice of addressing the inhabitants with quotations so inconvenient that they could not answer him, and it was on this basis that they were made to pay out money and grains.[150] In Izé, in 1232, a man was fined by agents of the King "for wanting to make them gifts," and this pretext of a strange simplicity was used to cause grain extortion in Langeais, in 1227.[151] Finally, I cite, in investigations of Touraine and Poitou, a certain number of fines inflicted on people who had refused to help royal agents pay the expenses of their *prévôtés* and other farmed out charges.[152]

Legitimacy of a fine can be allowed when it is necessary for persons who subcontract payment of a toll, and examples of this offence, real or supposed, were rather frequent in the years of the regency; in other words, when a man assigned to preside over the court of the provost was shown to have left without permission; but a Poitevin, taxed four *marcs* for saying "that royal jurisdiction is neither right nor good," protested against this allegation.[153] People were put in forfeiture or imprisoned for lucky finds; people were mistreated by royal officers for having arrested a robber on the King's road, or under pretext of having encroached a garden.[154] It was rather natural that one might be punished for having displaced boundary stones placed between the fiefs of the King and those of the Archbishop of Tours, but it would still be necessary to charge the culprit.[155] One of those persecuted for this false reason protested, moreover, against the charge of having stolen money pertaining to the King and that he transported outside the country.[156] A man was accused of having taken stones from the King's road; another was fined ten *sous tournois* for having cut a rod he wanted to use for whipping his horse.[157] Let us pass over the offences of pasture and hunting, often mentioned in the investigations, and the accusation of using false measurements. In every case, the name which should have been regarded by all as supreme in representing justice was only a mask to cover violence and extortion.

There were circumstances where claims of royal agents were truly exorbitant: think of the bourgeois in Tours who was fined because he refused his daughter to a sergeant, or another levied fifty *sous tournois* because the provost wanted to take a share of the dowry of his wife.[158] They imputed to people, to plunder them, violence and crimes that they claimed to have made: a fine of sixty *sous* was inflicted on Guillaume Boileau, parishioner of Saint-Symphorien of Tours, under pretext that he robbed a merchant and that another merchant's head was broken under the pent-roof of his house.[159] A parishioner of Azay, that they wrongfully accused of having killed a man and making another fall into the water, had to pay thirty-six *livres*.[160] People of Breuil-l'Abbess paid fourteen *livres* to the provost of Poitiers because a man was killed in a nearby wood.[161] Murders thus gave a pretext for punishments which, in many cases, appear to have been false; it was the same for brawls, when even those who had been beaten were not blamed. A girl accused Martin Frottecoine, of Mateflon, of rape, and the King's men, who provoked this denunciation, transported the alleged culprit to Beaufort-en-Vallée, where he appeared on a summons before a Jew linked to him for ransom.[162] A man and his wife were struck with a fine of twenty *livres* because their niece was accused of clandestinely giving birth in their house and killing her infant.[163]

The imagination of royal officials was fertile in expedients when it was necessary to press the population; sometimes the complaints which served as a pretext for their accusations were more strange than odious. Mathieu de Saint-Venant, provost of Tours, extorted a small sum from an inhabitant of this city, who refused to hang a robber.[164] An inhabitant of Saint-Maixent was subjected to a fine of sixty *sous* because his servant disturbed the water of a well to which the maidservant of a royal sergeant was going to draw.[165] In 1235, a drunkard of Chinon, drinking at the cabaret, told the crier of the place that he would cut his foot off for a *denier* of wine. Another paid for the wine and took to quarreling with his comrade, who naturally refused to let himself be mutilated. But the royal provost, who did not hear the joke, benefited from the occasion to extort from this singular punter a sum of forty *sous*.[166]

The situation was hardly better in the dioceses of Laon and of Rheims, and Gontier, *châtelain* of Laon, sadly famous for his violence, was implicated at least during a part of the regency.[167]

As for the provinces of the South, added in 1229, they were to feel even more sorry than the remainder of the kingdom; it is true that Blanche of Castile could not have been reproached for the sufferings that they had endured in a war started under Philippe Auguste, continued under Louis VIII, finished, if one wishes, by the Treaty of Paris, but whose after-effect was felt at least until 1243. In these half-conquered countries, invaded and plundered by people of the North, where many of the former owners were reduced to the adventurous and miserable condition of *faidits* [banished Albigeois], where an unceasingly reappearing war prevailed there, the Queen could not do a great many things to stop the overzealousness or interested violence of her agents. And in general, how does one charge all evil in France to her, while her enemies left her hardly any time to breathe, who fought Blanche, often on several sides at the same time, struggling against the great vassals and the English?

In Languedoc, miseries born of the civil war had not ceased when the Count de Toulouse lay down his weapons, because heresy, the primary cause of all evil, had not disappeared yet. The Church continued to fight it with a rigor which never disarmed, and Blanche of Castile, who could never go against the mores of her time, lent to this contest the sovereign power and the support of the secular arm to those who supported this inhuman fight in the name of faith. It was Blanche who, in the famous ordinance of April 1229, speaking in the name of her son, had formally prescribed to her agents and her barons to aid in the pursuit of heresy, regulating the sum which was to be paid by the royal bailiffs to those who would have taken *hérétiques*.[168] This ordinance, emanating from a princess who on so many occasions was notable for her justice, was the index of an extremely violent state of affairs. But the responsibility for what passed then in Languedoc goes back much less to kings than to the Church.

It was not only in the countries upset by the war of the Albigensians for whom the defense of the Catholic faith caused a cruel repression. In France itself, in Flanders and in the adjoining countries, out of Champagne, in Burgundy, heterodox doctrines were spread during the last years of the regency; those who practiced them were confused, according to the usage, under the names of Patarins and Bougres (Bulgarians), and one must admit that their beliefs actually made real progress then, because the Holy See moved in and took, to stop them, severe measures.[169] Gregory IX, who did not cease to push the King of France to fight heresy in the south of his estates, encouraged pitiless inquisitions and persecutions, whose principal author was a Dominican, then famous under the name of Robert le Bougre.[170] This fanatic, after having lived in Milan in the midst of non-believers of whom he had, says one, divided their errors, had entered the order of the preaching friars, and was dedicated to the destruction of heresy. From 1234, supported by the secular clergy and the most elite representatives of the laity, he prevailed against heretics with an amazing fury.[171] In Châlons, Péronne, Cambrai, in Douai, the bloody inquest of which he was charged was marked by executions; many of the men and women were made to ascend the *bûcher* [faggots and stake]. Princes gave their support to these acts of savagery, but those who witnessed it did not all believe in the sincerity of Brother Robert, and the chronicler Philippe Mousket did not hesitate to declare that he pursued under the inculpation of heresy a nobleman to whom he wanted "for a lady of Milan."[172] He continued his work for several years, whose last act was the torment of 183 heretics, burned in 1239 in Champagne, at Mount-Aimé, in the presence of the King of Navarre, of Alphonse of Portugal, Mahaut, Countess of Boulogne, the Archbishop of Rheims and an enormous crowd, in the midst of which stood a great number of bishops and nobles.[173] Louis IX, at least at the beginning, approved Robert le Bougre, and gave him, says one, guards to protect him from the indignation raised by his violences; but he appears to have made it possible to save from death certain heretics that he could bring back.[174] One of those who had been stopped in Hainaut was reclaimed by him, and he was not handed over for execution.[175] On the same occasion, Blanche of Castile saved the life with a woman of noble condition whose father, Mathieu de Lanvin, had been burned in Péronne; the Queen made this unfortunate, who was pregnant, promise that she would live as a good Christian woman.[176] Here all the most just and enlightened princes gave their presence to cruelties to which religion was used as pretext; still one must know their accord in not having assisted, like so many others, in the executions. For the rest, Blanche, who still had government in her hands at the time when Robert le Bougres made his appearance, had ceased to be Regent a long time before the end of the pursuits to which the name of this man remained attached.

      Peace and public prosperity could not be established in France other than by the triumph of royalty; before thinking of repression of abuses, it was necessary to overcome, and it is that point to which Blanche of Castile put all her care to maintain the royal army in a good state. For the period of the regency, the military institutions are the only ones for which we have precise and abundant information, because what we know of the legal organization and of finances is reduced, all in all, to a little thing. It was only at the end of the reign, after the return of Saint Louis to France, that the operation of the Parlement begins to be revealed to us in an important series of documents; I however know by an act written in 1230 that when in Paris this court sat at the Palais.[177] As for finances, the royal accounts teach us something, not however enough to allow us to arrive, in what relates to them, at general data. Recent discoveries clarify the important role of the Templars, at the time of the regency as before and later, in the administration of royal income; but the finances of Saint Louis cannot be studied with profit for the totality of his reign.[178] It was not so with the royal army: we know it extremely well, such that it was in the time when Blanche ruled alone, and nobody can deny that this princess did much to ensure for the royal power a well constituted military force.

General command of the troops was exerted, as much by great officers, as by men of war who did not have special titles or ranks. The charge of constable was held, at the time of Blanche, with much merit and devotion, by Mathieu de Montmorency, serving since 1218, dying at the end of 1230, then by Amaury de Montfort. Below this supreme leader were the two marshals, legatees for life since the reign of Philippe Auguste, but who during the regency numbered, without exception, three. Guillaume de Tournel appears as Marshal of France in a charter from 1221, and appears with his title, in June 1230, in the act of judgment drawn up against Pierre Mauclerc.[179] Robert de Coucy, brother of the famous Enguerrand III, was probably also marshal under the government of Blanche; in any case he was at the death of Louis VIII, with other barons when he promised this prince, then dying, to secure the crown to his son [Louis IX].[180] Jean Clement, also Marshal of France, sealed this same act, in the content of which he was not named elsewhere.[181] He was the son of Henri Clement, called the "small marshal," one of the servants devoted to Philippe Auguste, and belonged to one of those noble families of Gâtinais who showed themselves very faithful to royalty. Clements, for their part, count in their family four Marshals of France. Jean was extremely young when his father died, in 1214; in spite of that, and though this office was not hereditary, the King conferred it on him, and it was his cousin Gautier de Nemours who was charged in filling the duties until the new marshal had reached the age of manhood.[182] Jean Clément probably exerted the functions himself until August 1223 when he foreswore the retaining of *dextriers*, palfreys, or *roussins* which fell to him because of his office; at the same time he recognized he owed this office as a gift of the King, and promised that neither he nor his would pretend to hold it on a purely hereditary basis.[183] Perhaps it was during his minority, or because one of the two marshals did not render effective service, they had recourse to the nomination of a third marshal; Guillaume de Tournel, Robert de Coucy, and Jean Clément were marshals at the same time under the regency. On the other hand, Ferry Pâté appears as marshal in 1237, in three acts, as representative of the King and the Queen Mother; the document on which I could establish that he served since 1227 was badly dated by its editor.[184]

The office of Marshal of France was not a sinecure. In 1229, it was a marshal, perhaps Jean Clément, who directed the operations of the royal army at the siege of Bellême.[185] The marshals did not restrict themselves to leading the troops; they occupied themselves with their maintenance; one can cite, in this respect, the example of a knight who, having lost his war horse in the service of the King, estimated the price for the Marshal of France.[186] The marshal sometimes named, without any other indication than his title, in the royal accounts and investigations of 1234 was probably Jean Clément who, by the traditions of his family, was extremely close to the royal house.[187] It was undoubtedly him, in 1231, who under his orders had a company of sergeants with horse.[188]

Guy de Lévis, marshal *de la foi* [of the faith] in the war of the Albigensians, does not have to be confused with the Marshals of France; he commanded the crusaders, and it was Imbert de Beaujeu who had royal troops under his orders in Languedoc, since the departure of Louis VIII until the Peace of Paris; he was lieutenant of the King, and, in this command, he rendered signal service. Later, Jean de Beaumont was charged to reduce lower Languedoc in the revolt of Trencavel. Blanche of Castile and her son found in their entourage many brave and skilful officers to whom they could entrust control of an expedition. It was thus that in 1229 Jean des Vignes, one of the royal bailiffs in Normandy, was charged with reducing Haie-Paynel.

It was natural that one profited, in time of war, the talents of bailiffs and seneschals; they were men of the sword and had mainly military functions. In the case of expeditions or general levies, they recruited nobles and the communal militia.[189] We see, in 1242, Guillaume des Ormes, Seneschal of Carcassonne and Béziers, order knights to seize the garrison in the castle of Roquebrun.[190] Guillaume de Thézan, knight, attested that until he returned to the royal army, he was under orders of the Seneschal of Carcassonne.[191] During the Regency, men of Colombiers, gone to besiege Brusque with the army of Imbert de Beaujeu, being advised to return to their homes with the militia of Béziers, the seneschal Pierre Sanglier imposed a fine on them for having left the army without his authorization.[192] On the occasion of this same siege, the inhabitants of Roujan were also punished because the seneschal did not find them in their quarters.[193]

Blanche of Castile went herself to war, and at the headquarters of Bellême she transacted, in person, details relating to the campaign.[194] She took the young King to war, and he was with her twice, when she helped the Count de Champagne, in 1229 and 1230. She consulted, for control of operations, all the men of experience, and in 1230 the King of Jerusalem, Jean de Brienne, returned invaluable services for the army of Brittany.[195] With regard to command, it seems that certain feudatories had special rights; in the campaign of 1230 against Mauclerc and the English, the counts of Flanders and Champagne disputed the advance-guard and rear-guard; this quarrel finished, on 8 June, 1230, by an arrangement, and I must note, on this subject, that rights or claims of the Count of Flanders were undoubtedly old, because in the previous century, when, in 1124, Louis VI had joined together all the forces of his kingdom to push back an invasion of the Germans, it was to the Count of Flanders, Charles the Good, that command of the rear-guard had been reserved.[196]

The royal army, of which the command was not fixed by immutable rules, was composed of very diverse elements, in the midst of which an important element belonged, under Blanche of Castile, to hired troops. Frequent employment of these bodies of cavalry and infantry was one of the certain marks of real progress, and, under this aspect, Blanche certainly deserves praise. It had been, to tell the truth, extremely difficult, if not impossible, to expedite business with the help of feudal levies, when it was necessary to combat feudality.

Homage given by vassals generally involved, in the thirteenth century, the obligation to serve the King, in his wars, for forty days. It was not much, when it was necessary for operations the duration of which might be much longer, and still more, the care with which vassals answered the royal convocation varied much, according to their fidelity, their resources, their interests and the state of their relationship with the crown. Was it not told that, in one of the expeditions against Pierre Mauclerc, the majority of *les grands* sent each one two knights to Louis IX, and that without the quota provided by Thibaud de Champagne, the King and his mother would then have been in great perplexity?[197] There were cases where the military obligations of vassals were extremely slackened; naturally, lords of the royal domain, especially those of the ancient domain, filled their duty more regularly than the others. As for remaining beyond the forty days mandated by feudal usage, it was for nobles an affair of good will, of moral obligation, or of interest, and it often happened that they hired their service out, following the term to which it was permissible for them to be withdrawn. The annoying example of Thibaud de Champagne in the siege of Avignon, and by many barons in 1230 at the time of an expedition against Pierre Mauclerc, proves that one could with impunity, at forty days expiry, desert the King in all out war; in this last case *les grands* profited, they say, because they were joined together to go against their common enemy Thibaud. The military service of great vassals was thus a resource on which one could not always count; that did not prevent convening them; but, apart from rare circumstances where national feeling triumphed over selfishness or imposed silence on covetousness and resentments, the feudal levies were, for the crown, a support far from certain.

Ecclesiastic vassals, in spite of the opposition that they often made against the mother of Saint Louis, perhaps fulfilled their military obligations with more fidelity; the Regent took the precaution of summoning them when she prepared an expedition, and the convocations made in 1234, when Mauclerc revolted for the last time, indicates, as having to come with the royal army, the bishops of Auxerre, Châlons, Amiens, Coutances, Evreux, Avranches, Troyes, Langres, and Autun.[198] Furthermore, bishops did not all owe military service; an act of Louis VIII, in 1223, recognized that the Bishop of Angers was exempt, and the Bishop of Mans likewise.[199] There were however some exceptions, because the convocation addressed to bishops was not a simple formality. In June 1234, the *préchantre* of Amiens, wrote to Jean de la Cour, canon of Paris, to thank him for exempting the Bishop of Amiens to go with the royal army, with the help of a payment of one hundred *livres parisis*. If the other bishops could be exempted from their military service and expenses that it caused, the Bishop of Amiens was recommended to the good offices of Jean de la Cour.[200] In May 1226, Jacques de Bazoches, Bishop of Soissons, had recognized that he owed the King 120 *livres parisis* for his service from this year.[201] The chapters, like the bishops, sent their people to the royal army; in 1237, Louis IX restored the pledges that had been made by the chapters of Sens, Orléans, and Auxerre, about their military service, that without doubt they had not filled.[202]

We will see later that religious communities sent mainly troops of infantry to the army, generally accompanied by carts. In 1234, abbeys of the Laonnois were required to provide carts and ladders, those of Lyons and Mortemer only carriages.[203]

The main advantage of mercenary troops was that they could be relied on; Blanche also employed, in her wars, companies of knights, sergeants, and crossbowmen on foot and with horses, regularly paid.[204] They had nothing in common with hordes rented *en mass* and only placed under control of their chiefs, such as bands of wagon drivers and cotters who appeared at the end of the twelfth century, and large companies of the fourteenth. It was smaller corps, under recognized men, for whom one was sure, and made up of a number of men exactly stipulated in royal accounts.[205] Blanche did not, it goes without saying, invent this mode of recruitment, but at the beginning of the thirteenth century, and especially during her regency, it tended to become frequently used. A chronicler of the time, describing the land battle that followed the 1213 naval defeat of Dam, said that on this occasion French crossbowmen began combat, which advanced in small groups of two, five, eight; then came assault troops, after which entered a line of sergeants on horseback, soon followed by nobility.[206] The minstrel of Rheims, when he recounts the wars of Philippe Auguste, speaks of crossbowmen who were with the advance-guard and rear-guard.[207] Let us pass to the middle of the thirteenth century; at the end of 1245, when Louis IX and Blanche of Castile found Pope Innocent IV at Cluny, three bodies of troops preceded them; one hundred sergeants were at the front, assembled on magnificently harnessed horses; then a hundred other riders came dressed in armor; these carried round bucklers and shields, and their horses were covered with chain mail; a hundred well-armed men followed, with swords in hand, and only after them did the King and his many knights advance.[208] All of these elements, and others still, can be found in the royal armies of the regency.

The document which gives the most precise information on

troops in the pay of Blanche of Castile is drawn up in an account of Antrain on 23 July 1231; it mentions the payment of knights, sergeants, and crossbowmen either mounted or on foot, and the expenditure made for convoys.[209] At the head of the sums are a certain number of knights, probably representing the expenses of their armament and their maintenance, or balances due to them and their people. There one meets the names of the Count de Bigorre, the Viscount of Limoges, Guillaume and Pierre des Bars, Henri de Sully; as it became necessary to fight Pierre Mauclerc, who started to be abandoned by his vassals, Blanche took into her pay many Breton lords. Sums allotted to these various people vary much, according to the number of men-at-arms that each one had with him; Geoffroy de Pouencé received 500 *livres tournois*.[210]

Mentioned after this first article, under the name of loans, 700 *livres tournois* paid to Jean d'Affricamps, 600 to the Count de Champagne, one hundred to the Marshal of France, undoubtedly Jean Clement; of these three loans, the first two were made in the name of the Queen, the third in the name of Pierre de Chambly.[211]

In addition to the nobles indicated above, the Count d'Antrain enumerated, as hired by the crown, 146 knights, 135 mounted sergeants, twenty-one mounted crossbowmen, eighty-six infantry crossbowmen, forty-four foot soldiers, 1,600 infantry sergeants, and thirty-two carts with drivers. These figures represent the total manpower, because the men who belonged to the mercenary troops intended for the war in Brittany in 1231 did not all serve during the same number of days.

Mercenary knights in the pay of the King were paid little more than sergeants and mounted crossbowmen; however, the difference was very considerable between their remuneration and that of simple men-at-arms. Each one received six *sous* of money per day. Some had service only six, eight, and ten days, but they were exceptions, and their service, in general, varied from fourteen to twenty-nine days. Some arrived alone, others brought one, two, or several knights with them. Henri d'Avaugour and Guiomar de Léon, enemies of Pierre Mauclerc, engaged, with thirty-eight others, for a period of ten days. Among the nobles whose services were thus bought for rather moderate pay, one meets known names: Guillaume des Ormes, Mathieu de Roye, undoubtedly a relative of the chamberlain Barthelemy, Hugues d'Athies, several Normans and a Breton, the *châtelain* of Péronne.[212]

The mounted sergeants, a little less favored than knights, sometimes received four *sous* or four *sous* six *deniers* per day, and generally five *sous*.[213] They entered service either separately, or in small groups; the first mercenary company in the pay of the King was composed of thirty sergeants under the orders of a noble; the majority of the others were recruited along the way, in Vincennes, Mantes, Anet, Mans, Brulon, and Laval. The Marshal had a small company of mounted sergeants under his orders, of four riders, then of six, finally of twelve.

Like the mounted sergeants, the mounted crossbowmen formed an elite troop. Their pay was five *sous* per day, and they were paid in the same way, as well as the sergeants, in an account of 1234. The majority were engaged for a period from twenty-five to thirty days, some for a shorter time.[214] Usage hardly changed during the thirteenth century in the remuneration of mounted crossbowmen; a few years after the regency, Alphonse de Poitiers gave them five *sous tournois* per day.[215]

Evidently, relatively high pay for mercenary knights, mounted sergeants, and crossbowmen, was especially intended for the maintenance of their horses, because crossbowmen on foot mentioned in the account of 1231 received only a *sous* per man per day; forty between them were used during twenty-seven days, forty others during two weeks.[216] The pay of *léquillons* or *lacueillons*, foot soldiers of whom I am unaware of their role and armament, was a little lower than that of infantry crossbowmen; they had only eight *deniers* per day, that is to say two thirds of a *sous*.[217]

As for the sergeants on foot, they were engaged, in 1231, in companies of one hundred, 200, 300, and even 600 men; each one of these companies had its own wagons, at a rate of two per hundred men or approximately, probably intended to carry either weapons, or baggage. These small bodies of infantry, in 1231, were in general paid for their return.[218] An account of Alphonse de Poitiers, in 1245, seems to prove that this prince gave to his infantry crossbowmen five *sous* per day, his sergeants eight *deniers* only; in another document, dated to 1300, one sees that the mounted crossbowmen then received for each day of service twelve *deniers tournois*, or one *sous*.[219] The prices adopted under Queen Blanche for the payment of infantrymen thus varied little until the end of the thirteenth century.

Part of the sergeants on foot were armed with bows, and to these crossbowmen were reserved arrows called *carreaux* [squares].

The accounts of Alphonse de Poitiers, in 1245, mention two kinds of crossbows: one known as *arbalètes à deux pieds* [crossbows with two feet], the other intended for crossbowmen on horseback.[220] This distinction undoubtedly existed before 1235, because it was hardly possible that riders and infantrymen made use of the same process to draw their bows.

The master of crossbowmen, who had under his orders the bowmen, certainly had a big role in the royal army, but we do not know if he ordered, during the regency, foot sergeants, engineers, carpenters, and miners.[221]

It is probable that the knights taken into the service of Louis IX had the right to count on an allowance when they fell between the hands of an enemy who put them at ransom. In any case, we know that knights taken along by Prince Louis in England and made captive in his service claimed, in 1247, a subsidy; their deposition does not tell us they were addressed before, to obtain payment, from the widow of their former master.[222]

Accounts of the royal household in 1234, and of others still, contain interesting and diverse information on the price of horses. Not being able to enter here into a study for which the data is all together lacking, I will limit myself to note that war-horses or *dextriers* were of a price much higher than that of palfreys, reserved to ordinary use, and the saddle horses, and that this price often varied much according to the color of the horse.[223] It was undoubtedly to facilitate remounting cavalry and the acquisition of draught horses that at the moment of beginning a campaign bailiffs removed horses from their *bailliages*.[224] Knights, in time of war, had, at least in some cases, their palfreys with them; perhaps they also took a pack horse to carry their equipment.[225] Such was, in 1234, the case of mounted crossbowmen in the King's service. In an account of this year, there was care to mention those who lacked pack horses.[226] On the other hand, the knight, the mounted crossbowman, and the mounted sergeant entered service with only one *dextrier*. The account of 1231 cites, as an exception, a crossbowman with two horses; also this man received, per day, nine *sous*, double what was usually paid to one mounted crossbowman in addition to what a single crossbowman on foot received.[227]

Royal officers took care that horses of the cavalry were in top shape. One sees, under Saint Louis, a farrier of Saint-Maixent complained about not having received any wages for eighty horses which the bailiff of Poitou gave to him to look after.[228] The King was greatly interested that the men engaged in his service did not lose their mounts, since any man whose horse had perished with the royal army had a right, by this fact, to an indemnity known as *restaur de chevaux*. The *restaur*, if we judge it by the royal accounts, constituted one of the largest expenditures of wartime; in certain cases, it could happen that the owners of horses killed or that died in service were not compensated; but their right was manifest if, even after several years, it could serve as the basis for complaints. Here, after the royal investigations of 1247, are some of the facts relative to this right. In 1223, Louis VIII having passed by Alencon, his people took, to carry the baggage of the King, the horse of an inhabitant; this horse having died, the heir to its owner asked for, from this fact, a sum of twelve *livres* from the royal investigators.[229] At the time of the expedition which was marked by the siege of Avignon, a certain number of horses were requisitioned in Normandy, and complaints on the subject were addressed to investigators.[230] Among many of those injured appear two Norman knights, whose *dextriers* had been killed at the siege of Avignon and who required for this fact, in 1247, an indemnity of thirty *livres* each.[231]

People who requisitioned draught horses and wagons for military operations naturally had financial claims, especially in the event of loss; a certain number of Normans or inhabitants of Perche asked, in 1247, for various sums related to horses and wagons that had been taken from them when Louis VIII had left for the expedition to Avignon.[232] There were also, in Artois, many complaints about horses and carts which had been taken along to England by Prince Louis and to Poitou by Louis IX: "The number of plaintiffs is large," with respect to this inquiry, "great also is the sum of money that is claimed."[233] It was regrettable that circumstances in which Blanche of Castile found herself in upon the succession of her son did not allow her to pay, at that time, the sums due to those who had undergone losses in the service of Louis VIII. In 1247, two inhabitants of Beaumont-en-Auge complained to royal investigators about five horses, belonging to their father, formerly taken to Paris to carry from the Albigensian campaign equipment of the late king; four of these horses remained there; the fifth alone was returned, but without harness. Plaintiffs demanded to be compensated, like the companions of their father, to whom restitution was made, by order of the King, for the damage that they underwent in this expedition.[234]

Wagon trains of the state revenue formed, in the account of

1231, a special article; one finds mentioned the horses, saddle horses, horse guards and foot guards attached to this service, as well as pledges of the clerk and the servant employed to count the sums of money, and the expenses of the treasurers.[235] We know that at the time of Philippe Auguste the money was transported in barrels and the charters in bags; Alphonse de Poitiers had iron-hooped barrels for the transport of his money.[236]

The royal army, at the time of the regency naturally had for sieges a considerable personnel and material. Miners, that one sees at work on the siege of Bellême, were certainly not men taken randomly, but were people of the trade.[237] Machines or engines [of war] were trailed following the army, and when they lacked stones to serve them, they did not hesitate to demolish houses.[238] In 1236, when Thibaud de Champagne rebelled for the last time, the King of France brought with the army some *pierrières*, *mangonneaux*, and hauled from Aumale a large *trebuchet*, built by the Count de Boulogne.[239] People of the country could be necessary to help with transporting machines.[240]

The *maître des engins* [master of the machines] was appointed for guardianship and service of the machines; he also had miners under his command; he appears in the royal investigations, relating to a campaign of 1242.[241]

Carpenters were engaged for pay when there was a siege to make; some are found, in 1242, in the royal army, and, about the same time, in the service of Alphonse de Poitiers.[242] They also envisaged the case when bridges would have to be built; in 1213 or 1214, Philippe Auguste bought timber "to make bridges in time of war."[243]

The accounts of 1239 speak about iron for arrows bought for the King, of cords and keys for crossbows.[244] A factory of crossbows was established in Melun; there was in Louvre a store for them, entrusted to the guard of "the artillerist of the Louvre."[245]

Beside the feudal quotas and mercenary troops, most of the royal army, at the beginning of the thirteenth century, was made up of people who were not paid. We saw that Blanche of Castile had in her pay some companies of crossbowmen and foot sergeants; the remainder of the royal infantry was trained by the communal militia, by people of the abbeys, and by men taken, from the communes, in the royal domain.

Royal agents assembled the communal militia, which came to the army under the control of their municipal officers.[246] They consisted of infantry, in which the manpower was fixed, and which generally had foot sergeants, just as mercenary companies, and a number of carts. Service by commoners was not, like that of nobles, restricted to forty days; note that in the wars of Philippe Auguste it was, for some years, four or five months.[247] Following two statements, or appraisals, which are well-known, and the oldest goes back to Philippe Auguste, in the thirteenth century the quotas provided by the communes were extremely numerous, even by taking into account a certain number of communes or other localities that were hired with important sums.[248]

The value of these troops was extremely various in the Middle Ages. Some persons affected to scorn them; but others spoke about them in eulogistic terms.[249] Undoubtedly, one could not always find in the militia the same brilliant value which was the rule among the nobility, nor the regularity, the discipline that one was in right to ask from mercenary companies; however communal militias, which had a permanent organization, were not, necessarily, a simple mob. Although they had not been brilliant at Bouvines, on more than one occasion they did well.[250] Blanche of Castile always employed them. At the time of the sacring of Saint Louis, she found them useful to prevent the Count de Champagne from entering Rheims and to expel some of his people. Shortly afterwards, communes of the Paris environs were united, at the same time as the bourgeois of this city, to come seek the young King, threatened in Montlhéry. Communes sent their battalions to the siege of Bellême; they were convened in 1234 to go against Pierre Mauclerc; when the King wanted to restore order in Beauvais, he moved against this city with the militia of nineteen communes; later these same troops took part in the war of Saintonge.[251] In 1246, by way of a quarrel between the prior of Notre-Dame de Maigre and the convent of Signy, the provost of Laon occupied Signy by "the communes of the King," who for three days committed damage and depredation there.[252]

The royal infantry also included bodies provided by abbeys or raised, apart from the communes, on the domain.[253] These troops were united under the command of the bailiffs and seneschals; at the end of the war against Raimond VII, the people of Roujan and Colombiers were thus brought before Brusque, where Imbert de Beaujeu laid siege.[254] Commoners from the royal domain were exposed to fines when they did not come to the army, and this charge of having eluded the obligations of military service, even when it was unfounded, served as a pretext for acts of rigor and extortion. Without going all the way to 1240 and 1242, for which the investigations of Saint Louis reveal much of this behavior, I found that since 1227, in Touraine, inhabitants were struck with more or less rigor under pretext that they did not satisfy the obligations of their military service.[255] The men of the prioress of Miré, in the diocese of Tours, protested against a fine which the royal provost extorted from them, alleging that they were not in the army; however they were there, and offered to prove it.[256] In 1233, a royal sergeant arrested an inhabitant of Bléré, and detained him in Tours for three weeks, because he refused the service of *ost et de chevauchée*, from which he said he was free, as tenant of the Lady of Amboise.[257] A fine of twenty-five *sous* was imposed by Mathieu de Saint-Venant, provost of Tours, on a man who had not returned to the army of the King; the plaintiff managed to prove that he was sick at the time of quotation, and received eighteen *sous*.[258]

The military service of the commoners sometimes included the obligation to assemble guards or to hold garrisons in fortified places.[259] People were to present themselves to the watches or passed reviews by royal agents, in order to show the state of their weapons.[260] Thanks to these precautions, troops of unpaid infantry could present certain guarantees under the aspect of armament and discipline, in order not to make too bad a figure beside the companies of sergeants. All in all the royal army, though formed of unequal and disparate elements, represented a considerable force; Louis IX could count on it to continue and consolidate the work of his mother.

1 *Historiens de France*, t. XXI, p. 243; accounts of 1234.

2 Ibid., p. 245 c.

3 Ibid., p. 238 J, 239 c, 244 l.

4 In 1234, *Historiens de France*, t. XXI, 247 h, and elsewhere ; in 1237, same collection, t. XXII, p. 581 b, 582 d ; in 1239, ibid., p. 601 9, 008 J, h, l, 610e, j, h, 620 h.

5 Joinville, ed. of 1874, § 006-608.

6 Aubry de Trois-Fontaines, *Historiens de France*, t. XXI, p. 021 d; *Monumenta Germaniæ*, scriptores, t. XXIII, p. 942.

7 *Historiens de France*, t. XXII, p. 622 h.

8 Archives nationales, JJ, 26, fol. 351 recto, col. 1 July 1232 : Louis IX confirmed a gift made by Ingeburge to Marie de Corbeil.

9 *Historiens de France*, t. XXII, 610 a, 1239; p. 610 d.

10 *Historiens de France*, t. XXI, p. 247 f.

11 Ibid., p. 244 l; « *Justa argenti.* » 245 9; 236 9; 229 j.

12 Ibid., p. 247 9; 246 d; 247 f, 241 h.

13 Ibid., p. 241 a; 237 c, p. 238 e.

14 *Historiens de France*, t. XXI, p. 236 e; p. 234 c, 241 c.

15 Ibid., 241 c.

16 Ibid., p. 229 b; p. 234 j.

17 Ibid., p. 235 e; p. 245 h; p. 242 c.

18 Ibid., p. 236 c; p. 237 d; p. 246.

19 Ibid , p. 235 9; p. 236 h; p. 229 l, 237 b, 239 g-h.

20 Ibid., p. 241 d; 235 f.

21 Ibid., p. 247 d; 236 f; 248 j.

22 Ibid., p. 248 j.

23 Ibid., p. 239 f.

24 Ibid., p. 242 m.

25 Ibid., p. 237 e, « *et aliorum puerorum.* » p. 244 h, l; p. 230 b; p. 246 f.

26 *Historiens de France*, t. XXII, p. 566 f.

27 *Historiens de France*, t. XXI, p. 230 b.

28 Ibid. p. 239 c, h; p. 238 9; p. 249 a.

29 Ibid., p. 247 e.

30 Ibid., p. 231 f, h.

31 Ibid., p. 238 f (Martinus Alfonsus); 235 9, 236 h (Michael Hispanus); 248 f (Guarsias de Paciaco) ; 249 d (Rodriques) ; 241 a (Munusius Guarciæ domini Roberti).

32 Ibid., p. 231 c; p. 233; p. 241 9; p. 244 m; p. 228 j, 236 j; p. 240 c; *Historiens de France*, t. XXI, p. 233 h; p. 245 c, 238 e.

33 Ibid., p. 230 g.

34 Ibid., p. 249 : « *Balistarii et servientos equites.* »; p. 243 f; *Tablettes de cire de Jean Sarrasin* (*Historiens de France*, t. XXI, p. 360 ff., § 217 a, b, d, 218 a, b, 219, 220).

35 *Historiens de France*, t. XXI, p. 244 f, 245 e, 249 9, 230 a.

36 *Historiens de France*, t. XXII, p. 575 c; t. XXI, p. 232 f, 235 a, 248 h.

37 Ibid., p. 230 j; p. 230 h, 232 l, 233 d.

38 Ludewig has published, in his *Reliquise manuscriptorum* (t. XII, 2nd part, p. 3), a list of cloaks given, on the occasion of Pentecost 1231, to the knights, clerics and other men of the household : « *Pallia militum et clericorum aliarumque gentium hospitii domini regis Ludovici, ad terminum Pentecostes 1231.* » The texts relative to this usage are numerous for the thirteenth century; I need not cite them here.

39 Léon Gautier, *La Chevalerie*, nouvelle ed. (Delagrave), p. 250-252. The *adoubement* [dubbing] is the ceremony in which one arms a knight; Aubry de Trois-Fontaines, *Historiens de France*, t. XXI, p. 619 e, *Monumenta Germaniæ*, t. XXIII, p. 941.

40 *Historiens de France*, t. XXII, p. 589.

41 *Historiens de France*, t. XXI, p. 229 l, 230 I, 231 d, 246; *Historiens de France*, t. XXII, p. 580.

42 Aubry de Trois-Fontaines, loc. cit. It is not always possible to know if the *ménestrels* designated by the texts are singing jugglers, musicians, or jugglers juggling. See in this regard the facts alleged by Léon Gautier in *La Chevalerie* (table, at the word *jongleurs*).

43 *Historiens de France*, t. XXI, p. 246; p. 229 c, 231 a, c, e, 9.

44 Ibid., p. 231 e, 245 b.

45 *Historiens de France*, t. XXI, p. 228, 230 a, 241 e; p. 230 d, 233 j.

46 Ibid., p. 239 g; without doubt Nogent-le-Roi; *Histor. de France*, XXI, p. 235 h.

47 Ibid., p. 240 d.

48 Ibid., p. 409-411.

49 Ibid., p. 232 a (*malades*); 230 i (*pauvres*); *Historiens de France*, t. XXI, p. 230 c; Archives nationales, J. 1035, no. 22; Febraury 1234.

50 *Historiens de France*, t. XXI, p. 232 b.

51 Ibid., p. 230 h; p. 231 f, 232 f.

52 Ibid., p. 229 d, 231 9, 232 h, 234 e, f, h, m, 238 d, 239 f, 244.

53 Ibid., p. 229 a, 231 d, 234 c, f, 236 f, 237 e, 238 l, 241 f.

54 *Historiens de France*, t. XXI, p. 234 j.

55 Ibid., p. 232 d.

56 Ibid. p. 233, etc.; p. 244 l.

57 Ibid. p. 244 l; p. 232 j; p. 229 m; p. 236 d, i; p. 233 l; p. 230 c.

58 Ibid., p. 232 m, 237 a, 238 j, 239 j, 241 9, 243 f; p. 235 l.

59 Ibid., p. 234 b; p. 232 b.

60 *Historiens de France*, t. XXI, p. 232 h.

61 Ibid., p. 235 j; p. 243 j; p. 235 e.

62 Ibid., p. 235 d.

63 All that one can read on the subject of buying horses is borrowed from the accounts of 1234 and 1239, published in *Historiens de France*, t. XXI, p. 248-249; t. XXII, p. 611-613.

64 *Historiens de France*, t. XXII, p. 612 d.

65 *Historiens de France*, t. XXI, p. 249 b; *Historiens de France*, t. XXII, p. 613 e; p. 611 f, h.

66 *Historiens de France*, t. XXI, p. 248 h.

67 *Historiens de France*, t. XXII, p. 611-612.

68 *Historiens de France*, t. XXI, p. 249 e.

69 *Historiens de France*, t. XXII, p. 611; *Historiens de France*, t. XXI, p. 248; *Historiens de France*, t. XXII, p. 611.

70 « *Strepæ,* » t. XXI, p. 239 m.

71 *Historiens de France*, t. XXI, p. 243 f.

72 Ibid., p. 229 i, 244 9; p. 231 a, j.

73 *Histor. de France*, t. XXI, p. 239 l; t. XXII, p. 601 e-f, 606 d; t. XXII, p. 592 f.

74 *Historiens de France*, t. XXI, p. 232 h, 236 d, 239 b, 245 f.

75 Ibid., p. 232 c; p. 232 a, f, 239 e; p. 231 h, 232 j, 241 d, h, j.

76 An account published by Ludewig, *Reliquise manuscriptorum*, t. XII, 2nd part, p. 3, we learn that during Pentecost of 1231 there were, in the household, huntsmen and their servants, falconers, fishermen, bird-catchers, and furriers; services of the bakery and *échançonnerie* [wine cellar] are mentioned, as well as runners, *fruitiers* [fruit preservers], ushers, dog handlers. Instances related to the various services of the household are scattered in the accounts going back to the regency of Queen Blanche; I will abstain from entering a study here which, for the following years and the end of the reign of Saint Louis, would present a true interest.

77 *Historiens de France*, t. XXI, p. 226-251.

78 Potthast, *Regesta*, 8430; 18 July 1229.

79 Potthast, 8455-56 ; 28 and 30 September 1229.

80 Potthast, 9791 ; Rodenberg, *Epistolæ sæculi XIII e regestis pontificum Romanorum selecæ*, t. I, p. 501, n. 612; 5 December 1234.

81 Rodenberg, t. I, p. 541, n. 645; 16 and 15 June 1235.

82 Aubry de Trois-Fontaines, *Historiens de France*, t. XXI, p. 604 b; *Monumenta Germaniæ*, scriptores, t. XXIII, p. 927; *Willelmi chronica Andrensis, Monumenta Germaniæ*, t. XXIV, p. 769; d'Achery, *Spicilegium*, in-4°, t. IX, p. 662, in-folio, t. II, p. 868.

83 Huillard-Bréholles, *Historia diplomatica Friderici Secundi*, introduction, p. ccxcvin-ix.

84 Letter from Frederick II to Louis IX, Huillard-Bréhollos, t. IV, p. 539; Ficker, *Regesten*, n. 2087; 25 April 1235; Potthast, 9879; 16 April 1235; Gregory IX to the King of France; Henry III to Frederick II; Shirley, *Royal and other historical letters*, vol. I, p. 475.

85 Ficker, *Regesten*, n. 2099 a. It was with the story of this marriage that Roger of Wendover finished his chronicle; ed. Hewlet, t. III, p. 108-114. Cf. Mathieu de Paris, ed. Luard, t. III, p. 318-327; Mathieu de Paris, t. III, p. 340; Ficker, n. 2136.

86 Le Nain de Tillemont, t. II, p. 240-241.

87 Mathieu de Paris, t. III, p. 336.

88 Letters of the Pope to Pierre de Collemezzo and Louis IX; 13-15 February 1235; Rodenberg, *Epistolæ sæculi XIII*, p. 510-513, no. 624-626; *Layettes du Trésor des Chartes*, t. II, p. 2413-14; December 1235.

89 *Layettes*, t. II, p. 2332; January 1235.

90 Ibid., 2353; February 1235.

91 *Layettes*, t. II, p. 2335-2352; February 1235. See in the same collection another obligation of Mahaut (2368) and documents relative to the marriage of her daughter Jeanne to Gaucher de Châtillon (2173-74) ; Gaucher, who had married the first cousin of Saint Louis, was faithful to him and died, in defending him with a heroism that made him famous, on the retreat from Egypt.

92 *Layettes*, t. II, p. 2356; 21 March 1235.

93 Du Cange, *Des fiefs jurables et rendables*, 30th dissertation, at the end of the edition of Joinville (in-folio, 1668, p. 349-362).

94 Potthast, *Regesta*, 9131; 26 March 1233; *Layettes du Trésor des Chartes*, t. II, 2264-65; 2 January 1234.

95 Favors accorded to Louis IX and Blanche by the chapter general of Prémontré, 1232. *Layettes*, 2213-14. Letter of the prior and convent of the church of Christ, Canterbury, 1232. Ibid., 2221.

96 Le Nain de Tillemont, t. II, p. 143; *Historiens de France*, t. XXIII, p. 147; *E libro mortuali Sanctæ Catharinæ Vallis Scholarium*, etc.

97 Félibien, *Histoire de l'abbaye royale de Saint-Denys*, p. 227. Le Nain, t. II, p. 118. Guillaume de Nangis, *Vie de saint Louis* (*Historiens de France*, t. XX, p. 320).

98 See among the others Guillaume de Nangis, *Historiens de France*, t. XX, p. 320. Attribution of this story to Philippe de Grève is found in Aubry de Trois-Fontaines, *Monumenta Germaniæ*, scriptores, t. XXIII, p. 931; *Historiens de France*, t. XXI, p. 608. Another relation, for whom the author is unknown to me, but which is certainly the work of a nun from Saint-Denis, has been utilized by Félibien, *Histoire de l'abbaye royale de Saint-Denys*, p. 228-233.

99 See however, in the *Layettes du Trésor des Chartes*, documents 1987^2 and 2262^2.

100 *Table chronologique des diplômes*, t. V, p. 370.

101 *Willelmi chronica Andrensis*, *Monumenta Germaniæ*, scriptores, t. XXIV, p. 771, 1231.

102 This affair is known to me only by the *Inventaire des archives de l'Aisne*, t. III, série G, p. 8-9; G 2, register, charters 66 and 263; *Layettes*, t. II, 2228; January 1233.

103 Gregory IX to the King; injuries made against the monks of de Saint-Valory-sur-Somme by the people of this town; 15 July 1233; Martène, *Thesaurus anecdotorum*, t. I, p. 978.

104 Denifle, *Chartularium universitatis Parisiensis*, t. I, p. 148-150, n. 96-97.

105 2 May1234. Rinaldi, *Annales*, t. II, p. 103. Potthast, *Regesta*, 9452.

106 *Historiens de France*, t. XXIV, p. 71, n° 537. The Bishop of Séez complained himself that the King did not want to force the excommunicated knights to make absolution; enquiry of 1247. See, on the resistance of Saint Louis to this pretention of the clergy, the famous passages of Joinville, ed. of 1874, §§ 61 to 64 and 669 to 671.

107 Paul Fournier, *Les Officialités au moyen âge*, p. 98-99.

108 The quarrel between the King and Archbishop Maurice has been recounted at length by Le Nain de Tillemont, t. II, p. 150-156. See on this subject the *Chronique*

de Rouen (*Historiens de France*, t. XXIII, p. 334-336).

109 Rinaldi, *Annales*, t. II, p. 63-64. Potthast, 9051.

110 Valois, Guillaume d'Auvergne, p. 357, justification documents, n. XLII 26 August 1233; Rinaldi, *Annales*, t. II, p. 95; Potthast, 9283; 1 September 1233.

111 Potthast, 9317-9318; 23 October 1233.

112 Chronique de Rouen, *Historiens de France*, t. XXIII, p. 334.

113 *Historiens de France*, t. XXIII, p. 355 : « *nunquam vixit sine pœnis.* »

114 The quarrel between Louis IX, his mother, and the Bishop of Beauvais has been recounted by several modern historians, among others, Le Nain de Tillemont, t. II, p. 156 ff. For a reprise of this affair from the time of Bishop Geoffroy and his definitive rule, see the same author, p. 251- 258. Paul Viollet has summarized this difficult question, with much concision and clarity, in his *Examen critique d'un ouvrage de M. Gérin sur la Pragmatique sanction de saint Louis ; Bibliothèque de l'École des Chartes* , 1870, p. 181-182. See also the account of Labande, *Histoire de Beauvais et de ses institutions communales*, Paris, 1892, in-8°, p. 69-77. The texts from which I borrow my account, from the Council of Saint-Quentin, in August 1231, is found for the most part in the collection of Varin, *Archives administratives de Reims* (*Documents inédits*), t. I, 2nd part, p. 548-606. The most important of all is the inquest on the troubles in Beauvais, ibid., p. 593-601.

115 For the story of this insurrection, see the inquest, 2nd *témoin* [witness], p. 595; 3rd *témoin*, p. 596; 6th *témoin*, p. 597.

116 Inquest, 6th *témoin*, p. 597 : « *quia episcopus fuit in defectu.* » ; Letter of the King, Varin, p. 572.

117 Inquest, 2nd *témoin*, p. 595.

118 Ibid.

119 Aubry de Trois-Fontaines, *Monumenta Germaniæ*, t. XXIII, p. 931; Inquest, 8th *témoin*, p. 598, et al.

120 Inquest, 1st *témoin*, p. 594.

121 1st *témoin*, p. 594; 2nd *témoin*, p. 595.

122 1st, 2nd, 6th, and 8th *témoins*; Aubry de Trois-Fontaines, *Monumenta Germaniæ*, scriptores, t. XXIII, p. 931.

123 8th *témoin*, p. 598.

124 1st *témoin*, p. 594; 3rd *témoin*, p. 596.

125 Varin, p. 571-572; letter of the King to the superior and the chapter of Laon, December 1233.

126 *Layettes du Trésor des Chartes*, t. II, no. 2279 and 2280; Varin, p. 575, 6 April 1234.

127 Le Nain de Tillemont, p. 257-258.

128 Story of Le Nain de Tillemont, t. II, p. 262 ff; epitome of Viollet, *Bibliothèque de l'École des Chartes*, 1870, p. 178-180. See the documents on this affair in Varin, *Archives administratives de Reims*, t. I, 2° partie, p. 560 ff.

129 Varin, p. 581.

130 *Layettes du Trésor des Chartes*, t. II, no. 2404; September 1235.

131 *Layettes du Trésor des Chartes*, t. II, no. 1979-1979.

132 Ibid., no. 1959^2 and 1959^3, 1960.

133 Ibid., no. 1830 ff, 1912; no. 2108 ff.

134 *Chronicon Gerardi de Frachete*, *Historiens de France*, t. XXI, p. 3 and 4. See, in the same volume, texts relative to this famine, p. 764, 800, 807.

135 *Historiens de France*, t. XXIV, royal inquests, p. 117, n 201.

136 *Historiens de France*, t. XXIV, p. 110, no. 135.

137 Ibid., p. 120, no. 228; no. 226.

138 Ibid., p. 33 a; inquest on the vicomté de Verneuil and de Breteuil. For the sojourn of the King at Breteuil in 1234, see the same volume, p. 16, no. 103.

139 The lands of Guillaume d'Ouilly, Archdiocesan of Angers, were confiscated by the bailiff Jean des Vignes, under pretext that the closest heritors were in England; *Historiens de France*, i. XXIV, p. 50, no. 370-371 ; p. 51, no. 383; p. 55, no. 410. Diverse confiscations on the same theme, in depositions relative to the same inquest, no. 46, 52, 271, 311, 346, 390, 456.

140 Ibid., p. 59, no. 447; p. 68, no. 510.

141 Ibid., p. 50, no. 373; p. 62, no. 469, and in many other places.

142 Ibid., p. 64, no. 480. See also no. 479.

143 Ibid., p. 37, no. 281; p. 59, no. 443; p. 71, no. 540; p. 68, no. 513; p. 61, no. 458.

144 Inquest on Bernay, same collection, t. XXIV, p. 14, no. 85.

145 *Historiens de France*, t. XXIV, p. 146, 563; p. 202, n 1288.

146 Ibid., p. 118, 210.

147 Ibid., p. 118, 209.

148 Ibid., p. 179, 957.

149 *Historiens de France*, t. XXIV, p. 121, n 239.

150 Ibid., p. 197 ff, nos. 1176, 1188, 1193, 1255, 1267.

151 Ibid., p. 90, no. 214; Izé, in Mayenne, arrondissement of Laval; p. 142, no. 496.

152 Ibid., p. 142, no. 497; p. 152, no. 636; p. 153, no. 639; p. 194, no. 1144; p. 203, no. 1299, etc., etc.

153 Ibid., p. 142, no. 500; p. 145, no. 558.

154 Ibid., p. 153, no. 637 : « *falso imponens ei quod fortunam invenerat.* » ; p. 205, no. 1324 : « *quod invenerat pecuniam in terra absconditam.* » ; p. 169, no. 803; p. 166, no. 766.

155 *Historiens de France*, t. XXIV, p. 209, no. 1396.

156 Ibid., p. 207, no. 1350.

157 Ibid., p. 206, no. 1334; p. 180, no. 965.

158 Ibid., p. 169, no. 818. p. 121, no. 231.

159 Ibid., p. 193, no. 1133.

160 Ibid., p. 202, no. 1272.

161 Ibid., p. 226, no. 1561.

162 *Historiens de France*, t. XXIV, p. 79, no. 72.

163 Ibid. p. 115, no. 180.

164 Ibid. p. 163, 737.

165 Ibid., p. 224, no. 1536.

166 Ibid., p. 196, no. 1166.

167 Ibid., p. 289, no. 105.

168 *Ordonnances des rois de France*, I, 51; Du Chesne, *Historiæ Francorum scriptores*, V, 816 a.

169 Annales de Saint-Médard de Soissons, *Monumenta Germaniæ*, scriptores, t. XXVI, p. 522; d'Achery, *Spicilegium*, in-4o., II, 795; in-folio, II, 491; Mathieu de Paris, ed. Luard, t. III, p. 361.

170 Rinaldi, *Annales ecclesiastici*, t. II, p. 94; see Potthast, *Regesta*, 9993-9995.

171 For the persecutions of which Robert le Bougre was the principal author, consult Philippe Mousket, ed. Reiffenberg, t. II, verse 28871 ff; Mathieu de Paris, ed. Luard, t. III, p. 361, 520, and t. V, p. 247; Aubry de Trois-Fontaines, *Historiens de France*, t. XXI, p. 614 and 615, and *Monumenta Germaniæ*, t. XXIII, p. 936 and 937; the chronicle of Baudouin d'Avesnes, *Historiens de France*, XXI, 166, and *Monumenta Germaniæ*, scriptores XXV, 455; Epitome Andrese Silvii, prioris Marchianensis, *Historiens de France*, XVIII, 559, and *Monumenta Germaniæ*, XXVI, 215; the annals of Saint-Médard de Soissons, ibid., p. 512, etc.

172 Verse 28996.

173 D'Arbois de Jubainville, IV, 296-297; Le Nain de Tillemont, 11,289-293.

174 Mathieu de Paris, ed. Luard, III, 520; V, 247. Philippe Mousket, verses 28881 and 28912.

175 Philippe Mousket, verse 28899.

176 Idem, verse 28901-28910. An act concerning the persecutions of Robert le Bougre is mentioned in the inventory in-4 in the archives of the Pas-de-Calais : série A, p. 18, col. 2, liasse A. 10.

177 Boutaric, *Actes du Parlement*, t. I, p. CCCIII, n. 14; Boutaric, *Recherches archéologiques sur le Palais de Justice de Paris* (*Bulletin de la Soc. des Antiquaires de France*, t. XXVII, 1864), p. 7.

178 Léopold Delisle, *Mémoire sur les opérations financières des Templiers*, *Mémoires de l'Académie des Inscriptions*, t. XXXIII, 2nd part, 1889.

179 Lèopold Delisle, *Catalogue des actes de Philippe Auguste*, n. 2034; March 1221; *Layettes du Trésor des Chartes*, t. II, n. 2056.

180 *Layettes du Trésor des Chartes*, II, 1811; 3 November 1226.

181 Ibid.

182 Guillaume le Breton, ed. Delaborde, t. I, n. 180.

183 Martène, *Amplissima collectio*, I, 1175; Anselme, *Histoire Généalogique de la maison de France*, VI, 621.

184 *Layettes du Trésor des Chartes*, n. 1911.

185 Chroniques de Saint-Denis, *Historiens de France*, t. XXI, p. 105.

186 *Historiens de France*, t. XXIV, p. 71, n. 539.

187 *Historiens de France*, t. XXI, p. 239 b; same collection, t. XXIV, p. 68, n. 518; p. 82, n. 116.

188 See further. Marshal Jean is named in an account of the royal household returning at Pentecost 1231 : Ludewig, *Reliquiae manuscriptorum*, t. XII, 2nd part, p. 3, col. 1.

189 Boutaric, *Institutions militaires*, p. 274.

190 *Historiens de France*, t. XXIV, p. 345, n. 121.

191 Ibid., p. 332, n. 51.

192 Ibid., p. 376, n. 81.

193 Ibid., p. 368, n. 42.

194 See ch. 5.

195 *Willelmi chronica Andrensis, Monumenta Germaniæ*, scriptores, t. XXIV, p. 770.

196 D'Arbois de Jubainville, t. V, no. 2037 and 2037 bis. Archives nationales, KK, 1064, f. 279 V; Suger, ed. Lecoy de la Marche, p. 118.

197 Joinville, ed. of 1874, n. 74.

198 *Historiens de France*, t. XXI, p. 240.

199 D'Achery, *Spicilegium*, in-4o., t. X, p. 284; Le Nain de Tillemont, t. I, p. 296.

200 *Layettes du Trésor des Chartes*, t. II, n. 2285.

201 Ibid., n. 1782.

202 *Layettes du Trésor des Chartes*, t. II, n. 2557.

203 *Historiens de France*, t. XXI, p. 241, l-m.

204 Léon Gautier, *La Chevalerie*, new ed., p. 745.

205 Boutaric, *Institutions militaires*, p. 247.

206 *Histoire des ducs de Normandie et des rois d'Angleterre*, ed. Francisque Michel, p. 133.

207 Wailly, nos. 98 and 104.

208 Guillaume de Nangis, *Vie de saint Louis*, *Historiens de France*, t. XX, p. 352.

209 *Historiens de France*, t. XXI, p. 220-226.

210 P. 221-222.

211 P. 222.

212 P. 220-221.

213 *Historiens de France*, t. XXI, p. 222-223.

214 Ibid., p. 222.

215 *Archives historiques du Poitou*, t. IV, p. 25.

216 *Historiens de France*, t. XXI, p. 223.

217 Ibid., p. 223; *Historiens de France*, t. XXII, p. 207, note 19.

218 Tome XXI, p. 224.

219 *Archives historiques du Poitou*, t. IV, p. 96; Du Cange, glossaire, *Balistarii*, article on the *Balista*, p. 553, col. 2.

220 *Archives historiques du Poitou*, t. IV, p. 107.

221 *Historiens de France*, t. XXI, p. 243 d; Boutaric, *Institutions militaires*, p. 272.

222 *Historiens de France*, t. XXIV, p. 18 d, 18 t.

223 Léon Gautier, *La Chevalerie*, nouvelle édition, p. 722 ff, note. Color of the

horses, ibid., p. 724.

224 *Historiens de France*, t. XXI, p. 241 a.

225 Guillaume de Puylaurens, *Historiens de France*, t. XIX, p. 216 a.

226 *Historiens de France*, t. XXI, p. 249-250.

227 Ibid., p. 223, § 8. See, on the *règle du Temple* (*Soc. de l'histoire de France*, ed. H. de Curzon), articles concerning the number of horses that were for dignitaries and knights of this order, articles 51, 77, 99, 110, 120, 125, 130, 132, 138; the *bulla* of Urban IV carrying the conditions to which Charles d'Anjou was to obtain the kingdom of Sicily said that each knight brought by this prince was to have with him at least four horses: Archives nationales, J. 512, Sicile, n. 26.

228 *Historiens de France*, t. XXIV, p. 222, n. 1515.

229 *Historiens de France*, t. XXIV, p. 70, n. 528; 1223.

230 Ibid., p. 13, n. 77; p. 38, n. 282.

231 Ibid., p. 70, n. 531; p. 71, n. 539.

232 Ibid., p. 7, n. 38; p. 17, n. 117: p. 22, n. 157; p. 29, n. 230; p. 72, n. 543.

233 Ibid., p. 258, n. 47.

234 Ibid., p. 4, n. 17.

235 *Historiens de France*, t. XXI, p. 225.

236 Guillaume le Breton, *Philippide*, l. IV, v. 544-545, ed. Delaborde, p. 119; *Archives historiques du Poitou*, t. IV, p. 170.

237 *Archives historiques du Poitou*, t. IV, p. 44; accounts of Alphonse de Poitiers : « *Item pro II cementariis, II minatoribus...* »

238 This waas at the siege of Bellême; see above, ch. III.

239 *Ménestrel de Reims*, Wailly, n. 357.

240 *Historiens de France*, t. XXIV, p. 84, n. 139; 1242.

241 Philippe Mousket, ed. Reiffenborg, t. II, verse 25868; *Historiens de France*, t. XXIV, p. 251, n. 1914.

242 Ibid., p. 52, n. 391; p. 114, n. 175; *Archives historiques du Poitou*, t. IV, p. 86.

243 *Historiens de France*, t. XXIV, p. 257, n. 34.

244 Ibid., t. XXII, p. 589 9, 590 f. 593 e.

245 Ibid., t. XXI, p. 239 m ; t. XXII, p. 589 d, 608 c; t. XXI, p. 262 I.; Ibid., t. XXI, p. 239 h.

246 Boutaric, *Institutions militaires*, p. 156-160; Giry, *Établissements de Rouen*, t. I, p. 23 and elsewhere, t. II, p. 30 (text).

247 Boutaric, p. 208.

248 Boutaric, p. 203 and 206.

249 Léon Gautier, *La Chevalerie*, new ed., p. 744, note.

250 Guillaume le Breton, ed. Delaborde, t. I, p. 282.

251 *Historiens de France*, t. XXI, p. 241 I, 244 I; Aubry de Trois-Fontaines, 1233. See above; Mathieu de Paris, ed. Luard , t. IV, p. 195 and 218. Philippe Mousket, verse 31053.

252 *Historiens de France*, t. XXIV, p. 274.

253 See the two estimates published in Boutaric, p. 203, 206.

254 *Historiens de France*, t. XXIV, p. 368, n. 42; p. 376, n. 81.

255 *Historiens de France*, t. XXIV, p. 123, n. 252; p. 206, n. 1345; p. 209, n. 1383.

256 Ibid., p. 157, n. 675; 1235.

257 Ibid., p. 147-148, n. 579.

258 Ibid., p. 160, n. 709.

259 Ibid., p. 249, n. 1886 : « *eo quod non fuerat in excubia per unam noctem.* »

260 Ibid., p. 154, nos. 649 and 654; p. 171, n. 837; p. 248, n. 1862; p. 249, n. 1893.

Chapter Seven

Role of Blanche under the Personal Rule of her Son

Powerful influence of Blanche. – Her domains and her personal fortune. – Her pious foundations; Maubuisson. – Marriage of Robert d' Artois. – Alphonse of Portugal marries Mahaut de Boulogne. – Blanche and her children; princess Isabelle. – Relation of Balnche with her sister Bérengère and the house of Castile. – Her role at the court of France. – Jeanne of Flanders marries Thomas of Savoy. – Pierre Mauclerc quits the government of Brittany. – Solicitude of Blanche for Raimond de Toulouse and for Baudouin II, Emperor of the East. – Acquisition of the relics of the Passion. – Robert d'Artois refuses the imperial crown. – Blanche and the Jews; the Talmud. – Revolt of Trencavel; siege of Carcassonne. – Alphonse of France becomes Count de Poitiers. – Revolt of Lusignan. – Coalition against the King; campaign of Saintonge. – Submission of Raimond VII. – Innocent IV in Lyon. – Illness of Louis IX; he takes the cross. – Chartes d'Anjou becomes Count de Provence. – The King and his mother save the Pope threatened by Frederic II. – Death of Jeanne of Flanders; her sister Marguerite succeeds her. – Distress of Baudouin II. – Louis IX leaves for the Holy Land while entrusting France to his mother.

Louis IX had all that was necessary to govern. To the qualities of his heritage, to precocious virtues, he united the experience of his youth, doubled in value by the counsels and examples of his mother. He could not leave Blanche out of the way; he could not remove the most useful of all supports, and if the feeling of public interest did not push him to consult his mother in every great affair of state, he would have done so out of affection without limit, from the recognition and of the respect that he owed to her. Also, from 1236 to 1248, the Queen Mother never ceased to play a part of more importance in France; she was no longer, as at the time of the regency, made to carry all the responsibilities, all the labors of government, but preserved in the kingdom a place of honor, close to her son in completely predominant influence.

Freer than in the past, she consequently devoted a large part of her activity to the administration of her property, to the welfare of her house, to works of piety, especially to the establishment of her children and to their relation with the many members of her family, the interests of which she never forgot; but in everyone's eyes she remained the Queen of France. One can say without exaggeration that her son did not do anything without her; Blanche followed him everywhere, and nobody, even among the elite, neglected recourse to her intervention; on more than one occasion, in grave circumstances, it was she to whom agents of royal authority directly addressed themselves. Unceasingly invited to rule on the most important affairs, remaining beside her son at the head of government, she continued her working life; although not obliged, she profited her country of adoption with resources, experience, intelligence, and energy. This role was imposed on her by her son and by circumstances. Did she finally regret being able to deliver herself from toil? Must one think on the contrary that power, to which this great queen was for a long time accustomed, was so dear to her that she made a point of preserving it for the longest possible time? No one knows. What is certain, is that her powerful and wise activity did much good in France. She was the true agent of the tradition bequeathed by Philippe Auguste; like him, she was dedicated to the achievement of three goals: to fight the Plantagenets, to prevail over *les grands*, and to organize the state, against the needs of the Church, for the rights of the Crown. Would Louis IX not have, at certain points, renounced this tradition too soon, if the voice of his mother had not brought him back? Historians of the time represent him as having had some scruples in his youth, perhaps exaggerated, to which the Queen did not yield. It was told that Blanche, this grand-daughter of Henry II, this niece of Richard the Lion-hearted and King John, was opposed to the desire of the King, when pushed by reasons of conscience he had thought of restoring Normandy, removed to the English by his great father; thus, I can affirm that Blanche did well, and who knows if she had made it possible for her son to sign with Henry III the Treaty of

Paris, useful and glorious, but not less disastrous, when he left the enemies of France in possession of several provinces? Louis IX had not ceased showing an absolute respect for her, while all of the French and the foreigners continued to treat her as chief of state.

Blanche of Castile, after 1236, generally lived at the court of France. She had however, as Queen dowager, a fortune independent of her domains. Recall that in 1200, with the Treaty of Goulet, King John yielded to Prince Louis, on giving him his niece, the fiefs of Issoudun and Graçay, with those of Andre de Chauvigny, Lord of Châteauroux, held by the crown of England. Elsewhere, the *douaire* [dowager's inheritance] of Blanche included the three *châtellenies* of Hesdin, Bapaume, and Lens, assigned to her. Louis VIII, in his will, mentioned this *douaire*, in possession of which Blanche remained until the moment when she exchanged them against other fiefs.[1] In the same region she had again acquired from Thomas of Ham, Constable of Tripoli, the land of Vilaines.[2] Blanche acted on more than one occasion as lord of these various fiefs; she was rendered homage by Baudouin, lord of the manor of Lens, and in the document concerning the royal investigations of 1247 are a rather great number of depositions concerning her fiefs of Bapaume, Lens, Vilaines, and Hesdin.[3]

But in June 1237 Louis IX, executing the will left by his father, gave Artois in prerogative to Prince Robert, the eldest of his brothers; to enlarge this great fief, he thus formed from several pieces, the associated fiefs of Arras, Saint-Omer, and Aire with their dependences, three *châtellenies* which had until then constituted the *douaire* of Blanche and her acquisition of Vilaines; at the same time, it was agreed that the Queen Mother would be compensated by a concession for equivalent suitable fiefs.[4] This business was definitively regulated in 1240; Blanche accepted Meulan, Pontoise, Étampes, Dourdan and its forest, Corbeil, Melun and its *châtellenie*, with all their appurtenances. Louis IX, by the same act, gave her more with Crespy-en-Valois and its forest, Ferté-Milon, Pierrefonds and their dependencies; this concession was made for life. Moreover, the King granted his mother an annual rent for life of 4,500 *livres parisis*, perceived in these accounts as three ordinary settlements. He authorized to give the amount of 800 *livres parisis* in annual income, for alms, under conditions which would please her, by including a hundred *livres parisis* revenue given to the abbey of Maubuisson, and which was to be derived from the income of the fief of Meulan. In exchange for these important concessions Blanche renounced not only her *douaire*, but her dowry, formed, as one can see, by Issoudun, Graçay, and the fiefs of Andre de Chauvigny.[5]

Blanche continued to manage her fiefs in Berry until 1240; charters of March and April 1236 speak about markets that she established in Issoudun, and in the month of January 1238, Philippe, Archbishop of Bourges, attested that Guillaume de Huriel had sold for sixty *livres parisis* to Blanche some houses located in Issoudun, close to the square.[6] As for many fiefs of which she had acquired the enjoyment for life, they remained in her possession as long as she lived, as proved in examination of her accounts and some other documents. In March 1244, she bought revenue located in the *prévôté* [jurisdiction of a revenue collector in a royal domain] of Pierrefonds.[7] In May 1248, Simon de Boutervilliers sold *droits de cens* [quit-rent] to her which he held in Étampes; three years later, in 1251, the land of Valois seems to belong to her; finally, as Lady of Melun in 1243 she had recourse, by agreement with the King her son, to an arbitration between them and Count Thibaud de Champagne, to regulate the extent of their respective possessions between Melun and Brie.[8]

Beyond these possessions representing the equivalence of her *douaire* and of her dowry, Blanche had in Paris one or more houses that Jean de Nesle and his wife, in 1232, had yielded to the King as much as to herself.[9] In November of the same year, Louis IX had given up to his mother the rights that he had in this building, located at the place where the Halle des Blés [wheat exchange] exists in our day.[10] The hôtel de Nesle, which one should not confuse with the house of the same name located on left bank of the Seine, carried successively, starting from the fourteenth century, the names of hôtel de Bohême, d'Orleans and de Soissons.[11] Though Blanche probably inhabited it, I am unaware of up to what point and at which times she made her residence in it.

Accounts of the royal household provide the names of many people who were in her service; but in these documents the articles relating to the Queen Mother are seldom indicated in a precise way, so I cannot use them to reconstitute the personnel of this house. Charters belonging to different times name its chamberlain Renaud de Montargis, one of its ladies, Eudoline, who married Robert de Montfort, Jean de Cépoy and Agnes de Fallouel, both rewarded by Louis IX for services they rendered to his mother.[12] I do not know if it is necessary to recognize one of the familiars of Blanche in the unknown character who dedicated a mystical work to her, the *Miroir de l'âme* [Mirror of the Soul], in which are exposed with a certain elegance the reasons that a Queen must have to practice the Christian virtues.[13]

The personal income of Blanche was managed by Templars, and we have an account of the receipts and expenses made for her by the treasurer of the Temple in Paris; she did not depart from the usage then observed, in France and England, by the majority of princes and great lords.[14] For accounts which were made for her household or her domains, they undoubtedly employed *jetons* [metal counting tokens], unless however examples of these *jetons* known to us are considered as pertaining to one of her children.[15] The treasurer of the Temple, in the account drawn up for Candlemas (2 February 1243), mentions receipts for Étampes, Dourdan, Corbeil, Pontoise, and Meulan. These various domains represent the acquisitions made by Blanche in exchange for her *douaire* (Hesdin, Bapaume, and Lens); also one finds, at the end of the article which relates to them, "total for the *douaire*." The next article includes details of the income from Crespy and Pierrefonds. In the chapter of expenditure, it is necessary to cite important loans to the abbot of Pontigny, to the treasurer of Notre-Dame, the lady of Beaumont, the Countess of Flanders, a gift to the abbey of Maubuisson, the purchase of animals and sums allotted to the personal expenditure of the Queen. Again I cite a general list of sums due then to Blanche of Castile by a certain number of people and religious communities.

The account of expenditure made by Blanche of Castile in 1241 and until Ascension of 1242, presents a more lively interest, where one finds enumerated, according to custom, the places the Queen traversed and the sums disbursed during this period.[16] Here are yet the names of the personal domains of Blanche which appear most often. At first glance, one sees that this document differs from the accounts of the royal household drawn up about this time. First, there were expenses made for the King, the princes, the people who were at court, and the servants of the royal household. Second, in the accounts of Blanche, there are names of ladies and persons in service pertaining to her retinue, but these mentions are few compared with the abundant enumerations in royal accounts. The expenses made for the Queen Mother occupy themselves, in the accounts written on her behalf, in a rather not very important place; however, I cite some purchases of dresses, furs, fabrics, linen, even jewels and gold objects; the acquisition of a psalter was also mentioned, a small gift made to a scribe of the Queen, in Paris.[17] Evidently, these articles represent a very weak part of what was spent by Blanche, for her maintenance, and for her entourage. She lived most often at the court of her son, and I know that in many circumstances the purchases made for her use were carried on the royal accounts.

What predominates are the generosities made by the Queen, especially the donations of cash and in kind to a great number of religious establishments, including the abbey of Maubuisson, the monasteries of the Trésor-Notre-Dame, Villiers-les-Nonains, Parc-aux-Dames. The Queen gave much to the almshouses and devoted important sums to the indigent. In Vernon, she distributed bread to the poor in her chamber.[18] Then the generosities made to private individuals: gifts to a niece of St. Thomas of Canterbury, to the Viscount of Melun, for his knighthood, and to several other people, a gratuity for the messenger who aprized Blanche on the lying-in of the Queen of Navarre; gifts for the marriage of people from various conditions in life.[19] Blanche showed herself, as always, generous towards her compatriots: a Spanish knight received thirty *livres*; ten *livres* were allotted to a priest of the same country, who returned beyond the Pyrenees.

Money placed in the coffers of the Queen is mentioned, in her accounts, at regular intervals, generally in sums of 10 *livres*, probably destined for spending and gifts that she had to make on her travels. A smaller sum was registered as pocket money. It is enough to glance at the accounts of Blanche to note that her generosity was expressed in donations and very many foundations. Louis IX, wanting to support the liberality of his mother towards churches and convents, allowed her, at an unknown date, to spend each year in alms a perpetual sum up to 300 *livres*. At the same time, he reserved a faculty to her for laying out an advance of two years income which would follow her death, either *civile* [dead in law] or natural.[20] These expressions prove that Blanche had every intention to withdraw herself sooner or later into a convent.

Blanche had a marked predilection for the order of Citeaux, and it was in a Cistercian monastery where she dreamed of finishing her life.[21] She wanted this house to be raised by her and equipped from her purse. From the year when she definitively gave to her son the care of public affairs, she devoted a share of her time and income to the implementation of this project. Work relating to the construction of the abbey of Notre-Dame-la-Royale, more famous under the name of Maubuisson, began with her order on the territory of Aulnay, close by Pontoise, in the month of May 1236, in the first week after Pentecost. The abbey, for which property and revenues increased via a series of purchases and donations, was finished in 1242, before Easter.[22]

Most of the funds employed in the establishment of the abbey of Maubuisson were issued, from 1236 to 1242, by Brother Gilles, treasurer of the Temple in Paris, to Master Richard de Tourny, director of the work, who, during these six years, accepted from the Temple the considerable sum of 24,431 *livres*, 15 *sous*, 4 *deniers* of money, without speaking of what reached him elsewhere.[23] In 1239, Blanche founded for Maubuisson a revenue of 100 *livres parisis* to be taken on its *prévôté* of Meulan; she added to this rent the tithes of wheat and wine of Étampes, Dourdan and in the other *châtellenies* of her *douaire*. Louis IX confirmed this donation, and allotted, for his part, 100 *livres parisis* of revenue to the new abbey, from the *prévôté* of Mantes.[24] On his side, the Archbishop of Sens, Gautier Cornu, ratified, in February 1241, the concession of the tithes of Étampes.[25] In 1239 and starting from Ascension, Master Richard mentioned in his accounts the sums coming from these diverse sources; at the same time, he increased his resources by selling pigs, charcoal, leeks, iron, lime, structural timber, the whole provided by the domain of the new abbey. It was with the Queen herself that he established his accounts, beginning on 30 November 1237, then, under the terms of payment then in use, at Chandeleur [Candlemas], Ascension, and Toussaint [All Saints' Day].

Master Richard enumerated the expenditure of all kinds that he made in each term; I pay attention most closely to the construction and interior installation of the abbey. In the beginning all appears that relates to the building itself, frames, woodwork, doors and windows, lead, tiles, paving, timber structures for the dormitory, the vault, the abode of the priests and one part of the cloister, cords, panes of the convent and stained glass of the vault. He purchased 41,000 slats; he built a fountain, and bought manure for the garden where work began. Then furniture appears: thirty quilts, thirty cushions, 141 *aunes* [ells] of fabric, parchment, leather for shoes, boilers, cloth intended to furnish the cart of the abbess, and saddles. Part of the purchases were made at the Lendit [the fair at St. Denis], and the enumeration of Master Richard gives a variety of objects found at this singular grand fair. The account mentions, in the last place, land acquisitions.

The abbey of Maubuisson, with its many dependencies, gardens, enclosures, grounds, and properties of all kinds allotted to it from earliest times, became in a few years one of the most beautiful monastic establishments of the kingdom; frequent stays that Blanche and Louis IX made in Pontoise increased its reputation and its prosperity. Blanche established Cistercian sisters drawn from the abbey of Saint-Anthony, close by Paris, under the direction of Sister Guillemette, their first abbesse. It was in March 1242 that the Queen officially noticed the foundation of the monastery, which was consecrated, on 26 June 1244, in the presence of Louis IX and his mother; they placed it under the invocation of the Holy Trinity, Mary, and Saint Jean-Baptiste.[26]

The foundation of the abbey of Maubuisson was an object of special study, and I must not fail to mention all that Blanche of Castile and Louis IX did to equip and to expand it. Blanche never forgot her nuns of Pontoise; her accounts and those of the royal household prove it. Once she paid a workman to "illuminate and recover a prayer-book intended for the abbey of the Queen," sometimes bought fabrics for clothing of the nuns; she bought cheese for them.[27] Examples of her generosity were many and varied. The King, the Pope, lavished privileges upon this prosperous establishment from its birth, and accomodated within its walls ladies of the highest rank; witness the Countess Alix de Mâcon, who withdrew there in 1239, after having sold her county to the Crown.

This same countess of Mâcon was intended to become the first abbess of another house of Cisterciennes, also established on the domains of the Queen Mother. It was, indeed, close to Melun that Louis IX and Blanche of Castile founded the abbey of Notre-Dame du Lys; in June 1248, before leaving for his crusade, the King confirmed the donations which his mother had made to the monastery, and two years later Blanche established, for the nuns of Lys, a rent on her *prévôté* of Pontoise. Religious orders thus took a large part for the mother of Saint Louis in the division of her considerable fortune, and Gregory IX, reasonbly for his part, only did justice when, in 1237, he granted the doamains of Blanche immunity from interdict without a special permit from the Holy See.[28] Charters of the convent of Vézelay, the Dominicans of Rouen, the chapter of Soissons, attests to their devotion or their recognition in this connection, and the act of filial devotion that Louis IX achieved each time that he associated the name or the memory of his mother with one of his good works was as much justified as Blanche, in a crowd of circumstances, in being protector and benefactor of the churches.[29]

It was not with pious works, however, that most of her activity went; above all, she remained mother of the family and Queen of France; it was she, at least as much as Louis IX, who directed the royal house. The elder of her sons became men; she governed their establishment while raising the juniors. In June 1237, Prince Robert married Mahaut, daughter of the Duke of Brabant; he was knighted, named Count d'Artois, and it was the *douaire* of his mother which was used to supplement his appanage.[30] On this occasion, splendid festivals were given in Compiègne, and household accounts show us, once more, what princes of the house of France spent when they tried to cut a good figure; together they describe "dresses for the children," a fabric of scarlet with lines for "lord Charles," ermine for the young Countess d'Artois and "mademoiselle de Toulouse;" the royal children of France, their wives, their betrothed in marriage, remained grouped around the Queen Mother, and the luxury of a day on display removed nothing from the patriarchal paces of this family life.[31]

The daughter of Raimond VII, one raised at court, had not married yet, in 1237, Alphonse of France; they did not wait until this young prince had accepted knighthood to assure him the rich heritage of Toulouse. After the death of Prince Jean, to whom Louis VIII, by his will, had allotted Anjou and Maine, these two counties were reserved for Charles, first intended to enter holy orders, and Prince Alphonse preserved the expectancy of the county of Poitiers. He was not invested until 1241, but his marriage was probably celebrated in 1238.[32] On 27 May 1236, Gregory IX had granted for this purpose a new dispensation for engagement, resulting from the problem of their being first cousins.[33]

About the same time, Blanche was occupied to make a situation for her nephew Alphonse of Portugal, this orphan who appears, in the accounts of 1234, under the name of "messire Alphonse her nephew," as the childhood companion of Alphonse de Poitiers. In 1239, she made him marry Mahaut de Boulogne, widow of Philippe Hurepel; the Prince of Portugal became, by this fact, one of the wealthiest lords of the kingdom.[34] They celebrated his establishment with sumptuous festivals; at Pentecost he was knighted, with many noble young people, at the head of which figured Baudouin II of Courtenay, Emperor of Constantinople, doubly dear to

Blanche by the bonds which linked the houses of France and Castile.[35] It was then that Alphonse of Portugal and Mahaut de Boulogne were married. Important expenditures were made for the costume of the new Count de Boulogne, for the purchase and maintenance of his horses, for clothing his retinue.[36] The household accounts cite the minstrels who appeared in the festivals of his knighthood and marriage, and the King gave him, the same year, as pledges, the sizeable sum of 195 *livres*.[37] In August, by a new favor, Louis IX conceded *fouage* to him on lands held in Normandy.[38] Alphonse was a good relative and faithful vassal; in 1212, he played a big role in the victory of Saintes, but soon after (1245) he left France to exert regency in Portugal; we have an account of the expenditure that Alphonse of France made on his return, his passage through Poitiers, Saint-Maixent, Niort, Benon, and a contemporary text speaks of a detachment requisitioned to carry to La Rochelle a barrel filled with silver belonging to the Count de Boulogne.[39] Lastly, the nephew of Blanche of Castile became King of Portugal in 1248; his wife Mahaut, forsaken by him, did not have circumstances which had been worthy of the crown. Blanche of Castile assisted, within reason, with the marriage of this young prince whom she had raised; she registered on this occasion, from the accounts of the King, important sums for his robes and those of his people; expenditure, following the use then observed, merged with those of the young Queen, of the Countess d'Artois, the royal children of France; her name returns at every moment, in 1239, in the royal accounts.[40]

Undoubtedly Charles and Isabelle of France were called "*les enfants*" at court. Charles had, in 1239, a sickness on the occasion of which Blanche went to see him at Melun near Vincennes.[41] Accounts of the household name two men attached to his service, as well as the servant responsible for the palfrey of "Mademoiselle."[42] Princess Isabelle, usually indicated by this title, gave early marks of burning piety. Blanche kept her close, and it is told that at the time a serious malady struck Isabelle, her mother, obliged to go away, gave her to the guardianship of Marguerite de Provence; the state of the small princess became all the more worrying; Blanche had called for prayers for the re-establishment of her daughter's health, and she announced when there would be a cure, she would never belong in the world. This prediction was carried out; even in the first time of her life, Isabelle did not associate with the pleasures of her sisters-in-law and other ladies; she preferred to remain in her room, to study Holy

Scripture; she spent a good part of her time devoted to embroidering in silk the stoles and ornaments of the church. Her spirit was so strongly carried to pious thoughts, that often, for the refusal to eat, or to speak a word to the King his brother, Blanche was reduced to promise money for the poor.[43] Destined, by the Treaty of Vendôme, to marry Hugues le Brun, son of the Count de La Marche, Isabelle de France was then sought by Emperor Frederick II for his son Conrad; but she did not follow these projects, and the sister of Saint Louis passed all of her life in the practices of the most austere devotion.[44] Also as educated as her brother, she did not hesitate to devote itself, like him, to the achievement of the humblest duties, and her biographer Agnes d'Harcourt tells us she also washed the feet of the poor on Maundy Thursday. Pope Innocent IV, who at first had determined to marry her off, seeing this resolution, wrote her a new letter in which he relented without reserve for her to be dedicated to the state of virginity. These two letters were preserved in the abbey of Longchamp, in the foundation of which Isabelle de France, according to the examples given by her mother, employed the last years of her life.[45]

Concurrently with the love that she showed to her children, Blanche had preserved thoughts of constant fidelity for her family in Spain. Since her entry in France, she did not appear to have seen her older sister, the wise and valiant Bérengère, Queen dowager of Leon, once called the Queen of Castile, although she had voluntarily placed the crown on the head of her son Ferdinand III. There were frequent exchanges of presents and messages between these two women who resembled each other so much in their character and by the role they had to play, at the same time, in two kingdoms. At various points the accounts of Blanche name the servants of Queen Bérengère sent to her sister the Queen of France; undoubtedly it was the sister, who at that time, dispatched horses and pomegranates to Blanche of Castile.[46] Blanche sent to Spain textiles and furs, sometimes an object of imagery, silver vases, and a *hanap* [drinking bowl].[47] At one time impossible to specify, she forwarded to Bérengère a whole set of sacred vessels and sacerdotal habits; the richness of such a gift proves once more that Blanche of Castile, generous by nature, economical when it was necessary, but broad in expenditure when she found it useful, did not spare money when it came to her family.[48] Bérengère died November 1246 and was buried in the royal monastery of Las Huelgas, where her parents rested. Four years later, her youngest daughter, also named Bérengère and a nun in this same convent, made her a more beautiful tomb, and Pope Innocent IV came to her assistance by promising indulgences to those who would visit this tomb.[49]

It was Bérengère who, in 1237, married Jeanne de Ponthieu to her son, King Ferdinand III, become widowed on the death of Béatrix de Souabe, his first wife. Jeanne was grand-daughter to a sister of Philippe Auguste; her mother, the Countess Marie de Ponthieu, was thus cousin of Louis VIII and Saint Louis; her father was Simon de Dammartin, to whom Blanche had returned her favor after a long disgrace.[50] The King of England had sought this beautiful princess; she had even married her by proxy, but the opposition of the King of France, suzerain of the Count de Ponthieu, had prevented this marriage, of which Gregory IX and Innocent IV successively proclaimed nullity.[51] Jeanne de Ponthieu, famous for her virtues and beauty, married the nephew of Blanche in Burgos. Soon after, Ferdinand III wrote Louis IX to request him to confirm an agreement concluded between him and Simon de Dammartin for the succession of Ponthieu; the new Queen did the same; the presence of their chamberlain at the court of France, in 1239, proves that she was in diplomatic relations with Blanche of Castile and Louis IX.[52]

A sister of Ferdinand III, called Bérengère, like her mother, had married the King of Jerusalem, Jean de Brienne, and we will see what Blanche of Castile did for their daughter Marie and her husband the Emperor of the East, Baudouin II. In 1237 Baudouin came to France, and brought his beautiful young brothers, Alphonse, Jean, and Louis, that Jean de Brienne sent to the King and Blanche their grand-aunt, to request of them a guardianship.[53] They were given the most affectionate reception, and soon afterwards, when they lost their father, it was Louis IX and his mother who provided for their maintenance. They were called, at the court of France, "the children of Acre," an allusion to the city which was used as capital of the kingdom over which Jean de Brienne had reigned.[54] Blanche of Castile, absorbed with so many great affairs of state and in charge of a family, still found time to be devoted to the children of others.

She had a younger sister, Aliénor, married on 6 February 1221 to the King of Aragon, Jacques the Conqueror, who repudiated her in 1229. Alphonse of Aragon, born from this union, was recognized heir to the crown, but remained close to his mother, who withdrew to the court of Castile.[55] It was there, undoubtedly, where she remained, until

1239 when one of her envoys came to find the Queen Mother in Saint-Germain-en-Laye.[56] Blanche did not forget her sister Aliénor, and some time after she carried on her accounts a belt purchased for the high price of fifteen *livres*, and textiles, intended for the Queen of Aragon.[57] After the death of Aliénor in 1244, Alphonse came to visit his aunt Blanche, and, after having been received in Poitiers by Alphonse of France, he followed him to Cluny, where Pope Innocent IV was.[58] One of the sons of the King of Castile also visited the court.[59] As for the Prince of Aragon, I do not know if he subsequently returned to Spain; he was in France in 1248.[60]

To finish with the nephews of Blanche, I must note that Aliénor of Portugal, daughter of Queen Urraque and sister of Alphonse, later Count de Boulogne, had been given in marriage to Waldemar of Denmark, who carried the title of King even during the life of his father Waldemar II. She died in 1231.[61] Two years before, Waldemar II had ratified arrangements relative to her *douaire*.[62] The fact that this document was sent to France and deposited in the Trésor des Chartes, would be enough to show that Blanche of Castile kept an interest in the children of her sisters.

Apart from her family, throughout the kingdom, the reputation of Blanche remained so high one could have taken her for the true sovereign. Louis IX almost always had her nearby; he "required her presence and counsel, when he could profitably have it."[63] Royal authority was constantly delegated to her, in ordinary circumstances as in the most important affairs; like her son, and often with him, she traversed the kingdom and rendered justice. In 1235 or 1236, having at her sides the chamberlain Barthelemy de Roye, she arbitrated a quarrel between a Norman knight and the bailiff Jean des Vignes, and, on this occasion, the plaintiff addressed his request to the Queen Mother at the same time as the King.[64] Passing through Caen, she restored thirty *livres* to people who had been injured by agents of the crown.[65] Inhabitants of Arras complained about the damage caused to them by the King and his mother; they appeared before Louis IX and Blanche of Castile at Saint-Germain-en-Laye, in the apse of the church, and they promised to make it right.[66] Blanche traveled with the court, to one and another province; in 1242 we find her in Tours, and on 27 April 1244 in Limoges, she passed through with the King, her other son and the Count Alphonse de Boulogne, to go on pilgrimage to Rocamadour.[67] In the opinion of several people, she was associated with complaints addressed to the King as to acts of justice that they sought from him.⁶⁸ Public opinion was made, with a quite strange frankness, by the seneschal Pierre d'Athies, one of the hardest agents of royal authority. A man who appeared before him desired to call in the name of the King, but the seneschal answered harshly: "Say what you wish, and quickly! I would pay a hundred *marcs* to hear less of the King, and more of the Queen."⁶⁹

Thus, it was still Blanche of Castile to which one addressed oneself or that one feared. Her power in the kingdom was such that great lords attached a strange importance to her favor. It was because of her bad relationship with Simon of Montfort, Count of Leicester, refugee for a time in France after a quarrel with his brother-in-law Henry III, and crossing again to England in the month April 1240.⁷⁰ Later, without doubt in 1243, the Count of Leicester, having difficulties with Raimond VII, the Franciscan Adam March wrote on this subject to the minister of Trinitaires, in Paris. He requested him to act on his behalf to petition Blanche, for which she assented by an effect of her leniency, to restore peace between these two great lords, thus demonstrating her influence. Adam March added that only reasons of modesty prevented him from writing directly to the Queen.⁷¹ No foreign prince would have had the idea to journey through France without seeing the mother of the King. When, in 1240, Richard de Cornouailles crossed the continent to crusade in the Holy Land, Louis IX and Blanche received him with honor and gave him the hospitality of the palace.⁷² The same year, Edmond, Archbishop of Canterbury, fighting with the King of England, withdrew to Pontigny; and visited the Queen Mother and blessed her and her children.⁷³

The homages which people made to the old Regent were due not only to the nobility of her character and the role she had played; they are explained by the power Blanche still had. At every moment, she intervened in the relationships of the Crown with *les grands*, advising and assisting her son in all things, and especially when he acted to regulate one of the questions which realted to when she ruled France. She continued to supervise those who had formerly fought, and was named in public acts to point out the commitments which the barons had undertaken towards the King during the regency. It was thus that her name was given, in 1237 and 1238, to acts concerning the affairs of Flanders and Brittany.

In Flanders, Countess Jeanne, widow of Ferrand of Portugal, thought of remarriage. Remember the constancy with which Blanche had formerly served the cause of this princess; it was to the Queen

Mother that Ferrand owed his delivery from prison, and it was to Blanche, as to Louis IX, that the Flemings had sworn fidelity, when their count had left prison. When it was necessary to take new sureties for the second union that Jeanne was going to contract, Louis IX wanted his mother involved. It was a rule that the King closely supervised the marriages of his vassals, even when he could rely on their attachment. Louis IX and with him Blanche of Castile took very serious measures concerning Jeanne. From the first days of January 1237, Ferry Pâté, Marshal of France, Master Raoul de Meulan, clerk of the King, and the bailiff of Arras rode to Flanders. Marguerite la Noire, daughter of Emperor Baudouin I of Constantinople and younger sister of the countess, aldermen and the commune of Douai, the seneschal of Flanders, all renewed engagements taken formerly by the Flemings with regard to Louis IX and Queen Blanche.[74] In preparation for the case where Jeanne would not observe conditions subscribed after the delivery of Count Ferrand, they swore to hold against her for the party of the King, his mother and his brothers. They had spoken to make her marry Simon de Montfort, Count of Leicester; but the King could not admit that one of the principal English feudatories became the master in one of the largest fiefs of his kingdom. Simon de Montfort, after having at one time had to give up Mahaut, Countess de Boulogne, whom Blanche had married to her nephew Alphonse of Portugal, could no longer become Count of Flanders. In April 1237, by the Convention of Péronne, Jeanne issued the King a new act of fidelity and formally renounced any plan of marriage with the Count of Leicester. A great number of lords and cities under the Countess of Flanders individually ratified this promise.[75] In October, Jeanne married Thomas de Savoy, uncle of Queen Marguerite de Provence, and in December, having come to Compiègne to lend homage to their sovereign, the new husbands solemnly associated the name of Blanche to that of the King, in their promises of fidelity.[76] In consequence of an engagement which was then imposed on them, the nobles and towns of Flanders provided, before the royal envoys, some new guarantees.[77] Blanche was named, beside her son, in almost all of these charters.

  Her name also appeared in a public act when Pierre Mauclerc gave to Jean le Roux the estates that he had controlled for a long time. Pierre had never ruled Brittany; in November 1237 he had to yield the place to his son, who attained his majority. Since then this man, who had played for so long a time in the kingdom one of the primary roles, bore the title Pierre de Braîne, knight. In April 1238, Jean le Roux came to ratify in Pontoise an old transfer of Saint-James-de-Beuvron, Bellême, Perrière, and the lands that his father had taken from the crown in the counties of Anjou and Maine; Pierre de Braîne is mentioned in a treaty he had concluded in Paris, in 1234, with Louis IX and Blanche of Castile. For the second time he promised to give, if he could find them, to Louis IX, to Blanche or to the heir of the crown, letters by which the King had formerly conceded the fiefs to him from which he came to ratify their abandonment.[78]

For this untiring conspirator as for the other barons, the time of revolts seemed quite over. Mauclerc, reconciled with the King, with the Pope, then took up the cross; the same movement towards the Holy Land involved the former Count of Brittany, Count Jean de Mâcon his brother, King Thibaud, Duke of Burgundy, Count de Bar, Amaury the Constable of Montfort, Robert de Courtenay, and a whole army of great lords. I shall not recount the history of this lamentable crusade, during which Robert de Courtenay, Henri de Bar, Amaury de Montfort, and Jean de Mâcon all died; this last, before leaving, in February 1239 had sold his county to the King of France. His widow, Countess Alix, became a nun at Maubuisson soon afterwards, waiting for Blanche of Castile to make her Abbess of Lys. Everything leads me to believe that the Queen Mother was not a stranger to this important annexation.

There was, among the former enemies of the crown, one man to whom Blanche was more interested than all the others, the Count de Toulouse. She had more reason for not remaining foreign to the affairs of this prince; since the succession of her son she had done everything for the submission of Languedoc, and Raimond VII was her first cousin. However, Blanche of Castile, gifted in public affairs with untamable tenacity, always showed in her family relations a truly extraordinary fidelity of feelings. Whatever were their merits, those who were linked to her by the bonds of blood could be sure that despite faults of a despairing gravity, they would never miss her in time of need. Raimond experienced this more than once.

He had formerly taken the cross, after his discharge, to go five years into the Holy Land, and this engagement had been cited in the Treaty of Paris. It was, certainly, a hard obligation for a prince half despoiled, whose domains were impoverished by a long war. Since then, in France, a great number of barons made crusade, and if the situation of Count Raimond had been really difficult, they would have owed themselves to wait until he took serious measures to leave with them. However, the Count de Toulouse never left. Gregory IX had to thoroughly know the intentions of this man, conspiratorial by nature, which hardnesses of fate had made calculating and devious, and for whose spirit, shared in addition to ambition and fear, constantly sought means of missing the execution of some promise. On 28 April 1230, in an extremely severe letter, the Pope ordered him to set sail for the Holy Land the following March.[79] This injunction seemed to drive the Count de Toulouse back to an inescapable need; but he had at the court of France some sympathetic friends. The King, pushed by Blanche of Castile, intervened in his favor, and Gregory IX had to reverse himself. On 9 February 1237, he wrote Louis IX to consult on this subject his mother and some bishops; he declared himself ready to give respite to the Count de Toulouse until the feast of Saint-Jean-Baptiste the following year (24 June 1238). The King remained free of to take any measures he liked so that this time Raimond did not fail in the execution of his engagements.[80]

Raimond VII was not one of those whose experiences, even the more frightening, made him careful and scrupulous. At the moment when he claimed to be not preparing for the Holy Land, he attacked the Count de Provence, father-in-law of the King, devoted servant of the Church, and accepted against this prince the homage of Marcheilles. The King of Aragon, Jacques the Conqueror, who had taken up the cross and prepared to fight against the Moors, was thwarted in his projects by the aggression of which he was victim along with Raimond-Bérenger; both wrote Gregory IX to denounce the Count de Toulouse. The Pope lost all patience by seeing this crusader attack Christians; in a missive dated 18 May 1237, he recalled in strong terms to Raimond de Toulouse that he had enabled him to delay his departure [for the Holy Land], at the request of Louis IX and Blanche: "Be careful," he said, "that you do not reduce us to revoke the grace that we granted to them, and that we made for you in their honor."[81] Two days later, Gregory wrote in the same sense to the King of France and his mother.[82]

Those who so liberally employed themselves in pleading the cause of a former enemy were not satisfied; their reiterated examples finally prevailed on the head of the Church against the Count de Toulouse. On 9 June 1238, Gregory IX authorized Raimond VII to remain only three years in the Holy Land, and two months later he wrote Louis IX that upon his request he had ordered the Bishop of

Sora to give the Count a discharge.[83]

The efforts Blanche made in favor of Raimond VII often had a cost. In spite of the interest attached to his misfortune, I am reduced to ask whether this prince deserved anything awarded to him. Very different was the case of a man whom the mother of Saint Louis always treated with a touching solicitude, Baudouin II de Courtenay, Latin Emperor of Constantinople. Great-grandson of Louis le Gros, and consequently a distant cousin of the King of France, Baudouin had married Marie, niece of Blanche, daughter of Jean de Brienne and of Princess Bérengère of Castile. Called, at ten or eleven years, to the throne that his father and brother had successively occupied, Baudouin was not, for a long time, of sufficient age to rule, when fortune, by a frightening favor, put him at head of an empire which collapsed. One needed a man, a soldier, to defend the empire of Constantinople threatened by the Greeks; the barons called the wise and valiant Jean de Brienne, father-in-law of their sovereign, and gave him, with the regency, imperial honors. But the situation of the Empire of the East was almost without remedy; to face the danger, they needed money and troops; in 1236, Jean de Brienne sent his son-in-law to seek help in the Occident. Baudouin II was legitimate heir to the county of Namur and seigniory of Courtenay; he counted on the King of France for help to take possession of it.[84] The young emperor, then eighteen or nineteen years old, passed to Italy, where the Pope saw him and endeavored to interest in his fate the Western princes, and so he came to Paris. He had with him his three brothers-in-law, Alphonse, Jean and Louis, "the children of Acre," that Jean de Brienne sent to Blanche and her son. Baudouin accepted at the court of France a most affectionate reception; the King facilitated the means of returning his inheritance; the Queen Mother treated him, as much as one can judge about it, as family; she detained him for a long time, but she "found him childlike in his speech; because for an empire to hold it was appropriate to have a wise and vigorous man."[85]

Baudouin was for some time in France, when they learned, in spring of 1237, about the death of Jean de Brienne. It was for the Empire of the East an irrevocable loss. In the presence of increasing dangers to this state founded by Westerners and by the French, the Pope and King Louis took all measures possible to hasten relief. Gregory IX evinced active solicitude on this business, and the pressing letters that he addressed several times to Blanche of Castile show how much he was concerned to support the Latin conquerors of the Greek Empire, reduced to defend itself.[86] A first raising of troops, that Baudouin had prepared with the assistance of his protectors, having failed, partly by the ill will of Emperor Frederick II, the King of France encouraged his protégé to return to the Pope. Baudouin, who had been collecting some subsidies in England, had set out again for Italy in August 1238, and worked actively, here and there, to set up all available resources, when barons of the Empire of the East had recourse, to get money, to a desperate expedient.[87] To a representative of the Doge of Venice they pawned the most venerated souvenir which the Christians could possess, placed before the frontier of the Muslim world, the sacred Crown of Thorns, and, on September 4, 1238, this relic was given, under certain conditions, to the Venetian Nicolo Quirino, who had advanced the stipulated sums.[88]

Informed of the distress in which his people and the Empress Marie found themselves, Baudouin II redoubled his efforts with Louis IX, Blanche, and the French barons. The King and his mother gave him great sums, disbursed to hire troops and to bring together knights intended for the relief of Constantinople. Then the young Emperor, knowing their devotion to his cause, avowed to them that Crown of Thorns was committed to the Venetians. At the moment when it was to cease belonging to him, he expressed a keen desire to see it between the hands of a prince who was at the same time his King, his relative, and his benefactor. Fearing to offend the conscience of the King by speaking about selling an object also venerated by him, he offered to make a gift of it. Louis IX understood that he was acting to repurchase the Crown of Thorns; he could not be insensitive to this proposal.[89] Without speaking about his well-known devotion, possession of one of the principal relics of the Passion, given the ideas of the time, was to be a great honor for his kingdom; for her part Blanche, who did not lose sight of the fact of the interests of her niece, and who was doubly eager to see a remarkable bargain concluding itself, she used her influence so that the King made the acquisition of the Holy Crown.[90] Louis IX evinced the sharpest recognition of Baudouin, and soon two Dominican monks, Jacques and André, left for Constantinople, charged with releasing the Holy Crown to the authority of the King. They fully succeeded in their mission; we still have the charter by which the bailiff and great officers of the Empire of the Orient ordered Nicolo Quirino to hand over to the envoys, against payment, the holy Crown of Thorns (December 1238).[91] Repurchased by them and brought back to Venice, the crown remained there some time, while Brother Jacques hastened to return to France, to alert the King and Blanche about the result of his mission.[92]

Louis IX had given orders for everyone to come before the Crown of Thorns.[93] When those who brought it announced their arrival in Troyes, the King got under way with Blanche and went in haste to Villeneuve-l'Archevêque, having with him the metropolitan of Sens, Gautier Cornu, who we owe the detailed account of this transaction, the Bishop of Puy, and all the barons and knights that he had been able to gather. Arrived at Villeneuve, Louis opened the successive cases containing the reliquary, then the silver box contained in this case and on which were affixed, with the seal of the Doge of Venice, those of the barons of the Empire of the Orient; when the seals of the barons had been compared with those which hung on their letters patent, they broke them; a gold box appeared and the King contemplated the Crown of Thorns that it contained, the object of his desires and sacrifices. That was on 10 August 1239; there remained no more than to bring back the invaluable relic to Paris, whose transfer to France had been the object of so much meticulous precaution.[94] The royal accounts confirm all of these details, which are known to us by the account of Gautier Cornu; they speak of a sum allocated to the Lady of Beaujeu for its voyage to Villeneuve-l'Archevêque, of expenses paid to a servant on horseback, who brought the Crown of Thorns to Villeneuve, of a clerk who carried the cross before it, between Villeneuve and Sens.[95] It entry to this city (11 August) was very solemn; the King and Count Robert, barefoot and wearing hair shirts, carried the Crown on their shoulders; the following day they put themselves on the road to Paris. Beyond the gates, near the abbey of Saint-Antoine, in a place called La Guette, they built a platform; it was from there that, on 18 August, the reliquary was exposed to the eyes of an enormous crowd, the largest, according to one, that ever left Paris. After a short speech, the procession, in the midst of which was Blanche, the procession began again; at the head advanced a multitude of prelates, clerics, monks, knights, carrying candles and all barefoot, after the example of Louis IX and the Count d'Artois, who had again assumed their invaluable burden.[96] It was to the song of anthems that they entered Paris while moving towards Notre-Dame; finally, after an imposing Mass, celebrated in this church, the procession gained the palace. The Crown of Thorns had arrived at the end of its journey; it was introduced into the residence of the King of France, where it was placed in the Saint Nicolas chapel, decorated for this occasion, like the palace itself, with tapestries provided from the abbey of Saint-Denis.[97]

While the Holy Crown was brought to France, Baudouin II, at the head of an army, had again taken the road to Constantinople. After Midsummer's Day, he was advanced through Germany; the troops which accompanied him were numerous, and in 1240 he informed the King of England that with his assistance he had gained some advantages; but this help come from the Occident could not delay his ruin.[98] Towards this same year, Baudouin, always short of money, saw himself constrained to pawn a considerable portion of the True Cross, as guarantee of an enormous sum that he had borrowed from the Templars of Syria.[99] This time Blanche of Castile and her son came to the assistance of their unfortunate relative, and it was by the counsel of the Queen Mother that Louis, in 1241, made the acquisition of this relic which was going to escape the Emperor of the East. The wood of the True Cross was brought to France and solemnly received on its entry to Paris by the King, his mother, the young Queen and the princes. Blanche of Castile and Marguerite de Provence accompanied the foot the True Cross, when Louis IX transported it from the abbey of Saint-Antoine to Notre-Dame and then to the palace.[100] Other relics of the Passion, namely the iron of the Holy Lance and Holy Sponge, were still acquired in the following year, received with the same ceremonies and placed in their turn in the palace chapel.[101] It was when Louis IX, entrusted to possess these relics, of which the authenticity inspired doubts in nobody, and which he considered, in his naive piety, as the most invaluable of his treasures, built in their honor the richest and most elegant monument that the art of this time has left us, Sainte-Chapelle.

In spite of the uncontestable sincerity of her piety, Blanche always remained foreign to the fight which the Popes supported against Emperor Frederick II. Placed by the fact, even while she was Regent, at the head of a dynasty and of people with private interests, she did nothing to involve them in a war which France deplored without wanting to become entangled. She could regret as a good Christian woman that the head of the Church was threatened by the house of Souabe, but in a particularly serious circumstance, where it was a question of saving Innocent IV, she never pushed Louis IX to compromise himself in favor of the Holy See. If, on the other hand, she preserved courteous relations with Hohenstaufen, she could not encourage them in their violent campaigns against the Papacy. In March 1239, Gregory solemnly excommunicated the Emperor, then sent to France, as legate of the Holy See, the cardinal bishop of Préneste.[102] He wrote Louis IX recommending to him, and knowing the influence of Blanche, pressed her, in a flattering letter, to exhort her son to give a warm welcome to the Cardinal, to confuse the calumnies and lies of Frederick II, "who treated Jesus-Christ, her vicar and the Church, as mortal enemy."[103] These requests of the Pope did not lead to anything; the legate drew some money from the French clergy, but when Gregory wanted to go further, he worked alone.[104]

Towards the end of 1240, after having vainly offered to other princes the imperial crown, he wanted to name the King of the Romans, Count Robert d'Artois; negotiators appear to have been engaged on this subject by the legate Préneste; they failed, because Blanche did not want to leave her second son to engage in a similar adventure.[105] In this occurrence, she was certainly in agreement with the King, and undoubtedly she also approved when, the following year, he fiercely summoned Frederick II to release French prelates taken at sea when they went to the council convened by Gregory IX.[106]

The King and his mother were much less occupied with the struggle between the Empire and the Holy See than with the general interests of Christendom; Blanche felt, for her part, the widespread disquiet throughout Europe when it was learned that the Tartar hordes devastated Poland and Hungary.[107] What was to become of the Christian religion and civilization, if they could not stop these barbarians? As she posed this frightening question to her son, he reassured her, with this serenity of heart which later made so large a part of his misfortunes: "We are sustained, dear mother, by the hope of celestial consolations. If they come, we will cast them into hell from whence they left, or they will send us all to heaven."[108]

People, if we believe Mathieu de Paris, did not have as much calm; then, as always, their terror generated inept charges; it was said that the Jews provided weapons to the Tartars.[109] If Blanche partook of this prejudice, she would not have, in a public circumstance, used towards the representatives of Jewish doctrines a moderation that one hardly finds among her contemporaries. Like her son, like the Holy See, like almost all the princes and the lords of her time, she professed an aversion for the usurious practices of the Jews and Lombards, and it was with her approval during the regency that great barons of the kingdom, joined together at Melun in the presence of Louis IX, engaged not to allow the Jews to make any more loans.[110] It is necessary to acknowledge that this measure conformed to the spirit of the age. Blanche, born in a country where the Jews were better treated than in France, was opposed to persecuting them for the exercise of their worship. Such appears, at least, to have been her opinion at the time of the legal debate which gave way to an examination of the Talmud. Doctrines exposed in the Talmud having been denounced to Gregory IX by a converted Jew named Donin, and baptized under the name of Nicolas, the Pope, in 1239, had ordered prosecutions tending to seek out and destroy the writings which composed it.[111] These legal proceedings do not appear to have been carried out in France, where Louis IX seized all the manuscripts of the Talmud to which one could lay hands. During the lawsuit which resulted from this confiscation, several Jewish rabbis appeared in Paris, to defend their books, before the court of the King, chaired by Queen Blanche.

It is necessary to read from the Jewish records some details of this discussion, where the word was carried, in the name of the Jews, by one of their more erudite savants, Rabbi Yéhiel, from Paris.[112]

Pressed closely by his indicters, Yéhiel, on several occasions, directly addressed the Queen: "I beg you, Madam," he said, "do not force me to answer their charges."[113] One of the royal officers having said to the rabbi: "Nobody will make evil of you. " - "You will not be able," answered Yéhiel, "to defend us against the people in a fury. " - Then the Queen said: "Do not speak any more of that to me. We are resolved to protect you, you and all your goods, and they who would persecute you would be held for criminals. We know, because we have read them, about immunities that popes themselves granted to you."[114] The dispute being envenomed, and the Queen having requested the rabbi to swear an oath requested by his accusers, he protested that his conscience prohibited him from making it: "Since that is so painful for him," said Blanche of Castile, "and since he was never sworn, leave it."[115] For some time, she engaged in person in the controversy, arguing like a theologian, and to preserve at this debate an appearance of impartiality worthy of her presence, she reproached the Christian doctors for the violence of their attacks.[116] The quarrel was not finished by Blanche, and we do not know if the Queen was satisfied with the sentence which condemned the Talmud, including a large of number of specimens that were then delivered to the flames.

But, at a time when the idea and even the name of tolerance did not exist, it is interesting to see an enthusiastic Christian woman, the Queen, maintaining in a religious lawsuit the rights of defense.

Thus Blanche constantly was consulted, prompted by her son; she judged, she received the promises of barons and letters from princes; she decided the most serious questions. It was quite other thing when there appeared, in 1240 and 1241, new and pressing dangers. All attention was cast upon those who had saved the country and royalty; it was directly to her that royal agents addressed themselves, in the most critical circumstances of the wars against the Viscount of Béziers, the Count de La Marche, the King of England, and the Count de Toulouse.

Raimond VII, for whom Blanche and Louis IX had interceded so many times with the Pope, was scarcely devoted to them. In 1239, with the strong approval of the Emperor, returned to war with Raimond-Bérenger, invaded Provence, devastated it, beat the nobility of the country and the French established on the edges of the Rhone, that Raimond-Bérenger had called to help him. He took the castle of Trinquetaille in the Camargue and, with the assistance of the Marcheillais, besieged Arles, to restore it under obeisance to Frederick II. The intercessions of the King of England and the armaments of the King of France disengaged in time the Count de Provence. After an exchange of explications between Louis IX and Frederick II, Raimond VII raised the siege of Arles, devastated the Camargue, withdrew beyond the Rhone and took again the road to Toulouse.[117] This attack of Count Raimond against Provence had undoubtedly been concerted with authors of another expedition, to which he was not foreign.[118]

Son of the unhappy Raimond-Roger, Viscount of Carcassonne and of Béziers, who had died at the beginning of the war of the Albigensians, excommunicated in 1227 and despoiled, for several years, of the fiefs that he had one time recovered, the Viscount Raimond Trencavel was in exile at the court of Jacques the Conqueror, King of Aragon. It was there in 1236, undoubtedly, that he prepared from long distance to again take his estates. In 1240, he suddenly reappeared in the dioceses of Narbonne and Carcassonne, at the head of some Aragonese or Catalan knights, around which a section of his old subjects were not slow in forming. Several castles and fortified cities, Montreal and Limoux among others, soon fell into his hands, and it was with considerable forces that at the end of summer he presented himself before Carcassonne.[119]

It was a redoubtable place, this ancient city, defended by an enclosure which still evokes our admiration today, by a castle and several advanced works or *barbacanes*. Its garrison was rather strong, because after the first successes of Trencavel, Seneschal Guillaume des Ormes, the Archbishop of Narbonne, the Bishop of Toulouse, had come there to throw in their lot with several nobles of the country and a great number of clerics; but the defenders of Carcassonne had to take into account the feelings of the southernmost populations and with the desperation animating Trencavel and his partisans. Near Carcassonne there was a borough whose protections extended, in case of attack, until a point where its houses touched the strengthened enclosure of the city. Also the Bishop of Toulouse often went down to the borough to exhort the inhabitants to fidelity, while in Carcassonne they piled up wheat and the harvest of the vines, and put the walls in a state of defense; wood works and war machines were built. At the approach of enemies, Guillaume des Ormes sent word to Penautier to ask for help from Raimond VII, who returned from the Camargue; but the Count answered that he could do nothing until he returned to Toulouse and heard counsel. It was to acknowledge his complicity or at least his real disposition. Some days later, the Seneschal and the Bishop of Toulouse returned to this suburb, gathered the inhabitants in the church of Sainte-Marie and made them swear, on the altar of the Virgin, to remain faithful to the King. But as of the following day, 8 September, during the night, Trencavel was introduced into the borough by his partisans. A rather great number of clerics, who had taken refuge in the church, wanted to leave on the faith of a safe conduct; they were attacked and more than thirty perished in a massacre close to the Narbonnese gate, while the lords of Penautier, violating their word, joined the attackers. A few days still separated the occupation of the borough by Trencavel and the siege properly speaking.[120]

Carcassonne was besieged from 17 September to 11 October 1240. The details of this keen fight are known to us by a letter of extreme interest, addressed on 13 October to Queen Blanche by the Seneschal of Carcassonne, Guillaume des Ormes.[121] In this relation, the Seneschal explained all the incidents of siege, exposed all attacks, enumerated all measures taken by the besieging; assaults repulsed, mines and countermines, fortifications raised in haste behind places broken in breach, effectiveness of besieging fire and that of the garrison, names of those who were distinguished, missing nothing; it was the journal of siege that the commander of an invested place addressed, at the end of operations, to his hierarchical superior. It could be said that Louis IX had given over to his mother all the care of this business, because his name did not even appear in the report of the Seneschal. When Guillaume des Ormes speaks of the Constable of Carcassonne, of which he announced sterling service, he recalled, in addressing to Blanche, "your constable of Carcassonne; " with each line, the Queen was personally greeted: "We were, by the grace of God, well in measurement of awaiting your help. As for the other affairs of the country," Guillaume noted upon concluding, "we will be able to expose them to you when we will be in your presence." Blanche was treated here as a sovereign who acted on her own authority, and better yet, as a woman who could command armies. In truth to say, it was natural that they told the details of war to she who had taken Bellême, who during the minority of her son had so often accompanied armies in the field.

Relief sent by Blanche to the besieged of Carcassonne was under command of the Chamberlain, Jean de Beaumont, and the Viscount of Châteaudun.[122] Henry de Sully, Adam de Milly, the Marshal of France, Ferry Pâté, and Guy de Lévis, marshal of a crusader army, formed part of it or rejoined it, because they were in the country the following November.[123] With the approach of the royal army, said to have been numerous, at the arrival of which threw terror into all surroundings, Trencavel and his partisans took refuge in Montreal, a strong place from whence the Viscount left by capitulation at the approach of winter, with weapons and baggage, thanks to the mediation of the counts of Toulouse and Foix.[124] His partisans were not long in submitting themselves; as for him, he crossed the Pyrenees again and never regained possession of its estates, even after he had definitively returned to obeisance under the King of France.

In Béziers the alarm had also been sharp. Someone had written the bishop that Trencavel secreted himself into the city, disguised as a Franciscan; on this news the population, joined together by the bishop and royal officers, uttered cries of death against those who would betray the King; they closed all the gates and the keys had been given to the bishop, who kept them, during the night, at his bedside or at his feet, never giving them to any but loyal hands.[125] Blanche of Castile, for whom Guillaume des Ormes had noted the good behavior of

Béziers, wrote to them in October to thank them and commit them to remain faithful.[126]

Among the accomplices of Trencavel, the last who returned to duty was Olivier de Termes, a valiant lord, famous later for his exploits in the Holy Land; he only submitted in the following May.[127] Olivier became, rebel that he had been, Seneschal of Carcassonne, remaining in correspondence with the Queen Mother, and we still have a letter by which, at an unknown date, he addressed Blanche of Castile as widow of a noble family, requesting the Queen to grant, for love of him, requests that she must present to him.[128]

The conduct of the Count de Toulouse had been quite equivocal during the siege of Carcassonne, but it did not cost him anything in the course of events. Some months afterwards, he was at court in Montargis, and swore to the King to be useful against one and all; Raimond showed loyalty while awaiting an opportunity for rebellion; the occasion was not long in presenting itself.

The third son of Blanche, Prince Alphonse, had been in his majority for more than six months when he was given a fief. On 24 June, in Saumur, the King knighted him and invested him as Count of Poitiers and Auvergne; superb festivals were given in honor of the new count, and we know the details of the cost; we especially have, in the memoirs of Joinville, a very colorful description of the banquet offered by Louis IX in the markets of Saumur.[129] The King chaired this festival, surrounded by almost all that there was of the nobility in his kingdom, his brothers, the King of Navarre, Count de La Marche, Pierre Mauclerc, Count Jean de Dreux, who had also just been knighted with many others. The lords of Beaujeu, Coucy, and Bourbon, having behind them a large procession of knights and sergeants, kept the table of the King, which served the Count d'Artois, and, as *écuyer tranchant*, the Count de Soissons, while opposite Louis IX, Thibaud de Champagne was served by his seneschal, the Baron Joinville. Another table had twenty bishops and archbishops, and not far from them, opposed to the royal table, sat Queen Blanche, served by her nephew Alphonse of Portugal, Count de Boulogne, by the Count de Saint-Pol, and by a young German lord of eighteen years, son of Saint Elisabeth of Thuringia: "because of what was said Queen Blanche kissed him on the face with devotion, because she thought that his mother had kissed him many times." The luxury of this banquet, shared with an innumerable crowd of knights, exceeded anything seen of this kind. Blanche, from the place she occupied, contemplated with pride this imposing assembly.

King Louis, who had knights and 300 foot sergeants in Saumur, went to Poitiers in the month July; there, he invested his brother and constituted to him, under some reserves, liege homage, and revenue of 6,000 *livres parisis*.[130] A son of France was going to have this county that had been under Richard Coeur-de-Lyon and Otto of Brunswick, and whose title was still carried by Richard de Cornouailles, brother of Henry III. The vassals of Count Alphonse came to do homage; most important of all was the Count de La Marche and Angoulême, Hugues de Lusignan, who has so often been referenced since the commencement of the reign; it was not without sorrow that he filled, with regard to Alphonse, his obligations of vassal.

Now reappearing on the scene was a proud and violent woman, entering public life at the same time as Blanche of Castile, and showing evidence of a long contained resentment. Isabelle d'Angoulême, widow of King John and wife of Hugues de Lusignan, was more than a countess, because she always carried the title of Queen, and she exercised over her son, the King of England, a dangerous influence. Opposed to her, above her, Blanche dominated a kingdom over which John had had half; the contrast of these two fortunes was to appear cruel to her, and now she had to do homage, in the person of her husband, not only for a King that she hated, but as vassal of this King, a cadet of France, a third son of her rival. If the Count de La Marche suffered a mortification with his affirmation as vassal of Alphonse, it had to be undoubtedly difficult to achieve this act under the eyes of his proud wife. He had troops in Lusignan, and several times Joinville, who had been in Poitiers, saw him coming to speak to the King, always accompanied by Isabelle; the attitude of Lusignan had to be then nothing less than respectful, since our great historian believed that, during his stay in Poitiers, Louis IX, by fear of their conspiracies, was blocked in this city.[131] Hugues and Isabelle however ended up resigning themselves, and in July 1241 Hugues gave homage to Count Alphonse; it was necessary for him to go further, to restore Saint-Jean-d'Angely and the fief of Aunis, because the marriage formerly projected between his son and Princess Isabelle de France had not taken place.[132] Thus the Count de La Marche subjected himself for a time to the will of his King and his lord suzerain, as said by contemporaries and several modern historians. It was for the former Queen of England a cruel moment when she had to accept her shame, but when she saw her husband received in the castle of Lusignan by Louis IX and Alphonse de Poitiers, she could not be contained anymore.

The facts that I will expose are known to me by a sealed letter, celebrated from now on, that an inhabitant of La Rochelle addressed a short time later to Blanche of Castile. This document is in all ways of major importance.[133] We see the mother of Saint Louis keeping an eye on all that occurred in parts of the kingdom where her son was threatened with attack, informed of the smallest details by a secret agent, who came to see her in Vincennes, at the moment when she did not know about Aunis, in the midst of those prepared to revolt, an unknown man like him, charged to spy on hostile Poitevin barons. The anonymous author of this letter thoroughly knew the resources and dangers of his city, the situation of adjoining countries, characters, conversations, projects and acts of people he suspected. He gave to his sovereign the most intelligent counsel, he thought of everything; he was a careful servant, perspicacious and faithful. Setting aside the details, his letter proves to us in 1242 the most serious affairs were in the hands of Blanche, who treated them directly, as if they had been in her exclusive competence, and who could skillfully choose the instruments of her policy.

Learning that Louis IX and his brother had been received in Lusignan, Queen Isabelle returned; beside herself, she removed part of the furniture, bed linen, crockery, ornaments of the chapel, and shipped them to Angoulême.[134] To the astonished observations of the Count de La Marche she answered with insults. Hugues, very eager to appease her, wanted to come see her at the château of Angouleme; after three days of quarantine, he was grudgingly admitted to the presence of his wife, who, after having cried much, exclaimed: "Infamous man, you did not see what passed in Poitiers, when I had to wait three days to make my court with your King and your Queen; then, when I entered near them, in the room, the King had sat, on the side of the royal bed, and the Queen on another side, with the Countess of Chartres and her sister the abbess.[135] They did not call me; they did not offer a seat, and that well purposely, to humiliate me in front of the people. I remained there, like a poor wretched maidservant, upright opposite of them, in the middle of a crowd. At my entry, and upon my exit, they did not rise, in contempt for me just like you, if you could see it."

The Count was humiliated, made promises, left his wife,

accompanied by a last and insulting threat. On the advice of Isabelle, in Parthenay he assembled the barons and the *châtelains* of Poitou. It was there that hatred against France was given free reign, that objections were exposed without the least care: "The French always hated us... They will treat us worse than Normans or Albigensians." Poitevins united by oath, came to Angoulême to meet Queen Isabelle, who, against her practice, treated them with honor, even those that she liked less, and in her presence they renewed their conventions.

Then they went to Pons; in this new assembly, they not only called for revolt, but invited a foreigner to join them. The English seneschal of Gascogne was there, and with him, barons and *châtelains* of his government, mayors of Bordeaux, Bayonne, St. Emilion, Réole, and their aldermen, Count de Bigorre and all lords of the Bishop of Saintes, except Geoffroy de Rancon, personal enemy of the Count de La Marche. After being agreed that they were all lost if they fell under French domination, they confederated under oath. The detailed measures adopted by the conference of Pons were duly noted added by the agent of Blanche, in a postscript written after the return he had sent to the assembly of Poitevins and Gascons. It was nothing less than to blockade and starve La Rochelle, by ground maneuver, whereby the Count de La Marche must leave his castle at Frontenay, then go over water, with the help of the sailors of Bayonne, these masters of sea, and the people of Bordeaux, enemies of Rochelle, would pay very much for this alliance. All would be done without declaration of war, without warning Henry III; the barons would initiate hostilities on all sides, while protesting that they were informed of nothing. The communes of Gascogne played a key role in this plot, Bordeaux at the head; they promised 500 mercenary knights, 500 sergeants and mounted crossbowmen, and 1,000 foot soldiers.

The agent of Blanche intermingled his account with counsels which indicate a precise spirit, from a steady and well informed man. Against Hugues de La Marche and Queen Isabelle, it was necessary to proceed with energy, but one should try hard to avoid war, "because your land of Poitou is in a better state now than it would be at the time of the Kings of England." The letter ended with opinions full of wise measures that it was advisable to take with organization and defense of La Rochelle. The faithful agent of Blanche would have said all of this to the *châtelain* and the mayor of his city, but he feared discovery; already unknown persons had informed Queen Isabelle that he had spoken badly of her in Vincennes.

To prevail against Louis IX and Blanche of Castile in avenging his wife, Hugues de Lusignan could thus count on Poitevins and Gascons. Sure of the King of England, he had combined with King Jacques of Aragon, the Count de Toulouse and won over Raimond Trencavel.[136] Without doubt the plotters made too quickly with their work; they were flattered, as one claimed, to include in their party the King of Navarre and even the King of Castile.[137] On the other hand, public rumor showed Frederick II to be favorable to them.[138] It goes without saying that, in the fantasy of the Count de La Marche, the King of England had, more than any other, to fund the expenses of war against the King of France. However, it was necessary that Hugues trusted in his own funding and the provisions of the plotters, because he would not wait, to throw off the mask, until his son-in-law was able to support it.

After having accepted an invitation to Poitiers, to assume his rank at the court of Count Alphonse for the festivals of Christmas (1241), he changed his mind, in the night which preceded the day fixed for his departure. Isabelle of Angoulême had decided to brusque with all. She came to Poitiers with him, but it was for the intention to declare to the brother of the King of France, in abusive and violent terms, that she withdrew herself from his homage and held him to be a usurper. Then Hugues and Isabelle abruptly left the city, surrounded by their people, burning the house where they had lodged.[139] After this bloody insult, war became inevitable, and after Alphonse denounced to Louis IX the insolent provocation of his vassal, the latter hastened to inform the King of England. It was not without sorrow that Henry III managed to involve his subjects against France, tired to always pay, eager to respect a truce which was not yet expired, and not very anxious to renew the sad experiments that he had made twelve years before.

I do not have to recount the war of 1242 here.[140] While Henry III landed in Royan, Louis IX, who took the initiative, removed from the rebel Poitevins almost all of their strongholds. Then he marched against the English; the Charente passed to the royal army at Taillebourg; a great battle raged, on 22 July, under the walls of Saintes, and the King of England, after having given up this city to the victorious French, went to Barbezieux, thence to Blaye after a disastrous retirement. Obliged to take refuge in the south of the Gironde, given up by Count de La Marche, who made his submission, having no more of a really useful ally than the Count de Toulouse, he still sought to be maintained, blockading La Rochelle in vain, seized for some time the Ile de Ré. But his situation was without exit; he recognized it, and finished by concluding, on 7 April 1243, a truce which must last until next 29 September, with the possibility of being renewed for five years.

The account of these events belongs much less to the life of Blanche of Castile than to the history of Saint Louis; however, the anonymous letter which I analyzed is not only to teach us that the Queen Mother played a great role in 1242. Joinville did not forget in his account:

> And in this expedition against the King of England and against the barons, the King gave great gifts... But neither for the gifts, nor for the expenditure that one made in this expedition, or for others on this side of the sea and beyond, the King did not require nor never took, neither from his barons, neither from his knights, neither from his men, nor from his good cities. And this was no wonder, because he did that by the counsel of the good mother who was with him, by the counsel of which he acted, and by that of the men who remained with him from the time of his father and the time of his grandfather.[141]

In the mind of her contemporaries, the memories of this war remained fully with the name of Queen Blanche; the author of the *Grandes Chroniques de France* lent the following words to the widow of King John, arriving to meet her son Henry III at the time of his landing in Gascogne: "Good son, you are of good nature, come to aid your mother and your brothers, against that foul and evil Blanche of Espaigne."[142] One claims that Isabelle, feeling lost, paid people to poison the King of France and his brothers; their plot was discovered in time. What a contrast between these abominable proceedings and the moderation of Louis IX, who saved the life of his prisoners and did not allow any jokes to be made before his vanquished enemies![143] The Count de La Marche and Queen Isabelle, who had deserved at the very least to lose their freedom and their fiefs, were free on conditions too good for them, after such a revolt and such a defeat. Blanche of Castile, if she was then at the side of her son, had to be sufficiently avenged, when she saw the Count de La Marche, his wife, and his children, kneel in front of the King, and shout "thank you" to him.[144]

The Count de Toulouse was even less worthy of pity than Hugues de Lusignan. To join the enemies of the kingdom, he had forgotten every promise, relationship, and intercessions of the Queen to the Pope; but it was necessary for him to well remember when, after an unhappy war, he came to beseech peace. Betrayed by his ally the Count de Foix, and having no more hope to await any help either from Poitevins, nor from the English, nor from the King of Aragon, he saw peace proposals as the only option. He was going to be attacked by an army under the command of Imbert de Beaujeu and the Bishop of Clermont entering Languedoc, when, on 20 October 1242, he wrote Louis IX to offer him submission.[145] This time again, it was Blanche who interceded for him. The unhappy man had, the same day, addressed his too lenient cousin a begging letter: "After God," he said to her, "it is in the leniency of Your Serenity which we have special confidence."[146] And he wrote to her about the affection he had received in so much evidence, called upon the memory of his mother, aunt of Blanche, asked for humbly; he hoped for grace in consideration of his daughter who was in France. He gave himself entirely to the counsels of the Queen, and called upon her mediation. Decided to subject himself, his lands, and his partisans, he gave up heretics without shame to services of which he had been able to resort, subjected himself without conditions, launched protests of eternal fidelity. From the first word that Blanche would condescend to write him, he was ready to approach the King.

Raimond would have been twice as guilty, twice more shameless in the platitude of his protests, if pardon had been granted to him. He made his peace at Lorris, in January 1243, and, on the 19th of this month, he gave letters patent to Blanche of Castile in which he engaged, in the most categorical terms, to destroy heresy.[147] I cannot reproach Blanche for having, once more, given the Count de Toulouse evidence of her moderation; it is true that Raimond was her cousin, but he was also the father of the Countess de Poitiers; and elsewhere, if his character did command respect, his long misfortunes could be worth a little compassion to him; moreover, it was important not to treat the provinces of the Midi with too much hardness.[148] Why strike, when one was strong enough to forgive?

It was the last revolt of the barons that the King of France had to cut down. This time, all was finished; the work of Blanche appeared complete, since high feudality could not do anything more against the crown. Was Queen Blanche going to finally rest, to live in peace in the kingdom that she had been useful to with such an amount of courage and intelligence, beside this admirable prince? For some time one could believe it. France was quiet, and it was necessary to go beyond its borders to find discord and war. Although in England Henry III saw dissatisfaction growing around him, the fight between the Holy See and the Empire began again with a despairing roughness. Gregory IX had died on 22 August 1241, and after an interregnum of approximately two years, hardly stopped by the transitory pontificate of Celestin IV, the Genoan Sinibalde Fieschi climbed, on 25 June 1243, the throne of Saint Peter; he took the name Innocent IV. The terrible mission of destroying Frederick II fell to a man with the glance of a sure eye, a master, gifted in policy of an audacity full of resources and frightening tenacity. He had until then passed as favorable to moderate ideas, but such illusions hardly survived his ascension. Shortly after this day, the Pope and the Emperor measured and recognized each other as mortal enemies. At the beginning, there were negotiations imposed by the need to show the world at least an apparent good will; the King of France, this man of peace, supported them; but there was nothing to hope for. After a temporary bringing together, the Pope, seeing himself more and more threatened by Frederick, secreted himself in Sutri, gained Cività-Vecchia, then Genoa, determined to take refuge beyond the Alps. Then began, between the head of the Church and its great adversary, a relentless war. I do not know up to what point Blanche of Castille endeavored to reconcile them; perhaps in this respect she did not have the same hopes as her son. During this fight, she placed herself only once before, in 1247, on a day when the interest and the dignity of France was obviously concerned. Besides this circumstance, the role she played between Innocent IV and Frederick II is hardly known to us.

It was with Louis IX, with the counts of Artois and of Poitiers, in the general chapter of the order of Cîteaux, in September 1244, that Innocent required the King of France to defend him against the attacks of Frederick II and to accommodate needs of his kingdom. Mathieu de Paris recounted this really imposing scene.[149] The King came to sit with his retinue in the chapter room, leaving from a feeling of respect to Blanche the most honorable place, when all the abbots and monks, bending their knees and clasping hands, begged him to be favorable to any request from the Pope. Louis IX, in spite of the benevolence of his attitude, did not give them at the time a formal answer, and whatever his decision, Innocent IV, instead of establishing himself in France, fixed his residence in Lyon, which was within two steps of the kingdom, in the vicinity to which the French and their prince could bring him in the event of distress. He arrived there on 2 December 1244.

The pontifical court barely established itself in Lyon, when an event whose consequences were quite serious, after causing in Blanche of Castile the cruelest of emotions, changed with one blow her projects and hopes.[150] Louis IX caught, during the expedition to Poitou, a fever which decimated his army. Of a delicate constitution, he had only imperfectly recovered his health, and as of the year 1243, he felt enough suffering to ask prayers from the general chapter of Cistercians.[151] At the end of 1244, the disease reappeared under the form of a violent fever, accompanied by dysentery.[152] With the news of the danger which threatened the life of the King, consternation was general; a crowd of archbishops, bishops, abbots, and barons ran to Pontoise, where Louis was; they all sent prayers to prescribe his cure, in processions and in public prayers; but the evil worsened.[153] Etienne de Bourbon said that Louis IX was placed, out of humility, on a bed of ashes; in his sufferings he said to those near him: "See me; I am a rich man and noblest of the world, most powerful of all by my treasures, my power and my friends, and here I cannot shed this disease one hour. What was all of it worth?"[154]

Blanche and the one of her sons, undoubtedly the Count d'Artois, stayed near the King; but their care could not prevent him nearing death. He was believed lost, and although he was there, unconscious, abandoned by the doctors, funeral news was spread throughout the palace; a chronicler even alleged that the clergy was ordered to come to pray near his body and to proceed to his funeral.[155] "He was in such extremity," says Joinville, "that one of the ladies who kept watch over him wanted to draw a cloth over his face, and said that he had died. And another lady, on the other side of the bed, did not suffer it; but she said that he still had a spirit in his body. And during the debate of these two ladies, Our Lord operated in him and sent health to him. And as soon as was in a position to speak, he required that they give him a cross; and this they did. Then the Queen Mother said that speech had returned to him, and she showed great joy. And when he took up the cross she appeared to be in mourning."[156]

This account does not agree in all points with that of Mathieu de Paris; for after Mathieu, at the moment when all hope seemed lost, Queen Blanche brought in relics of the Passion, and touched some to the body of her son, hoping that if Louis returned to life, he would take up the cross and visit the Holy Sepulcher. Suddenly, the King made a sigh, had a contraction in the arms and legs, so that he rose at once, and in a loud and sepulchral voice, he said: "By the grace of God, the rising sun has come to find me at the top of the clouds, and recalled from death."[157] The bishops of Paris and Meaux were at his side, or very close; he requested a cross, and in spite of their objections, the begging representations of his mother, the bishop of Paris, Guillaume d'Auvergne, acceded to his desire.[158]

No event, save the death of her son, could have caused Blanche a similar pain. The crusade, was for her a terrible concern, for the King, who hardly escaped death, the prospect of dangers and incalculable sacrifices; it was the interest of Christendom substituted for that of France, this war against infidels absorbing all the resources which the war against the English had claimed; it was the policy of Philippe Auguste, Louis VIII, his widow, sacrificed to one of these remote and arduous campaigns absorbing the armies and wealth of Western princes, to say nothing of the hazard to life. From that moment, Blanche lived in worry, while waiting to die in sorrow. For the rest, her son did not recuperate in a day, and towards Christmas, the Queen, indicating he remained in danger, requested Eudes, Abbot of Saint-Denis, to expose in public the remains of Saint Denis, Saint Rustique, and Saint Eleuthère, so that, by their intercession, Louis IX would obtain from heaven his revival. The exposure of these famous relics took place in the royal basilica, on 23 December, in the midst of an enormous crowd; a historian of Saint-Denis dated from this day the final improvement which occurred in the health of the King.[159]

The Pope was extremely moved by learning of the illness of the King of France; as head of the Church, he could not remain indifferent to the fate of a prince who, by his virtues, was used as model for all others.[160] From this moment, by the fact that Louis IX was now a crusader, a new bond linked him to the Holy See, protective of all those who had made a pledge to fight the infidels; one also sees Innocent IV, between 1245 and 1248, constantly occupied with preparations made in France for the crusade, and under his aegis he rendered services of which the importance cannot be disputed. His relations with the King carry the mark of sincere and constant cordiality; but he did not forget that Blanche was very powerful in France, and he often addressed her for resolution of questions which were usually submitted to sovereigns alone. He took the precaution of writing to her when he elevated the Bishop of Noyon, Pierre Charlot, natural son of Philippe Auguste; he often did so, when he wanted to obtain rights of election restored to archbishops or lately elected bishops; in 1246, the Queen Mother was associated with her son in complaints that the Holy See made to them about measures taken in Languedoc by royal officers relative to the property of heretics.[161]

Innocent IV would have liked for the King of France and his mother to openly take sides against the Emperor. But he could never arrive there; neither the one nor the other believed their duty was in the Council of Lyon, where they condemned Frederick II; however, from this moment until his departure, Louis IX forever ceased working to reconcile the Holy See and the Empire; his good will was recognized by Innocent, who, in return, showed himself generally favorable to French policy; he had the proof of it, when the house of France pressed on the court of Rome to ensure Provence for the youngest brother of Louis IX.

Raimond-Bérenger, father of the young Queen of France, Queen of England, and of the Countess of Cornouailles, died in Aix on 19 August 1245, leaving in his will his estates to his fourth daughter, Béatrix, to the detriment of the three others. However, it was known that Count de Toulouse sought the hand of the young princess, while the King of Aragon intrigued on his side to attract the succession of Provence to himself. But Blanche and Louis IX had thrown their choice to this wealthy heiress, from whom they wanted to obtain a hand for Prince Charles of France. They were seconded in their project by the pontifical government, which helped to abort the plans of Raimond VII, not giving him a timely exemption which he needed to marry Beatrix. This marriage question of Provence was certainly one of those which Louis IX and Blanche of Castile adjudicated with Innocent IV at a conference in Cluny.

It was in 1245, at the end of November, when the Pope met them in this abbey. Louis IX had brought to Burgundy a small army corps whose beautiful disposition made a deep impression on those who saw it. He had with him his mother, his sister Isabelle, the Count d'Artois, perhaps also his two other brothers, the Emperor Baudouin II, the son of the King of Aragon, one of the royal princes of Castile, the Duke of Burgundy, a crowd of great barons and knights. The entourage of Innocent IV was hardly less brilliant; but it was not a simple courtesy call or a solemn pageant; Louis IX and Blanche had come to Cluny to treat with Innocent IV on the most serious questions. For seven days they had between them, without witnesses, three secret conferences, whose mysteries were never, to my knowledge, revealed to anyone. By only the fact that he invited his mother to such an interview, Louis IX showed the world what authority she had kept in the kingdom. They probably spoke, in Cluny, of the crusade in preparation, of this war between the Holy See and the Empire which made a misfortune for the Christian world, and of which the appeasing was ardently wished for by the King of France. It is also beyond doubt that the project of linking Prince Charles with Béatrix of Provence was not forgotten.[162] The Pope, while regaining Lyon, went to Mâcon, where he celebrated the dedication of the church of Saint-Pierre (8 December 1245), in the presence of the King, his mother, and his brothers.[163]

The first result of this interview was not long in waiting; withdrawing himself from there, Louis IX sent towards Provence, to guarantee the young Countess against the enterprises of the King of Aragon, some troops that he had brought to Cluny. Then he left his brother Charles at the head of an army; the blow, elsewhere, was prepared in advance, with the assistance of the regents to whom Raimond-Bérenger had left the guard of his estates. This marriage so greatly desired at the court France was celebrated on 31 January 1246; Charles accepted Maine and Anjou from the King; his wife brought to him Provence; it was a wealthy portion that Blanche of Castile left for the youngest of her sons.[164] At the same time French influence became prevalent on left bank of the Rhone, in the Kingdom of Arles which for a long time was a dependence of the imperial crown. From an account whose value is doubtful enough, the new Count de Provence, recognizing the poor service that had just been given to him, would have complained to Blanche about the fact that celebrations of his marriage had not been equal in splendor to those which had been celebrated for the weddings of Louis IX: "I am son of a King and Queen, and he was not," referring to his brother's birth when Louis VIII was only crown prince.[165] If this unpleasant word had been pronounced, it would not be to the honor of Charles; Blanche of Castile, while contributing to his establishment in advantageous conditions, had deserved well of him and of France.

To help a French prince to become master in Provence, was for Innocent IV to ruin in this county the authority of Frederick II, who was the suzerain. Always and everywhere he kept in mind a war with the house of Souabe, the destruction of a great and frightening prince who in his eyes became evil genius incarnated. In his mind, there was little safety for the Church other than in the defeat or death of Frederick; one preached conciliation to him in vain, he remained deaf and walked right in his way, striking, exposing himself to blows, making use of all weapons and stopping anybody. At the end of 1246 (5 November), he rejected once more the mediation of Louis IX; he did so in extremely measured terms, while saying he was ready to try a new peace effort; but, in a correct reading of this missive to the King of France, his acceptance was equivalent to a refusal. Blanche of Castile received a letter from the Pope designed in same the terms.[166]

The Emperor, also, for a long time led his party to go until the end; but in 1247 he wanted to carry a mortal blow to his adversary, and this blow was to reach France. Remaining until this point on the sidelines in this duel between Christians, Louis IX and Blanche of Castile rose up; they issued loans to support Innocent IV, and the Pope was saved.

Combined with the Count de Savoie, who controlled the passages of the Alps, relying on the neutrality or even on the consent of the French nobility, whose principal representatives were confederated in November 1246 to oppose the clergy, Frederick had resolved to cross Mount-Cenis, go down to the valley of the Rhone, retaining in his host the Count de Savoie and the Viennese Dauphin, to attract those of the French barons that he knew were favorable to his cause, and to go thence to Lyon. It was a master stroke; Innocent would have been constrained to run away or accept conditions of the Emperor, become again, by this victorious appearance, the Almighty in the Kingdom of Arles. In presence of this danger, largest perhaps that he had ever experienced, Innocent IV took some measures for self-defense, and at the same time he informed Louis IX and Blanche of the plot against him.[167]

In the first days of June 1247 the King of France found himself in Pontigny, where he had returned with his mother to attend the transportation of the remains of Saint Edmond, Archbishop of Canterbury.[168] Around him were the Cardinal-Bishop of Albano, Cardinal Eudes de Châteauroux, the Bishop of Tusculum, legate in France for the preparation of the crusade, the Archbishop of Sens and a crowd of prelates, the nobles, come from France and England. Blanche had a particular devotion to the memory of Saint Edmond, and we saw that the Archbishop of Canterbury had come to see her, when he had to retire to France. Mathieu de Paris represented her praying, in the midst of lit candles, near the tomb which contained the body of this saint, pointing out the blessing that had given her, and her children, and requesting him "to confirm the Kingdom of France in its peaceful and triumphant prosperity."[169]

Charged with apprizing the King of projects from the Emperor and calling upon him in the name of the Pope to help, the cardinals of Tusculum and Albano did not have to negotiate a long time.[170] Louis IX deplored the fight of the Holy See and the Empire; just like his barons, with much moderation and piety, he sometimes had to defend the rights of his crown against the enterprises of the clergy; but he could not let the Pope succumb to the blows of Frederick II, at the gates of his kingdom. How to allow that the Emperor appeared at the head of an army in Lyon, in complicity with the vassals of the Crown, to again became absolute master in the Kingdom of Arles where Charles d'Anjou had just been given a place? It had been for France at the same time a political disaster and a dishonor. Louis IX, Blanche of Castile, Robert d'Artois, Alphonse de Poitiers, Charles d'Anjou, at once informed the Pope that they were ready to get under way with an army, to help him. This time acting not to interpose, but to fight, Blanche of Castile was not satisfied to send her sons before the Imperial power; she left herself in spite of her fifty-nine years. Already the Lord de Bourbon, whose domains were not far away from Lyon, prepared to support Innocent IV; the Emperor had already moved towards the Rhone, and if he wanted to deal with the French they were ready to receive him.[171]

This decisive attitude from people who until then evinced strong reservations, reassured Innocent IV. This recognition was dictated in letters addressed to Louis IX, Blanche, the three brothers of the King, and Chamberlain Jean de Beaumont.[172] That which reached the Queen Mother was, like the others, full of thanks and praises.[173] For the rest, the demonstration that the house of France came to make in favor of the Papacy was enough; Innocent knew his enemy enough to know that he would not come, in cheerfulness of heart, to fight a battle against the army of Louis IX; he requested his generous defenders not to put themselves on the way to Lyon before a new appeal. Events justified his precaution; Frederick II, at the time of passing to the execution of his great project, was recalled by the revolt of Parma; from this day, misfortune never left him.

Apart from this case of extreme gravity, he had better things to do in France than compromise himself in quarrels foreign to the interests of the kingdom. Great affairs did not cease, and while Louis IX prepared his expedition to the Orient, the Queen Mother had other occupations to give her activity. During the disease of her son, she governed. The Countess Jeanne of Flanders died in December 1244, leaving all her estates to her sister Marguerite.[174] When this princess came to Paris to give to homage to the King her cousin, she found him sick. Blanche, with assistance from her sons Robert and Alphonse, and from the royal council, made her swear an oath on the Gospels and admitted the right of relief, by the new vassal to her suzerain; Marguerite was then authorized to receive the homage of the Flemish.[175] But at the same time the Queen, remembering the precautions that she had taken with the regard to Jeanne and Ferrand, sent Marshal Ferry Pâté with other envoys to Flanders; they were charged to receive sureties from the cities and the lords, who had engaged, at the beginning of 1245, to serve the King, Blanche, and the princes, against their new countess, if Marguerite were unfaithful to conventions passed with the Crown, in other words, if the treaty concluded formerly with Jeanne and Ferrand was not observed.[176] It was the question of the Flemish succession, confused by the children that Marguerite had with two husbands, Bouchard d'Avesnes and Lord Dampierre, that raised menacing difficulties. In July 1246 Saint Louis and the legate of the Holy See, Eudes of Châteauroux temporarily alleviated this disagreement by an award which allotted Hainaut to Jean d'Avesnes and held Flanders for Guillaume de Dampierre.[177] The public acts do not speak of the role Blanche of Castile played in this first arrangement.

It was also necessary for him to work unceasingly for his protégé the Emperor Baudouin II, because this poor prince was really not in a state to conduct affairs. Straightened closely and always short of money, he had arrived at the saddest of expedients. In 1241, it had been necessary that Louis IX told him to give up the seigniory of Courtenay to the prince of Achaïe, who had come to secure it; letters that he wrote on 5 August 1243 to Blanche of Castile give us an idea of the quite poor situation to which he was reduced.[178] In one, after having congratulated the Queen on how counts de La Marche and Toulouse had made their submission, he answered modestly to her counsels and reproaches; Blanche having informed him that people had accused him of allowing the Greeks to dominate him, he thanked her for this warning, protested that he only had advisers from the nobility of France, and promised the Queen to always tell the truth: "If you find in us something to be reproached, then we beg you to tell us and we will correct it; you will see us always ready to follow your counsel and to accept your command, begging in any devotion Your Serenity to have pity on us, because all our confidence, all our hope is in the favor of the King our lord, your son, and in yours."[179]

The second letter of Baudouin, written the same day, is still more curious. After having thanked Blanche for sending money, the Emperor of the East spoke, extremely seriously, of a project of alliance with the Sultan of Iconium. It was necessary to link with this prince against Vatace and the Greeks; the Sultan asked in marriage a relation of Baudouin, and the Emperor had acceded to this desire. As well the young princess was to remain Christian and Catholic, to preserve chaplains with her, her clerks, the people of her household. And on top of this he explained to the Queen of France that many infidels, in Asia, had Christian wives, that the Sultan, for love for his wife, was going to raise churches in his cities, and to ensure revenues for the clergymen who were to serve them. The emir charged to negotiate this business had even affirmed that the Sultan could even be converted by a Christian princess. The Emperor of the Orient accepted all these beautiful assurances with the credulity of child; to achieve his project he counted on one of the daughters of his sister Isabelle, Lady Montaigu, and her brother-in-law Eudes; and it was Queen Blanche who was to give the responsibility to determine them to make such a sacrifice.[180] What was Blanche of Castile to think, when a man who had an empire to control came to tell her such odd stories, to address such a strange request to her?

While waiting to find sure allies among the Muslims, Baudouin II had only one thing to do: beseech once more the generosity of Christian princes. He returned to the Occident at end of 1243; in spring of the following year he was in Rome, then with the council of Lyon, in Cluny, in Saint-Germain-Laye, near the King of France, in June 1247.[181] More than ever Blanche and the King of France supported him and took care of his affairs; on 12 June 1247, about to leave the county of Namur, he made his people swear to keep this fief for him, to name and to revoke the lords of the manor and the sergeants at the will of the King, of Blanche, and of the counts Robert,

Alphonse and Charles de France. If rumors of his death had suddenly been spread, the return of his castle of Namur to anybody would be nullified, by the command of the King, his mother, and his brothers.[182]

The good will of Blanche did not manage to raise prospects for the young Emperor. Returned to Constantinople, he still had, the following year, to give his wife full powers to engage the lands that he yet possessed in France.[183] Letters that the Empress Marie wrote in January and February 1249 to her grand-aunt, show that at that time Blanche of Castile still took active interest in the affairs of Baudouin II.[184] But the problems of these unhappy relatives could not occupy more than a secondary place in the concerns of the Queen.

She saw the approach of her son's embarkation for the the East with increasing emotion. She feared this departure was to be a true misfortune for the entire kingdom; each one in France returned an account of themselves, but Louis IX kept nothing more in mind than the delivery of the Holy Land; the combined efforts of his mother and her best advisers found him inflexible in his resolution.[185]

As he wanted to be in a state of grace from the moment of his departure, to carry into the Holy Land a satisfied conscience while leaving behind him a kingdom as happy as possible, he resolved on one of the most beautiful measures a King ever took. By his order, investigators were commanded to traverse, in 1247, all provinces annexed to the royal domain since the succession of Philippe Auguste. All those who had been maltreated or plundered by the bailiffs, the seneschals, the provosts, the sergeants and the other representatives of royal authority, came to express their objections to these impromptu judges and to ask for repair which was due them; their number was large, because they had suffered much, over the past forty years, in the countryside and even in the cities. The royal power was shown strong, at the beginning, after the reunion of the countries removed from the English; there had been many passages of armies under the "Conqueror" and at the time of his son Louis VIII; in time had come this horrible war of the Albigensians, making so many ruins and giving pretext to such abominable violence, and, after it, the civil wars, the revolt of Trencavel and the great rising of Poitevins and the Count de Toulouse, in 1242. The royal agents had acted too often as in a conquered country; they were scantly supervised and hardly obstructed. What sufferings accumulated during these forty years! But what a noble idea was this spontaneous and meticulous reparation! Had anyone ever seen a prince rectifying himself, at his expense, the wrongs caused to the populations under the reigns of his father and his grandfather? The impression was immense; it persisted for centuries; the son of Blanche was more than only a good King, he became the sovereign *par excellence*, the impeccable judge, the consolator, and the friend of his subjects.

The conscience of Louis IX was so well known, so dominated by the idea of duty, that the English wanted to benefit from his delicacy. Richard de Cornouailles, exposed, on his behalf and on behalf of Henry III, rights of the crown of England to provinces that King John had formerly lost.[186] It was claimed that the King of France was prepared to make him concessions; Blanche had to quiver when she saw that perhaps someone was going to take from her hands this patient and glorious work since the beginning of the century, of which the achievement ensured the unity of France and highlighted the glory of the reigning dynasty. Undoubtedly, she was among those opposed to the King yielding his scruples; without even mentioning the excellent reasons which explained the dispossession of King John, they had a hundred times more reason to say that there was prescription on this, and the bishops of Normandy rendered a service to France, the day when they declared to the King that the country was well with him.

The preparations of Louis IX continued until with the summer of 1248. The King of France was more than three years into arming for the Holy Land; all was ready for the departure; he had made immense provisioning; a port, arranged purposely at Aigues-Mortes, was to receive the Genovese fleet, chartered for the passage of the crusaders; the Pope gave to his legate in France, Eudes de Châteauroux, a new mission close to the Christian army in the East. On 12 June, Louis IX went to Saint-Denis; there, Eudes of Châteauroux gave him a sash and a pilgrim's staff, as to his brothers the counts of Artois and of Anjou; Queen Marguerite was to imitate their example two days later.[187] To leave Saint-Denis, the King went barefoot to Notre-Dame, to pray and to hear Mass; then, leaving Paris the same day, he went, always barefoot and dressed as a pilgrim, until the abbey of Saint-Antoine, accompanied by processions and the people, who could not be persuaded to leave him. He entered the abbey, was recommended with prayers of the nuns; riding a horse then, after having taken leave of the people who accompanied him, he gained Corbeil, where undoubtedly he spent the night. Since this day, he renounced without regret the sumptuous clothing that princes and the nobles carried; this father of a whole people, voluntarily imposing on himself a modesty that he did not require of others, was rather more than enough to make a beautiful figure under humble clothes.

In spite of his prayers, Blanche accompanied him for three or four days.[188] In Corbeil, or rather in the hospital which was very close to this city, she accepted regency. By this act, the King gave her the right to employ anyone she would like in the affairs of state, and to dismiss them at will, to institute and relieve royal agents, to confer dignities and vacant ecclesiastical benefices, to receive the promises of fidelity from bishops and abbots, to restore them, to give to the chapters and the convents the right to elect their chiefs.[189] Louis IX left to the Queen Mother the guardianship of his children. Soon the cruel moment came; he had to leave; words that one generally ascribes to Blanche at the time of this farewell cannot be textually exact, and I prefer not to bring them back; no account could give an idea of such painful feelings. It is said that the Queen fell into a swoon, that her son raised her, they embraced and he took leave of her while crying.[190] She would not see him again.

Saint Louis crossed Burgundy, stopping in the churches and monasteries; the Franciscain Salimbene, who saw him passing to Sens, left us a striking portrait of him: "The King was fragile and rather thin and tall; he had the face of an angel, a gracious figure. He came to the church of the Minor brothers, without princely luxury, in the garb of a pilgrim, carrying a staff and bread basket, which decorated with wonder his royal shoulders; he did not advance on horseback, but went on foot. His brothers, who all three were counts, followed him, humble like him in their attitude and their costume... And really, to have so devout a King, one would have thought him a monk, in spite of his weapons of war, moreso than a knight."[191] The King passed by Lyon, to take leave of the Pope, to confer one last time with him and to receive his blessing; then he descended the valley of the Rhone, moving towards Aigues-Mortes. He took with him to the East his wife, Robert d'Artois, Charles d'Anjou, and Béatrix de Provence, Countess d'Artois, who was pregnant, and could not embark, and had to remain behind, with the Count de Poitiers, who differed his departure until the following year, to help Queen Blanche in government of the kingdom.[192] Lastly, on 25 August 1248, the King boarded his vessel; during three days, the fleet of the crusaders had to wait in place, then, on 28 August, the wind being raised, Saint Louis and his companions set sail for the island of

Cyprus.¹⁹³ For more than two months the last test of Blanche had begun; since then, dedicated until the end of her days to work and the anguish of a separation made a hundred times harder by the conscience of the dangers her son faced, she had no more consolation in this world than achievement of a great duty.

1 *Layettes du Trésor des Chartes*, II, 1710; July 1225.

2 Archives du Pas-de-Calais, série A; Trésor des chartes d'Artois ; inventaire in-4, p. 13, col. 2; actes de July et October 1228. Cf. Archives du Nord, Chambre des comptes de Lille, inventaire in-4, t. II, p. 101, col. 2 (Registre B. 1593).

3 Inventaire des archives du Pas-de-Calais, p. 14, col. 1; inv. des arch. du Nord, t. II, p. 101, col. 2; September 1234; *Historiens de France*, t. XXIV. The three *châtellenies*, p. 260, n. 54; Bapaume, p. 259, n. 49; ibid., n. 50; Lens, p. 256, n. 28; Vilaines, p. 259, n. 51; Hesdin, p. 259, n. 52; ibid., n. 53.

4 *Layettes*, II, 2562; July 1237.

5 *Layettes*, II, 2885 ; 1240.

6 Ibid., 2441 et 2446; March and April 1236; Ibid., 2692 ; January 1238.

7 *Layettes*, II, 3173 and 3174; March 1244.

8 *Layettes*, III, by M. J. de Laborde, 3671, May 1248; 3959, August 1251; D'Arbois de Jubainville, *Histoire des comtes de Champagne*, V, art. 2646; *Layettes*, II, 3131.

9 Archives nationales, JJ. 31, fol. 66 V; 1232.

10 Guérard, *Cartulaire de Notre-Dame de Paris*, t. III, p. 12-13; November 1232.

11 *Histoire de l'Académie des Inscriptions*, t. XXIII, p. 202-271 (1756). Cf. *Mémoires de la société de l'histoire de Paris*, t. VI, p. 180 (1879, M. Anatole de Barthélemy), and *Bulletin* of the same society, t. VII, p. 50 (1880, M. Bonnassieux).

12 Cartulaire de Saint-Étienne-des-Grés, Archives nationales, LL. 465, fol. 45, April 1232; Archives nationales, JJ. 26, fol. 239, July 1234; Archives nationales, JJ. 30 A, fol. 104 V, 1263; 97 V, July 1261.

13 *Histoire littéraire de la France*, t. XXX, p. 325-329.

14 Léopold Delisle, *Mémoire sur les opérations financières des Templiers*, p. 32; Archives nationales, J. 1030. n. 9.

15 Jules Rouyer and Eugène Hucher, *Histoire du jeton, au Moyen age*, Paris, 1858, in-8, p. 78.

16 Bougenot, *Comptes de dépenses de Blanche de Castile (1241)*, in the *Bulletin historique et philologique du Comité des travaux historiques et scientifiques*, 1889, no. 1 and 2, p. 88, after a MSS in the British Museum. The rest of this account is found in the ms. latin 9017 of the Bibliothèque nationale, fol. 69.

17 Bougenot, p. 89-90.

18 Ms. latin 9017, lines 31-32.

19 Ibid., line 20; Bougenot, p. 90.

20 Archives nationales, K. 531, n. 13; minute in parchment.

21 Here are some examples of donations and favors accorded by Blanche to Cistercian monasteries: Trésor-Notre-Dame, Archives nationales, K. 191, n. 15; L'Amour-Dieu, *Gallïa christiana*, X, instruments, col. 137; Villiers-aux-Nonains, *Table chronologique des diplômes*, VI, p. 148, etc., etc.

22 A. Dutilleux and J. Depoin, *L'abbaye de Maubuisson* (*Notre-Dame-la-Royale*), *histoire et carlulaire* ; see especially in the collection *Histoire de l'abbaye et des abbesses*.
    Épinois has published (*Bibliothèque de l'École des Chartes*, 1858, p. 550) the *Comptes relatifs à la construction de l'abbaye de Maubuisson*.

23 Delisle, *Mémoire sur les opérations financières des Templiers*, p. 32-33.

24 Archives nationales, JJ. 26, fol. 164 r.

25 *Layettes du Trésor des Chartes*, II, 2896; February 1241. In May 1240, Blanche made a gift to her abbey from a new rent of one hundred *livres parisis* from her *prévôté* in Pierrefonds; Archives nationales, K. 191, 47, n. 118. I do not propose to enunciate here the titles concerning the donations of Blanche to the abbey of Maubuisson; this work would tend to carry me outside the limits which I would care to impose. All that which follows is found in the accounts published by Épinois and to the work of Dutilleux and Depoin.

26 Dutilleux and Depoin, *Histoire de l'abbaye et des abbesses de Maubuisson*, p. 7.

27 *Historiens de France*, XXII, 605 e; Bougenot, *Comptes*, p. 80 and 90.

28 Le Nain de Tillemont, III, 172; Joinville, § 724; *Layettes du Trésor des Chartes*, II, 2575; 6 October 1237.

29 Vézelay, *Layettes*, 2461 and 3197; Dominicains de Rouen, ibid., 3119; Chapitre de Soissons, ibid., 2786.
    The Bibliothèque nationale has a bible, of very beautiful execution, given by Queen Blanche to the nuns of de Saint-Victor (ms. latin 14397).

30 Le Nain de Tillemont, II, 300. *Historiens de France*, XXII, 579-583.

31 *Historiens de France*, XXII, 582 e.

32 Le Nain de Tillemont, II, 321; Aubry de Trois-Fontaines, after having recounted the marriage of Robert, in 1237, reported that of Alphonse « *eodem fere anno.* » The

passages of Guillaume de Nangis, cited on this subject by Dom Vaissète, are not contrary to this date (Vaissète, t. VII , p. 96-97).

33 *Layettes du Trésor des Chartes*, II, 2448; 27 May 1236.

34 Le Nain, II, 333.

35 *Historiens de France*, XXII, 589 b. The Courtenays descended from Louis VI, and Baudouin maried Marie de Brienne, youngest niece of Queen Blanche.

36 Ibid., 588 h, 590 h, 591 c, 595 9, 609 J-9, 611, 620 l.

37 Ibid., 589 e, 591 d, 586 b.

38 *Layettes du Trésor des Chartes*, II, 2833; August 1239.

39 *Archives historiques du Poitou*, t. IV, p. 108; 1245; *Historiens de France*, XXIV, p. 163, n. 734.

40 *Historiens de France*, XXII, 607 h, 604 j, 610 a.

41 Ibid., 598 h, 599 a-b, 600 a, 600 e.

42 Ibid., 595 9, h.

43 *Vie d'Isabelle de France*, by Agnès d'Harcourt, published by Du Cange, following his edition of Joinville, 1668, p. 169.

44 Huillard-Bréholles, *Friderici II historia diplomatica*, t. VI, p. 97; July 1243.

45 *Vie d'Isabelle*, p. 170.

46 Bibliothèque nationale, ms. latin 9017, fol. 69, lines 9 and 27.

47 Bougenot, *Comptes de Blanche*, p. 90; Bibliothèque nationale, ms. latin 9017, top.

48 Archives nationales, J. 103-i, n. 8.

49 Florez, *España sagrada*, l. XXVII, col. 611, and *Memorias de las reynas catolicas*, t. I, p. 483; Potthast, *Regesta*, 14184; *Registres d'Innocent IV*, n. 5100.

50 Rodrigue de Tolède, ed. of 1545, fol. LXXXIV verso, liv. IX, ch. xvm, 1237; Florez, *Memorias*, t. I, p. 469.

51 Mathieu de Paris, *Chronica majora*, t. III, p. 327-328; Le Nain, t. II, p. 239 ff.

52 *Layettes du Trésor des Chartes*, II, 2699-2700, 23 March 1238; *Historiens de*

France, t. XXII, p. 602 b.

53 Guillaume de Nangis, *Chronique*, ed. Géraud, t. I, p. 187.

54 *Historiens de France*, t. XXII (1239), p. 591 c, h, 604 h, 612 a.

55 Florez, *Memorias*, t. I, p. 455; Schirrmacher, *Geschichte Castiliens*, p. 349, 369-370. Alphonse died in 1260 : *Art de vérifier les dates*, ed. of 1750, p. 681.

56 *Historiens de France*, t. XXII, p. 598 d-e.

57 *Comptes de Blanche*, Bougenot, p. 88, and ms. latin 9017. fol. 69, line 33.

58 *Archives historiques du Poitou*, t. IV, p. 108.

59 *Chronicon Cluniacense, Bibliotheca Cluniacensis*, p. 1666.

60 *Historiens de France*, t. XXI, p. 276 h, 1248.

61 Florez, *Memorias*, t. I, p. 415; Johannes Meursius, *Historia Danica*, 1638, 2nd part, p. 21. Aliénor de Portugal died in childbirth 13 May 1231 and her husband succumbed, 28 November 1231, to a wound received while hunting. One must not confound Aliénor with her aunt Bérengère de Portugal, who had married King Waldemar II.

62 *Layettes*, II, 2005, 25 July 1229.

63 The confessor of Queen Marguerite, *Historiens de France*, t. XX, p. 65. On 3 May 1236, Louis IX, having Blanche of Castile at his side, took the advice of his counsellors, knights, and clerics, who composed his Parlement, on a request of the Comtesse de Boulogne. Boutaric, *Actes du Parlement*, t. I; *Arrêts et enquêsts antérieurs aux Olim*, n. 16.

64 *Historiens de France*, t. XXIV, p. 4, n. 19.

65 Ibid., p. 3 g.

66 Ibid., p. 254, n. 9, 11.

67 Ibid., p. 111, n. 148; *Grande chronique de Limoges, Historiens de France*, t. XXI, p. 766.

68 *Historiens de France*, t. XXIV, p. 42, n. 316: another deposition concerning Queen Blanche, ibid., p. 194, n. 1141.

69 *Historiens de France*, t. XXIV, p. 393-394.

70 Guillaume de Nangis, *Chronique*, ed. Géraud, t. I, p. 191; Thomas Walsingham,

Ypodigma Neustriæ, p. 142.

71 *Monumenta Franciscana* (collection of the Master of Rolls), letters of Adam de Marsh, p. 381. Bémont, *Simon de Montfort*, p. 16.

72 Mathieu de Paris, *Chronica majora*, t. IV, p. 45.

73 Mathieu de Paris, t. IV, p. 631.

74 *Layettes du Trésor des Chartes*, t. II, n. 1911; 2 January 1237 and not 1227, as the previous edition; the date is in every letter in the original charter (J. 534, n. 15); *Layettes*, II, 2476, 4 January 1237; 2478, 10 January 1237.

75 *Layettes*, II, 2491-2509, 2519-2556.

76 Le Nain de Tillemont, t. II, p. 311; *Layettes*, II, 2583-2584, in Compiègne, December 1237.

77 Ibid., 2585-2605, 2611-2691, 2695-2697; Aubry de Trois-Fontaines, *Monumenta Germaniæ*, scriptores, t. XXIII, p. 940.

78 Ibid., 2705-2706; April 1238.

79 Rodenberg, *Epistolæ sæculi XIII e regestis Romanorum pontificum selectæ*, t. I, n. 688; Potthast, *Regesta*, 10151; 28 April 1236.

80 Rinaldi, *Annales*, t. II, 1237, n. 33; Potthast, 10295; 9 February 1237.

81 *Layettes*, 2514; 18 May 1237.

82 Rinaldi, *Annales*, t. II, 1237, 35-37; 20 May 1237.

83 Rinaldi, 1239, 71-73, 9 July 1238; *Layettes*, 2736 and 2738; Potthast, 10641 and 10644; 10 and 20 August 1238.

84 Guillaume de Nangis, *Chronique*, ed. Géraud, t. I, p. 187; *Opusculum Galleri cornuli, archiepiscopi Senonensis, de susceptione coronæ spineæ* Jesu Christi, Historiens de France, t. XXII, p. 28. The texts related to Baudouin II and the transfer of relics from Constantinople have been examined with care by Le Nain de Tillemont, t. II, p. 307-311, 336-345, 409-410.

85 *Le Ménestrel de Reims*, ed. of Wailly, n. 438.

86 Lettres à Blanche de Castile, 30 October 1237 and 20 July 1238, *Layettes du Trésor des Chartes*, 2577 and 2729.

87 Mathieu de Paris, t III, p. 481.

88 *Layettes*, 2744; 4 September 1238.

89 Relation of Gautier Cornu, p. 29.

90 Gautier Cornu, p. 27; Mathieu de Paris, t. IV, p. 75; *Johannis Longi chronica Sancti Berlini*; *Monumenta Germaniæ*, scriptores, t. XXV, p. 842.

91 *Layettes*, 2753; December 1238. Aubry de Trois-Fontaines indicates the total amount of the sums expended on this occasion by Saint Louis (*Monumenta Germaniæ*, scriptores, t. XXIII, p. 947.)

92 Gautier Cornu, p. 29-30.

93 Philippe Mousket, verse 30598.

94 Gautier Cornu, p. 30-31.

95 *Historiens de France*, t. XXII, p. 600 h. This very account confirms several others relative to the Crown of Thorns, p. 601.

96 Philippe Mousket, verse 30611.

97 Gautier Cornu, p. 31; Aubry de Trois-Fontaines, *Monumenta Germaniæ*, t. XXIII, p. 947; Deuxièmes annales de Saint-Denis, *Bibliothèque de l'École des Chartes*, 1879, p. 291; Guillaume de Nangis, *Vie de Saint Louis*, *Historiens de France*, t. XX, p. 326, and the *Chronique*, ed. Géraud, I, 191; *Récit du XIII siècle sur les translations faites en 1239 et en 1241 des saintes reliques de la Passion*, published by Wailly, *Bibliothèque de l'École des Chartes*, 1878, p. 409-410.

98 Aubry, *Monumenta Germaniæ*, scriptores, XXIII, 946, 1239; *Annales Erphordenses*, *Monumenta Germaniæ*, scriptores, XVI, p. 33; Mathieu de Paris, *Chronica majora*, IV, 54-55.

99 Léopold Delisle, *Mémoire sur les opérations financières des Templiers*, p. 17.

100 See, for this second translation, the *récit* published by de Wailly, *Bibliothèque de l'École des Chartes*, 1878, p. 410-412; *grande chronique* of Mathieu de Paris, t. IV, p. 90-92; Nangis, *Chronique*, ed. Géraud, t. I, p. 191; *Johannis Longi chronica S. Bertini*, *Monumenta Germaniæ*, scriptores, t. XXV, p. 842.

101 Wailly, *Récit du XIII° siècle*, etc., p. 412-415; "Traité sur la translation de Sainte-Geneviève," *Historiens de France*, t. XXIII, p. 141; 1242.

102 Le Nain de Tillemont, t. II, p. 349.

103 *Layettes du Trésor des Chartes*, II, 2835 and 2836, 21 October 1239.

104 Le Nain de Tillemont, t. II, p. 367.

105 Aubry de Trois-Fontaines, *Mon. Germaniæ*, scriptores, t. XXIII, p. 949,1. 31.

106 *Saint Louis et Innocent IV*, ed. in-8, Thorin, 1893, p. 5-6.

107 Le Nain, t. II, p. 403.

108 Mathieu de Paris, *Chronica majora*, t. IV, p. 111.

109 Mathieu de Paris, t. IV, p. 131-133.

110 *Layettes*, II, 2083; December 1230.

111 Potthast, *Regesta*, 10759 and 10760, 10767 and 10768; 9 and 20 July 1239. I have supplied elsewhere the bibliography of this question (*Saint Louis et Innocent IV*, in-8, p. 303). It is sufficient to indicate here the works of Isidore Loeb (*Revue des études juives*, 1880 and 1881) and of Noël Valois (*Guillaume d'Auvergne*, p. 118-137).

112 Wagenseil, *Tela, ignea Satanæ*, Altorf, 1681, 2 vol. in-4; t. II, 2nd part : *Disputatio R. Jechielis cum quodam Nicolao*. The catalog of Hebrew property in the Bibliothèque nationale, n. 712, indicates a manuscript more complete on this tract; see also *Histoire littéraire de la France*, t. XXI, p. 507.

113 Wagenseil, *Disputatio*, p. 7.

114 *Disputatio*, p. 8.

115 Ibid., p. 12-13.

116 Ibid., p. 13-14, 22.

117 D. Vaissète, *Histoire de Languedoc*, in-4, t. VI, p. 717-718.

118 Aubry de Trois-Fontaines, *Monumenta Germaniæ*, scriptores, XXIII, p. 948: « *et comes Tolosanus dicebatur cis occulte consentire.* »

119 D. Vaissète, t. VI, p. 718-719.

120 D. Vaissète, *Histoire de Languedoc*, in-4°, t. VI, p. 720. Douët d'Arcq, *Siège de Carcassonne, Bibliothèque de l'École des Chartes*, 1845-1846, p. 363 ff.

121 Douët d'Arcq, loc. cit., p. 371-375, text of the letter.

122 *Chronique de Saint-Médard de Soissons* (d'Achery, *Spicilegium*, in-4°, t. II, p. 797). I cannot relate here the texts relative to the role played on this occasion by Jean de Beaumont.

123 D. Vaissète, *Histoire de Languedoc*, t. VIII, col. 1047; charter of Nov. 1240.

124 Aubry de Trois-Fontaines, *Monumenta Germaniæ*, scriptores, t. XXIII, p. 948; Douët d'Arcq, *Bibliothèque de l'École des Chartes*, 1815-1846, p. 377; deposition of a witness before the royal inquisitors.

125 Archives nationales, J. 1028, n. 3; inquest relative to the keeper of keys in Béziers.

126 This letter has been published by Bourquelot, *Revue des sociétés savantes*, 4th series, t. V, p. 447.

127 *Layettes du Trésor des Chartes*, t. II, 2914 and 2918, May 1241.

128 Archives nationales, J. 1022, n. 37.

129 *Bibliothèque de l'École des Chartes*, 1853 ; accounts of expenses on the knighthood of Alphonse, comte de Poitiers, published by Boutaric, re-edited in *Historiens de France*, t. XXII, p. 615-022. Joinville, ed. of 1874, no. 93-97.

130 Boutaric, *Saint Louis et Alphonse de Poitiers*, p. 46; *Layettes*, 2926, Poitiers, July 1241.

131 Joinville, ed. of 1874, 98-99.

132 *Layettes*, II, 2928; July 1241.

133 Léopold Delisle, *Mémoire sur une lettre inédite adressée à la reine Blanche par un habitant de la Rochelle* (*Bibliothèque de l'École des Chartes*, 1856, p. 513-555). Delisle established that this letter was written between the months of July and December 1241.

134 All that follows is borrowed from the letter published by Delisle, *l. c.*, p. 525-529.

135 See, on the subject of Isabelle, comtesse de Chartres, and her sister Alix, Abbess of Fontevraud, the dissertation of Léopold Delisle, l. c., p. 518.

136 Mathieu de Paris, t. IV, p. 179; D. Vaisséte, t. VIII, col. 1067; *Layettes*, II, 2941; 15 October 1241; Vaissète, VIII, col. 1067; 17 October 1241.

137 Mathieu de Paris, *Chronica majora*, t. IV, p. 184; IV, 204.

138 Philippe Mousket, verse 30851.

139 Mathieu de Paris, *Chronica majora*, t. IV, p. 178.

140 Ch. Bémont, *La campagne de Poitou*, 1242-1243 (extract from the *Annales du Midi*, t.V). Bémont has summarized the diverse phases of this war with a grand

precision, rendering its true character to the event generally known as the Battle of Taillebourg, and demonstrated that the debacle of the English was the result of not only leaving Saintes, but of abandoning the Barbezieux.

141 Joinville, ed. of 1874, n. 105.

142 *Historiens de France*, t. XXI, p. 112; *Les Grandes Chroniques de France*, ed. Paulin Paris, IV, 268.

143 Mathieu de Paris, *Chronica majora*, t. IV, p. 207; IV, 231-232.

144 Joinville, ed. of 1874, n. 104. Cf. Guillaume de Nangis, *Vie de saint Louis* (*Historiens de France*, t. XX, p. 338).

145 *Layettes du Trésor des Chartes*, II, 2995; 20 October 1242.

146 *Layettes*, 2996, 20 October 1242.

147 *Layettes*, II, 3012, 19 January 1243.

148 Guillaume de Puylaurens, *Historiens de France*, t. XX, p. 769 e.

149 Mathieu de Paris, *Chronica majora*, t. IV, p. 391-393.

150 Le Nain de Tillemont has assembled in his *Histoire de saint Louis*, t. III, p. 58-63, all of the testimony related to the malady of the King. See also *Saint Louis et Innocent IV*, in-8, p. 36-39.

151 Mathieu de Paris, t. IV, p. 225; IV, 257.

152 Ibid., IV, 397. First annals of Saint-Denis, *Bibliothèque de l'École des Chartes*, 1879, p. 281.

153 Guillaume de Nangis, *Vie de saint Louis* (*Historiens de France*, XX, p. 344).

154 Lecoy de La Marche, *Anecdotes d'Étienne de Bourbon*, p. 93.

155 Mathieu de Paris, IV, 397; *Chronicon hanoniense quod dicitur Balduini Avennensis* (*Monumenta Germaniæ*, scriptores, XXV, 453-454).

156 Joinville, ed. of 1874, no. 106-107.

157 Mathieu de Paris, IV, 397.

158 *Boniface VIII, bulle de canonisation de saint Louis* (*Historiens de France*, XXIII, p. 155); *Beati Ludovici vita, e veteri lectionario extracta* (ibid., p. 162); Johannis *Iperii chronicon Sancti Bertini*, dans Marténe, *Thesaurus novus anecdotorum*, III, col. 723.

159 Guillaume de Nangis, *Vie de saint Louis* (*Historiens de France*, XX, p. 344).

160 Ibid.

161 *Registres d'Innocent IV*, t. I, no. 255 and 263; same collection, nos. 1057, 1152, 1301, 3640; Potthast, *Regesta*, 12165, 19 July 1246.

162 *Saint Louis et Innocent IV*, in-8, p. 154-160.

163 *Gallia christiana*, t. IV, col. 1080; Mathieu de Paris, IV, 485.

164 *Saint Louis et Innocent IV*, p. 165.

165 Mathieu de Paris, t. IV, p. 546.

166 *Registres d'Innocent IV*, t. I, n. 2948; 5 and 6 November 1246.

167 For the detail of these events, see *Saint Louis et Innocent IV*, p. 244-266.

168 Annals of Waverley, in the *Annales monastici*, ed. Luard, t. II, p. 338 (collection of the Master of Rolls); Mathieu de Paris, t. IV, p. 631. Cf. *Saint Louis et Innocent IV*, p. 261-262.

169 Mathieu de Paris, IV, 631. Blanche, during the translation, covered the body of Saint Edmond with ornaments and weapons; Quantin, *Répertoire archéologique de l'Yonne*, p. 48.

170 Letter of Innocent IV, 17 July 1247, *Registres d'Innocent IV*, n. 3042.

171 Nicolas de Curbio, *Vie d'Innocent IV*, ch. 24 (Muratori, *Rerum italicarum scriptores*, t. III, p. 592); *Registres d'Innocent IV*, 3040 and 3041, 3043 and 3044.

172 Letters of 17 July 1247, *Registres d'Innocent IV*, 3040-41, 3043-44.

173 Letter 3041.

174 Le Nain de Tillemont, t. III, p. 129; Anonymous fragment from the 13th century (*Historiens de France*, t. XXIII, p. 134).

175 Le Nain de Tillemont, III, 130-131.

176 *Layettes du Trésor des Chartes*, t. II, nos. 3231 to 3240, and 3243 to 3337; January to March 1245. See nos. 3456 to 3458 and 3475; February to March 1246.

177 Layettes, 3534; July 1246.

178 Du Chesne, *Historiæ Francorum scriptores*, t. V, p. 423-424; 20 February 1241.

179 *Layettes*, t. II, n. 3123; 5 August 1243.

180 Du Chesne, *Historiæ Francorum scriptores*, t. V, p. 424-426; 5 August 1243.

181 Le Nain, t. III, p. 7 and 161.

182 *Layettes*, t. III, n. 3604; Namur, 12 July 1247.

183 Ibid., 3727; Palais des Blaquernes, October 1248.

184 Ibid., 3737, 3740, 3741, 3745; letters to the Empress Marie de Brienne; see the receipts delivered to Queen Blanche by the creditors of the Empress, in May 1249; *Layettes*, 3772 to 3775.

185 Mathieu de Paris, t. V, p. 3.

186 Mathieu de Paris, t. IV, p. 646.

187 See, for the departure of Saint Louis, Le Nain de Tillemont, t. III, p. 176 ff; *Saint Louis et Innocent IV*, ed. in-8, p. 323-324.

188 *Récits d'un Ménestrel de Reims*, ed. Wailly, § 370; anonymous work titled *Anciennes chroniques de Flandre*, *Historiens de France*, t. XXII, p. 331.

189 *Ordonnances des roys de France*, t. I, p. 60; July 1248.

190 *Ménestrel de Reims*, *l. c.*; *Anciennes chroniques de Flandre*, *l. c.*

191 *Chronique de Salimbene*, p. 94.

192 Guillaume de Nangis, *Vie de saint Louis*, *Historiens de France*, t. XX, p. 356.

193 Ibid; Guillaume de Nangis, *Historiens de France*, t. XX, p. 552; Mathieu de Paris, t. V, p. 24.

Chapter Eight

The Second Regency. Death of Queen Blanche.

Alphonse de Poitiers delays by one year his departure for the East. — Interested Policy of the King of England. — Stay of Louis IX in Cyprus. — Crusade of Alphonse. — Death of the Count de Toulouse. — Damietto and Mansourah; captivity of Louis IX. — Improvement of the relationship with Henry III. — Louis IX in Syria. — Return of Alphonse and Charles d'Anjou. — Death of Frederick II. — Affairs of Provence. — Illness of Queen Blanche. — Innocent IV returns to Italy. — Situation of the King in the Holy Land. — Crusade of the Pastoureaux. — Avesnes and Dampierre. — Advisers of the Regent; Parlement. — Blanche and the clergy. — The Queen delivers the serfs imprisoned by the chapter of Notre-Dame. — Emancipations — Illness and death of Blanche. — Conclusion.

      Piety had swept away filial love. While going beyond the seas to fight the enemies of Christ, Louis IX did not only subordinate the interests of France to his faith; he imposed silence on the sentiment which for a long time had dominated his life. It was Blanche of Castile he had sacrificed. Let us forget for a moment the sufferings of this crusade; they only made it more illustrious, and without them her role would not have the inclination for which it gave extraordinary proofs, supported with a superhuman patience and courage. But what became, upon his departure, of that which she had raised, maintained on the throne, protected during so many years against all their enemies, and now severely tested like a soldier? At sixty years of age it was necessary for her to go back to work and to take up once more the burden that she had so courageously carried before. Concerns and pains were to succeed in a mother's heart without a truce; could she at least, to forget them, seek rest in the solitude of Maubuisson where she had planned for her last days, the reward for a whole life of abnegation and fatigue? Everything depended on it.

If ever Blanche had had passion for power, she had to make sad reflexions on human grandeur, and, one cannot doubt that it was not personal ambition which drove her during these last years when she once again took up this trade of Queen, putting her experience at the service of France, with dignity and strength worthy of admiration. Constrained with this last sacrifice, it was not seen that she complained; she did not condemn her son, she continued to serve him, and she did not have the right to blame him; Saint Louis was too grand to be put in the same rank as everyone else, and what in others had been a fault, had only placed him at the first rank among the noblest representatives of humanity.

While allowing the Count de Poitiers to delay his departure until the following year, Louis IX wanted not only to give his mother a consolation. The presence of Alphonse was, for the Regent and the Kingdom, a pledge of safety; the Count was nearly twenty-eight years old; placed since 1241 at the head of a great fief, gifted with an intelligence whose superiority was not late to affirm, he could offer his mother a very useful cooperation, a guarantee of real value in the event of serious difficulties or of conflicts with foreign powers. It is probable that during this year, while preparing his crusade, he was often found beside Blanche; he was found then in Paris, in Pontoise, and certainly the Regent could not have an adviser more capable of assisting her.[1] She could also Count on the good will of the Pope, who, more than ever, was going to be the protector of France. After the departure of Louis IX, of Robert and Charles d'Anjou, Innocent IV had written the Queen to engage her to take courage and to promise her to take care that the safety of the kingdom was not compromised; this insurance could not be an indifferent thing to Blanche of Castile, who knew how foolish it was to count on the good disposition of the King of England.[2]

Peace had not been restored between France and England after the war of Poitou, and the truce to which they had agreed was nearing its end; however, Henry III did not want to conclude a final arrangement with his brother-in-law at the price of impossible restitutions. He had just made with Louis IX, via mediation of his young nephew Henri , son of Frederick II and Isabelle of England, a new attempt to obtain the old French fiefs of his house. Frederick II remissly allowed himself to support this untimely demand. As for the King of France, for whom reconciling provisions were however well-known, he had answered at the time of his departure that he could not go against the wishes of all his subjects, of his mother, and of his vassals.[3] After the departure of the King, Henry, passing from requests to hostile measures, pretending to want to start war again. He would undoubtedly not have been in a state to make it, and, among his subjects themselves, they hardly took his quarrelsome intentions seriously; behind these preparations, the English foresaw a determination to ask new sacrifices of money.[4] However, Henry III appears to have taken some measures to attack France, or at least to bring disquiet; it was probably for this reason that troops were gathered in England from Gascogne; a certain number of knights had orders to be in London on the 15th and 22nd of August, and on 15 September in Portsmouth, where vessels intended for their transport were assembled.[5]

Was this project really intended to threaten France? Innocent IV appears to have believed so, when he intervened at once in favor of Louis IX. Two pontifical envoys, the notary Albert and Master Paul, found Henry III in Windsor (14 September 1248), and urged him not to attack any of the lands possessed by the King of France. Rumors abounded that they had even threatened to smite England with an interdict; but Henry III did not wait for this injunction of the Holy See to give France a few months respite.[6] On 20 September, his brother-in-law Simon de Montfort, Count of Leicester, came to Lorris to extend until 29 December the truce which was on the point of expiring.[7] It would have been more dignified to declare in all honesty that they would not undertake expeditions against Louis IX while he was in the Orient; but the King of England, in place of proceeding without ulterior motive to such a natural concession, held himself to half-measures. The final time limit of the truce was deferred, a little later, to All Saints day of 1249, then to 24 June 1250.[8] During this time, negotiations continued between the two crowns. In the spring of 1249, an adviser of the King of England, Barthelemy Pèche, left on embassy for France, and it was undoubtedly about the same time that Simon de Montfort, being in Paris, wrote to Henry III to say that his affairs were progressing well.[9] The Count de Toulouse having died, Henry, at the end of the year, charged the Count of Leicester to claim from his testamentary executors the land of Agenois, to which the Crown of England had rights.[10] As for seriously assisting Louis IX in his crusade, he probably never thought of it. While posturing intentions to send reinforcements into the Holy Land, he did not want

English crusaders to leave at the same time as the King of France; they only joined the French in Egypt, under the command of Guillaume Longue-Epée, Count of Salisbury.[11]

Blanche had reason to be cautious against England; but whatever the concerns, even the most serious, they were little things compared with the emotion of waiting in France for news from the Orient. Having decided to open his efforts against Egypt, Louis IX first directed himself towards the island of Cyprus, and it was Limisso that he approached about the middle of September 1248; he saw himself constrained to await in Cyprus for those who were to join him, and events brought him to remain there until next spring; it was there that he accepted an embassy of Tartars, about which he wrote his mother; at the same time he sent a Latin translation to her of a letter that the Great Khan had addressed to him.[12] He stated that diseases were rife in his army, taking many victims, removing several great lords who surrounded him. Blanche had to learn from him that Queen Marguerite had fallen ill, and that Charles d'Anjou suffered from quartan fever. Unfortunately for us, letters written by the King were not preserved. When Blanche learned that Frederick II had sent supplies to Cyprus, she wrote, like her son, to Innocent IV to request that he reconcile himself with the Emperor, and forwarded to this prince, with presents, expressions of her gratitude.[13] The continuation of events showed that Frederick, Emperor of the Occident and King of Jerusalem, could not do more for the holy war; he was too preoccupied fighting the head of the Church to spend his money and his men in the service of Jesus Christ, and it was from neither Germany nor Italy that the King of France could wait for reinforcements.

It was important that his brother, the Count de Poitiers, joined him with a good army. During the year which followed the departure of the King, Count Alphonse did not cease to prepare his own expedition; the Pope assisted him, and took, as of the end of October 1248, all possible measures to ensure aid worthy of his enterprise.[14] The good will of Innocent IV, in this circumstance, was undeniable, but it is permitted for one to believe that the results obtained did not entirely answer his call; a letter of 20 April 1250 to Count Alphonse from Treasurer Saint-Hilaire de Poitiers, says that at this date the Treasurer, ordered to gather revenue assigned to the crusade, had received nothing of the 6,000 *livres parisis* promised by the Holy See.[15] Alphonse, happily, had other resources; before leaving, his mother loaned him 4,400 *livres parisis*.[16] He needed supplies for the voyage; the Queen and her sons had requested Frederick II to give them to him. Frederick answered Blanche in extremely courteous terms, speaking about his attachment to the house of France, of interest that he carried for the crusade, of the desire that he would have had to take a part in it; he excused himself from it, and cast responsibility upon the Pope for his situation; he added that the scantiness of supplies, extremely poor for the previous two years in the Kingdom of Sicily, had prevented him from sending all that he would have wished; but in answer to the prayers of Blanche, to which he could not, nor did not, want to remain deaf, he came to dispatch for the Count a thousand loads of wheat, as many loads of barley taken in from his stores, and fifty good *dextriers*. He gave the Count the right to buy, in the Kingdom of Sicily, all that he could need for himself and his people. Louis IX accepted from the Emperor a letter designating the same terms; the generosities of Frederick were not, it should be said, likely to facilitate very much the expedition of the Count de Poitiers. Alphonse left for Lyon, where he was in July 1249, reached Aigues-Mortes, and embarked on 25 August, one year to the day after the departure of the King his brother; he took along with him his wife, Jeanne de Toulouse, the Countess d'Artois, and a whole body men that Joinville called the *arrière-ban* [general levy] of France.[17] We still have accounts drawn up by these people at the time of departure, and a charter relative to the armament of a Genoese ship chartered for this fleet.[18] Blanche of Castile had her sorrow increase by this last separation; she was neither at the beginning, nor at the end of her sufferings; but she felt rather strongly in control of a kingdom whose fate was entrusted to her. Her strong spirit was at the height of all difficulties.[19]

The Count de Toulouse, a crusader for many long years, had left neither with the King, nor with the Count de Poitiers; he had however made his preparations; the King and Blanche lent him money for his voyage to the Orient. But when he reached Aigues-Mortes finding Alphonse and Countess Jeanne, it was only to take leave of them.[20] Instead of weighing anchor, he returned via Rouergue, to Milhau, where the fever took him; he died in this town on 27 September 1249, one month after his daughter and son-in-law had left France.[21] This death, which certainly pained Blanche, was to create new concerns, since Alphonse de Poitiers was, as heir of his wife, the only heir to Raimond VII. As for the departed, I am embarrassed to judge him; the misfortunes of his youth, the partial dispossession to which he had been subjected, the ambition that he always had to regain lost domains, explain, without excusing it, a fickleness of which he gave too much evidence. The sentiments of Blanche in this regard had always been faithful, and even after his last revolt, he found methods to employ to make a return to grace. It is true that Raimond was her first cousin, that he perhaps tested these sentiments by threatening domains removed from this close relative that had come to enlarge the inheritance of Louis IX; but she had not plundered Raimond VII; she benefited, and profited royalty, from a situation created by others. Consequently, she had never given up on him since the Treaty of 1229, while Raimond had not hesitated to betray her in combining with the Count de La Marche and the English. Blanche of Castile was a great queen, and Raimond VII a poor *politique*; he seems to have been a rather weak character, and the rigors of fate had perhaps caused in him an attenuation of moral direction.

It was necessary to ensure the Count de Poitiers in possession of domains left by Raimond VII; Blanche had naturally to take care of this business, and elsewhere Alphonse, upon leaving, had sent Saint-Hilaire de Poitiers to remind the Queen that he counted on her to take care of his interests. The trusty servant was carefully discharged from this care: "And when I was before Madam," wrote he to his master, "I told her how much you were detained at port, and the day and hour of your passage, and the great expenditure that you had needed to make; I prayed her on your behalf to direct, as mother, counsel in your affairs, because she has your confidence, all your attention. She answered me that she would happily do so."[22] It was certain that Blanche would take this role seriously, and the technicalities of the succession of Toulouse was not only to reveal to us her solicitude for the rights and the interests of her third son. Archambaud de Bourbon, who for certain fiefs recovered the county of Poitiers, had died on Cyprus, leaving for heir his son-in-law the young Odand de Bourgogne. In October 1249, Blanche received from the new Lord de Bourbon homages that he made to the King and to Count Alphonse, and gave all the necessary guarantees for Odand to meet his feudal duties.[23]

For the succession of Toulouse, Blanche took from the first days all possible precautions. Soon after the death of Raimond VII, the seneschal of Carcassonne, to whom she had given instructions, left for the court, in order to report and to take orders.²⁴ Blanche did not lose a moment to place in her son's hand the lands of the deceased; she took possession of it, not under the terms of the will left by Raimond VII, but under the terms of the Treaty of 1229; only she took the precaution to associate with her action Sicard Alaman, the most important of those to whom the Count de Toulouse had entrusted the execution of his last will.²⁵ In October, she commanded Guy and Herve de Chevreuse, and with them the Treasurer Saint-Hilaire, to recognize the authority of Alphonse in his new estates.²⁶ These three commissaries went to Toulouse and, on 1 December, in the castle of Narbonnais, they accepted the oaths of the Count de Comminges, and a quantity of nobles and municipal magistrates.²⁷ Five days later, the consuls and the town of Toulouse lent oaths in their turn; but before, the agents of Blanche declared that, by order of the Queen, they had entrusted the government of the country to Sicard Alaman; Sicard, for his part, swore to observe, until the return of the Count, the freedoms and customs of the city.²⁸ During all the winter (December to March), a great number of nobles and municipalities made acts of fidelity towards their new lord, maybe between the hands of the three commissaries sent by the Queen, maybe before other representatives of the Count and Sicard Alaman.²⁹ This last, in his acts, noticed that he was the lieutenant of Alphonse by the will of Queen Blanche.³⁰ There was at some point an inclination to resist. Consuls and bourgeois of Agen refused to swear oaths; but on February 1250, they sent to the Queen two of their number, along with two bourgeois of Condom, to offer their submission.³¹

In the Comtat Venaissin or Marquisate of Provence the situation was more complicated. The Holy See, while leaving Raimond VII in possession of this country, had not made any formal abandonment. After the death of Raimond, Cardinal d'Albano had come to take possession in the name of the Church; also the commissaries of Blanche took care not to pass on the left bank of the Rhône.³² On 9 March 1250, Innocent IV had not yet given up his claims, when he wrote the Bishop of Carpentras to reserve the rights of the Church on Comtat Venaissin.³³ The city of Avignon, wedged in the Comtat of which it was not supposed to form a part, belonged undivided to the counts de Toulouse and of Provence; they refused to recognize Alphonse and maintained independence, under protection of their *podestat* Barrel des Baux, most powerful among the lords of Provence.³⁴ But Barral was not late in seeing the risk he ran while playing this part; on 1 March 1250, he came to find the Queen and pledged all his efforts to make Avignon submit to Count Alphonse, and Arles to the Count d'Anjou; he went so far as to promise to make war on these two cities, required by the Queen.[35] Alphonse de Poitiers, who fought then in Egypt, could hardly suspect that, thanks to the skill of his mother, his affairs were in such good order.

The King of France and his army had started from Limisso in the second half of May 1249; but a violent storm had dispersed the Christian fleet.[36] It had been necessary to return to Cyprus, to gather the scattered vessels; finally, after an easier crossing, they had arrived on the coast of Egypt. The disembarkation had taken place on 5 June and, as of the following day, the crusaders had entered Damiette.[37] It was a great success; Louis IX informed his mother, and Robert d'Artois, for his part, wrote Blanche of Castile a relation of the victory that the crusaders had just gained.[38] This letter is extremely interesting; the Count d'Artois, a good son, gave Blanche news of family members: the King, Marguerite, Countess Béatrix, all were in good health; the Count d'Anjou still felt his fever, which however was on the decline. "The Countess d'Anjou," continued Robert, "gave to the world, in Cyprus, a small extremely beautiful boy, very well made; she left him there with a nurse."[39] Blanche transmitted this good news to the King of England, in a letter where one finds, beside very precise details, marks of personal attention; she finished in telling Henry III that his sisters-in-law, Queen Marguerite and the Countess d'Anjou, were expecting: "Give, as you wish, this news to your very dear spouse the Queen of England, and please offer her salutations on our part."[40] Blanche was not the only one to be delighted. In France, in England, they learned by many letters that Damiette was conquered; one even went so far as to say that Alexandria and Cairo had had experienced the same fate.[41] The Queen hastened to send to her son money and supplies, and the sums that she dispatched were considerable, because to transport them to the sea, it was necessary to harness eleven carriages each with four horses, without counting several beasts of burden.[42] The reinforcements arrived too. These were the first English crusaders, under the command of Guillaume de Longue-Épée, and then, on 24 October 1249, Alphonse de Poitiers and his fleet.[43]

The Regent was to be informed of all that occurred in Egypt; but voyages were long, and such that people in France were under the impression of a first success, when great and painful struggles had started for the crusaders. Advancing in the direction of Cairo, they had delivered, on 8 February 1250, a terrible battle. Robert d'Artois was carried away, in spite of the orders of the King, through his ill-considered valiancy, and perished, encircled in Mansourah; Louis IX, after having run greater dangers, had remained master of the field of battle; but the French army, stopped in its tracks, obliged to fight unceasingly, could not leave the camp that he had established close to Mansourah.[44] It was from there that Louis wrote his mother (March 1250), to request her to ensure the heirs to the Count d'Artois the rights which their father had to the county of Ponthieu.[45] The letter by which he told Blanche about misfortunes that reached them both would interest us even more; it exists no more. Blanche was cruelly struck. Robert appears to have been a very devoted son; there was proof of his violence when he insulted the Count de Champagne, forgetting his duties towards Blanche of Castile, showing that he did not take lightly the insults made against his mother. He was very brave, even too brave a man, since his death was atonement for heroic imprudence. The King, who could not restrain his tears, on the evening of the battle, when one asked for news of his brother, envied the fate of the one who had just died sword in hand.[46]

The death and horrors of the battlefield were nothing in comparison to what awaited Louis IX. After remaining stationary for some time, he had to beat a retreat, in the midst of an army decimated by diseases, seriously afflicted himself with dysentery which had carried off his soldiers, and finished by falling, on 6 April, under the power of the Sarrasins.[47] He had withdrawn to the rear guard, exhausted, when Geoffroy de Sargines came along, protecting him with great difficulty, until the village where the infidels had seized him. Could there be a more lamentable spectacle than this great king, overcome, dying, prostrate in a meager house in the midst of his despairing companions in arms, while in the street outside the last of his defenders, Gaucher de Châtillon, was cut down fighting for him. Blanche was not there, this time, to look after and comfort her son; a bourgeois woman of Paris, encountered in the rout, supported on her knees the head of one who had comforted so many miseries.[48]

Louis IX did not die; he regained enough vitality to be able, in the lamentable weeks which followed, to appreciate a disaster without precedent. It was his courage, his dignity, the calmness proved in the middle of dangers and sufferings which would have thrown others into a panic, which excited the admiration of his enemies. It was necessary to return Damiette, to give up Egypt which was covered with corpses, by leaving thousands of prisoners there, to pay an enormous ransom; Louis endured all of that without weakening. Finally he could embark for Syria: he approached the port of Saint-Jean-d'Acre about the middle of June, overcome, but larger in his defeat than ever a prince had been following the day of victory.[49]

The Christian world, France especially, learned with consternation what had just occurred. It was claimed that Queen Blanche and *les grands* of the kingdom, refusing to believe the messengers of this lamentable news, took them for impostors and hanged them.[50] It must be a fable. Blanche had enough strength of character to preserve her mental and spiritual presence in the midst the most serious circumstances; but one can appreciate her pain.

Leaving to others the care to discuss the causes of this misfortune which struck her son, the Regent occupied herself more than ever to come to his assistance. She sought help everywhere, in France, and abroad, and did not meet with good will or useful cooperation other than that of the Pope. Still, the effective action of the head of the Church did not occur immediately. Upon learning of the destruction of the Christian army and the reverses of its chief, Innocent had written to the King to comfort him, to the French clergy to order prayers and to press the preaching of crusade; but Blanche and her son desired from the Holy See something other than marks of sympathy, and one must recognize that Innocent made serious efforts to help them.[51] At the end of November 1250, perhaps stimulated by the entreaties of Alphonse de Poitiers and Charles d'Anjou, who had just returned to France, he prescribed new measures for the collection of funds intended for the holy war and the departure of crusaders at the time of the next passage, whose date was to be fixed by Blanche of Castile. Instructions having the same goal were given, in Germany, to the provincial prior of the Dominicans and to the minister provincial of Franciscans concerning crusaders from Friesland and Norway. At the same time, lifting of the tenth [extraordinary tax] previously granted to Louis IX, for three years, on the incomes of French clergy, was extended for a new period of two years.[52]

It was all that one could ask of the Holy See in situation where it was struggling with the Empire. The kings were less generous; they felt sorry for Louis IX and let him conclude his own business. In Norway, Hakon IV was for a long time pledged to crusade, but his intention to go to the Orient had never been serious.[53] It is said that

Ferdinand III of Castile, the nephew of Blanche, touched by the misfortunes which overpowered his cousin, took up the cross, but this fact has never been formally established, and Ferdinand, to suppose that he made such a wish, died without executing it.[54] The hopes that were placed on England were also disappointed.

Since the Count of Salisbury and his small body of troops had left for Egypt, where the Count found death at Mansourah, pledges for the cross were multiplied in the domains of Henry III. On 6 March 1250, this prince himself made a pledge to go to the Holy Land; but, from the earliest days, his intention inspired little confidence, in France as in England; Treasurer Saint-Hilaire de Poitiers, writing to Count Alphonse, said straightforwardly that persons believed Henry to have taken up the cross only to delay the departure of English pilgrims. Blanche of Castile, following this letter, had written to the Pope to demand that these crusaders be threatened with excommunication if they did not leave by August (1250). She obtained more enthusiasm for her cause and, on 9 June, Innocent IV gave orders so that their departure not be delayed. But after the disaster in Egypt had been learned of, the Pope, not wanting to leave scattered reinforcements intended for the Holy Land, opposed in an absolute way for English crusaders to travel in small groups or one after the other, and enjoined them to await his orders. Henry III did not ask for anything else; because he did not cease proposing his projects of crusade, to which he had obtained a tenth that the Pope granted, twice, for one five year period. In spite of honest intentions on the part of his subjects, in spite of calls of Louis IX and efforts of the Holy See, his preparations led to nothing.[55]

Taking up the cross by Henry III had at least finally improved his relations with France. On 5 March 1250, he charged Richard de Cornouailles and two of the uncles of Queen Aliénor, Philippe and Pierre de Savoie, to extend the truce for a period of sixteen years and beyond that; he gave them full powers to restore peace; letters of 8 March accredited them to the Regent.[56] Undoubtedly this step was not yet made when Blanche of Castile, to determine her son's return, believed that she had neither peace nor truce with the King of England.[57] The conclusion of the truce is a certain fact; during the next winter, twice, Henry III for his part appointed commissaries charged to take care that it was observed.[58] On 6 January 1252, he again conversed with "his very dear cousin" the Queen of France. Various infringements of the truce having been made to the detriment of Gascons, subjects of the Crown of England, Blanche had promised indemnities; Henry requested her to indicate a day when the figure of sums to be paid could be regulated in a conference, for which he sent two deputies to Gascogne.[59] Two months later, these commissaries informed their master that they awaited the opening of the conference, whose place and date had been fixed by the Queen of France.[60] About the same time, the mayor and aldermen of Bordeaux sent ambassadors to Henry III, to speak with him about the seizure, arrests, or spoliations, made to the detriment of their fellow-citizens on the lands of the King of France and of the Count de Poitiers.[61]

Thus relations established became easier between the two countries since the spring of 1250. On 2 February 1252, Henry III restored to the French the cargo and armaments of a vessel shipwrecked on the coasts of Sussex.[62] Four month later, answering a complaint of Blanche, he informed her that he delivered Anseau de Trainel and two other knights, all three liege men of the King of France, arrested in Gascogne when they went on pilgrimage to Saint-Jacques de Compostelle. Towards the end of this year (23 November), he learned that Guy de Lusignan asked, before crossing to England, authorization from Blanche.[63] Failing this final peace, one did not think any more of seeing kings quarrel. But Louis IX could not suspect that things would go so well, when, in June 1250, he put forward the danger of a conflict with England as one of the reasons which could determine him to return to France.[64]

The King of France and his companions in misfortune had approached Acre at Midsummer's Day about the middle of May, in a state of weakness and destitution which was pitiable. Whatever was the size Louis IX's heart, the sight of those who surrounded him was enough to remove any idea of immediate revenge. Exhausted by deprivations and diseases, sometimes covered in miserable clothing, they brought to Syria, with the memories of their sufferings, a feeling of poignant emotion, while contemplating that a great number of their comrades were still prisoners.[65] What a contrast between the state of heart of these unhappy men and the pride of an Arab poet who, about same time, addressed to them, in the manner of a farewell, these cruel mocking remarks:[66]

> Say to France when you meet him, these words of truth, which come from a sage man: That God rewards you for having killed the admirers of Jesus, the Messiah! You went to Egypt

intending to conquer this kingdom; you believed you would encounter nothing but horns and drums. A sortie was conducted into the multitudes which appeared in your eyes as a space too narrow. You carried out your companions, by your beautiful councils, to the doors of the tomb. There are fifty thousand that one will see nothing more of but dead, captive, or wounded. God grant success for similar expeditions! Perhaps Jesus will be taken from you. If your Pope grants it, often treason comes to a man of good counsel. Tell them they think of returning to be avenged for a wiser intention: The house of the son of Lokman still exists; the chains are always there, like the eunuch Sabih.[67]

This insolent challenge shows that the Muslims of Egypt had no fear of the French. The people overcome at this point seemed to have, for the moment, nothing to lose, in returning home, and Louis IX hoped, indeed, to re-embark himself for France as soon as the Christians remaining in Egypt would have recovered their freedom. This return was the best hope Blanche; for some time already, and undoubtedly before learning of the captivity of her son, she had written to him to speak to him about the dangers which the kingdom ran and to request he return.[68] Louis IX had already prepared his vessels, when new arrivals in Egypt changed his plans. The King of France, his two brothers and those of the Christians who had returned to Syria had been delivered by virtue of a treaty concluded with Sultan Almoaddham; after this prince had been massacred, under the eyes of the French, by the Mamelukes, the emirs who had taken the government in hand were engaged to carry out the conditions stipulated in one part or the other, and it was as Louis IX had bought, by a first payment and by the rendering up of Damiette, the right to embark for Saint-Jean-d'Acre. But after his arrival in Syria, the emirs, in answer to the ambassadors that he had sent, refused to keep their commitments and delivered only four hundred prisoners out of twelve thousand who were still in Egypt.[69]

To leave, under such conditions, was for Louis IX to give up to slavery, apostasy, or death, the thousands of men for whom he was the last hope, it was perhaps also to dedicate to the destruction of what remained of the Kingdom of Jerusalem. The King united with his barons all those who could clarify their opinions; he informed them of his perplexity, asked their advice, and, though after a time, in a new assembly, siding with opinion expressed by the majority, he declared that he was decided to remain in Syria: "I warned myself," he said, "that if I remain, I do not see my kingdom in danger, because Madam the Queen has many people to defend it."[70]

To comfort his mother, to assist in the government of the kingdom and to give to France a greater security, the King commanded the return to Europe of the counts of Poitiers and Anjou. It had been really cruel to absolutely leave Blanche alone, at the moment when the new resolution of her son fell to despair; and what would have become of France, if the Regent had folded under the weight of her age, tiredness, and emotions? Louis IX also hoped that his two brothers could organize the relief which he needed and to press the levy of subsidies; elsewhere, it was vital that Alphonse de Poitiers regained as soon as possible the states fallen into his hands by the death of Raimond VII. At the beginning of August, the two princes embarked with the Duke of Burgundy and a great number of barons.[71] The King, who remained isolated, stripped of resources, charged them with carrying to his subjects a letter in which he made them an account of his misfortunes and exhorted them to holy war.[72] After having related the fall of Damiette and the battle of Mansourah, he gave of Robert d'Artois a touching memory: "It was there that for a time we lost this famous and beloved man, our brother the Count d'Artois, of good memory, let us remember with bitterness and pain, although we are foolish to not be delighted about it rather than to cry, because we have hope and the conviction that he is flown away with the crown of martyrdom towards the celestial fatherland, in the eternal joy of the saints."[73] He finished while exposing the reasons which prevented him at present from passing again to France, and pressed all those of his subjects who were crusaders to come or to send help in the month of April or May, at the time of the next passage, or at least at the following Midsummer's Day.

Some time before, Louis IX, in reply to a letter of his mother, had written to her about business concerning the abbeys of Royaumont and Lys. Two monks of Royaumont, that the Regent had sent East, were probably charged with carrying this letter to France before the departure of Alphonse de Poitiers and Charles d'Anjou.[74]

Blanche was finally going to see two of her sons; autumn began when the princes arrived in France. Lyon was on their way; they came there with the Duke of Burgundy, to speak with the Pope and to undoubtedly ask him to finally make with Frederick II a peace which would have made it possible for the Holy See to devote part of its resources to help their brother.[75] One does not accord more than a mediocre confidence in an account which says Innocent IV, threatened by them to be driven out of Lyon if he did not go along with their opinions, would then have projected to withdraw himself to Bordeaux.[76] It is against what is known about Louis IX to ascribe to him, especially in his rapport with the Pope, processes as violent as this one. Moreover, Alphonse and Charles, who had never been in fights with Innocent, and who soon went to support him in Provence, were too skilful politicians to treat him this way; it may be however that, without going so far, they testified to him their dissatisfaction. They arrived in Paris, and were accepted by their mother with a joy which would attenuate their bitter concerns.

One claimed, perhaps wrongly, that after their return both counts showed themselves not very assiduous in arranging the intended relief of Louis IX; that which could make one believe, for their part, in serious interests to defend him, especially in Provence and in Comtat Venaissin, where the cities of Arles, Avignon, and Marseilles still ignored their authority.[77] The Emperor was assured fidelity of the Avignonnais and Arlésiens, and one was in right to fear that, in this area, he opposed the final establishment of influence of the French, when his death, arrived on 13 December 1250, and all changed.[78]

The disappearance of Frederick was not a misfortune for France, neither for the King, nor for Blanche of Castile. Many people thought he was the only one able to save the Holy Land, and only hostility of the Holy See prevented him from going to the aid of the King of France; but for a long time there had been no possible compromise between Rome and the Empire, and so even if Frederick had the sincere desire to do something for Louis IX and crossed, he could never have distracted a notable part of his forces from the fight against Innocent IV. Blanche had some experience of this; she and her sons had obtained from the Emperor for the crusade a really small thing. Ancient ally of the house of France, he showed for a rather long time a worrying preference for England; however it seems difficult to admit that during the crusade to Egypt he had, in spite of his protests of friendship with regard to the French princes, voluntarily played the Muslims off against the Christians. This suspicion, about which Joinville already mentioned, and which seems justified by the assertions of Arab historians, is so odious that one must not defend it.[79] While waiting for new evidence, one can believe that Frederick, for whom tepidity in matters of faith and good relations with the sultan of Egypt were well-known, was compromised in spite of himself by the intrigues of his subjects or of his partisans.[80] It was especially for the Holy See that the death of the Emperor was going to profit; Innocent IV was triumphant; "he had confounded the enemy of Christ, Frederick the snake."[81] At least, the death of his adversary, while giving him relative safety for some time, allowed him to link with the sons of Queen Blanche, to triumph in the valley of the Rhône in a cause which was at the same time that of France and that of the Church.

Not only had the Pope given up speaking about his claims on the Comtat Venaissin, but he intervened with strength in the business of Provence in favor of Charles d'Anjou, dispatching the Dominican Etienne, his chaplain and his adviser, to restore peace there in accord with the Count, writing on this subject to the Marseillais, Arlésiens, and people of Avignon, some sharp letters and, one that scoured the inhabitants of Avignon, is even threatening.[82] The French princes were soon on top, thanks to the alliance with the Holy See and to their military action. Arles submitted to the Count de Provence on 30 April 1251; on 7 May it was Avignon which made peace with Alphonse and Charles, the two lords.[83] The resistance of Marseilles was to be more prolonged.[84] Barrel des Baux who, in spite of his promises to the Regent, remained contrary to Count Alphonse, was not to return to grace until in January 1253; Alphonse then forgave him, in memory of Blanche, who had interceded for him, and to the prayers of Charles d'Anjou.[85] It was the obstinate hostility of the Marseillais which determined the Pope to prolong or to renew in Provence the mission of Brother Etienne.[86] The two counts were thus in uncontested possession of all their estates; as for their return, they were led by practical people: Charles divided his time between the inheritance of his wife and the prerogative of Anjou; Alphonse visited Languedoc, came to Toulouse with Countess Jeanne and abrogated, in spite of rights, the will of Raimond VII, to exempt, so it seems, the pious legacies that this prince had made.[87]

It is probable that in all these affaires Blanche could hardly assist her sons; she was very sick towards the beginning of 1251. A bit late, she learned that Innocent IV was going to leave Lyon and return to Italy; she made him offers of service and testified her desire to see him again. Innocent IV did not think it wise to expose the Queen to the fatigues of a voyage too dangerous for her health; perhaps he also feared that Blanche would not miss the opportunity of addressing him in favor of Louis IX and the Holy Land. Taking care not to hurt her feelings he wrote to her, on 18 March 1251, a letter full of praises. He did not want the Queen, exhausted by the long sufferings of disease, to get under way for Lyon; he marked his regret not to be near her himself, but the urgent business which recalled him to Italy did not allow him not to delay his departure: "What still opposes," said he, "with the desire that we both have to see each other, it was the just concern for your weakness, fear that your convalescence be not delayed by some movement of emotion, your health exposed, as God does not like, a relapse. Your life is the safeguard of the people, as you must put all the care possible to preserve or recover health, which is the good of all."[88]

Blessings and vows which accompanied this letter could only be sincere; Innocent IV had much to thank Blanche for, at the very time that he had not been extremely eager to be at this time opposite her. He closed after thanking her in extremely affectionate terms and avoided the embarrassment of an interview. Furthermore, he was upset with her for remaining in courteous relations with Frederick II and to have continued to treat with the Emperor after his condemnation at the Council of Lyon. On 24 March, the Bishop of Paris accepted orders to give, for this fact, absolution to Blanche each time that he would judge it necessary.[89]

King Thibaud de Navarre was then in Lyon; Henry III had also expressed the desire to come, but the Pope could not to wait; he accepted at the time of his departure the visit of Guillaume of Holland, King of the Romans, who he raised to the throne of Germany to compete with Frederick II. Lastly, on 19 April 1251, he left forever the city which had been his refuge for more than six years.[90] Though removed from his great enemy, the Pope was still much too worried about finally destroying the house of Souabe, so that his return to Italy had an appreciable influence on the destinies of France.

Relief from the Occident was quite necessary to Louis IX who, reduced to his own resources, could hardly benefit from his stay in Palestine. While waiting for assistance, he remained on the defensive, occupied with strengthening places remaining to the Christians, to supervise the struggle against Muslim princes. The Sultan of Aleppo was then at war with Egypt, and it was through the favor of their discords that the King of France had finally obtained release of all the prisoners. At the end of winter, he left Acre for Caesarea, about which he began to raise walls. Blanche did what she could to help, but the Holy Land was very far away; great sums of money that she sent about this time to her son were lost with the ship that carried them.[91] The letters from the East were frequent, and during the summer, the Patriarch of Jerusalem wrote Blanche to give news of the King and Queen Marguerite, of her grandchildren born in the East, and of the running fight among the Muslims of Egypt and Syria.[92] The incidents of this war were addressed in a letter from Caesarea, 1 August 1251, by Louis IX to his brother Alphonse; the King gives details about his situation reassuring enough: the Christian army was not worried, supplies were not lost, communications by ground with Saint-Jean-d'Acre were open, and at sea the ships of Louis IX drove out the Arab corsairs; the King was well and the fortifications of Caesarea were being built; Louis insisted that they send him without delay the aid which he required to make profitable divisions among the infidels and finished by requiring frequent news of his mother, Charles d'Anjou, and his sister Isabelle. This letter teaches us that the correspondence between the King of France and Blanche were frequent; he wrote about his previous envoys, in another missive addressed by him to the Count de Poitiers.[93] No doubt he often wrote his mother, as he did it even for business of a secondary importance; it was thus that he was seen to address her, on 25 September, about loans made to some of his barons and knights, in October, by way of an arrangement at one time concluded between him and the monastery of Grasse.[94]

If calls sent by Louis IX to the Regent had nothing lamentable in them, they were not less pressing, and by a misfortune Blanche could hardly count on anyone but herself for aid sacrificed in a pious obstinacy to defense of Christian interests. The Pope, returned to Italy, continued against Conrad IV the war to which the death of Frederick II had not put an end, and to support this he preached a crusade in Brabant and Flanders against the house of Souabe. When Blanche, pushed by the requests of her sons, assembled *les grands* of the kingdom to call upon their devotion to the King, they resisted Innocent IV with violence who, in place of working for the crusaders of the Orient, used his forces against Christian princes. Blanche was undoubtedly of their opinion, and it was even said she went to confiscate the goods of the French who would have taken the cross against the sons of Frederick II, while saying: "That those who fight for the Pope are maintained by the Pope."[95]

While recriminating against the Church, *les grands* were not at all disposed to help their sovereign; the clergy, religious orders even, did not think of putting themselves in motion to avenge the defeat of Christian arms, and yet Louis IX was not forgotten by all his subjects. His misfortunes had caused in all the kingdom a major emotion, and when they knew where he was abandoned, though poor, the disinherited thought of him. With the voice of an unknown, they saw all shepherds and poor people of the country rise and get under way to find in the East this great friend of the unfortunate ones. In a few weeks, all of France was covered with true armies, joined together by enchantment, which traversed the country, involving with their continuation thousands of women and children. At the beginning, these poor people, in their naive enthusiasm, did not want anything but to help their good King. They were sincere, whatever were the intentions of their obscure leaders; but soon impure elements mingled with these troops of improvised crusaders, leading to disorder and violence. Representatives of the Church, often wealthy persons and in positions to seldom defend themselves, were the first victims of this singular movement. For a long time, the prestige of the clergy was gained through their opposition to the nobility; they were reproached, wrongly or rightly, for devoting to the quarrels of the Holy See the resources which had been better placed in the hands of the King of France; so the Pastoureaux, while waiting to fight Sarrasins, started to fall upon clerics and monks; this quickly proceeded to murders and scenes of plundering, in which the laity was not spared. Blanche of Castile, for one moment hesitant, saw the danger and dispersed these bands who, under pretext of delivering the King, ransacked the kingdom. It seems that on this occasion she had initially lacked perspicacity. The rising of the Pastoureaux could not have resulted in a true crusade. It was not 1095. The Holy See, the high clergy, the nobility of France, were not disposed to lay out expenses for the conquest of Jerusalem. Alone, what could these mobs of coarse people accomplish, so miserable, badly led, barely armed?

It was in the north of the kingdom that there appeared, towards Easter, a man with a strange allure, said to have been sent by the Virgin Mary to preach the crusade among the shepherds.[96] He appeared to be sixty years old, with a long beard, pale and meager in visage.[97] His contemporaries usually called him the Master of

Hungary; but his name is not known to us. Two or three chroniclers claim that he was named Jacques and had been a Cistercian monk; another called him Roger.[98] Nothing is more varied than the epithets which historians, all being clerics or monks, were pleased to call him, thus having excellent reasons not to spare him. He was thus a ribaud, a necromancer of shameful life, cursed by the sages and honored by the ignorant, an apostate, a heretic and pagan, educated in the occult sciences at the schools of Toledo and passed from Christianity to the law of Mahomet.[99] They repeated in his time that he was solemnly engaged under the Sultan of Egypt to deliver masses of Christians, and to him; and one recognizes in him one of these adventurers who, forty years earlier, had caused in France, among the children, the most peculiar of crusades.[100] Let us take these fables for they are worth; it is not less true that the reasons or the feelings which inspired the Master of Hungary remain unknown to us. Was he an impostor, enlightened, ambitious? He spoke several languages, was very informed, endowed with an eloquence which can only explain the temporary but extraordinary success of his enterprise.[101] The people believed that one with his hands, constantly closed, contained the charter by which the Mother of God had imposed his mission to him.[102]

He began his preaching in Picardie, traversing the countryside; according to him, the angels and the Virgin had appeared to him and God had chosen the shepherds, they had announced to him the poor, the common people, must deliver the Holy Land and come to the aid of the King of France.[103] At his word, shepherds gave up their animals, left the country without taking leave of their parents or their masters, and followed him; he crossed [enlisted] them all, men, women and children, on his own authority, without any coming from the Church, to which this right was always reserved.[104] The movement took in a few days the most amazing proportions, extended to Picardy, Flanders, Brabant, Hainaut, then gained Lorraine and Bourgogne; on all sides, the "Pastoureaux" got under way; in less than one week, they were thirty thousand, organized as a kind of army, commanded by chiefs and arranged under banners on which the vision of the Master was represented.[105]

This *levée en masse* of poor people who, undoubtedly, were sincere, inspired from the first a mistrust among the clergy.[106] Everywhere laymen were favorable to the crusade of the Pastoureaux and took their chiefs for saints. Nobody warned to resist them; quite the contrary, supplies were given to them. Those who received at their table the leaders of this unexpected rising affirmed, in their stupidity, how the dishes from which they ate grew instead of decreasing.[107] "People of France," says a foreign chronicler, "believed in them; rose in a terrible way against the monks, especially against preaching friars and minors, because these monks had preached holy war and crossed people to pass the sea with the King, who had been overcome by Sarrasins. The French who remained in their country agitated against Christ, at the point of blasphemy this name blessed of all; and in these days, when the minor brothers and preachers asked for alms, people clenched their teeth, and at their sight, calling some other poor, gave sums of money, while saying: 'Take that, with the name of Mahomet, which is more powerful than Christ.'"[108] The Franciscan Salimbene, author of this strange account, perhaps exaggerated; but it is certain that, as from the first days, the Pastoureaux showed themselves very hostile to the clergy and mainly to the begging orders. The first big city they crossed was Amiens; "those of the city gave up their wines and supplies, and all this for them; they asked them, because they were bewitched, at the point to find that a holier race there could not be." The bourgeois appeared before the Master of Hungary, and several knelt in front of him, "as if he were a saint."[109]

    A similar agglomeration was naturally to attract to it all the vagrants and people *sans aveu* [without a fedual patron] from the countryside where it was formed; soon armed Pastoureaux enlarged themselves with a quantity of unfortunates, the excommunicated, robbers, murderers, fallen women, and the number of people it involved with its continuation augmented without measure; they were not long in being sixty thousand, armed with swords, pitchforks, axes, large knives, and *bisaiguës* [mattocks, or perhaps large carpenter's chisels]; when they crossed the cities, carrying their innumerable banners, holding up their weapons, the fear that they inspired was so great, that no one representing legal authority dared to resist them.[110] The audacity of the Master and his lieutenants was growing; they preached as if they had been priests, vigorously declaiming against monks of all kinds, against bishops and canons, against the court of Rome, granted absolution, distributed the cross to those who wanted it, made and unmade marriages, not prohibiting a link between nine men and only one woman. They simulated miracles, praised themselves to cure patients, returned sight to blind men, health to the impotent. The people let them do this; priests and the clerks wanted from the first to oppose the diffusion of dangerous errors; they wanted to kill them.[111]

On approaching Paris, the chiefs of the Pastoureaux had some reasons to be anxious; who was not going to examine their actions in this city which was at the same time the center of royal power, the fatherland of the liberal arts and theology?[112] They could wait until the Regent, while seeing them so near, pass from indulgence to severity. Until then, Blanche had done nothing to stop their progress, that is to say she did not realize their excesses, that is to say rather she hoped to use this formidable movement to the profit of her son and the Holy Land.[113] She had given orders to let them pass, telling her agents to not oppose them. She commanded the great Master to speak with her, either in Maubuisson, or in one of the royal residences located around Paris, questioned him, treated him with honor and returned him with gifts. The Master of Hungary returned to his trusted companions and made known to them they could now kill priests and monks, "because he had so well enchanted the Queen and all her race, that she held for good all that they would do."[114] From that moment they believed all was allowed; the Master went up in pulpit at Saint-Eustace and preached in the costume of a bishop, a miter on his head; during this time the Pastoureaux, supported by the population, attacked the clergy, the mendicant orders, and even the bishop himself.[115] Blood ran; many clerics were killed or wounded, several among them were thrown into the Seine; a priest, saying Mass, was stripped of his chasuble and was crowned in derision with roses. To prevent a collision between these brutal masses and the clerics of the Université, it was necessary to close the Petit Pont, which gave access from the City to the left bank of the Seine.[116]

The Pastoureaux left the city, enjoying the height of impunity which they had found in Paris, where all was the source of science.[117] But they had become so numerous that no city was large enough to lodge them and nourish them; the Master of Hungary divided them into several corps, which then went in various directions, producing the same excesses everywhere, sowing terror.[118] In Rouen, the cathedral and the archiepiscopal palace were forced; the archbishop and all his clergy, joined together in synod on the occasion of Pentecost (4 June), were thrown outside.[119] Orléans was the scene of a bloody fight. It was against the opinion of the bishop and the clergy that the bourgeois had opened the doors to an army of Pastoureaux; these entered the city on 11 June, and to start, the Master of Hungary announced that he was going to preach. The bishop had prohibited all of his clerics to go to this scandalous ceremony, and the majority, obeying his orders, were held carefully barricaded in their houses; but Orléans, being a university town, housed quantities of students come from everywhere; some of these young people yielded to temptation to go hear the preaching of the Master, and as if mad, from the top of the pulpit, launched his violent words, when someone had the audacity to reproach him aloud for his imposture. He had hardly spoken when one Pastoureau, with a blow of his axe, split his head; the battle commenced at once; twenty-five clerics were killed or precipitated into the Loire, many were wounded; a great number of Pastoureaux also perished, and we still have one *bulla* addressed, the following year, by Innocent IV to Berthoud de Linange, brother of the elected Bishop of Spire, who had taken part, while a student, in this fatal brawl.[120] The civil population had done nothing to defend the clerics; the bishop and clergy escaped the danger by hiding; but soon the Pastoureaux, fearing reprisals, withdrew.[121]

In Tours, the violent scenes recommenced, facilitated as everywhere by the indifference of the bourgeoisie. The school and convent of Dominicans were taken by main force, several monks were wounded, others were dragged through the city half naked; Franciscans were not treated better; the churches were profaned and Pastoureaux were amused to mutilate a statue of the Virgin. All that did not prevent people from still accepting the virtue of these rowdy characters and to bring patients to them to cure.[122] Here is how their chief treated the lame: "he grasped them by the legs and all the other members, and tightened them so extremely that, thorough the pain, they were said to be cured to be able to escape his hands."[123] Other bands went into Anjou and Bretagne.[124]

All these excesses ended up worrying the laymen and drawing them from their strange indifference; when they believed themselves threatened, they resolved to make common cause with the clergy.[125] Royal officers received an order to oppose odious disorders; Blanche recognized she had been misled; she made no difficulty in acknowledging her error, ordering the pursuit of these people who acted in truth like brigands, to excommunicate them, to seize them, to destroy them.[126] The largest troop of Pastoureaux came to enter Berry, when their larcenies and their homicides for a long time finally caused a deserved repression; twelve of their chiefs were captured and hanged at Cosne.[127] As the majority of this army moved on Bourges, the clerics of this city went to speak to the royal officers and declared themselves ready to show to them facts that the Pastoureaux were villainous criminals; the bailiff and the provost heard them and the proof was not long to appear.[128]

Not finding in Bourges either clerks or priests, the Pastoureaux threw themselves on the goods of the Jews, which were in the guard of the King, invaded their synagogues, tore their books [religious texts] to pieces.[129] The bourgeoisie, who had given them all they could wish, were not better treated; these pretend crusaders broke into cupboards and trunks, to take gold and silver; "and with all this, they took young ladies and virgins, and they reveled in bed with them."[130] They made so well, that finally the royal officers opposed these bands who were given over to audacities with impunity for too long. They wanted to lock them up in the city; they [Pastoureaux] broke down the gates and precipitated outside. But the bourgeois launched an attack and reached them at some distance from there, between Morthomiers and Villeueuve-sur-Cher.[131] The Master of Hungary was killed, torn to pieces, and they plundered those who surrounded him. A great number found death in this combat.[132] The majority fled. They were hunted like rabid dogs; they were hung. In little time, all this multitude dispersed "like smoke."[133] Some of their bands had gained the valley of the Rhone; some reached Beaucaire, Aigues-Mortes and Provence, in Marseilles, where the *viguier* [provost] had been informed by the messengers of the bailiff of Bourges.[134]

Others advanced in the direction of Guyenne; they passed to Limoges, entered onto the lands of the King of England, arriving in Bordeaux.[135] Simon de Montfort, the Count of Leicester and brother-in-law of Henry III, controlled this country; he ordered them to withdraw, threatening to be at their heels with his knights and the militia of Bordeaux. They were dispersed at once; their chief, having wanted to take the sea, was recognized by the crew of his boat for an accomplice of the Master of Hungary and thrown into the Gironde, feet and wrists tied together. In the popular imagination, he was an ally of the infidels, and Mathieu de Paris says in good faith that they found in his baggage money, poisons in powder form, and letters from the Sultan.[136]

The fate of the Pastoureaux was no better in England. One their chiefs disembarked in Shoreham and had collected around him five hundred poor wretches, shepherds, ploughmen, pig-keepers, herdsmen, and other people of this species. But soon it was learned that the Pastoureaux were excommunicated, that the Master of

Hungary and his lieutenant had perished, one in Berry, the other in Gascogne, and that their troops were dispersed. This audacious man who had crossed the sea to gain for his cause a new kingdom, tried to preach, but his listeners rose against him and forced him to seek refuge in a wood, where he was seized and cut to pieces.[137] Henry III had no desire to allow this new sort of plague to flourish in his domains; on 8 July 1251, he commanded the guard of the Cinque-Ports that if bands of Pastoureaux formed in his jurisdiction, they had orders to immediately cross the English Channel and leave England without delay. In the event of resistance, he would call to his assistance the Viscount of Kent. The Viscounts of London and all the kingdom accepted similar orders for the repression of this dangerous movement.[138]

A certain number of Pastoureaux, recognizing the vanity of their enterprise, took up the cross, placing their hands between those who had the right to grant it, and voyaged to aid Louis IX in the Holy Land.[139] It was all that remained of this spontaneous crusade, formidable at its beginnings, and on which Blanche of Castile had, says one, hoped to raise in the East the fortunes of her son.

One can hardly explain the patience with which Blanche tolerated the devastations of the Pastoureaux for some time. Should it be believed that age and sorrow had ended up prevailing over her firmness, or that, discouraged from seeing her son abandoned by the Church and by *les grands*, she counted on the chances of this enterprise without hope, tried in favor of Louis IX by the poorest people of the kingdom? This assumption itself has only a poor probability, because such a failure had been in contradiction to the instinct for authority which was the dominating feature of Blanche's character. Until the end of her life, she remained as she had always been, an active woman, energetic, a Queen both severe and right, who wanted to do everything by herself, and intended nothing to be neglected unless it acted to maintain the rights and majesty of the Crown.

Even during the hard years of the crusade, her court appears to have remained as it had been in happier days. Blanche kept the house of France in a dignified status. She gave hospitality to her small niece, Marie, Empress of Constantinople, received in Pontoise the visit of the King of Navarre, whom she formerly protected, treated the brother of the King of England with a munificence which astonished foreigners.[140] During Lent of 1250, Richard de Cornouailles crossed to

France to be near the Pope; he had with him his wife Sanche de Provence, sister of Queen Marguerite, his oldest son, forty knights equipped with the greatest luxury, accompanied by a crowd of carts, fifty horses, and a great number of servants. Richard found a most flattering reception from the Regent; she gave them rich presents, treated the Count de Cornouailles as a relative, almost as a son.[141] Blanche had a hundred reasons to devote expensive generosity to this first cousin who was a rich and powerful lord, the son of a king. I do not know if she often had grandchildren with her; she undoubtedly had them raised in the Louvre, since Innocent IV, in 1252, wrote that the *châtelain* of this fortress had the care of the children of the King of France.[142]

Her relationship with nobility had little interest. The great barons could not think anymore of revolting, and all the lords remained, as regards the Crown, in their natural rapport. Blanche was sometimes named in charters by which nobles made acts of vassalage.[143] She entrusted the guard of Sablé and three other castles to knights of the Lady of Craon, against commitment to return them, if they were required, to the Queen or the Count d'Anjou.[144] Among the great fiefs, only one was in circumstances able to cause Blanche serious concerns.

The oldest son of Marguerite le Noire, Guillaume de Dampierre, who carried while his mother lived the title of Count de Flandre, died in a tournament, shortly after having returned from crusade. Guy, his younger brother, was admitted by the Queen to make an oath of fidelity for Flanders; in February 1252, he came to Paris to engage himself to fulfill towards the Crown all the obligations that fell to his house.[145] But at the same time with a new gravity there appeared difficulties born of antagonism between Avesnes and Dampierre. On 11 July, the King of the Romans, Guillaume of Holland, accepted vassalage from Jean d'Avesnes, his brother-in-law, to the detriment of Marguerite and Guy de Dampierre, the fiefs that the house of Flanders held from the Empire.[146] Jean d'Avesnes broke his word, thus renewing some old quarrels, because he had come to Paris, in November 1248, with his brother Baudouin, promising to observe the arbitration deal made in 1246 with Louis IX and the legate of the Holy See.[147] War began, and Marguerite, seeing that all was called into question, went to find Blanche. She begged her, as cousin and vassal, to support her in her rights. Blanche was at this moment weakened enough by disease to not be able to occupy herself with such a serious question. She directed Marguerite to the counts of Poitiers and Anjou. These two princes were then at Saint-Germain-en-Laye, where Count Alphonse was ill; they did not supply the Countess of Flanders with anything but an evasive answer. Seeing this, Marguerite took matters separately to the Count d'Anjou, and made him an offer of the county of Hainaut, to engage him in her interests.[148] Charles could not give this business much attention until after the death of his mother. This circumstance is almost the only one where Blanche gave to others the authority to settle an important matter.

For the rest, she did not lack good servants; in many cases, I see her surrounded by her council, of which the composition could vary, though certain people had almost always formed part of it. At Vernon, on 8 April 1252, she held court, having around her the bishops of Bayeux, Lisieux, Évreux, Séez, Coutances, and the Countesses of Boulogne and of Ponthieu, the abbots of Saint-Riquier, Saint-Victor de Paris, bailiffs of Caen, Amiennsss, Vermandois, and several of her ordinary advisers, among them the *panetier* Geoffroy de Chapelle and the deacon of Saint-Aignan d'Orléans.[149]

Her council was fewer when, on 23 February of the same year, she publicly reserved the rights of her sons Alphonse and Charles to the succession of Jeanne de Boulogne, daughter of Philippe Hurepel and widow of Gaucher de Châtillon, while putting under the King's authority any litigious consequences of this succession.[150]

Blanche also appears in the royal council, when the bourgeois of Paris and masters of the Université came to swear oaths (19 June 1251) to her. The bourgeois swore to keep peace in the city, to obey the Queen and her representatives, not to conceal what was necessary in testimony against the authors of crimes committed in Paris, to denounce secret criminals and disturbers of the peace to those who would keep their city under the name of the Queen. By requiring this oath, Blanche did not take a superfluous precaution; the recent disorders which were produced in Paris, in the passing of the Pastoureaux, justified serious precautions. The same day, masters of the Université appeared in their turn before the Queen and the royal council, and read the oaths they were held to make from all of their colleagues and students. The bishop, an official and chancellor of the church of Paris, denounced before clergy and laymen, men or women, anyone of bad morals who would disturb the public peace or studies; the masters engaged not to claim as being students the people found guilty of frequent quarrels, of abduction, infraction, vagrancy, flight, armed robbery, or homicide. Moreover, the Queen took a series of provisions which, while respecting a certain measure of privileges for the University, would be used as a guarantee against excesses that abuse of these freedoms had too often engendered.[151] For twenty-two years, Blanche had not changed her relationship with the students; she wanted respect, order, and in the schools they hardly helped; turbulence remained the rule in the Université; the Pope himself had to prevail, at this same time, against students who carried weapons.[152]

Among members of the royal council, one sees in their number Philippe Berruyer, Archbishop of Bourges, the bishops of Evreux and Orléans, the *panetier* Geoffroy de Chapelle, Guy de Chevreuse, one of those whom Blanche had sent to take possession of the Toulouse succession, Pierre d'Ernencourt, one of the most active agents of royal administration, the Deacon of Saint-Aignan d'Orleans, Étienne de Sancerre; but this presents a difficulty. When the acts of the Regent are studied, it is sometimes difficult to know if one is in the presence of the royal council properly speaking, or of the Parlement. Those who composed the first jurisdiction of the kingdom appear in several documents where this jurisdiction was not named, and not necessarily being judicial documents. It may be that delimitation of capacities and functions had not always been definitely established; nothing prevented a king, a regent, from having recourse successively to the same men as political advisers, as businessmen, or as judges.

The role of the Parlement was consequently rather considerable, and enumeration of some affairs, brought before it, can give an idea of its activity. On 13 February 1250, "at the court of the king, in Paris," the bishop and bourgeois of Châlons, in a lawsuit about the weavers of this city, finished their disagreement by an accord, "at the day which was assigned to them by the Queen on several disputes"; we still have the depositions of the witnesses produced by the bishop against the bourgeois, and the role of guarantors provided by the weavers who were in prison.[153] In 1251, another agreement put an end to the lawsuit of Hugues Tirel, Lord of Poix, against the mayor and the commune of this locality; it had been judged "in the court of the King" that Lord Imbert de Temploi would make an investigation in Poix; it transcribed the charter by which various people notified Blanche and her council of the agreement that occurred in their presence.[154] In September 1252, a similar Parlement in Pontoise noted an agreement between the Abbey of Saint-Éloi and the commune of Noyon; the intervention of the Queen was stipulated in this act, made before "the masters of the court of the king" and transcribed "in the register of the King."[155] On 22 November 1252, "when the illustrious Queen Blanche, of good memory, still lived," the prior of Saint-Martin-des-Champs and the provosts of Paris appeared before the advisers of the King. "The aforementioned advisers, after terms of the act, were in the cabinet of the royal palace, close to the court, opposite the door of the King." The lawsuit finished only the following 25 February, "in Parlement."[156] These acts, and an award, delivered to Melun on 25 June 1251, prove that this Parlement followed the Queen, at least in certain cases.[157]

The majority of investigations in lawsuits before Parlement or other royal jurisdictions were in the name of Blanche; inquiries made in Falaise by the bailiff of Rouen; inquiries between the Countess d'Artois and the solicitor of Béthune; inquiries of Pierre d'Ernencourt and Etienne, Deacon of Saint-Aignan d'Orléans, to know if clothiers of Paris had the right to hold open shop during the fair of Lendit.[158] Blanche pronounced, in August 1249, an agreement between the abbots of Cluny and Sainte-Genevieve; it was before her that a lawsuit relating to the Viscount de Turenneis was finished with an award, in Parlement.[159] An examination of all these acts appears to show that the intervention of the Regent in legal affairs was not purely nominal.

Bailiffs and the seneschals, who were not hesitant in addressing Blanche, even at the time when she was not Regent, were from 1248 to 1252 her faithful agents and sometimes her advisers. One finds several bailiffs with her in Vernon; the seneschal of Carcassonne addressed a report to her on the rights that the Viscount of Béziers possessed in the town of Albi; it was by order of Blanche and Alphonse de Poitiers that Pierre de Voisins, seneschal of Alphonse in Toulouse, enjoined the Count de Comminges to give his daughter to him.[160]

The temperament and the feelings of Blanche are especially put in light, during the second regency, by her relationship with the clergy. The ministers for religion too often had a tendency not to take account of royal prerogatives; in this case, Blanche was inflexible, required the submission of those who, in spite of the sacred character of their function, were only subjects. Her relationship with the Holy See was always correct, pleasant even; however Innocent IV did not make the mistake of loading her with complaints, when he believed that she wronged the Church. It was thus that in 1251 he transmitted to her the complaints of Danish prelates about the right of toll that royal agents had habitually levied on clerics, pilgrims, and scholars of their nation come to France.[161]

In the high clergy of her kingdom, Blanche found many devoted servants and several of her ordinary advisers. She treated them with favor, witnessed by the Bishop of Paris, to whom she lent money to help pay the debts of his church; but there was not an archbishop, bishop, prelate, even among the privileged people, who was exempted from fulfilling his duties towards the Crown; Blanche, like her son, held absolutely to the rights of the sovereign over the churches, advowsons of ecclesiastical dignities or of vacant benefices, oaths of fidelity required of the bishops and the abbots, permission to proceed with elections given by the King to the chapters and convents, *saisie de la régale* [royal right to revenue from vacant bishoprics], or of the perceived ecclesiastical incomes between election and confirmation of an archbishop, bishop, or head of a monastery subjected to this right.[162] In these kinds of questions, Blanche was just and benevolent, but did not leave anything to chance. The bishop elect of Soissons, archdeacon and procureurs of the chapter, had come to Paris to declare before the Queen that in their church the collation of prebends, vacant at that time, did not belong to the King, but the Queen and Parlement opposed them in formal denial, and obliged them to submit.[163]

The restitution of *régale* being a gracious act on behalf of the King, Blanche might grant an answer to a request conceived in most respectful terms.[164] In January 1252, at Maubuisson, four bishops attested in the presence of Pierre Lamballe, archbishop elect of Tours, asking the Regent to return to him certain incomes; the Queen having agreed to it, he answered: "Madam, we extremely thank you for this good deed, and for all the others which we await from you."[165] Her provost, the senior and the chapter of the church of Soissons demanded twice that *régale* be restored to their elected bishop; after a first failure, they address the Queen again, "on bended knees."[166] The Pope knew that in these kinds of questions he did not have influence enough to put forward, and Blanche was already gone, when on 7 December 1252, being unaware of her death, he requested her to give *régale* to the Bishop of Téronanne.[167]

The rights of the Crown, in these matters, was well

established, but on other questions there could emerge, between the royal power and ecclesiastical authority, serious difficulties. It was especially in connection with conflicts over jurisdiction that there appeared antagonism of the civil and the religious powers; yielding to their natural inclination, obeying their interests, perhaps gained from doctrines which Emperor Frederick II had been the most famous and more violent defender, the lay subjects of Louis IX, in very great numbers, by no means hid their irritation against the encroachments more or less proven when they reproached the churches.[168] The nobility was at the head of this movement which, sometimes slowed down, began again without warning, and with various recoveries, since the beginning of the century, in consideration of the great barons of France confederating against the clergy. Their hostility appeared under the second regency of Blanche with a new roughness; it was to some extent a general war, whose episodes were sometimes long and impassioned, as for example the quarrel between the Archbishop and the Viscount de Narbonne, in which Blanche, in her capacity as Regent, found fray. In the middle of the thirteenth century, *les grands*, the lords, were not the only ones fighting against the rights or the legal claims of the churches; inhabitants of the cities were following their example, so that the Council of Valence, in 1248, condemned the leagues and the brotherhoods trained by the bourgeois and the nobles to fight with the clerics. We come to see that during the rising of the Pastoureaux, people in cities allowed all kinds of violence against the clergy, and never came to help them very much; they had not seen themselves as threatened. In 1252, Pope Innocent IV intervened, in France, in favor of the clerics; he fought with energy the authors of fines or contrary statutes to the privileges of the clergy; but while condemning facts and tendencies that he found reprehensible and dangerous, he avoided, when he could, to enter in open fights with royal agents; this reserved attitude had sometimes cost him.

  In 1251, the Bishop of Laon complained to him about what Parlement and the bailiffs of the King, among others, made in illicit competition with his jurisdiction. On the occasion of these conflicts, they seized, he said, his goods and those of his clergy, his men and his servants. In answer to this complaint, Innocent IV ordered the deacon of Saint-Etienne de Troyes to prevail, when he would take place there, against the barons, bailiffs and other representatives of the temporal jurisdictions; he stated to him that no one was to cite in court any clergy of the diocese of Laon for the business of the churches and for personal actions.[169] I will not examine whether the Pope was right or wrong, but it is necessary to acknowledge that bailiffs and royal seneschals sometimes used, towards the churches, rather rigorous processes. Sometimes Innocent IV complained to Charles d'Anjou of how the seneschal of Carcassonne put his hands on castles formerly yielded by Louis IX to the predecessor of the Archbishop of Narbonne; sometimes he charged this Archbishop and the Bishop of Elne to engage royal officers with moderation, who, under various pretexts, maltreated the churches.[170] It was in the prayer of the Bishop of Albi that, on 18 May 1252, he enjoined the Archbishop d'Auch to employ ecclesiastical censures to put the agents of the crown at reason.[171]

An example that I give will however shows that in certain cases the royal power was in its right. One knows that the clergy of France had granted to Louis IX a tenth on the occasion of his crusade; however the abbot and the convent of Cluny allowed the arrival the end of 1251 or the beginning of 1252 without being discharged themselves from this obligation towards the crown. This not very excusable negligence ended up being expensive; while the abbot was in England, the bailiff of Mâcon, without having, it appears, received any special order from the Regent, seized the château de Lourdon, which belonged to the abbey of Cluny. Innocent IV believed it his duty to protest against this process; he claimed an evacuation of the castle from Louis IX, from Blanche of Castile, wrote the Archbishop of Bourges, who however was one of the principal advisers of the Crown, to pronounce, in the event of refusal, an interdict against the château de Lourdon and all those who held it, kept it, or lived in it. However, he had the care to stipulate that this sentence could reach neither the King, nor his mother, nor his brothers.[172] Blanche did not yield; the abbot of Cluny returned to possession of his castle only at the price of heavy sacrifices; but the measure of coercion taken against him was not merited, and the Pope would have perhaps done better not to support parties until the end who had owed something. After the death of Blanche, at the proper time he claimed compensation for the abbot of Cluny, based on how the Regent had ordered compensation on goods to which she had done wrong.[173] I like to believe that the children of Blanche did not take any account of this inadmissible claim.

Blanche, once engaged in conflict, did not like to yield, and her officers were not more accommodating than her, as could be noted with the monks of Lire on the occasion of their difficulties with the royal abbey of Maubuisson.[174] However, it would be very unjust to represent the Regent as absolutely opposite to any idea of conciliation.[175] The year of her death, she gave a proof of moderation while intervening, at the request of the Pope, between Eudes Rigaud, Archbishop of Rouen, and the bailiff of Caux. This officer refused to deliver to the archiepiscopal prison those of his prisoners who were free of the ecclesiastical jurisdiction; Blanche promised to give orders for them to be conducted by the bailiff or his sergeants, but at the expense of the Archbishop, during a limited time, and without damage to royal rights.[176]

But it was not necessary for the clergy, defending their interests, to show disrespect, because Blanche of Castile was decidedly not going to tolerate insolent resistance. The chapter of Paris arrested *en masse* the men of Orly, Châtenay, and some other villages of which it was the *seigneur*, undoubtedly because they had refused to be subjected to the payment of the *taille* [tithe]. They were imprisoned in the house of the chapter, and they remained there in such a state of destitution, "that they were also as unto dying." When the Queen learned of it, she humbly requested the canons deliver them, saying that she would readily investigate this business; but the canons answered her that she did not have to interfere with their serfs and their villains, "of whom they could take and kill and make such justice as they would like." They went further and, to be avenged for the complaints that the prisoners had deposed to the Queen against them, they locked up with the prisoners their wives and their children; these unhappy people "were so distressed by the heat one after the other, that several died from it." The Queen had great pity for these people, "who were so tormented by those who were supposed to help them;" she ordered her knights and bourgeois to take up arms, come to the prison of the chapter, and demand its men force the gate, and struck the first blow with a baton she had in her hand; the door was opened at once, the prisoners put outside; Blanche took them under her guard and, to punish the canons, confiscated their temporal revenue.[177]

The historian to whom we owe this account, adds that she kept the goods of the chapter in her control until full satisfaction and that the serfs delivered by it were freed with the help of the payment of an annual right, but we know from another source that Blanche, after having filled her duty of sovereign while helping people who were her subjects, took care not to strike as a blind man the canons who stood her at defiance. She so mastered herself that instead of seeking to make them expiate their control, she ordered, shortly after, the bishops of Paris, Orleans, and Auxerre, to make an investigation to know if the people of Orly owed, yes or no, the *taille* to the chapter. The interested parties had accepted this mediation before a representative of the Queen and in presence of her council, and royal justice was then so not very partial that, on 1 December 1252, at the moment when Blanche came to be deposited in the tomb, the three bishops restored to the chapter the right to tax people in Orly for the business of the church of Paris, and not only for the military service which they owed the crown.[178]

It was necessary, in this affair, for a cause which Blanche particularly had to heart. She was interested in these populations to which their servile condition sometimes rendered their lives quite harshly. This excess of inequality shocked her, "and as this Queen had pity on people who were serfs, she ordered in several places they be freed on paying rights. She partly did it because of pity that she had for girls of this condition, for no one would have them in marriage, and having been spoiled."[179] Royalty, which marched then at the head of all progress, accomplished a wise act of policy and filled a duty to humanity by drawing the serfs from their lamentable situation. It was from the example of the King of France and various prelates that in 1247 the Bishop of Paris, Guillaume d'Auvergne, sage, a friend of Blanche, requested the Pope to help gain manumission for the serfs of Wissous.[180] His project, of which the execution was undoubtedly blocked by the chapter of Notre-Dame, was not carried out until 1255, but Blanche, in this work of justice and charity that she had undertaken, did not let herself yield to difficulties.[181] She liked the humble, for whom her throne was the only recourse; she had compassion for their sufferings, and they always found her ready to help them. In March 1252 she ratified an act by which the abbot and the convent of Saint-Maur-des-Fossés freed, for 2,100 *livres parisis*, the entire population of serfs, men, women and children, which they owned in Saint-Maur-des-Fossés, in Paris, in Varenne-Saint-Maur, and in Chennevières.[182]

The care and defense of the weak, more than anything else, could distract and comfort Blanche of Castile in the midst of sorrows which obscured her last days. This intrepid woman, dominated unceasingly by the noblest of ambitions, would have been able to find that, in spite of her age and disease, her place was still quite beautiful, if she had only been Queen; but she was a mother, and that was what made her suffer. After the tirednesses and the tribulations of her life, she would have deserved two rewards, to govern the kingdom in peace and to see her son again; this second satisfaction was not granted to her. The King did not speak of return; he appeared so distant that one assumed of him even, wrongly undoubtedly, an intention to finish his days in the Holy Land; and what was the profit of this sacrifice?[183] One moment he had hoped that the alliance of Muslims in Egypt would enable him to reconquer the Kingdom of Jerusalem; then events over which he could do nothing had destroyed this illusion.[184] Despite everything, he still remained, always awaiting relief from the Occident, pressing Henry III to finally carry out his vow for crusade, and receiving, in answer to his calls, only egoist protestations. In June 1252, Henry wrote to Louis IX and Queen Marguerite, to demand once more the French provinces that his father had lost; at this price he was prepared to begin his departure.[185] Undoubtedly he exempted himself from addressing these interested requests to Blanche, because he knew the scorn that she would not fail to heap on them; as for the account which says Louis IX, without consulting *les grands* of his kingdom, would have promised to restore Normandy and the other fiefs of Plantagenets, it can be only the echo of false or exaggerated gossip.[186]

Thus Louis IX, deaf to the calls of his mother, remained in the Orient.[187] Torments and mournings followed one another for Queen Blanche with a rigor which tried but failed to discourage her; after her sisters, it was her nephew Ferdinand III, King of Castile, who died on 30 May 1252, carrying to his tomb the hope that perhaps she would see him take up arms for the Holy Land.[188] She still had her daughter, Princess Isabelle, her niece, the Empress of Constantinople, Marie de Brienne, her two sons Alphonse and Charles. But Charles d'Anjou was absorbed in negotiations by Innocent IV for the Kingdom of Sicily; Alphonse de Poitiers was ill; he had, they say, paralysis, and we know that about this time his sight was threatened.[189] Hardly well, he again took up the cross.[190] Blanche, as a mother who always sacrificed, could wish that the Count de Poitiers was going to join his brother in Syria; but with what emotion did she see the approach of this new separation? The crusade, which had removed Robert d'Artois from her, which in her old age condemned her to live without Louis IX and would martyr her with ceaseless concerns, was still going to involve the son which remained to her. Human power has limits; Blanche succumbed.

It was in Melun, when about November 1252 the heart disorder of which she suffered suddenly took on such a serious character that she had to be transported in all haste to Paris.[191] She lay down never to rise.[192] Having premonitions of death, she had set her affairs in order, and prescribed that, at the expense of her personal fortune, all those were compensated to whom she had wronged.[193] Then she forgot her life of tirednesses and pains to think no more; at rest in another existence.

Five or six days before her end, she received communion by Renaud de Corbeil, Bishop of Paris, and the same day she accepted from his hand the garb of a Cistercian, which the nuns wore in Maubuisson. To the bishop, on imposing these poor garments on her, she told him she would keep them on if she suddenly died, declaring she wanted to be a nun in life and in death; and indeed, as from this hour, she was, until her last sigh, like the humblest of her sisters, under the obedience of the abbess of Maubuisson. After she had accepted the last sacraments, those who surrounded her, seeing that she had lost speech and appeared at an end, transferred her onto a bed furnished with straw that had been covered in simple serge. Priests and clerics who assisted believed her dead and kept silence, when suddenly, in a weak and low voice, she recited prayers for the dying: "*Subvenite sancti Dei*; come to my help, saints of the Lord!" They followed her; but she had hardly murmured between her teeth five or six verses, when her spirit left her."[194]

It was the 26th or 27th of November 1252, probably in the evening, that Blanche of Castile found in death a peace of which her life had almost always been deprived.[195] She had lived a little less than sixty-five years. She was covered in royal vestments; on her nun's veil they placed the crown of a queen, and Blanche of Castile was carried, on a litter decorated in gold by her sons and the greatest lords of her court, through the streets of Paris, then to the abbey of Saint-Denis. The bier was deposited in the chorus of the church and enlightened with a quantity of candles. They stood watch over the body of Blanche during the whole night. Finally, on the morning of 29 November, after the Mass and offices for the dead, the funeral procession, with crosses and processions which accompanied it, took the road to Maubuisson. A service was celebrated (29 November) in the church of this abbey.[196] Blanche had reached her last residence.

Above the vault in which her body was deposited, they built, in the chorus of the nuns, a tablet of copper approximately two feet in height, decorated with an epitaph and bearing a carved image of the Queen, in the habit and coat of a nun, a crown on her head and supported by two angels.[197] On 13 March of the following year, the heart of Blanche was carried solemnly from Maubuisson to the abbey of Lys, close to Melun, by Countess Alix de Mâcon, whom Blanche had made abbess of this convent.[198]

The Regent was in the tomb for a long time, when the news of her death came to Jaffa, where Louis IX was. It was the legate of the Holy See, Eudes de Châteauroux who, accompanied by the Archbishop of Tyr and Geoffroy de Beaulieu, confessor of the King, took care to apprize the son of Blanche that the greatest and surest affection was removed from him. Upon the first words, Louis IX could not restrain his lamentations; then, falling to his knees, he accepted, with humble and grateful thanksgivings, the blow that struck him down.[199] But his pain was so deep that during the following days one could not speak to him. Finally, he sent for Lord de Joinville and, as soon as he saw him, embraced him: "Ah! seneschal, I lost my mother!" - "Sire," he answered as a good and hard soldier, "It does not astonish me, because she was to die; but I am astonished that you, who are a wise man, showed so deep a mourning; you know that saying of the sage, for any sorrow that man has in the heart, nothing must appear on his face; because it makes his enemies merry and embarrasses his friends." For Queen Marguerite, who cried, this man, who had a good heart but frankness of speech, held out consolations of another kind: "This was the woman whom you hated most who died, and you show so much mourning!" - "And she said to me," adds Joinville, "that it was not for the Queen that she cried, but for the sorrow which the King in mourning had showed, and for his daughter who remained in the guard of men."[200] Here, it is necessary to acknowledge, a little summary funeral oration, and many people in France had to find something moreover to say when they learned that their great Queen was taken from them. Services that her son made in the Holy Land, the prayers which he sent to ask for her in the churches, would not have caused Blanche as much satisfaction as the regrets of her subjects. For the majority of them, she remained "the wise one, the valiant one, the good Queen of France," and many could have subscribed to this judgment of an eloquent simplicity: "Her death troubled the humble folk, because she pressed the rich and upheld justice."[201]

All historians of the time honored Blanche of Castile, and since then, through the ages, in spite of all the divergences of opinions, public recognition rewarded only insufficiently the services that she rendered, expressed in splendid praises; but more than all the words, a simple expression of this fact can immortalize her memory. The action of Blanche on men and events was personal, decisive. One can say that all was called in question following even the triumphs gained by Philippe Auguste, when he made her Queen of France, content in dying to leave a whole family to raise, entrusting the government of the kingdom to her. How the people then wished for his loss and counted on his failures! But Blanche was of strong race; she had already proven reliable at a time when prince Louis fought in England for a desperate cause; she was raised by Philippe Auguste, the guardian of this royal heritage and this tradition of the Conqueror. Stronger from all that she had learned from studying this great prince, assisted well by the servants he had gathered, knowing at bottom the resources and the dangers of her situation, she accepted the fight; it was a war of royalty against great feudality, of order against anarchy, of freedoms then possible against oppression, of progress and civilization against brutal and retrograde ambitions. This war was worth the sorrow to be fought, and she disdained defeat; elsewhere, the children of Blanche were there; they had to be defended.

In various degrees, with more or less violence or cheating, the large feudatories, once overcome, had a horror of royal power. The high clergy, too often torn between practices of devotion to the Crown and a natural aversion for the prevalence of civil authority, promised much useful cooperation, but foresaw threats of opposition. But people of the cities and the countryside placed their hopes in royalty, which, while showing itself sometimes severe and even harsh, was their only defense. Blanche fought the great vassals, who were almost always against her, supervised the clergy, among whom she found representatives of faithful and intelligent collaboration, applied herself to the people, who liked her, defended her, and did not separate from her on the rare corrections she had to inflict on them. Furthermore, in France there were regions where everyone, large and small, were for her and her son, the old royal domain and also possessions of certain churches, certain abbeys. As for the great lords, she found a way to divide them, to arm one against the others, to combine with anyone who the day before was her adversary.

As a practitioner of a system, while bringing it into play, following circumstances, the flexibility of her spirit and the tenacity of her character, she dissolved coalitions of the great, thwarted their plots, reduced the Count of Brittany and defended the Crown against a formidable league under Thibaud de Champagne, her inconstant admirer. The English, descending upon France to profit from our discords, were set at a distance, and their invasion reduced to useless comings and goings. During the bad years, Blanche was everywhere; she led the armies, made camp with the troops, and besieged castles, only quitting an enemy to run after another. In the midst of this storm, she still found the means to overpower the Count de Toulouse, and to put an end to the war of the Albigensians by the Treaty of Paris, ensuring the Crown a great part of Languedoc, and making what remained of it the heritage of a son of France. When the danger decreased, she married Louis IX to the daughter of the Count de Provence, and extended the influence of France by this marriage to the left bank of the Rhône. She struck a last blow against the Count of Brittany, still inflicted salutary lessons on the turbulent Thibaud IV, whose several fiefs passed under the direct control of the Crown, then, gradually, without trauma, she gave power to the most admirable prince that the Christian Middle Ages knew.

The education of Saint Louis alone, for Blanche of Castile, would be a more than sufficient claim to fame. Those of her children that death did not remove at too early an hour were, a skilful administrator who knew to how to make of Languedoc a French province, another this conqueror of whom ignorant or partial critics wanted to see the defects, but that all Frenchmen should love for having carried well beyond our borders the arms and fame of France. Her daughter Isabelle was a saint. Her court was distinguished among all by order, the spirit of harmony, and inalterable affection which reigned between royal family members, between masters and servants. She expended enough sums to cut a fine figure, but without extravagance; it is enough to glance at the accounts of this noble house to see in which place charity held for her. Blanche, who traversed France in all directions, went nowhere without giving alms; when she arrived in a place, the poor who had not, on the royal path, received money, came to her court at a castle, in her room, to ask for bread. Hadn't the King who she had raised, although not able to go himself, searched to the ends of the kingdom for all those to whom his grandfather, his father, and his agents had done wrong?

Such was the spectacle offered by the royal house during the time of the first regency. Things did not change when Blanche left power. Elsewhere, she was not retired from activity; she remained mixed up in all affairs, responsible for the most serious interests. After 1236, as before, she judged, managed, worked for France, and, in the most critical moments, it was towards her that one turned to naturally. The repression of insurrection led by Trencavel and the defeat of the dissolved coalition after the Battle of Saintes was mainly her work. In the eyes of the French and foreigners alike, she was always the Queen of France, and this was only just, because soon enough she had to resume government of this kingdom again, of which she safeguarded the size and independence.

The last years of her life, during which she suffered so much, completed her glory. Left alone after the departure of Louis IX for the Holy Land, she returned to work, having for a distraction her fears and sorrows without truce, having no reward other than the feeling of her utility, without any hope other than peace and happiness for France. While unceasingly preparing reinforcements and money which her son needed, she prevented the resumption of hostilities with England, ensured the Count de Poitiers the succession of Toulouse, taking care of the interests of her children apart from the kingdom. Horrible news, come from Egypt, struck her heart but did not cut her down; after this blow, to which another would have succumbed, she continued to go, bearing her sufferings proudly, preserving a strong heart in an exhausted body. Majestic and charitable, she imposed on all, even to the representatives of the Church, respect for the Crown, and showed unhappy serfs, by drawing them from prison, in freeing them, that the most humble, in the Kingdom of France, could always count on protection from the sovereign.

Concurrently in their history, great kings and great queens have almost always made legends. Blanche of Castile had one, a legend born of jealousy which sought to make her odious, derived from impotent wrath directed against her in revolts that were put down. The students, whom she repressed in their vagrancy and disordered imaginations, comforted in their mishaps by giving her a lover in the Cardinal of Saint-Ange. Partisans of Pierre of Brittany and the English diverted themselves much at the expense of her alleged affair with Count Thibaud; and since, without claiming to make him wrong, many people, amateurs of more or less gracious anecdotes, found time to transform her into the heroin of a novel.

When these interested calumnies spread themselves for the first time, Blanche, at least forty years old at the time, surrounded by her children, fought in the midst of a kingdom afflicted with civil war, invaded by foreigners. To support herself in the middle of innumerable dangers and concerns, she had only the feeling of crushing responsibility, joined to the ambition of a prince when he carries out a great war, when he fights for the throne or for his life. At the moment when they believed her close to succumbing, her enemies could be forgiven for assuming she had been skilful enough to attach herself to a great lord, who was at the same time her relative and vassal.

One would also be wrong to represent Blanche as a woman dominated in all circumstances by conventual concerns. She was undoubtedly pious, as much and more as any princess of this era; her alms, her foundations, her generosity towards the churches, calm and touching enthusiasm of her last moments, suggested the sincerity of her Christian feelings. But she never sacrificed the dignity of the secular power to the interests of the Church, and if Louis IX had taken her advice, he would not have left France, which needed him, for the Holy Land, which he could not save. Her conscience, however delicate, would never make it necessary to return the English provinces whose conquest had been more than legitimate. Innocent IV, whom she pledged to defend, did not involve her in his fight against Frederick II, and despite the respect she demonstrated to the Pope, as to all the representatives of the Church, she did not want to allow the bishops and the priests of her kingdom to forget that they owed obedience to the King.

Endowed with a will before which all were to submit, arrogant when they sought to humble her, and sometimes too prompt to fly into a passion, she lost dignity, charity, and justice, when she made malicious and pitiless quarrels with her daughter-in-law Marguerite de Provence. Marguerite, who was a respectful wife and sometimes devoted to the point of heroism, suffered more torments under the Queen than she deserved. Blanche feared that this new person would steal away her influence? Was she simply irritated about having to divide with another person the love of her son? There are things that can be explained, but which cannot be excused.

She had however, an excellent heart. Faithful in her affections, always happy when she could help, the tenderness that she displayed to the King her son and to her other children could not fault the maternal feelings she had for the children and the grandchildren of her sisters. She treated as a son her nephew Alphonse of Portugal, as a daughter her niece Marie de Brienne. Devoted to her sisters, to her cousin Blanche of Navarre, the mother of Thibaud de Champagne, she forgave him more then once for his not very loyal behavior, pulled Ferrand of Flanders from prison, relative of her sister, husband of a niece of Philippe Auguste, pardoned Raimond de Toulouse, son of her aunt Jeanne of England, but her feelings of family never pushed her to neglect the interests of France. She resisted all the claims, all the attacks of her cousins Henry III and Richard de Cornouailles, treated them with courtesy in moments of calm, and for whom she was always, in the event of conflict between the two kingdoms, a keen adversary.

Her kindness, her recognition of Crown servants, extended to all members of the royal house, French or Spanish. They could, without wounding her, give her not very pleasant counsels, or even address her with unjust reproaches. One day when she prepared at great expense to leave on pilgrimage for Saint-Jacques de Compostelle, Bishop Guillaume d'Auvergne told her that it would be much better to give all this money to the Dominicans of Paris. She listened without ill humor, and accommodated herself to his advice.[202] And what must one think of the humble leniency with which this irreproachable mother received the admonition of a stupid monk, come to tell her that she was funding the debauchery of her son? Another ruler would have at the very least thrown him out; Blanche of Castile was too much above such an insinuation to become angry. It was very difficult to forgive, as she had often done to fallen adversaries, to show after victory that she was without resentment and could save, following their defeat, those whom she had been afraid of.

When one studies the history of the wars or the revolts which have disturbed France from the advent of Philippe Auguste to the middle of the thirteenth century, one is astonished how rare it is a question of the tyrant. Apart from cases of heresy, part of the hateful war of the Albigensians, for which the responsibility does not adhere to the kings France, the scaffold and the gibbet hardly applied except to criminals. They could have had recourse to more or less summary executions, whilst repressing rebellion of a city, or to put an end to excesses of armed bands; but in general they respected prisoners of war. As for the chiefs, even when they had been the worst of rebels, they never paid with their heads for rising against royal authority or for infidelity to the fatherland. The guiltiest and most harshly treated, Renaud de Boulogne, died in prison, at the same time as the Count of Flanders was liberated. Philippe Hurepel easily returned to grace, after having directed against Blanche the most dangerous of the coalitions; Thibaud de Champagne, more than once forgot the services he had received, and did not lose his fiefs; the Lord of Coucy and several others, against whom it had been necessary to lead armies to make them return to their duty, had not even been inconvenienced. There had been no torments for Pierre Mauclerc and Hugues de Lusignan, both guilty for having twice conspired with the English, for lying, for perpetually revolting against Blanche of Castile and Louis IX, and no prison, no exile for the proud and violent forces of Isabelle d'Angoulême. Blanche, who could push them out of her kingdom, throw them in dungeons, or send them to their deaths, found it natural to spare them. She did nothing but conform, in this as in so many other things, to the traditions always followed by Capétiens of the first race, which made France avoid spilling blood.

After the great crises, after alarming dangers, in the presence of more or less unforgivable crimes, the winner, to prevent the return of evil, has to necessarily choose between cruel repression and forgiveness. In other epochs, those who ruled our fathers applied, by principle, a system of rigor. An apology for the scaffold, on the whole, could well have its *raison d'être*, and, in a country transfigured by Richelieu, it would be at the very least imprudent to claim that political executions were never used for nothing. I will restrict myself to note, to the glory of Philippe Auguste, Blanche of Castile, and Saint Louis, that they never had recourse. Had their indulgence caused a weakening of royal authority, to compromise France in the maintenance of order and peace? Among these great lords that Blanche did not wish to strike, more had since then fought, in Egypt, beside Saint Louis; all finished, sooner or later, by being peaceful, returning to their role of feudatories. What would one have gained to persecute them or to make them perish? Blanche of Castile, whom her adversaries maltreated so much, was satisfied to overcome them; she was too strong not to scorn violence, which often comes from weakness, too skillful to needlessly persecute those from whom she had nothing more to fear. She left to her son examples of leniency; what she founded lasted, because she did not misuse her power, and acts of moderation ensured the durability of her work.

There are figures that the centuries do not manage to destroy;

they seem to grow as their entourage disappears by the fatal action of indifference and lapse of memory. Queen Blanche of Castile, who worked, fought, and suffered for old France, who Spain gave us for the triumph of civilization, was not foreign to anybody; even the ignorant know her name. This posthumous popularity, for which nobody knows the cause, but which no one thinks of disputing, is the reward for services that she rendered to her second fatherland.

1 *Layettes du Trésor des Chartes*, t. III, n. 3728, Paris, 13 November 1248; Ibid., 3754, Pontoise, March 1249.
2 Du Chesne, *Historiæ Francorum scriptores*, t. V, p. 412.
3 Mathieu de Paris, *Chronica majora*, t. V, p. 71.
4 Mathieu de Paris, t. V, p. 51.
5 Record office; Close rolls, 32nd year of Henry III, roll 62, membr. 5 *in dorso*; Close rolls, 62, membr. 4 r, 17 August 1248 : « *De navibus arestandis and galeya.* » ; Ibid., 3 r, 10 September 1248 : « *De navibus liberandis.* »
6 Mathieu de Paris, V, p. 23 and 51.
7 *Layettes*, t. 111, n. 3713; Lorris, 20 September 1248.
8 Rymer, ed. of 1816, t. I, p. 270 : « *De treuga cum Francia juranda.* »
9 Record office; Patent rolls, n. 58, membr. 5 r (above) : « *Pro Bartholomeo Pecche*; » 1 May 1249; Shirley, *Royal and other historical letters*, t. II, p. 52-53. Letter given in Paris on *veille de Pâques* [Easter Eve], without doubt in 1249.
10 Kymer, t. I, p. 271 (below); 23 December 1249.
11 *Saint Louis et Innocent IV*, in-8, p. 221-223.
12 Wallon, *Saint Louis et son temps*, t. I, p. 227; Guillaume de Nangis, *Vie de saint Louis* (*Historiens de France*, XX, p. 358); a French translation of this letter is given in Mathieu de Paris, *Additamenta*, t. VI, p. 163-165.
13 Mathieu de Paris, t. V, p. 70.
14 *Layettes*, t. III, 3720-3726, 26-28 October 1218; 3828; *Registres d'Innocent IV*, 4295, 9 January 1249; *Layettes*, III, 3781; 9 July 1249.
15 Boutaric, *Saint Louis et Alfonse de Poitiers*, p. 75.
16 Arch. Nat., J. 748, n. 17; accounts of Alphonse de Poitiers established 26 August 1249. « *Hoc sunt que debebat dominus comes anno et dio supradictis. — Domine regine, IIII IIII 1. par.* »
17 Huillard-Breholles, t. VI, 5th part, pp. 746-748, and 748-750; July 1249; *Layettes*, t. III, n. 3783; Lyon, July 1249; Guillaume de Nangis, *Vie de saint Louis* (*Historiens de France*, XX, p. 372; the same, *Chronique*, ed. Géraud, I, 204); Joinville, ed. of 1874, n. 179.
18 Arch. nat., 3. 748, n. 17; accounts of 26 August; *Layettes*, 3788, 13 August 1240; Layettes, 3789; 18 August 1249.
19 « *Blanchia... virili animo gubernante.* » E chronico Normanniæ (*Historiens de France*, XXIII, p. 214).
20 *Layettes*, 8802, testament of Raimond VII; see also 3672.
21 Guillaume de Puylaurens, *Historiens de France*, XX, 772.
22 Boutaric, *Saint Louis et Alfonse de Poitiers*, p. 70.
23 *Layettes*, 3812-3819; October 1249.
24 D. Vaissète, *Histoire de Languedoc*, t. VI, p. 809.
25 *Layettes*, III, 3829; oath of the comte de Comminges; see the testament and codicil of Raimond VII, *Layettes*, 3802-3803.
26 Catel, *Histoire des comtes de Tolose*, in-folio, 1623, p. 378; October 1249.
27 *Layettes*, III. 3829; 1 December 1249.
28 Catel, *Comtes de Toulouse*, p. 378; *Layettes*, 3830; 6 December 1249.
29 *Layettes*, 3831, 3832, 3839 to 3843, 3855, 3856.
30 *Layettes*, 3863; 4 April 1250.
31 *Layettes*, 3833 and 3845; 16 December 1249 and 3 February 1250.

32 Boutaric, *Saint Louis et Alfonse de Poitiers*, p. 74.
33 Muratori, *Antiquitates*, t. VI, col. 142, 9 March 1250.
34 D. Vaissète, ed. in-4, t. VI, p. 814.
35 *Layettes*, III, 3854; 1 March 1250; Boutaric, p. 74; letter of the Treasurer Saint-Hilaire de Poitiers.
36 This tempest struck on 23 May 1249.
37 Wallon, *Saint Louis et son temps*, t. I, p. 238-246.
38 « *Prout ex litteris ipsius filii nostri regis intelleximus.* » Mathieu de Paris, t. VI, p. 166.
39 Mathieu de Paris, t. VI, p. 152-154.
40 Mathieu de Paris, t. VI, p. 165-167.
41 Ibid., t. VI, p. 155 to 163; p. 167 and 169.
42 Mathieu de Paris, t.V, p. 110-117. I follow here the account of an English historian, without claiming to affirm that sums collected by Blanche were indeed disbursed; it seems that they had been able to simply give them to Templars against payment orders sent by them to their brothers in Syria. This idea comes naturally to mind when reading Delisle on the financial transactions of the Templars.
43 Guillaune de Nangis, *Vie de saint Louis*, *Historiens de France*, t. XX, p. 372.
44 Wallon, *Saint Louis et son temps*, t. I, p. 267-277.
45 Arch. nat., JJ 26, fol. 384 recto; March 1250.
46 Joinville, n. 244.
47 Wallon, t. I, p. 293-295.
48 Joinville, ed. of 1874, n. 308-310, 390-392.
49 Wallon, *Saint Louis et son temps*, t. I, p. 328.
50 Mathieu de Paris, t. V, p. 169.
51 Du Chesne, *Historiæ Francorum scriptores*, t. V, p. 413; 12 August 1250; Du Chesne, t. V, p. 415; Innocent IV to the Archbishop of Rouen and his suffragans.
52 *Saint Louis et Innocent IV*, p. 344; *Historiens de France*, t. XXI, p. 532-540; *Triennis and biennis decima ab anno MCCXLVII collecta.* The *biennis decima* was the new *dixième*, established for two years, the documents which concern this subsidy are quite numerous; I will cite here a letter of Innocent IV to Blanche: *Layettes*, III, 3924, 18 March 1251.
53 *Saint Louis et Innocent IV*, in-8, p. 223-227.
54 *Saint Louis et Innocent IV*, p. 345, note 1. Don Martin Fernandez de Navarrete, historian of the Spanish crusades, did not believe in this projected crusade of Ferdinand III : *Memorias de la real academia de la Historia*, t. V, Madrid, 1817; *Disertacion historica sobre la parte que tuvieron los Españoles en las guerras de ultramar o de las cruzadas*, p. 88, J 48.
55 See, for the details relative to this projected crusade of Henry III, *Saint Louis et Innocent IV*, in-8, p. 345-351.
56 Rymer (ed. of 1816), I, 272; 5 March 1250; Shirley, *Royal letters*, II, p. 59; 8 March 1250; Henry III to Blanche.
57 Joinville, n. 419.
58 Patent rolls, n. 60, membr. 12 recto (towards to top); 21 January 1251 : « *De dictatoribus treuge constituas.* » Rymer (1816), I, 277; 1 March 1251.
59 Shirley, *Royal letters*, t. II, p. 69; 6 January 1252.
60 Shirley, t. II, p. 81; 6 March 1252.

61 Shirley, t. II, p. 84; 1252, towards the middle of April.
62 Close rolls, n. 66, membr. 26 in dorso; 2 February 1252 : « *De quadam navi confracta in costera Sussexie.* »
63 Patent rolls, n. 6l, memb. 7 recto; 5 June 1252 : « *Pro Anselme de Trengniel et aliis ultramarinis.* » Cf. Shirley, II, p. 86-88; two letters patent of 6 June.
64 Close rolls, n. 67, membr. 26 in dorso; 23 November 1252 : « *De Guidone de Lezingn[iaco].* » Guy de Lusignan had received *en garde*, from Henry III, a part of the island of Oléron; Shirley, II, p. 85; 28 April 1252.
65 Joinville, nos. 407-409.
66 Bedr-eddyn Alaïny, *Le Collier de perles* (*Historiens des croisades* ; *historiens orientaux*, t. II, 1st part), p. 214.
67 "The King of France," says Bedr-cddyn Alaïny, "was placed in chains and conducted to the house occupied by the secretary of the divan, Fakr-eddyn Laan. The eunuch Sabih Almoaddhami was ordered to take care of him." *Le Collier de perles*, p. 110; see note 1.
68 Joinville, n. 419.
69 Du Chesne, t. V, p. 431 a : letter of Saint Louis to his subjects. Wallon, *Saint Louis et son temps*, t. I, p. 329.
70 Joinville, n. 436. Wallon, t. I, p. 330-334.
71 Wallon, p. 337.
72 Du Cange., ed. Joinville (1668), *Observations*, p. 384, and Du Chesne, t. V, p. 428; this letter, dated from Saint-Jean-d'Acre, in the month of August 1250, was dispatched by the King of France to Queen Blanche, who promulgated it in November, by letters patent given at Pontoise. Bibliothèque nationale, ms. latin 8865, fol. 188 r-189 v.
73 Du Chesne, t. V, p. 429 a.
74 Archives nationales, JJ. 26, fol. 349 r; Acre, July 1250. Martène, *Amplissima collectio*, t. I, col. 1306-1307.
75 Mathieu de Paris, V, p. 175.
76 Mathieu de Paris, p. 188-189. Mathieu speaks in several places of the project that had the Pope retire to the lands of the King of England (t. V, p. 112 and 118).
77 Idem, V, p. 203.
78 Idem, V, p. 146.
79 Joinville, n. 443; Michaud, *Bibliothèque des croisades*, t. IV, p. 448; Bedr-eddyn Alaïny, *Le Collier de perles* (*Historiens des croisades* ; *historiens orientaux*, t. II, 1st part), p. 201.
80 Villani recounted (liv. VI, chap. xxxvi) that upon learning of the defeat of Saint Louis, the Gibelins of Florence were filled with joy.
81 « *Stravit inimicum Christi, colubrem Fredericum* », says the epitaph of Innocent IV.
82 *Registres d'Innocent IV*, 5294 to 5298; 16 February 1251.
83 Le Nain de Tillemont, III, p. 423; *Layettes*, III, 3937, 7 May 1251; ibid., 3938, 10 May.
84 Le Nain de Tillemont, III, p. 425.
85 Layettes, III, 4036 ; Vincennes, January 1253. see also 4037 to 4039.
86 Potthast, *Regesta*, 14340; 21 June 1251.
87 *Layettes*, III, 3925; Charles d'Anjou à Saumur, 21 March 1251; 23 May 1251;

Boutaric, *Saint Louis et Alfonse de Poitiers*, p. 80-85. The conduct of Alphonse, in this affair, was scandalous.

88 *Registres d'Innocent IV*, 5329; 18 March 1251.

89 *Registres d'Innocent IV*, 5332; 24 March 1251.

90 D'Arbois de Jubainville, t. V, pièce 2971; 18 March 1251; *Registres d'Innocent IV*, 5337; 2 April 1251; *Saint Louis et Innocent* IV, p. 366-367.

91 29 March 1251; Mathieu de Paris, V, 239. This fact is not reported by other historians; I cannot regard it as absolutely certain.

     An assertion of Fontanieu, that I have no control of, would lead one to believe that in France they then sought to collect money by all means, to assist the King. Following a Norman chronicle that cites this scholar, Blanche would have taken a silver box in which the heart of Richard Cœur-de-Lyon, was kept locked up in the cathedral of Rouen (Bibliothèque nationale; Fontanieu, *Portefeuilles*, t. XL; *Cartulaire historique de saint Louis; des croisades. Remarques historiques sur les croisades, etc.*).

92 Annals of Burton (*Annales monastici*, ed. Luard, t. I, p. 296).

93 *Layettes du Trésor des Chartes*, III, 3956; 11 August 1251.

94 *Layettes*, III, 3960; 25 September 1251; Martène, *Thésaurus anecdotorum*, t. I, col. 1047; *ex autographe*; October 1251.

95 Mathieu de Paris, V, 259-261.

96 Mathieu de Paris, V, 248, « *post Pascha* » ; Easter fell, this year, on 16 April.

97 Mathieu de Paris, V, 246; *Chroniques de Saint-Denis, Historiens de France*, XXI, p. 115.

98 *Continuatio chronici S. Martini abbreviati*, *Monumenta Germaniæ*, scriptores, XXVI, p. 476; *Chronica minor auctore minorita Erphordiensi*, same collection, XXIV, p. 200; *Flores temporum auctore fratre ordinis Minorum*, ibid., p. 241; anonymous chronicle finished in 1286; *Historiens de France*, XXI, p. 83.

99 *Continuatio chronici S. Martini, loc. cit.*; *Chronicon Gaufridi de Collone, Historiens de France*, XXII, p. 3; Letter written to Adam de Marsh by the guardian of Franciscans of Paris, in the *Annals of Burton* (*Annales monastici*, ed. Luard, t. I, p. 290); cf. Denifle, *Chartularium Universitatis Parisiensis*, t. I, pièce 198; Mathieu de Paris, V, 246.

100 Mathieu de Paris, V, 246; *Chroniques de Saint-Denis* (*Historiens de France*, XXI, 115); Baudouin de Ninove, *Monumenta Germaniæ*, scriptores, XXV, p. 544; Mathieu de Paris, V, 247.

101 *Chronica minor*, etc. (*Monumenta Germaniæ*, scriptores, XXIV, 200); Mathieu de Paris, V, 246.

102 Mathieu de Paris, V, 247.

103 *Chroniques de Saint-Denis*, loc. cit., p. 115.

104 *Chroniques de Saint-Denis*; Mathieu de Paris, V, 247; Guillaume de Nangis, *Chronique*, 2nd ed. (Delisle, *Mémoire sur les ouvrages de G. de Nangis*, p. 41); *Chronique anonyme finissant en 1286* (*Historiens de France*, XXI, p. 83 c).

105 Primat, *Historiens de France*, XXIII, p. 8; Richer de Senones, *Monumenta Germaniæ*, scriptores, XXV, p. 310; *Chroniques de Saint-Denis*; Primat, p. 8; *Chronique anonyme, etc.* (*Historiens de France*, XXI, p. 83 c).

106 Guillaume de Nangis, *Chronique*, 2nd ed. (Delisle, *Mémoire*, etc., p. 42) : « licet... bona intentione hoc facerent. »

107 Primat, p. 9. The happy disposition of the people towards the Pastoureaux is attested by all historians of the time.
108 Salimbene, p. 225.
109 *Chroniques de Saint-Denis* (*Historiens de France*, XXI, p. 115).
110 Primat, p. 9; Mathieu de Paris, V, 248; *Chronica minor auctore minorita Erphordiensi* (*Monumenta Germaniæ*, scriptores, XXIV, p. 200) : « *sequobantur meretrices.* »
111 Primat; *Chroniques de Saint-Denis*; Guillaume de Nangis, 2nd ed. of the *Chronique*; Mathieu de Paris; Salimbene; Annals of Waverley, *Annales monastici*, ed. Luard , II, 344; letter to Adam de Marsh, *Annales monastici*, I, p. 291 (Denifle, *Chartularium*, I, pièce, 198).
112 Primat, p. 9.
113 Primat; G. de Nangis, *Chronique*, 1st ed. (Delisle, *Mémoire sur les ouvrages de G. de Nangis*, p. 42).
114 *Chroniques de Saint-Denis* (*Historiens de France*, XXI, p. 115).
115 *Chroniques de Saint-Denis*, loc. cit., p. 116.
116 *Chroniques de Saint-Denis*, p. 116; Guillaume de Nangis, *Vie de saint Louis* (*Historiens de France*, XX, 382); letter written from Paris to Adam de Marsh (Annals of Burton, *Annales monastici*, I, 291); *Annales de Oseneia*, *Annales monastici*, IV, 100; *Annales Hamburgenses*, *Monumenta Germaniæ*, scriptores, XVI, p. 383 : « *in ipsum episcopum fecerunt insultum.* »
117 Guillaume de Nangis, *Chronique*, 2nd ed. (Delisle, *Mémoire*, etc., p. 42).
118 *Chroniques de Saint-Denis*, p. 116; Mathieu de Paris, V, 251.
119 Letter to Adam de Marsh; *Chroniques rouennaises de Saint-Laud et de Sainte-Catherine-du-Mont* (*Historiens de France*, XXIII, 396 and 401).
120 *Registres d'Innocent IV*, 6162; letter of 17 December 1252.
121 Mathieu de Paris, V, 249-250; Primat, p. 9; Guillaume de Nangis, *Chronique*, 1st ed. (Delisle, *Mémoire*, etc., p. 42); the same, *Vie de saint Louis* (*Historiens de France*, XX, p. 382); letter to Adam de Marsh, p. 291; *Annales de Oseneia*, *Annales monastici*, IV, 101; Thomas de Cantimpré, *Bonum universale de apibus*, ed. of 1627, book 11, ch. 3, § 15; *Johannis de Tayster annales* (*Monumenta Germaniæ*, scriptores, XXVIII, p. 589).
122 Letter to Adam de Marsh by the guardian of Franciscans of Paris, *Annales monastici*, 1, 291-292.
123 *Continuatio chronici S. Martini abbreviati* (*Monumenta Germaniæ*, scriptores, XXVI, p. 476).
124 D. Morice, *Histoire de Bretagne*, I, 189.
125 Thomas de Cantimpré, book II, chap. 3, § 15.
126 Letters of Adam de Marsh, *Monuments franciscana*, in the collection of the Master of Rolls, p. 109; Mathieu de Paris, V, 251.
127 Primat, p. 9.
128 *Chroniques de Saint-Denis* (*Historiens de France*, XXI, p. 116).
129 Primat, p. 9-10; Guillaume de Nangis, *Chronique*, 2nd ed. (Delisle, *Mémoire*, p. 43); the same, *Vie de saint Louis* (*Historiens de France*, XX, p. 382).
130 *Chroniques de Saint-Denis*.
131 Guillaume de Nangis, *Vie de saint Louis* (*Historiens de France*, XX, 382). Cf. Wallon, *Saint Louis et son temps*, I, p. 364.

132 Primat; Guillaume de Nangis, *Vie de saint Louis*, and 2nd ed. of the *Chronique*, and several other chroniclers.
133 « *quasi canes rabidi.* » Mathieu de Paris, V, 251; Guillaume de Nangis, *Vie de saint Louis*, and the *Chronique*.
134 *Johannis Longi chronica Sancti Bertini* (*Monumenta Germaniœ*, scriptores, XXV, p. 846); *Chroniques de Saint-Denis* (*Historiens de France*, XXI, p. 116).
135 *Historiens de France*, XXI, p. 807 and 808; *Anonymi chronicon rhytmicum austriacum* (*Monumenta Germaniœ*, scriptores, XXV, p. 361).
136 Mathieu de Paris, V, 252.
137 Mathieu de Paris, V, 253.
138 Record office, Close rolls, 65, membr. 8 in dorso; 8 July 1251.
139 Mathieu de Paris, V, 253.
140 Marie, after being taken to find Louis IX on Cyprus, was repatriated to France. Joinville, n. 140; D'Arbois de Jubainville, t. V, catalog, piece 3039.
141 Mathieu de Paris, t. V, pp. 97 and 110.
142 *Registres d'Innocent IV*, piece 6064; 28 October 1252.
143 *Layettes*, III, 3971, 3973.
144 *Layettes*, III, 3896; September 1250.
145 *Layettes*, III, 3981 ; February 1252.
146 Ficker, *Regesten*, 5107-5109; 11 July 1252.
147 *Layettes*, III, 3730; Paris, November 1248.
148 *Le Ménestrel de Reims*, n. 401-403; *Anciennes chroniques de Flandre* (*Historiens de France*, XXII, 338); *Istore et croniques de Flandre* (*collection de chroniques belges*), t. I, p. 165.
149 Archives nationales, JJ. 26, fol. 323 V, col. 2; 8 April 1252.
150 *Layettes*, III, 3978; 23 February 1252.
151 Denifle, *Chartularium Universitatis Parisiensis*, t. I, n. 197; d'Achery, *Spicilegium*, in-f, III, 630.
152 Denifle, *Chartularium*, t. I, n. 213 ; 6 June 1252.
153 Boutaric, *Actes du Parlement*, t. I, p. cccx; 13 February 1250; p. cccxi; Arch. nat., J. 1028, n. 8.
154 Boutaric, p. cccxvn.
155 Ibid., p. cccxx.
156 Marrier, *Monasterii regalis S. Martini de Campis Parisiensis historia*, p. 206-208.
157 Justel, *Histoire Généalogique de la maison de Turenne*, preuves, p. 52.
158 Arcb. nat., JJ 26. 285 r, and 344 r; Boutaric, *Actes du Parlement*, I, p. cccxi, ccxxi.
159 Du Chesne, *Bibliotheca Cluniacensis*, col. 1516; Justel, *Maison de Turenne*, preuves, p. 52.
160 Vaissète, *Histoire de Languedoc*, in-4, t. VIII, cols. 1301-1305, 1312.
161 A *bulla* of Innocent IV, 13 June 1249, attested to the regard that the Pope had for Blanche of Castile on that which concerned collations of benefices; *Registres d'Innocent IV*, 4583, 5163-5164, 5181; 18 March 1251 (Denifle, I, n. 195-196).
162 *Registres d'Innocent IV*, 4931; *bulla* of 29 November 1250; Blanche expressed absolutely that permission to proceed with elections in this case depended on on her; *Layettes*, III, 3906 and 3937.

163 Boutaric, *Actes du Parlement*, I, p. cccxix; Baluze, *Miscellanea*, III, p. 101; 12 February 1252.
164 *Layettes*, III, 3893, 3894, 3906, 3914 to 3916, 3975.
165 *Layettes*, III, 3977; January 1252.
166 Ibid., 3976; 30 January 1252.
167 *Registres d'Innocent IV*, 6131.
168 Paul Fournier, *Les officialités au Moyen âge*, p. 105; *Saint Louis et Innocent IV*, in-8, p. 376-379.
169 *Registres d'Innocent IV*, 5120, 1 March 1251.
170 *Histoire de Languedoc*, in-4, t. VI, p. 827.
171 Potthast, *Regesta*, 14596, 18 May 1252.
172 *Registres d'Innocent IV*, 5597 to 5599, 28 March 1252.
173 Potthast, *Regesta*, 15078, 3 August 1253.
174 *E chronicis Lyrensis monasterii, Historiens de France*, t. XXIII, p. 469.
175 *Layettes*, III, 3714, 3853.
176 *Layettes*, III, 4011, 13 July 1252.
177 *Chroniques de Saint-Denis ou Grandes chroniques de France, Historiens de France*, XXI, p. 117, ed. Paulin Paris, IV, 331.
178 Dubois, *Historia ecclesiæ Parisiensis*, t. II, p. 418.
179 *Chronique anonyme finissant en 1380; Historiens de France*, t. XXI, p. 141.
180 *Registres d'Innocent IV*, 3445, 13 November 1247.
181 Dubois, *Historia ecclesise Parisiensis*, t. II, p. 418; Bibliothèque nationale, collection De Camps, t. XXXV, fol. 162.
182 Archives nationales, L. 457, pièce 5; LL. 46, fol. 62 verso; LL. 48, 2nd part, fol. 29 verse.
183 Mathieu de Paris, t. V, p. 311.
184 Wallon, *Saint Louis and son temps*, t. I, p. 365-367.
185 Rymer, ed. of 1816, t. I, p. 282.
186 Mathieu de Paris, t. V, p. 280.
187 *Anciennes chroniques de Flandre, Historiens de France*, t. XXII, p. 338.
188 Schirrmacher, *Geschichte Castiliens*, etc., p. 429; Mathieu de Paris, t. V, p. 311.
189 *Saint Louis et Innocent IV*, in-8, p. 398-400; Mathieu de Paris, t. V, p. 311; *Layettes*, III, 4055; 31 May 1253; letter of the seigneur de Lunel to the comte Alphonse.
190 *Layettes*, III, 4030; letter written to Saint Louis by the Treasurer Saint-Hilaire de Poitiers.
191 *Chroniques de Saint-Denis, Historiens de France*, t XXI, p. 116; ed. Paulin Paris, IV, 330.
192 *La déposition de Charles d'Anjou pour le procès de canonisation de Saint Louis*, published by Riant (*Notices et documents publiés pour la société de Histoire de France, etc.*, 1884, p. 175), say that Blanche died at Maubuisson; it is probable that Charles confused it or badly interpreted it; we will see that the body of the Queen was brought back from Paris to Maubuisson.
193 The confessor of Queen Marguerite, *Historiens de France*, XX, 64; *Bulla* of Innocent IV; Potthast, *Regesta*, 15078.
194 Deposition of Charles d'Anjou; the confessor of Queen Marguerite. D' Auteuil says, on the faith of a text that I do not have, that Blanche had called the abbess and

nuns of Maubuisson, as well as the nuns of Lys (Blanche de Castile, livre III, p. 120, 125).

195 Dutilleux and Depoin affirm, after a necrology of Maubuisson, that Blanche died on 26 November (*Histoire de abbaye and des abbesses de Maubuisson*, p. 13, note 1). The date of 27 November is given by the *chronique de Normandie* and by an obituary of Mont-Saint-Michel (*Historiens de France*, t. XXIII, p. 214 and 581); obituary from Notre-Dame de Paris, without doubt a confusion between the day of her death and the first day of her obsequies, places her death on 28 November (Guérard, *Cartulaire de Notre-Dame*, t. IV, p. 192); the chronicle of Sainte-Catherine-du-Mont, in Rouen, says that she died on 29 November (*Historiens de France*, t. XXIII, p. 402); this was the day of the funeral at Maubuisson, at the same time Eudes Rigaud attested, present at this ceremony (*Journal des visites pastorales d'Eudes Rigaud*, p. 150). The date of 1 December is given by Mathieu de Paris (*Chronica majora*, V, 354); for the hour of her death, see Le Nain de Tillemont, III, 455, and VI, 268).

196 I assume from diverse authors the details relative to the funerals of Queen Blanche; these are : Mathieu de Paris (V, 354) ; *Chroniques de Saint-Denis* (*Historiens de France*, XXI , 116-117, and Paulin Paris, IV, 330); Primat (*Historiens de France*, XXIII, 10); Eudes Rigaud (*Journal des visites*, p. 150).

197 Dutilleux, *Inventaire de l'abbaye de Notre-Dame-la-Royale, dite Maubuisson-lez-Pontoise*, introduction, p. 2, p. 16; Dutilleux and Depoin, *Les bâtiments, église et les tombeaux de Maubuisson*, p. 106 (2nd part, tombs of the church). The epitaph given by the authors of this work is found in *Histoire Généalogique de la maison de France*, par Scévolo and Louis de Sainte-Marthe, in-f, 1647, t. I, p. 504.

198 D'Auteuil, *Blanche de Castile*, book III, p. 132.

199 Geoffroy de Beaulieu, *Historiens de France*, XX, 17.

200 Joinville, ed. of 1874, n. 603-605.

201 *Chronique anonyme finissant en 1286* (*Historiens de France*, XXI, 83); *Chroniques de Saint-Denis* (*Historiens de France*, XXI, 117).

202 Lecoy de la Marche, *Anecdotes d'Étienne de Bourbon*, p. 389, note.

Printed in Great Britain
by Amazon